Historical
Vines

SMITHSONIAN SERIES IN ETHNOGRAPHIC INQUIRY

William L. Merrill and Ivan Karp, Series Editors

Ethnography as fieldwork, analysis, and literary form is the distinguishing feature of modern anthropology. Guided by the assumption that anthropological theory and ethnography are inextricably linked, this series is devoted to exploring the ethnographic enterprise.

Advisory Board

Richard Bauman (Indiana University), Gerald Berreman (University of California, Berkeley), James Boon (Princeton University), Stephen Gudeman (University of Minnesota), Shirley Lindenbaum (City University of New York), George Marcus (Rice University), David Parkin (University of Oxford), Renato Rosaldo (Stanford University), and Norman Whitten (University of Illinois).

Polly Wiessner and Akii Tumu

Historical Vines

ENGA NETWORKS OF EXCHANGE, RITUAL, AND WARFARE IN PAPUA NEW GUINEA

With translations and assistance by
Nitze Pupu

Illustrations by Akii Tumu

SMITHSONIAN INSTITUTION PRESS
Washington and London

COPY EDITOR: Jane Kepp
PRODUCTION EDITOR: Duke Johns
DESIGNER: Janice Wheeler

Library of Congress Cataloging-in-Publication Data
Wiessner, Pauline Wilson, 1947-
        Historical vines : Enga networks of exchange, ritual, and warfare in Papua New Guinea /
    Polly Wiessner and Akii Tumu ; with translations and assistance by Nitze Pupu.
        p.   cm.
    Includes bibliographical references and index.
    ISBN 1-56098-792-8 (cloth : alk. paper). — ISBN 1-56098-767-7 (pbk. : alk. paper)
        1. Enga (New Guinea people) — History. 2. Enga (New Guinea people) — Rites and ceremo-
    nies. 3. Enga (New Guinea people) — Warfare. 4. Ceremonial exchange — Papua New Guinea —
    Western Highlands Province. 5. Ethnohistory — Papua New Guinea — Western Highlands
    Province. 6. Oral tradition — Papua New Guinea — Western Highlands Province. 7. Western
    Highlands Province (Papua New Guinea) — Social life and customs. I. Tumu, Akii. II. Pupu,
    Nitze. III. Title.
    DU740.42.W49   1998
    995.3 — dc21   97-33620

British Library Cataloguing-in-Publication Data available

Manufactured in the United States of America
05 04 03 02 01 00 99 98   5 4 3 2 1

⊖ The paper used in this publication meets the minimum requirements of the American
National Standard for Information Sciences — Permanence of Paper for Printed Library Materials
ANSI Z39.48-1984.

Contents

Maps

Tables

Preface

There are projects that one would never have the heart to begin if one knew just how much lay ahead. This was one of them. Fortunately, the realization of just how large a job Akii Tumu and I had taken on came little by little as the material became too engaging to permit us to turn back.

We began in 1985 with no specific research project in mind; I had come to Enga Province in Papua New Guinea with my family when my husband, Flemming Larsen, was offered the job of assistant secretary of health there. Having previously worked with the !Kung San (Ju/'hoansi) of the Kalahari (southern Africa), and having come to Papua New Guinea on rather short notice, I had no previous experience in Enga and little time to prepare. Akii, director of the Enga Cultural Centre and an accomplished artist, introduced me to the community of Kundis in the Ambum valley, where I began to learn Enga, conduct studies of time use, and record topics of conversation. Given the excellent anthropological work that had already been carried out in Enga, it seemed best to look and listen carefully before choosing a research topic. Akii also asked me to collaborate in cataloguing and gathering further information on the superb artifact collection in the Enga Museum founded by Paul Brennan. The Enga Provincial Government hired two museum trainees, Alome Kyangali Kyakas and Pesone Munini, to assist and participate in developing a broader cultural program.

Both lines of investigation led in the same direction. Public discussions and court cases at Kundis usually turned back to the past. We did not get far with the museum collection before we realized that the richest component of Enga culture lay not in the material but in the oral record. We then shifted direction and initiated what we thought would be a small-scale project to collect the "origin" traditions of all Enga tribes and to look at their role in orienting Enga actions and identity.

Our initial plan was short-lived, for it soon became evident that Enga history contained far more than "origins" and was more central to Enga society than I had recognized. It was composed of a wide array of oral traditions, from sacred poetry and charter myths for tribes and cults to more factual historical traditions recording a wide variety of events of the last two hundred to three hundred years. In generations past, these oral traditions had provided a framework within which Enga could orient their actions and sense of identity. That is, when faced with problems, Enga turned to history to find their bearings. A wealth of information was there to guide them, both in historical traditions passed down in the men's houses and in the ritual poetry and sacred rites of ancestral and bachelors' cults. Decisions could be made with respect to past relations, events, experiences, and values that had been transmitted over generations.

Today this is no longer possible. Enga rush headlong into the future with little time and ever-decreasing sources with which to look back. The replacement of men's houses by family houses has removed the primary setting for historical education, leaving many traditions to pass away with the men who held them. History is still called on at clan meetings and in court cases, but with no coherent framework in which to place it, such information has little meaning for the younger generation and is easily forgotten. Performances of ancestral and bachelors' cults are held infrequently, if at all.

Our goals expanded greatly when we realized that as the oral record vanished, only the written record would remain for future generations. With the exception of the historical investigations of Roderic Lacey, Kundapen Talyaga, and a few Enga who have published short articles on their clan histories, the written record documents the postcontact period only. If this were not corrected, future generations of Enga would derive their sense of tradition and identity from studies carried out in recent decades by non-Enga, each with his or her own approach. We felt that if we could record and write down Enga historical traditions, future generations would have a history told by Enga, for Enga, documenting both the failures and the accomplishments of their ancestors and the processes through which the accomplishments were realized. We hope this effort will provide a balanced and inspiring source of orientation and identity for future generations.

Between 1985 and 1988 we conducted research among more than one hundred tribes of Enga. We worked intensively in each area, moving back and forth among the tribes living there until some coherent picture began to emerge and then moving on to the next area. By the middle of 1987, many connections between the areas had become evident, particularly in the history of the trade, exchange networks, and cults that linked eastern, central, and western Enga. In

April 1988, after three years of joint fieldwork, I returned to the Max Planck Institute, where I had worked since 1981, and began to compile tribal histories. Akii came to the Max Planck in early November, and after six weeks of translation, review, and discussion we realized that our interviews contained many intriguing leads. These indicated that the rise and development of the Tee ceremonial exchange cycle, the Great Ceremonial Wars, and a number of the larger ancestral cults—all massive exchange networks that circulated pigs and valuables—were well within the scope of Enga oral history. We felt that we had just begun to understand the precolonial history of Enga and set to work formulating new questions.

In December 1988 Akii returned to Enga and began to work on those new questions, sending me translations of the interviews as they were completed, so that I could write a draft of the book. Nitze Pupu, who had translated most of our interviews, collected an outstanding history of his family in the Great Ceremonial Wars and Tee exchange cycle. In 1990 Akii returned to Germany with the additional material. Together we tried to compile a history of the Tee exchange cycle, the Great Ceremonial Wars, and the major cult networks and to work out their relationships to one another. At this point, information from different sources fell together to provide a relatively coherent picture. Nonetheless, we realized that it was necessary to treat our syntheses as hypotheses and test them systematically in the major clans involved.

Between July and September 1991 I went to Enga to do this with a draft of our book and many questions. Our work proceeded with ease owing to the knowledge we had already acquired. Interviews that had previously taken the form of questions and answers turned into lengthy and fascinating discussions of broader issues. At Tari we visited Chris Ballard, who was working on similar problems for the Huli, and together we gained much insight into ritual links between Huli and Enga. After seven weeks of intensive research, returns began to become redundant or to diminish greatly, a general indication that we had collected a significant part of the information still available. The end result of these nine weeks of research was a substantial body of testimony on ritual and exchange displaying a high degree of consistency and closely linking the Tee exchange cycle and Great Ceremonial Wars with each other and with the ancestral and bachelors' cults. It was at this point that we decided to draw the line and complete the book—research on Enga historical traditions could continue for a lifetime.

Schemes that seem clear and logical in discussion can cloud and disintegrate when put to paper. When Akii came to Germany in the fall of 1993 to read and correct a draft of the book, a number of things did not add up, and new questions arose, setting off a "final" bout of interviews that Akii carried out in Enga between December 1993 and February 1995. In March 1995 he came to Germany once more to read the "final" draft of the text, and again he returned with more questions. Further joint fieldwork, including a grueling journey into northwest Enga to track down traditions concerning the arrival of the sweet potato, was carried out in July and August 1995 to answer the "very last questions."

A note on cooperation is warranted. Few joint projects hold together over the long run, particularly when the researchers are from different cultures. We actually managed to work well together from start to finish, with intermittent breaks of six months or so required by our own schedules and the great distance between Enga and Germany. There was from the outset a division of labor according to our skills. Akii dealt largely with interviewing, translating, and checking translations, and I worked more with research problems and design, compiling the material, and writing. Had this division remained in force, it would have produced a disjointed book with data collected by a member of the culture and an analytical framework imposed from outside. But it did not—there were no interviews during or after which I did not ask or send (too) many questions. Conversely, my syntheses and initial drafts, directed by my anthropological education, were but a starting point for both of us. Akii took off from and developed the ideas and orientation much further or differently, directed by his experience in the complexity of Enga politics and exchange, among other things. Usually this would initiate discussions over hours, days, or even weeks, followed by new hypotheses, rounds of interviews, and synthesis. The most insightful connections were often made by Akii.

Our research was held together by more than a division of skills (and the fax machine). The intrinsic interest of the material drew us on, and for Akii in particular there was the desire to preserve the history of his own people. During the frustrating days and weeks when we pursued dead ends and the information stopped flowing, we were rescued by a shared, offbeat sense of humor—more than a few times we had to pull off the road after a long and fruitless day's work to recover from laughter.

For the first three years, we carried out most interviews jointly in Enga, never in Melanesian Pidgin. Akii explained the purpose of our project and asked the relevant questions in Enga. I followed as best I could, and Akii then summarized or clarified the more complex points during or just after each testimony, so that we could both ask questions on the spot. For the few areas that Akii had to avoid because of clan conflicts, I interviewed with the help of others, in most cases with much less success. It was essential that the interviewing be done by someone fluent in Enga language, culture, and metaphor who also had a good grasp of all the information collected in previous discussions. After 1988 Akii carried out interviews alone, except during our nine weeks of intensive work together in 1991 and our three weeks in 1995. Additionally, Nitze Pupu collected oral traditions of the Yakani tribe, and David Hamal, who had regularly helped us during university holidays, gathered some information on the Kepele cult and leadership in the Kandep and Tumundan areas.

Enga history is largely a matter for men; women are reluctant to speak about it. To gain a female perspective on the past, Alome Kyangali Kyakas accompanied us on the majority of trips during the first three years and interviewed women about their lives and traditions (Kyakas and Wiessner 1992). This work added women's views of historical events that occurred after approximately 1920, but it did not extend further than the limits of living memory. Pesone Munini of the Enga Cultural Centre conducted numerous interviews on ancestral cults and healing rituals. During school holidays we were joined by university students from various parts of Enga who were of great help in identifying knowledgeable men, establishing contact with them, and making preliminary translations of recordings.

During each interview, genealogies, names and locations of all branches of the tribe, and lists of cult performances held were noted by hand. Major testimonies were recorded on cassette, as were important parts of discussions. Inevitably, many interesting remarks were added after the recorder was switched off—these were noted later. Akii listened to the cassettes after interviews, designated rotations for translation, and translated some important testimonies himself, as well as all spells, songs, and poetry. The majority of the historical narratives were translated by Nitze Pupu.

All formal and some important free texts were transcribed, but not the entire contents of cassettes. (Those contents, available at the Enga Cultural Centre, will not lie dormant on cassette but will be used in other publications, including ones for Enga schools and radio programs.) Nitze's translations were made directly from the cassettes into English, as he is blind. Translations of informal testimonies were free, with repetition omitted when it made the English text too tedious. In this book, only formalized traditions such as songs, incantations, and poems are given in both Enga and English. To have done the same for all historical narratives would have nearly doubled the length of the book.

All Enga names and texts are written in the central Enga dialect (Mai). Throughout the book we have tried to conform to the orthography presented by Adrianne Lang (1973) in his Enga dictionary, with the exception of place names given on maps. To avoid confusion, we have adopted spellings for these from standard Enga maps—spellings that sometimes depart from Lang's orthography by dropping silent vowels at the ends of words: for instance, Lagaip rather than Lagaipa, and Kandep instead of Kandepe. Greater departures from Lang's orthography do occur, however; for instance, maps use the popular Wabag for the capital city rather than Wapaka. In narratives, Enga persons are usually referred to by first name or first name preceded by clan name. In credits for the narratives quoted in this book, we have given the narrator's first name followed by his father's name, along with the narrator's tribe (and sometimes clan) and place of residence.

We were extremely fortunate to have Nitze Pupu's assistance. Nitze had completed the first half of his studies in law at the University of Papua New Guinea in the late 1970s and then took a year off to help draft the first Enga provincial constitution. A car accident left him blind, and he returned to his home in Wakumale village near Wabag. In 1986 he began translating for us with the assistance of Meck Kepai to write for him. After completing typing and Braille courses at the Centre for the Blind at Goroka in 1988, he continued with translation work, using a word processor with voice playback, and conducted interviews on the Tee exchange cycle, the Great Ceremonial Wars, leadership, and war reparations within the Yakani tribe. He resumed his law studies at the University of Papua New Guinea in 1991, continuing translation work during his "free time" and over the holidays, and graduated in 1994. We now have nearly one thousand pages of translations. Without such a competent and energetic colleague, the project would have been much more formidable and the quality of translation poorer.

Polly Wiessner

Acknowledgments

In some highland New Guinea societies, small ceremonies are held and magic words recited so that nobody will be overlooked in a distribution of wealth. We sought such formulas for our "distribution of thanks," but Enga leaders just shook their heads and said that these matters were too important to be left to magic words — that such knowledge was held deep in the head and heart. And so we must try to match the best of Enga big-men in recalling all those who helped us so generously over the last ten years, hoping that where the head fails, the heart will not.

First and foremost, we would like to extend our gratitude to the hundreds of Enga who generously gave us their time and knowledge. We cannot name all of them. Very special thanks go to a few who became our teachers in oral history, devoting days of their time to helping us understand: Leme Poul of Kaekini, Ambone Mati of Nemani, Yopo Yakene of Kamaniwane, Kopio and Kambao Lambu of Timali, Kyakas Sapu of Lanekepa, Saiyo Tondea of Sakate, Alo Peter of Kelyanyo, Tindiwi Loape of Yomondaka, Pakea Yakani of Yakumani, Saiyakali Patao Yaki of Yana, and Yakapus Mioko of Kamaniwane.

We were assisted in our data collection by many literate Enga: David Hamal, Paul Steward, and Sakias Tamao of Kandep, Thomas Waip of Laiagam, Yoan Lapi and Peter Thomas of Mulitaka, Joseph Lakani of Par, James Mongola of Tari, Maria Kimala of Irelya, Robert Pyaso of Wabag, and Danny Kili Nembo of Awalemanda. Theodore Mawe of the Mendi Cultural Centre was of great help in tracing ties between Enga and Mendi, and Jo Mangi of the University of Papua New Guinea advised us on connections between Tari and Porgera and on matters concerning prehistory. Others working at or in association with the Enga Cultural Centre contributed significantly to research and translation: Alome Kyakas,

Pesone Munini, Meck Kepai, Lelyame Yoane, Kuna Masili, and Andy Utuwai. For their assistance we are most grateful. Lazarus Endikio accompanied us on many trips, providing help and humor on all occasions.

Particular thanks are due to Fr. Philip Gibbs, Chris Ballard, and Rod Lacey for sustained interest during our research and for reading and commenting on the entire manuscript as it developed. Fr. Doug Young gave us numerous insights from his participant studies and programs in conflict resolution. Fritz Robinson generously provided us with his notes and thoughts from his personal experiences in the Sangai cult. Many people helped us with advice, problems, and practicalities, including Leo Ango, Paul Brennan, Ruth and Paul Wohlt, Lois and David Birner, Gelma and Graham Taylor, Josie and Peter Mommers, Alois Hemetsberger, and Elias Posi. During July and August 1995, Sr. Katherine Mair, Fr. Tony Kröl, Fr. Doug Young, and Sr. Henrilena v.d. Laar at Par Catholic mission kindly hosted Polly with good food, lodging, and conversation. Gelma and Graham Taylor, Frank Faulkner, and Alo Peter repeatedly provided us with warm hospitality.

In 1995, when we returned with additional questions, several Enga asked, "Haven't you two been at this for an awfully long time?" They seemed uncertain whether to wonder at our diligence or despair at our dull pace. Those who supported us over all these years must have felt the same. The project began with minimal resources but gained funding as it grew. For the first three years we worked using our own resources and Polly's private vehicle. The Department of Enga paid the salaries of Akii Tumu, Alome Kyakas, and Pesone Munini throughout the course of our work and gave us a generous publication subvention for this book. (The Enga Provincial Government is one of the few in Papua New Guinea that supports an active cultural program on a long-term basis.) From 1988 to 1995 the Forschungsstelle für Humanethologie in the Max Planck Society provided Polly with an honorarium to work up the material and generously funded four trips for Akii to come to Germany and two trips of Polly's to Enga. We are grateful to the Department of Enga for its patience and to the Max Planck Society, and Irenäus Eibl-Eibesfeldt in particular, for understanding just how much time a project of such scale and complexity requires.

Over the years we received encouragement or assistance from many people in the Department of Enga, the Enga Provincial Government, and the Enga local government councils: Kundapen Talyaga, Mark Yappao, Tao Liua, Danley Tindiwi, Anguu and Philip Kyakala, Regina and Luke Kembol, Graham Taylor, Diri Kobla, Rance Mimi, Nah Tao, Anderson Aipiti, Henry Kyakas, Patricia Rimbao, Daniel Kumbon, Margaret and Pato Potane, Michael Mangala, Don Archibald, Albert MacSaen, Jeffrey Balakau, and Anson Isingi.

This project would have been impossible without the foundation built by those who went before. The outstanding studies of Mervyn Meggitt, Roderic Lacey, Paul Wohlt, Paul Brennan, and Kundapen Talyaga provided us with a solid starting point. Many others contributed helpful comments or discussion at various stages in the preparation of the manuscript: Anton Ploeg, Irenäus Eibl-Eibesfeldt, Frank Salter, Brian Hayden, Andrew Strathern, Gabriele Stürzenhofecker, Volker Heeschen, Wulf Schiefenhövel, Maurice Godelier, Pierre Lemonnier, Pascal Bonnemere, Mervyn Meggitt, Pamela Swadling, Robin Hide, John McComb, John Waiko, Doug Young, John Burton, and Ray Kelly. James Watson, Roderic Lacey, and Andrew Strathern made very helpful comments on the entire manuscript. We thank Bill Merrill at the Smithsonian Institution for a careful reading of the manuscript and good suggestions for revision, Daniel Goodwin and Bob Lockhart at the Smithsonian Institution Press for continual help with the many details of production, and Jane Kepp for copy editing that straightened the many twisted paths that might have led readers astray.

The anchor necessary to complete any project comes from home, and we appreciate the sustained patience of Flemming Larsen and Yakolapae Tumu and of our children, who had to put up with their parents being occupied in the field or on the computer: Silas, Niko, Woody, Salin, Sylvia, West, Nia, Pauline, and Alice.

Introduction

This book presents the results of a ten-year study of the precolonial history of the Enga of Papua New Guinea as portrayed in a wealth of oral traditions. The period covered is extraordinary for its rapid rate of change. Among other things, it saw a shift from hunting, gathering, and shifting horticulture to intensive agriculture and the emergence of what were to become some of the largest networks of warfare, cult performances, and ceremonial exchange known in prestate societies. Our intent is twofold: first, to compile the history of these events for future generations of Enga, and second, to use anthropological methods and perspectives to explore the social processes involved in the formation of these broad-reaching networks.

The Enga, who today number about two hundred thousand, inhabit the valleys and mountainsides of the western highlands of Papua New Guinea (PNG). Their highland neighbors include the Melpa and Kakoli to the east, the Mendi and Wola to the south, the Huli to the southwest, and the Ipili to the west (map 1). All of these western highland peoples are known for their endemic warfare as well as for their far-flung and elaborate networks of ceremonial exchange involving hundreds or even thousands of participants and the distribution of massive numbers of pigs, pearl shells, and other valuables. Warfare, ceremonial exchange, and the activities of large ancestral cults were orchestrated by powerful big-men who were brilliant orators, flamboyant performers, and skilled economists. These men juggled complex financial obligations in their heads, commanding such principles as credit and payment of interest to assemble large amounts of wealth for public distribution in the pursuit of prestige ("name") and political goals. Virtually anybody contemplating these great networks, whether Enga, anthropologist, or layperson, wonders, "How and why did they come to be?"

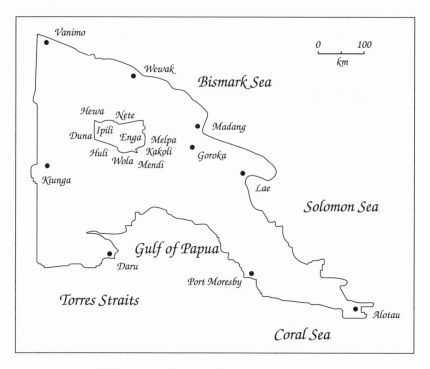

Map 1. Locations of the Enga and their neighbors on the main island of Papua New Guinea.

Enga, too, appear to have been long concerned with this question, for beginning some eight to ten generations ago they began systematically to keep track of pertinent events through a body of historical traditions, *atome pii*, which are distinct from myth or story, *tindi pii*. The regular transmission of historical traditions begins, for the most part, after the introduction of the sweet potato some 250 to 400 years ago, an event described in a narrative that goes as follows: Two sisters and their useless brother, orphaned and mistreated, packed up their possessions and set out from the Sepik to start a new life. In their net bags they carried seeds and cuttings, among them sweet potato vines. Over the years they worked their way southward through the foothills and into the highlands, settling at various places and planting lush gardens. One day when they were living in Hewa territory, an Enga hunter came across their homestead, marveled at the sea of sweet potato vines in the surrounding gardens, and tried the new crop for the first time. Pleased by its taste, he brought some back to Walia, later returning to get the two sisters. The sweet potato grew well at Walia. When it was plentiful, they held a distribution, handing out vines to people from near and far, an event that was to be commemorated repeatedly over the next two hundred to three hundred years in a ritual called "the bridge of the sweet potato vines" (*aina pungi toko*).

With the introduction of the sweet potato, constraints on production were released and a new era of opportunity began. Most importantly, the sweet potato permitted people in many areas of Enga to settle more permanently, practice intensive agriculture, expand into higher altitudes, and produce a substantial surplus "on the hoof" in the form of pigs. Following the logic of distribution at Walia — that name and prosperity come to those who give rather than to those who retain — innovations that sprang up in subsequent generations and the "vines" of oral tradition that recorded them were circulated widely. The outcome was twofold. First, far-reaching networks of social, economic, and ritual interaction developed. So great was the flow of wealth and information within and among these networks that they were restructured with each new generation. Second, a factual body of traditions recording the history of each tribe (or phratry) and its constituent clans,[1] ordered by genealogies and extending back at least eight to ten generations, began to be systematically transmitted in men's houses. The many topics covered included tribal origins, genealogies, migration and dispersal, natural disasters, warfare, innovations in communication, agricultural techniques, styles of dress, and the development of major cults and ceremonial exchange networks. The material on which this book is based consists of the historical traditions of 110 Enga tribes.

The course of events described by these traditions presents a unique situation in which the sweet potato was introduced within the span of historical traditions (that is, some 250 to 400 years ago), but the arrival of the first Europeans occurred only within living memory (during the 1930s). Hence the Enga oral record (and those of other highland societies as well) allows us to work with questions that are usually relegated to archaeologists: What happens to a society when, in the absence of influence from foreign populations, constraints on production are released by the introduction of a new crop and substantial surplus production becomes possible for the first time? How is the potential of the new crop exploited and by whom? What had to be done to bring about change in social, economic, and ideological terms? Who did this, how, and with what outcome?

At the heart of this book is an ethnohistory of the Tee ceremonial exchange cycle, from here forward referred to simply as the Tee cycle or the Tee.[2] It was (and still is) a complex institution involving sequential, interlocking clan distributions of pigs and valuables. It circulated wealth throughout central and eastern Enga in a three-phase cycle financed by both home production and credit and involving subsequent repayment, preferably with interest.

The Tee had quiet origins in some twenty clans along the trade routes of eastern Enga approximately eight to ten generations ago. By the onset of the colonial era it had grown into a regular, three-phase exchange cycle in which pigs, goods, and valuables moved through clan after clan from east to west and then from west to east and back again, linking some 355 clans, or a population of about fifty thousand to seventy thousand Enga. Although we did not devote more effort to the history of the Tee cycle than to other subjects, the Tee occupies a central position in Enga history, because in crafting its course, collaborating big-men and their families drew in participants, wealth, ideas, and ritual from eastern, western, and central Enga as well as from surrounding areas. We are particularly fortunate to have a good oral history of the social, economic, political, and ritual aspects of the development of the Tee cycle. Although outstanding descriptions and analyses of exchange networks in New Guinea are available (Malinowski 1922; Rappaport 1968; A. Strathern 1971; Young 1971; Meggitt 1974; Weiner 1976; Hughes 1977; Sillitoe 1979; Feil 1984; Lederman 1986; Healey 1990), their history, which is the key to further understanding and comparison, usually lies beyond reach of the ethnohistorian and evades the trowel of the archaeologist.

First Phase: Tribal Histories

Our initial research design drew on Roderic Lacey's (1975) excellent analysis of Enga oral traditions as history. In planning our research, we faced some difficult choices, owing to the large volume of historical traditions available and the terrain to be covered. Enga is a large province with more than one hundred tribes and eight hundred clans, many of them living in very remote areas. All clans of a tribe share a common origin tradition, but in addition, clans, subclans, lineages, and even families have their own histories that tell of more recent local events. It was necessary to set some limits.

The first was to restrict our research largely to precolonial times, because precolonial history is essential to understanding colonial history and because precolonial traditions were rapidly being lost.[3] The second was to cover the more general history of all Enga tribes rather than collect detailed histories of tribes in one area or from a sample of tribes spread out over the province. This would permit us to record the basic histories for all tribes before they were forgotten, obtain an overview of interaction between different areas in the past, and gather data in a way that would enable as much verification as possible. The last was essential: on one hand, the material could not simply be taken at face value, but on the other, it is all too easy to dispossess a people of their history when they indeed have good oral records by assuming that these have been distorted in order to legitimate current relations, to retell events the way people would have liked them to be, or to please the anthropologist.

The most appropriate methodology for Enga seemed to be to evaluate and interpret the oral record by using converging lines of evidence (Rosaldo 1980:97). This approach has been successful in the work of John Waiko (1982, 1986) with the Binandere and in that of Klaus Neumann (1992) for the Tolai, both of Papua New Guinea. These studies relay history from the perspective of its "owners," thereby preserving its own structure and perspective, and then lay it parallel to the yardstick of the written record. Alas, for precolonial Enga history we had no written records as guides. Yet because tribal histories are passed on more or less independently of one another, because most clan histories have been transmitted separately for at least the past five to six generations, and because very different kinds of information are contained in historical traditions, it was possible to draw converging lines of evidence from the oral histories themselves.

We examined internal consistency and reliability on four levels. First, we compared versions of the same traditions as told by persons from different clans of a tribe to see whether they concurred on the essential points or, if not, how they differed. Presumably, what is shared most likely stems from an original version (Vansina 1985). Second, we confirmed accounts of events such as wars and migrations at both ends and with neighboring groups. Third, we sought regional trends by looking at whether themes and events in the history of one tribe entered into the histories of others during the same time period. Finally, we examined evidence for developments in one area of life in the context of others. For example, growth in ceremonial pig exchange was expected to be accompanied by developments in agricultural production, land use, or both.

Our decision to include all tribes of Enga turned out to be more productive than we expected. Over the course of our research we found that Enga historical traditions were highly consistent on many topics and that events reported in the history of one tribe often clarified or added to the histories of others. It would have been impossible, as it turned out, to understand the history of any single tribe without considering the histories of other tribes in the same region and surrounding ones. Furthermore, tribal histories are by no means equivalent in quality and content—some are extremely complex and rich in detail while others are sparse. Had the histories of a few key tribes been omitted, regional developments would have remained incomprehensible.

Our initial research design involved surveying all Enga-speaking tribes in the province and collecting information on the following topics:

1. Tribal origin traditions, places of "origin," and past subsistence strategies and lifestyles.

2. Tribal genealogy.
3. Locations of all branches of a tribe at their "times of origin" and today.
4. Tribal dispersal and migration, including the cause of each major migration and the generation in which it occurred. Information on migration was obtained for all branches of a tribe that were not currently at or near their places of origin.
5. All major cult performances held by a tribe (we made lists of these and in some cases obtained descriptions), and the ways in which groups obtained sacred objects for bachelors' cults.

When time permitted and the context was favorable, we also explored the following:

6. The origins and histories of major cults.
7. The history of trade and ceremonial exchange (*tee*).
8. Agricultural developments and natural catastrophes.
9. Whether there were other important traditions that we had overlooked.

Although we set out on this task with optimism, logistical problems at times became overwhelming. Covering the history of the entire province with its remote areas, poor roads, wet weather, incessant tribal fighting, and occasional highway holdups was an absurd undertaking, as anyone who knows the area can well imagine. Once we managed to reach the desired clan, it was not unusual to find that the people thought to know the history best had left to visit relatives, attend pig exchanges, or—worst of all—go to Wabag, from where we had set out in the first place. Hours could then be wasted interviewing those who knew "half the story" or returning again and again to find the right person. Owing to shortage of time, family obligations, and difficulty of travel, it was necessary to restrict most of our research to areas within a two- to four-hour walk of roads or airstrips serviced by government charters.

For groups living in places we could not reach ourselves, we enlisted the help of mature, literate Enga from those areas to obtain names of clans there, their current locations, their origin and migration traditions, and their major cults.[4] Danny Kili Nembo was successful in collecting such information for the Maramuni region and for parts of northern Kompiam that we could not reach. We were unable to cover the Waga valley of western Kandep, the Lyalam-Yeim area north of the Lagaip, and parts of the Wale-Tarua region.[5] Nonetheless, in the initial three years of the project we covered ninety-two Enga tribes and branches of eighteen immigrant tribes from neighboring linguistic groups, and we interviewed briefly in twenty-three clans of the Porgera valley that had Enga or mixed Enga-Ipili origins. Our information was much better for some tribes than for others; we obtained but sketches of the histories of twenty-three of the Enga tribes and six of the immigrant groups, largely those in outlying areas.

Fortunately, in interviewing we encountered no obstacles comparable to the logistical ones. Information contained in tribal histories is generally told openly unless it concerns land that is under dispute, current interclan tensions, or some details of sacred rituals. We steered well away from all of these. After Akii explained our project and goal—to preserve oral traditions for future genera-tions—older men were genuinely pleased and cooperative. The twenty-five-year colonial period was something of the past, and the government was no longer regarded as a force outside the towns, except to provide services. Fears that we were part of a government plan for land redistribution could be quickly dispelled.

Because we interviewed hundreds of people, it is hard to make blanket state-ments about how people viewed us. People of outlying areas were surprised by our arrival, curious, and somewhat wary in the beginning, but appreciative that we had come so far. In more central areas, word of our work spread rapidly, and often people anticipated our arrival. Akii is a fellow Enga, and expatriate women are associated with health and education, so people tended to accept our goals as sincere. Once an interview had progressed into serious testimony, attention was directed to Akii. At the end of the interview, the presence of a foreigner seemed to make people more tolerant of seemingly endless and sometimes meaningless questions. People addressed us as equals. Rarely did we get the impression that they told us what they thought we wanted to hear, and they let us know if they thought we had collected incorrect information.

The events of the colonial era had great impact on the oral history of that period, as we discuss in chapter 2. We found little indication, however, that the influence of the colonial administration had been projected back into the pre-contact period, other than for the occasional reinterpretation of specific pre-contact events as predictive of the coming of the white man or other recent occurrences. This is probably because direct contact with the colonial adminis-tration was largely limited to legal action and the organization of public works. In contrast, there were many resourceful missionaries in Enga who established warm personal contact and ran extensive religious, health, and education pro-grams (Gordon and Meggitt 1985). The influence of Christianity was great, and though Enga almost always drew a distinct line between their own tradition and that introduced by missionaries, biblical stories were occasionally told in place of origin traditions or were woven creatively into Enga oral tradition. For example, some elders, both eccentrics and those whose thoughts had been muddled by age, were convinced that they had found the spot on their sacred Mount Mongalo in western Enga where the Lamb of God had been sacrificed, or that it was really Jesus who had been killed in former performances of the traditional Dindi Gamu cult. When elders launched into reiterations of Bible stories, we explained that these had already been written down and that we did not need to record them again. We did, however, record traditions that combined Enga history with biblical stories, because of the fascinating collages that resulted and because some may be the sources of future religious movements. We have not used them in this book but reserve them for work on the postcontact period.

We did not pay informants, for a number of reasons. First, we did not want to establish a relationship of inequality—of employer-employee or buyer-seller. Second, it is impossible to put a price on information: "What you have to say is worth two kina, thank you." Finally, to pay might have incited embellishment of old traditions or fabrication of new ones. In most cases, both old and young helped us graciously after we explained why we could not pay.

Our research stimulated an interest in history on the part of younger Enga, who then went out of their way to help us make contact with appropriate elders. Tribal genealogies and origin and migration traditions were not endless to collect, because once we had managed to interview three to five of the most knowledgeable men from different clans of a tribe, further interviews yielded redundant and rapidly diminishing returns. Doubtless this was in part because we were working in the eleventh hour. Had we started our work forty years earlier, our results would have been much richer. There seemed to be little problem with intentional deceit—those who did not want to answer a question generally said they did not know anything about the subject. When people did not know an oral tradition well, they readily referred us to others who might.

Initial interviews were carried out in public at the market, after village court sessions, or at other gatherings where it was possible to assemble a group of knowledgeable people and make contact with those whose houses were far away. Many passers-by would stop and listen briefly; those who had something to add remained, gave their testimonies, and commented on the narratives of others. Often, group interviews in the marketplace degenerated into a squabbling chaos and everybody gave up. Still, public interviews were an efficient and open way of informing people of what we were doing, identifying knowledgeable people, and stimulating interest in our project. Private interviews were carried out in many different settings—ideally, on ridgetops with magnificent views, by blazing fires in Enga houses, in our own houses, or beside the stream at the Enga Cultural Centre. As often as not, however, informants were waiting for us at village centers far from their own houses. As the weather turned, we had to continue discussions huddled damp and cold under the overhang of the corrugated roof of a defunct store or crammed inside our Nissan double-cab with tape recorder on the gearshift and windows fogged or plastered from the outside with the faces of curious children.

Over the course of our research we experienced two major setbacks. The first was an armed holdup in 1987 in which we lost all our equipment as well as confidence to move about as freely as we formerly had. In 1988 the Enga Cultural Centre was robbed and approximately one hundred cassettes containing Enga oral history were stolen. We had translated or taken notes on most of these, but for those that had not yet been copied, the original Enga versions were lost. It is a sign of the times that these cassettes will be taped over with rock music.

Second Phase: The Tee, the Great Wars, and the Cults

In 1987 we held an oral history seminar with ten of the top "men of knowledge" in central Enga to explore the potential of group discussion for verification and synthesis. Although the seminar stimulated interest, participants felt over-whelmed, said less than they did in private discussions, and expressed a desire to discuss historical problems later individually. What it did achieve was to make us realize that the history of the Tee cycle, bachelors' cults, some ancestral cults, and Great Ceremonial Wars was covered comprehensively in the Enga oral record. (The Great Ceremonial Wars, *yanda andake,* which are hardly mentioned in the literature on Enga, were spectacular, semiritualized "tournament" wars between two tribes or pairs of tribes fought repeatedly over generations to forge alliances, formally display strength, and enable the exchange festivals that fol-lowed.) We had included questions on these topics in some of our interviews, but apparently we had not had or displayed adequate knowledge to elicit such information. In Enga history, as in all fields, simple, superficial explanations are given to beginners. Only if one demonstrates knowledge sufficient to under-stand certain information and place it in its proper context do elders go into greater depth.

From this seminar forward, we concentrated on the history of the Tee cycle, the Great Ceremonial Wars, and the cults. The most significant break came from conversations with Leme Poul of the Kaekini clan in the middle Lai valley, a former organizer of the Tee cycle. Leme had begun to work on Enga history decades before we had, collecting the oral traditions of tribes during campaigns to organize the Tee cycle. With an extraordinary memory for detail and a keen mind for synthesis, he had acquired in his lifetime a hawk's-eye view of the history of eastern and central Enga. Over the long run, many of his ideas were supported by our research, though others were not; regardless, they pointed to invaluable sources and lines of investigation.

Most narratives that we had recorded in response to our original questions described what happened, when it happened, and what the outcome was. They concerned one event or subject only, giving few answers to the "why" questions and rarely telling how past events were organized or linking different kinds of events. We now realized that new questions were required to understand the history from a viewpoint of social action—how individuals and groups brought about change. These "why," "how," and "in which context" questions elicited discussions in which individuals offered knowledge, experiences, analyses, observations, and opinions of their own or those relayed to them by their fathers or grandfathers. They provided a much better understanding of the dynamics of change over approximately the past hundred years.

During the course of our discussions with certain men, sometimes in a series of five to ten interviews, we asked directed questions, shared information given by others, and tried out our own ideas.[6] Reactions were, for the most part, frank. For instance, people informed us that what we had been told was interesting but that they had never heard anything like it before; that what we had collected was likely to be more complete than what they knew; that they could add more; or that the information we provided opened a new perspective for them. People did not feel uneasy if their testimonies differed from those of others. Enga historical traditions are not formalized, and it is accepted that different accounts of a single event exist because of diverse experiences and vantage points. There is little competition between "men of knowledge" to be considered "right" or to be the only one to really know history. Knowledge is used competitively only in public disputes when land, wealth, or relationships are at stake. In such contexts, attempts may be made to twist information to serve immediate ends. We steered clear of all issues of current contention.

We often returned to elders to present our syntheses and see how they reacted to the placement of their ideas or testimonies in a broader scheme. Elders did not hesitate to let us know when they thought we were wrong—they were the teachers in our long sessions together. Our grand schemes drawing on information that linked the Tee cycle, Aeatee cult, and Great Wars, compiled from numerous interviews, were refuted at least three times. Each time we returned to the drawing board in desperation, mitigated only by laughter, to come up with further questions for a new round of interviews. We made an effort to hear out sidetracks (and there were many) with enthusiasm for the new perspectives they might open.

The Narrators

During our fieldwork we encountered extraordinary differences between individuals in the kinds and amounts of knowledge they retained and in personal approaches to history. This alone would make an interesting topic of study. Were it possible to classify, one might say that there were, for one type, the "gardeners"—men who had kept their hands in the soil or on the ax handle while the important events of their clan unfolded and who thus were able to give us only undigested fragments of oral traditions. There were knowledgeable men who had mastered tribal traditions to the last detail but who accepted them as closed fact. There were others who knew the same traditions but who had also spent much time rethinking their contexts, meanings, and implications without confusing inherited knowledge with their own reflections. With such men, discussions of historical traditions were as valuable as the narratives themselves. There were "specialists" who had a wealth of knowledge on certain subjects only—for instance, origin myths, the Tee cycle, or bachelors' cults. Some knew early traditions best, whereas others were more fluent in events of the last three to four generations. Finally, there were a very few extraordinary men who had collected historical traditions from surrounding tribes and pieced together the history of their regions. When setting out for a day's work, it was difficult to predict what was to come, for knowledge is not vested in certain chosen people, nor do Enga have a uniform attitude toward their history: some reflect deeply on the meaning of the past, and others accept what they hear at face value.

From all men who had an interest in the past it was possible to obtain some information of historical import. We interviewed people from all walks of life and looked for consistency and confirmation in the totality of the material. By doing so we avoided the problem of having to judge the reliability of single testimonies. If a person could give a coherent account (and quite a number of older men were too confused to do so), we considered his contribution to be a valid rendition of what he had heard. Testimonies that provided exceptions could be identified as such when compared with others, sometimes with interesting implications. For example, knowledge of how the exchanges of the Tee cycle and the Great Ceremonial Wars were coordinated was held by the big-men of certain clans only. It was almost as revealing to learn what some people did not know about such matters, and who did not know it, as it was to discover what others did know.

Transforming the Enga oral record into a written one, though necessary if the information is to survive, leaves us with doubts and reservations. The oral record is usually taken with some leeway, as "so-and-so's version or opinion," but what enters the written record is all too often received as fact. The reader should be aware that although our medium is the written word, our methods closely mirror those of local Enga historians. That is, when a new historical tradition is established or an existing one transmitted, information and analysis from the accounts of others may be incorporated to put it in a broader perspective. If certain points or topics do not draw the attention of the receiver, they may be lost. Similarly, in researching and compiling this book we have chosen certain subjects, gathered information on them from different sources, and presented what we found to be the most authoritative and interesting testimonies. Because we could not interview all knowledgeable men and have selected some questions to the neglect of others, information has been lost, as it has been in the men's houses over generations. Enga renditions of historical events are put to the test and corrected when presented in public forums; we tried to duplicate this process by laying out our syntheses to elders for critique.

The essential difference between our work and that of local Enga historians is one of scale. Thanks to technology, modern transportation, and our freedom of movement, we were able to collect and compile information for the entire province rather than for a single tribe. This means that the material is no longer structured from within but must be compiled and ordered from outside. Nonetheless, like all Enga oral traditions, the history presented here can be seen as merely one rendition at the end of a long chain of transmission that has put the information through processes of selection and interpretation. It should be read and understood as such.

1

The Enga, Their Historical Traditions, and Our Approach

When we began our research in 1985, the roads and paths of Enga led us on a journey through a diversity of terrains, each challenging the foot or wheel in a different way. Traveling from the southeast to the west (map 2), the road leaves the steep, narrow valley of the Minamb with its seemingly endless bridges, crosses the deep gorge where the Lai river takes a sharp turn to the north, and then climbs the winding curves into the lush, rolling valley of the Lai. There the landscape is a patchwork of houses, small trade stores, gardens, casuarina forests, grasslands, and ceremonial grounds with their ancient trees and long rows of wooden stakes to which pigs will be tied in an upcoming *tee* exchange.

At Wabag the valley narrows and the road gradually climbs into the high, open, and starkly beautiful grassland of Sirunki, which separates the valleys of the Lai and the Lagaip, Lake Ipea shimmering in its midst. After a rapid descent to Laiagam, where the headwaters of the Lagaip converge to form a basin that seems to contain a whole world within its mountain walls, the road begins to wind its way along the southern slopes of the Lagaip valley. At a number of points where it forms the border between conflicting clans, armed warriors linger by the roadside or pace up and down keeping sentry. Though the characteristic

Enga garden mounds, houses with sloped, thatched roofs, ceremonial grounds, casuarina groves, and foraging pigs measure out the landscape here as in the Lai, there is not the same feeling of abundance in these high, steep valley settlements.

At Mulitaka, the sacred mountain of Mongalo dominates; then the valley narrows and deepens and the road skirts the slopes, yielding spectacular views of valleys to the north. After Tumundan (see map 3) there begins a long, slow climb through the high-altitude rain forest with the anvil-shaped Mount Tongopipi hovering to the south. Upon descent from Mount Maipa the road becomes a terrifying track cut into the mountainside, suspended above the Porgera valley. In 1985 the Porgera valley, a melting pot of Enga, Ipili, and Huli, seemed to be a quiet world of its own, with the smoke of morning fires marking scattered homesteads in the mist. Ten years later the roads were highways, and the valley had been transformed by gold into a bustling mining community almost beyond recognition to those who knew it before.

A trip from north to south yields even greater diversity. To the north of the central valleys is lower, remote, semitropical country, inaccessible by road and merciless on the traveler because of the great distances between communities and the rugged terrain. There is some compensation in its varied gardens and local markets, which offer a wide selection of fruits and vegetables exotic to other regions of Enga. In stark contrast, to the south of the central valleys lies the high country of Kandep with its vast grasslands, forests, and swamps, ever changing in appearance with the cloud cover. The high altitude is immediately apparent from the cold and the sparse distribution of gardens amid acres of long fallow. Signs of wealth are evident only in the long houses constructed for the *yae* pig exchanges and in the monstrously large pigs that emerge from time to time after foraging amid swamp grasses. These are first impressions, and for the visitor who knows that Papua New Guinea is a land in which more than eight hundred different languages are spoken, it is hard to imagine that such a diversity of landscapes could be the home of some two hundred thousand people who share a single language and culture.

The Enga who inhabit this country are a highland agricultural population settled between altitudes of approximately 1,200 and 2,500 meters above sea level (Tumu et al. 1989). First contact with Europeans in major valleys occurred in 1934 when the Leahy brothers ventured briefly into central Enga and the Fox brothers crossed through northernmost Enga while prospecting (Connolly and Anderson 1987; Ballard 1995).[1] Neither party found gold, and so there was a lull in contact with visitors from the outside until Taylor and Black set up a base camp and airstrip at Wabag during their legendary Hagen-Sepik patrol of 1938–39. From 1942 until the end of World War II, Wabag served as a patrol post to keep lines of communication open and provide escape routes for allied troops (Lacey 1982:14–15). In

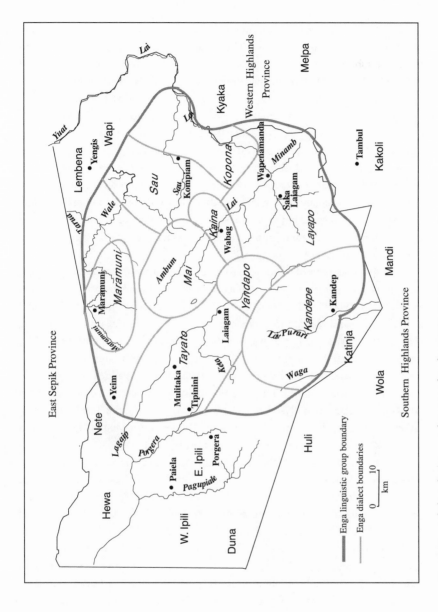

Map 2. Enga dialect divisions and surrounding linguistic groups.

the late 1940s and early 1950s, patrol posts were established at Wapenamanda and Laiagam, and in 1960 at Kandep. The colonial administration appointed local leaders, established a police force, instituted the Australian legal system, and enforced an end to warfare. People were censused and recruited for public works projects such as building roads, patrol tracks, and airstrips (see Gordon and Meggitt 1985). Missionaries simultaneously established churches, schools, agricultural projects, and clinics. In 1975, after Papua New Guinea became independent, Enga was declared a separate province from Western Highlands.

We refer to the period from first contact until 1945-50 as the contact period, because in these years new crops, tools, and ideas were introduced and anticipation of imminent change prevailed, but there was little direct colonial domination. We call the decades between 1945-50 and independence in 1975 the colonial era, for during these years Enga was directly under the rule of the Australian Colonial Administration.

Virtually all aspects of Enga life have been described in the anthropological literature. The comprehensive publications of Mervyn Meggitt (1956, 1957, 1958a, 1964a, 1964b, 1965a, 1965b, 1971, 1973) cover most geographical areas and aspects of life and contain in-depth analyses of social organization (1965a), exchange (1971, 1972, 1974), and warfare (1977). The work of Ralph Bulmer (1960, 1965) has covered the same for the Kyaka Enga of Western Highlands Province (map 2). The studies of Paul Wohlt (1978; 1986) and Eric Waddell (1972) provide a sound understanding of Enga agricultural systems, and those of Daryl Feil (1984) give a detailed analysis of the Tee exchange among the Tombema Enga. Other important works cover Enga religion (Bulmer 1965; Meggitt 1965b; Gibbs 1975, 1977, 1978; Brennan 1977), Tee exchange (Bus 1951; Elkin 1953; Bulmer 1960), kinship (Meggitt 1964b; Feil 1978a), land rights (Lakau 1994), women (Kyakas and Wiessner 1992), environment and health (Feachem 1973, 1975; Sinnett 1975), oral traditions (Lacey 1975, 1979; Talyaga 1975, 1982), and law and order from the beginning of the colonial period until the 1990s (Gordon and Meggitt 1985; Wormsley and Toke 1985; Young 1995).

Considerable regional variation does exist within Enga, as the geography suggests. The linguist Paul Brennan (1982) has divided the current population of Enga into nine mutually intelligible dialect groups (map 2): the Layapo, Kopona, Sau, Kaina, Mai, Yandapo, Tayato, Malamuni (Maramuni), and Kandepe. Nonetheless, different areas share many aspects of economic, social, political, and ritual life. Most Enga subsist as agriculturalists, relying heavily on the cultivation of the sweet potato in an intensive system of mulch mounding to feed pig and human populations. In all regions of Enga, a variety of greens makes an important contribution to the diet, and in regions lying below 2,000 meters there is an ample supply of yams, taro, bananas, and sugarcane. At higher altitudes, where yams and bananas do not survive and taro and sugarcane grow more slowly, the limited range of domestic crops is partially offset by the large tracts of forested land that abound in pandanus and other wild plant foods and shelter marsupials and cassowaries. Throughout Enga great value is placed on pigs, the major social and political currency.

Enga households are well distributed over tribal land, with population densities in 1980 varying from 159 persons per square kilometer of usable land in the central valleys to 5 per square kilometer in fringe areas (Lea and Gray 1982). Land, every person's most precious asset, is owned both individually and by the clan. It is owned individually in that it is passed from father to son or, in some cases, to daughter's descendants. It is owned by the clan in that it may not be transferred to people outside the clan who do not become permanent members, and infringement on the land of individuals is taken as an act of aggression against the clan as a whole. Though there are extensive uninhabited areas at high altitudes and in outlying areas, all land is owned, and little, if any, remains free for the taking.

Politics occupy much of men's time and effort and involve a strong preoccupation with land and exchange. Whereas frequent and destructive warfare creates sharp divisions between clans and claimed the lives of about 25 percent of the male population between 1900 and 1955 (Meggitt 1977), ceremonial exchanges of pork, live pigs, shells, salt, oil, and foodstuffs (and in recent decades, cash) forge alliances and are used to reestablish peace. Ceremonial exchange, which confers prestige on individual families and clans, demands the continual supervision of men as well as the attention and diplomacy of women, who form bridges between groups (Feil 1978b; Kyakas and Wiessner 1992).

Male-female relations are characterized by a separation of the sexes that is more pronounced in the west than in the east. The social evaluation of women is lower than that of men, in part owing to the stigma associated with menstruation. Men operate in the public realm; women exert their wills largely through the private. Until the last few decades, the division between the sexes was strengthened by the existence of separate men's and women's houses. Though Enga adults of the same sex are considered potentially equal, men can make names for themselves, become big-men (kamongo), and wield considerable influence by displaying skill in mediation, in public oration, and in manipulating wealth, among other things. Competition for status and leadership in these arenas is intense. Tolerance for big-men's having several wives, more wealth, and greater influence than others depends heavily on the benefits they provide to their fellow clan members; should they fail to deliver, their demise is rapid. Women generally do not engage in overt competition except during courtship and are not accorded similar public name and fame, though their accomplishments as mothers, gardeners, pig raisers, and private mediators in exchange are acknowledged (Kyakas and Wiessner 1992). Men's status in relation to other men, then, is achieved, in contrast to the status of men and women relative to each other, which is set by ideology.

Political units are stipulated by a segmentary lineage system that divides groups into tribes or phratries (*tata andake*), clans (*tata*), subclans (*yumbange*), and lineages (*akalyanda* or *yumbange yakane*). The basic territorial and cooperative unit is the clan, though clans are part of larger units that we call "tribes."[2] Clans of a tribe are associated by a common origin myth and genealogy that links all members to a tribal founder. In most cases there is no concept of a tribal territory, though fellow clans of a tribe may come to one another's defense when they are attacked by clans from other tribes. All Enga tribes and their constituent clans share a common language.

At the time of Meggitt's studies in the 1950s and 1960s, tribes (phratries) of central Enga (map 3) were composed of between 920 and 5,400 people divided into an average of 7.8 clans with a range of 100 to 1,000 members each (Meggitt 1965a:6–9). Today they are substantially larger. All male members of a tribe trace their genealogies back eight to twelve generations to a common tribal founder through the male line or, in the case of immigrants, through the relevant females or hosts. Until the 1940s to 1950s, many tribes participated as a whole in fertility cults and cooperated in making general plans for the Tee cycle. In central Enga, tribes united to stage the Great Ceremonial Wars. Severe damage to "brother" clans during warfare was avoided. Today, tribal collaboration is generally restricted to elections. Clan members cooperate to defend clan land, to make war, to pay war reparations, and, in most cases, to hold festivals of the Tee cycle; in the past they also staged performances of the bachelors' cults and cults for the ancestors. Subclan and lineage members assist each other in agricultural undertakings and raise bridewealth and funerary payments, among other things.[3]

Marriage is clan exogamous with two exceptions: when a clan has grown very large and is about to split, marriages may occur between people of different subclans; and clan members may marry women from immigrant segments of other subclans. Ideally, descent and residence follow the male line, though in practice there is much flexibility depending on the region and the demographic status of a clan. For eastern and central Enga, about 90 percent of marriages are patrilocal (Meggitt 1965a); in western Enga, the figure is about 70 percent.

Although most Enga are Christians today, their former cosmology and religious beliefs were dominated by two sets of spirit beings: the sky people and their descendants, the ancestors. Though cult performances were held for both, the greatest efforts were directed at communicating with the ancestors, who were believed to play a more active role in the affairs of the living.

The foregoing are features of life familiar to all Enga; they provide common grounds for interregional understanding and cooperation. Many differences also

exist in dialect, dress, subsistence, beliefs, cults, bridewealth payments, war reparation exchanges, large-scale ceremonial exchange, and leadership. We detail
these differences later in their historical contexts.

Origins

Enga historical traditions take the listener on quite a different journey from that
of the roads and paths, one that ventures back over the ridges of time into the
misty past of seven and eight generations ago and sometimes beyond. The time
depth of such traditions is great in comparison with those of most New Guinea
societies, many of whom do not systematically recall events before the time of
their grandfathers or great-grandfathers. Yet archaeologically speaking, this time
span is but a thin layer on top of thick deposits.

The first settlers, immigrants from Asia, are currently thought to have arrived
on the main island of New Guinea from Asia about fifty thousand years ago
(Groube et al. 1986; Swadling 1986). Presumably they reached New Guinea by
island-hopping in crude seacraft at a time of intense glaciation when sea levels
were low. There they encountered unfamiliar mammalian fauna composed almost
exclusively of marsupials, including the now-extinct "giant" wallaby and marsupial
wolf. The climate was much colder than it is today, the high mountains were
permanently snowcapped, and the tree line lay at 2,000 meters, in contrast to
3,500–4,000 meters today. The geography of the main island was also significantly
different. For example, much of what is now the Sepik-Ramu lowlands was
flooded by an inland sea that gradually began to fill in some six thousand years
ago, and the main island of New Guinea was linked to Australia by a land bridge
to form a continent called Sahul. A flora abundant in food sources awaited the
immigrants — sago, coconuts, breadfruit, local bananas, yams, pitpit, sugarcane,
pandanus, other nuts, and a variety of edible greens (Swadling 1986).

Though evidence is scant, it appears that these seafaring people settled in the
lowlands near the coast, where their descendants remained for the next ten thousand to twenty thousand years (Swadling and Hope 1992:23). The earliest known
highland occupation sites, such as Kosipe in Central Province at 2,000 meters, date
back to 24,000–30,000 B.P. (before present). Their inhabitants must have been
primarily hunters and gatherers, though there is also some evidence for early plant
manipulation (Swadling and Hope 1992:27). After 14,000 B.P., the climate began to
warm and highland settlements spread; by 10,000 B.P., most of the major highland
valleys were occupied and some of the world's oldest agriculture was being
practiced in the Waghi valley (Golson 1977, 1981, 1982). The presence of seashells
in archaeological sites indicates that trade between the highlands and the coast

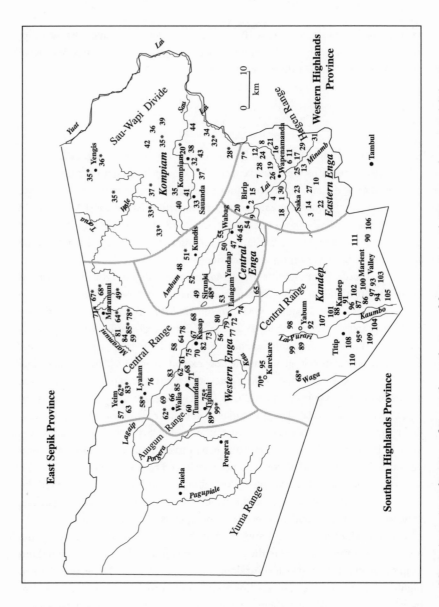

Map 3. Approximate locations of Enga tribes at the time of first contact with Europeans, by area and dialect group.

EASTERN ENGA

Layapo
1. Aluni
2. Depe
3. Gipini*
4. Itokone
5. Kandawalini
6. Kumbi*
7. Lungupini (2)
8. Lyakani* (Sikini)
9. Lyipini
10. Lyomoi
11. Maini*
12. Matea* (Sikini)
13. Nenaini
14. Pauakaka
15. Pumalini
16. Pyaini
17. Pyapini
18. Sikini
19. Sinyi
20. Tinilapini (2)
21. Tokopetaini
22. Ulidane*
23. Waimini

24. Waipalini* (Depe)
25. Wauni
26. Yakumane
27. Yambatane
28. Yandamani (2)
29. Yatapaki
30. Yoko
31. Yoponda

KOMPIAM

Sau and Kopona
32. Aiyamane
33. Aiyele (3)
34. Inapini
35. Kungu (4)**
36. Ingi (2)
37. Lakani (3)
38. Lyongeni
39. Nenge*
40. Pumane
41. Tiaka**
42. Waitini
43. Yangutini*
44. Yangini/Pakaini (Yakani)

CENTRAL ENGA

Mai and Yandapo
45. Apulini (2)
46. Awaini
47. Itapuni
48. Kunalini (2)
49. Lyaini
50. Malipini
51. Potealini
52. Sakalini
53. Tia
54. Yakani
55. Yanaitini

WESTERN ENGA

Upper Lagaip/Tayato
56. Angalaini
57. Auwini
58. Kaiya (2)
59. Kamani
60. Kisipini
61. Konemane
62. Kundiki (3)
63. Lambuaka
64. Limbini (2)

65. Lote
66. Maeyango
67. Monaini (2)
68. Mulapini (4)
69. Pandame
70. Piandane (2)
71. Pumane (2)
72. Pyaini
73. Sakate
74. Sambe
75. Tekepaini (2)
76. Tiwini
77. Tombe*
78. Tupini (2)
79. Walini
80. Waitini
81. Wawini
82. Yambanima
83. Yandape (2)
84. Yangi
85. Yangutini (2)

KANDEP

Atone and Katinja
86. Aimbatepa

87. Akulya*
88. Alitipa
89. Bipi (3)
90. Enza*
91. Ima
92. Kamani
93. Kambia*
94. Kambitipa
95. Kapini (2)
96. Kototepa
97. Kupatopa*
98. Kunalini
99. Kuu (2)
100. Lyatepa*
101. Lyumbi
102. Mamba*
103. Masa*
104. Maulu
105. Mondatepa*
106. Pima*
107. Tatali
108. Timitopa
109. Yalipuni
110. Yamape
111. Yamatepa*

Note: Many tribes are dispersed; only major branches in outlying areas are shown on the map. Numbers in parentheses indicate the number of branches shown. We hope to have covered 90 percent of the tribes in Enga. Tribes of the Waga valley are excluded, as may be some tribes of outlying areas.

*small groups
**Kungu-Tiaka are also known as Sene-Yokasa.

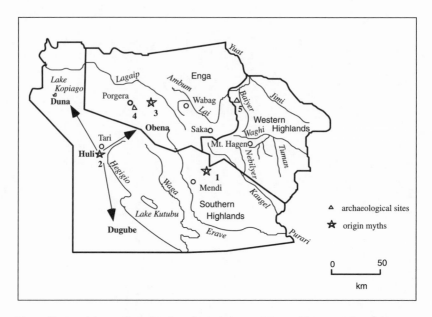

Map 4. Enga origin myths and archaeological sites. 1, Mount Giluwe origin myth; 2, Hela origin myth; 3, Mount Mongalo origin myth; 4, Kutepa rock shelter; 5, Yuku rock shelter.

was well established by this time. When and how pigs, Asian taro, yams, and bananas first reached New Guinea are matters of debate, although these items are known to have been present for at least five thousand years. Since feral pigs were not found in Australia at the time of European colonization, it is likely that pigs were introduced after about 6000 B.P., when rising sea levels at the end of the last glacial had flooded the Torres straits, separating New Guinea from the continent of Australia (White and O'Connell 1982).

Enga provides no exception to the general prehistory of highland valleys. Excavations carried out by Sue Bulmer at Yuku rock shelter (1,300 meters above sea level) in the Baiyer region on the eastern border of Enga have reached basal layers that were occupied twelve thousand years ago; remaining ones may go back another five thousand years (White and O'Connell 1982:57) (map 4). Those at Kutepa rock shelter in the Porgera valley excavated by Jo Mangi have revealed at least ten thousand years of periodic occupation at 2,300 meters. Debris in the early levels of Yuku and in most levels of Kutepa suggests that the sites were occupied by hunter-gatherers or people on hunting-gathering or trading expeditions.

Pollen evidence from Lake Birip in the middle Lai valley has been interpreted as indicating that forest clearance began approximately four thousand years ago as the result of agriculture, most likely that based on taro (Golson 1977, 1982).

Some thousands of years then passed until the sweet potato was introduced between about 250 and 400 years ago. In the mid-1600s came the "time of darkness," *yuu kuia*, when the volcano on Long Island erupted, covering the highlands with a layer of ash and blocking out the sun for two to four days. Around the time of these two events or shortly after, Enga historical traditions, *atome pii*, joined the stream of Enga oral tradition and began to record history in a more systematic manner.

Enga myth and cosmology posit quite different beginnings. Though myths explaining the origin of the Enga are numerous, we will mention three central ones that influence Enga perceptions of their past. The first comes from the origin tradition of the Maragomoye tribe, Kakoli speakers in the Kaugel valley of Western Highlands Province near the eastern border of Enga. It has been adopted by the Enga as well, because it provides the origin tradition of the major Enga tribes in the Saka valley. The mythical ancestor of the Maragomoye, Anda Kopa, lived on the slopes of Mount Giluwe (map 4), from which he mastered the land and bush, cultivating all kinds of food crops (see Didi 1982a, 1982b). When he was ready to harvest, he sent a message to all corners of the "world" for people to come to a giant feast just above the tree line on Mount Giluwe. Hundreds of people turned up, and since Anda Kopa did not have accommodations for all of them, he uncovered some of his earth ovens at daybreak and distributed different kinds of food to people from the various regions—Mendi, Ialibu, and Mount Hagen, among others—so that they could return home that day. Other pits were never opened. Humps found in the local landscape and depressions that hold water are said to be the unopened and opened earth ovens, respectively. This myth is used to explain, among other things, the distribution of peoples and the foods they cultivate.[4]

The Enga version follows a young man named Kiualumaita and his sister, who set off in the direction of Tambul in the upper Kaugel valley. The young woman is said to have chosen the "heavy" foods that grow well at high altitudes. She settled at Tambul, where she gave birth to the founders of the Yanuni and Kisane tribes. Her brother, bearing the "lighter" foods, went to the Saka valley and eventually established his permanent residence at Alumanda. He married and had a son named Pembe, the founding father of most Saka valley tribes.

Although the details of the Anda Kopa myth are not widely known in Enga today, its influence is still great. There is a pervasive belief in easternmost Enga that all Saka tribes, some Layapo ones, and most cultural innovations ultimately came from the direction of Mount Giluwe (see also Lacey 1975:98). As we shall see later, there is no evidence whatsoever that this was the case, though certainly the long history of interaction between the people of the Saka, Kaugel, and north Mendi regions expressed in the myth is substantiated by historical narratives.

Western Enga tell another story, with humor. It begins with a man named Andaita and his sister, Itame. Itame had neither a vagina nor a urinary opening. She found that if she rubbed her vaginal area against a *matopa* tree, it gave her a pleasant warm sensation and relieved an itch, so she began to do so regularly. When her brother discovered what she was doing, he planted a sharp chip of stone in the tree that opened her vagina. As the myth goes, without embarrass-ment or fear of incest she showed him her wound, he comforted her, they slept together, and over the years they had three children, the first of whom was called Tita. Tita was said to have come up from the west and settled for some time in the Kiunga area (see map 1) near the Ok Tedi mining site, where his wife gave birth to a son, Hela. Hela had four sons—Hela Kuli (Huli), Hela Opone (Obena), Hela Dugube, and Hela Duna. They shared a men's house until one day Opone and Kuli discovered that their brothers were consuming human flesh. Instantly they spoke different languages and separated. Hela Dugube became the forefa-ther of peoples on the Papuan plateau whom Enga call Duguba, and Hela Duna became the forefather of the Duna near Lake Kopiago (map 4). Hela Kuli and Hela Obena went to the northeast, Hela Kuli staying near Tari and becoming the founding ancestor of the Huli. Obena, his brother, settled in the Kandep region of Enga and became the founder of the western Enga.[5] Among other things, the myth is used to validate the close relationship between the Enga and Huli that exists today. Different versions are told by the Huli and Duna (Glasse 1965; Ballard 1995); modern ones relate it to the distribution of mineral wealth at Ok Tedi, Porgera, and the oil fields of Southern Highlands Province.

Other origin myths place Enga origins in Enga, claiming that they descended from the mythical sky people (Meggitt 1965b:49–52).[6] Among these, one of the most popular tells of a man and woman, the first people, who lived near Mulitaka in the Lagaip valley. The woman gave birth to a son, and when the baby cried, her husband told her not to breast-feed it but to wait until he fetched a gourd of water from the sacred spring on Mount Mongalo. She waited and waited, growing impatient as the baby cried. The husband reached the spring and filled the gourd, and before he began his journey home, he called down from the mountain:

"Katambii [stay or live]?" When the woman didn't answer, he called the same again twice.

Then he called, "Kumambi [die]?" and she answered, "Yes." He then knew that he had fetched the *yalipa endake* [water of life] too late—that the baby had been given breast milk instead. And so humans became mortal.

There is no way to determine from the scant archaeological evidence available whether Enga descended from those who had inhabited the province for thousands of years, as the Mount Mongalo myth implies, or whether they came in later migrations from the east or west. Certainly, by three hundred to five hundred years ago the central valleys were well populated with the ancestors of the current Enga. It is at this time that oral traditions begin to describe past events in more factual terms.

Before turning to these events, we discuss the value of different kinds of Enga oral traditions as historical sources by examining their contexts of production, their transmission, function, structure, chronological framework, and historical content, and their apparent strengths and biases. Our aim is not to classify and analyze oral sources; such work has been done by Roderic Lacey (1975, 1979, 1980, 1981) with great clarity, sensitivity, and appreciation. It is, rather, to offer some idea of the material that is available and how we used it.

Enga Oral Traditions as Historical Sources

History underlies all matters of public concern in Enga and therefore surfaces continually in public forums. Land disputes cannot be resolved outside of their historical contexts, the settlement of wars hinges to a large degree on the history of relations between opposing groups, exchange often follows the paths of those who went before, and lessons of the past are recounted to those who threaten to make rash decisions. Historical knowledge is thus an important source of power and influence for Enga people. It is imparted to male clan members who seek it and demonstrate that they are competent to understand it, place it in its proper context, and use it for the benefit of the group. Today, few young men take an interest in history, but in the past, most young men learned their basic tribal history informally in the men's houses from their fathers, uncles, or grandfathers. Those who sought more active public roles continually built upon this corpus of knowledge whenever the opportunity arose: during bachelors' initiations, visits, clan meetings, exchange festivals, and many other occasions. Aspects of history that do not touch on issues of current contention may be told to relatives in other clans or tribes but rarely are retained by them in any detail. This diverse body of information, passed on by so many people in a multitude of different contexts, has been an important part of Enga cultural heritage for generations.

Enga distinguish between myth (*tindi pii*) and history (*atome pii*), and only in origin traditions are the two intertwined: widely known myths are fitted with factual details relevant to tribal identity. The following list gives a working classification of oral traditions. We did not systematically collect myths, poetry, magic formulas, songs, or proverbs, and so these are combined into general categories. Systematic investigation of their structure and content, a fascinating topic, awaits future work.

1. Myth (*tindi pii*). Free text, preferably told in rhythmic chant.
   a. Myths and tales.
   b. Origin myths for cults.
2. Historical traditions (*atome pii*).
   a. Tribal origin traditions (*tee pia*). Free text with stories embellished by narrators, but historical information such as names of tribal founders and their spouses, places of origin, and subsistence strategies of tribal founders are transmitted with little alteration. Approximately one-third of origin traditions are told via myth.
   b. Genealogy linking the narrator to the tribal founder. Fixed sequence extended with each new generation.
   c. Historical narratives concerning any historical events of interest. Free text.
   d. Metaphorical legends recording historical events. Free text.
   e. Historical traditions of the colonial era. Free text.
3. Other forms of oral tradition.
   a. Praise poems from the bachelors' cults recording the history of the sacred objects (*sangai titi pingi nemongo*). Fixed, formalized text with generational additions made by senior bachelors.
   b. Magic formulas and sacred poetry for cults (called *nemongo* prefaced by words indicating the cult or cult rites during which they were recited). Fixed, formalized text.
   c. Magic formulas for private, personal ritual (*nemongo*). Fixed, formalized text.
   e. Songs (*wee*). Lyrics fixed, although names and places may be changed to fit the occasion.
   f. Proverbs (*kongali pii*). Fixed text.

Note that *pii*, as in *atome pii* and *tindi pii*, means "word" in Enga. *Tee pia* is a form of the verb *tee pingi*, which means to begin.

Myths

Myths or tales (*tindi pii*) make up the largest body of Enga oral traditions and deal with a broad range of subjects (see Meggitt 1976). They are told in the evening while people lie around the fireside with eyes closed. When narrated by masters, they are recited in a poetic chant with repetitive rhythmic patterns and rhyme. Complex and colorful images are used to challenge listeners and hold their attention. A single myth can go on for over an hour, requiring extraordinary verbal skill on the part of the narrator.

Myths are stories that do not claim to record actual historical events. Because they are embellished by skilled storytellers, they can increase in length and detail over time, whereas historical traditions tend to dwindle. In most cases, myths are of value for disclosing attitudes and worldviews, but because they are not associated with a particular tribe or period of time, they remain out of historical context. It is thus difficult to say whether the conditions, events, and relationships they describe were of significance in the past, and if so, when, where, why, and to whom. Some myths may indeed encode valuable information which predates that contained in historical traditions. Unfortunately, it is difficult to determine whether a myth or passages of it are ancient or relatively recent, since myths appear to be continually updated.[7]

Myth and history run parallel to one another and overlap only in tribal origin traditions, where myths may be used as vehicles to transmit historical facts about tribal lifestyle, location, neighbors, and political ties at the time when historical narratives began to be regularly transmitted in men's houses. Similarly, cult origin myths may provide valuable information on a cult's underlying ideology, basic tenets, and historical spread. Later in the book we use some information from tribal origin traditions to construct a baseline from which to look at change. We analyze cult origin myths in the chapters on ancestral and bachelors' cults. We restrict our use of myth largely to these two applications, and we always specify when we have derived information from mythical rather than from historical traditions.

Historical Traditions

Historical traditions (*atome pii*) are narratives that originated in eyewitness accounts and have been passed down over the generations. They are intended to relay factual information about conditions, events, and relations of the past. The skeleton of Enga historical traditions includes an origin tradition for each tribe— *tee pia* ("beginnings")—and a genealogy tracing tribal members to the founding ancestor through the male line. The earliest generations of persons named in the genealogies are fictive and serve to define tribal structure, and the accompanying oral traditions are often, but not always, mythical in nature. During or immediately after the generation of subclan founders (about seven generations ago), there is a noticeable break, and brief, somewhat dry historical traditions begin to record real people and events, particularly those concerning relations of people to land: major battles, dispersal within tribal lands, migrations, and the generations in which they occurred. The core of tribal histories thus defines Enga social and political divisions from the tribe down to the individual family. It gives them an identity, ties them to specific tracts of land, and recalls important relations with surrounding groups. A wide range of information on other topics—subsistence, agriculture, cults, ceremonial exchange, trade, and environmental crises—is included in many clan histories.

The point at which historical traditions began to be systematically passed on in the men's houses in their current forms is hard to establish, though certainly they were well grounded by the seventh generation before the present (which we consider to be 1990), and they continue into current times. Historical traditions do not begin where myths leave off, but rather join the stream of oral tradition around the seventh to eighth generation before present and run parallel to myth from that time onward. Mythical and historical traditions intertwine only briefly in tribal and cult origin traditions.

Genealogies

Genealogy is an essential feature of all Enga tribal histories. It establishes social and political divisions, ties groups to certain tracts of land, and specifies relations to one or more other tribes. For individuals it confers identity and defines obligations as a member of a certain tribe, clan, subclan, and lineage. All Enga genealogies trace men to the founding ancestors of their tribes through the male line, although female links are often remembered if a man joined the clan of his wife, mother, or some other female relative. In eastern and central Enga, where land inheritance is more strictly patrilineal, sons, but not daughters, are systematically remembered unless marriages of daughters created important exchange ties or brought new members into the clan. In western Enga, where bilateral land inheritance is more common, both sons and daughters may be remembered, but genealogies still follow the male line. Genealogical knowledge is passed on from father to son in the men's houses, so few women have in-depth knowledge of genealogies, though they are fluent in the complexities of current kinship relations.

Enga genealogies extend back approximately ten generations, the shortest that we collected being eight and the longest fourteen. They can be divided into two parts: the first appears to record fictive or "representative" founding ancestors—tribal, clan, and sometimes subclan founders—and the second, real persons born into the subclan from the sixth or seventh generation until the first, or most recent. Most of the variation in the lengths of genealogies comes from the number of generations for the first part.

A typical Enga genealogy begins with a founding ancestor, often nonhuman, who is said to have given birth to a human ancestor. Nonhuman ancestors, including marsupials, snakes, birds, and insects, are more common in the genealogies of western Enga tribes. The sons of founding ancestors may be the tribal founders, or there may be one or two generations between the founding ancestor and the tribal founders, particularly when the founding ancestor is nonhuman. Clan founders are usually the sons (or, in some 10-20 percent of cases, daughters) of the tribal founders. In fifteen out of eighty tribes (19 percent) for which we have good information, there exists an additional generation between tribal and clan founders. These are all large tribes with more than six constituent clans.

A few genealogies, known only by tribal leaders, are much more encompassing. For example, that of tribes in the Saka valley, following the Mount Giluwe origin myth given earlier, links the tribe descended from Pembe's sons (Yambatane, Pauakaka, Waimini, and Sikini) to the descendants of his sisters in the Tambul region (Yanuni and Kisane) as well as to immigrants from Tambul (Lyomoi) and Mendi (Aiyamane, Ulidane, and Gipini) who moved to the Saka valley to join in-laws.

When learning their genealogies, men follow a direct line from the founding ancestor down to themselves, listing all sons and sometimes daughters born to their forefathers of each generation. An example is the following genealogy of Kakyo, a man from the Yanaitini tribe near Wabag, with the generations numbered in descending order:

11. Sons of Pondoliane
    (founding ancestor)
    a. Itokone
    b. Namuni
10. Sons of Namuni
    a. Yanaitini (tribal
       founder)
    b. Kainawaingya
9. Sons of Yanaitini
    a. Kepa
    b. Paule
8. Sons of Paule (clan
    founders)[8]
    a. Kalinatae
    b. Piao
    c. Neneo
    d. Kokope
    e. Kondakana
7. Sons of Neneo
    (subclan founders)
    a. Tepetae

    b. Epolo
6. Sons of Tepetae
    a. Wangalya
    b. Kupakapo
5. Sons of Wangalya
    a. Aiya
    b. Kalyenge
4. Son of Aiya
    a. Naoene
3. Sons of Naoene
    a. Kapyakotae
    b. Lyopolo
    c. Wakaitane
    d. Mendalane
    e. Aiyuni
2. Son of Kapyakotae
    a. Kakyo
1. Sons of Kakyo
    a. Tanoa
    b. Pilipus
    c. Leas

Other men give short forms of their genealogy, listing only the one son of each forefather in their direct line. For instance, for sons of Yanaitini, only Paule would be given, and for sons of Paule, only Neneo, and so on. Discrepancies in the exact relationships of persons in the founding generations of genealogies are fairly common, because, as many informants recognize, they are simply formalized schemes that represent groups and alliances in the past.[9] Different versions rarely display major contradictions, however. One version might list the founders of associated tribes as "brothers" while another lists them as "cousins," but the fact of positive affiliation remains constant. Seniority in the early generations has little import. That an independent clan today claims to be founded by the tribal founder's son rather than by a grandson, for example, implies neither dominance nor superiority within the tribal structure.[10] From the generation of subclan founders on, far fewer inconsistencies are found.

Enga genealogies raise some difficult questions. On one hand, we know, and many Enga also recognize, that the early generations are formalized schemes for defining social and political organization. Parts of Enga have been inhabited for at least ten thousand years, and certainly the population of Enga did not stem from a few persons who lived some eight to ten generations ago. On the other hand, genealogies of more recent generations seem to keep fairly accurate records of males, and in some cases females, born into a tribe who survived at least to late adolescence or early adulthood. To see whether we could find a cutoff point between the formalized sector that lays out tribal structure and more factual portions of genealogies, we analyzed 166 personal genealogies collected from eighty-six tribes. This analysis, described in Appendix 1, indicated that the break fell between the generation of clan founders and that of subclan founders, and that fairly accurate recording of males born into a tribe began to be kept either in the generation of subclan founders or in the next. This is also implied in accompanying oral traditions: superhuman deeds are attributed to founding ancestors, tribal founders, and sometimes clan founders, but the characters and exploits of men in subsequent generations are more mundane.

The structure of genealogy raises the question of why most clans began systematically to pass on records of their members and major events starting around the sixth to eighth generation before the present. That is, if historical traditions had always been told by father or grandfather to son to specify kinship relations and relate life experiences, then why, at a certain point, was the time span they covered greatly lengthened? One possible answer is that this is the time when the effects of the sweet potato were beginning to take hold—when people began to garden more intensively and so were concerned with establishing rights to tracts of land. Genealogy has everything to do with land inheritance.

Carefully collected genealogies of entire clans can provide a wealth of information on matters such as the growth or decline of clans, immigration, emigration, mortality rates from tribal fighting, and polygamy (for example, see Meggitt 1958a; Wohlt 1978; Talyaga 1984). To have systematically collected such genealogies, however, was beyond the scope of our project. We were able to record only the personal genealogies of individuals interviewed, restricting our use of genealogy to (1) establishing a chronological framework by which to order past events; (2) charting tribal composition in early generations to better track subsequent growth (or decline) and dispersal of tribes; and (3) estimating the size of the population of Enga in the generation of subclan founders. Let us first take a look at genealogical chronology.

GENEALOGICAL CHRONOLOGY   Enga measure the passage of time over the short and the long run. For short-term time reckoning, there is a calendar that divides the year into twelve paired lunar months.[11] Enga do not keep track of years, even though the counting system used in the Tee cycle has the capacity to do so. Rather, events within a lifetime are ordered by life stages, and beyond that they are sequenced by generation in genealogies. Enga are aware of the number of generations in their genealogies and during recitations often count them off on their fingers to make sure they have omitted none. To use genealogy to order events by generation, together with using stages of the life cycle to place them within the span of a generation, is thus consistent with Enga time reckoning.

The idea underlying genealogical chronology (Vansina 1985:183-85) is that one generation—the time from the birth of a person to the birth of his or her first surviving child—represents a certain number of years on average. The number of years per generation for any society depends on who is given in a genealogy—men or women—and the average age at which they marry. For Enga, only sons who survive to adulthood are systematically recorded, and thus a generation in Enga genealogy is the time from the birth of a man to the birth of his first surviving son. Average age at marriage in the past was about twenty-five for men (Meggitt 1965a; Wohlt 1978); accordingly, it would be reasonable to say that a generation should be approximately thirty years (Lacey 1975:27).

The application of genealogical chronology to Enga historical traditions must take different time periods into consideration. For the first three to four generations before the present, it is possible to date events roughly using first contact as a benchmark for verification. We used the following reasoning to do so: most of the men whom we interviewed were between sixty-five and eighty and had adult sons between thirty-five and fifty. We defined the latter as the first generation. When an event was placed in somebody's lifetime, informants usually meant the most socially and politically active period of his life—between the ages of about thirty and sixty. Otherwise they said, "When so-and-so was very young or very old," and so on. If members of the first generation were, on the average, forty-five years old in 1990, then events placed in their adult lifetimes would extend back fifteen years and continue fifteen years on into the future—in other words, between 1975 and 2005. By the same logic, events placed in the adult lifetime of the second generation would have occurred between 1975 and 1945, and so on.

Theoretically, one could continue with this method of dating, but we are reluctant to do so beyond the fourth generation.[12] Events of the fourth generation occurred when the grandfathers of most men interviewed were adults, and so they are often remembered in some detail. In the fifth or sixth generation before the present, events become truly third- or fourth-hand, something that can be immediately sensed from the decline in detail. It is very possible that some telescoping occurs from the fifth generation on back—that more distant events are pulled forward and compressed into a single generation. At any rate, one can no longer assume that generations spanned approximately thirty years. Yet because events ascribed to the fifth, sixth, seventh, and sometimes eighth generations before the present do show chronological consistency (that is, one tradition does not place a migration in the seventh generation while another describes the same group in its place of origin in the sixth), it appears that genealogy can still be used to sequence events of this period.

After the seventh or eighth generation, one arrives in the time of clan founders, tribal founders, and founding nonhuman ancestors. We refer to this period as the time of the "founding generations." Some important events are attributed to the founding generations, such as the introduction of the sweet potato and the renowned "time of darkness" mentioned earlier. The latter, which Russell Blong (1982:193) has dated to the mid-1600s on the basis of radiocarbon analysis, provides the only fixed date we have for the founding generations. Unfortunately, there is no way to sequence events from this era or to know how long a time span it covers. Our best guess, based on analogy with the current pattern—that memory is fairly vivid until grandfather's or great-grandfather's generation—is that historical traditions attributed to the founding generations would be unlikely to stretch more than three to four generations beyond that of subclan founders, or to the mid- to early 1600s. Certainly, some kinds of historical records were kept prior to that time, but whether or not any of this information is still retained in myth is an intriguing question.

With fixed dates available only for the beginning and end of the period considered, the best chronology we can provide is shown in Table 1. One further note of caution: we found that genealogical chronology stood up to some tough tests for internal consistency if, and only if, the informant's genealogy had been recorded on paper and the event placed during the lifetime of a specific named person. Statements that an event occurred in the lifetime of

Table 1

Methods Used for Dating Events in Enga Historical Traditions

Generation	Approximate Date	Method of Estimating Time	Event
1	2005–1975	Fixed events	Independence, 1975
2	1975–1945	Fixed events	Numerous events of colonial era
3	1945–1915	Fixed events	Leahy brothers, 1934; Taylor, 1938-39
4	1915–1885	Estimated from age at time of first contact with Europeans	
5	1885–ca. 1855	Events sequenced	
6	Unknown	Events sequenced	
7	Unknown	Events sequenced	
Founding	Unknown	None	Time of darkness, mid-1600s

somebody's grandfather or great-grandfather were often just another way of saying, "It happened long ago."

TRACKING TRIBAL DISPERSAL   A second and important use of genealogy was to track the growth (or decline) and dispersal of tribes. For the founding generations, constituent clans of a tribe are named and their general locations indicated in accompanying origin legends. By comparing this genealogical information with lists of current clans and their locations, we were able to systematically map structural and locational changes. For instance, if a tribal founder was said to have had five sons but the descendants of only four could be located, then we knew to ask about the descendants of the fifth: had they died out, joined another group, or migrated to another region? This method uncovered cases of immigration and emigration and of groups that had died out or fragmented that otherwise would have been overlooked.

ESTIMATING POPULATION SIZE   The third use of genealogy was to obtain a rough estimate of the size of the population of Enga in the seventh generation before the present—the generation of the subclan founders. Briefly, we calculated the number of subclan founders from genealogies for the tribes of different areas of Enga, because subclan founders appear to have been the first real individuals recorded in genealogies. Then, assuming that these men were heads of households, we multiplied the number of subclan founders by average household size for Enga to obtain a minimum estimate of average clan size. Our methods are described in greater detail in chapter 2 and Appendix 2.

Origin Traditions

All Enga tribes have origin traditions, *tee pia*, that give the name of the tribal founder, the names of his children, his place of origin or residence, and often additional information about his lifestyle and relations with surrounding groups. Tribal traditions are free texts passed on informally in the men's houses, and they provide powerful symbols of group identity. Origin traditions do not always describe "beginnings": of ninety-eight origin traditions that were confirmed by several elders, thirty began with historical narratives concerning migration, fourteen with legends concerning the exploits of tribal founders,[13] and twenty-nine with mere identification of the tribal founder, his location or original place of residence, and the names of his siblings and children. For the remaining twenty-five, elaborate myths were used to transmit similar information. Migration traditions give place of origin, reason for and generation of migration, final destination, and sometimes description of the journey. Such information could usually be confirmed at both ends, unless the point of departure of the migrant group was far outside the study area.

Narratives about tribal founders include their places of residence, exploits, marriages, lifestyles, and relations with others, and they appear to have been based originally on real conditions or events. Myths used to transmit origin traditions are usually adapted from traditional stories told throughout the highlands and fitted with facts to make them relevant to tribal identity. Enga regard the plot of the myth as fiction but the added information as history. For example, one myth told in many parts of the highlands has been adopted as the origin myth for two separate Enga tribes. It begins with a hawk who finds a baby hanging in a net bag, kidnaps him, and brings him up as his son. When it comes time for the young man to marry, the hawk flies out to find him a wife. Feigning injury, he lures the woman to the house of the young man. They fall in love, get married, and have sons who become tribal founders.

When this myth was borrowed by the Sambe-Kunalini tribes, important additions were made: the hawk kidnaps the baby from Kandep, brings him up on marsupial meat, and builds him a house where he can settle permanently at Papyuka near Laiagam. He steals tools from agriculturalists in the Lai valley and teaches his son to become a gardener. When his son grows up, the hawk lures a wife for him from the Lai valley; they marry and have two sons, Sambe and Kunalini. Informants generally agree that the added facts have significance: that the baby was stolen from the Kandep area points to early associations with Kandep. That the hawk taught his son to be a gardener and built him a permanent house may imply a change in lifestyle from heavy dependence on hunting and gathering to sedentary agriculture — certainly other Sambe-Kunalini historical narratives suggest a strong dependence on the forest in the past. The luring of the wife from the Lai valley represents past marriage ties with tribes of eastern Enga, a claim confirmed at both ends. The origin myth of the Yalipuni tribe of southwestern Kandep is based on the same myth, but fitted with different details suggesting migration from the Aenda *semonda* (tribe) of the Nipa area in Southern Highlands Province (see Sillitoe 1979:43).

To obtain further insight into the historical value of origin myths, we collected several versions of the same myth from different branches of a tribe and compared them for internal consistency. We then sought confirmation in the traditions of neighboring or related tribes and contrasted the relations between groups as described in origin traditions with those of recent decades. The last method in particular gave some measure of whether origin traditions had been updated to legitimate current relations.

The results from comparing versions of the same origin myth from different clans of a tribe revealed great variation in length and complexity of the plot, but information concerning residence of tribal founder, place of origin, environment, and lifestyle was remarkably consistent. "Cousin" or "brother" affiliations with surrounding tribes were almost always agreed upon. There were no cases in which two tribes claimed the same place of origin unless they were brother tribes, and brotherhood in the past was always acknowledged by both parties. Brother tribes or neighboring ones described either similar modes of subsistence for their tribal founders or a division of labor — one brother a gardener and the other a hunter. As for the wives of tribal founders, for complex tribes with several branches there was sometimes inconsistency in the wives' clans of origin but not in the region from which they came. This is not surprising, because tribal founders' marriages presumably represent more general alliances of the past that may have differed from clan to clan. Interestingly, the marriages of tribal founders, though undoubtedly representative and not real, could usually be confirmed in the tribes of wife-givers, reaffirming that alliances did exist in the past. Thus, it is probably fair to say that though the plots of origin myths in and of themselves have little to do with history, they are vehicles for communicating information about past tribal composition, location, relations, and identity.

We then compared the present-day locations of and relations between twenty-three pairs of tribes that claimed to have been "brothers" in the past: six were still closely allied, ten had separated in space and had little to do with each other, and seven had clearly hostile relations. With regard to residence, of eighty tribes that were in the province at the beginning of their oral histories for whom we had good information, fifty-six still had major groups near their place of origin, whereas twenty-four had been almost totally displaced. Displacement was always acknowledged by both those who were expelled and by the victors who took the land. In short, certain facts added to Enga origin traditions seem not to have been revised from generation to generation to provide charters for the present. Rather, narrators often related differences between present and past with considerable interest. On these grounds we used information contained in origin traditions to (1) map the composition and locations of tribes in about the seventh generation before the present, (2) describe their subsistence bases, when possible, and (3) obtain a rough sketch of each tribe's relations with surrounding groups.

Historical Narratives

Factual historical narratives, *atome pii*, in free texts that have neither mythical qualities nor formal structure make up the greater part of historical traditions. They begin in the founding generations and continue into the present. The bulk of *atome pii* concern matters related to land, such as tribal dispersal, migration, and warfare, though they contain information on a variety of other topics as well: *tee* exchange, trade, environmental disasters, construction of new men's houses, ceremonial grounds, and gardens, bachelors' cults, ancestral cults, and developments in songs and forms of dress, among other things. Historical narratives may be held by families, subclans, clans, or tribes. They are passed on in men's houses for education, interest, or entertainment and are used actively in discussions during clan meetings and in a variety of other contexts. All men have more or less equal access to such information if they seek it. Unlike myths, which may be told by men or women, historical traditions are men's domain, and beyond events that took place within living memory, it is impossible to uncover women's perspectives.

The sources of historical traditions are eyewitness accounts that are broadened in the years that follow. For example, if a young man takes part in a war, he will come home from battle with a limited view. Experiences shared in the men's house during evening discussions will widen his perspective. Because most wars have lasting political implications, the subject will crop up again and again over the years, and he will place the event in an ever broader political framework. The testimony that he passes on to his sons, his grandsons, or researchers is an eyewitness account analyzing and vividly portraying his own experiences along with what he has learned from others throughout his lifetime. We make extensive use of such expanded eyewitness testimonies in the chapters on war reparations, leadership, cults, and the Great Ceremonial Wars.

Sons and grandsons tend to take a genuine interest in the exploits of their fathers and grandfathers, and so some of them are likely to pass on eyewitness accounts accurately and in detail. What is transmitted is neither a fixed text nor an entirely free personal rendition, but something in between. One might say that people try to reproduce historical narratives as accurately as possible without resorting to rote memorization. If they get something wrong or bend the tradition to suit their interests, they are corrected by others when their versions surface in public discussion. The corrective factor must have been strong in the past, because versions of a given historical tradition collected in different clans or subclans rarely contradict one another on major points. Though historical narratives seem not to be revised to legitimate current schemes, the addition of each new tradition to the repertoire puts former ones in a different perspective — farther back in that chapter of Enga history, so to speak. For instance, a narrative describing war between two groups might be eclipsed by another concerning subsequent *tee* exchange, or vice versa. That both are maintained provides a broad historical repertoire that can be called on selectively to serve the interests of the moment. For example, either hostile relations of the sixth generation or friendly ones of the third could be evoked to justify current action.

What might be called an "egalitarian" effect also comes into play. Though some family traditions may boast of the accomplishments of their forefathers of recent generations, these are underplayed when told to broader audiences who might otherwise ridicule them. Following the Enga norms that all men are in principle equal and that those who gain the status of big-men represent their clans, individual names in history are often replaced by clan names, and individuals are credited with successes but not elevated to the status of heroes. Myth has its heroes and heroines in the immortal sky people, but seldom is such status attributed to their mortal descendants.

By the next generation, the event has become more remote — few people, if any, know someone who was directly involved in it, and so the fate of the narrative is left up to chance. Should it fall on the ears of an avid local historian or somebody with a particular interest in what it describes, it may continue to be transmitted painstakingly. This is by no means always the case. With each generation that passes, information that fails to draw attention is lost, and many historical traditions become shorter — by the sixth or seventh generation they are often, though certainly not always, mere sketches. Comparison of different testimonies indicates that it is loss of information rather than distortion that creates the most severe biases, often very frustrating ones. Whereas questioning could fill in gaps for more recent occurrences, it drew blanks for earlier ones: the narrator had heard only what he told in his testimony and could say no more. As one moves back into the founding generations, however, historical narratives stop dwindling, perhaps because it is only highly significant events from this period that are transmitted.

Historical narratives or, for recent times, eyewitness accounts provide the backbone of information on which we draw. They are not uniform: their nature, quantity, quality, function, and biases vary with each topic we discuss. The language of eyewitness accounts and historical narratives is conversational, and words are not carefully chosen. Rather than ponder the implications of a single word and draw conclusions from it, it was more productive to return and ask the narrator what he meant. We often did so.

Historical Traditions of the Postcontact Era

Historical traditions (*atome pii*) continue up until the present, though they underwent change with the foreign events that occurred after first contact and in the colonial era. After the arrival of the Leahy brothers in Enga in 1934 and the ruthless slaughter at Tole near Wabag (Connolly and Anderson 1987), what might be considered a new chapter of historical traditions began. Whereas formerly most of the events people experienced made sense within their everyday lives and cosmology, this one and many that followed were inexplicable. What is totally foreign is subject to unrestrained personal speculation and interpretation. Thus, whereas one can collect the names of men killed in the Great Ceremonial Wars of the 1930s and obtain remarkable consistency between testimonies, it is difficult to get similarly coherent information about those shot by Leahy in the same decade. When a man was killed in the Great Wars, songs of victory were sung, mourning and funeral ceremonies were held, and later, war reparations were paid. These events remained in memory and were recorded in historical traditions. After the Leahy shootings, fewer formalities were observed, and so the dead were more easily forgotten except by those who buried them and mourned their passing.

The same principle — that accounts of what is poorly understood vary greatly — holds true for many other incidents in the colonial era. For the first time Enga narratives recorded historical events that were not internally generated, and a new genre of commentary came to life — one that marveled at changes coming from the outside, tried to explain the incomprehensible from the vantage of Enga worldview and experience, protested the brutality of the colonial administration, and integrated biblical traditions, among other things. Though we found postcontact narratives difficult to order from within, with the help of the written record it is possible to compile them into a fascinating portrait of responses to the entirely new: admiration, protest, bewilderment, and, above all, attempts to forge connections between the new and the old. The richness of the postcontact narratives also enables comparison of testimonies by numerous people regarding the same event.

Metaphorical Legends

There is a subcategory of historical narrative that deserves separate mention because it is easily confused with myth: it is what we call metaphorical legends. Rather than recording specific factual events, metaphorical legends give a broader view of past trends and relationships, particularly developments associated with exchange. For example, they may deal with the origins of chains of finance in the Tee cycle or with incidents that portray the relationship between two clans. These are matters that Enga usually discuss using figurative speech (*kongali*). Such narratives are told in extended metaphor, parable, or analogy to encapsulate a development or relationship. Often it is only the fact that they are specified as historical rather than mythical traditions, placed in a certain generation, and interpreted by the narrator that identifies them as history instead of myth. Because key developments such as the origin of the Tee cycle are conveyed in metaphorical legends, we cite them occasionally throughout the text, together with explanations by elders.

Praise Poetry from the Bachelors' Cults

There is one form of oral tradition that does not fall within the category of *atome pii* but that has a distinctly historical intent (see also Lacey 1975). This is the *sangai titi pingi nemongo* of the bachelors' cults, sacred poetry that describes the series of transactions by which a cult's sacred objects were purchased from another clan of high repute, brought secretly to the cult house after perilous journeys by night, and passed on through the generations. At each step of purchase or transmission, new lines or verses are added. Recitations can last up to thirty minutes, albeit with much repetition. Only ambitious and capable young men learn the poetry in its entirety; most remember only the fragments that contain essential historical information. It is possible to use this material to trace the spread of the sacred objects and even of the cults themselves. Much of the history of the bachelors' cults given in chapter 8 is based on information from *sangai titi pingi nemongo*.

Magic Formulas and Poetry

Sacred poetry, magic formulas, and incantations were essential parts of bachelors' and ancestral cult performances, with specific formulas used at virtually every step. Their accurate recitation was believed to be essential for the cults to be effective. When cults were bought and sold, as they frequently were in Enga, the ritual experts of the purchasing groups had to learn these incantations with precision or else invite competent experts from other groups to recite them. Such poems and formulas were chanted in run-on lines in what is sometimes archaic language, an indication that they are old, though there is no way to date them by generation. Complex imagery and figurative language can pose difficulties for translation today, and it seldom can be done without the help of ritual experts. Although some cult formulas are simple and repetitive, others add much to an understanding of the purposes and underlying beliefs of different rites. Some sacred poems describe the extent of cult networks. We used these oral traditions whenever possible to help clarify key elements of different cults. Some are presented in the text with their format restructured from that of a run-on chant to lines and verses for clarity of presentation. Others, such as those of the Kepele cult, are not given, because Enga felt that a written presentation of these sacred formulas for the public might bring misfortune to the clan or tribe.

Personal Formulas

In the past, magic formulas (*nemongo*) were recited to support almost any undertaking of importance, from making a net bag or planting a garden to dressing for a dance or preventing a wig from becoming disheveled during sleep.[14] They were obtained by individuals to achieve personal goals. They had to be purchased and learned with great precision to be effective, though once owned they could be passed on in a family without payment and still maintain their power. The principle behind most magic formulas was that the recitation of the names of objects, plants, or animals with desired properties, accompanied by the performance of specified actions, would result in the transfer of those properties to the designated subject. Some invoked the help of the ancestors or sky people and others were simply thought to work by "magic." Nobody could tell us about the original sources of *nemongo*, nor did they know anyone who claimed to have authored new ones. The structure of magic formulas used for personal goals is similar to that of formulas used in cults, except that personal ones are usually much shorter and have little historical content. Numerous examples can be found in the book *Inside the Women's House: Enga Women's Lives and Traditions* (Kyakas and Wiessner 1992). Some personal formulas can yield keys to understanding beliefs, whereas others, perhaps most, hold no historical information and yield no insights for historical investigations.

Songs

Songs (*wee*), though often of no more than two or three lines, deliver potent messages. They may inflict heavy insult or challenge, be used in one-upmanship, tantalize, or break the ice in tense relationships. They are rich in symbolism, and their meanings can be intentionally ambiguous to suggest openings in social or political relationships while remaining noncommittal. Their composers are the quick-witted. People throughout Enga claim that songs used to communicate political messages are a development of the past five generations; before then there were only work jingles and songs for entertainment and courtship. Indeed, we were given no songs associated with political events prior to the fifth generation, although from then on songs sung during events were often remembered better than the events themselves. Together with place names and features of the landscape, songs invoke memories of historical occasions; they often capture their core issues or spirit. Whenever possible, we collected songs associated with events, and we give some of these in both Enga and English in the text.[15]

Proverbs
Enga is rich in proverbs that can be instructive in clarifying norms, values, and meanings. Sometimes people quoted proverbs as they recounted historical narratives, others Akii already knew, and still others were solicited from elders. Some Enga proverbs are included in the text to illustrate Enga conventional wisdom.

Historical Traditions as Agents of Social Change
The wide array of Enga oral traditions with historical content was transmitted from generation to generation as knowledge used to guide decisions and educate the younger generation. The very material on which this book is based was thus an important vehicle for bringing about change. Whereas certain kinds of oral traditions, such as myths and magic formulas, seem to have deep roots in Enga culture and to be used as anchors for certain values and aspects of identity, others, such as historical traditions, poems from the bachelors' cults, and songs geared toward intergroup communication, were developed after the introduction of the sweet potato to bring about change or mediate its effects. Some were highly factual, laying down fixed points, and others left much room for interpretation and creativity. Some reinforced traditional values and others introduced the new. Perhaps most importantly, historical traditions did not eclipse the past by portraying it similarly to the present but conveyed a sense of the rapid developments that were taking place. And so in former times, just as today, young people were attuned to expect change in their lifetimes and to participate actively in the process.

We have tried to put some of the oral traditions upon which this book is based within the reader's reach. In either the text or the appendixes we offer translated passages from some of the relevant testimonies in order to convey how Enga portray their own history and to document our reasoning.[16] We chose this format because even though it is easy for us to say that two hundred to three hundred cassettes are available for others to use, it is hard to work with the material of others, as we discovered in trying to use recordings made by Paul Brennan and Roderic Lacey. In the absence of contextual information, subjective impressions, evaluations, nonverbal clues, remarks made after interviews, and the possibility of asking questions at the end, testimonies collected by others are incomplete. A series of interviews yields far more than "texts." Rather, it reflects the cultural heritage and life experiences of an individual. Without a sense of the person, one has fewer guidelines by which to evaluate testimonies and place them in a broader scheme.

On that note, we close our general discussion of Enga oral traditions as history; for each topic, internal consistency, biases, and problems are discussed chapter by chapter closer to the subject matter. We now turn to the approach we took in compiling and analyzing Enga historical traditions.

Theoretical Orientations

In decades past, Western scholars generally regarded preliterate societies as "people without history" (Wolf 1982). Prior to the work of Jan Vansina (1965), attempts to systematically make use of oral sources to explore history were few. As a result, written information on a society's "cultural heritage" often began with the accounts of the first Western anthropologists, who were concerned with documenting the ethnographic present and analyzing their observations according to theoretical concerns of the day. "Tradition" was defined as the way things were around first contact, and postcontact history recorded the changes that followed. If the dominant anthropological theory of the time was materialism, most aspects of society were presented in light of economic goals and functions; if structuralist analysis was the focus of interest, quite a different view of the society emerged. Ironically, if this trend continues, it means that future generations' sense of identity and understanding of their cultural heritage will depend in part on an accident of timing: at which point in the development of anthropological theory the first dedicated anthropologist arrived in a given culture.

To avoid this outcome, in our studies of Enga history we drew on a number of theoretical frameworks, in order to be able to write both a "historical ethnography" and an "anthropological history." For historical ethnography, we sought approaches that would elucidate broader forces underlying change, both those generated from within and those coming from without. First, we tried to understand the role of ecological factors in the equation of change: the initial impact of the sweet potato, short-term and long-term responses to the potential it offered, and, most importantly, the implications of environmental differences for cultural adaptations in eastern, central, and western Enga. Next, we employed a variety of techniques for obtaining some measure of demographic growth, its causes, and its impact. A vast literature exists for these two issues, beginning with the work of James Watson (1965a, 1965b, 1977). Ecological and demographic hypotheses were thus in place to be tested with data from Enga history.

External and internal changes are inextricably linked. Just as environmental change can set off developments in social and political relations, so too can new social or political orders have environmental impact. Therefore, as our next step in working toward a historical ethnography, we posed questions derived from Marxist perspectives to examine change generated from within (Terray 1972; Friedman 1974; Godelier 1977; Modjeska 1982). We asked how change is induced by conflicts over the means of appropriating and controlling land, tools, raw materials, labor, and the products of labor—such as kinship, political relations, gender relations, and religious associations. We also considered whether changes in the position of Enga in the broader economy of Oceania affected precolonial history, for traders and settlers had reached the coast of what is now Papua New Guinea long before they entered the highlands.

Finally, in order to comprehend strategies employed throughout Enga history to cope with what Meggitt (1977) has presented as the Enga people's major preoccupation—territorial boundary maintenance—we drew on concepts from human ethology (Peterson 1975; Eibl-Eibesfeldt 1989).[17] Strategies for territorial maintenance identified in ethology go beyond physical defense via warfare to include the maintenance of boundaries through social advertising, ritualized aggression, and exchange. An ethological approach offers the potential to situate the chosen strategies in a wider evolutionary perspective.

All of the foregoing approaches, except perhaps human ethology, are primarily materialist. They have been used by numerous researchers to account for developments that took place in the New Guinea highlands after the introduction of the sweet potato. By following these lines of investigation, we were able to come up with comparable results that shed light on the findings of other studies. Nonetheless, these approaches offer limited potential for more fine-grained analyses that concern *how* individual and group action within a given cultural context affected relations among people, land, and resources. Specifically, broad materialist frameworks, parsimonious though they may be in their explanations, often obscure the cultural processes behind change, such as how cultural orientations guide actors and how actors in turn alter norms, give things new meaning, or coalesce their actions into resulting group responses. Herein lies the cultural pulse of change. To bring out these aspects of Enga history and write an anthropological history that elucidates the role of cultural factors in the process of change, we drew on some concepts from "practice theory" (Ortner 1984) for collecting, organizing, and analyzing our material.

Essentially, the stance we took from practice theory (Bourdieu 1977, 1990; Giddens 1979, 1984; Sahlins 1981, 1985) looks at how culture both restricts and enables social action. It proposes that the actions of individuals or groups are guided by and interpreted within the framework of cultural structures and orientations—what might be called "cultural heritage." Whether we look at how history is portrayed, at the incorporation of a new crop in a subsistence scheme, or at the formulation of a new means of conflict resolution, cultural concepts, values, and meanings play a formative role. An understanding of preexisting conditions is thus an essential starting point from which to clarify the options and orientations of the actors. In turn, social action is seen as constituting, reproducing, or altering aspects of culture through the intended and unintended consequences of individual or group projects, such as the schemes of Enga big-men. Sometimes unintended consequences arise when actions guided by cultural orientations meet contradictions from the external world. The concept of social action that we used was similar to that formulated by Bruce Knauft (1993:13)—"the interplay between cultural orientation and individual motivation, on the one hand, and the contingencies and constraints of the nonsymbolic world on the other." An understanding of the latter is essential, because environmental limitations changed significantly throughout the period considered.

Though practice theory has generally been applied to daily or short-term interaction, it is perhaps most interesting when applied to history, particularly oral history based on firsthand or secondhand eyewitness accounts, for there the processes and consequences of social action can assessed. To analyze the Enga material, we first tried to reconstruct environmental potential and constraints at the time Enga historical traditions began and then to understand how these were altered through time, drawing on findings from current research on agriculture and environment in New Guinea. Next, we established a "baseline" for cultural orientations by compiling information on past social organization, intergroup relations, exchange, and accompanying rules and values for different areas of Enga from the earliest Enga historical traditions. We also tried to reconstruct basic features of cosmology and ritual life.

It was then possible to organize the historical narratives from subsequent generations to look at how cultural orientations and structures existent at the outset restrained, guided, or shaped social action over the period considered, and to what extent individual and collective action altered economics, ideology, and society. This endeavor demanded careful documentation of Enga history and analysis of what indeed changed, the first objective of this book. The results raised two other issues that also became central themes.

One of these is the question of how change was brought about. It can be argued that accelerating competition was a driving force behind change, but such competition cannot simply be taken as a given. Although competition is a force found in all societies—one with deep evolutionary roots—certain parameters must be set before it can unfold. There must be agreement to compete rather than simply to squelch those who try to get ahead; in many prestate societies, competition is severely constrained. Certain things must be socially stipulated: what is competed for, who competes with whom, when, how, in what context, and over what, and what the privileges and prerogatives of the winners will be. If competition is allowed to accelerate, its results, such as emerging social inequalities, must be mediated. And in the face of great diversity between areas, homogeneity in concepts, rules, and values must be established before regional exchange networks can develop. To demonstrate how such new parameters are defined, where they come from, how they are integrated into the broader population, and by whom they are integrated is our second objective and central theme. Understanding how norms, values, and meanings are altered to bring about change provides an essential complement to existing ecological and economic models (Watson 1965a, 1965b; Modjeska 1982; Feil 1987).

Our third objective is to assess the relationship between quantitative and qualitative (structural) change — that is, how much growth can be assimilated before major features of a cultural system are overturned by internal contradictions? Specifically, at the beginning of the period considered, Enga society was organized along lines of kinship and principles of potential equality between households. As the pace and scale of economic activity increased with the construction of large exchange networks, at what point did it bring tensions, overload, or contradictions into Enga society? Did these pressures cause principles of equality and structures of kinship to break down, leading to centralization of power and a formalized social hierarchy, or did the former curb the latter?

To look at change from the foregoing perspective is far more than a theoretical exercise. Knowing which cultural orientations persisted over the last few centuries and why is essential for predicting problems and possibilities likely to crop up in the future. Furthermore, it is only against the background of history that one can evaluate what is being altered and accomplished by contemporary developments, how it is being done, and whether the means and outcomes are indeed taking the desired course. Our intent in calling on concepts from practice theory was to draw out aspects of change that would complement materialist models previously applied to the Papua New Guinea highlands. We did not intend to further develop practice theory itself. Nonetheless, our use of practice theory should offer some insights into its value for historical studies based on oral traditions.

History has both particular and general import, and so this case study has bearing on broader issues. First, we hope it will stimulate parallel research in New Guinea and eventually open the way for intercultural comparison of historical processes. It is difficult to see how our understanding of the similarities and differences between New Guinea societies can go farther without including a dynamic historical dimension. Second, for those in archaeology, anthropology, and political science interested in the evolution of more complex political organization, the Enga case provides a good example of how change is brought about, as well as an example of the resistance of "egalitarian" systems to alterations in sociopolitical structure, even in the face of rapid demographic and economic growth. In doing so, it helps identify the ingredients necessary for social transformation to occur. Third, analysis of the process of individual initiative and group response in setting the parameters for and bringing about change raises some interesting questions for evolutionary biologists. And finally, by specifying spatial and material correlates whenever possible, we hope to make our findings more accessible to archaeologists.

When Roderic Lacey (1981:55) had completed his investigations of Enga oral traditions as history, he wrote: "Where, then, are the historical conclusions from these explorations? The answer is that they still lie dormant, because more evidence is needed by which claims of origin traditions can be tested and interpreted. Now it is necessary for Enga, with guides and maps like these, to gather evidence together so that the history of their people can be written." This was our goal and the aim of the many Enga who helped us. We realize that on our journey back through time we have left much ground uncovered and have raised more questions than we have answered. Nevertheless, we hope the material presented here will make it possible for Enga to look back into their past and encourage the younger generation to build on our research, just as we have built on Lacey's, and to go farther.

TOP: Pig stakes being set out for an upcoming Tee exchange in central Enga, 1950s.
Photo by Norma L. Heinicke.

BOTTOM: A *tee* exchange held for war reparations at Kundis in the Ambum valley,
1986. Today, sheep and cows are sometimes included in *tee* exchanges because Seventh-
Day Adventists do not raise pigs or eat pork. Photo by author.

Dressing for a traditional dance at Tetemanda, near Wabag, 1986. Dancers must be dressed and painted to perfection, for elders observing the dance make predictions about a dancer's future and fate from his or her appearance. Photo by author.

Warrior with blackened face, spear, and shield, 1971. The shield is made from a strip of bark stretched tightly over a wooden frame. Photo by Paul W. Brennan.

Men crossing a bridge over one of the many torrential rivers of Enga, 1950s. Photo by Norma L. Heinicke.

Traditional dance performance held in Kompiam, 1979. The wig style of these dancers indicates that they are from the Saka-Layapo dialect group. Photo by Paul W. Brennan.

Orator making his point during a *tee* at Lakemanda, central Enga, 1971. Photo by Paul W. Brennan.

Typical Enga landscape with houses nestled on hillsides among groves of casuarina trees and mounded sweet potato gardens. Ambum valley, 1987. Photo by author.

Saa yangenge, a marsupial feast at Tiakamanda, Ambum valley, 1971. Photo by Paul W. Brennan.

Parade of pearl shells before a line of traditional dancers and the public during a Tee cycle of the 1950s. Photo by Norma L. Heinicke.

Tee exchange at Lauwanda, central Enga, 1970s. Photo by Paul W. Brennan.

Laisa and Nita presenting axes and cash during a *tee* exchange at Wakumale, 1977. Note that the bills are tacked to bamboo poles for display. Photo by Paul W. Brennan.

Yombone handing over a cassowary during a *tee* exchange at Wakumale, central Enga, 1977. Photo by Paul W. Brennan.

Young men cleansing their bodies before entering the Sangai hut at Laialama, Kompiam district, 1969. Photo by Paul W. Brennan.

Mioko presents pearl shells during a *tee* exchange at Lenge, central Enga, 1974. Photo by Paul W. Brennan.

TOP: Kyakas and Akii holding a sacred ancestral stone from central Enga. This is actually a cast; the original is in the Australian National Museum. Photo by Fr. Philip Gibbs, 1976.

BOTTOM: The bachelors' parade: young men emerging from the Sangai cult house at Mulisos, central Enga. Photo by author, 1986.

Young women using traditional tools to break ground for a garden, Saka Valley, 1971.
Photo by Fritz Robinson.

2

Environment, Population, and Subsistence in the Early Generations of Oral History

No matter what region of Enga is considered, ecological conditions reported at the time of first contact with Europeans were very different from those portrayed in oral traditions going back earlier than the sixth generation. Contrast, for example, the description of the Lai valley in J. L. Taylor's Hagen-Sepik patrol report of 1939 with one from Lyipini tribal history some six to eight generations earlier:

We were now in the heart of the valley, one of the most beautiful in New Guinea, if not in the world. Everywhere were fine well-laid out garden plots, mostly of sweet po-

tatoes, and groves of casuarina. Well cut and graded roads traversed the countryside and small parks or "playgrounds," the "bena" of the Mount Hagen people or the "kama" as they are called here, dotted the landscape, which resembled a huge botanic garden. It may well be called the garden valley of the Lai. (Taylor 1939:29-30)

Lyipini [after leaving his home in the Yandap region] climbed up to Yawalemanda and to the top of Mount Munimanda. There he planted the *tato* stick he had brought with him, and today *tato* trees grow at that spot. Dawn was breaking when he came down to Lepalemanda, and in the early morning light he could see the valley below. He saw smoke rising in the distance above the treetops and felt sure that it was a sign of human life. He hurried down in the direction of the smoke and came to a house. The door was closed and nobody was home. Overcome by exhaustion, he pushed aside the door of banana leaves and went in. With his eyes red from lack of sleep, he found a suitable spot and went to sleep. . . .

[Depe then comes home and discovers Lyipini sleeping in his house.] "I am glad that you have come," said Depe. "I have been living alone on this land. Now that you are here, we can live together, and in the course of time we shall be known as Depe and Lyipini," Depe said enthusiastically.

With these words, he embraced Lyipini and took him to the top of a hill to look over the landscape. They could see that there was plenty of land for both of them and they were satisfied. "I'll work the land to the left, and the land to the right is all yours," Depe told Lyipini.

Lyipini built his house at Pyolapya on the land that Depe had given to him. He married and had five sons: Diuapini, Malo, Ambetane, Kepeokini, and Wiokini. His sons grew up and became the founders of the clans of Lyipini. Wiokini was a trapper and claimed the forest land around Yawalemanda. Kepeo was a gatherer of mushrooms and pearl shells. Diuapini was a gardener and wore *kyangali* leaves to cover his buttocks, which identified him as such. Malo and Ambetane were also gardeners. (Lanyia Kingi, Lyipini tribe, Rakamanda)

In telling the Lyipini tribe's origin legend, Lanyia Kingi was well aware that it had been simplified and made representative over generations. Certainly Depe was not the only man living in the area, and Lyipini had not arrived in the Lai valley unaccompanied but with his family and relatives. As the rest of the Lyipini origin tradition claims, they were refugees seeking a new home following a conflict in the Yandap region. The point remains that there was enough free land at the time for Depe to welcome newcomers.

The situation changed rapidly. Some four to six generations later, the Depe and Lyipini tribes had grown to the point that they were no longer content with their land on the southern slopes of the Lai valley. They gradually fought their way down into the bottom of the valley, displacing other clans and occupying the fertile land around Birip. By the time the first patrols arrived in the Lai, Depe and Lyipini were too large to be willing to share the beautiful gardens and ceremonial grounds described by Taylor and were fighting bitterly for land with surrounding tribes and even among themselves (Allen and Giddings 1982). Most of the land in the Lai valley, as Taylor noted, was garden land, and the descendants of Lyipini's sons Wiokini and Kepeo were no longer gatherers and trappers.

Differences in descriptions of population, subsistence, and environment between early and later generations, such as those just quoted, permeate Enga historical traditions. How much confidence can one have in such descriptions?

Can they be used to reconstruct a picture of the past? As we outlined in chapter 1, analyses of Enga origin myths and early narratives indicate that they have a sound historical basis with regard to certain types of information and are not continually restructured to form a charter for current relations. Furthermore, the change described in the historical traditions is gradual and continuous. There is no abrupt jump from an ideal past with few people and plenty of land to a time of dense population and struggles over land. Hunting and taro decline only gradually in the oral record as sweet potatoes and pigs assume increasing importance. Finally, we see considerable consistency in early oral traditions in the portrayal of environment, subsistence base, and population density by region.

On these grounds we feel it is worthwhile to compile from the early historical narratives all available information on population, subsistence bases, specific resources utilized, early agricultural systems, and relations of production for the various regions of Enga. Doing so provides a baseline from which to look at subsequent changes and makes it possible to use the Enga case to examine hypotheses about pre-sweet potato agriculture that have been presented by others (Waddell 1972; Golson 1977, 1982; Kelly 1988).[1] Our main points are (1) that pre-sweet potato diversity between eastern, central, and western Enga was substantial, so that there existed very different starting points and options for change after the introduction of the new crop; and (2) that resources, goods, and luxury items were valued differently around the time of the introduction of the sweet potato from the way they were in later generations. As we shall see, much effort was required to change the worth attributed to certain products, particularly pigs, after the the sweet potato made its appearance.

Population Distribution and Size

Oral traditions from the founding generations depict a sparsely populated landscape—there were vast tracts of uncleared land, immigrant groups were readily welcomed, distances between settlements were much greater than they are today, and spouses were difficult to find. There is, however, absolutely no reason to believe that most of Enga was unpopulated and was colonized only later by immigrants. By approximately 250 to 300 years ago, all of the central valleys of Enga, some of the adjacent high country, and the region around the Kandep swamps were inhabited by groups who intermarried, traded, and participated in joint feasts and rituals. This probably had been the case for thousands of years.

Map 5 gives the distribution of Enga tribes in the founding generations by plotting each at its claimed place of origin. We found no conflicts or inconsistencies in this information. It illustrates that eight to ten generations ago, Enga

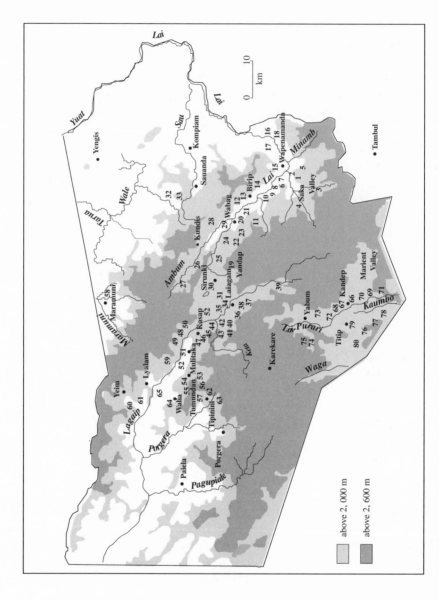

Map 5. Enga-speaking tribes claiming origins in Enga Province.

Saka and Layapo Enga

1. Yambatane
2. Waimini
3. Pauakaka
4. Sikini
5. Inapini
6. Aluni
7. Yoko
8. Itokone
9. Yanaitini
10. Lyongeni
11. Depe
12. Pumalini
13. Tinilapini
14. Lungupini
15. Yandamani
16. Pyaini
17. Tokopetani
18. Sinyi

Mai-Yandapo Enga

19. Lyipini
20. Apulini
21. Yakani
22. Itapuni
23. Awaini
24. Malipini
25. Potealini
26. Pumane
27. Aiele
28. Sene
29. Yokasa
30. Lyaini
31. Tia
32. Waitini
33. Lakini

Upper Lagaip

34. Waitini
35. Walini
36. Pyaini
37. Sambe
38. Kunalini
39. Lote
40. Pumane
41. Wau
42. Andamane
43. Angalaini

Tayato Enga

44. Sakate
45. Yambanima
46. Piandaine
47. Monaini
48. Limbini
49. Kaiya
50. Tupini
51. Konemane
52. Mulapini
53. Pumane
54. Yangutini
55. Yandape
56. Kundiki
57. Kisipini
58. Wawini-Yangi
59. Tiwini
60. Auwini
61. Lambuaka
62. Mondatepa
63. Kapini
64. Maeyango
65. Pandane

Atone and Katinja Enga

66. Ima
67. Alitipa
68. Lyumbi
69. Aimbatepa
70. Kototepa
71. Kambitipa
72. Tatali
73. Kamani
74. Bipi
75. Kuu
76. Yalipuni
77. Tieni
78. Maulu
79. Timitopa
80. Yamape

were truly a highland people showing a strong preference for areas above the malaria belt.[2] Although population at that time is said to have been sparse, most of the land within reach of the central valleys was claimed either as residential and garden land or as forest land for hunting and gathering.

In contrast to the situation during the twentieth century, few of the fringe areas were inhabited by Enga tribes. The northeast corner of Enga was home to the Wapi and Lembena and possibly other small groups now in the Sepik, and the southern portion of the Kompiam area was largely uninhabited.[3] The Maramuni and Yeim areas were the home of Nete- and Penale-speaking peoples. Enga living in the Lagaip valley mentioned periodic trips to the north to trade with and obtain food from the Nete and Penale, as well as frequent intermarriage with them, but according to our brief investigations, only two Enga groups, Wawini and Yangi (map 5:58), claim to have originated there.

The western boundary between the Enga and the Ipili was probably around Tipinini,[4] and only in subsequent generations did Enga clans move farther into the Porgera and Paiela valleys. We have little information from the southwestern corner of Enga, where Enga and Huli linguistic groups meet, but no Enga tribes that we encountered claimed to have originated west of the Waga river (see also Meggitt 1956). Finally, most of the Marient valley of southern Kandep was the forested hunting territory of Mendi clans and was said to have had few permanent residents, if any.

The distribution of tribes shown in map 5 gives the misleading impression that the Lagaip valley was more densely populated than the Lai and Ambum valleys. In fact, this was not the case, for Lagaip and Kandep genealogies indicate that clan size was smaller in the west than in the east.

Dialect Divisions of Enga

The encompassing term "Enga," used by people of the Mount Hagen area to refer to their eastern neighbors, was first applied by Taylor (1939) in his Hagen-Sepik patrol report. Though it seems that the Enga had shared a common language throughout the span of their oral history, the cultural landscape of Enga was subdivided into named groups, as it is today, distinguished by variations in dress style, ritual, exchange, subsistence, relations between the sexes, and, in some instances, dialect, among other things. Map 2 shows the major dialect divisions that existed in the 1970s, according to Brennan's studies (1982:fig. 11.1). Table 2 summarizes dialect groups and their cultural subdivisions.

Before the development of large-scale cult and exchange networks that drew together people of neighboring areas, dialect and other cultural divisions appar-

Table 2

Enga Dialect Groups and Cultural Subdivisions

Dialect Group and Subdivision	Location/Composition
1. Layapo Enga	
a. Layapo Enga	Lai valley
b. Saka Enga	Saka valley
2. Mai Enga	
3. Yandapo Enga	
4. Tayato Enga	
a. Tombeama	North side of Lagaip river
b. Wakema	South side of Lagaip river
c. Teketopa	From Keta river to Mulitaka
d. Yoleyopa	Mulitaka to Tumundane
5. Kandepe Enga	
a. Atone	Northeast side of Lai-Purari river
b. Kandep	Southeast side of Lai-Purari river
c. Katinja	West side of Lai-Purari river
6. Maramuni Enga	Immigrants from upper Ambum valley, Sirunki, and Lagaip to Maramuni area
7. Sau Enga	Immigrants from Ambum valley to area north of Sau river
8. Kopona Enga	Immigrants from Saka and Lai valleys to area south of Sau river
9. Kaina Enga	Immigrants from Layapo clans to Mai areas plus Mai-Layapo integration with the rise of ceremonial exchange networks

Note: Numbers 1-5 are pre-sweet potato divisions. Numbers 6-9 are dialect divisions that formed as a result of post-sweet potato migration or integration. The Teketopa-Yoleyopa division appears to be a very old one; people no longer know its cultural meaning.

ently were even more pronounced. Eastern Enga was divided between the Saka Enga, comprised of tribes in the Saka valley and those on the south side of the Lai whose territory bridged the ridge separating the Lai and Saka valleys, and the Layapo Enga of the middle Lai, lower Lai, and Minamb valleys. Significant differences appear to have existed between the Saka and Layapo Enga in the founding generations, although these are minimal today.[5] Saka tribes were closely tied to the Kakoli of Tambul and through trade ties had imported much of their ritual and myth, among other things. The expansion of the Tee cycle from the Saka to the Layapo Enga in subsequent generations did much to integrate the two.

Five to ten kilometers west of Wabag, the Layapo and Mai Enga dialect groups meet. Although this boundary is not sharply defined, distinctions do exist. Layapo and Mai Enga speak different but mutually intelligible dialects and vary in dress styles, rituals, procedures for paying bridewealth, women's traditions, and bachelor's initiations. The central Enga can be subdivided into the Mai and Yandapo Enga, the former inhabiting the Wabag-Ambum region, the upper Lai valley, and parts of Sirunki, and the latter, the high country southwest of Wabag called the Yandap. There are indications that prior to the seventh generation, the Yandapo Enga lived in regions above about 2,100 meters and were more depen- dent on hunting than the Mai, who were settled in the upper Lai and Ambum valleys. Central Enga went through such turmoil, however, in the sixth to seventh generations that Mai-Yandapo relations before that time are unclear.

Bridging the Layapo and Mai-Yandapo today are the Kaina Enga, *kaina* mean- ing middle. The Kaina Enga are composed of tribes at the Mai-Layapo border and Yanaitini, a large tribe of Layapo origin that migrated to central Enga. Brennan (1982) identified the Kaina as a separate dialect group, but they receive no mention in early oral traditions and Enga generally do not regard them as a culture group like Layapo or Mai. Because the Kaina are made up of clans that linked the Great Ceremonial Wars of central Enga to the Tee cycle of eastern Enga, it is likely that this dialect division formed within the span of historical traditions.

Between the high country of the Yandap and the Lagaip-Keta river junction are a number of tribes that span the east and west; most prominent among them are the Sambe (map 5:37). Culturally these groups are closer to the Yandapo Enga, though Brennan's (1982) linguistic map places them with the Tayato, and their early history ties them to tribes of northern Kandep. There is no Enga designation for these people,[6] but we will speak of them as the Enga of the upper Lagaip. They were and are middlemen between the Lai valley and the Lagaip and Kandep regions, sharing traditions with all three.

At the junction of the Keta and Lagaip rivers begins the country of the Tayato Enga. Early oral traditions hint of former subdivisions within the Tayato, but these are difficult to define today. One was between the Tombeama Enga on the north side of the Lagaip and the Wakema on the south side. Myths that are not tied to the history of any particular generation or group describe hostilities between the Tombeama and Wakema; a cultural boundary is also suggested by the fact that the Kepele cult, the central ancestral cult of the Wakema for at least the last six generations, did not spread into Tombeama areas. A second distinc- tion existed within the Tayato Enga between the Teketopa Tayato, which in- cluded groups from the Keta river to Mulitaka, and the Yoleyopa Tayato west of Mulitaka. People today know little about the past meaning of this division — whether it was merely descriptive terminology for eastern and western Tayato or whether it was accompanied by other differences as well. Just as the Tee cycle reduced some differences among eastern tribes, the Kepele cult network did so for western Enga.

The Kandep region is dissected by the Lai-Purari river, which runs from north to south. Although Brennan's linguistic map places most of the peoples of the Kandep area in one dialect group and locates Katinja language speakers in the southwest corner, cultural distinctions are otherwise. Enga on the northeast side of the river are called the Atone (Aruni in Meggitt 1956), and those on the southeast side, the Kandep Enga. These people keep alternate residences in the Lai and Saka valleys and in the north Mendi area for times of frost. People living on the west side of the river are generally called Katinja Enga. Because of their close association with the Wola and Huli, they are usually fluent in three languages: Enga, Huli, and Katinja. The last is said by Enga to be a mixture of Enga and Wola. Many differences exist between the Atone-Kandep and the Katinja in styles of dress, dialect, and rituals, among other things. To the west of the Katinja are a few Enga groups in the Waga valley who are not included in this study (see Meggitt 1956).

As we discuss in chapter 5, further dialect divisions came into being when Saka-Layapo clans migrated and settled south of the Sau river in the Kompiam region and when Mai clans from the Ambum occupied the headwaters of the Sau and the north side. The distinction between those with Mai origins and those stemming from Layapo-Saka areas is still recognized today and is reflected in dialect and ceremonial dress. The former are Sau dialect speakers, and the latter, Kopona speakers (Brennan 1982:200); differences between the two dialects are not great. Feil (1984) calls Kopona speakers living southeast of the Sau river "Tombema," the Kopona pronunciation of Tombeama. We avoid using Tombema to refer to Kopona inhabitants because it is a geographical designation with much wider usage—for instance, it is applied to Layapo Enga living north of the Lai river (Waddell 1972:15), to Enga of the lower Ambum (Meggitt 1958a:258), and to Tayato Enga living north of the Lagaip river.

Population Estimates for the Seventh Generation

In the founding generations, Enga tribes are said to have been small, with constituent clans composed of but a few men's houses whose locations are sometimes recalled. This begs the question, how small? In Appendix 2 we estimate the size of the Enga population in the seventh generation from genealogical information, in the hope that our method yields more realistic figures than would pure speculation. The result is that some seven generations ago Enga had a minimum population of 8,860. If we include the fifty-seven immigrant clans to the Lai, Saka, and Minamb valleys and a few of those to Kandep who may already have been settled in Enga by this time, the minimum population increases to 9,500. Even if our estimates are off as much as 100 percent and the population was closer to 19,000, the point remains that seven to eight generations ago Enga population was small in comparison with the 150,000 counted in the 1980 census.[7] It should be clear that these are our best estimates and no more; the reader may take them, leave them, or modify them. None of the arguments in this book is built on these figures.

Environment, Subsistence, and Production

How did these small tribes of the central valleys of Enga live prior to the introduction of the sweet potato? In the following sections we compile descriptions of subsistence bases and lifestyles as portrayed in the origin traditions of each region and discuss specific resources and relations of production. Though evidence in any single origin tradition is sparse, interesting trends emerge on the regional level.

Eastern Enga

The fertile lower valleys of eastern Enga were the most hospitable in the province even before the introduction of the sweet potato. They were high enough (between 1,500 and 1,900 meters) to be above the malaria belt but low enough to permit the reliable cultivation of crops such as yams, winged beans, bananas, and sugarcane. All of these matured relatively quickly at such low altitudes. The forested valley slopes and ridgetops offered a variety of wild game, food plants, and construction materials. No historical traditions mention severe food shortages.

There is every indication that Layapo and Saka Enga fully exploited the agricultural potential of the region prior to the sixth to seventh generation. Sixteen out of twenty origin traditions from eastern Enga contain some information on subsistence. Of these, all sixteen mention gardening, six mention pigs, three trapping, two hunting, and two the gathering of pandanus nuts. In nine out of sixteen, specific crops are named: taro in nine, yams and bananas in four, and sugarcane, winged beans, spinach, and ginger each in one or two. The sweet potato enters into only one—clearly it was either not yet available or not widely cultivated during this period. The general pattern depicted was one of the tillage of gardens on river terraces, the utilization of valley slopes for pig forage, and preservation of the higher forests for hunting and gathering. Men hunted, but hunting was not prominent; additionally, there are several references to the collection of frogs, birds' eggs, caterpillars, and honey. Pigs are also there, but in the background and attributed little symbolic importance. The feasts specified are either taro feasts or cult feasts provisioned with marsupial meat, not pork feasts. It is the trade of salt, axes, shell headbands, and tree oil rather than hunting or pig exchange that adds intrigue to historical narratives of this area.

Origin traditions for tribes or clans that claim to have migrated into eastern Enga from surrounding higher-altitude areas paint quite a different picture. The majority of these people appear to have moved from the Kaugel and Nebilyer valleys into the Tambul-Tomba region (Kola) after the introduction of the sweet potato to gain better access to hunting grounds, to situate themselves at the crossroads of the trade, or to take refuge after tribal fighting. Finding the environment too harsh, many of them moved down into the eastern valleys of Enga. In eight out of ten of their origin traditions, there is some mention of subsistence. Gardening enters into all eight, but only two of these name specific crops — taro, sweet potato, sugarcane, spinach, yams, and bananas. Three out of eight mention pigs, and six out of eight have hunting as a focal point. This conforms to the pattern found throughout the province — the origin traditions of groups in higher altitudes focus on hunting and those from lower altitudes on gardening.

Central Enga

Central Enga, home of the Mai and Yandapo, offered both stretches of fertile gardening land in the Lai and Ambum valleys below 2,100 meters and an abundance of cassowaries, marsupials, and pandanus in the adjacent high country of Sirunki and the Yandap.[8] Here the focus shifts to hunting: fourteen out of fifteen origin traditions for tribes in the Ambum, upper Lai, and upper Sau areas include some description of subsistence activities, and of these, hunting and trapping are mentioned in eleven and gardening in eight. Unlike the origin traditions of eastern Enga, in which references to hunting are few and casual, those from central Enga stipulate that a man of worth could provide his family with an ample supply of marsupial and cassowary meat. Accordingly, clan lands often included hunting territories in the high country of Sirunki and the Yandap.

Tribal and clan founders of central Enga were also gardeners. The importance of both hunting and gardening is sometimes conveyed through the portrayal of one brother as the hunter and the other as the gardener. The houses of tribal and clan founders represent the ideal — they were stocked with abundant supplies of raw or steamed meat and surrounded by lush gardens:

In the beginning, a long time ago when there were few people, there was a man named Kindole Puu. He had a beautiful house surrounded by gardens with all kinds of food and *sambisambi* grass. He had made the inside comfortable with marsupial furs, cassowary feathers, and the feathers of other birds. He ate well, living from fresh marsupial meat, the meat of cassowaries, and smaller birds, as well as the food from his gardens. (From the Malipini origin legend, Ambaipu Yakene, Malipini Kamaniwane clan, Kundis)

Specific vegetable foods are named in five origin traditions—taro, sugarcane, and pandanus. The only reference to sweet potato is in the Yanaitini origin legend, which describes experimentation and the discovery that the sweet potato grew well at higher altitudes. Finally, pigs are cited in five instances, although as in eastern Enga, little importance is attached to them.

The Lagaip and Porgera

Moving westward into the high country of Sirunki-Laiagam, one enters the land of legendary great cassowary trappers, and gardening virtually drops out of the picture. Hunting appears in all ten origin traditions, often at the center of the plot, and gardening in only three of the ten. Specific garden crops are not named. Pigs are not mentioned at all. Nonetheless, no sense of hardship is portrayed in these groups that form the crossroads between east, west, and south.

Among the Tayato Enga west of the Keta-Lagaip river junction, where the Lagaip valley begins to deepen and steepen, the slopes provide a number of different ecological zones. Interestingly, tribes of this area appear to have been divided by niche rather than to have regularly exploited the full spectrum of possibilities. Those with origin locations over 2,100–2,200 meters describe a predominantly hunting and gathering lifestyle, enjoying a huge range of movement; if they kept small gardens, these receive no mention. Those claiming origins below 2,100–2,200 meters were gardeners, keepers of pigs, and hunter-trappers, though again pigs are in the background. Unfortunately, subsistence is infrequently detailed in Lagaip origin traditions, and so it is impossible to give a more precise picture. Shortage of garden food is cited in three origin traditions. The Tayato say that formerly they had an active food trade with the Nete and Penale to the north, namely in *itatu* (*Pangium edule*) and sago, and that they were dependent on those groups for supplementary food in times of hardship. From just west of Mulitaka to the Auu-Koma range, where the soil is so poor that taro does not grow well on the lower valley slopes (see Meggitt 1973), no origin legends concern gardening. The tribes who claim origins in this region apparently were hunter-gatherers of the high country who had strong ties with the Yamape tribe of western Kandep, a group that spans Enga and Huli. Finally, pandanus receives more attention in the origin legends of western than of eastern Enga.

In the Porgera valley, the division of niches between hunters and gardeners was similar to that of the Lagaip. Pandanus was a major resource of the region and appears in several origin traditions: seasonal gatherings in pandanus groves provided an opportunity for Enga, Ipili, and Huli to meet. Taro is the predominant crop in early myths and legends (Gibbs 1975), and Porgera is one of the few areas of Enga that has a historical narrative pertaining directly to the arrival and spread of the sweet potato. As in other regions of Enga, pigs receive little attention.

Kandep

Of all the areas of Enga, Kandep is one of the harshest, and no doubt life was even more precarious prior to the introduction of the sweet potato. Though its forests provided ample game and pandanus, virtually all of the land lies at over 2,300 meters and is susceptible to regular frosts and periodic severe "killer frosts" (Waddell 1975). Still, its oral traditions from before the sixth generation show great vitality, and at least fourteen tribes claim pre-sweet potato origins there. There were two mitigating factors: one was the possibility for Kandep families to move to alternate residences in surrounding lower areas during periods of frost, which they did regularly. The second was the small pocket of low fertile land in the Kaumbo valley of southern Kandep, lying at 1,800-2,000 meters, where taro, bananas, and sugarcane could be reliably cultivated. Many of the groups who resided near the southern end of the Kandep swamps kept gardens there prior to the introduction of the sweet potato. Without ties to people in surrounding valleys and access to their resources, Kandep people probably would have used most of the region only as hunting grounds.

Details of subsistence are included in most Kandep origin traditions. Hunting forms a part of eight out of fourteen origin traditions for Kandep tribes. It assumes particular importance among groups at the northern end of the swamps, who appear to have relied almost totally on hunting and gathering over a vast high area that stretched north to the Lagaip and west to the Porgera valley. Kandep origin traditions are among the few that do not underestimate the importance of gathering — harvesting pandanus plays a significant role in six out of fourteen origin traditions, and tribal ancestors are said to have gathered desirable wild foods such as mushrooms, greens, and edible beetles.

Six out of fourteen Kandep origin traditions portray tribal founders as agriculturalists — those of southern Kandep who had access to land in the Kaumbo valley. Even tribes claiming origins near present-day Kandep station kept taro, banana, and sugarcane gardens there, though they also cultivated small gardens near the edges of the swamps. Greens called *auwa* in Enga (*Rorippa* sp.) are the only domesticated foods named by groups living north of Kandep station for the early generations. Finally, the sweet potato enters into the origin traditions of three tribes. Two of these concern the introduction of the sweet potato; there is no other indication that sweet potatoes were cultivated in the Kandep area during the founding generations.

Interestingly, Kandep, the only area of Enga where considerable social and symbolic value is attributed to pigs in this early period, is also that with the harshest environment for gardening: pigs play a role in twelve out of fourteen Kandep origin traditions. There is no description of pigs being fed with domesticated crops, only with forage. Presumably the land in and around the swamps provided enough forage so that only minimal supplementary feeding was required to keep pigs tame. Incentives for pig keeping may have had to do with the higher social, symbolic, and exchange value attached to them by the Kandep people's Mendi or Huli neighbors. Alternatively, because relations with relatives in lower valleys were maintained through reciprocity (Waddell 1975; Wohlt 1978), and because the Kandep region did not provide any of the most prized trade goods, residents may have relied on pigs as a major currency of exchange.

Pre-Sweet Potato Agricultural Systems

The information just compiled gives some idea of subsistence bases in the different areas of Enga during the founding generations, but it says little about agricultural systems at the time. Before reviewing the scant oral evidence, we first consider the interpretation of pollen diagrams that extend back far beyond the oral record. Jack Golson (1977, 1982), interpreting phases of swampland utilization at the Kuk archaeological site near Mount Hagen, has put forward a scheme that argues for the development of intensive agriculture in the Kuk area long before the introduction of the sweet potato. He then uses evidence from other areas of the highlands to suggest that this was more than a local phenomenon. For Enga, Golson (1977:622, 626; 1982:121-22, 131) uses the pollen studies of Donald Walker and John Flenley (1979) to piece together a picture of the development of agriculture in Enga which parallels that at Kuk. He proposes that at Birip Crater lake (1,900 meters) in the middle Lai valley, a decrease in forest taxa indicates the beginning of forest clearance approximately four thousand years ago. Then, around 2000-2500 B.P., a recovery of forest taxa occurred, possibly as a result of soil tillage and more intensive agricultural practices that required less forest to be cleared. At 1200 B.P., an increase in casuarina pollen implies tree fallowing, a method that is fast and effective in restoring soil structure and fertility.

In response to the question of why agriculture was intensified, Eric Waddell (1972) proposed that highland societies originally practiced shifting cultivation, causing progressive transformation of the natural vegetation into grassland unfavorable for that kind of agriculture. In an attempt to restore equilibrium in the ecosystem, the staple, taro, was separated from subsidiary crops and cultivated in open field systems with intensive methods that allowed for more permanent use. This released land for subsidiary crops and allowed for longer fallow and forest regeneration.

What perspectives can the oral evidence add to this? For eastern Enga, oral traditions give no reason to doubt that soil tillage and intensive agriculture were well established by the time the sweet potato was introduced. Though we have no detailed descriptions of pre-sweet potato gardening, origin traditions mention tribal founders clearing areas of grassland for taro gardens and suggest that gardens on the rich soils of the valley bottoms were cultivated repeatedly. They describe slash-and-burn techniques, tillage in association with taro, and large gardens planted for taro feasts. Controlled tree fallowing by planting casuarina is said to have been intensified in recent generations; nonetheless, there are at least two historical narratives from the sixth and seventh generations that explicitly mention the planting of casuarina — one comes from eastern Enga and the other from central Enga.

Since the oral record begins more than a thousand years after what is interpreted as the first traces of intensification, it is impossible to provide further evidence pertinent to Waddell's hypothesis. We can add only that within the span of oral history, reasons given for concentrating the staple in more permanent open fields include the desire to preserve a lifestyle that optimally utilized the resources of different niches in valley systems — fertile garden land near the valley bottoms, mixed gardens and secondary growth for pig forage on the slopes, and forests for hunting, gathering, and obtaining construction materials on the upper valley slopes.

Golson (1982:131) goes on to interpret the pollen results from Lake Sirunki (2,500 meters) and Lake Inim of central Enga similarly, though the area is near the altitudinal limits of the sweet potato, not to mention taro, and is frequently stricken by frost. Historical traditions give little support to Golson's scheme of permanently settled agriculturalists prior to the introduction of the sweet potato for Sirunki or any other area of Enga above roughly 2,200 meters, as is clear from the material presented earlier.[9] Such are the pitfalls of applying models from one area to another without careful consideration of interregional diversity.

This brief analysis gives but a sketch of subsistence, lifestyle, and agricultural systems for the founding generations. Certainly, many origin traditions from which we obtained information present the ideal. Nevertheless, that the ideals vary by area and altitude zone is itself instructive: tribes "originating" below approximately 1,900 meters, regardless of region, tend to have origin traditions that revolve around agriculture, those of tribes located between 1,900 and 2,200 meters give roughly equal importance to gardening and hunting, and those of tribes originating above 2,200 meters are almost solely concerned with hunting and gathering pandanus. There is no mention of the sweet potato in any area during the founding generations except in a few traditions that deal with its introduction or with experimentation, and pigs are given much less social and symbolic importance than they receive during later periods. Further understanding of subsistence during the founding generations can be obtained by exploring each resource individually: its natural attributes, the context in which it is mentioned, and its social, symbolic, and ritual significance.

Resources of the Early Generations

Taro

Taro (*Colocasia esculenta*), called *maa* in Enga and sometimes referred to as *akali waingi*—metaphorically, "life giver"—is the number one crop of early oral traditions. Its importance as a staple food is recalled in the traditional *enda lyonge* ceremony performed by newly married couples before they engaged in sexual relations: husband and wife exchanged and planted taro seedlings as a sign of commitment to provide for their family in the future (Kyakas and Wiessner 1992). Taro remained an important crop after the introduction of the sweet potato and is still a preferred food for ceremonial occasions throughout Enga, except in bachelors' cult performances. Even in the 1970s, people of the middle Lai valley were able to name twenty-three different varieties of taro, all of which they had planted in the recent past (Waddell 1972:63). For areas below approximately 2,000 meters, taro provided a reliable crop that matured within nine to twelve months and was produced in sufficient abundance to hold large taro feasts. Though historical narratives do mention the destruction of taro by beetles, no devastating regional crop failures are described.

Taro can be grown up to approximately 2,400–2,600 meters, but in areas above 2,000 meters with poorer soil, the crop takes up to one and a half to two years to mature and has a low yield. Thus, for parts of western Enga, problems with taro gardening and accompanying food shortages were matters of concern owing to both high altitude and poor soil. Origin legends for tribes from Kandep, Sirunki, Lagaip, and Porgera, whose land lay above 2,300 meters, contain little indication that taro was grown extensively prior to the introduction of the sweet potato. Certainly the combination of poor soil, slow growth, and susceptibility to frost would have made it a most unreliable staple.

Taro was cultivated by both men and women, each of whom had their own complementary magic spells to promote its growth. As a delicate crop subject to damage by beetles (*Papuana* spp.) and blight, it was planted with ritual precautions involving magic formulas that varied from area to area. Interestingly, similar folklore never developed around the cultivation of the sweet potato: of over one hundred women interviewed (Kyakas and Wiessner 1992), most knew the magic spells for planting taro, but not a single one knew any for sweet potatoes. The productivity of the sweet potato was promoted only via the large cults directed toward the fertility of humans, pigs, all crops, and wild foods.

Bananas, Sugarcane, Yams, and Other Subsidiary Crops

Other crops are mentioned in origin traditions but only in passing—most frequently, yams (*amu*), bananas (*angato* or *sae*), and sugarcane (*lyaa*). These were cultivated by men and were important for ceremonial occasions. Short magic formulas were used for planting these crops, but procedures were much less elaborate than those for taro. Additionally, ginger (*ita mai*), winged beans (*alyongo* [*Psophocarpus tetragonolobus*]), and highland pitpit (*mina* [*Setaria palmifolia*]) appear in the origin traditions of some groups in the central valleys. Greens that fall into the general category of spinach (*auwa* [*Rorippa* sp.; see Wohlt 1978:393]) are the only crops cited in the origin traditions of tribes living above 2,300 meters.

James Watson (1968) has proposed that *Pueraria lobata,* a tuber cultivated in small quantities throughout the highlands, might have been an important food source prior to the introduction of the sweet potato. In Enga it is called *kotena* and was planted within living memory as a minor crop. It is said to grow on slopes in well-drained, dry, loose soils, sometimes together with bananas or sugarcane. Strong poles were fixed to support its climbing vine. In areas below 1,900 meters it matures into a huge tuber within five months; at higher altitudes maturation is much slower. After harvest, the best tubers were preserved, cut into four pieces, dried, and stored for planting at a later date. People liked it but pigs did not. It was regarded as a valuable food for times of shortage, and curiously, it was one of the essential foods consumed during seclusion for the *take* ritual to attract wealth. *Kotena* receives little attention in Enga history; presumably it was always a secondary crop.[10]

Game Animals

Of all subsistence activities mentioned in origin legends, hunting receives first priority except in the middle Lai and Saka valleys. A man's ability to provide game meat is presented as a fundamental skill for attracting a wife, supporting a family, and gaining status in the community. Sharing of game meat was essential hospitality, symbolically extended to the ancestors during fertility cult performances. All aspects of hunting were closely connected to a man's sense of possession, pride, and self-respect; accordingly, a good proportion of the quarrels and wars that split up groups in the founding generations began with disputes over hunting areas, hunting implements, products of the hunt, or hunting dogs.[11] Hunting remained a significant subsistence activity in the central valleys at the beginning of the twentieth century. Until contact it made an important contribution to the diet outside of the major valleys and to ceremonial purposes in all regions: hunting for marsupials was an essential phase of most large fertility cult performances, and in western parts of Enga marsupials were a component of bridewealth payments.

Game animals named in origin traditions include cassowaries and a variety of marsupials: ring-tailed and phalanger opossums (*Petaurus* sp., *Pseudochirops* sp.), tree kangaroos (*Dendrolagus* sp.), bandicoots (*Perameles* sp.), spiny anteaters, and bush rats (*Uromys* sp.). These were either snared, trapped, or shot with bows and arrows. Cassowaries, which weigh up to thirty kilograms, were the largest game procured and could provide meat for several families. Trapping these dangerous birds, an activity carried out with the aid of magic formulas, required skill and courage. Success conferred prestige. Cassowary meat was the delicacy par excellence, and failure to share the savored cassowary intestines is mentioned as a common cause of disputes in origin traditions. Aside from cassowaries, most game hunted or trapped weighed under four kilograms, but when human populations were sparse, apparently game size was compensated for by abundance. Early historical traditions describe a supply of marsupials in the high forests sufficient to provide a regular contribution to the diet. A variety of birds and their eggs, lizards, frogs (*monge*), tadpoles (*amonangai*), grasshoppers (*aimbu*), beetles, caterpillars (*saunana*), and grubs (*pombata, mumu*), collected by women, children, and elderly men, are also named.

It is impossible to estimate approximately how much food hunting and trapping contributed to the diet—no doubt origin traditions, in order to make good stories, exaggerate the numbers of game animals killed. Nonetheless, recent studies of hunting in PNG offer some indication of the amount of game that can be obtained from the forest in sparsely populated regions (Dornstreich 1973; Hyndman 1984; Dwyer 1985). Peter Dwyer, for example, in his detailed study of the Etoro of the Mount Sisa area, found that Etoro got on the average 40-50 grams of meat per day (6 grams of protein) from nondomesticated animal foods. Even though the Etoro had a ratio of pigs to humans of 1.3, wild game provided twice as much animal protein as did pork and made up a much more regular part of the diet. The Etoro are not primarily hunters but rather devote most of their energy to gardening. A lifestyle involving more frequent hunting trips and movement of households to areas rich in game, as is suggested in the early historical traditions of groups living above 1,900-2,200 meters, could have brought hunting success two or three times greater than that of the Etoro.

Pandanus and Other Wild Plant Foods

Saa mendapu Ayandaka pilyamo upa kepa lao lalo konja.
Kuima tangaipa kepa lao lalo konja.
Lia aia kepa lao lalo konja.
Upa ingitange manditina nalimba bona,
Upa itaka manditina nalimba bona.
Sundu yaki upa pima patamba,
Aiyoko yaki upa pima patamba.
Anga sai upa lyao manditamba bona.
Yaka leno.

The opossums at Ayandaka are the *kepa* opossums I was talking about.
I was talking about the *kuima tangaipa* opossum.
I was talking about the *lia aia* opossum.
You'll have them all with intestines so let's go,
You'll have them all with excreta so let's go.
We'll wrap them with *sundu* leaves on our way,
We'll wrap them with *aiyoko* leaves on our way,
We'll cut down the bright pandanus so let's go.
That's right.

As expressed in this traditional love poem from the Lagaip valley, harvesting pandanus nuts, in conjunction with hunting and collecting bush foods, drew people from many different directions to the high forests for weeks or months at a time, sojourns that brought relaxation, socialization, and opportunities for courtship. The productivity of pandanus was enhanced both in private rituals and in the performances of large fertility cults. A fertility ritual for pandanus described to us in the middle Lai valley covered not only pandanus within the tribe's own range (middle Lai to Yandap) but also that in the Waka (western Kandep) and Tari-Margarima areas, for a bumper harvest could draw guests from afar.

Three species of pandanus trees are found in Enga, but one of them, *Pandanus conoideus* (*nitupa* or *alemokoi* in Enga), grows only in the lower reaches of the province and does not enter into any historical traditions that we collected. Of the remaining two, each of which has many varieties, *P. brosimos* (*wapena*) grows wild in the high forests and *P. julianeti* (*andaka anga*, literally "house pandanus") is currently planted around human habitations. *P. julianeti* has more mesocarp, softer nutshells, and sweeter, larger nuts than *P. brosimos*. It is not known whether *P. julianeti* is a different species or a domesticated variety of *P. brosimos* (Monro 1980). Some Enga say that the planting of pandanus trees near houses is relatively recent—certainly it is not described in early historical traditions, when hunting and gathering trips to the high forest were more common. *P. brosimos* produces only one crop annually, but since altitude affects rate of maturation, the pandanus season in the high country can last for five to six months. *P. julianeti* has a shorter growing season than *P. brosimos*—approximately two months—and occasionally trees bear nuts biannually. Both cassowaries and marsupials feed on pandanus nuts, so gathering them could profitably be combined with hunting.

Of all the vegetable foods available in Enga, pandanus was nutritionally the richest, particularly with respect to the amount of effort expended in harvesting it. Pandanus nuts contain approximately 12 percent protein, 66 percent fat, and 22 percent carbohydrates (May 1984). The mesocarp, the middle section in which the nuts are embedded, is also eaten by pigs and humans. It contains 8.46 percent protein (Rose 1982) and is said by some Enga to be a starchy food like root crops.[12]

In addition to pandanus, the forests of Enga offered a wide variety of other foods for gathering. The importance of these plant foods in the past, together with the insects, amphibians, and reptiles already mentioned, and their nutritional value to children of recent generations who gather them as snacks while playing in the bush should not be underestimated. They include ferns (*tambu, kelemane,* and others); chestnuts (*pai*), acorns (*lepa, tuu*), and other nuts (*ambuma tuu, yumbi tuu, lipai tuu*); *itatu* (*Pangium edule*); breadfruit (*kupi, kauma, kaima*); berries (*mamuni*); mushrooms (*waitu, mongenane, sumba, menalyaa, angaliti*); greens (*auwa, takae*); and seeds (*kanata, waku dii, sambai*), among others.[13] Some of these made up an important part of the diet for adults and children alike. For example, large quantities of chestnuts were harvested seasonally in western Enga. Ferns, breadfruit leaves, and greens were regularly cooked in earth ovens.

Pigs

In numerous origin traditions and early historical narratives, men and women are said to have owned pigs,[14] and in some they attend pig feasts and use pigs as one of several valuables for bridewealth exchanges or war reparations. As with wild game meat, the sharing of pork facilitated social relations. Nonetheless, in comparison with narratives from later generations, relatively little importance is attached them. To give some examples: though many tribes trace their origins to nonhuman ancestors, the majority of these are birds or marsupials; only three tribes of Enga attribute their ultimate origins to pigs. We recorded many accounts of quarrels and wars that broke out over hunting during the early generations, but only one that started over a pig. No large ceremonial *tee* exchanges of pigs and wealth are described in origin legends; the major social gathering was the traditional dance (*sing-sing* in Melanesian Pidgin, *mali* in Enga), which does not require pork consumption. Whereas there is only one origin tradition from an immigrant tribe in which pigs are mentioned as markers of social standing, hunting, particularly cassowary hunting, is mentioned as a high-status activity in several. Salt, stone axes, tree oil, shell headbands, and bark twine for net bags are the stuff of early historical traditions on the trade, not pigs. In short, during earlier generations pigs were slaughtered for feasts or given away as part of bridewealth payments, but until four to five generations ago, when there was a boom in various forms of *tee* exchange, pigs were fewer and of less significance. Wealth and social status depended not on agricultural production but on products like axes, net bags, salt, and cosmetic oil that involved other forms of labor.

In addition to *tee* exchange, there are at least two reasons for the lesser importance of pigs. First, more game was available, and so pigs were not the primary source of meat for daily subsistence or ceremonial occasions. Second, a much greater proportion of pig fodder came from forage, and thus less labor was invested in them than it was during the twentieth century, when up to two-thirds of the sweet potato crop in the Lai valley was fed to pigs (Waddell 1972:66). No origin tradition that we collected described pigs being fed regularly on garden produce. For example, the origin myth for the Atone Enga of eastern Kandep tells of a woman who domesticated the first pigs. She dug baby bush rats out of their burrow, raised them to discover that they were really pigs, and then bred them. It is said that "when the piglets were old enough to forage on their own, she bred the sow again and raised more piglets." The Malipini tribal origin legend gives a similar description: "Meanwhile, farther down the Lai valley there was a man named Sikini. This man had a huge pig that he had taken care of for his whole life by taking it out to root for worms in the morning and bringing it home at night. One day when Sikini was off doing something, the pig got lost." Sikini then tracked his pig, but the moment he discovered a salt spring, he instantly forgot about the animal, a passage that draws hilarious response today. Because Enga value pigs more for the labor that goes into them than for the pork that comes out, if pigs were raised largely on forage in times past then presumably they were once less expensive than they are today—as was the case in many other parts of New Guinea (Kelly 1988; Lemonnier 1995).

How feasible is it, if land is available, to raise pigs largely on forage? Certainly in some parts of New Guinea with low population densities, pig husbandry with very little supplementary feeding is still practiced profitably, as Ray Kelly (1988) has shown for the Etoro of the Mount Sisa area. The Etoro domesticate piglets by fondling and feeding them for the first three months and then feeding them with scraps to keep them tame.[15] In this way, the Etoro manage to keep a ratio of 1.3 pigs per person, as the Enga do today (Wohlt 1986). Etoro pigs are part of bridewealth payments and are slaughtered at funeral feasts, but they are not a major currency of wealth and status. Kelly (1988) and George Morren (1977) give similar examples from other PNG societies. Kelly suggests that in highland societies before the introduction of the sweet potato, when the population was much smaller and less garden food was available, pigs may have obtained the bulk of their fodder from foraging and, as semidomesticated animals, would have been more difficult to exchange live.

The Enga historical record lends some support to Kelly's hypothesis. Early historical tradition suggests that pigs indeed relied heavily on forage in the past and that only with increasing population, shortage of land for forage, and acceleration of pig production to meet the pressures of *tee* exchange were pigs' diets supplemented heavily with sweet potatoes. The result was an increase in their value. Furthermore, the exchange of live pigs became more frequent the growth of the Tee cycle of eastern Enga and the Great Ceremonial Wars of central Enga. No men or women whom we asked, however, had heard of a time before pigs were brought into houses at night or were not tame enough for live exchange.

In the twentieth century, there were women's magic formulas to speed the growth of pigs, men's formulas to tame wild pigs, a range of medicaments to treat pig diseases, and ceremonies to drive off ghosts that were believed to cause pig maladies (Kyakas and Wiessner 1992). There is nothing in the procedures, metaphors, or language of pig lore that gives any clue to whether these were age-old recipes or more recent ones.

Trade in Foodstuffs

The sharing and exchange of food was the social cement of Enga and a significant leveler of variation in food supply from area to area. Pandanus, taro, and yam feasts were held to gather people for specific purposes or merely to share a bumper harvest. Ancestral cult performances drew people from near and far, all bringing the specialty foods of their area to contribute to the feast. When food ran short, people of the high country sought refuge in lower valleys, where they were fed by their hosts; they had opportunities to reciprocate when the forest provided an abundance of pandanus nuts and other wild foods or by contributing labor when new gardens were cleared.

Though food sharing permeates early historical traditions, the Lagaip is the only region of Enga for which a regular trade in foodstuffs with people from other language groups is described. So essential was this trade that some Tayato Enga groups were called the "food seekers" by their Nete- and Penale-speaking trade partners to the north. Intermarriage with Nete and Penale paved the way for visiting, exchange, and the migration of Lagaip families to the Maramuni area, where they had access to lowland foods for the duration of their stay. Apparently, however, only two foods were actually traded on a regular basis and brought back on the long and rugged journey to the Lagaip: *itatu* (*Pangium edule*) and sago, both of which can be grown only below 1,200 meters. The sago trade was discontinued after the introduction of the sweet potato, and so little is known about it, but it must have provided the Tayato with an excellent supplementary source of carbohydrates.

Itatu, by contrast, was widely traded from lower regions into all the central valleys of Enga throughout the span of oral history and was included in bridewealth and other ceremonial exchanges. *Itatu* is made from seeds of the fruit of *Pangium edule*, a tree that grows below approximately 1,000 meters. These seeds contain poisonous substances belonging to a cyanide complex and require elaborate preparation to be made edible. *Itatu* is traded into the central valleys of Enga in three different forms according to the way it is processed: *kapale*, *ambelyo*, and *kindi*. *Kapale*, which means clay or mud in Enga, was made by boiling the fruit, soaking the seeds, and then burying them for up to a month to ferment. Strict ritual procedures were followed during *kapale* production. The resulting product was a foul-smelling, muddy-looking substance that was packaged and given in bridewealth payments. *Itatu* was also processed, dried, and sliced into a form called *ambelyo* used widely in ceremonial exchanges, for it is light, compact, and nutritious. To make the third form, *kindi*, the seeds were steamed overnight in an earth oven and eaten the next day. All forms of *itatu* were rich in energy and protein, with 244 kilocalories and 6.8 grams of protein per 100 grams of fresh weight (John McComb, personal communication, 1990; Bonnemere 1993).

Environmental Failure and Food Shortage

In the central valleys of Enga, severe environmental failure and food shortages are rare. When shortages do occur, they are the result of either warfare or poor planning. In areas above 2,200–2,300 meters, frost (*pipya* or *kinduta*) is prevalent, killing some of the crops, if not all, and making it necessary to establish alternate residences (Waddell 1975). Fortunately, the lower valleys provide havens, for they are frost free and only rarely affected by other climatic fluctuations such as drought or flood. At the onset of heavy frost, many families move to lower regions, leaving a sparse population to live on remaining garden and bush foods. Periodically, the frost is extremely severe, prolonged, and preceded or followed by a long drought and forest fires. It affects not only crops but also food-bearing trees, pigs, and game animals. Those who do not leave higher areas in time find themselves caught short and too weak from hunger to manage the two- to three-day trip to lower valleys. Wohlt (1978) found that forty-six out of approximately five hundred members of the

Bipi Kapii clan at Yumbis perished in the frost and drought of 1941, mostly children and very old people.[16] Meggitt (1958a) reported that Lai residents were affected by the drought, although not by frost.

The earliest report we collected of extreme frost that in combination with drought caused widespread famine pertained to the founding generations and was associated with the subsequent rapid acceptance of sweet potatoes in high-altitude regions. Other periods of severe frost are reported in oral histories, but it is difficult to construct an accurate chronology of frosts over the last two centuries because they are remembered only if they caused significant events such as migrations. For the twentieth century, we know that severe frosts occurred in 1900, 1941, 1972, and 1990 — approximately once a generation (Wohlt 1978:110).

In addition to accounts of frost and drought, there are legends concerning other natural disasters that occurred "long ago" which can not be placed in any specific generation. Presumably they happened in the founding generations. In Kandep, for instance, a historical narrative from "long ago" describes a heavy flood that wiped out gardens and most trees directly surrounding the swamps. When digging ditches near the swamps today, people still find the trunks of trees that died at that time. For the Lagaip, a storm that covered the valley in a thick blanket of snow is recalled. From that time on, as the narrative goes, gardens were built on slopes so that in the event of a reoccurrence, the snow would melt before it destroyed the crops. A great forest fire is said to have swept through the northern Lagaip many generations ago, leaving the entire region a wasteland. At another point in history, the entire Lagaip river is said to have dried up.

The most dramatic natural event recalled in Enga oral history is the "time of darkness," *yuu kuia,* when a volcanic eruption on Long Island off the northern coast of PNG blanketed the highlands with ash and blocked out the sun. Time-of-darkness legends from different parts of the province emphasize different themes, but those that we recorded, along with those collected by Meggitt (1973) and Mai (1981), depict people as staying in their houses, terrified. Pigs, dogs, and rats sought the shelter of houses, and wild animals, bewildered, came out into the open. A few courageous men went out to scavenge food from the gardens or clear the ash from the roofs so it would not break through the thatch. For a reason that is not remembered, these could only be men from families with one son. People who could not find food slaughtered pigs and ate them. After a few days people were desperate, but then rain fell and cleared the sky. Streams and rivers were temporarily blocked with ash, and gardens were covered.

Russell Blong (1982) found that the Enga time-of-darkness legends accurately described the nature and effects of the ash fall. Only the generational dating was questionable. Paul Mai (1981, cited in Blong 1982:178), on the basis of twenty-four Enga oral traditions on the time of darkness collected by Enga-speaking oral history students, found that most legends placed the event between 1840 and 1880, or approximately four to five generations ago. We received similar answers upon first questioning, but when we asked whether it occurred around the same time as better-known events in these generations—major wars or migrations— informants immediately retracted their statements and said that it had occurred much earlier, sometime in the founding generations. In this respect our findings agree with Meggitt's (1973:124): "Nobody was prepared to suggest just when the darkness came. The most common response was, 'My father's father told me this story, and he learned it from his father.'"

Blong (1982:193), on the basis of radiocarbon dating, among other methods, estimated that the time of darkness occurred in the mid-1600s, a date that would fall within the founding generations of Enga oral history. Golson (1982:130), in his analysis of archaeological material from Kuk, found that the ash fall coincided with environmental changes that indicate the introduction of the sweet potato. If these dates are accurate, then it means that Enga historical narratives describing extraordinary events can be passed on in some detail for at least three hundred years.

Division of Labor

Kimape cut down strong trees like *pipi* and *maukele* to build a fence around his garden. When he finished, the fence looked like opossums' teeth. He grew taro and these grew like rats' tails. So much green food appeared that it looked like a lake.

However, Kimape was not happy. He used to think about where he could find a woman to share the fruits of his labour. (Gibbs 1975:167)

This passage, taken from a myth recorded in the Porgera valley, sums up a problem conveyed in many tribal origin traditions—that tribal founders had to make efforts to attract wives who would bear their children, share the wealth of the land, and provide kinship ties. For example, the founder of the Lyomoi tribe in eastern Enga hunts and plants gardens to nurse a leper woman back to health so that he can marry her. The founder of the Malipini tribe in central Enga convinces the wife of another man to stay with him by lavishly providing her with the products of his hunting and gardens. And the founder of the Waitini and Lakani tribes of Kompiam wins his wife by impressing her with the richness of his forests and gardens. Not a single origin myth or legend that we collected states that tribal or clan founders sought wives who could cultivate gardens and raise pigs.

In stark contrast is the attitude expressed in the following passage, taken from the life story of Lambu, one of the great big-men of the Yakani tribe, who was born around the beginning of the twentieth century.

I told you earlier that my father was married to many wives. Well, all the rest were married to look after his pigs and gardens except for my mother. He married my mother solely for the purpose of doing *tee* exchange with her relatives. That was the initial reason. However, after marrying all of those women, obviously he did *tee* exchange with many of their relatives. (Kambao Lambu, Yakani Timali clan, Lenge)

Lambu's grounds for marrying ten of his eleven wives are clearly laid out: they would cultivate gardens and raise pigs to make him a wealthy man. Such attitudes are common in narratives of the past four to five generations.[17]

It could be argued that the viewpoint expressed in the first quotation is the product of myth alone, were it not for other evidence suggesting a real change in the division of labor through time. In ten out of forty-two origin traditions or early historical narratives, women play no role at all, whereas men engage in both hunting and gardening or else one is a gardener while his "brother" is the hunter. In another eleven traditions, men are said to be hunters, and gardening is not discussed at all. There are ten origin traditions in which men and women share the garden work, four in which only women are mentioned as gardeners, and five in which women are described as gatherers. In only two cases are men described as hunters and women as gardeners. Though women are underrepresented, the overall impression given is that men hunted, women gathered, and men and women worked gardens together, men clearing and planting and women tending and harvesting. Later, with the development of complex ceremonial exchange, the image of the self-sufficient male hunter-gardener vanishes, and emphasis is put on the importance of female labor for cultivation.

The division of crops into men's crops and women's crops gives further insight into the past work routine. Bananas, sugarcane, ginger, and yams were crops cultivated exclusively by men, and only men had the magic formulas with which to plant them. The staple crop for most areas, taro, was cultivated cooperatively by men and women. Thus, men hunted, did a good part of the garden work, and did all the work involving wood—chopping firewood, fencing, and house building. Women cultivated taro (together with men), grew other minor crops, gathered, and were responsible for the time-consuming work of extracting fibers from bark, twisting it into twine, and making frontal aprons (*yambale*) and the large net bags (*nuu*) used to carry everything from meat and garden produce to infants. Such a division of labor would have given men a greater work load—in view of this it is not surprising that the sweet potato became primarily a women's crop in both eastern and western parts of Enga.[18]

Relations between "Hunters" and "Gardeners"

As we discussed earlier, for the Lagaip, Porgera, and some parts of Kandep, origin traditions describe a division of niches between "hunters" of the high country and "gardeners" of the lower valleys, accompanied by cultural differences.[19] Unfortunately, neither myths nor historical narratives give a good picture of the lifestyle of the hunters, their residential arrangements, or their male-female relations. Probably there was no clear line between the two groups in terms of subsistence — all "gardeners" had some dependence on hunting and trapping, and though it is not stated, the "hunter-gatherers" of the high country must have supplemented their diet with garden foods, either grown in small plots or gotten in exchange with horticulturists. The result could have been a relatively homogeneous population with a continuum of adaptations ranging from heavy dependence on gardening to heavy dependence on hunting-gathering, but the oral record indicates otherwise. Rather, a conceptual distinction between "hunters" and "gardeners" permeates myths and origin traditions. It is accompanied by mention of intermarriage and exchange between the two, on one hand, and by tension and misunderstanding, on the other. We summarize four examples of well-known origin traditions couched in myth that have at their center relations between "hunters" and "gardeners."

The first is the lengthy origin myth for the Pokalyanda, or Aeatee, fertility cult of the Potealini tribe.[20] It opens by describing two brothers who live in the high country near Laiagam, the older of whom keeps pigs and hunts cassowaries and marsupials. The younger brother eats the lowly foods: lizards, snakes, and food scavenged from the bush. The younger brother goes out looking for food, gets lost, and travels eastward to the Lai valley, where he meets a beautiful "sky woman" who takes him to her well-kept house surrounded by flourishing gardens. He marries her and is transformed into a handsome and wealthy man. They make arrangements to pay the bridewealth so that his brother can marry another woman from the east. A very complex plot follows having to do with misunderstandings and quarrels over a *kundu* drum given as bridewealth. In the end, the marriages are broken, and the younger brother turns into a snake that becomes the protector of the Potealini tribe. Among other things, the entire myth dwells on the differences in lifestyles of people in the different niches of the area where the fertile Lai valley meets the rugged high country of Sirunki and the Yandap, and with misunderstandings that develop between them.

Another myth that has been adopted as an origin tradition by the Tatali tribe of Kandep and the Payame clan of Porgera concerns the difficulties of a marriage between a gardener and his wife, who is from a hunting-gathering group. It tells of a man who captures a beautiful woman in the forest. To escape, she turns herself into a number of different animals, but he does not release her. She agrees to go with him if he promises never to call her the daughter of a pandanus tree. One day when he is away, she becomes enthralled by *yae* birds dancing in the forest and neglects their child and household chores. In anger, the man breaks his promise, and she disappears with their son into a river. After a long period of mourning and pursuit he recovers his family. She then admonishes him: "Look at all the trees you have cut down. You have destroyed the forest. Never say these bad things to me."

In addition to themes concerning tension in marriages between "hunters" and "gardeners" is that of the exchange of labor for agricultural products, as is played out in the origin myth of the Bipi tribe (see Appendix 7 for the full version). A "gardener" from the southern part of Kandep comes to a place called Bipi Lendea at the northern end of the swamps, looking for someone to help him cut the branches off the trees in his garden. There he encounters snake people who live in temporary shelters, and much is made of the difference in housing between "hunters" and "gardeners." Molopai, the snake man and "hunter," reluctantly allows his favorite son, Bipi, to go with the "gardener" to help him. Molopai's son moves through the forest with ease, kills an impressive number of marsupials along the way, and then skillfully cuts the branches from the trees in the garden. The "gardener" prepares domesticated foods for him, they eat their fill, and they go to sleep. During the next days he discovers that the young man turns into a snake at night, and one night he clubs and tries to roast him. The snake boy escapes, returning home to tell his father what happened. The father takes revenge and then warns his other sons to disperse so that the same will not happen to them.

Other versions of this story are told by Bipi and by most agricultural groups of southern Kandep. The latter's versions are reciprocal and admit to the attempted murder of Molopai's son but attribute it to a misunderstanding—they did not realize that the snake was Molopai's son. All versions suggest that men from "hunting" groups exchanged labor for domesticated foods, and all imply that relations between the two groups were fraught with misunderstanding.

Finally, there are a number of myths that center on fear of the deep forest. They contrast the safety of cleared land with the dangers of the high forest and the demons believed to inhabit it. Fear of forest demons and respect for the forest demanded a change of language during hunting expeditions to a ritualized, indirect form of speech that was used throughout Enga and in many other highland societies (Franklin 1972; Pawley 1992).[21] There are some suggestions in Enga myth that such fears were not pure superstition but were based in part on tense relations between "hunters" and "gardeners." For example, at the end of the origin myth for Bipi, the founding ancestor, Molopai, takes revenge on the gardener who attempted to cook his son. He assumes the form of a forest demon and devours the gardener's son, directly acknowledging association between "hunters" and forest demons.

A similar concept—that hunters of the high country were cannibals with magical powers—is found in the origin legend of the Lote tribe near Laiagam. A handsome and skillful cassowary hunter comes down into the valley to attend a dance, adorned with necklaces of cassowary claws. The crowd watches with horror as one of its young women gets up and dances beside him, for people believe that he is a cannibal and that the cassowary claws are human toenails. She marries him in the end, and they prosper and found the Lote tribe, proving everybody wrong.

Summary

The portrayal of population, environment, and subsistence laid out in the preceding pages must be regarded as a tentative baseline from which to look at change, for in the oral traditions about the founding generations it is difficult to separate fact from fiction. Within these limitations, the following picture emerges. Approximately eight generations ago, the valleys of the Lai, Saka, Minamb, Ambum, Lagaip, Porgera, and Lai-Purari (Kandep) rivers were inhabited by some ten thousand to twenty thousand people who were divided internally by differences in subsistence base, dialect, dress, and ritual, among other things. Most of the land within reach of these valleys was already claimed as hunting territory. In the fertile valleys of eastern Enga, under approximately 1,900 meters, lived sedentary agriculturalists who cultivated taro, yams, bananas, sugarcane, and other crops, supplementing their diet with hunting. In central Enga, between 1,900 meters and 2,200 meters, hunting/trapping and gardening seem to have been roughly equal in importance. For western Enga, gardening virtually drops out of the picture among groups originating at about 2,200–2,300 meters, and precarious, shifting horticulture together with hunting and trade in foodstuffs seems to have provided the mainstay for groups living below 2,200 meters. Men hunted, cleared gardens, fenced, built houses, chopped firewood, and defended clan or tribal land. Women tended gardens, gathered wild foods and materials, and produced net cloth for bags and clothing. The brunt of the work load appears to have fallen on men. Pig husbandry was based largely on forage, and game animals rather than pigs provided the major source of meat for daily and ritual consumption. Early myths and narratives depict culturally recognized distinctions between "agriculturalists" and "hunters" accompanied by ambiguous relationships of tension and misunderstanding, on one hand, and marriage and exchange, on the other. Neither hunters nor agriculturalists emerge as dominant. These differences in lifestyle throughout Enga, and particularly those between east, center, and west, strongly affected the course of developments even after the sweet potato provided a common denominator for production in all areas of Enga.

3

Social Organization, Leadership, and Trade in the Early Generations of Oral History

To sketch a starting point from the material contained in Enga historical traditions on kinship and intergroup relations, leadership, and trade is not an easy task. Myths are of little use in reconstructing social relations, for they are often updated to entertain. Personal syntheses of what people have heard about the distant past can yield valuable insights but must be evaluated with information from historical narratives that describe concrete events. The two remaining sources, nonmythical origin traditions and early historical narratives, often have no definite anchoring point in time and can be greatly abbreviated.[1] Still, it is

possible to glean some valuable information from these sources concerning the marked differences that existed between eastern, central, and western Enga, important relationships and their meanings, and the significance attached to the many forms of material goods that were circulated to maintain these relationships. In order to have sufficient material, it will be necessary to draw on historical narratives from a period of unknown duration spanning the time from the founding generations until the sixth to seventh generation before the present. We call this period the "early generations"; it covers the time just before and just after the introduction of the sweet potato.

Patrilineal Descent: Tribes and Clans

The ideal basis for Enga social and political organization during the early generations, as today, appears to have been the patrilineal tribe and its respective clans,
whose members claim descent from a common ancestor. According to historical
narratives and our estimates from genealogy, tribes were much smaller at the
time and appear to have cooperated in a broader range of activities. Clans, in
turn, appear to have been composed of but a few men's houses, subclans receiving virtually no mention. How long this organizational model has been prevalent
in Enga is impossible to determine, simply because the delineation of patrilineal
tribes and clans is the very subject matter of Enga origin traditions and genealogy — it is the given ideal structure from the outset. It defined land-holding
groups and established corresponding rights and obligations for cooperation,
defense, and exchange. It delimited units of competition, each with its own
leaders: tribes competed with other tribes, clans with other clans, and so on.
Loyalties within clans (and, in the earlier generations, within tribes) were strong.
Fellow clan members helped fill each other's needs for defense, cooperation in
agricultural enterprises, and the raising of payments for war reparations. They
gave assistance to individual households in need, whether or not this aid could
be reciprocated.

For the early generations, our data do not confirm the strict patrilineal norm
for clan membership laid out by Mervyn Meggitt (1965a): historical narratives
and genealogies indicate that maternal kin and in-laws were regularly recruited
from outside to increase clan size, forge trade ties, assist with defense and land
clearance, and so on. This was particularly true for the more mobile groups of
western Enga (Wohlt 1978) and for migrant groups who established new communities. For example, genealogies from the founding generations for some
tribes of central Enga, Kandep, and the Lagaip valley trace up to 30 percent of
their clans to daughters or granddaughters of tribal founders or to "adopted"
males. Immigrants were assimilated quickly and called by agnatic kin terms after
the second generation.

Early oral traditions depict tribal organization as having been more centralized
in the east than in the west. Eastern and central Enga tribes, whose members
were clustered in more sedentary communities, apparently had much better
opportunities to coordinate their exploits than did their dispersed, mobile neighbors to the west. This difference is expressed in a number of ways. Origin
traditions for some tribes of the east and center include descriptions of the tribal
founder's dividing up wealth and land between his sons, conveying the image of
a centralized family. For western regions, in contrast, family images of tribal
organization, though present in genealogies, are entirely absent in origin tradi-

tions. Whereas it is often tribes that are the protagonists in eastern Enga, the principal actors in the west for the same generations are clans or subclans. Furthermore, different units were rallied to fight in the east and west: narratives from eastern and central Enga report a high frequency of intertribal conflicts, whereas those from western Enga describe predominantly inter- or intraclan conflicts.

Leadership

The nature of leadership in patrilineal tribes and clans of this period is difficult to assess, because oral traditions give credit to groups, not to individuals, and express equality of male clan or tribe members. For this reason we make only a few observations. First, Enga do not make heroes of their distant forefathers.[2] To the contrary, egalitarian ethics structure oral traditions to the point that founding ancestors may even be ridiculed. In the tribal founder "hall of fame" are such characters as Lungupini of the middle Lai valley, who uses his own leg as a block against which to cut grass. Upon his wife's first menstruation he shows great pity for her "wound," binding it with grass and leaves. Yanaitini of Tetemanda, though the putative founder of a large and powerful tribe, is said to have had a disagreeable character. Ima Kano of the Ima tribe in Kandep, a man caught between a former world of hunting and a modern one of agriculture, is at once idiot, trickster, fool, and conservative. He is too primitive to observe the restrictions on sexual behavior and has intercourse with his wife while her parents are present, and he is too stupid to realize that his net bag is not a person, cutting it up when it does not obey his orders. An entire repertoire of Ima Kano stories has entertained people throughout Enga for generations.[3]

Despite this blanket of egalitarianism thrown over early historical narratives, concepts of low and high status are not totally lacking. In the east, it is said that men who controlled the salt-ax-stone trade at Tambul and in the Saka valley had always been influential managers of wealth, like their descendants of later generations. Interindividual competition for attained positions of status and wealth thus appear to have been accepted from the early generations onward. By contrast, in western areas of Enga, both myths and historical narratives portray social relations as more egalitarian. The only mention of wealth or status is in conjunction with hunting: good hunters, particularly cassowary trappers who could provide meat for the group, are credited with high regard in several historical narratives. Take, for example, the ending of the origin legend for the Lote tribe of the Laiagam area, which describes the marriage of a Kunalini woman to the tribal founder, Lote, a great cassowary trapper believed to be a cannibal:

The Kunalini woman was named Tamako. Because she was one of the most beautiful women in the area, she attracted many suitors and was the subject of much gossip. Nobody had the courage to approach her and ask her for marriage until Lote did, and so she became his wife.

Lote and his wife moved to Mamale and had a son. Tamako discovered that Lote was not a cannibal but a great trapper of cassowaries. She named her son Kaiti [woven cassowary feather headdress] for the cassowary meat that she ate regularly, which was considered by others to be the food of wealthy families. She named their second son Kamapu [ceremonial ground] as an indication that he was born to a family of high status. Her third child, a daughter, she named Kandelyo [to look at, be in high regard] so that she could become wealthy and be highly regarded. After that she had three more children, Watiti, Ipane, and Kepe. (Sipisipi Pote, Lote Ipane clan, of Kupitu, Mapumanda)

Furthermore, in western Enga but not in the east, ritual experts who presided over ancestral cults were highly feared and respected, though they were men who possessed neither the wealth nor the mediation and organizational skills of big-men.

How much fame was attributed to war leaders of the past is uncertain. Until the fifth or sixth generation before the present, no war leaders, heroes, or organizers of war reparations are lauded. Only then do the names of some fight leaders begin to appear in conjunction with certain wars, but their military achievements receive little eulogy except in first- or secondhand accounts from recent generations. No doubt these were men with "name," though their status and influence seem not nearly to have matched those of the war leaders described for eastern highland societies (e.g., Berndt 1971; Watson 1971; Godelier 1982). In the religious realm, ancestral cult performances of the east were conducted by elders, not by specialists. In the west, ritual experts of inherited position, who commanded considerable fear and respect within their immediate realms of specialization, presided over the performances.

Polygamous marriages, perhaps the most objective universal markers of wealth and status, also indicate social inequalities from the early generations onward, with some men in each generation having two to four wives. The accomplishments of polygamous men are not specified, though there can be little doubt that proficiency in mediation and oration, like all abilities that benefited the group, were part of their repertoires.

Personal statements concerning the development of leadership, founded on information passed on by people's fathers and grandfathers, give a similar impression. Prior to the expansion of the Tee cycle, the Great Ceremonial Wars, and war reparations, status differences were recognized but leadership was less strongly developed and was executed largely through quiet mediation and persuasion. Public boasting displays and quasi-coercive actions such as preferentially giving and withholding wealth, so characteristic of more recent generations, were few. Like early historical traditions, personal statements underscore the principle of potential equality of all male clan or tribe members that was to be an important force throughout Enga history.

Whether or not leadership is said to have been weakly or strongly developed in any given generation, the Enga term for leader, *kamongo,* is applied throughout to men of influence, with the exception of ritual specialists. It can best be translated as "big-man," a term that came into regular usage with Marshall Sahlins's (1963) classic paper on Melanesian leadership. It applies to enterprising men who have created rather than inherited their name, fame, and influence through their ability to manage wealth, mediate, orate in public, and organize — in other words, to deploy a variety of skills that benefit the group and thereby elicit the loyalty of others. Because their leadership operates by "the creation of followership" (Sahlins 1963:290), it is based on power to achieve, not on power over others, and must be constantly maintained by words backed with deeds.

The vast amount of research and discussion of Melanesian leadership over the past four decades (for good summaries, see Lindstrom 1981, 1984; Brown 1990a, 1990b) and in recent years (e.g., Lemonnier 1990; Godelier and Strathern 1991) has shown that the category of big-man encompasses a great diversity of leadership styles, extent of power, and spheres of influence. This generalization applies not only cross-culturally but also within single cultures. For example, even in the twentieth century there were different degrees of "bigmanship" in Enga. Big-men ranged from competent organizers of subclans with limited followings to the great *kamongo* of the Tee cycle who had great influence beyond the boundaries of their clans, assembling and distributing hundreds of pigs in any one Tee festival. There were different styles of *kamongo,* from quiet men whose words were few but carried much weight to flamboyant showmen and orators. Even economic strategies varied, some men drawing a good deal of wealth from home production and applying much of it to clan needs, and others building far-ranging networks financed through regional exchange systems. With such diversity possible in Enga concepts of *kamongo,* it seems reasonable to use the term "big-man" for leaders in all generations who were self-made and who elicited followers through actions beneficial to their groups. At no period in history do criteria for leadership appear to have been otherwise.

Relations with Affinal and Maternal Kin

Because the affairs of patrilineal tribes and clans are the very subject matter of historical traditions, one might expect that people's relations with affinal and maternal kin would be eclipsed. That they are not attests to their centrality in Enga society. Enga sometimes portray their social universe as a spiderweb of delicate strands, the outer tiers spun through marriage ties. The importance of relations with affinal and maternal kin is laid out from the beginning in narratives from the east, center, and west, even though relations between the sexes differed greatly by area, being much more relaxed in the east. Numerous origin traditions not only explain how tribal founders came to be but also describe their search for spouses outside the clan and the establishment of relations of mutual support with in-laws.[4] For those that begin with myth, the means of finding a spouse are simply episodes in entertaining stories—a hawk luring a wife for his adopted son or a man capturing a female forest spirit. The majority are more down-to-earth. They tell of men encountering women on journeys, or of love at first sight during dances when marriages forging important interregional ties were contracted. For instance, the union of one of the sons of the Apulini tribal founder with a Sambe woman whom he met at a dance in Laiagam created a major link between the Lai and Lagaip valleys. That of the daughter of the Limbini tribal founder at Mulitaka to a man from the Bipi or Kuu tribe of northern Kandep paved the way for the Tekepaini, a large branch of Bipi, to migrate to the Lagaip.

No matter how young men and women meet in myths or early narratives, the subject matter generally turns to relations with in-laws initiated through bridewealth exchanges. Though such exchanges are rarely described in detail in early narratives, it is clear that in the past, as today, bridewealth payments involved two-way exchanges between the families of the bride and groom. Most elders interviewed stated that even in the third to fifth generations, bridewealth payments were smaller than in recent decades and included fewer pigs in proportion to other goods or valuables—salt, stone axes, net bags, and processed *itatu* seeds, among other things. This claim is supported by the texts of traditional songs sung by brides (Kyakas and Wiessner 1992). It is emphasis on long-term relationships of mutual support rather than on bridewealth payments that prevails in a number of early historical narratives. For example, when Lyomoi of Tambul marries Sangamawana, daughter of Pembe, the founding father of Saka tribes, the negotiations are described as follows:

In the morning, when Lyomoi and Sangamawana prepared to leave, her parents gave her a net bag and a pregnant sow to take with them. Her father said, "Keep this pig and do well with it. One day I will come and visit you and then you can give me bridewealth."

Lyomoi took Sangamawana back the way he had come and they arrived at Kalintesa [Tambul] and lived there. The pig they had brought with them had five piglets, two females and three males. When the piglets were big enough, they castrated two of the males and kept one as a boar. The mother pig became pregnant once more and gave birth to three male piglets. Sangamawana's father came to visit them, and they gave the piglets to him as bridewealth. (Takuna Wapo, Lyomoi Tendepo clan, Kalintesa, Tambul)

The result of the marriage, whether representative or real, was a close association between Lyomoi and the Pembe tribes, who permitted six Lyomoi clans from Tambul to migrate to the Saka valley.

On the other side of Enga, the Kisipini origin legend from Tipinini in the Porgera valley tells how the tribal founder, Kisipini, fell in love with a young woman during a sojourn in the high forest to harvest pandanus nuts. He fed her mildly poisonous mushrooms to keep her from returning home and then asked her parents if she could stay with him while he nursed her back to good health. When she did not return home, they sent a message asking for bridewealth. Kisipini brought the bridewealth to Tari, and exchange relations between the two families began.

Incidents of more formalized bridewealth exchange also exist in early historical traditions. For instance, in the history of the Depe Waipalini clan, some seven generations ago a Waipalini man married a woman from the Ima tribe in Kandep, and the pigs for the bridewealth were staked out on the top of Mount Wambumanda, midway between the two regions. The spot is still marked and remembered. Over the next generations, the ties formed by this marriage facilitated the movement of people between the Lai valley and Kandep.

An interesting didactic narrative concerning the importance of marriage ties comes from the founding generations in Lyipini history. It cautions against holding back young women who want to marry and thereby forfeiting the enduring and profitable links that are established by formal marriage:

We [Lyipini] are not related in origin to Kepe and Aluni, but let me tell you the story. There were two girls who were dancing. Two young men from nearby saw them. Lyipini said, "They are dancing because they are moved by a young man's leg" [an expression describing sexual interest or promiscuity]. Kepeo, a son of Lyipini born of a woman from the Yandap, took a stick and beat them. The two girls became very frightened; maddened by pain, they fled in terror. They arrived at Sambakamanda, the place of the Aluni Kepe clan, and stayed there. They became the mothers of fertility and bore children. When they went to Sambakamanda, they brought net bags of wealth with them, and so their descendants are said to have easy access to wealth. For instance, even at a young age their children could handle a stone ax and own pigs or other forms of wealth.

Aluni Kepe was one of the sons of the two women. The two girls were daughters of Lyipini and sisters of Kepeo and Diuapini. One of the girls said to her brothers, "You two of the loincloth, stay here and leave us in peace since you have beaten us." The girls did not put their hands in the soil, they continued dancing. Kepeo was embarrassed because he had beaten them up and done a foolish thing. (Lanyia Kingi, Lyipini Diuapini clan, Rakamanda)

In his explanation, Lanyia said that the sons of the two women who eloped with men of the Aluni tribe became big-men who controlled the Sambaka trade route. Because the brothers of the girls did not support their desire for marriage and pay bridewealth, but instead beat them for promiscuity, potentially valuable exchange ties were never established.

The foregoing tradition is an exception for its time in that it centers on provision of wealth as one of the components of maternal and affinal relationships. Of twenty-three origin legends and historical narratives that have relevant information, only four emphasize wealth exchange, and all of these come from clans of eastern Enga directly on trade and early Tee cycle routes. The remaining nineteen briefly describe the bride's family as helping the young couple to get started by giving the two a garden, a pregnant sow, assistance in forest clearance, or an alternate residence after they are ousted in warfare. These, together with food sharing and general hospitality, seem to have been the most common stuff of relations with in-laws in the early generations. Only in the fourth to fifth generation, when war reparations and Tee exchange expanded greatly, did the provision of pigs become a regular obligation of affinal and maternal kinship.

Bridewealth is followed by a series of other payments to wife's or mother's kin: *wane kenge singi*, gifts for the growth of children; *beta pingi*, payments for children's injury or illness; and *laita pingi*, substantial death payments of pigs to maternal kin for every person who dies, whether man, woman, or child. Wife's and mother's kin do not have the same formal obligations to husband's kin but reciprocate when appropriate — in the Tee cycle, to help with war reparations, or to provide alternate residences in times of hardship. We cannot say on the basis of historical traditions anything about payments for children's growth and injury in the early generations; these are familial concerns, not subjects of historical tradition. Men and women interviewed claimed only that in the time of their grandfathers these payments were made with simple things — for instance, bark fiber for making net bags, small packages of salt, or black palm wood. Only with the expansion of *tee* exchange and subsequent integration into the cash economy were they dramatically inflated to include live pigs and cash. By contrast, funeral feasts during which pork or pigs are given to maternal kin are one of the age-old events that people of the early generations are said to have traveled long distances to attend. They are the most common context in which pigs are mentioned.

In summary, the dominant impression conveyed by early historical narratives concerning affinal and maternal ties is the wide range of possibilities they opened for alliances, trade, assistance, and socializing. Trips to attend feasts, traditional dances, and other social occasions held by clans of in-laws broke the drudgery of daily life and provided opportunities for innovations to spread. Such open relations stood in contrast to agnatic relations within the clan, which established boundaries on the basis of brotherhood, and with them, a certain degree of closure. Both were essential to the welfare of families, though they sometimes brought about conflicts of loyalties. As we shall see, both provided important orientations in steering the course of history.

Land and the Maintenance of Boundaries

Meggitt's studies (1972, 1977) have portrayed the Enga as a people preoccupied with the acquisition and defense of land through physical means, that is, warfare. To better understand the relations of people to each other and to land, as well as choices available for the defense of land, it is important to extend the concept of territory maintenance to include social and ritual means. Social boundary maintenance (Peterson 1975; Eibl-Eibesfeldt 1975, 1989:321–39) is an idea drawn from ethology that provides a much broader concept of territoriality. Through social or ritual territory maintenance, people advertise and draw respect for their group and its boundaries. Once this is accomplished, access to resources can be opened to outsiders who show respect for possession and enter into relationships of exchange. Cooperation and respect, in turn, reduce motivation to take the property of others by force.

In the Enga case, although physical defense of clan boundaries was practiced throughout history, social boundary maintenance was equally important. Traditional dances, ancestral cults, and war reparation payments advertised territorial possession, and then access to clan resources was extended to affinal or maternal relatives from other clans, who entered into mutual exchange. Through such relationships people obtained wealth in the form of pigs, goods, and valuables from affinal relatives, assistance of many forms, and, in some cases, garden land to cultivate on a temporary basis. With labor rather than land in short supply throughout most of Enga history, obtaining wealth produced outside the clan through exchange offered much greater opportunities than did usurping the land of others and having to produce the same products oneself. The relationship between physical and social-ritual boundary maintenance for the early generations is discussed in detail in chapter 5.

War Reparations

Warfare, as a form of intergroup competition and as a means of boundary maintenance, has been endemic to Enga since the very beginning of historical traditions, in the form of both spontaneous clashes and systematic efforts to expel other groups. With perhaps the exception of strategies in early trade alliances, wars and subsequent reparations are the only truly political events described for the early generations, in the sense that they involved relationships of alliance and competition between entire groups. Whatever the cause of a war, the outcome usually was dispersal within clan or tribal lands or migration to fringe areas—not staying put and making peace with the enemy via reparations. Reparations appear to have been paid only to allies, for no origin traditions or historical narratives from this period report both parties remaining, engaging in formal peace negotiations, and exchanging wealth.

War reparations to allies for men lost or property damaged were paid as a matter of course, for it was recognized that allies did not join wars out of the goodness of their hearts but to receive similar help when they were in trouble, to avenge old grudges in somebody else's war, or to obtain part of the spoils of war, including land. Of fourteen legends from the early generations that give some idea of the contents of war reparations paid to allies, land was given in all fourteen, and in two, steamed food and live pigs or pork in addition to land. For the victors, the giving of land not only discharged part of their debts to allies but also secured friendly neighbors, making social boundary maintenance possible. If the losers were completely ousted, they often had the opportunity to give a portion of their land to their allies before leaving, thereby assuring a foothold should they try to return or, if they did not, friends and trade partners in their former homeland.

The following passages give two accounts of war reparations paid to allies as described in early historical traditions. The first comes from the war between the Aimbatepa and the Yamape (map 5:69, 80) some seven to eight generations ago in southern Kandep. After this war, the Aimbatepa reluctantly gave most of their land in the fertile Kaumbo valley to their ally Maulu, moving up into their former hunting territory.

A long time ago in the generation of Aimbatepa and Yamape [founding generations], there was a quarrel between two young men over a bow.[5] Each wanted the bow and neither would give in, so they began to fight. The fight escalated, and soon they had wrestled each other to the ground. Somebody came by, noticed that the fight was serious, and broke the bow in half, giving one-half to each of the young men.

This did not end the brawl, and soon others joined in. The quarrel escalated into a full-fledged tribal war between the Atone and Katinja people. Maulu, who lived in the higher country north of Kaumbo, supported Aimbatepa against Yamape and Yalipuni, the battles taking place on Maulu's land at Maulu Pau. In the end, Yamape retreated, and Aimbatepa moved to where they are settled now near Lakalapa. Aimbatepa gave his [their] original land to Maulu, who had helped in the war and whose land had been devastated.

Aimbatepa did not actually plan to give away his land, but it happened like this. After the war Maulu came to Aimbatepa and gave him a pig, a piece of sugarcane, and a banana leaf. He did this several times. Aimbatepa was puzzled by these gifts and tried to figure out their meaning. Later Aimbatepa realized that this was an indication that Maulu wanted to settle on his land where he could grow all of the things he had given Aimbatepa and take possession of his pigs, bananas, and sugarcane. Aimbatepa gave up his land and moved eastward to his hunting country near Lakalapa, where they are today. (Tumbili Meane, Aimbatepa tribe, Lakalapa)

The second account comes from a Yoponda legend collected by Roderic Lacey describing how the Yoponda and Nenaini tribes, both of Kakoli-speaking origins, were driven out of the Tambul area approximately six generations ago. Before migrating to the Minamb valley, the Yoponda paid war reparations to allies in the form of pigs, marsupials, and garden produce along with a good portion of their abandoned land, thereby maintaining friends and allies in Tambul. Their allies were two Kakoli clans—Aiyokoni of the Lyomoi tribe in Tambul and Kengetapae, a "brother" clan of Yoponda and Nenaini. The lands given in compensation listed at the end are all local places in the Tambul area.

In those days warfare was prevalent and it was in one of these wars that the sons of Yoponda and Nenaini became involved. The war by which they were forced out of their territory was against the Tendepa people and one other group whose name I cannot recall. The war broke out after a quarrel about a stolen boar and a tussle over a piece of land through which one man was building a garden fence.

The war that followed was one of the longest that was ever fought in the area. It went on and on until there was no more food left and all the pig stock was destroyed too. When the war was over, compensation payments still had to be made, but Nenaini and Yoponda had no pigs with which to pay and so they were faced with another problem besides war. Nevertheless, my grandfather's father's grandfather [Kapia, the grandson of Yoponda] asked the Saka people to hunt and kill some possums and bring them down to Kola to help him make his compensation. All that Nenaini and Yoponda could gather for these payments was possums; however, the Saka people brought along pigs, bananas and other foods besides possums. Among those who came from the Saka area the leading group was the Sassipakuni people and they came to the rescue of the Nenaini and Yoponda people.[6]

Compensation was then paid with possums and a few pigs. When they saw the plight in which the Nenaini and Yoponda found themselves, spokesmen from Sassipakuni said:

"These lands are caught up in warfare and are conquered by your enemies. Why do you allow your feet to be caught in such a troubled place as this? We are seeking new members and have much land that is vacant. Pay off your compensation debts and come to make a new home for yourselves in our territory."

Without any hesitation or reluctance on their part, Nenaini and Yoponda paid off their compensation debts: one to Kengetapae for their loss of two men named Umjape and Kambualo who were killed while fighting on Yoponda and Nenaini's side; and another to Aiyokoni for the loss of another two men who died while fighting on their side.

After making these compensation payments to the Kengetapae and Aiyokoni people, representatives of the Nenaini and Yoponda *palu* [lineage] spoke thus:

"These friends have come to rescue us from this troublesome place, so let us go. We have given you the pigs and possums for compensation and now we leave our territory to you."

When they had spoken in this way, they gave away those lands which made up their territory in Kola: Aiani, Kombolya, Sakala, Polyapu, Sokaenge, Wapulao, Nipilya, Ambano-Kungu, Lumbu-Pange, Molo, Mutumutu and Pokosaka. These lands made up their original territory but they gave it away before they left Kola.

When they arrived here [in the Minyamp (Minamb) valley], they were given territory by the Sassapakuni people and were left there by them to live on their own. (Lacey 1975:259–60; narrated by Kale, Yoponda, Walia, in November 1972; translated by Nut Koleala)

How important the transfer of goods and valuables was in war reparations to allies is difficult to discern from oral records. That land transfers are mentioned preferentially may be in part because they were remembered better than were exchanges of food and goods. Apparently, too, prior to the expansion of the Tee cycle clans living off the early Tee routes held war reparations at men's houses, implying that they were smaller-scale events than those of later times:

In the times of his ancestors before Yama first made the *mena tee pingi* [Tee cycle] they had a form of exchange called *tee pingi* also. This was a compensation payment made by one group to another after death in warfare. When these exchanges occurred, their ancestors would mark the event by planting a commemorative cordyline bush [*akaipu tipu wai*] at their ceremonial ground. At these earlier *tee pingi* men would perform these pig exchanges at their men's houses [*akalyanda*], not in public on the *Kamapi* [ceremonial grounds]. (Lacey 1975:166; interview with Kepai of the Apulini tribe)

In these parts [near the Mai-Layapo border], meetings were held at the men's house prior to war reparations. Small sticks were bundled to represent each pig. They made sure that each person in the clan, particularly the men, contributed something. Pigs were preferred. The actual reparations were distributed on the ceremonial grounds, unlike in many other places, especially areas to the west. For instance, people of the Yandap and Kandep areas [to the west] brought pigs to the men's house, where they tied them. Then the would-be recipients were invited to the men's house to look over the pigs and were given the pigs at the men's house. (Kambao Lambu, Yakani Timali tribe, Lenge [Wabag])

In short, although the evidence is sparse, war reparations of the early generations appear to have had the following characteristics: First, they were paid only
to allies on a regular basis; enemies solved problems by separating from each
other in space, either through the outmigration of one party or dispersal within
tribal lands. Second, land was a major component in war reparations,[7] whereas
steamed marsupial meat, pork, and vegetable foods, plus a small number of live
pigs, were supplementary components to meet social and emotional needs.
These features were to change as the land filled.

Trade

In the early generations, trade was active, as it probably had been for thousands
of years.[8] It is mentioned in a variety of contexts: bridewealth exchanges, barter
of salt for stone axes and other trade goods, and the exchange of foodstuffs.
Tribal founders are said to have made long journeys to obtain salt, axes, foodstuffs, and valuables.[9] Goods and valuables were traded for purely utilitarian
reasons—to procure ax stone, black palm wood, or foodstuffs; for social reasons—to be used as gifts that fulfilled obligations to affinal and maternal kin; and
for personal reasons—to procure items for self-decoration that increased social
esteem and chances of attracting spouses. One criterion of a big-man that is
frequently mentioned is that he have an ample supply of decorative items to lend
to fellow clanspeople who wanted to attend dances. Unlike the case in later
generations, transfer of nonagricultural products such as wild game meat and
trade goods, rather than transfer of pigs, appears to have formed the backbone
of exchange.

Early oral traditions give no detailed descriptions of exactly how trade was
carried out, nor do they stipulate the exchange values of different goods and
valuables. Long journeys for the purpose of trade are, however, depicted as more
regular events than they were in recent times, when the Tee cycle, Great Ceremonial Wars, and other exchange networks delivered trade goods to people's
own ceremonial grounds. Early oral traditions tell of trade trips from Tari to the
salt springs at Pipitaka in the upper Lagaip, journeys of north Mendi traders to
the salt springs of the Yandap, and travels of Nete and Penale people from the
Maramuni area to the Lagaip (map 6). Early traders were said to have traveled
alone, in groups with other men, or in parties with men, women, and children.

Salt
The major trade good produced in Enga was salt, sodium chloride. Enga craved
salt to enhance the taste of food and appreciated the labor that went into pro-

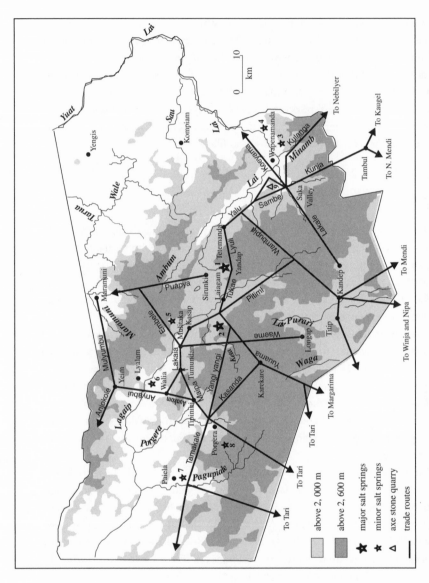

Map 6. Major trade routes and salt springs mentioned in early Enga historical traditions. 1, Yandap; 2, Pipitaka; 3, Nulupelemeposa; 4, Ketane; 5, Auketa; 6, Walia; 7, Paiela; 8, Kumbirae; 9, Kamongo creek quarry.

cessing it. Whether it was also a necessary nutrient is not yet well understood; there are highland populations such as the Eipo of Irian Jaya whose diet is similar to the Enga's but who manage well with no supplementary sodium chloride (Koch 1984:86). Its importance is summed up in the following testimony from central Enga:

The pack of traditional salt [salt wrapped in pandanus leaves] opened up areas such as the Layapo [eastern Enga], the Sau [Kompiam], Kandep, and regions to the west. The salt brought us cosmetic oil, the stone ax and its binding materials, and *itatu* fruits [*Pangium edule*], along with fibers for making women's net bags and men's aprons and bags. I was told by my father that if you do not have anything to do with the salt trade, then you will not meet new people bringing other goods that you yourself cannot produce here. All the major trade routes were established by salt going out and other valuables such as *mamba* oil, stone axes, *itatu* fruits, and other minor trade valuables coming in.

Had it not been possible for us to get what we needed with local salt, I cannot think of anything else that would have taken its place in doing just what it did. My father also told me that in finding marriage partners for my daughters and sons, I should try to establish links with respectable families on each of the major exchange routes that I have mentioned earlier. In doing so, one obtained access to the most valuable trade items traveling on each route. (Ambone Mati, Itapuni Nemani clan, Kopena [Wabag])

The largest salt springs were located in the center of Enga: throughout the Yandap and at Pipitaka near the Keta-Lagaip river junction (map 6).[10] Although the two locations are less than 20 kilometers apart as the crow flies, in the early generations the Yandap springs were owned almost exclusively by clans in the upper and middle Lai valley,[11] whereas those at Pipitaka belonged to clans settled directly at the springs and their relatives in the Porgera valley. Accordingly, much of the Yandap salt moved eastward while that from Pipitaka was traded westward; salt from both circulated to the north and south. There were smaller salt pools at a place called Nulupelemeposa at the intersection of the Lai and Minamb valleys; at Auketa on the north side of the Lagaip near Pipikungusa; at Walia in the Lagaip; at Paiela (Mangi 1988:64–65); and at Kumbirae west of Porgera near Aijama creek (Meggitt 1958b:312).

Detailed descriptions of making salt, a task carried out by men and women, can be found in the excellent accounts of Meggitt (1958b) and Jo Mangi (1988:63–64). Briefly, soft wood was cut into billets, dried, placed in the salt pools to soak for one to four months, and then removed, drained, and burned in special shelters containing fire pits. After about twenty-four hours the wood was reduced to ash comprising the final salt. The hot salt-ash was wrapped in large leaves before it could absorb moisture and then was bound with 10–12 meters of dried pandanus leaves to form a waterproof package. Because this process was slow, those who did not live nearby returned home after they had put their billets in the water to soak and came back after a few months to process them, a recurrent theme in myths and early historical narratives. The Yandap salt pools were generally fenced off into squares owned by individual families. At Pipitaka, access to the pools was organized differently: lineages or subclans had rights to different sections of a pool's edge. If people came to soak billets when the pools were full, they would lay them at the appropriate point along the edge to reserve a place. When a second party arrived, it put its billets behind those already on the shore in order to claim next priority, forming lines that radiated out from the pool's edge.

Although salt springs were owned, outsiders easily obtained access. People interested in trading for salt came to the Yandap and Pipitaka from such distant places as Tari, north Mendi, Tambul, Maramuni, and eastern Enga. In recent generations they often traveled in large, well-armed parties and stayed near the springs with friends, relatives, or trade partners with whom they traded piglets, shells, axes, or other goods and valuables either for packages of salt or for the right to use the pools (Meggitt 1958b). Specialist salt makers from clans that owned springs were also available to fill orders placed by trade partners. The area surrounding the salt springs was a peace zone—it was strictly forbidden for residents or visitors to assault men from enemy tribes who came to trade. Once travelers were outside of the clan boundaries of the owners of the springs, dangers were greater, but it is said that efforts were made nonetheless to solve problems between tribes on the major trade routes and keep them open and safe for travel. To give some examples of just how far salt traveled: salt from the Yandap springs reached the Lake Kutubu region to the south, the Jimi and Waghi river valleys to the east (Hughes 1977), the Sepik to the north, and the Lake Kopiago area to the west (see map 4).

Early oral traditions describe a process of making salt identical to that just given. Prior to the introduction of the sweet potato, however, seasonal residence was impossible in the direct vicinity of the Yandap pools, owing to the high altitude (2,600 meters or more), harsh climate, and poor soil.[12] Thus, members of tribes from the middle and upper Lai valley who held rights to various springs periodically traveled to the Yandap carrying stocks of food with them, placed the billets in the pools to soak, and returned to process the salt at a later date. At Pipitaka (2,200 meters), permanent settlement appears to have been possible even before the introduction of the sweet potato, and owners could provide accommodation for traders who came to buy or make salt.

No mention is made in early oral traditions of major tribal wars that took place over salt springs in the Yandap. There could be a number of reasons for this. First, without permanent settlements near the pools it would have been difficult to hold the land even if it could have been taken. Second, since there were many salt pools in the Yandap, they were not a scarce resource. Third, clans owning the pools gave access to visitors and traders without charging exorbitant prices; traders in turn made their own profits by bartering the salt at higher prices elsewhere. In contrast, the history of the Pipitaka area, which has fewer salt springs and suitable surrounding land for permanent settlement, recounts numerous and vicious tribal clashes.

Axes

Salt was exchanged for a variety of other trade goods, the most important being stone axes. There was only one ax-stone quarry in Enga, at Kamongo creek on the land of the Itokone tribe (map 6), where good quality ax stone was quarried from exposed boulders in the bed of the creek.[13] Axes from this source, called *sambe* or *motokea*, were used by surrounding tribes but were less important both qualitatively and quantitatively than axes obtained via trade networks from quarries in what is now Western Highlands Province. John Burton (1984:218), who sorted 623 axes in a collection made by Paul Brennan from all regions of Enga, found that only 4 percent were *sambe* axes from the middle Lai valley. Thirty-five percent were from the Tuman quarries in the Jimi valley, and the remaining 61 percent came from other quarries in Western Highlands.

Burton (1984, 1989), in a fascinating study of stone ax production and trade, located the major sources of ax stone in Western Highlands Province and gave a vivid description of quarrying procedures. Establishing a new quarry required an enormous amount of labor, first to remove the overburden and then to quarry the ax stone. The job was carried out by a labor force of up to two hundred men working full-time for up to four months at a time and following strict ritual procedures. Mobilizing and feeding such a large workforce, combined with the risks of following unproductive seams of stone and of shaft collapse, made the venture an expensive one.

Quarrying was only the first step, for blanks then had to be ground down, polished, and sharpened, tasks that together required thirty-five to forty-five hours of hard work on the grindstone. Then the axes were hafted, another forty-hour job for a skilled craftsman (Burton 1984:121, 134). Axes were valued for both their functional properties and their labor input. Out of the association between labor and value came the ceremonial ax, a decorative item of no functional value worn on ceremonial occasions as a symbol of wealth. It was one of several forms of wealth, together with salt and spun fibers for net bags and frontal aprons, that was labor intensive but not based on agricultural production.

Those who could not get stone from the Itokone quarries or Western Highlands made do with small, poor-quality axes fashioned from river pebbles. Although these were used throughout Enga, larger and stronger quarried blades greatly facilitated the felling of large trees and building of houses and so were highly desired components of bridewealth payments. Even in the generation before contact, only the wealthy men in each clan regularly possessed such axes. Through preferential lending, they could affect the production of others:

Before the coming of the white man, we used stone axes to build houses, make fences, and clear gardens. Kalia Pawata and Kalia Polane were among the very few in the clan who owned big stone axes. Everybody had his own small axes, but when we had to cut down large trees, it was necessary to borrow large ones. Sometimes the owners of the big stone axes would lend one, but only grudgingly. They would say, "If you don't use it correctly the binding material will break and the edge will become dull faster than it should. If you want to use it, then be sure to take care and use it properly." (Pambene Ayakali, Yakani Laita clan, Yatulama [Wabag])

Burton found that stone from modern quarries, including those that supplied ax stone for Enga, entered the archaeological record between twenty-five hundred and one thousand years ago (1984:228, Table 10.7). The provision of large work axes for forest clearance in areas like Enga, in exchange for salt, may have added an incentive for people to open quarries so long ago.

Net Goods

Strings spun by hand from bark fiber were a third significant, labor-intensive, utilitarian trade good (see Mackenzie 1991 for a thorough discussion of net goods). When woven into frontal aprons, they constituted an important element of ceremonial dress, and when made into net bags, they enabled their bearers to transport everything from infants to pork and garden produce over rugged country with both hands free. Different qualities of strings and weave determined whether a frontal apron or net bag was for everyday or ceremonial use. So important were they in early oral traditions that women were as frequently described in the context of collecting bark fibers as they were in gardening, suggesting that women were the producers of a major source of wealth even before the intensification of pig husbandry. As a good that could be made in all regions of Enga, net cloth was a currency of exchange for those who had no other highly desired resources in their areas.[14]

Social Valuables

In addition to valuable utilitarian goods and foodstuffs, other prized items circulated over early exchange networks. Most of those named in myths and legends were items of decoration to be worn at traditional dances, the major occasions during which people met, engaged in social activities, and arranged marriages. Dances were also the great social levelers in that everyone could borrow ornaments and participate; men could dress as women, and women as men. A good appearance during a traditional dance was an indicator of social and moral standing and enhanced the possibility of attracting a spouse. Accordingly, the appropriate items of dress were highly valued and took on myriad symbolic values.

Items traded included *mamba* and *topa* oil, which was rubbed on the skin to make it glisten; ochre, used for face painting and other ritual purposes; plumes from cassowaries or birds of paradise; shells; and cane for belts and armbands. Perhaps the most important of these in the trade was *mamba* tree oil, which could be obtained only from lower altitudes. Most *mamba* came from the Lake Kutubu region, where local residents tapped it from large lowland forest trees, *Campnosperma brevipetiolata*. It was transported north by Huli, Wola, or Mendi traders, exchanged for salt or other products by people throughout the southern Kandep area, and then circulated northward into all areas of Enga (Mangi 1988). After the Kompiam area was settled by Enga tribes, *topa* tree oil, also made from a species of *Campnosperma*, was traded into the central valleys of Enga. Additionally, highly desired drums (*laiyene*) used in traditional dances were produced by the Ipili and circulated eastward over trade networks (Meggitt 1957). The stealing of such drums during dances and their retrieval constitute the plots of a number of well-known myths and legends. *Mamaku*, gold-lip pearl shells cut into crescent shapes, were rare until the fourth to fifth generation before the present, and other shells receive little note in early oral traditions with the exception of *angata tenge*, strips of opossum skin embroidered with *Nassa* shells.

Trade Routes

Map 6 offers a rough reconstruction of the major trade routes of importance in early oral traditions.[15] It shows only the general direction of each route, not its specific course, and only a small fraction of all the routes that crisscrossed Enga. All clans were connected by local paths, and there were multiple links over ridges between valleys, making it possible for travelers to avoid enemy territory and lessen the risk of ambush.

In the east, two major routes, the Kunja and the Kulanga, were used for the importation of stone axes. Several ran from the Saka valley down the lower Lai, the Koeyama being the most prominent in the early generations. Though certainly the Layapo tribes had some knowledge of the Sau valley, early historical traditions record no major trade with peoples of this area. A number of routes, including the Lakale, Wambupia, and Apole (the last not shown on map 6), led from the Saka and Lai valleys to Kandep and on to areas of the southern highlands. Over these, salt and axes were sent south, and cosmetic oil and other goods moved north. These were also the paths traveled by Kandep residents seeking refuge from frost.

Axes and other goods were sent up the Sambe and Yalu routes into central Enga, from where numerous branches led to the Yandap salt springs. Only one of these, the Lyuli, is shown. Salt was brought to Laiagam via the Tukae route and the Suku (not shown). A similar convergence of trade routes occurred near Pipitaka, from where salt was exported to the south and west. Such paths, too, were traveled by peoples of the high country seeking refuge from frost.

A number of routes linked Laiagam with Porgera. Along them, salt and axes, among other things, moved west, and drums, feathers, and shells received from the northwest moved east. From Porgera, several trade routes led south into Huli regions and west into the Paiela area and on to Kopiago. In contrast to eastern Enga, people of Sirunki and the Lagaip and Porgera valleys had strong ties to the north, from where they obtained foodstuffs and other lowland products from Nete, Hewa, and Penale peoples.[16] From Yeim, Maramuni, and other communities in the north, people made voyages north into the Sepik and west into Hewa territory.

Populations of the main island of Papua New Guinea were in contact with traders throughout the period considered in this book, and with colonists since 1884 (Waiko 1993). The many trade routes leading in and out of Enga certainly brought Enga people into interaction with surrounding highland and highland fringe societies, but how far did this broad sphere of interaction extend? Did it bring new items or ideas from traders, European explorers, and colonists long before contact? We looked carefully for signs of influence from outside and identified three effects. One was epidemics that preceded first contact. For example, a severe epidemic, perhaps smallpox, that ravaged entire groups is reported to have occurred in the Kompiam area during the fifth generation. The social impact of such epidemics, however, is hard to assess from the historical record. A second effect was an increase in trade items, such as cut pearl shells, coming from the coast after European contact. A third was rumors of new and strange happenings relating to encounters with Europeans, probably heard tenth-hand. Some echoes of these rumors, particularly those regarding European material possessions, appear in myths and stories, in accounts of dreams, and in visions reported by cult participants. There is little evidence, however, that the few material goods or ideas that filtered up from the coast had a substantial impact on the economy, society, or politics of Enga, other than to enable anticipation of things to come.

Trade Alliances

Early historical narratives give some clues to how the trade was organized, all agreeing on one point—the existence of a central axis that extended from the Tambul area of present-day Western Highlands Province, along the Kunja and Kulanga routes into the Saka valley, and over the ridge on the Ome route to the middle Lai valley (map 6). The major participants were Yanuni clans of Tambul, Yambatane of the Saka, and Itokone and Yanaitini originally of Tilyaposa and Lamandaimanda (mid-Lai). The descendants of all of these tribes symbolically express their close relationship in a number of common origin traditions.[17]

The Yanuni-Yambatane-Itokone-Yanaitini alliance worked as follows: Yanuni and other Tambul tribes stood in the middle of trade networks that drew axes, shells, oil, and other goods from regions to the south and east up through the Kaugel, Nebilyer, and north Mendi valleys. As middlemen, they took these goods and valuables down the Kungu bush route to their "cousin" tribe, Yambatane, in the Saka and exchanged them for salt from the Yandap, among many other things. From the Saka, the trade alliance proceeded northwest along the Ome route to the Itokone and Yanaitini people of the middle Lai valley, who had laid claim to some of the major salt springs in the Yandap, some thirty to forty kilometers to their west as the crow flies. After the introduction of the sweet potato, Yanaitini moved to Tetemanda in central Enga to be closer to the salt springs, extending the alliance along the Sambe and Yalu routes (see map 11). Focal clans in these tribes are said to have had the salt–stone ax trade firmly in their grip. Other routes branched out from the Saka valley, but these appear to have been without major alliances.[18]

Within the Yanuni-Yambatane-Itokone-Yanaitini alliance, trade is said to have been carried out on the basis of individual ties, with members of these four focal groups acting as agents to obtain goods for people off the central trade route:

Bartering was done with members of Yanaitini, Itokone, Yambatane, and Yanuni, all of whom had strong links and easy access to each other's resources. People from surrounding areas would bring to their relatives in these four groups whatever they had to offer in exchange for what they wanted to obtain. For example, if a person from the Aluni Waiminakuni clan wanted to trade a stone ax for a pack of salt, he would get in touch with an Itokone man. The Itokone man would then arrange to have a pack of salt brought down to Tilyaposa from Tetemanda to trade for the ax. Or the Itokone man would take the Waiminakuni man with his ax to a Yanaitini family at Tetemanda and exchange it in Yanaitini territory. The arrangements for the exchange were usually made through kinship connections. In this way, people surrounding Yanaitini, Itokone,

Yambatane, and Yanuni traded and got what they needed from distant areas. (Tipitape
Kaeyapae, Itokone tribe, Pompabus)

   Although this description is recent in that it comes from personal recollections
of Tipitape's forefathers as well as from his own experience, it does agree with
descriptions in early historical narratives that tell of people from the south or
west going to one of the four focal tribes in the Lai valley with goods to exchange
for stone axes. The extent to which the trade alliance was in the hands of big-men
and created social and economic inequalities is unclear; early historical narratives
mention only that there were always big-men at the focal points who had influence over the flow of goods and valuables.

   In western Enga, traders from the Mendi, Wola, and Huli people journeyed
to the Keta river to obtain salt or to eastern Kandep in quest of axes from the
Lai valley. This trade seems to have been carried out largely by parties or individuals on the basis of kinship relations; with perhaps a few exceptions, it seems
not to have been fixed by trade alliances. In one exception, the Pumane tribe at
the Keta-Lagaip junction and its "uncle" clan, Maipange, at Porgera may have
had a more structured alliance through which salt was sent westward to Porgera
and then on to the Huli.[19]

   As ceremonial exchange networks such as the Tee cycle and Great Ceremonial
Wars expanded, pigs became numerically the most important items of wealth.
Nonetheless, essential trade goods — salt, axes, net bags, tree oil, and decorative
items for ceremonial dress — retained their social and utilitarian value and continued to be important components of most exchanges until contact. From
approximately the fifth generation onward, the Tee cycle and Great Ceremonial
Wars circulated goods and valuables, and so the need to engage regularly in
trading expeditions decreased. The traditional trade, *aloa pingi,* did continue, but
its most active participants were people outside of the major exchange networks
who profited by bringing goods and valuables into the central valleys at the peak
of the exchange cycle. A good example was traders from the Mendi area who,
before periods of ceremonial exchange in eastern Enga, came to the Yandap,
purchased salt, took it south, and traded it for cosmetic oil. They then returned
to Enga to sell the oil at much higher rates than had been required to purchase
the salt (Meggitt 1958b:312). Before the Great Ceremonial Wars, similar trade
transactions provisioned warriors with plumes.

   Over generations, existing trade paths became trampled into wide "roads,"
with new routes branching off from them as Enga migrated into fringe areas.
Throughout history, the salt springs drew people to the center of Enga, providing
channels for the spread of new developments and ideas. Some Enga suggest that

without the integrating effect of the salt trade, regional differences might have been much more pronounced than they were at first contact.

Summary

Although information on social organization, leadership, and trade prior to six or seven generations ago is sparse, it is possible to reconstruct a sketch of Enga society in the early generations. Such a sketch highlights a number of points that were significant for setting the course of Enga history. Had Enga organization at the onset been less open, more egalitarian, and less structured—or, conversely, more hierarchical and centralized—the course of events after the introduction of the sweet potato would undoubtedly have been very different. As it was, oral traditions portray a society divided into localized, land-holding tribes and clans whose membership ideally, but often not in practice, was determined by patrilineal descent. The small tribes of eastern and central Enga appear to have formed cooperative units for some enterprises, while those of western Enga were more diffused. An ethic of potential equality of all individuals (within the sexes) prevailed, and leadership was not strongly developed, though some men were recognized as *kamongo,* big-men. Marriages contracted with persons outside the tribe or clan formed the bases for enduring intergroup alliances, and bridewealth exchanges initiated lifelong relationships of exchange, assistance, and mutual support with maternal and affinal kin.

These two axes of kinship, agnatic and affinal, embedded each person in a network of supportive relationships that filled his or her needs. Clan membership, based primarily but not solely on descent from common ancestors, defined social and spatial boundaries and furnished a pool of men and their families who, as potential equals, cooperated in agricultural enterprises, defense of land, procurement of spouses, and appeasement of the ancestors, among other things. It assured security—from the net bag (in which babies were carried) to the grave, so to speak. Whether individuals' actions were right or wrong, they were supported and defended. On one hand, clan membership limited individual enterprise in that the products of efforts had to be returned to the clan. On the other, when this was successfully done, clan leaders acquired powerful backing.

The second axis of kinship, that established by marriage, had to be created and maintained. It opened boundaries and was virtually the only path to obtaining resources or assistance from outside the clan. Efforts to build and maintain networks based on affinal or maternal kinship depended on family enterprise as well as on social and economic competence—whereas all people in principle could reap similar support from their clans, ability to successfully manipulate maternal and affinal relationships was the key to furthering the social and economic standing of the family.

Marked differences existed in social relations between east, center, and west. In the east, for example, patrilocal residence after marriage was more pronounced, tribes and clans were more unified, status differences were more pronounced, relations between the sexes were more relaxed, and the trade was more formally organized. These differences set different courses for change in the three areas and provided an important source of variation from which the large exchange networks were later crafted.

In the realm of intergroup relations, boundaries and rights to resources were maintained by both social means, advertisement and exchange, and physical ones, armed aggression. The former offered great potential for innovation on the part of individuals and groups while the latter employed more conservative means: spacing or replacing neighbors. War reparations were paid to allies for men lost but rarely to enemies. A major component in reparations was land, supplemented by the distribution of cooked food and small numbers of live pigs. People gathered to socialize at traditional dances, rituals, pig feasts, and funeral gatherings, and they undertook long journeys for the purpose of trade.

In keeping with principles of potential equality, status came from the distribution, not the accumulation, of wealth. There is little evidence for intensive agricultural production to create a surplus in the form of pig herds, or for social inequalities based on pre-sweet potato agricultural production, as Golson (1982) and Feil (1987) have proposed for other parts of the western highlands. Rather, the focus of economic interest (beyond subsistence production) was on the trade that circulated nonagricultural products—salt, ax stone, strings of bark fiber, articles for self-adornment, and wild foodstuffs—and other forms of wealth, many of which required intensive labor input. The field for economic competition was open, and because wealth, whether in the form of pigs, land, or goods, could be transferred for women given in marriage or lives of allies lost in battle, competition for wives and allies thus implied wealth competition (Godelier 1991). Certain clans and individuals exerted a stronger hold on the trade than others, and these were in a better position to profit from the potential for increased production after the arrival of the sweet potato. A broad network of trade routes traversed Enga, integrating the people of different regions. It was along these paths that sweet potato vines passed from hand to hand to bring changes to the lives of highlanders some two to three centuries before contact with Europeans.

4

The Introduction of the Sweet Potato

The introduction of the sweet potato remains an enigma in many respects. When did it arrive in highland New Guinea? Was it first brought from South America along eastern routes or western ones? What was its immediate impact? Another aspect that is initially puzzling is why the sweet potato, though it was to become the staple crop, slipped into Enga with relatively little note in oral traditions, particularly in the eastern and central regions. When one asks about the sweet potato today, some say that it was always there, whereas others list the varieties that were first cultivated, name somebody in the clan who was the first to plant a large mounded sweet potato garden, or cite a discovery that it grew well at high altitudes. That the sweet potato is a relatively new crop is not common knowledge: only a few know oral traditions that pertain directly to its origin.

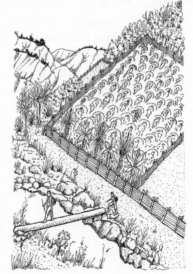

Upon closer reflection, perhaps this is not so surprising.[1] First, sweet potato vines, unlike crops brought by Europeans, were not introduced by a dramatically intruding population but were quietly passed along existing local trade routes. The plant came from lower-altitude areas where it did not grow especially well and offered few advantages, if any, over taro and yams, and so it would not have been presented as a "wonder crop." Second, Enga historical traditions tend to focus on who did what and when, and to relegate origins, other than tribal origins, to the domain of myth. How sweet potatoes were used and by whom thus receive more attention than the fact of their arrival. It might be added that the gray area concerning the introduction of the sweet potato is not without parallels today, for many young Enga cannot distinguish major crops introduced by Europeans from traditional ones.

There are two competing ideas about the introduction of the sweet potato. The most widely held view (Yen 1974; Watson 1977; Golson 1982; Swadling 1986; Golson and Gardner 1990) is that it was brought from South America to Indonesia some 350 to 400 years ago by Portuguese explorers and passed via the local trade to the island of New Guinea. An alternate hypothesis argues for an earlier introduction from the east, on the basis of linguistic studies (Scaglion and Soto 1994) and evidence for the presence of the sweet potato in Polynesia by 800-1500 B.P. (e.g., O'Brien 1972; Yen 1974; White and O'Connell 1982:183; Bellwood 1987; Hather and Kirch 1991). Had it arrived via the eastern route, it *could* have reached the highlands earlier than it might have by the western route, although an eastern introduction does not necessarily imply anything about its time of arrival in the New Guinea highlands. Though charred sweet potato tubers from around 800 B.P. have been found on Mangaia Island in central Polynesia, some 4,000 kilometers east of New Guinea (Hather and Kirch 1991), many factors could have speeded or retarded its diffusion. Sweet potato is a high-altitude crop that in coastal areas does not grow as well as other crops, and so it may have been slow to spread from island to island. Social and ideological factors must also have played a role, because even though sweet potatoes were cultivated in western parts of the New Guinea highlands for at least the past 250 to 400 years, some groups in the eastern highlands obtained it only between 60 and 100 years ago (Watson 1965a; Sorenson 1972, 1976). Among the Mountain Ok, taro remains the staple crop, though sweet potatoes have long been available (Hyndman and Morren 1990).

Attempts to determine when the sweet potato was introduced to the highlands on the basis of the archaeological record and pollen analysis have been inconclusive, for both methods yield only indirect evidence. No fragments of sweet potatoes have been found in archaeological sites dating earlier than 250 years ago, so only the changing use of swampland as revealed by archaeological excavations can be interpreted as an indicator of its introduction. Pollen analysis also gives no definitive results, since sweet potato pollen is not preserved. Pollen diagrams give relative frequencies and not absolute counts of forest taxa, and thus are but general measures of decline in primary forests owing to either natural or human agents. As a result, the evidence has been subject to very different interpretations (see, for example, Golson 1977, 1982).[2] At the moment there is more support for a later than for an earlier introduction (Golson and Gardner 1990).

Fortunately, the oral record is somewhat stronger, though it, too, is inconclusive. First, there is negative evidence, such as that presented in chapter 2, that the sweet potato does not enter into early oral traditions. Second, there is the positive evidence elicited by questions such as, "Do you know anything about the origin of the sweet potato?" The most explicit oral traditions on the subject come from the Huli, who divide their history into three periods (Ballard 1995): (1) *ira goba naga,* when ancestral *dama* spirits are held to have eaten wild foods only, (2) *ma naga,* when people who were fully human ate taro, cucumbers, bottle gourds, and yams but dug no ditches for proper gardens and raised no pigs, and (3) *hina naga,* when people ate sweet potatoes, cultivated proper ditched gardens, and raised pigs. This scheme of staple phases is complemented by a genealogy extending back some twenty generations, with three to five generations of *dama* spirits, four to eight generations of taro eaters, and eight to ten generations of sweet potato eaters. First possession of the sweet potato is attributed to a woman from the Digima clan who obtained it within the temporal scope of Huli history. Most other clans then trace their ancestors' acquisition of the crop from Digima (Ballard 1995:85).

The Enga oral record also holds traditions concerning the introduction of the sweet potato, but they are not formalized like those of the Huli: Enga do not divide their history up into periods on the basis of subsistence strategies, nor do they associate the cultivation of the sweet potato with the origin of truly modern humans or pig husbandry. The cultivation of the sweet potato bears no direct relation to genealogy. That few persons whom we interviewed knew sweet potato origin traditions attests to the fact that its arrival was seldom given a central place in the overall cosmological or historical scheme.

In the rest of this chapter we present the oral and ritual evidence for the introduction of the sweet potato into Enga country by area and then draw on material from historical narratives concerning experimentation with the new crop, initial uses and impact on subsistence systems, and settlement of different regions. In contrast to approaches used by others, ours concentrates on people's acceptance of the sweet potato, for attitudes differed greatly according to altitude, other environmental conditions, and social factors. We close with estimates of population growth within the span of historical traditions.

The Arrival of the Sweet Potato in Enga

Of the oral evidence that does exist in Enga, all testimonies point to an introduction of the sweet potato into the Lagaip and Porgera valleys from the north prior to the generation of subclan founders. The historical narrative summarized

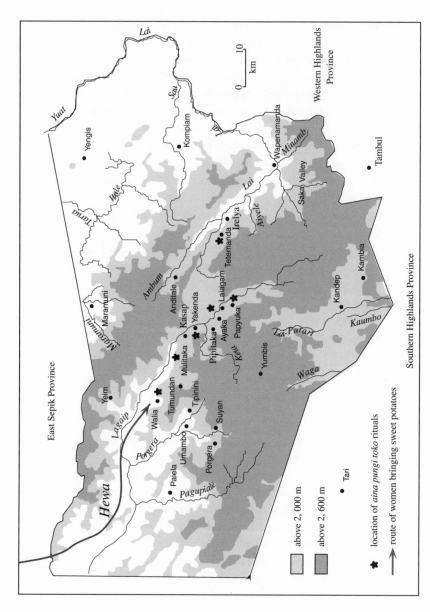

Map 7. Locations of *aina pungi toko* ("bridge of the sweet potato vines") rituals.

in the introduction, which tells of the two sisters bringing sweet potato vines from the east Sepik and distributing them at Walia (map 7) in western Enga, is a straightforward account devoid of mythical overtones (see Appendix 3 for the full version narrated by Alo Peter). Although the two women are probably "representative" of a more complex process of transmission, what is fascinating is that the plant's arrival was commemorated in a ritual held periodically in the Lagaip and upper Lai valleys from its time of introduction until first contact. The following passage picks up where Appendix 3 leaves off:

So because the women brought the sweet potato here, this is what we did at Walia when there were severe food shortages. We constructed a bridge [aina pungi toko, the bridge of the sweet potato vines] across the Yolo river, which flows past Walia, in commemoration of the two women who came with the sweet potato vines for the first time and in an attempt to get them to come once again, bringing fertility.[3]

On the day the bridge was constructed, all the women came dancing in from both sides carrying sweet potato vines with tubers on them, taro, and sugarcane, with which they wrapped the ends of the log to be placed across the Yolo. The ends of the logs, enveloped in crops, were then covered over with soil to fix the ends of the bridge firmly in place. When this was done, they sang the following songs [the first by men and the second by women]:

> Papa kaki niina andaka iki lopo sipya lao lelepe, nana andaka opaka pipya, yolo toko kee-waa.

> My sister, don't say that your house was the only one that experienced food shortage. My house was the same. Yolo bridge, kee-waa.

> Manja pote nyo pelyamo akimeaka nyo pelyape, sio, pungi tange minapeta sio.

> Manja sweet potato being taken out by what? Stayed, holding tightly to the vines.
> [Manja refers to the Maeyango tribe at Walia, who hosted the aina pungi toko celebration]

In memory of the man who went down and brought up these two women [sisters] with the sweet potato vines, the men hunted opossums and steamed them in an earth oven. They did nothing else but eat them [that is, it was a memorial feast with no ritual acts performed or spells recited]. In memory of the sisters they built two large earth ovens lined with hot rocks, and they steamed sweet potatoes in one and marsupials in the other. They took all of the steamed sweet potatoes to the ceremonial grounds and distributed them to everybody who was there, calling the names of clans and areas of Enga [and surrounding language groups] to commemorate the distribution and spread of sweet potatoes. Even if nobody from one of these areas was there at the ceremony, somebody would always come forward saying, "Peakape" [an expression of gratitude], and receive them with appreciation. After distributing the sweet potatoes to everyone present and [symbolically] to all areas of Enga that they could think of, they said, "Ongo pitaka bipa wapipi" [it has been distributed to all].

Here are some names of the areas to which they symbolically gave sweet potato: Tari, Kola, Mendi, and so on. Many people gathered for this event; it was like a very large traditional dance and not restricted to one small group. (Alo Peter, Pumane Kelyanyo clan, Tumundan)

And so it was that through the *aina pungi toko,* the introduction of the sweet potato and the subsequent distribution of vines was remembered.[4] The symbolic distribution of sweet potato vines furthermore expresses an important theme that appears again and again in Enga history: that prosperity comes to those who distribute and share, rather than to those who retain wealth for themselves— whether the wealth is in vines, food, cults, ideas, or goods and valuables. During a later interview, Alo Peter added that when the women brought the sweet potato to Walia, they found the soil so poor and stony that they built mounds to facilitate its growth.

From Walia, the sweet potato vines were passed on to neighboring clans, to people from other parts of Enga, and to members of surrounding linguistic groups who came to visit relatives or barter for salt at Walia's salt springs. One of the recipients was probably the Ipili-speaking Mayuni clan of the Porgera valley, whose history tells how it spread the crop to other groups in the Porgera valley:

A long time ago a wind named Pulaipa gave birth to Mayuni and Tanakae, who lived as brothers in one house. Mayuni stayed at home in the valley at Umambo [map 7] making gardens, digging sweet potatoes, and building houses, while Tanakae was a cassowary hunter. Tanakae went everywhere hunting cassowaries because all of this forest land was his. He often slept in Kutepa rock shelter [near Tipinini].[5] When he killed cassowaries, he roasted and ate them all by himself. Mayuni was not happy with his brother Tanakae because most of the time he didn't share with him. Sometimes he thought about leaving his brother and going off to live on his own.

One day, Mayuni went to his gardens and Tanakae went out hunting after they had a quarrel about sharing. Tanakae returned home and found that his brother was gone. Thinking that he might have left for good, Tanakae went to Tari, where he got married and became the founder of a large clan.

Mayuni came home very late and found that his brother had gone, so he set out after him. It was late and darkness fell, so he spent the night at Suyan [map 7] with an old man and his daughter. He had brought a bag of sweet potatoes with him, which he hid outside the house to save for his journey.

The old man told his daughter to go out to get some food early in the morning. At daybreak she took her net bag, went out, and came back with a bag full of earth-worms.[6] The young woman cooked the worms and gave some to Mayuni.

"I don't eat this kind of food," said Mayuni, "but I'll get you some sweet potatoes that I left outside the house. He brought them in and gave some to the old man and his daughter. They cooked the sweet potatoes and found that they tasted very good.

"Since you are young and unmarried, you can take my daughter with you," the old man offered after they had eaten.

Mayuni took the young woman back to his home, and they planted sweet potatoes together. They also brought some vines back to the old man and planted them at his place. That is how sweet potatoes spread to the Suyan area. Before they did not eat sweet potatoes, but only earthworms. (Aiyo Anginape, Mayuni clan, Umambo, Porgera)

A reciprocal version of this story is told by the recipient, the Aipakane clan at Suyan, as part of its origin tradition. It not only confirms the event but also adds a new dimension—that the sweet potato arrived during a period of famine. At the end of this version, the girl turns into a sacred stone used in the Kepele ancestral cult, expressing a widespread theme in western Enga ritual associating the introduction of the sweet potato with the advent of sacred fertility stones.

From Walia, where sweet potato vines were first distributed, the tradition of the wandering women bringing sweet potato vines was both integrated into the Kepele cult of some Lagaip tribes and commemorated in related *aina pungi toko* performances. For example, historical traditions from the Monaini tribe near Kasap (map 7) acknowledge that there was a time before people had sweet potatoes, when taro grown in the Lagaip and sago received in trade "took its place." Monaini people recall the arrival of the sweet potato in the origin myth for the ancestral stones used in their Kepele cult. These stones are said to have originated when a woman or a woman and her daughter traveling from the north or northwest (depending on the specific version of the tradition) brought sweet potatoes and other foods to the Lagaip. She (or they) settled at Kasap and turned into sacred fertility stones. Two women from Kasap traveled on to Keokungusa near Ayaka, where the daughter was seduced by the Walini tribe's founding father. The mother went on to Kanake near Laiagam, the Kepele cult site of the Sambe tribe. Both are believed to have turned into sacred Kepele stones. Two women then left the Sambe site and journeyed to Tetemanda and Irelya, territory of the Yanaitini and Apulini tribes, respectively, where they were seduced by tribal ancestors and later were transformed into the fertility stones used in the Aeatee cult, a version of the Kepele. In no oral tradition is it stated that these were the same women, though the continuity of the tradition from Walia to Irelya is recognized.

Wherever the women bearing sweet potatoes are alleged to have traveled, *aina pungi toko* celebrations similar to the one at Walia were held, usually prior to

Aeatee-Kepele performances, to commemorate their journey and bring fertility. In addition to the bridge built over Yolo creek near Walia, *aina pungi toko* were built over Andane creek near Mulitaka (map 7) by Tekepaini, Limbini, Aiele, Monaini, and Kaya clans; over Lematu creek near Yakenda by Monaini, Tupini Sakate, and Yambanima clans; over Yapu creek near Ayaka (Laiagam) by Walini clans; over the Lagaip river near Papyuka by Sambe clans; and over the Lai river near Tetemanda by Yanaitini clans.

The following is a description of the *aina pungi toko* performance near Yakenda and its association with the Kepele cult:

There was a creek near Yakenda called Lematu that ran from the high ground toward the Lagaip river. It was influenced by the Kepele. When the Kepele was hungry, it gave a sign by flooding the creek and causing landslides that damaged homesteads and the natural environment.

When this occurred, the ritual expert called for the ceremony to determine whether it was time to hold the Kepele cult. This was done because it was believed that the Kepele man stayed at Kasap and his wife at Pipitaka. When the man was hungry, he wanted his wife to come from Pipitaka and bring him food, particularly sweet potatoes. She did not go secretly to Kasap but caused the creek to flood as a sign that people should prepare the way for her to bring food to her husband.

Messages were sent out to the Sakate and Monaini people, and then the ritual experts told certain men to go to the bush and chop two *ipiliaka* trees that had been designated for the bridge. The logs were carried down from the bush accompanied by a singing and dancing procession. When the ritual experts had laid them across the creek, subclans of Monaini and Sakate organized themselves in groups and danced to the construction site bearing food and sweet potato vines with which to decorate the bridge and singing the following song:

> Aina pungi nyoo pata, aki mendeme nyo pata? Aina pungi ongonya tange minapeta sio.

> If anything will take the sweet potato away from Yakenda, what would it be? I hold on to the vines tightly.

A similar song was sung for pandanus.

People waited to see if the Kepele man at Kasap was satisfied with the food that had been provided. They waited for a month and watched to see whether their gardens grew well and pandanus trees bore good nuts. If conditions improved, this meant that the male Kepele had been hungry only for garden foods and that the woman had provided them. If conditions did not improve, then it meant that both the male and female Kepele were hungry for meat, and it was necessary to kill pigs and hold the larger cult performance. Monaini and Tupini then performed their Kepele, and Sakate held theirs at Pipitaka. (Saiyo Tondea, Sakate Ipane clan, Yakenda, Lagaip)

The association of the *aina pungi toko* and the Kepele cult varies from place to place, and only in areas around Walia is the tradition of the two women bringing sweet potatoes from the Sepik known today. Despite local variations, all *aina pungi toko* performances had the following points in common. They were held during times of food shortage, in memory of the wandering women, with the intent of bringing about renewed fertility. They all involved the building of a bridge over a creek or river that was subject to flash flooding. The log was put in place with great festivity: its ends were fixed in beds of sweet potatoes and other food crops, or the log was decorated with sweet potato vines, or both. *Aina pungi toko* celebrations were big events gathering people from many different clans and tribes for a traditional dance during which songs identical or similar to those just quoted were sung. They had the celebratory air of feasts without the solemn rites of ancestral cults.

Kandep

The arrival of the sweet potato in the Kandep area is reflected in myths and rituals as it is in the Lagaip valley, but not in the historical narratives we collected. We encountered no mention of the Walia distribution or the *aina pungi toko*. A myth from the Kambia tribe of southern Kandep (map 7), however, has two aspects that may have historical bearing, for, like traditions from the Porgera valley, it claims that the sweet potato was acquired during a period of famine.

In the beginning, there was no sweet potato in this land. There were vast areas of forest, and the people lived on nuts and fruits that they gathered from trees in the forest. At that time there lived a man and his wife; like everybody else they too lived from gathering. Then there came a time when there was a long dry spell, and all the fruits and nuts dried up and died. There was nothing around to eat, and they thought that it would not be long until they starved to death.

One day the woman disappeared, leaving her husband alone in his house to die of hunger. Later she returned with some white roots. He wondered what these could be. His wife hastily cooked them in the fire and told the man to eat them. They tasted so good that he asked his wife where she had gotten them. She told him that she had gathered them out in the bush.

The dry spell lasted for months, but the wife repeatedly brought home sweet potatoes for both of them to eat. Then one day she complained that she had a stomachache, and the next day she died. Just before she died, she told her husband that he was to bury her in a certain place and was to visit her grave four to five months later. He did as he was told, and to his astonishment he found sweet potato vines growing on her grave. He then dug into the grave and found many tubers. He then collected the vines and distributed them to his friends living around Kandep and Mendi. The sweet potato actually grew from the sexual organs of a woman,[7] and so even today, if there is no sweet potato around, women can always find some, because it is thought that sweet potato originated from a woman.

Though we recorded no historical narratives concerning the introduction of the sweet potato in the Kandep area similar to those given for the Lagaip and Porgera valleys (and we did not ask very widely), those asked said they had heard that it came from the direction of Tari. Traditions from the Ima tribe near Kandep station claim that the sweet potato arrived from the direction of Tari in the generation of Ima Kano, the tribal founder. Ima Kano, the trickster, idiot, and conservative, was said to have been ridiculed by others for being "old-fashioned" and rejecting the new crop, stubbornly refusing to eat anything but taro.

After the introduction of the sweet potato, southern Kandep clans that had been settled in the lower Kaumbo valley cleared land and planted sweet potato gardens in their former high-altitude hunting grounds. This shift in subsistence base is reflected in a small garden ritual called *aina yoko wapuingi saa ingi waitaka pingi,* "the feast to create the sweet potato leaf and to forget about eating the innards of marsupials."

Eastern and Central Enga

For the eastern and central valleys of Enga we recorded only one testimony that told directly of the acquisition of the sweet potato.[8] Apparently the new crop was integrated into the garden repertoire so gradually that its arrival was not regarded as a significant "event" to be passed on in historical traditions. Pre-sweet potato agriculture was productive and secure and incorporated a much broader range of crops than did agriculture in the west. There is little evidence that pig forage was heavily supplemented with garden produce, and so pig fodder was not in high demand. Crops such as taro and sugarcane were deeply entrenched both economically and for their prescribed roles in social and ceremonial events. For all these reasons, some time was required before the sweet potato found its place in the gardening regime. The one testimony that we did record on the introduction of the sweet potato describes its reception in precisely this context — that of a new food that incited mild curiosity. It comes from a clan that formerly inhabited the high country at the headwaters of the Aiyele river (a tributary of the middle Lai), spanning the east and center of Enga (map 7).

My early forefathers did not eat sweet potatoes; sweet potatoes were introduced only some time later. That is what my father told me. It is said that many years ago there arrived a food called *moro.*[9] Some people asked what it was, but those who knew something about it just said that it was called *moro.* Later it was called *mapu.* Depe [the tribal founder] had a grandson whose name was Kikula. When he grew up and married, he and his wife had a son whom they named Mapu after this new food called *mapu*. Of course, they were referring to the sweet potato. So the founder of my lineage was Mapu, and all the other lineages in my subclan were founded by sisters of Mapu. We are usually called Maputae. . . . It [the sweet potato] was called *Mai moro* [after the Mai Enga], so it must have come from the west. It is said in these parts that they were eating only breadfruit; they also ate the fruit of *sundu* [that is, wild foods], but they did not eat sweet potatoes. It was during this time that the sweet potato came into these parts. (Lyala Anjo, Depe Kowepa clan, Wapomanda-Birip, middle Lai valley)

There are, in addition, two narratives from the central Lai valley that deal with the experimental phase in which the potential of sweet potatoes in higher altitudes was realized. Both come from branches of the Yanaitini tribe that migrated from the middle Lai valley to central Enga to be in a better position in the trade once they realized that agriculture there would be productive.[10]

Collectively, the oral evidence for the introduction of the sweet potato leaves two central questions only partially answered: From which direction did sweet potatoes come, and when? In response to the first, a northern introduction through Walia seems most plausible from the available information, although we cannot rule out the possibility that the crop had several different points of entry into Enga. The second is more difficult, because all relevant oral traditions come from the founding generations and therefore evade genealogical dating. We can say only that the sweet potato arrived before 220–250 years ago but within the span of historical traditions, which we seriously doubt stretch back more than 400 to 500 years at most.[11] The uncertainty of the time of arrival of the sweet potato makes it impossible to relate its introduction to other changes on a precise temporal scale. That is, we do not know whether certain changes unfolded over a few decades or or over centuries. We have tried, however, to present the material in such a way that it can be subjected to further interpretation once a more secure date is established.

Advantages of the Sweet Potato

Whether or not the superiority of the sweet potato was immediately recognized and recorded in oral history, its advantages over taro were great. Sweet potatoes grow better at higher altitudes and in naturally poorer or more agriculturally degraded soil than does taro. Consequently, the plant opened up much of the land in Enga above roughly 2,000 meters for productive gardening. Because it grows on degraded soils, it can be used as a follow-up crop in a system of crop rotation. Sweet potatoes mature more quickly than taro. In the middle Lai valley, for instance, at 1,700–1,900 meters, taro takes a year to mature and sweet potatoes only six to eight months. At Yumbis (2,550 meters), sweet potatoes take approximately nine months to mature, in comparison with nineteen to twenty-eight months for taro (Wohlt 1978). This attribute is extremely significant in areas susceptible to frost, where rapid recovery of crops is critical.

Sweet potatoes are also more productive than taro, yielding between 10 and 37 metric tons per hectare in different parts of Enga, depending on soil and altitude (Bourke and Lea 1982:81).[12] After the first harvest, sweet potato vines put down secondary roots and new tubers develop that allow for subsequent harvests over the next one and a half years. Although both taro and sweet potatoes may be damaged by rodents and insects, taro crops are subject to destruction by blight and beetles that do not attack sweet potatoes. Finally, the sweet potato is a greatly superior food for pigs, because, unlike taro, it does not need to be cooked.

All of these advantages released the constraints that had previously bound Enga agriculture and brought about many changes. Most notable among these were that people were able to settle in areas formerly suitable only for hunting and gathering and that the potential was created for producing a much larger surplus of wealth in the form of pigs once the demand for them was in place.

James Watson (1965a:442), who was the first to point out the impact the sweet potato had on New Guinea highland societies, argued that its effect was "revolutionary" and that the situation at contact in the highlands was not a long-established cultural or social one. He gave as probable motives for change adaptive strategies, environmental stress, dietary advantage, and conscious intergroup competition played out through pig exchange. The acceleration of pig exchange was made possible by the greatly superior qualities of the sweet potato as pig fodder. Central to Watson's insightful arguments were the effects of social and political competition: if some people expanded pig production, others would be forced to keep up or else lose in such essential matters as finding spouses or recruiting allies in warfare (Watson 1977).

Harold Brookfield and Peter White (1968:47), conversely, argued against a revolutionary effect and proposed a simple "evolutionary" hypothesis based on energetics to explain the sweet potato's displacement of taro and other staples in the highlands: the sweet potato offered higher returns for comparable inputs of land and labor. That is, changes brought about by the arrival of the sweet potato built on previously established cultural and social trends and thus were less radical than those proposed by Watson.

The debate has spurred valuable research on many topics, from the productivity of different agricultural systems (Waddell 1972, among many others) to pre-sweet potato social conditions (Golson 1982; Feil 1987). A conclusive answer will never be reached, for at least two reasons. First, the impact of the sweet potato differed greatly between and even within highland societies, depending on preexisting environment, subsistence base, society, politics, and symbolic values attached to certain crops. Second, the proponents of the two sides follow different agendas and do not really engage: Watson's proposal for revolutionary change centers primarily on the social and political, whereas Brookfield and White's concentrates on agricultural development, essentially missing the thrust of the former.

In the remainder of this chapter we add what we can to knowledge concerning the reception of the sweet potato in each area of Enga, the resulting changes in settlement patterns, and the crop's possible effects on population. In the next chapter we look at its direct and indirect effects on the broader redistribution of people in space. The social, political, and ritual developments that took place after the introduction of the sweet potato are the subject matter of the rest of the book.

Reactions in the West

As we have seen, early oral traditions portray the population of western Enga as being divided by niche into "hunter-gatherers" and "agriculturalists."[13] How pronounced this difference was in terms of actual subsistence is uncertain, but a social distinction was recognized. Relations between the two were characterized by trade and intermarriage as well as mistrust. Food shortages were frequent and people were plagued by leprosy, a nutritionally related disease. As if these hardships were not enough, severe frost or drought caused periodic killer famines. Apparently it was during one of these that the sweet potato arrived in higher-altitude regions of western Enga.

Although we cannot give definitive evidence, certainly some historical traditions portray the acceptance of the sweet potato as immediate. The most common response for mobile clans in the high country was to settle as agriculturalists in the lower reaches of their land or on land in the valleys acquired through marriage ties. For instance, after the famine described in the Aipakane legend given earlier, its neighbor, Maipange, along with other Porgera-area groups — Tokeala, Yawanakali, and Pakoa — who also had been living from famine foods, settled farther down in the valley and became sweet potato agriculturalists. The Makepa clan near Mount Pakapu tells a similar story. After severe losses from starvation, its members scattered to the four winds to resettle with affinal kin: some to Tari, some to Laguni in southern Kandep, and others to Yulindaka near Tipinini.

The history of the Bipi and Kuu tribes of northern Kandep, who also hold that their forefathers belonged to a hunter-gatherer tradition, indicates a similar trend toward dispersal and downward movement. In the Laiagam basin, a number of tribes such as Sambe, Pyaini, and Lote describe a parallel shift to more sedentary agriculture within the lower reaches of their tribal lands around the same time, although they do not relate this directly to the introduction of the sweet potato.

Not all movements were downward; some small groups took advantage of the sweet potato to move up in elevation (see Wohlt 1978:27–29). Other upward migrations were motivated by necessity, such as the Aimbatepa tribe's move up out of the Kaumbo valley into its former hunting grounds (2,300 meters) after its devastating war with Yamape described in chapter 3. Such upward migrations were relatively few, however, until the fourth and fifth generations before present, when the central valleys had filled and greater numbers of people struck out seeking new land. For the Bipi Kapii clan at Yumbis (2,550 meters), for example, Wohlt (1978:208) found a population increase of 7.5 percent per year beginning around 1900, owing to the influx of immigrants from the Lagaip valley.

Reactions in the East

The sweet potato made its entrance into an entirely different setting in eastern Enga, where it was not urgently needed as a staple crop for humans or pigs and so required some time to take hold. It might have taken even longer if the Enga had not been compulsive agricultural experimenters, as Waddell (1972) noted. In the generations after its arrival, its attributes were explored and its suitability as pig fodder and as a high-altitude crop was discovered.

Social acceptance seems to have lagged behind agricultural acceptance, a trend illustrated in two historical narratives from the Itokone tribe of the middle Lai valley. The first recognizes a dietary difference between eastern and central Enga that persisted until approximately the fourth generation. It tells of a vow made by a family that left Itokone for the wife's natal clan at Tetemanda after a tribal war: that they would never again see the sugarcane, yams, and bananas of the east but would spend the rest of their lives eating the salt and sweet potatoes of central Enga. The second describes an Itokone big-man of the fourth generation, Tuingi, as being the first to plant a very large mounded sweet potato garden. When he harvested the garden, he held the first sweet potato feast in place of the usual taro or pork feast. He called it *mapu yae,* following the term for a pig feast, *mena yae.* Among some clans of the lower Lai, acceptance of the sweet potato was even slower, and taro remained the staple food until the second to third generation before the present.

Mounding is said to have begun when the sweet potato was brought to Walia, but we came across no traditions describing the development or diffusion of the large mulch mound, *mondo*. There is some evidence that it was developed in western or central Enga, for in the histories of some tribes of the Lai valley it is claimed that formerly people planted sweet potatoes in small mounds, *yukusi* (see Waddell 1972:42 for a description of these). The Itokone leader, Tuingi, for instance, is said to have been the first man in his tribe to build *mondo* rather than *yukusi*. One point on which people agree almost unanimously is that *mondo* were developed to make multiple harvests possible.[14] With the ample, loose soil and the work space provided by *mondo*, it is possible to unearth large tubers without disturbing the immature ones and the vines. If harvesting is done skillfully, one can get three to five harvests at approximately one- to two-month intervals.[15]

The acquisition of the sweet potato in the east, unlike the west, seems to have had little immediate impact on the distribution of people over tribal land. Only gradually was the crop's potential to grow at higher altitudes and on poorer soils exploited, when increasing human and pig populations pushed homesteads and gardens higher and higher up the valley sides. A testimony describing this process for a branch of the Lungupini Yakau clan of the lower Lai valley is given in Appendix 4.

One of the outcomes of the progressive establishment of homesteads over a greater proportion of tribal land was a decline in game. Hunting receives less attention in oral history as each generation passes. Game was reduced earliest in the Lai valley, and by the 1970s Waddell found that only 5 percent of land of the Aluni tribe (middle Lai) was forested (Waddell 1972:174). Game was slower to dwindle in central and western parts of the province, and older men of central Enga claim that marsupials and even cassowaries could still be hunted in the higher reaches of clan territory at first contact. At the time of Meggitt's studies in the late 1950s, 20 percent and 23 percent, respectively, of the land of two clans in central Enga was forested (Meggitt 1958a:311). For the Tumundan area of the Lagaip, hunting remained important until recent decades.

It has been proposed that with the shortage of protein brought about by the decline of game in the major valleys, pigs were raised more intensively to fill dietary needs (Watson 1965a, 1965b; Morren 1977; Modjeska 1982). Though plausible, this idea is supported neither by information from Enga history nor by recent practice (Meggitt 1974). Despite a shortage of animal protein, pork was not consumed regularly but in great quantities at rituals and ceremonial exchanges, often with extravagant wastage. This unlikely situation may have come about because the use of pigs for social and political purposes was established while hunting still provided a regular contribution to the diet. By the time game had seriously dwindled, pigs had gained too high a value as social and political currency to be slaughtered regularly for household consumption.

What one sees for eastern Enga, then, is a very gradual change in subsistence systems and settlement patterns over the generations after the arrival of the sweet potato. Formerly, the preferred settlement pattern was one of gardens on the lower valley terraces and slopes in which the staple crops were grown, swidden gardens and pig forage on the middle slopes, and hunting-gathering land on the forested upper slopes. The salt-for-axes trade appears to have dominated interclan economic exchange, and hunting contributed substantially to the diet. As the population expanded, as ceremonial exchange networks grew, and as pig production was intensified, homesteads were built and gardens cleared throughout clan land. Game then declined, and with it, the contribution of hunting to the diet. The result was a different subsistence system and pattern of land use — one based on intensive sweet potato cultivation and pig husbandry rather than on taro cultivation supplemented by hunting and gathering.

Population Growth

Population growth is a dominant theme in Enga historical traditions. It is directly named by Enga as the cause of clan fission, emigration, and the need for more complex forms of communication, among other things. Clan or subclan histories include oral records of new gardens cleared (Wohlt 1978), men's houses built, or ceremonial grounds established with each generation (Lacey 1979) as groups expanded. Population growth is, for most Enga elders, the context in which their history was played out.

Using the estimates of population size seven to eight generations ago made from genealogies, one can get some idea of the rate of growth from the generation of subclan founders until the present, although it should be taken only as a "best guess." In chapter 2 we calculated that the population of Enga was between 9,500 and 19,000 around 220 years ago. According to the national census (excluding areas that are largely inhabited by non-Enga, namely, the Porgera, Paiela, Hewa, and Wapi census divisions), the population of Enga was 153,323 in 1980. Even though the expansion of the Enga population from an absolute minimum of some 10,000 to more than 150,000 over a period of 220 years seems very rapid, it requires only a moderate annual growth rate of 1.25 percent. If the initial population was more like 20,000, and if the period from subclan founders to 1980 was more than 220 years, the growth rate would have been below 1 percent. In the 1980s, with availability of modern medical facilities and vaccination programs, annual population growth was estimated to be 2.0 percent by the national census and considerably higher — at least 2.3 percent — by more precise surveys such as Wohlt's (1986). Wohlt's work in the Bipi Kapii clan (1978), Lacey's investigation of the establishment of ceremonial grounds in the Yakani tribe of the Wabag area (1979), and Bowers's study of the same for the Kakoli of Tambul (1968:225-27) make projections that parallel ours for past population growth.

The question of what brought about the population growth experienced within the span of Enga history is not an easy one to answer. Certainly, in areas above approximately 2,000 meters, the agricultural and nutritional properties of the sweet potato would have contributed significantly. A shift from a mobile lifestyle to a more sedentary one would have permitted a reduction in birth spacing, and the availability of a reliable staple food suitable for young children might have contributed to a decline in child mortality.[16]

Below 2,000 meters, the sweet potato provided some of the same advantages over former crops but probably not enough to greatly affect fertility and mortality. There, cultural factors may have played a significant role. In the face of mounting competition in both warfare and ceremonial exchange, high priority was put on increasing the size of the family, subclan, and clan. Both male and female children were desired—males to assure the future strength of the clan and females as producers and links for exchange networks outside the clan, among many other things. Protective measures were instituted for the benefit of women and children: infanticide was abhorred and child neglect discouraged by the obligatory compensation payments to maternal kin for children's injury and illness. Concerns over menstrual pollution separated the sexes, but there were no beliefs about female sorcery that legitimated punitive violence toward women. During warfare, families were sheltered—women and children were removed from the area of conflict and generally were not targets of aggression. Widows of reproductive age were soon remarried. Such measures to protect women and children, strongest in eastern Enga and declining toward the west (see also Meggitt 1977), are correlated with the importance of ceremonial exchange, agnatic versus cognatic kinship, and severity of pollution beliefs, among other things. We cannot say with any assurance how long such measures have been in practice, but mythical traditions indicate that infanticide was practiced in western regions before the span of historical traditions, and accounts of vicious wars shortly after the introduction of the sweet potato suggest that women and children may not always have been sheltered.

The potential for such cultural practices to affect population become evident when the Enga are compared with other PNG societies. For example, in the past the Etoro of the Papuan plateau, southern neighbors of the Huli who do not have competitive ceremonial exchange, believed that large newborns were witches and accordingly killed up to 30 percent of infants (Kelly 1977:52n2). Women who were suspected of sorcery were executed, and during retaliatory night raids, entire longhouses of men, women, and children were burned and occupants slain as they tried to escape (Kelly 1977:19). Before and after contact the Etoro experienced radical population decline owing to European-introduced epidemics in the 1930s and 1940s, other biological factors, and cultural factors (Kelly 1977:25–31). This experience stands in stark contrast to that of the Enga, who also suffered severe epidemics in the 1940s but whose population continued to grow steadily.

Attitudes and practices concerning health may also have contributed to growth among the Enga. People with obviously contagious diseases were isolated, and lepers were either driven out of the community or put to a cruel death. Those afflicted with skin diseases were isolated in bush camps to either die or return when they recovered. The potential for the sweet potato to grow at higher altitudes enabled households to spread out widely over the countryside, slowing the spread of epidemics and the pollution of water sources. Had taro remained the staple, it would have been necessary for homesteads to be clustered in lower, more fertile parts of valleys. We certainly have not identified all possible causes of decline in mortality and increase in fertility, but the foregoing should suffice to make the point that the nutritional and agricultural attributes of the sweet potato were not the only significant factors.

Summary

The sweet potato appears to have first reached Enga from the north prior to 250 B.P. and probably no earlier than 400–500 B.P. When more precise dates become available from archaeological evidence, they will greatly advance our understanding of the developments that took place in the early generations: how long it took for the sweet potato to affect subsistence, settlement patterns, population size and distribution, and the intensification of pig production. The initial acceptance and use of the sweet potato appears to have depended heavily on the preexisting environmental and social conditions of different regions—an observation that calls for revision in arguments that speak of *the* effects of its introduction. Nevertheless, throughout Enga it eventually led to the adoption of new subsistence systems and patterns of land use and to the more intensive production of a common currency for exchange—the pig. Though it displaced taro as the staple crop in all but the lowest altitudes, it never took over taro's social and ceremonial functions. Initial changes were much more profound in the west than in the east, though probably the reverse can be said for later generations: changes in the west were eventually curbed by environmental constraints, but once the sweet potato was rooted as the staple in eastern and central Enga, the fertile environment there permitted almost unrestrained development.

5

Tribal Migrations and Warfare

When tribal genealogies and subsequent records of growth and dispersal began some seven to eight generations ago, they intersected a process that had been going on for thousands of years. There is no way to determine how quickly groups had grown and dispersed prior to this time, but within the span of oral history the process was rapid. Among other things, it saw the reshuffling of people within the central valleys and the expansion of Enga tribes into outlying areas that previously had been uninhabited or occupied by people from other language groups. These movements, which disrupted people's relations to social and natural

resources, are key to understanding many of the developments that took place later, because they provided the stimulus for the rise of large systems of ceremonial exchange and the integration of eastern, central, and western Enga.

In this chapter we first trace the history of Enga migrations by area, outline the settlement of outlying areas, and discuss the consequences of population redistribution from the founding generations until the third to fourth generation. From that time onward the topic becomes too "hot" to include in interviews. After looking at migration, we discuss the causes and outcomes of warfare and how these changed through time, questioning

Meggitt's (1977) thesis about land and Enga warfare from a historical perspective and by drawing on concepts from ethology and practice theory.

The subject of tribal migrations and warfare is extremely complex. For example, of eighty tribes who claim to have "originated" in Enga, forty-six have major branches located far outside their areas of origin. In view of this, we have tried to make our synthesis detailed enough to be comprehensive for Enga yet general enough to be comprehensible to non-Enga by presenting much of the data in maps, tables, and appendixes. We restrict our discussion to general trends; only the few wars and migrations that were critical to later developments in ceremonial exchange are discussed in some detail. What should come through, however, is a sense of the extraordinary variety in the causes, courses, and outcomes of Enga warfare. Each generation saw wars ranging from skirmishes between subclans or contests for establishing a balance of power between neighboring clans to full-blown destructive wars that displaced entire clans or tribes. Only with such a broad perspective is it possible to grasp the complexity of Enga warfare that so evades both anthropologists and politicians today.

Tribal Migrations

To trace migrations, we are fortunate to have a rich and factual body of material at hand. At its base are genealogies that describe tribal structure some seven to eight generations ago and stipulate tribes' relations to land. Such information is both internally consistent and in accordance with claims of neighboring tribes. The twenty-two tribal histories that begin with migration traditions also seem to record events with a firm historical basis. Only six could not be confirmed at both ends; for these, the immigrants came from areas outside of Enga where we did little or no research. Beginning with the generation of subclan founders, oral histories become dynamic, recording tribal growth, dispersal, and migration by generation. We tried to check all migrations of entire tribes or clans that took place within Enga (except those to the Paiela, Lyalam, Yeim, and Waga areas), as well as those to or from the north Mendi and Kola areas, at both the point of departure and the current place of residence. For the many that could be followed up, we encountered no major discrepancies regarding cause, generation, and outcome. For larger migrations, current place names, creek names, house sites, or trees planted to commemorate people who were previously settled there lent further support.

There are a number of reasons why migrations are carefully remembered in Enga. First and foremost, they justify current claims to land by both parent and migrant groups. It is accepted that if one group completely ousted another prior to two or three generations ago and the latter resettled in another area, the land is no longer a matter of contention. The victors have rights to the territory they gained, and the migrants to their new area of residence. Both are eager to register these claims. Parcels of land taken from groups who were not completely displaced, however, can remain matters of contention for generations. Second, no particular honor is associated with the winning of battles that occurred before the lifetime of the narrator; indeed, battles lost are often recalled to provide "lessons" for the future. The basic facts of battle legends thus tend to be similar in the oral histories of both sides, although the winners dwell more on details of the war and the losers shift their attention to settlement of their new area of residence. Third, a tribe can achieve a position of strength either by holding a large block of land in one area or by being widely dispersed and thereby gaining access to the resources of several regions. Accordingly, when asked about branches of their tribe living in other areas, people did not hesitate to give their locations and reasons for migration. Fourth, migration histories are used as a basis for maintaining links with people in other areas who could provide alternate residences in times of conflict or environmental failure, particularly frost.

Information on migration was not hard to collect.[1] What is rarely given in tribal histories, however, is information about subclans, lineages, or clusters of families who were driven out of their homelands and subsequently disbanded. The dissolution of subclans and particularly lineages to settle with relatives in other clans occurred far more frequently than their migration and successful resettlement as independent groups.[2] Tracing these former units was beyond the scope of our project, but bearing this limitation in mind, let us take a look at tribal dispersal and migration by area.

Eastern Enga: Immigration

The early history of eastern Enga was marked by an influx of groups from the south and the adjacent high country to the east (map 8; Table 3). From the time of tribal founders until the sixth to seventh generation, the ancestors of twelve tribes migrated into Enga, six from the north Mendi area and six from the Kola area (which includes Tambul, the upper Kaugel valley, and the upper Nebilyer valley). Because the migrations from north Mendi (map 8:1-6) occurred in the founding generations, narratives describing them are sketchy at best. Apparently, three of these immigrant tribes—Wauni, Yakumane, and Kandawalini—were recruited from the Kupa and Yakumba tribes of north Mendi by dwindling groups in the Wapenamanda area. They grew to be some of the largest and most influential tribes of eastern Enga, as well as major producers of pigs. It is tempting to speculate that they spurred interest in pig production, because their origin traditions place a heavy emphasis on pigs, in contrast to the traditions of tribes

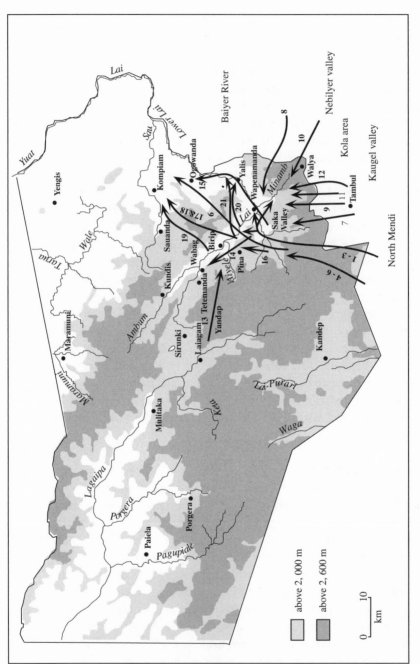

Map 8. Major migrations in eastern Enga from the founding generations until approximately the fourth generation before the present.
Key to tribes: 1, Yakumane; 2, Kandawalini; 3, Wauni; 4, Ulidane; 5, Gipini; 6, Aiyamane; 7, Lyomoi; 8, Pyapini; 9, Maini; 10, Yatapaki and Kumbi; 11, Nenaini; 12, Noponda; 13, Lyipini; 14, Yanaitini; 15, Inapini; 16, Sikini; 17, Lyongeni; 18, Waingini; 19, Tinilapini; 20, Yandamani; 21, Lungupini.

Table 3

Major Migrations in Eastern Enga from the Founding Generations until Approximately the Fourth Generation

No. on Map 8	Tribe	No. of Clans	From[a]	To[a]	Reason	Distance[b]	Alt.[c]	Generation[d]
Immigration to Enga								
1	Yakumane	4	N. Mendi	Wapenamanda	Unknown	45 km	-300 m	F
2	Kandawalini	7	N. Mendi	Yaibos, middle Lai valley	Unknown	45 km	-300 m	F
3	Wauni	2	N. Mendi	Yatamanda, Minamb valley	Unknown	45 km	-200 m	F
4	Ulidane	4	N. Mendi	Saka valley	Joined relatives in Sikini	38 km	-100 m	F
5	Gipini	3	N. Mendi	Saka valley	Joined relatives in Sikini	38 km	-100 m	F
6	Aiyamane	10	N. Mendi	Saka valley	Joined relatives in Sikini	38 km	-100 m	F
7	Lyomoi	6	Upper Kaugel or Tambul	Saka-Minamb	Given land by relatives	27 km	-300 m	F
8	Pyapini	6	Western Highlands, Mt. Ambra	Minamb valley	Salt trade	48 km	+200 m	5–6
9	Maini	1	Sakaleme (Kola)	Minamb valley	Unknown	25 km	-300 m	8
10	Yatapaki and Kumbi	2	Togoba, upper Nebilyer	Minamb valley	Frost	20 km	-250 m	8
11	Nenaini	5	Tambul area (Kola)	Minamb valley	Conflict	17 km	-300 m	7–8
12	Yoponda	3	Tambul area (Kola)	Minamb valley	Conflict	15 km	-300 m	6–7
Migration within Enga								
13	Lyipini	5	Yandap	Birip, middle Lai	Conflict	25 km	-500 m	F
14	Yanaitini	6	Tilyaposa, middle Lai	Tetemanda, Wabag	Salt trade	20 km	+200 m	F
6	Aiyamane	10	Saka valley	Kompiam, Sau Valley	Conflict	35 km	-400 m	7
15	Inapini	9	Saka valley	Ogowanda & Yaemanda, Kopona	Conflict	22 km	-500 m	F

Continued on next page

Table 3 continued

No. on Map 8	Tribe	No. of Clans	From[a]	To[a]	Reason	Distance[b]	Alt.[c]	Generation[d]
16	Sikini	3	W. Saka valley	Pina, Lai valley	Conflict	8 km	-200 m	5
17	Lyongeni	3	Pina, middle Lai	Sau valley, Kompiam	Conflict	23 km	-250 m	4–5
18	Waingini	1	Pina, middle Lai	Winikosa	Conflict	23 km	0 m	4–5
19	Tinilapini	2–3[e]	Pina, middle Lai	Sau valley, Kompiam	Conflict	23 km	-250 m	4
20	Yandamani	12	Bilimanda, middle Lai (near Pompabus)	Yalis, lower Lai	Natural expansion	12 km	-200 m	7–8[f]
21	Lungupini	2–3	Yaibos, middle Lai	Tupikores-Yalis, lower Lai	Natural expansion	12 km	-200 m	7–8[f]

[a]Locations are given as general areas or as well-known places shown on maps.

[b]Approximate distance of migration. Note that terrain is rugged, characterized by ridge after ridge, and so real distance traveled is generally 50-100 percent more than the "as the crow flies" figures given here.

[c]Approximate difference in altitude between new and old residence. These are very rough estimates owing to poor altitudinal information on maps, insufficient knowledge of precise location for many past and present settlements, and the altitudinal range of 300 meters or more covered by the land of some clans.

[d]Approximate generation of migration. F indicates founding generations, prior to the seventh to eighth generation.

[e]Large segments of clans.

[f]Migration continued over several generations.

of the Lai and Saka valleys that are oriented to the salt-ax-stone trade. The other three tribes—Aiyamane, Gipini, and Ulidane—came from the north Mendi area to join relatives in the Sikini tribe of the Saka valley.

The migrations of the six other major tribes (map 8:7-12) from Western Highlands Province to eastern Enga were more recent and are generally well remembered.[3] Most of these tribes had moved up into the Kola area from the lower Kaugel or Nebilyer valley after the introduction of the sweet potato as refugees from warfare or as enterprising groups who sought to be permanently located at the crossroads of the trade and in places where hunting was good. When killer frosts hit, however, or when the land proved less productive than anticipated or the politics of the area thickened, the original immigrants or their descendants moved on into eastern Enga to places where they had hunting lands or were given land by people related through marriage ties.[4]

Historical narratives describe a steady trickle of immigrants who left their homelands for the fertile, frost-free valleys of eastern Enga. Population was sparse in the central valleys at the time, and apparently it was not difficult for immigrants to obtain land. Five out of nine migration legends that name hosts say that the immigrants were given land by their mothers' or wives' people, and the other four merely say that they were hosted by groups who were already settled in Enga. Reasons for welcoming immigrants were many: land was plentiful, and immigrants could provide their hosts with friendly neighbors, support in warfare, finance, help in clearing land, and trade ties. Once settled, however, immigrants recruited other families from their groups of origin, and support for their original hosts was short-lived. Numerous historical narratives tell of conflict developing between hosts and immigrant groups just a few generations after their arrival. Appendix 5 gives an example from the Yatapaki tribe of group migration, settlement, recruitment of new members, eventual division into independent clans, and conflict with hosts or neighbors.

Although the stream of immigrants into easternmost Enga was constant, farther up the Lai valley fewer migrations occurred, because the hinterland to the north and south was for the most part uninhabited hunting grounds. Some tribes of the middle Lai, mainly Aluni, Sikini, and Depe, did welcome Kandep immigrants who came as refugees in times of frost, and the Depe gave land to the Lyipini (map 8:13) when they fled the Yandap-Laiagam area after a conflict. Depe and Lyipini later fought their way down into the Lai valley, obtaining flat land in the valley bottom around Birip and generating great turmoil among the clans already settled there.

Immigration into eastern Enga brought significant population increases. According to our estimates from genealogies, it would have added at least six hundred to eight hundred people to a resident population of approximately thirty-five hundred,[5] almost doubling the population of the Saka and Minamb valleys in which most of the immigrants settled. After the first round of immigrants had arrived and filled much of the empty or sparsely populated land in the easternmost areas, concerns over new surges of immigrants arose and are reflected in some historical traditions. For instance, Yakumane (Wapenamanda) and Wauni (lower Minamb) histories tell of a war ritual held by the two tribes to pledge mutual support against intruders. Their neighbor, the Pyapini tribe, spied on the ritual but did not join the alliance. As a result, it is said, only Yakumane and Wauni grew into large, powerful tribes, while the Pyapini, who continued to welcome immigrants, eventually lost much of their land.

After the Yakumane-Wauni pact in approximately the sixth to seventh generation, no large groups of immigrants penetrated their boundaries to move into the Lai valley. Incoming groups who could not find adequate land in the Minamb or Saka valley were deflected into the lower Lai and then on to the Baiyer river area.[6] Other tribes, such as the Itokone, whose land bordered on areas in which immigrants settled also have early historical traditions in which their boundaries are clearly defined, in contrast to the histories of tribes farther up the Lai who were not confronted with immigrants.

Eastern Enga: Emigration

Immigration was not balanced by emigration in eastern Enga during the founding generations; only two major migrations out of eastern Enga are reported for this period. One was the departure of the entire Yanaitini tribe (map 8:14) from the Pompabus area (middle Lai) to Tetemanda near Wabag in central Enga to assume a more strategic position in the salt trade. The second was the expulsion of Inapini (map 8:15), a branch of the Waimini tribe, after an internal conflict over a bird trap in the Saka valley. The circumstances of this war and subsequent migration are poorly remembered, although the results were significant: the ancestors of nine present-day Inapini clans moved to the uninhabited area east of Kompiam station near Yaemanda and Ogomanda.

Waves of emigration out of eastern Enga did occur some generations later as a result of serious wars between original residents and descendants of immigrants. The most significant of these led to the expulsion of the former immigrant tribe of Aiyamane to the area south of the Sau river (Kompiam; map 8:6). Shortly afterward, a conflict between Aiyamane's brother tribes resulted in the return of many, but not all, of these new immigrants to their former homelands in the north Mendi area (map 8:4-5). Aside from clearing the western Saka of a significant portion of its new immigrants, the most notable outcome of these wars over the long run was that they initiated settlement of the area south of the Sau river, which was said to have been uninhabited when they arrived, except for scattered hunting huts.[7] Apparently the area was too low to have attracted Enga from the central valleys, particularly since parts of it were in the epidemic malaria belt, but it was also too high for growing some important foods of lowland peoples—sago, breadfruit, *Pangium edule,* and lowland pandanus, among others. People from other language groups were first encountered north of the Sau river.

The Aiyamane expulsion was followed by a second wave of emigrants in the fifth generation when serious trouble broke out in the Saka once again and three Sikini clans spilled over into the Lai valley (map 8:16). Their arrival displaced three tribes or large segments of them from the area near the junction of the Aiyele and Lai rivers (map 8:17-19). The displaced tribes settled near the Aiyamane in the area south of the Sau river. Most of these migrants thrived in their new settlements and kept up ties with tribes in the central valleys, first through trade of pigs and lowland products (black palm wood, tree oil, and *itatu* fruit, among other things) and later through the Tee cycle.

All other migrations out of the Lai valley recorded within the span of oral history were smaller in scale and involved only subclans, lineages, or families. With a few exceptions, these smaller groups were absorbed by their host tribes and did not establish independent clans.[8] Additionally, branches of the Yandamani and Lungupini tribes (map 8:20-21) on the north side of the middle Lai valley expanded into the lower Lai. In some cases they were given land by clans living in the area, and in others they fought vicious battles to expel the local clans and drive them eastward into the Baiyer area. That there were no further major migrations out of eastern Enga was certainly not because of a lack of warfare. It was either because the fertile valleys were able to support large populations and the resident clans were determined not to be uprooted, or because neighbors from "brother clans" were not eager to see profitable exchange partners depart.

To sum up, immigration into eastern Enga from the founding generations until approximately the sixth generation greatly increased the population of the easternmost valleys and spurred several major developments. Important among these were (1) the settlement in eastern Enga of north Mendi, Kakoli, and northern Melpa clans or subclans, all of whom had important trade ties to the east or south; (2) the settling of a large and influential Layapo tribe, Yanaitini, in central Enga where it could oversee the salt trade; and (3) the settling of the Kompiam district south of the Sau river, which opened access to new sources of wealth including great potential for pig production.

Central Enga

Central Enga did not experience waves of migrants similar to those in eastern Enga. Only two tribes are said to have moved into this area within the span of oral history: Yanaitini, as mentioned earlier, and Sakalini (map 9:3; Table 4),

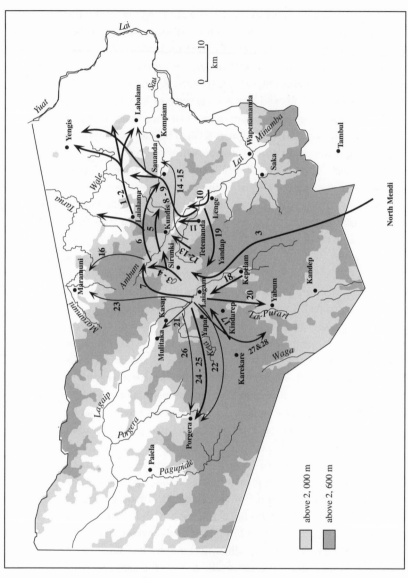

Map 9. Major migrations in central Enga and the upper Lagaip valley from the founding generations until approximately the fourth generation. Key to tribes: 1, Lakani; 2, Waitini; 3, Sakalini; 4, Lyaini; 5, Pumani; 6, Aiyele; 7, Kunalini; 8, Sene; 9, Yokasa; 10, Yakani; 11, Yanaitini; 12, Malipini; 13, Potealini; 14, Potealini; 15, Malipini; 16, Sakalini; Lyaini, Mulapini; 17, Pyaini; 18, Lote; 19, Apulini; 20, Kunalini; 21, Kunalini; 22, Kunalini; 23, Kunalini; 24, Pumane; 25, Wau; 26, Angalaini; 27, Walini; 28, Watini. Note that Sene and Yokasa are also called Kungu and Tiaka.

which left the Mendi area after a misunderstanding and journeyed northward to settle in the Sirunki area of central Enga. Both were welcomed and given land by local residents. Nonetheless, substantial internal population shifts occurred as those in higher altitudes fought to gain land in the lower valleys after the introduction of the sweet potato, setting off the migration of evicted groups into outlying areas. Let us take a closer look at these.

During the founding generations, Mai Enga tribes of central Enga were spread out over the upper Lai valley and throughout the Ambum. Additionally, two Mai tribes, Lakani and Waitini (map 9:1-2) had just begun to expand eastward into the upper Sau, aggressively displacing peoples of other language groups, including Lembena, Bulai, and Wapi speakers.[9] The Yandapo Enga, a subdivision of the Mai, inhabited the Sirunki plateau and parts of the Yandap, relying heavily on hunting and gathering.

In the sixth to seventh generation, two major wars broke out that profoundly affected the history of central Enga, for they provided the basis for two of the Great Ceremonial Wars fought in later generations. Prior to these wars, the "brother" tribes of Pumane and Aiyele (map 9:5-6) occupied land that stretched from the high, cold country of Sirunki down into the upper Ambum valley and parts of the upper Sau. Their neighbor to the west, Lyaini (map 9:4), had large tracts of land in Sirunki but few holdings in the upper Ambum. The early oral history of Lyaini tells how the tribe successfully recruited small groups from other tribes through marriage ties and the adoption of the Sakalini (map 9:3) as a "brother" tribe, in order to increase its strength and numbers significantly. It is not known how long after the arrival of the sweet potato Lyaini began to organize this larger alliance, but perhaps its efforts were facilitated by increasing sedentism in the wake of the new crop.

When a war with Pumane broke out over a trivial matter—the theft of a bundle of sugarcane—Lyaini and Sakalini took the opportunity to unite forces and expel virtually all the Pumane and Aiyele clans from the Ambum valley. The war took place on several fronts—around Sirunki, near Anditale in the upper Ambum, and near Kundis in the middle Ambum. The local battles are described as having been extremely vicious and destructive, but because they were fought over a broad area, specific incidents were not compiled in historical traditions to give a coherent overview. Most people agree that it was a relatively short war, lasting a few months to a year. In the end, most Pumani and Aiyele clans were driven down the Ambum valley to Kundis and then over into the upper Sau valley near Sauanda, where Aiyele had land.

Before leaving, Aiyele gave some of its forested land at Sirunki, as well as that on the eastern side of the upper Ambum, to Kunalini of Laiagam (map 9:7), to whom it was related through marriage ties. The victors, Lyaini and Sakalini, who

Table 4

Major Migrations in Central Enga and the Upper Lagaip Valley from the Founding Generations until Approximately the Fourth Generation

No. on Map 9	Tribe	No. of Clans	From[a]	To[a]	Reason	Distance[b]	Alt.[c]	Generation[d]
Central Enga								
1	Lakani	Many subclans	Laialam (Sau), Wale, Tarua	Throughout NE Kompiam	Natural expansion	25–30 km	-300 to -800 m	F[f]
2	Waitini	Many subclans	Laialam (Sau), Wale, Tarua	Throughout NE Kompiam	Natural expansion	25–30 km	-300 to -800 m	F[f]
3	Sakalini	4	Kandep	Sirunki-Ambum	Conflict	50 km	+100 to -200 m	6–7
4	Lyaini	4–5[e]	Sirunki	Upper Ambum	Take land	10 km	-100 m	6–7
5	Pumani	2	Middle Ambum	Upper Sau	Conflict	12 km	+200 m	6–7
6	Aiyele	4	Upper Ambum	Upper Sau, Wale-Tarua	Conflict	20 km	-100 to -250 m	6–7
7	Kunalini	5	Laiagam	Sirunki, upper Ambum	Conflict	10 km	+200 m	5–6
						20 km	none	
8	Sene	6	Lower Ambum	Dispersed north of Sau river	Conflict	20–50 km	+200 to -1000 m	6
9	Yokasa	6	Lower Ambum	Dispersed north of Sau river	Conflict	20–50 km	+200 to -1000 m	6
10	Yakani	5	Middle Lai, Lenge Rakamanda	Lower-middle Ambum	Conflict	8 km	none	6
11	Yanaitini	7[e]	Upper Lai, Tetemanda	Lower Ambum, south side	Land	6 km	-150 m	6
12	Malipini	7[e]	Upper Lai	Lower-middle Ambum	Land, conflict	6 km	-150 m	6
13	Potealini	3[e]	Upper Lai	Middle Ambum	Conflict, land	8 km	-200 m	6–7
14	Potealini	2	Upper Lai	Paipa, Sau valley	Conflict, land	30 km	-200 m	6–7

15	Malipini	2 subclans	Middle Ambum	Sau valley	Land	22 km	none	4-5
16	Sakalini, Lyaini, Mulapini	Many lineages/ families	Upper Ambum–Sirunki	Maramuni	Land, conflict	35 km	-800 m	7[f]
Upper Lagaip								
17	Pyaini	6	Yapai	Laiagam	Join relatives	8 km	-400 m	7-8
18	Lote	7	Kepelam	Laiagam (returned later)	Join relatives	12 km	-200 m	7-8
19	Apulini	3[e]	Irelya (Wabag)	Kepelam	Join relatives	23 km	+300 m	7-8
20	Kunalini	3	Laiagam	N. Kandep	Conflict	20 km	+200 m	5
21	Kunalini	1[e]	Laiagam	Mulitaka	Conflict	17 km	none	5
22	Kunalini	1-2[e]	Laiagam	Porgera	Conflict	40 km	none	5
23	Kunalini	1-3[e]	Laiagam	Maramuni	Conflict	40 km	-700 m	5
24	Pumane	1-2?	Keta river	Porgera valley	Conflict	35 km	none	5-6
25	Wau	1-2?	Keta river	Porgera valley	Conflict	35 km	none	5-6
26	Angalaini	1-2?	Keta river	Porgera valley	Join relatives	35 km	none	5-6
27	Walini	1	Laiagam-Keta	N. Kandep	Conflict	25 km	+200 m	6-7
28	Watini	1	Laiagam-Keta	N. Kandep	Conflict	27 km	+200 m	4-5

Note: Sene (8) and Yokasa (9) are also called Kungu and Tiaka.

[a] Locations are given as general areas or as well-known places shown on maps.

[b] Approximate distance of migration. Note that terrain is rugged, characterized by ridge after ridge, and so real distance traveled is generally 50-100 percent more than the "as the crow flies" figures given here.

[c] Approximate difference in altitude between new and old residence. These are very rough estimates owing to poor altitudinal information on maps, insufficient knowledge of precise location for many past and present settlements, and the altitudinal range of 300 meters or more covered by the land of some clans.

[d] Approximate generation of migration. F indicates founding generations, prior to the seventh to eighth generation.

[e] Large segments of clans.

[f] Migration continued over several generations.

also had friendly ties with Kunalini, were satisfied with this solution because they could not occupy all the land they had gained. For the evicted to give land to their relatives or allies before they depart and thereby keep some ties with their homeland is a solution mentioned in quite a number of historical traditions. It is said by some that Pumani and Aiyele hoped to muster forces and, with help of allies in the lower Ambum, return to retake their land. Before they could do so, their plans were cut short by warfare in the lower half of the Ambum.

The lower Ambum valley was home to the Sene-Yokasa (map 9:8-9),[10] "cousins" and allies of Pumani and Aiyele. Shortly after the Lyaini-Sakalini versus Pumane-Aiyele war, a fight broke out between men from the Sene-Yokasa clan Kukune and men from a Yakani subclan called Makumuni (map 9:10) over the stolen collar of a hunting dog. Many allies joined Makumuni, and the conflict escalated into a full-blown war, driving Sene-Yokasa groups up the lower Ambum to Kundis. The Kukune took their last stand at Powasa near Wabag, fled up the Lai, and crossed over the ridge to the Ambum through Yanaitini land. Yanaitini allied with Yakani and attacked them in their flight, slaughtering most of them as they tried to cross the river. It is said that their bones could be seen along the Ambum river until relatively recently. Other Sene-Yokasa men and their families escaped up the Ambum valley, where they were caught between Yakani, Yanaitini, and their allies to the southwest and Lyaini-Sakalini, who had just taken the upper Ambum. With no other possible exit, they moved on to the upper Sau valley and settled across the river from Pumani and Aiyele. It is doubtful that this war was over land, for most of the aggressors already had ample land. Other political motives must have been involved, though these are not spelled out in historical traditions.

The expulsion of Pumane-Aiyele and Sene-Yokasa groups from the Ambum is the largest coordinated effort of tribes to obtain land described in Enga oral history — twenty-three clans were driven out of the valley. Unlike the case in eastern Enga, where some 10 to 20 square kilometers of usable land were obtained in each of the major wars, during the Ambum wars some 160 square kilometers were taken,[11] including some of the best land in central Enga and large areas of high forest as well. The victors fulfilled their goal — to acquire garden land in the Ambum valley — but could by no means occupy all of it. Yakani clans settled throughout the middle and lower Ambum and, as was customary for the time, gave significant portions of the land they had gained to their allies, Yanaitini, Malipini, and Potealini (map 9:11-13).

If the defeated tribes ever rallied forces and tried to retake their land in the Ambum, there is no clear mention of it in the material we collected. Apparently the odds were so stacked against them that they set their sights elsewhere. Gradually they expanded north and east to settle widely throughout the northern

Sau, Wale, and Tarua areas, moving as far east as Yengis and Labalama (map 9:8-9), where they proliferated.[12] When they encountered Bulae, Penale, or Wapi speakers, they either drove them out or intermarried with them and integrated them into their communities.[13] Owing to their newfound wealth in this area (which is favorable for pig husbandry), along with good strategy, they grew rapidly in numbers and successfully put themselves back on the map of trade and exchange through the Great Ceremonial Wars and the Tee cycle.

After the Ambum wars, central Enga saw no more major migrations, although the resettlement of subclans, lineages, and families as war refugees or seekers of new land was constant—for instance, the migrations of Potealini and Malipini clans to the upper Sau (map 9:14-15). As the population of the upper Ambum-Sirunki area increased, a steady trickle of families moved north to join relatives in the Maramuni area (map 9:16). Finally, one significant migration occurred from lower to higher altitudes—a branch of the Apulini tribe of Irelya moved up into the Kepelam area (map 9:19) at the invitation of the Sambe tribe, to whom it was related through marriage, creating an active link between the Lai valley, Kandep, and the Lagaip.

The repercussions of post-sweet potato population shifts in central Enga were substantial, though we do not know how long these developments took to unfold. First, the migrations following the Ambum wars opened up the vast area to the north of the Sau river for Enga clans. These later provided significant numbers of pigs, black palm wood, tree oil, and *itatu* fruits to fuel the trade, the Great Ceremonial Wars, and the Tee cycle. Second, the reshuffling of groups initiated the integration of eastern, central, and western Enga that was to continue for generations. Yakani, a Mai tribe at the border of the Mai-Layapo dialect division, and Yanaitini, of Layapo origin, penetrated more deeply into central Enga. Yandap groups such as Lyaini and Sakalini, as well as Potealini of the upper Lai, moved closer to the Mai and Layapo. Clans of the Lagaip such as Kunalini became firmly rooted in former Mai regions, and Mai clans from Apulini migrated to the headwaters of the Lagaip.

The Upper Lagaip Valley

The upper Lai and Ambum valleys of central Enga are separated from the Lagaip by the high country of Sirunki and the Yandap. Because major tribes spanned the two valley systems, there is no clear division between the Mai-Yandapo Enga and the Enga of the upper Lagaip, which we define as the area between the headwaters of the northwest-flowing Lagaip and its junction with the Keta river (map 9). Prior to the introduction of the sweet potato, the Enga of the upper Lagaip appear to have been most closely associated with the peoples of northern Kandep, moving widely within the high country that separates the two valley systems. The largest of the upper Lagaip tribes, such as the Sambe and Kunalini, held land in both regions. Groups were well spaced, and although feuds and skirmishes are mentioned in oral traditions for this early period, there appear to have been few major wars. After the introduction of the sweet potato, upper Lagaip tribes, including Sambe and Kunalini, settled more permanently in the lower reaches of their own territories (not shown in map 9). Those with no land in the valley bottom obtained rights from in-laws. For example, the Pyaini and Lote tribes (map 9:17-18) were given land by the Sambe and Kunalini, with whom they had marriage ties.

Once the Sambe had established a more permanent residence at Papyuka, close to Laiagam, they made concerted efforts to become linked into the Lai valley trade. First, Sambe clans invited a number of Apulini subclans (map 9:19) from the Wabag area to settle on their eastern border, forming a bridge between the Lagaip and the Lai. Beginning around the sixth generation before the present, they hosted Yanaitini's Great Ceremonial Wars with Monaini, receiving great wealth from the reparation payments that ensued and drawing the Yanaitini more directly into the mainstream of the salt-stone ax trade. These initiatives redirected Sambe's orientation from the south and west to the east.

One of the first major intertribal wars reported in the oral history of the upper Lagaip was that between the "brother" tribes Sambe and Kunalini, who resided near Laiagam. It escalated from a dispute over a dog collar in the fifth to sixth generation (after Lyaini and Sakalini [map 9:3-4] had taken the land in the Ambum) and continued for a long time—some say ten years and others thirty. In the end, Kunalini was totally uprooted: three Kunalini clans fled to areas of northern Kandep where they owned land (map 9:20), and most of the remaining clans and subclans migrated to Sirunki or the upper Ambum, where they had obtained land from Aiyele (map 9:7). Others fled west to Mulitaka and Porgera or north to Maramuni (map 9:21-23), among other places, where they established new communities. Much of the land vacated was given to allies of defeated Kunalini clans.

Kunalini did not fare badly in the generations that followed, for land in other regions was plentiful at the time. Census figures from the early 1970s give a population of three thousand for Kunalini and thirty-five hundred for Sambe (as cited in Lacey 1975:94). Sambe's motives for this prolonged war remain unclear. Certainly, a cycle of runaway aggression was partly responsible. Garden land seems not to have been an issue, but hunting land within easy reach of settlements might have been one consideration. More likely, competition in the trade was a point of contention, for after Sambe ousted Kunalini, it became the central hub for the area.

Other wars took place in the fifth to sixth generation near the Keta-Lagaip river junction that drove Pumane, Wau, and Angalaini to the Porgera valley, where Pumane and Wau are called by their Ipili names, Pulumani and Waiwa (map 9:24–26). The migration of these clans laid the groundwork for the close relationship felt between clans of the Lagaip-Keta junction and Porgera today.

During the generations following the Sambe-Kunalini war, population increased and the upper Lagaip became riddled with conflict; it remains so today. With growing tension over land, some subclans and lineages (map 9:27–28) migrated southward into higher country or moved back into their former hunting grounds, setting up permanent settlements in the high country at Kindarep, Yapai, and areas of northern Kandep near Yabum and Karekare.

In general, then, after the introduction of the sweet potato, previously mobile groups of the upper Lagaip settled more permanently in the lower reaches of the valley. Although ties between northern Kandep and the Lagaip had always been strong, both migrations and initiatives in the trade brought some upper Lagaip tribes in closer contact with central Enga. Similarly, wars in the Keta area that expelled clans to Porgera increased the traffic between the two regions. Tribes of the upper Lagaip then became more firmly entrenched as middlemen for interaction between the south, east, and west.

The Middle Lagaip

West of the Keta river begins the country of the Tayato Enga. There, oral history portrays quite a different profile of tribal dispersal and migration, in both scale and causes. It no longer tells of large wars that displaced entire tribes but of smaller intratribal wars that uprooted clans or large subclans. For example, among the Layapo, Saka, Mai, and Yandapo Enga to the east, of twenty-one wars recorded after which clans were ousted and set up independent groups outside of tribal land, nine were intratribal and twelve intertribal. The average war led to the displacement of 3.3 clans or major segments of clans. In contrast, among the Tayato Enga, of fourteen wars recorded,[14] thirteen were intratribal and only one intertribal. The resulting migrations were much smaller, with an average of one clan or major segment of a clan displaced per tribal war. The high frequency of intertribal wars in eastern and central Enga, in contrast to intratribal ones among Tayato tribes, is closely related to the environment and to settlement patterns — recall that in the past, the Tayato were mobile and dispersed, with a less centralized tribal structure.

Not only did the scale of migration differ for the Tayato, but so did its causes. Again looking east first, of eighty-nine Saka-Layapo and Mai-Yandapo clans that established tribal branches in outlying areas, seventy-one were displaced by warfare and only eighteen departed on their own accord seeking new land. Six of the latter were Yanaitini clans who moved to central Enga for the purpose of manipulating trade. In other words, most left their homes in the central valleys only when forced to do so. The Tayato, on the other hand, were more willing to strike out voluntarily. Of forty-two clans or major clan segments that left their homelands to settle elsewhere, fourteen were uprooted by warfare and the other twenty-eight left in search of new land. Migration to the north by those "seeking food" is said to have begun long before the introduction of the sweet potato.

Migrations of Tayato clans occurred in all directions, although the predominant orientation was to the north, where the Tayato had a long history of productive exchange and intermarriage with Nete and Penale peoples. Some northern migrants continued on into the Sepik, the Gadio Enga being one example (Dornstreich 1973). Map 10 (1-17) and Table 5 give some of the major ones reported to us.[15]

The initial migrations of Tayato clans into outlying areas are said to have been small, though in later generations, as new members were recruited from the Lagaip, new settlements steadily grew. Paul Wohlt's (1978) excellent historical study of the Bipi Kapii clan's settlement at Yumbis provides an good example of the processes involved. Some 170 years ago the Kapii migrated from Telyatesa at the northern end of the Kandep swamps to Yumbis (2,550 meters) near Karekare. Yumbis had been their former hunting and pandanus territory, and upon discovering that sweet potatoes grew well there, they decided to settle permanently. Wohlt estimated that the original immigrant group consisted of three to four families. Through genealogy, he reconstructed population growth at Yumbis from the time of first settlement until the present. He then marked out different plots of land with the aid of aerial photographs, collected information about who had cleared them, and related natural population growth and acceptance of immigrants to patterns of land clearance.

Wohlt's results show that from approximately 1805, when Yumbis was first settled, until 1895, population growth was gradual and largely owing to natural increase. Around 1885 Kapii clansmen began to recruit numerous immigrants, mostly from the Lagaip valley. Their willingness to come indicates mounting conflict and pressure on resources in their homelands. At the turn of the century, Kapii experienced a small decline in population because of a severe frost, but in 1905 the population recovered and then boomed over the next generations with the acceptance of many immigrants. It peaked in the 1930s and then declined with death and emigration after the severe frost and epidemics of the early 1940s. Between 1805 and 1975 the population of the Kapii clan grew from around 20 persons to 398, although it would have been closer to 600 had it not been for the setbacks of the early 1940s.

By 1975 approximately 45 percent of the Kapii clan was made up of agnates

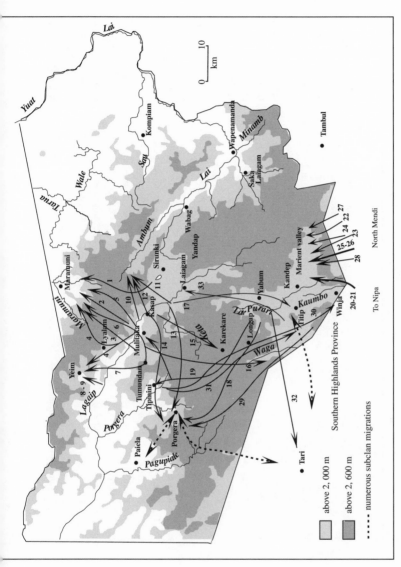

Map 10. Major migrations in the Lagaip valley and Kandep from the founding generations until approximately the fifth generation. Dashed arrows indicate frequent but undocumented migrations. Key to tribes: 1, Mulapini; 2, Limbini; 3, Pumane; 4, Kaiya; 5, Monaini; 6, Yangutini; 7, Kundiki; 8, Auwini; 9, Lambuaka; 10, Tupini; 11, Sakate; 12, Monaini; 13, Sakate; 14, Monaini; 15, Piandane; 16, Mulapini; 17, Sakate; 18, Bipi and Yomondaka; 19, Tekepaini; 20, Mamba; 21, Akulya; 22, Yamatepa; 23, Pima; 24, Enza; 25, Kupatopa; 26, Lyatepa; 27, Masa; 28, Kambia; 29, Tieni; 30, Mondatepa; 31, Kapini; 32, Tatali; 33, Timitopa Tombe.

Table 5

Major Migrations in the Lagaip Valley and Kandep from the Founding Generations until Approximately the Fifth Generation

No. on Map 10	Tribe	From[a]	No. of Clans	To[a]	Reason	Distance[b]	Alt.[c]
Middle Lagaip							
1	Mulapini	Sirunki, Tukusenta	5[d]	Maramuni	Land, conflict	30 km	-700 m
2	Limbini	Mulitaka	2	Maramuni	Trade, land	30 km	-600 m
3	Pumane	Mulitaka, Tumundan	3[d]	Maramuni	Land, conflict	30 km	-600 m
4	Kaiya	Mulitaka	2[d]	Yeim, Maramuni	Conflict, land	30 km	-450 m -600 m
5	Monaini	Mulitaka	2[d]	Maramuni	Conflict, land	30 km	-600 m
6	Yangutini	Tumundan	3[d]	Maramuni		32 km	-600 m
7	Kundiki	Wanepaka (Tumundan)	1[d]	Yeim	Conflict	23 km	-450 m
8	Auwini	North of Augum Mountains	5	Yeim, Lyalam	Land, conflict	17–22 km?	?
9	Lambuaka	North of Augum Mountains	4–5	Yeim, Lyalam	Land, conflict	17–22 km?	?
10	Tupini	Mulitaka	1	Upper Ambum, Maramuni	Conflict	22 km 30 km	none -600 m
11	Sakate	Keta river	1	Upper Ambum	Conflict	20 km	none
12	Monaini	Kasap	1[d]	Upper Ambum	Land, join relatives	26 km	none
13	Sakate	Keta river	1[d]	Porgera valley	Conflict	35 km	none
14	Monaini	Kasap	1[d]	Porgera valley	Join relatives?	33 km	none
15	Piandane	Kasap	2[d]	Karekare, NW Kandep	Conflict	27 km	+500 m
16	Mulapini	Yoko (west of Mulitaka)	2–3?	Wage valley	Unknown	37 km	+250 m
17	Sakate	Keta	1[d]	Titip, SW Kandep	Join relatives	44 km	+150 m
Kandep							
18	Bipi and Yomondaka	Telyatesa, Yabum, N. Kandep	1	Porgera valley	Land	42 km	-150 m

19	Tekepaini	2?	N. Kandep	Porgera valley, Mulitaka	Frost	42 km	-150 m
20	Mamba	1	Winja, SHP	Marient, S. Kandep	Land?	15 km	+400 m
21	Akulya	1	Winja, SHP	Marient, S. Kandep	Land?	15 km	+400 m
22	Yamatepa	1	Sumea, N. Mendi	Marient, S. Kandep	Land?	25 km	+400 m
23	Pima	1	Nene, N. Mendi	W. Marient	Land	14 km	+300 m
24	Enza	1	Nene, N. Mendi	W. Marient	Land	14 km	+300 m
25	Kupatopa	1	Pingitip, N. Mendi	W. Marient	Conflict	17 km	+300 m
26	Lyatepa	1	Pingitip, N. Mendi	Marient	Land	17 km	+300 m
27	Masa	3	Wailya, N. Mendi	Marient	Land	24 km	+300 m
28	Kambia	2	Pingitip, N. Mendi	Marient	Conflict	15 km	+300 m
29	Tieni	1	SW Kandep	Porgera valley	Land	52 km	-200 m?
30	Mondatepa	1-2?	Porgera valley	Winja	Conflict	67 km	-300 m
31	Kapini	2	Porgera valley	SW Kandep	Conflict	50 km	+150 m
32	Tatali	1	N. Kandep	Tari area	Join relatives	55 km	-600 m
33	Timitopa Tombe	1[d]	Titip, SW Kandep	Upper Lagaip	Conflict	44 km	-150 m

Note: Generation of migration has been omitted because, for Lagaip groups, migrant groups were often spread out over time. All migrations from one tribe to a specific area are summarized in a single row and represented by a single arrow on the map to avoid the maze that would otherwise result. For Kandep too, time of migration is difficult to specify for many groups, particularly those who moved gradually into the Marient, using new settlements first as alternate residences and later settling permanently.

[a]Locations are given as general areas or as well-known places shown on maps.

[b]Approximate distance of migration. Note that terrain is rugged, characterized by ridge after ridge, and so real distance traveled is generally 50–100 percent more than the "as the crow flies" figures given here.

[c]Approximate difference in altitude between new and old residence. These are very rough estimates owing to poor altitudinal information on maps, insufficient knowledge of precise location for many past and present settlements, and the altitudinal range of 300 meters or more covered by the land of some clans.

[d]Large segments of clans.

descended from the original settlers. Another 10 percent consisted of new immigrants, and the remaining 45 percent were descendants of past immigrants
who were fully integrated into the clan (Wohlt 1978:fig. 18). Most immigrants
were related through female ties—for example, over one quarter of all immigrants were daughters' husbands (Wohlt 1978:239). The Kapii's incentives for
inviting immigrants to join them were to obtain assistance in land clearance and
to establish new ties through which to finance ceremonial exchange. Because it
was families or lineages who recruited immigrants, new members were welcomed into lineages that had plenty of land even if other lineages were short of
it. Once lineages felt that they had enough members, they accepted fewer immigrants; descendants of immigrants then continued to help with land clearance
in exchange for additional garden land. Lineages thus went through open and
closed phases depending on the availability of land and the political aspirations
of their members.

Our genealogical data indicate that the model for community establishment
described by Wohlt has widespread application for groups that migrated into
outlying areas of western Enga.[16] It has some import for the formation of new
communities in outlying areas of eastern and central Enga as well, although the
first waves of migrations in the latter area were generally larger, and so a greater
proportion of clan members there are descendants of the original settlers.

The new Tayato communities in remote areas of the north were too small
and dispersed to be able to draw major *tee* exchanges or large-scale ancestral cults
into their areas. Their residents had little choice but to return to their tribes of
origin in the Lagaip to participate in these events. The traffic that resulted between the Lagaip and outlying communities greatly benefited both, with outlying groups fueling major cults and exchanges of the Lagaip with such goods and
valuables as pigs, black palm, *Panguim edule,* shells, and tobacco.

Kandep

Unlike eastern and central Enga, Kandep, with the exception of the Kaumbo
valley in the southern corner (map 10), is defined not by low fertile valleys with
adjacent high country but by a high, swampy basin at 2,300 meters surrounded
by even higher country. The introduction of the sweet potato made permanent
settlement and productive agriculture possible throughout the Kandep area.
Prior to that time, Kandep residents appear to have lived by hunting and gathering and by exchanging forest products for domestic ones with people in surrounding lower valleys, or, in the case of the tribes of southern Kandep, by
planting gardens in the lower Kaumbo valley.

In keeping with the region's unique physical and social geography, post-sweet
potato population shifts in Kandep differed substantially from those of other

regions of Enga. Three overlapping trends can be identified. The first was a continuation of what had been going on for centuries—the temporary migration of Kandep residents to and from lower areas to seek refuge from the ravages of frost. Temporary migrants often chose to settle with their hosts, and occasionally hosts in turn moved to Kandep if tension in their own areas ran high. The movements of individual families and lineages from Kandep to Margarima, Tari, the Lagaip valley, the Lai valley, and Mendi was so frequent that we have not even attempted to indicate them on map 10.

The other two trends in population movement appeared after the introduction of the sweet potato. One paralleled that found in other areas of Enga—the settlement of tribes in lower valleys. For Kandep, however, this was an option only for clans who had land adjacent to major valleys. Bipi, Yomondaka, and Tekepaini clans of northern Kandep, for example, moved down into the Lagaip and Porgera valleys (map 10:18-19). The Maulu of southern Kandep (not shown) settled on adjacent land obtained from Aimbatepa of the Kaumbo valley as war reparations. The other response was the establishment of permanent settlements in higher, forested regions where agriculture had formerly been too precarious, keeping alternate residences with kin in other valleys. Good examples from the founding generations are provided by the dispersal of the Bipi and Kuu tribes throughout northwestern Kandep, the movement of the Aimbatepa and Kototepa tribes out of the Kaumbo valley into their former hunting territories, and the migration of several clans of the Mamba and Akulya tribes from the Winja area of Southern Highlands Province into southern Kandep (map 10:20-21). In the fourth to fifth generation, when land in the Mendi area was becoming more densely populated, there was an influx of immigrants from north Mendi into the Marient valley of Kandep, their former hunting grounds (map 10:22-28). The cause of migration for most of these groups was the abundant game and pandanus in the Marient, together with flat land suitable for gardening. The immigrant clans from north Mendi remained closely associated with their tribes of origin, returning for major exchange festivals and cult performances.

Finally, it should be noted that there was frequent migration between western Kandep and the Porgera valley—by the Tieni, Mondatepa, and Kapini, for example (map 10:29-31)—and to and from Huli areas. Because we do not have good records of the latter, they are indicated roughly by the dashed arrows on map 10.

Post-sweet potato migration patterns within Kandep thus involved primarily dispersal into previously uncultivated areas, distributing people more widely over the landscape and thus avoiding the large-scale wars and displacements of population that occurred in eastern and central Enga. Although the sweet potato made agriculture in the Kandep area productive, it was not immune to the effects of frost, and its arrival did not reduce the traffic of temporary migrants to and from lower valleys. They remained long enough in alternate residences to become integrated linguistically and culturally, and thereby became important agents for fueling the exchange cycles of their hosts and for importing and exporting cults between linguistic groups. As masters of ritual life, middlemen in trade, and suppliers for ceremonial exchange, Kandep Enga kept themselves well placed on the map of social, religious, and economic events, despite the disadvantages of high altitude, relatively poor soil, and a dispersed population.

Summary

After the introduction of the sweet potato, though we do not yet know how long after, historical traditions report a substantial redistribution of the population of Enga. Some instances of resettlement within tribal lands or of out-migrations can be related more or less directly to the potential of the new crop; many others, however, were secondary effects occurring some generations later. Responses varied significantly from area to area. Migrations reported in historical traditions involving entire tribes of clans were largely from higher to lower altitudes. Individual families or lineages throughout Enga, however—particularly from the fifth generation on—settled higher and higher up the valley sides and into the hinterland.

The results of population shifts in some cases were disruptions of existing balances of power and relations to land, followed by warfare and expulsion of the defeated. Such migrations further integrated the different regions and initiated the settlement of outlying areas previously uninhabited by Enga: Kompiam, Maramuni, and Lyalam-Yeim, among others. The new communities thrived and attracted immigrants from the central valleys, and so their numbers grew; by 1980, settlements in outlying areas comprised approximately 20 percent of the population of Enga. The disturbance of former networks of trade brought about by migration, the increasing integration of the different regions of Enga, and the efforts of migrants to put their new communities on the map in turn provided stimuli for the development of exchange and cult networks.

Tribal and Clan Warfare

Historical narratives concerning warfare make up a significant part of Enga oral history from the founding generations until the present. Whereas Enga say that long ago, life was quite different from the way it is today—the Tee cycle did not exist, political songs were not yet well developed, population was sparse—we heard no claim that there was ever a time before warfare.

Considering that Enga historical narratives continually attest to the importance of warfare, it is noteworthy that war is rarely glorified in either myths or historical traditions. Narratives, songs, and poems do not praise war heroes or acts of valor in the distant past. Accounts of individual heroic exploits—and of crushing defeats—that occurred during the lifetimes of living individuals or their fathers are told and retold for education and entertainment in men's houses. But for events that took place before living memory, recollections of leaders and logistics tend to fade. Descriptions of tribal wars become cut-and-dried accounts of causes, course, and outcome. Some wars of the past are presented as the outcomes of hopeless misunderstandings, but most are portrayed as attempts to solve problems, reach goals, achieve balance, or uphold the honor of the clan—its ability to protect its members, resources, social alliances, and land.

The Causes of Enga Warfare

Although the fact of warfare remains a constant, the nature of the problems and goals that set off wars changed through time. This can be seen in Table 6, which summarizes the sources of disputes that triggered the wars reported in tribal histories. It should be cautioned that these data do not come from a systematic study of warfare and that tribal histories tend to record wars that had significant outcomes for tribal structure or land holdings: the splitting of groups, redefinition of their boundaries, expansion into adjacent territories, and migration of tribes or clans to other areas. Tribal wars that ended in stand-offs are underrepresented. Data on warfare for the second and third generations were taken from Meggitt's (1977:13) study of war in fourteen central Enga clans from 1900 to approximately 1950, since we avoided asking about warfare during recent generations. Meggitt's records are not directly comparable with ours; they are much more complete but apply to fourteen clans of central Enga only. In 55.9 percent of the wars recorded by Meggitt, however, the victors secured some land, and in 17.6 percent the losers were wholly evicted (Meggitt 1977:14), indicating that his figures, like ours, pertain to tribal wars whose outcomes involved redistribution of population over the land. We initially tabulated our figures for eastern/central and western Enga separately, with the result that conflicts over land, women, and pigs were slightly more frequent in the east and those over hunting and homicide slightly more so in the west. We later combined the two sets of figures, as given in Table 6, because the differences were not statistically significant.

Before considering the figures given in Table 6, we should emphasize that incidents that sparked wars do not necessarily reflect the underlying problems or goals, either those present at the outset or those that developed over the course of the fighting. Often, remarks added by elders, in addition to the context and

Table 6

Numbers of Tribal Wars in Different Generations, by
Source of Original Dispute

Source of Dispute	F–8[a]	7–6	5–4	3–2[b]
Hunting or meat sharing	12	4	4	0
Possessions or work sharing	14	5	3	2
Pigs	1	2	3	12
Pandanus	1	0	2	3
Homicide/political provocation[c]	1	5	7	11
Women[d]	2	3	4	2
Land[e]	0	2	9	41
Total	31	21	32	71

Note: Generation 1 is the present generation.

[a]Includes tribal wars from the founding generation to the eighth generation.

[b]Data in this column are from Meggitt (1977:13). Meggitt's categories "homicide payments" and "avenging homicide" have been combined into "political/homicide," and rape and "jilted suitor" into "women."

[c]Includes actions with the intent to provoke: homicide (sometimes executed by a paid killer), intentionally disrupting a funeral, refusing to help as allies, refusing to pay war reparations, hindering exchange, and so on.

[d]With the exception of three cases of adultery/competition for women, incidents in this category refer to rape. Rape that leads to tribal warfare can usually be considered an act of political provocation similar to assault or murder.

[e]Includes disputes over gardens or other infringements by one clan on the land of another. To take the land of others is rarely given as a cause of warfare in historical narratives, though informants may suggest that it was a primary underlying motive.

outcome of the war, provided insights into underlying tensions and objectives. In our discussion of Table 6, we make use of such contextual information.

From the generation of the tribal founders until approximately the eighth generation, the incidents that most frequently set off tribal wars were disputes over hunting and trapping, meat sharing, possessions, and work. These are better understood when broken down between intra- and intertribal wars. Intratribal wars are usually described within the framework of disputes over meat sharing, particularly the sharing of cassowary intestines, and those over work. Cassowary intestines were considered a great delicacy, and to exclude persons from a share of this desired food expressed personal or social rejection of them. Such conflicts usually took place within a small group, and the outcome was more often insult than injury, followed by the departure of the disgruntled party. Accompanying such narratives is the theme of hopelessness and despair felt by both parties over their misunderstanding and their inability to solve problems. For example, in the metaphorical Sakalini origin tradition, one "brother" follows his insulted sibling, trying to catch up with him, apologize, and persuade him to return. During the pursuit they sleep on opposite sides of a large boulder, neither one knowing the other is close by. The insulted brother gets up early and departs, never to return. One-third of the incidents counted as within-group wars prior to the seventh generation were resolved by a similar departure of the insulted party; no doubt many of these explanations are stereotyped.[17] The focus on meat sharing as a source of problems corresponds to the emphasis placed on hunting prior to the seventh generation.

Other incidents that triggered internal armed warfare in this period include failure to respect the possessions of another or to contribute to a group project such as building a house or preparing for an ancestral cult performance. These wars generally have more violent outcomes — opponents begin by wrestling, escalate to combat with sticks, and finally take up weapons of war, calling on relatives for support. The war continues until one party is displaced to another part of tribal land or completely ousted; allies may be invited to occupy some of the land acquired.

The nature of intratribal wars described in early historical traditions point to a number of underlying problems. The first and probably most significant was the growth of communities to sizes so large that their members could no longer cooperate effectively, leading to conflict and dispersal. This option, to "vote with one's feet," is used by many hunter-gatherers and shifting horticulturists as a means of resolving problems. The second may have been contention over hunting-trapping land within immediate reach of settlements. The frequency of hunting-related disputes suggests that even when the population of Enga was sparse and agricultural land plentiful, Enga were concerned with keeping others far enough away to maintain ample forested land nearby. A man of worth provided his family with game meat, and when hunters had to go farther afield to do so, tensions mounted and tempers flared. Internal group splits often resulted in the departure of one party to establish a new community in former hunting land of tribal territory. Depending on the sizes of the groups that split and how widely they dispersed, once resettled they often reestablished bonds of "brotherhood" and became allies.

In contrast, intertribal warfare in early generations was set off by more aggressive and provocative acts such as stealing, particularly theft of hunting implements or game from traps. The most common outcome was all-out war and the expulsion of one group. Again, historical narratives give the impression that one of the underlying reasons for such wars was the desire to keep troublesome neighbors some distance away. A good example can be found in the metaphorical account of a war between the Bipi and Kuu tribes of Kandep after a dispute over fire tongs. Not only did the ensuing war separate the two tribes, but it is also said that the animosity was carried over into subsequent generations. From that time on, when Bipi and Kuu groups met in the forest, they engaged in skirmishes that kept their settlements well apart.

In the less stereotyped legends of the sixth and seventh generations, problems concerning hunting-trapping, meat sharing, possessions, and work sharing remain sources of conflict but decrease in relative numbers. Incidents of tribal warfare sparked by homicide or political provocation and, to a lesser degree, disputes over land, increase. This trend continues, and by the fourth to fifth generation, homicide–political provocation and land disputes together set off 50 percent of tribal wars recorded. Problems over hunting, work sharing, and possessions diminish greatly in importance. The category "homicide/political provocation" in Table 6 includes all acts that provoke a response from the opponents — premeditated murder, sorcery, intentional disruption of a funeral, refusal to help as allies or pay war reparations, and hindering trade and exchange. Several accounts of the wars of this period describe how, if the enemy clan is not a neighbor and its men thus make difficult targets, a killer is hired and paid with a wife, goods, and land to provoke a war.[18] The category "women" is made up largely of rape cases in the context of political provocation and so could be combined with homicide and political disputes.

Wars resulting from premeditated homicide, rape, and other aggressive or insulting acts were sometimes engineered by big-men as parts of strategies to attain their own political goals, to test the strength of other groups, or to create exchange ties.[19] Failure to avenge aggression or insult indicated inability to defend one's members, hold one's land, and secure exchange ties; successful payback reestablished a balance of power and respect. The psychological wound following homicide or other provocative acts was thus deep:

Now I will talk about warfare. This is what our forefathers said: When a man was killed, the clan of the killers sang songs of bravery and victory. They would shout "Auu" [hurrah or well done] to announce the death of an enemy. Then their land would be like a high mountain [manda singi], and that is how it was down through the generations. The members of the deceased's clan would become small [koo injingi]. They would be nothing. But when they had avenged the death of their clansman, then they would be all right. Their hearts would be open [mona lyangenge]. In other words, when one fights and takes revenge for the death of a fellow clansman, then one gets even and back on equal footing. (Tengene Teyao, Yakani Kalia clan, Wakumale, Wabag)

Furthermore, it was believed that if a death went unavenged, the angry ghost would cause havoc.

Although cases of homicide that were not premeditated could be solved peacefully through negotiation and compensation, the fear always existed that failure to avenge a death would be taken as a sign of weakness. Vengeance was not designed specifically to punish the killer but to demonstrate the ability to respond and reestablish equal footing. Successful payback, as a symbolic demonstration of ability to defend, could thus be inflicted on any male member of the enemy clan or, in some cases, on an ally of the enemy; the mere fact of being a clan member labeled a person a potential target. With few ways to assure security against payback murders through one's individual actions, individual and clan interests became one and the same — to demonstrate the ability to avenge deaths of fellow clansmen in order to deter aggressive acts in the future. This factor had a profound impact on the unity of the clan and the loyalty of its members.

Obsession with revenge for upholding clan honor could result in what van der Dennen (1995) has called the "war trap": aggression to demonstrate strength, in the hope of assuring future security, in itself led to a cycle of war. This was exacerbated by the fact that under the cover of restoring clan honor, individual strategies were played out: a man might join a war in the heat of the original quarrel, to gain repute as a valiant warrior, to win a plot of land, to make a name during the process of peacemaking, to forge exchange ties via war reparations, to fight out old grudges in the war of an ally, or merely for the feelings of excitement and brotherhood that came with fighting.[20] Individual goals and actions greatly complicated the course of a war. Furthermore, homicide plots could and did escalate, creating their own problems, as is demonstrated in the following case from Monaini Diuatini clan history (Lagaip) of the sixth to seventh generation. Note here how failures as well as successes are remembered.

Maipu, a "son of Diuatini" [that is, from the Monaini Diuatini clan], lived at Poko near Mulitaka a long time ago. A man from the Diuatini Maipa subclan killed a man from the Kaiya tribe and a war broke out. During the war no Diuatini man was killed to avenge the death of the Kaiya man, and so when the war came to an end, Kaiya decided to avenge the death in a payback killing rather than in a tribal war. Kaiya offered a Diuatini man one of their women in payment if he killed a fellow Diuatini clansman. He accepted the offer and murdered a young man from the Diuatini Kakaipu clan by sneaking into his house and hacking him up with an ax while he was sleeping. The man who was murdered had just gotten married.

The Kakaipu subclan blamed the matter on the Maipu subclan, who had started the war in the first place. They told the Maipu subclan that they would later help them in their war against Kaiya, but first they needed to avenge the death of their own man. They did so one day when a man from another Diuatini subclan was building a house.

A Maipu man came over to help him thatch the roof of his house, and while they were working, a Kakaipu man, who had been hiding in the bushes, jumped out and split the Maipu man's head open with his ax. Shortly after, when a Maipu man met a Kakaipu man, he murdered him in payback. By this time the situation had gotten very tense and a tribal war broke out within Diuatini. Many people were killed. Maipu clansmen and their wives and children fled to Maramuni by the Molyoko track. Kakaipu and other Diuatini clansmen fled by the Pawapi track. Most of them later settled near Pasalakusa. (Apele Ipai, Monaini Diuatini Kakaipu clan, Maramuni)

The original war was thus between clans of two tribes, Monaini Diuatini and Kaiya. However, when Kaiya hired a Diuatini man from another subclan to execute the payback murder, it intentionally provoked warfare between the two Diuatini subclans, Maipu and Kakaipu. Kakaipu men expressed loyalty to their brother subclan by promising to help later in the war against Kaiya, but only after they took revenge against Maipu for the man who was murdered. The payback killing resulted in further homicide within Diuatini, intratribal warfare, and the dispersal and migration of the Diuatini clan. The Kaiya tribe, playing on the necessity for revenge, created havoc within Diuatini and emerged as the ultimate victor. As in many other wars, the ousting of one party was not a goal from the beginning but the result of anger brewed during the course of the war — anger that made one side want to banish the other from the neighborhood.

The increase in wars caused by provocative political acts accompanied three major developments that occurred between the seventh and fourth generations before the present. The first was the changing distribution of people over the land after the introduction of the sweet potato. The second was the emergence of the Tee cycle of eastern Enga and the Great Ceremonial Wars of central Enga, in which tribes and clans competed to gain control over the flow of goods and valuables. The third was the splitting of larger groups into separate clans who sought to establish their independence, subdivide tribal land, and maintain or extend their newly drawn boundaries. All of these developments required the continual exploration of the strength of neighboring groups and negotiation of power relations.

During the last two to three generations before the present, conflict over land became the major source of warfare, according to Meggitt (1977), although his findings have been disputed by Andrew Lakau (1994) and others.[21] Lakau, who also worked among the central Enga, not only disagrees with Meggitt's hypothesis but questions whether the central Enga ever fought over land during the twentieth century. He presents no figures to directly challenge Meggitt's claims, however, or any competing hypothesis backed by data. His critique is hard to evaluate because neither he nor Meggitt specifies interviewing methods. This is problematic because, on one hand, Enga will rarely say that they went to war to usurp the land of others—particularly not to an insider like Lakau. Political strategies are not laid out so openly on the table. On the other hand, if asked by an outsider whether land was a motivation, Enga might answer affirmatively, simply because once a war has broken out, gain and loss of land is a potential consequence as clans strive to rid themselves of hostile neighbors or take revenge. Land then becomes an issue. Furthermore, different people within a clan go to war for different reasons, even though the majority agree on the triggering incident, and new motivations arise during the course of the war.

Although many wars between 1900 and 1950 were mentioned in the context of other events, we did not systematically collect data on this issue for reasons mentioned earlier. However, a historical perspective with a focus on social action can be used to question some of Meggitt's fundamental assumptions and put his results in a different perspective. In support of Meggitt, precolonial narratives do confirm that the central Enga were preoccupied with land as the basis for sustenance. As such, it took on further meaning as a symbol of independence, equality, and the pride of each and every man. (We will return to this point later.) Men with land were potential equals; a man without land was a nobody. One cannot say that central Enga did not fight over land between 1900 and 1950, as Lakau claims; disputes over garden land near clan borders are cited as triggering incidents for some wars of this period. Some of these were interpersonal disputes that escalated into war, comparable to the theft of pigs or other property, and others were parts of broader plans to gain contested garden land.

Nonetheless, Meggitt's thesis can be questioned on two accounts. First, there is no evidence at any point in precolonial history that pressures on land caused food shortages for pig and human populations or other economic hardships (see also Lakau 1994). In the earlier generations, land won was often more than could be occupied and was given to allies or relatives recruited into the clan. In later generations, there was less land free for the taking, but even at the time of our study, when population had increased greatly and cash crops put extra demands on land, families in most (but not all) areas had more land at their disposal than labor with which to cultivate it.

Second, historical narratives from the second and third generations by no means portray Enga clans as perpetually poised to snatch the land of weaker groups, as Meggitt's work implies. It is this point to which Lakau also objects. As discussed in chapter 3, land was defended through both physical means (warfare) and social boundary maintenance (advertising and ritualized competition, exchange, and opening access to resources to kin who cooperated). Social boundary maintenance was by far the more expedient option because it avoided loss of life and property and because it was generally labor rather than land that was in short supply.

The Enga are hard workers with a long work week (see Waddell 1979:89) and would have had to work even harder before the introduction of steel tools (Wohlt 1978:430–35). Small household labor forces could not easily have increased production by cultivating more land, even if large plots of additional land could have been obtained. Thus, cooperative neighbors who could help finance *tee* exchanges were in many cases more valuable than the land they inhabited. History provides ample cases in which small clans existed for generations side by side with much more powerful ones in relations of cooperation, without fear of expulsion, because of the benefits that both obtained through exchange. Warfare was called upon when social relations became conflict-ridden, cutting short finance and other forms of support between groups.

In this context it is probably fair to say that the success of a clan over time was a matter of the way leaders played their cards to obtain a strategic balance between physical and social boundary maintenance and were able to construct new ways to achieve the latter. Many clans remained powerful throughout the span of historical traditions, others rose and fell, and still others were continually in a tight spot. In short, Meggitt's arguments (1977:9), which place all other Enga institutions, such as *tee* exchange, subservient to concerns over land and war,[22] give a one-sided view of the options employed by Enga to pursue economic and political goals and of their finesse in choosing between the two.

The Outcomes of War

Another important perspective for understanding the relation of Enga warfare to land can be obtained by analyzing outcomes of war through time. Owing to the contents of the historical record, discussed earlier, it is not possible to look at the outcomes of all wars but only at those in which the losing clan or large subclan was totally evicted from tribal land, migrated, and set up an independent branch elsewhere. Results are nonetheless revealing.

As can be seen in Table 7, during the sixth and seventh generations, migrations by defeated groups to areas outside of tribal lands were numerous, and their distances great. Simultaneously (but not shown in Table 7), internal conflicts caused families, lineages, and subclans to bud off from large communities and settle in what were previously forested areas of clan lands. Warfare during this period effectively solved problems by spacing conflicting parties across tribal land or by enabling one party to uproot the other and give part of the land gained to allies. Unfriendly neighbors were thus replaced with friendly ones.

By the fourth to fifth generation, as tribal lands filled and much of the land in fringe areas was already claimed, new solutions were sought to reestablish peace and allow social boundary maintenance to be resumed after disturbances— namely, the extension of war reparations to enemies, the topic of chapter 9. At

Table 7

Number and Average Distance of Migrations of Defeated Clans after
Warfare in Eastern and Central Enga

	Generations 6-7		Generations 4-5	
	Eastern	Central	Eastern	Central
Number of migrant clans	30	35	15	7
Average distance of migration (km)	25	25	15	13

Note: These data include only clans who were totally displaced from the eastern and central valleys
of Enga by warfare and who resettled as a group elsewhere, not clans who disbanded after losing a
war, who immigrated into Enga, or who made secondary migrations after establishing new residences in fringe areas. The total number of clans whose history is covered is approximately 250.
We may have overlooked some migrations, but these data should represent at least 80 percent of
the major ones whose groups persisted into the present.

this time one sees a marked decline in the number of migrations after warfare
and a significant decrease in average migration distance.

For the first half of the twentieth century (second to third generation), this
trend continues. Meggitt (1977:14), reporting on the outcome of thirty-four wars
with known outcomes between 1950 and 1955, claimed that one subclan and five
clans were wholly uprooted from their land, an exceptionally high rate of evic-
tion for Enga warfare.[23] The supposedly evicted groups, however, did not migrate as they might have in previous generations but dispersed to the four winds,
resettling in the clans of relatives, often neighboring ones. Though we have no
systematically collected data for this period, cases we were told about had similar
outcomes in both eastern and central Enga. That is, we were told of no migrations of entire clans or tribes out of the major valleys to set up independent
communities elsewhere in the second to third generation, although such migrations continued to occur in more sparsely populated areas such as Maramuni and
northern Kompiam. We do not intend to say that clans and even whole tribes
were not ousted from their land during this period; they certainly were.[24] However, evictions resulted in the dispersal of clan members to live with relatives
after long and costly wars.

What is perhaps most interesting in these figures is that they demonstrate the
historical basis for the close association between warfare and land and for the
Enga's preoccupation with land. Prior to the fifth generation, when land was
plentiful, complete routs of enemy groups were most frequent. Victors often
could not fill the land they had gained and had to invite friends and allies to do
so. Clearly, the objective of warfare was not to procure land but to get rid of

disagreeable neighbors and competitors—an objective often chosen in the heat of battle when tempers were raging. For warfare to be effective in solving problems by spacing querulous neighbors apart from each other, land had to be lost. Displacement of the enemy was the solution to a problem, not the "cause" of the war. It was in this context that the link between warfare and land developed, not in the context of land shortage.

As the population grew and land filled, warfare became a less effective solution to problems, because people had to stay put after they fought. In this fact may lie the source of the "traditional enmities" so common in Enga, for when neither party was displaced, many problems were never resolved. Though less effective, warfare persisted as a competitive strategy for a number of reasons. First, it continued to be successful in displacing enemies in some cases, albeit after lengthy struggles. Second, numerous personal strategies were embedded in warfare that made individuals eager to fight: making a name, foiling the plans of others, or forging new exchange ties via compensation to allies. Third, warfare had long been a part of Enga culture, and embedded motivations, emotions, and the apparatus of warfare were not easy to dismantle by individual initiatives.

The decreasing effectiveness of warfare in solving problems had its own repercussions. It required a whole new repertoire of strategies for solving problems peacefully or, if warfare proved unavoidable, for reestablishing peace and the balance of power and reinstating means of social boundary maintenance. These topics are the subjects of chapters to come.

Frequency and Scale of Tribal Wars through Time

Unfortunately, it is impossible to determine whether tribal wars increased or decreased in frequency through time, because memories of wars have faded with each generation. Certainly the total number of tribal wars in each generation increased, but considering the population growth in Enga, the number of wars per capita did not necessarily rise. Still, an increase in warfare proportionate to that of the population would have made armed conflict a much more common experience within the lifetimes of individuals. Nicholas Modjeska (1982) has proposed that with a growing population and more complex relations, warfare also increased, necessitating new ways to make peace. We cannot definitively confirm or refute this proposition for Enga, but it does appear that it was not so much an increase in warfare as a decrease in the effectiveness of tribal fighting for solving problems that demanded new solutions.

Interestingly, there seems to have been little change in the range of scale and viciousness of wars from the early generations until contact with Europeans. In all generations one finds small, restrained wars between "brother" groups as well as large wars featuring complex strategies, the enlistment of allies, the loss of many men, and the total ousting of the defeated. Additionally, the ethics of warfare, which stipulated that wars within tribes and clans should inflict minimal damage and that only intertribal wars should incur high losses, remain constant in all periods. Although it was often entire tribes or clusters of clans that fought in the early generations in eastern and central Enga — as opposed to clans in more recent generations — tribes at that time would have not been much larger than individual clans are today. The scale and viciousness of a tribal war thus appear to have depended on the goals of the war, not on the generation in which it occurred, with the exception of the Great Ceremonial Wars discussed in chapter 10. A significant factor in containing warfare in later generations was the heavy debts that could be incurred by allied deaths when land could no longer be given as part of reparations.

Summary

We do not want to overstep the bounds of our limited data, so let it suffice to emphasize a few points. First, throughout their history Enga were concerned with boundary maintenance and the spacing of other groups for social reasons (the growth of communities until they were too large to cooperate), political reasons (maintaining optimal positions in trade and exchange networks), or ecological reasons (the desire to have abundant hunting land or fertile garden land within easy reach of settlements). Boundaries were maintained through physical means (warfare) and social ones (advertising or ritualized competition followed by exchange and the opening of access to resources to those who cooperated). The former could be extremely destructive, whereas the latter were essential to clan welfare because they permitted income to be obtained from outside the clan. Tribal wars appear to have fallen within a constant range of scale and viciousness throughout the span of historical traditions, depending on the objectives of the conflicting parties.

Second, causes of warfare were complex, because different participants often had divergent goals that were further altered by anger developed during the course of a vicious war. Though land was certainly a factor in warfare, Meggitt's (1977) picture of clans poised to take the land of neighbors is based on the incorrect assumption that it was land rather than labor that most stringently limited production. The history of different strategies used in Enga does not conform to a model of aggressive materialism but reveals a complex interaction between strategies of physical and social boundary maintenance, the latter enabling households and clans to circumvent the constraints of local labor forces with finance from outside.

Third, tribal warfare appears to have been most effective in solving problems prior to the fifth generation because land was plentiful and groups could be widely spaced. Loss of land thus became inextricably linked to warfare before there was pressure on land. Warfare gradually became less and less effective as tribal lands filled and much of the fertile land in outlying areas was occupied. Problems could no longer be as easily resolved by driving out hostile neighbors and replacing them with cooperative ones. New solutions for reestablishing peace and balance through ceremonial exchange were constructed by tribal leaders so that boundaries could once again be maintained by social rather than physical means. Such solutions sowed their own seeds of change.

Finally, although the following chapters do not concentrate on warfare, readers should bear in mind that the attempts of groups to resolve problems, attain goals, and establish balance of power through warfare was a strong force and constant concern throughout Enga oral history. It should not be underestimated.

6

The Early Stages of the Tee Ceremonial Exchange Cycle

> The Tee was planned by Kitalini from the beginning so that the Saka would be the center for exchange goods, particularly pigs. That is why cooked pork and live pigs came from all directions into the Saka valley.
>
> Apanyo Mauwa, Yambatane Watenge clan, Saka Laiagam

Enga often describe the Tee ceremonial exchange cycle as a flooding river, and flooded it was. In the 1960 and 1970s it is estimated to have drawn in some thirty thousand to seventy thousand participants (Brennan 1982).[1] Its history could easily have become drowned in the mingling of its many tributaries, had it not been for two starting points agreed on by most elders: that the Tee originated in the Saka valley of eastern Enga and that it is relatively recent, beginning in the founding generations but expanding rapidly only after the fifth. Indeed, claims concerning its recency find overwhelming support in historical traditions. There is absolutely no mention of the Tee cycle in either myths or historical narratives prior to the sixth generation before the present, except in the histories of a few key tribes among whom it originated. Furthermore, participation in the Tee cycle is not said to be something "that was always done by the ancestors." To the contrary, many clans along major Tee routes have oral traditions describing in straightforward terms where

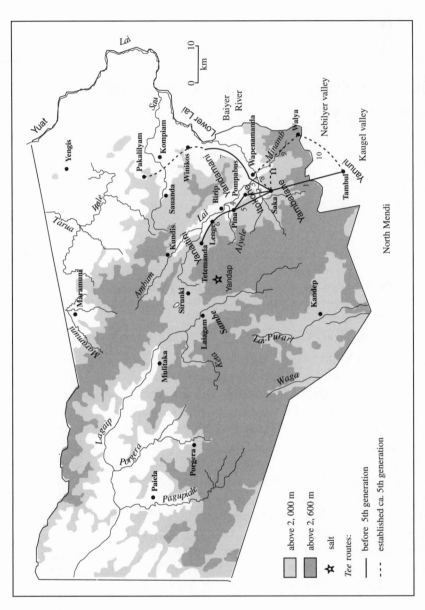

Map 11. Routes of the early Tee cycle. 1, Kunja; 2, Ome; 3, Sambaka; 4, Lyai; 5, Sambe; 6, Yalu; 7, Koeyama; 8, Kungu; 9, Kulanga; 10, several routes linking Walia to Tambul; 11, Walepa.

the Tee began and how they first came to take part in it. A reconstruction of the history of the Tee from historical traditions is thus possible, although it is extremely complex because of the many factors and parties involved. We begin with what elders lay out as its foundation: strategies for controlling the trade.

The Eastern Trade Alliance

Historical traditions dealing with the early trade agree on one point, the existence of a central alliance between Yanuni clans of Tambul, Yambatane of the Saka valley, and Itokone and Yanaitini of Pompabus and Tilyaposa in the middle Lai valley (map 11). This alliance worked as follows: Yanuni and other Tambul tribes stood at the junction of networks that brought axes, shells, oil, and other goods from regions to the south and east up through the Kaugel, Nebilyer, and north Mendi valleys. As middlemen, they took these goods down the Kunja bush route to their "cousin," Yambatane, in the Saka valley and exchanged them for salt from the Yandap area, among many other things. The Itokone and Yanaitini tribes did not serve as middlemen in the salt trade but acquired salt directly from the source 40–50 kilometers to their west in the Yandap, where they owned land containing some of the major salt springs. Their rights of ownership are validated in the following metaphorical legend telling how Sambe clans, who lived adjacent to the salt springs, "woke up too late" to lay claim to them:

Long ago, Itokone and Sambe [of Papyuku near Laiagam] made an agreement that they would meet and decide how to divide the land in the Yandap between them. They set a day and time to meet. Itokone got up very early and climbed a high mountain called Yakopyamanda. From there he looked around in all directions, saw all the land below him, and felt very content. He chopped wood, built a fire, and sat there waiting for Sambe to come. Sambe climbed the mountain very slowly, and arrived later. By this time Itokone had used up most of the firewood in the area.

When Sambe reached the top of the mountain, Itokone said to him, "I slept near here and came very early, but I see that you have arrived very late. It must be because you already have all the land you need." They decided to draw the boundary line from that point by putting a post in the ground as a marker. Itokone got the larger part of the land. Later Itokone went and talked to men from the Apulini clans of Maimai and Kopale who lived in the Yandap area to tell them of the agreement. (Pyaene Laowala, Yanaitini Kia clan, Tetemanda)

Sambe has a very similar, complementary historical narrative acknowledging that it "missed out" in this division of land.

The salt springs of the Yandap (map 11) were numerous and dispersed; Itokone did not have a monopoly on them. Clans belonging to tribes living closer to the Yandap (Itapuni, Awaini, Malipini, Sakalini, Sambe, and Apulini) also owned springs and manufactured salt, but they were not in the same advantageous position as members of the Itokone and Yanaitini tribes.[2] They lived farther to the west in a different dialect group and lacked direct ties with Tambul, the major point of entry for axes.[3]

After the introduction of the sweet potato, major trade alliances were extended up the Lai valley, possibly in response to an increasing demand for axes as a greater segment of the western Enga population engaged more intensively in gardening. The Yanaitini moved to Tetemanda, near present-day Wabag, to be in a better position to make salt, which they agreed to exchange with the Itokone for stone axes (map 11).

The origin tradition of Yanaitini begins with two brothers, Itokone and Yanaitini. They were originally from the area near Pompabus where Itokone lives today. When Itokone was on his way from his home at Tilyaposa to the Nakatima salt springs near Mulisos, he stopped at Tetemanda. Tetemanda at that time was a jungle of *yumbi* trees. There he built himself a small hut and continued on his journey to the salt springs. When he arrived, he cut up pieces of dry wood and put them in the pool of salt water to soak. Since they had to soak for months, he went back to Tetemanda, planted sweet potatoes and other crops at the back of his small house, and returned to his home at Tilyaposa.

Some months later Itokone got his mother, sister, and brother and returned to the salt pools to take out the wood and burn it into salt ash. When they had finished, they started home and spent the night at Tetemanda. Itokone saw that the crops he had planted earlier were growing well, particularly the sweet potatoes. He realized that the land was fertile and considered settling there.

The next morning Itokone told his brother of his plans to live permanently at Tetemanda and asked him to take their mother and sister back home to Tilyaposa. He urged them to cook and eat their breakfast quickly in order to get an early start for the long and tiring journey. When the food was ready, Itokone noticed that Yanaitini was not eating and asked him what was the matter. Yanaitini did not reply, so Itokone guessed what was on his mind. He asked Yanaitini if he himself would like to stay at Tetemanda instead, and Yanaitini said yes. So they agreed that Yanaitini should remain at Tetemanda and that Itokone should take his mother and sister back to Tilyaposa. [Yanaitini was known for his bad manners and his tendency to be a troublemaker. For these reasons, among others, Itokone was quite willing to live apart from him.]

Before they left, Itokone made the agreement that since the distance between Tilyaposa and the salt quarry was long, Yanaitini should make salt and send it to Itokone, and that Itokone would send Yanaitini stone axes in return. Itokone then left with his mother and sister, and Yanaitini stayed at Tetemanda. (Pyaene Laowala, Yanaitini Kia clan, Tetemanda)

After recounting this origin tradition, Pyaene went on to describe Yanaitini's distribution of wealth to his grandsons. The Kalinatae clans—Kia, Kalepatae, and Yapokone—received his bundle of charms, representing the focal role they played in the trade and Tee cycle:

While they were living there [at Tetemanda], Yanaitini fell ill, and Kalinatae, realizing that he might die, took his grandfather's bundle of charms [*takameyaki*] to attract wealth in *tee* exchange. Later, Lanekepa and Pauwale's other sons arrived. Seeing that Kalinatae had already taken the bundle of charms, Kepa took the pig rope and the club for killing pigs [skill in pig raising]. Neneo took the bamboo knife [skill in the art of public speaking and peacemaking, for the bamboo knife makes a clean, sharp cut]. Kokope took the spear [skill in fighting], Piao, the stick for planting taro [skill in the cultivation of taro], and Kondakana, Yanaitini's digging stick [skill in gardening].

Itokone and Yanaitini's possession of salt pools in the Yandap and Yanaitini's move to Tetemanda indeed seem to be firmly grounded in historical events; they are noted in the historical traditions of other tribes as well. For example, Yanaitini's former place of residence is remembered in the history of the Itokone and other neighbors in the middle Lai valley. Yanaitini's move to Tetemanda is also noted in the history of the neighboring Itapuni of Kamasa, near Tetemanda. That Yanaitini and Itokone had rights to salt pools in the Yandap is recorded in Sambe history and that of some other clans of central Enga. Exactly when Yanaitini moved to Tetemanda is impossible to estimate from genealogical chronology, because the tradition comes from the founding generations. However, it must have occurred after the introduction of the sweet potato and before the seventh generation.

Once settled at Tetemanda, Yanaitini extended its own trade links to the west, north, and northeast in a number of ways, including participation in the Great Ceremonial Wars that were forming in central Enga. Most notable among the alliances the tribe formed via the Great Wars was that with Sambe of the Papyuka-Laiagam area at the crossroads of trade routes coming from the south and west. Yanaitini big-men (*kamongo*) were then able to manipulate the flow of wealth in central Enga to their own advantage, with the Yambatane of the Saka valley having little influence over their decisions.

In approximately the same period, a second development took place that further threatened Yambatane's hold on the trade. As we discussed in chapter 5, large numbers of people from the Lyomoi, Kupa, and Yakumba clans left the north Mendi area to join groups near Wapenamanda (see map 8:1-3). Together they formed the Yakumane, Kandawalini, and Wauni tribes, who became prosperous neighbors of Yambatane. Kandawalini then moved farther on up the Lai, opening the way for a new trade route. Numerous other clans from the Nebilyer valley and Tambul migrated into eastern Enga within the next two to three generations, settling in the Minamb valley or pushing on into the lower Lai and Baiyer river regions (see map 8). Notable among these were Nenaini and Lyomoi clans whose "brothers" remained in Tambul at the heart of the trade. Most of these had strong connections to the east or south, and together with the wealthy Wapenamanda tribes they threatened to divert the mainstream of the trade through the Minamb valley directly into the Lai and westward to Tetemanda, bypassing the Saka.

Yambatane big-men, realizing that they were losing their hold on the trade in both eastern and central Enga, took action to broaden their sphere of social influence. It is as a result of their tactics that the Tee is said to have originated. Two metaphorical legends recall this origin: the Kitalini legend from the Saka valley and the Tiane's *kingi* legend from Tetemanda. Both refer to developments that took place after the introduction of the sweet potato and Yanaitini's move to Tetemanda and before approximately the seventh generation. We begin with the Kitalini legend.

Kitalini and the Origin of the Tee

The Kitalini legend is the only historical tradition we collected that is acknowledged to be the origin legend for the Tee cycle. That it is metaphorical, with Kitalini representing the big-men of the Yambatane Mama clans (Yana, Mama, Winau, and Yandamau) is recognized by Enga narrators. That powerful men in clans along the major trade alliances controlled the flow of wealth at this early date is also widely acknowledged.

After the dispersal of Saka Pembe's [the founding ancestor's] sons, Yambatane remained at Kukuma near Saka Laiagam. There he had two sons, Mama and Lyowangi, each of whom had four sons of his own. Later, three out of Mama's four sons died of *yama* sickness and only the youngest, Kitalini, was left.[4] . . .

[The next section, omitted for brevity, tells of the young Kitalini going to the bush with his father, getting lost, building a hunting hut, and living on forest products.]

Kitalini stayed in the bush and did not go home to visit his parents until he grew into a handsome young man, because he was afraid that if he did he might catch *yama* sickness. He was tall like a *pai* [chestnut] tree, and it is said that he was so strong from his life in the bush that ten men would not have been able to tackle him.[5]

One day Kitalini heard that there was a traditional dance at Alumanda and dressed himself for the occasion. When he entered the dance grounds, everybody rushed up to greet him. He joined the dance line and performed so impressively that all eyes were riveted on him. Young women from all over the area came, danced beside him, and tied strings around his belt as a form of love magic, each hoping that she would be the one to marry him even if he ignored her at the dance. After one day at the Alumanda dance, Kitalini went on to a dance held by Yandamani.[6] There he joined the line of dancers, and before long three extraordinarily beautiful women came over and danced beside him. Kitalini was so enchanted by these women that he whispered to each that he would take her back to his home. The three women, who were from Melyoposini, Yandamani, and Yandamani Yanana clans of the lower Lai, followed Kitalini to his house, where he told them to take a good look at his living conditions.

When they had seen everything, he said, "As you see, I have no pigs, no gardens, and not even a regular house. I have no brothers with pigs who might help me pay bridewealth. So what do you want to do?"

"We did not come here for the bridewealth," the three women replied. "We came here because we want to marry you."

Kitalini realized that it would be an insult to the women's parents to marry them without paying bridewealth, so he asked them to go back to their houses and wait for a message from him. He warned them, "If you do not hear from me in four days, then you will know that I could not raise the bridewealth, so you should go back to your other boyfriends."

Reluctantly the three young women went home, hoping that they would hear from Kitalini soon. During this time they neither ate nor slept but just waited anxiously. Kitalini had to think fast to come up with a way to raise enough bridewealth for three women in four days, particularly since he had no brothers to help him. He sent out messages along the Kunja, Sambe, Walepa, Sambaka, and Ome routes [map 11], saying, "If people are supposed to help and give, then do so, for I need pigs now."

During the days that followed people arrived with pigs from all directions, gave their pigs to Kitalini, and told him to dispose of them as he pleased. By the end of four days Kitalini had many pigs, enough to make a generous bridewealth payment for each of the three women. He took some of the pigs, divided them into three equal lots, and gave them to the parents of the three women, keeping the rest to thank the people who had helped him with the bridewealth. The parents, pleased with the bridewealth and marriage arrangements, gave Kitalini one pig in exchange for each pig he had given.

Kitalini gathered together all the pigs and sent messages back down the Walepa, Kunja, Sambe, Sambaka, and Ome routes that he was going to hold a Tee distribution to pay back those who had helped him.[7] People from all directions gathered on the Alumanda ceremonial grounds, and Kitalini lined up the pigs and gave them out, taking pigs that had come along the Sambe route and giving them to people from along the Kunja route, and so on. The people took their pigs home along the various routes, and over the years the exchange between these men, Kitalini, and others continued, the center being at the Alumanda ceremonial grounds.

In the beginning these exchanges involved a small number of people and few pigs, but Kitalini's wives gave birth to sons, and his sons to many grandsons, and so the exchanges grew. Even today it is according to this tradition that the leaders in the Saka gather when they want the Tee to start and discuss what they should do. Then they divide themselves into several groups according to the routes along which they have marriage links. If a man is married to an Itokone woman, then he and his group follow the Ome route; if a man is married to a Sikini woman, then he follows the Sambe route to Tetemanda. The different groups of men follow different routes to organize the Tee cycle. (Saiyakali Patao Yaki, Yambatane Yana clan, Kukuma, Saka valley)

During our interview, Saiyakali moved quickly from the Kitalini legend to the Tee cycle of more recent times. When he was finished, we asked whether the Tee cycle indeed began in Kitalini's time. To this he replied, "Not really," explaining once again that in Kitalini's time the Tee was held on a very small scale and that only in the generation of Kitalini's grandsons and great-grandsons (around the fifth to sixth generation) did it begin to expand into a true cycle that incorporated many clans in eastern Enga.

Like many oral traditions concerning trade and exchange, the Kitalini legend is symbolic and does not disclose political motives directly. Saiyakali added no interpretation.[8] Other Tee leaders, however, explained that Kitalini was probably representative of Yambatane big-men and that the legend described moves on the part of these big-men to expand their spheres of influence, thereby keeping control of the trade. Kitalini's "first Tee" was engineered by Yambatane big-men as a way of raising wealth to secure exchange relations along major trade routes, as well as a way of establishing a new branch of the trade alliance from the Saka across the Lai and into the lower Lai valley (map 11:7). This route cut off alternate ones that were forming down the Minamb valley directly into the middle or lower Lai and threatening to divert the mainstream of the trade away from the Saka. Later, Itokone, Yambatane's ally in the Tee, waged war on the Kandawalini,[9] taking a substantial portion of their land along the Lai and severing them from their "brother" tribes in Wapenamanda. This move further blocked the formation of a direct Lai valley route. The historical traditions of a number of clans of the middle Lai acknowledge that such efforts on the part of Yambatane were successful and that as a result they remained peripheral to trade and Tee alliances until the beginning of the fourth generation.

In initiating a form of exchange that later developed into the Tee cycle, Yambatane men combined the time-tested tactic of exerting influence through well-placed affinal ties with innovation — the establishment of chains of finance (A. Strathern 1969). The providing of goods on credit, as we have seen, had previously existed between clansmen and their affinal and maternal kin. However, Kitalini's taking wealth from exchange partners and relatives along one trade route and channeling it to those along another constructed chains of finance that transcended the bounds of immediate kinship ties. Formerly, for example, an individual, A, could have obtained finance from a close affinal or maternal kinsperson, B, and B could have gotten the same from his own relative,

C. Enchained finance meant that A could receive wealth from C through B, something that does not seem to have been done, at least on any regular basis, outside the Tee cycle. Enga describe these chains as stems of *lyongo lyongo*, a horsetail plant whose detachable segments make up the stem, just like segments fitted together in a Tee chain. Tee chains allowed families to draw on the wealth of a much broader segment of the population, including people who were unrelated by ordinary kinship reckoning. It should be emphasized that these chains of finance did not spring up "out of the blue" but were built upon on a well-established foundation of trade partnerships.

Maintaining Tee chains is a delicate matter, as an Enga proverb explains: "The Tee flows on a path no bigger than a single strand of a spider's web. All care must be taken not to break it."[10] Though Kitalini's campaign for wealth is abbreviated in the rendition given earlier, there is little doubt that he treated these fragile webs with care, going first to the houses of immediate affinal or maternal relatives, asking them to give, and then traveling on with them to their relatives or trade partners to ask for support, as Tee organizers of more recent generations did. When it came time to reciprocate, an essential part of Kitalini's strategy was to provide generous returns to those who had helped him, taking the exchange pigs contributed by his brides' parents, adding them to those he had judiciously set aside, and holding a public distribution to repay creditors along different routes. To reciprocate generously bound Tee associates through both the goodwill and friendship expressed and the prospect of financial gain. Furthermore, it incorporated the concept of earned interest: the receiver might use the gift as capital in other transactions in the meanwhile, and when possible should share some of the gain with the original giver. Generous returns should not be confused with the concept of "increment" used by Andrew Strathern (1971:216) for the Moka exchange system of the Melpa people around Mount Hagen, in which there is competition between partners and groups to give back more than one has received. In the Enga Tee cycle there is no such competition between partners—generous returns are desirable, though not necessary, and are aimed at strengthening the bond, not at winning in the "game" of giving and establishing temporary superiority.

The Kitalini legend gives the first description in historical traditions of a "Tee" exchange held for the general purpose of paying back creditors. Other narratives of the time concern distributions of wealth for specific events only: marriages, funeral feasts, or war reparations. It is also the first account of a public distribution of wealth in eastern Enga carried out on a clan's ceremonial grounds.[11] Prior to this time, traditional dances and cult feasts are said to have been situated on ceremonial grounds, but the locations of war reparations and bridewealth distributions remain unspecified. In central Enga before the Tee cycle, war reparation

distributions were held at men's houses (see also Lacey 1975:166). That the first
public distribution of wealth on a clan's ceremonial grounds was associated with
the establishment of finance through chains of creditors is not surprising, for in
addition to advertising ability to manage wealth, it allowed people to testify that
investments from many and distant sources had been justly repaid.

In short, the new elements in Kitalini's "first Tee" are finance through chains
of creditors and subsequent public distributions of wealth held to pay back
creditors along these chains. Its primary purpose was to secure alliances to
control the trade, and consequently, for the next two generations it remained
limited to clans directly on the major trade routes. This lent the Tee cycle its
linear form, which persisted even after it had encompassed the greater part of
eastern Enga and its role had broadened.

The beginning of the Tee cycle with its new strategies of finance had reverberations in the histories of neighboring tribes. For example, a fascinating historical narrative from Itokone documents the first use of chains of finance by
the Nenae clan.

In the past there lived a man named Itokone. He fathered Mupa, Nenae, Lanjetakini,
Lundopa, and Tandaka, and then he had two more children, Koeyakini and Napukini.
Mupa had pigs, but Nenae did not. At Lamandaimanda [middle Lai valley], the sons of
Itokone set out pig stakes on the ceremonial grounds [*mena limando*, stakes to which
pigs will be tied in an upcoming *tee*]. Nenae had no pigs, but he set out stakes on the
ceremonial grounds anyway [*mena kii*, stakes set out to plan a future distribution].
Their mother, a Kaekini woman, came that morning, checked each line, and asked
questions about the stakes. Somebody told her that they belonged to the sons of
Itokone, and that one row of stakes belonged to each of his sons.

One row was longer than the others, which prompted her to ask, "Whose stake is
this?"

"That belongs to Nenae," she was told.

"Why do you put up a row of pig stakes when you have no pigs in your house?" she
asked Nenae.

"I am not like Mupa, who only breeds pigs. I follow the Gote cult. You see, I go up
there [to the Saka valley and Tambul] and chase down the pigs. That is how I am going
to get my pigs. I am not so simple."[12]

So what they [Nenae, accompanied by his brothers] did was to slaughter pigs and
bring the sides to the Saka valley. That was called *saandi pingi* [to give initiatory gifts].
They did not do it directly but through the Aluni Kepa clan. They also gave sides of
pork to the Waiminakuni clan, who in turn gave them to Yambatane. Yambatane took
the sides of pork and went to Kuiamanda in the Kola [Tambul] area. That is the land
of Katimbi, the current Tee *kamongo* [big-man] of the Tambul area. In that place the
Tee cycle was launched. Yambatane then brought the Tee to the Saka valley, took pigs
from it, and gave them to the Waiminakuni, Kepa, and Maitepa [clans of the Aluni

tribe]. Then they gave pigs to men of Itokone, and the Tee came to rest at Tilyaposa. Itokone then held their Tee and gave pigs to the Timali clan, and so the Tee went up to Lenge. Itokone also gave pigs directly to the Yanaitini Kia clan [at Tetemanda]. That was how the Tee cycle was performed in the early stages. . . .

In those days only the clans that I mentioned participated in the Tee cycle, and that was the situation for some time. Later, as people in the neighborhood saw and heard about the Tee, they began to take part. All others learned from these people, and then they did Tee. That is how the Tee cycle expanded to other regions. (Palane Yakenalu, Itokone Nenae clan, Tilyaposa)

The key to this legend lies in the meaning of the two kinds of pig stakes. *Mena limando* are stakes sharpened to a point to which pigs are tied for distribution. These are the stakes that were set out by Nenae's brothers. Nenae, however, planted *mena kii,* stakes that are not sharpened on top and are used to designate how many pigs will be given in a future distribution. He set out his *mena kii* even though he had no pigs in his house, because he was already linked to the Tee and expected to receive pigs through chains of finance. Accordingly, he told his mother that he was not simple—he did not raise all his pigs at home like his brothers but caught onto new trends coming from the east. He then took his "brothers" to the Saka to introduce them to the new system of finance.

The Westward Expansion of the Tee Cycle

The Kitalini legend as told by Saiyakali primarily concerns the efforts of Yambatane men to expand their influence northward into the lower Lai valley. Other oral traditions place equal emphasis on ties with the west. For example, in a version of the Kitalini legend given by Apanyo Mauwa of the Yambatane Watenge clan, it is said that some Yanaitini of Tetemanda helped finance Kitalini's marriage, and that the skeletal remains of the exchange pigs given in the first Tee distribution held by Kitalini were kept in the men's house at Tetemanda as a symbol of their affiliation. From that time on, part of the men's house of the Yanaitini Kia clan was said to have "belonged" to Yambatane Watenge who stayed there on journeys to organize the Tee cycle.

The expanding westward influence of the Yambatane tribe and its efforts to organize the early Tee cycle in such a way as to tap into the wealth that Yanaitini had acquired in central Enga are told from quite a different perspective in the Yanaitini tradition of "Tiane's *kingi*" (see Appendix 6 for the full version). In it, Yanaitini of Tetemanda goes out hunting and comes across two opossums fighting in a pandanus tree. He attempts to capture one but ends up with only the "thumb" from its paw. In the morning he discovers that it is a human thumb, not an opossum's. Frightened by this strange event, he holds a small ritual for the spirits and calls a traditional dance at the end, inviting people from the neighborhood and all the way down the trade route to the Saka valley. People gather from far and wide and the dance begins. Yanaitini dresses in the finest ceremonial attire to participate, concealing the thumb, known as Tiane's *kingi*, in his headdress. It transforms him into an awesome, charismatic figure, to the wonder of the spectators. When his wife removes it between performances, however, he becomes an ordinary man once more.

Annoyed at her husband's intent to marry other women who are attracted by his newfound fame, Yanaitini's wife reveals the secret to Yambatane of the Saka valley. Yambatane steals the thumb and sends it eastward by relay runners from clan to clan along the western Tee and trade route to the Saka and on to the Yanuni tribe in Tambul for safekeeping. Remarks at the end of the story say that it is because Yambatane stole the charm to attract wealth that the center of wealth remained in the Saka and that the key clans in organizing the Tee were Yanaitini at Tetemanda, Yambatane Watenge of the Saka, and the Yanuni tribe of Tambul.

With the information provided by the Kitalini tradition — that the Tee cycle originated when Yambatane men initiated a new system of finance to obtain wealth for building alliances in the trade — it is possible to gain some understanding of the Tiane's *kingi* legend. The first half of the legend, in which Yanaitini acquires the charm, explains the success of Yanaitini clans after they moved to central Enga in terms of Enga belief that charms, spells, and rituals play an important role in attracting wealth. From other historical narratives we know that this was actually owing to their pivotal role in both the salt–ax-stone trade and the Great Ceremonial Wars with Monaini (see chapter 10). Most likely the fight of the opossums in the pandanus tree represents the Great Ceremonial Wars.

The central theme of the second half is self-evident: the arrival of Yambatane at the dance with a contingent of men from clans along the Tambul-Saka-Tetemanda trade route represents the Tee alliances that Yambatane had formed to tap into the wealth of central Enga. This theme becomes even more pronounced when Yambatane steals the charm to attract wealth and passes it by relay through a network of allied groups, drawing wealth into the Saka over the Yalu and Sambe Tee and trade routes (map 11:5-6) and sending it along the Kunja route to Tambul. The narrator, Anjo, did not hesitate to make this interpretation, but he went no further.

Note also the power of Yanaitini's wife in determining his success. This is not an isolated example, for women played important roles by creating and maintaining essential relationships throughout the history of the Tee (see also Feil 1978b; Kyakas and Wiessner 1992). Although conflicts between spouses in the

Tee did occur, men and women generally worked together for the good of the family. In the pages to come, we thus speak of the Tee initiatives not of individuals but of families.

The Tiane's *kingi* legend depicts the extension of the Tee cycle to central Enga as a dramatic affair. Such is the spirit of metaphorical legends, which are designed to capture the tensions of political struggles. Quite a different impression is received from the more factual histories of clans along trade routes who joined the Tee cycle in its early stages. These are straightforward accounts of specific marriages through which subclans or lineages first became involved.[13] Historical narratives from the Yanuni tribe in Tambul, for example, recount that long ago people from Tambul exchanged axes, cassowary feathers, necklaces, and other items with people of the Saka valley in the trade. Yet only with the marriage of a Yanuni man, Melene, to a Yambatane woman in the sixth generation was such exchange regularly integrated into the early Tee cycle. Elders from the Aluni Waiminakuni clan, a neighbor of Yambatane, pinpoint their entrance into the Tee to the marriage of an Aluni woman named Palu Taipu to a man of the Yambatane Watenge clan in the seventh generation. Their neighbor, the Itokone Nenae clan, traces its first Tee link to the marriage of Kitalini's "sister" to an Itokone man. The Sikini Lyonai Tee history that we collected does not identify a specific marriage but attributes the clan's entrance into the Tee cycle to marriages contracted with Itokone or Yambatane. The Yakani Timali clan of Lenge joined the Tee in its early stages through marriage links with Itokone; Itokone men acknowledge these early links with Timali and say that they were initiated because "the men from that clan were big, tall men and they were affluent. It was also the land of the large *waima* trees [indicators of soil fertility]. For these reasons they created Tee links."[14] The Lyipini Kepeo clan first participated in the Tee during the fifth to sixth generation after a Kepeo woman married Wambe of the Yakani Timali clan, an event confirmed in both Kepeo and Timali history.[15]

Routes of the Early Tee Cycle

From the oral histories of different clans, together with an overview given by Tee organizers, it is possible to put together a very general chronological geography of the spread of the early Tee. So far as we could determine, Yambatane clans began to hold Tee exchanges with clans along major trade routes some eight to ten generations ago.[16] The pivotal players were not entire tribes but clans among the Yanuni of Tambul, the Yambatane of the Saka, and the Yanaitini of Tetemanda. Other clans gave pigs, goods, and valuables to those who were involved directly in the Tee, who in turn passed the items down their Tee chains along the major trade routes. When the direction of the flow of wealth was reversed, those in donor clans were reciprocated. The following testimony describes this process:

> While Yanaitini was at Tetemanda, Yambatane stole the charm Tiane's *kingi* and fled. At that time people living to our north [in the Ambum and upper Sau valleys] and in the Lai valley did not give much thought to the Tee cycle. They just produced pigs for consumption and for the reasons that I mentioned earlier [funeral feasts and war reparations]. The only route that existed [to the west] at that time was the Yalu route; it was well known because of the Tee cycle. I [the Kandawalini Kaekini clan] would go up the Aiyele valley and set foot on the Yalu route to get goods from the Tee (because we did not join until later). People had pigs in the Lai valley, some even had large ones, but they did not participate in the organization of the Tee. They took part only in war reparation distributions with both cooked pork and live pigs. Tetemanda was the center for doing Tee. The clans living to the east of Tetemanda, such as Sapipi, Aipiyape, Yakale, and Kaeyalu, did not participate directly in the Tee but gave pigs to the Yanaitini Kia clan at Tetemanda [and, as he explains later, received pigs, goods, and valuables in return]. So the Tee from the beginning belonged to you, Yanaitini, and Yambatane.[17]
> (Leme Poul, Kandawalini Kaekini clan, Maeyokomanda [Yaibosa])

Approximately six to eight generations ago, the early Tee clung to the following trade routes radiating out from the Yambatane clans in the Saka valley:

1. The Kunja route (map 11:1) from the Saka valley to Yanuni clans in Tambul. Possibly some clans of Pauakaka and Lyomoi in the Saka were also included in the early phases of the Tee, but we were unable to confirm this.
2. The Ome route (map 11:2) over the ridge that separates the Saka valley from the Lai valley, leading to Itokone clans at Tilyaposa-Pompabus. From Itokone, the wealth was taken over the Lyai route (4) to Sikini Lyonai clans in the Aiyele valley.
3. The Sambaka route (3) over the ridge separating the Saka and Lai valleys, leading to Aluni clans at Sambakamanda. From there, as described in the Kitalini legend, Tee relationships were extended to the Yandamani Yokoenda clan at Bilimanda in the middle Lai valley and then along the Koeyama route (7) and on to Yandamani Yanana and Melyoposini clans in the lower Lai.
4. The Sambe route (5) from Saka Laiagam through some Sikini clans in the Saka valley and over the Sambe mountain ridge that separates Saposa in the Saka valley from the Aiyele river, a tributary of the Lai. In the Aiyele valley, the route passed through the Sikini Lyonai and Muitapa clans.

5. From the Ome-Lyai and Sambe routes, the Tee continued over
   the Yalu ridge that separates the Aiyele valley from the Lai valley
   and on to Yakani Timali and Yanaitini Kalinatae clans in the upper
   Lai and lower Ambum valleys (6). In the earliest stages, the Yalu
   route is said by some to have included only Yambatane, Itokone,
   Yakani Timali, and Yanaitini Kia, with the others — Sikini Muitape
   and Lyonai, Depe Koepa, Lyipini Wiyo, and Apulini Talyulu in
   the Aiyele valley — joining between five and six generations ago.

The Sphere and Scale of the Early Tee Cycle

During its early phases the Tee traversed a vast area and three language or dialect
groups — Kakoli, Saka-Layapo Enga, and Kaina-Mai Enga — although it incorporated but a handful of clans in each group. Within participant clans, the numbers
of individuals who took part were also few:

In the past [about the fifth generation], only a few people were involved in the Tee
cycle. Only a few promoted the Tee and actually took part in it. In those times there
were many who were "poor" [*tipya*]. The Tee cycle was held in the Saka valley and
branched off through the Kungu, Sambaka, and Sambe routes. . . . In those times
when the Tee routes that I have mentioned were opened up, only a few people were involved. For instance, here in Birip [Depe Liala clan] there were only a few who took
part in the Tee cycle; all of the rest did not have enough pigs to take part in the Tee;
they simply were not interested in doing so. Therefore in those times the Tee was done
on a very small scale. That is not to say that the Tee cycle did not cover a large area,
but that not many pigs were given away. Most people would give away one or two pigs
only, and if a person gave away more than ten pigs, he was regarded as a big-man. It
was only with the coming of the white man that the Tee cycle expanded greatly — now
you see many clans taking part. (Apakasa, Depe Lyala clan, Birip, middle Lai valley)[18]

The view expressed by Apakasa — that only a few men in each clan took part
in the early Tee cycle — is substantiated in other testimonies.[19] For example, each
subclan or lineage has its own history of the first families to take part, because
joining the early Tee was not a clan affair but something that individual families
did when the interest was there and wealth and ties permitted. Only as the Tee
cycle became flooded with wealth, first from the Great Ceremonial Wars of
central Enga and later with the new wealth introduced by Europeans, did more
and more families become interested in stepping up production so that they too
could participate.

It should also be noted that the "poverty" of many families mentioned by

Apakasa and a number of others interviewed is a subjective evaluation made relative to the standards of more recent generations and is not part of the historical narratives. It refers to poverty in goods, valuables, and particularly pigs, not to land, housing, and subsistence. It is one of several ways of saying that in the past there were fewer pigs and commodities in circulation, and it should not be interpreted to mean that social inequalities were greater in the past. To the contrary, elders say that social inequalities were less pronounced in the early generations. As Apakasa explains, many people had relatively few pigs because they were uninterested in the labor-intensive task of raising more. At the time, hunting provided meat for daily meals and ceremonial occasions, and attention was focused on the trade. Only as the Tee cycle grew and reached a certain threshold at which its benefits became highly visible did a broader segment of the population invest more effort in pig production.

In keeping with claims of lower levels of pig production in the past, Tee distributions held by clans prior to the fourth generation were said to be small in comparison with those of more recent times. Some idea of their scale is depicted in the preceding testimony by Apakasa and in a passage from Apulini history of the fifth generation recorded by Roderic Lacey:

When he first made the Tee, Yama may have placed six *mena limando* [pig stakes] on the center of the *kamapi* [ceremonial grounds]. His sons Masa and Wapuli, when they made the Tee, may have been able to go further and add another two to their father's record. Kepai was taught that Wapuli planted some of the large chestnut [*pai*] and beech [*tato*] trees which still stand on the southern side of the *kamapi*. Then Wako and Lemalu, their sons, may have added another three. They would then have reached a total of eleven *mena limando*. (Lacey 1975:166, referring to Kepai, Apulini Talyulu clan, Irelya)[20]

Furthermore, wealth distributions in the early Tee cycle were smaller because the Tee chains that radiated out from the Saka valley were short:

Nowadays people go to the Yandap area, they go to your side [the Ambum, referring to the territory of Akii's Yanaitini tribe], and they go in all directions to campaign for the Tee. That was not done before Pendaine's time [the fourth generation]. I do not mean that Tee cycles were not held before Pendaine's time, but they were carried out on a small scale and sequences of giving were short. (Kambao Lambu, Yakani Timali clan, Lenge)

Tee cycles initiated by Saka valley Yambatane clans would move into the Kopona area, Tambul, or Tetemanda, incorporating clans directly along the major trade routes and returning to their point of origin in the Saka. Tee cycles initiated by Yanaitini at Tetemanda or by Timali at Lenge traveled to the Itokone, the Yambatane, and perhaps on to the Yanuni at Tambul but did not link with the Tee cycles on other routes. Yambatane clans remained in the center of the system, manipulating the flow of goods via short Tee cycles that radiated out in a number of directions.

We know little about the sequences of Tee cycles prior to the fourth generation, by which time they had settled into a three-phase cycle involving initiatory gifts, main gifts that moved in the opposite direction, and steamed pork given in a return phase. It was not possible to ascertain whether the Tee had assumed this pattern in the very beginning or whether it developed over subsequent generations. Both historical narratives and personal testimonies claim, however, that the early Tee cycles were arranged on an ad hoc basis, as need arose. That is, when major clans in the Tee network needed to finance specific events such as war reparations, marriages, or funeral feasts, their members called on partners to initiate a Tee cycle, just as Kitalini had done for his marriages. As we will see later, it was only in the third to fourth generation, when so many clans became involved in the Tee that it would no longer respond to the needs of single clans, that it became a self-perpetuating cycle.

Expansion of the Early Tee: Cycle Routes and Reasons

The limited scale and scope of the Tee was not long-lived; in the fifth generation it is said to have expanded "like a bush fire" in some areas of the east. People in clans neighboring on the Saka valley (that is, in the Minamb valley and the Wapenamanda area) saw that those along Tee routes were enjoying greater access to cooked pork, live pigs, and other goods and valuables. They realized that they too must join if they were to acquire the wealth necessary to compete in almost any area of social and political life.[21] Entrance into the Tee was not difficult, owing to its organization along lines of affinal and maternal kinship. Those seeking to join arranged marriages with persons directly along Tee routes, informally sending wealth into the system and receiving returns from it. Later, when several families in a clan had established such ties and an occasion arose in which many pigs were to be given — such as in war reparations — these distributions were phased into a specific Tee cycle. Subsequently, members of the clan held regular distributions on their ceremonial grounds during the courses of Tee cycles.

From this time period forward, a distinction must be drawn between trade routes and the sequence of giving in the Tee cycle — what might be called the course of the Tee. Trade routes are named paths that link valleys. From the fifth generation on, the Tee cycle no longer clung to trade routes but meandered through many clans in an area (see Meggitt 1974:172–73; Feil 1984:63), the wealth being brought home along different trade routes. Though courses of the Tee were not named, its general route of progression was described by saying that it was moving along such-and-such a trade route.

The incorporation of clans off the usual trade routes broadened the Tee from a system of finance that served interests in the trade to a multipurpose system of finance for bridewealth, payments to affinal or maternal kin, and war repara-tions—obligations that secured the production and reproduction of families, subclans, and clans. Returns in the Tee were applied to individual and group needs alike, lending a group aspect to the system that developed hand in hand with the initiatives of individual families. Participation of many clan members in the Tee was then encouraged, because, owing to complex marriage prohibi-tions,[22] most subclan members had very different configurations of affinal and maternal ties from which they could draw finance. The more each family could glean through its own connections, the greater the wealth brought into the clan. Enga describe this relationship between the individual and the group in a meta-phor of birds in the nest or parrots that roost in the same tree. When morning breaks, they fly different ways, giving the impression that they are pursuing their own interests, but in the evening they return with food to the same roost. And so it is said to be with aspiring men in the Tee: each goes his own way seeking finance but returns with wealth to provide for clan needs.

As more families joined the Tee cycle, it branched out, taking the general direction of several other trade routes. The first was the Kungu route (map 11:8) that went from Yambatane in the Saka through its "brother" tribe, Waimini, and on into the Yakumane clans of the Wapenamanda area. Soon after Yakumane began to take part the Tee, families from clans of the Pyapini, Maini, Wauni, Yatapaki, Nenaini, and Yoponda tribes in the Minamb valley joined in, so that this branch of the Tee veered to the southwest following the former Kulanga trade route (map 11:9). From Walia, at the head of the Minamb valley, the wealth was sent across the Kola area to Tambul (map 11:10). Tee cycles that came down the Minamb moved into the Saka valley via the Walepa route (11), with some of the wealth going on to Wapenamanda. From Wapenamanda, it was sent along the Kungu (8) and Sambaka (3) routes to the southwest and north into the Sau-Kopona area via the Koeyama route (7), the Tonge, the Sapuiya, and the Waliema (the last three run more or less parallel to the Koeyama). Of these, the Koeyama route, which had been established by the marriages of Yambatane Kitalini, was the oldest. The course of the Tee no longer clung precisely to the old trade routes but zigzagged to and from clans in the vicinity.

The following testimony from Lete Aiyaka of the Yatapaki Palyamuni clan gives an example of how one Minamb valley clan joined the expanding Tee cycle, underlining the point that clans entered the Tee gradually on the basis of marriages arranged with those already in the mainstream:

My grandfather said that when he was a little boy he heard his grandfather talking about traveling to the Kopona [east Kompiam] area to trade. He asked them why they were going to that area, and they told him that they were going down there to barter for pigs, because they had lots of pigs down there. It was not Tee; they went down there only to trade with the things they had. Later, girls were given to young men from the Yandamani area [lower Lai] in marriage, and as a result social ties were opened up. Many people then used these ties to come up to our area as well. For example, a person from here would go down to the Kopona area with a shell headband woven on opossum hide (angata tenge) that he would give in exchange for a pig. When he was down there he saw many herds of pigs roaming around and returned home to tell others of how many pigs they had down there. They realized that if they gave their girls in marriage to people who had pigs, they would do better in acquiring pigs. As a result of marriages, many pigs began to come up, and only after that did the Tee cycle reach this area.

Before, all the people from here to Mount Hagen took part in traditional dances only, but did not participate in the Tee cycle. At that time pigs came from clans to the west of us. I was told that they had a lot of pigs around Wabag, that pigs went up from the Sau valley into the Ambum valley and on into the Wabag area, and that the pigs received in the Saka valley came from Wabag.[23] People bought pigs and then bred them. You know how we buy pigs today, well, that happened before [the Tee]. It [barter for pigs] is not new. My grandfather said that in the past [before the Tee cycle] they bought pigs with shell headbands. Now we use money to buy pigs. . . .

In the times of Watale, Kapiya, and Kalu, there was no Tee. Only in the generation of Kambi [fourth to fifth generation] did the Tee come from the western side. The Tee came from the land of the Yakumane and Yandamani clans, but it must have originated in the Saka valley. The Tee does not owe its origin to this part of the area; it was never mentioned in these parts until the time of Kambi, when it came up from the Saka valley through the Walepa route. . . . In these parts the Tee was done only in more recent times; it was not done here long ago. (Lete Aiyaka, Yatapaki Palyamuni clan, Yaramanda)

Other interviews in Minamb clans yielded similar information on the circumstances of the Tee, its timing, and people's entrance into it.

At the same time that the Tee cycle was spreading up the Minamb valley, it was expanding to the north following migrations of Saka-Layapo speakers into the Kompiam-Kopona region (map 11: continuation of route 7). By the fourth generation, this route had reached what is now Kompiam station and had crossed the river to end at Pakalilyam. Pakalilyam is near the border between the Kopona area, settled by Saka-Layapo immigrants from the south, and the Sau area, settled by migrant Mai clans from the Ambum valley to the west. Other branches developed in the Kopona and Baiyer areas as Layapo immigrants expanded and pushed to the north and east. A good example is given in the history of the Aiyamane Sauli clan at Luma for the fourth generation:

Our forefather Sauli was the first man to come this way [to the area around Kompiam station]. He claimed all the vacant land when he came. However, as time went on my forefathers were pushed further down [northeast to Luma] as the population increased.[24] After we settled here, we began to open up trade routes. When stone axes came from Kola, we exchanged them for pigs through traders who were middlemen between us and the Kola people. All trade goods came from people living in the Lai valley or in the Wabag area. We did not trade with people from the east, because at that time there were few people living directly east of us.

Trade became more and more frequent as we got to know people on the trade routes and we developed ties through marriage. Then the Tee came from the Kola area through the Saka and ended up here. We began to raise many pigs to give away in the Tee. I do not know who actually started the Tee cycle. . . . We consider ourselves to be closer to the people of the Wapenamanda area than to the people at Wabag. (Loke Itayango, Aiyamane Sauli clan, Luma, Kopona)

The proliferation of new routes to the north and east in the fourth to fifth generation established the Yakumane tribe of Wapenamanda as a new hub in the Tee. Whereas axes were the principle exchange items that came from the east and salt was the principle item from the west, for northern tribes, including those in the Wapenamanda area, the primary currency of exchange was pigs.

In contrast to the northern and eastern Tee and trade routes, no branches or extensions developed off the western Sambe-Yalu route to Tetemanda in the fifth generation, for the clans of central Enga were absorbed in their own networks of exchange via the Great Ceremonial Wars.

The Early Tee Cycle, the Moka, and War Reparations

In the preceding pages we have proposed a simple explanation for the development of the Tee: it grew from the tactics used by Yambatane men to develop new and longer pathways of finance in order to acquire the wealth necessary for contracting marriages and other forms of alliance that would help them expand their spheres of influence in the trade. The critical innovation of the Tee — chains of finance that tapped into the wealth of non-kin — was constructed on the basis of existing trade alliances, ties with affinal and maternal kin, or both. During the initial stages, few clans were involved, but nonetheless the sparse network that was formed covered a vast area, creating the framework for developments to come. The greater access to wealth provided by the Tee cycle was so compelling that neighboring clans sought to join in, and gradually the purpose of the Tee was broadened from one of controlling the trade to one of obtaining wealth for a wider variety of social and political needs.

Other researchers writing on the Tee cycle in the ethnographic present have come to similar conclusions concerning its general origin. For example, Mervyn Meggitt (1974:195) and Andrew Strathern (1971:133-34) both proposed that the Tee cycle was born out of tactics of big-men in eastern Enga aimed at controlling the trade. Additionally, two other suggestions concerning the origin of the Tee merit discussion, for they add interesting perspectives even though they find little support in historical traditions. The first of these is an idea introduced by I. E. Kleinig (1955) and taken up by Daryl Feil (1987:265)—that the Tee was "imported" from the Moka of the Mount Hagen area. We considered this possibility carefully in our interviews with prominent Tee cycle organizers. According to both Saka valley and Tambul informants, the Tee originated with the Yambatane tribe of the Saka and was extended to the Yanuni tribe of Tambul along the Kunja trade route through marriage ties in approximately the sixth generation.[25] Big-men of Tambul did not participate in the Moka at that time, nor are there any claims that the Moka was brought into Enga with migrant tribes from the east and subsequently developed into the Tee cycle.[26] It was only in the third to fourth generation that the Tee cycle was extended farther down the Kaugel valley and toward the north Mendi area, affording big-men an opportunity to receive wealth from one exchange system and invest it in the other.

Tee organizers from the Minamb valley gave similar views. For example, Kepa Pupu of the Yoponda Ipupa clan at Walia, an active agent in the Tee from the 1940s through the 1970s, said that only when he was a child did his father begin to go into the upper Nebilyer valley to get pigs from people in the Yangupini, Komakai, and Potepa tribes, who were within the sphere of the Moka.[27] These groups later participated in the Tee cycle directly, but Kepa insisted nonetheless that pigs given in the Moka were not channeled into the Tee or vice versa.

In short, all available information indicates that the Tee cycle was extended to groups in Western Highlands Province only within the last three generations, and that the Tee cycle and the Moka were not coordinated in any systematic fashion. There is, in fact, no reason to assume that the two should have a common origin, for their structural differences are substantial. To mention a few: the Tee cycle places a much greater emphasis on pigs, and the Moka on pearl shells; the chains of creditors and sequences of giving are much longer in the Tee cycle than in the Moka; and although there is competition in the Tee cycle to "do well" by giving and receiving more than others, the locus of competition is not between donors and recipients as it is in the Moka. Neither individuals nor clans in the Tee cycle try to "outdo" others by giving back more than they received. Finally, Moka payments, like Enga war reparations, are given largely by persons in one clan to partners in one recipient clan, whereas those in the Tee are distributed among Tee partners in several different clans. That is, Moka involves enchained distributions of pigs between groups, whereas Tee involves the same between individual families.

Archaeological and ethnographic studies (A. Strathern 1971; M. Strathern 1972; Hughes 1977; Golson 1982) indicate that people in the Mount Hagen area probably had a number of conditions similar to those in Enga which contributed to the rise of elaborate ceremonial exchange. These were (1) mutually supportive relationships with affinal and maternal kin who could provide finance from outside the group; (2) trade with surrounding groups for axes, salt, oil, and pearl shells; (3) intergroup competition in the form of warfare and war reparation payments to allies; and (4) the introduction of the sweet potato within the last 250–400 years, which released constraints on agriculture and greatly increased the potential for surplus production. Given these similar preconditions, it is not surprising that two large-scale ceremonial exchange systems developed independently after the introduction of the sweet potato in response to the cultural context, problems, potentials, and historical events of each area, with points of contact forming between them as they expanded.

A second proposal for the origin of the Tee cycle, made by Feil, is that it developed out of war reparation exchanges, as Strathern (1971) convincingly argued was the case for the Moka. As Feil put it (1987:265), "it seems undeniable that the Tee originated as a system of compensation payments." This view is not mere speculation but is based on the claims of many informants that prior to the Tee cycle there was another form of "tee" in war reparations (see also Lacey 1975), and on the fact that war reparations are often integrated into the Tee cycle (Meggitt 1974:174; Feil 1984). Nonetheless, Enga historical traditions do not describe the beginning of the Tee cycle as such; significantly, its origin is situated in the context of Kitalini's bridewealth exchanges and the trade, not of war reparations. Indeed, it would be very difficult to imagine how the Tee cycle, with its long chains of partners and carefully organized sequences of festivals, could have grown out of war reparations between individual clans. To say that the Tee did not originate from war reparations is not to say that war reparations did not have a substantial impact on its further development. They certainly did, for the Tee was a system of finance, and war reparations, particularly those from the Great Ceremonial Wars of central Enga, increased demands for finance. As we shall see, such demands greatly accelerated the expansion of the Tee and added flesh to the skeleton of an exchange system that had grown out of tactics for controlling the trade.

Competition in the Early Tee

The early Tee cycle was the result of tactics employed by big-men in the Saka valley who sought new sources of influence and finance to control the trade. It was constructed by a few individuals along major trade routes who discreetly concatenated preexisting trade and exchange relationships into chains of finance. The effects of the early Tee on production are not directly mentioned in historical traditions, but the impression given is that they were minimal. The Tee allowed big-men to assemble more wealth without greatly augmenting production or arousing the attention of fellow clansmen. Competition to control the flow of wealth was there, but merely as a current that ran under the surface. Only as demands for finance in other realms of life increased, particularly for war reparations, did the advantages of the Tee as a system that could provide capital for individual and group projects become evident to a broader segment of the population. In short, subtle individual competitive strategies played out within the framework of existing institutions and orientations led to the creation of a system of enormous potential. This potential, however, was to be fully realized only under the pressure of intergroup competition, altered values, and the impetus of developments in neighboring areas.

7

Cults for the Ancestors

The house stands,
Green food is here.
I give, you give, all must give.
Greens, wild *korokas* and cordyline shrubs grow well.
Everything grows well.
The *puli* tree grows well, come see it.
The *puli* tree is well, come and see.
I go to get good things, you follow.[1]

    Kepele cult spell published in Philip Gibbs,
    "The *Kepele* Ritual of the Western Highlands"

Few oral traditions are known as widely and told with as much enthusiasm as those concerning cults for the ancestors. Their place in Enga oral history is second only to that of tribal origin traditions, and in western Enga, origin myths for tribes and ancestral cults are often intertwined. The former tell how tribes came into being, giving them a sense of identity and tying them to certain tracts of land. The latter account for the tribes' continued existence, because the regular performance of cults for the ancestors was believed to be essential for group prosperity and fertility.

Cults for the ancestors were the anchors of society. In their performances, the ideal

relationships between various tribal segments were acted out and central norms reaffirmed, particularly the equality of male tribal members and households and the obligation of group members to share and cooperate. Although the emphasis was on internal solidarity, external kin were not excluded. Boundaries were opened and relatives from other clans and tribes came as invited guests to celebrate, bringing specialties from their own areas to help provision the feasts. Cults were also exchanged widely among Enga and with neighboring linguistic groups; in this context they became important forums in which leaders could set new directions. As integrative events, ancestral cults grew hand in hand with economic developments and must be counted among the greatest systems of ceremonial exchange.

Most ancestral cults were brought to an abrupt end with the arrival of the Christian missions in Enga. Elders recall watching with anxiety as missionaries or their converts smashed ancestral stones into the river or relegated them to the category of "museum pieces" to be sent for display at the Mount Hagen Cultural Show. As a result, few ancestral cults persisted into the era of ethnographic studies, and the few available eyewitness accounts by outsiders come from patrol reports (see Lacey 1975:ch. 3). The ethnographic works that do exist (e.g., Meggitt 1965b; Gibbs 1975, 1978; Brennan 1977) give valuable descriptions based on the memories of informants, but with some exceptions (Lacey 1975) they do not place the cults in the social, political, and economic settings from which they suddenly vanished.[2] As such, cult performances remain events apart, with the consequence that some of the most powerful rituals of sociability, equality, and group unity, as well as primary agents of change, are removed from analyses of Enga society. For example, in Feil's (1987) impressive synthesis of highland societies, virtually all aspects of economics, society, and politics are considered except the cults. Since cults were the principal means of expression of group interests, their omission allows a disproportionate amount of importance to be placed on the individual.

So intertwined were the economic and ritual aspects of Enga history that it was difficult to decide which to place first or whether the two should be presented in tandem chronologically. Because the latter would have obscured the stream of development in ancestral cults, we compromised and divided the history of ancestral cults between this chapter and chapter 11.[3] This chapter has four parts: the first outlines Enga cosmology and religious beliefs, and the second reconstructs a pre-sweet potato ritual map of Enga. Two very different worlds of ritual emerge related to local ecologies and spheres of interaction of the time: in the east, a relatively pragmatic one coordinated by elders and big-men, based on establishing cooperation with the spirit world; and in the west, one permeated by mystery, complexity, and appeasement, firmly in the grips of ritual experts.

The next section shifts focus to post-sweet potato developments in ancestral cults. By tracing the way cults or elements of them were imported and exported throughout post-sweet potato history, principles of cult transmission can be outlined. The fourth section gives the post-sweet potato history of the great Kepele cult network of western Enga, attempting to uncover how, when, and why each layer of beliefs and rites was added.

Enga Cosmology and Religious Beliefs

At the center of the Enga spirit world stood two sets of supernatural beings: the immortal sky people (*yalyakali*), who dominated Enga cosmology but were not linked to specific individuals, tribes, or clans, and their mortal descendants, the ancestors (*yumbange*), who were considered to be more directly responsible for the welfare of their living descendants and their land (see Meggitt 1965b; Brennan 1977).[4] According to Enga cosmology, Aitawe, symbolized by the sun, with the help of the female moon, created the sky people, who were believed to have a life similar to that of Enga on earth, but in a richer and more perfect sky world (Meggitt 1965b; Brennan 1977). Although the sky people are the subject matter of a large number of Enga myths, they receive only occasional mention in historical narratives. Rituals for the sky people, held uniformly throughout Enga, are said to have predated many of the cults for the ancestors. Consequently, historical traditions tell of the rise, development, and spread of some cults for the ancestors but take for granted the prior existence of rituals for the sky people.

Although beliefs about the omnipresent sky beings are vaguer than those concerning the ancestors, in general our informants felt that they were responsible for the destinies of humans.[5] Little could be done to influence their decisions directly, however. In a sense, the will of the sky people was regarded as fate, though Enga also saw sky people as protectors of humans so long as they conformed to basic moral codes. Should they fail to do so, the sky people would abandon them, laying them open to death. The sky people were also believed to be responsible for certain natural events such as the weather, landslides, and thunderbolts, and it was thought that they could assist in divination (Meggitt 1965b:108). Feasts called *yalyu*, or *gote pingi*, were held locally throughout Enga for the latter purpose.[6] There were, in addition, two major cults that we discuss later in which sky people were believed to help directly in the personal maturation of young men: the Sangai bachelor's cult (chapter 8) and the *mote* boys' initiation of the Kepele cult (this chapter).

In contrast to the sky people, the spirits of the ancestors (*yumbange*), composed of all deceased male (and perhaps female) tribe members,[7] were thought to affect the welfare and prosperity of their descendants. The ancestors resided in the clan's or tribe's sacred stones or forest pools, or wandered around clan territory, their presence manifested in visions or other unusual occurrences. Unlike the sky people, they were directly associated with clan or tribal land, influencing soil fertility and assisting in defense.[8] The largest cults were directed toward the ancestors.

Pre-Sweet Potato Cults

The Yainanda of Eastern and Central Enga

Oral traditions of eastern and central Enga prior to the seventh generation mention only two major religious events: *yalyu* feasts for divination aided by the sky people and the Yainanda cult for the ancestors.[9] No historical traditions tell of their beginnings or diffusion, and so it is reasonable to assume that they had been performed since at least the tenth generation and probably long before that. Groups who migrated to the Kompiam region as early as the seventh to eighth generation brought the *yalyu* feast and Yainanda cult with them to their new homelands, a further indication of their antiquity.

Despite the wide variety of terms used to refer to the Yainanda, performances and the reasons for holding them seem to have been rather homogeneous. Eyewitness accounts for most clans of eastern and central Enga included the following features; brief descriptions in early historical traditions suggest the same:[10]

1. Reasons for holding the Yainanda were invariably environmental imbalances: the poor growth of crops, pandanus, pigs, and children. Occasionally, small-scale Yainanda performances were held when wars took a turn for the worse. In addition, precautionary performances were held when strange occurrences signaled the unrest of the ancestors—for example, the unearthing of a new cult stone, the appearance of an old one on a path, or visions of humans or animals that appeared to clan members and subsequently vanished. First, small Yainanda ceremonies were held by subclans, and if conditions did not improve, larger ones were held involving the entire clan. Invited guests from other clans attended the latter, bringing specialties from their own areas.

2. The ceremonies were initiated by a bout of communal hunting to provide marsupial meat, the essential food for both the feast and the sacred rites. Afterward, men gathered for the formalized tram-

pling of the grass on the ceremonial grounds. Pigs were also slaughtered, although pork was not essential for Yainanda cults.

3. The feast was sponsored by the host group and partially provisioned by guests. Women were given raw food to take home and steam in their own earth ovens, but they strictly avoided food handled in a ritual context, because the power of the ancestors that permeated it was believed to cause birth defects.

4. Sacred stones,[11] representing the collectivity of the ancestors, were symbolically "fed" by elders (enveloped with leftovers or smeared with blood), wrapped in fat and leaves, and buried near the clan's ceremonial grounds—sometimes in small, temporary shelters—from where the ancestors could oversee conditions within clan boundaries.

5. Outside the small sacred area where the stones were kept, celebrants and guests feasted. Cult performances lasted one day only.

6. The Yainanda was an "egalitarian" cult affording few opportunities for personal display or competition. All men contributed more or less equally, and a group of elders, rather than ritual experts, presided.[12] Food was distributed freely and not used for economic ends such as incurring or settling debts.

Yainanda cult performances similar to those just outlined were held in most of central and eastern Enga.[13] Some elders speculate that the Yainanda cult may have come ultimately from the Kola (Tambul) region many centuries ago along the Tambul-Saka-Lai trade route. Certainly the Yainanda has many points in common with cults described by Strauss and Tischner (1962) for the Mbowamb (Melpa) people, and so it seems likely that the Layapo-speaking Saka Enga, the Kakoli, and the Melpa had lived within the same sphere of ritual interaction for centuries. The homogeneity of the Yainanda in space and its apparent continuity through time may be due in part to the fact that there were no ritual experts who sought to enhance their reputations by innovating.

Pre-Sweet Potato Cults of Western Enga

THE KAIMA CULT   Yainanda cults reach their geographical limit in the high country that separates the Lai and Lagaip valleys. To the west, one enters a different ritual sphere oriented more toward the Huli, Ipili, and perhaps peoples to the north. Prior to the seventh generation before the present, the only ritual that appears to have crossed this boundary was the *yalyu,* or *gote pingi,* feast for the sky people. Environmental problems in western regions were addressed in family- or lineage-based rituals held to improve hunting, pandanus harvests, and gardens. Groups of the high country south of the Lagaip performed a precursor of the Kepele ancestral cult directed at assembling youths for male initiation, among other things. The most widespread clan ritual, the *yaka kaima*, or *kaima*, was called when misfortune struck in the form of sickness or death, although it was not merely a healing ritual. Successful appeasement of the spirit world was believed to bring about general good fortune and prosperity for the clan.[14] The *kaima* was practiced over a vast area stretching from the northernmost borders of Enga through the Lagaip and Porgera areas and south into western Kandep. The spread of the Kaima cult continued until contact. For example, a narrow belt of clans in Sirunki, the upper Ambum, and northern Kompiam that held the Yainanda adopted the Kaima within the last five generations.

In contrast to the open, festive Yainanda cult, the oral traditions, beliefs, and rites of the Kaima were sinister and aimed at appeasement. Considerable variation existed in clan performances, but most had the following essential features:

1. The Kaima cult was called when sickness, particularly leprosy, struck clan members or when an important clan member died an untimely and ghastly death.
2. A long, rectangular cult house was constructed of hardwood, *dilya,* so that it would not catch fire when pieces of pork were roasted in it.
3. A ritual expert, usually from another clan, was summoned to conduct the ceremonies.
4. On the day of the ceremonies, celebrants dressed in special attire, and a few pigs were slaughtered.[15]
5. Two chosen young men opened the ceremonies by climbing a tree so that the sun could shine on them. One was a *mandipae*, a man who resides in his mother's place, and the other, a *tolae*, a man who resides in his father's place. While they were climbing the tree, the ritual expert took a bark plaque representation of the Kaima spirit,[16] an aggressive bird, painted with clay and ochre and trimmed with feathers, and made it "dance." As the sun shone on the boys, those standing around the tree howled, "Whoo, whoo, whoo!" to greet the Kaima spirit.
6. Next, two young women carrying the front legs and shoulders of a pork entered, went over to the tree, and scratched off some of the bark with the pigs' hooves while reciting spells to please the Kaima.[17]
7. The boys climbed down the trees, covered their heads with tradi-

tional rain capes, and were driven to the men's house, where
they remained for five days.

8. All of the pork fat was put aside to feed the spirits of the ancestors who resided in forest pools. Once it was divided, small
pieces were thrown into the fire in the center of the cult house,
and names of specific ancestors were called to receive them.

9. The next day, the ritual expert, sometimes accompanied by a
clan elder, went to the forest to feed the ancestral pools. There
were two pools, a red one and a black one. The red pool, where
the male ancestral spirits resided, was believed to rise up like a
snake and devour any human beings whom it encountered. The
black pool, where the female spirits resided, was thought to be
calm and harmless. Fat for the red male pool was tied tightly
onto the stick with strong *tatali* ropes, so that the pool would
have a hard time untying it and could not leap up and kill the
men. Fat for the black female pool was tied loosely to the stick
with breakable *guli* ropes, because the pool was said to concentrate on eating what it was given and not to try to kill the men
who fed it. (When clans moved, the pools were said to follow
them and reappear close to their new settlements.)

10. Meanwhile, male and female celebrants consumed the pork. The
ritual expert was paid with stone axes, net bags, and shells, in addition to pork.

The Kaima is acknowledged to be very old. In the 1940s, for example, pro-
scriptions espoused by the millenarian Ain's cult demanded the abolishment of
"new and alien" cults such as the Kepele but permitted the long-established
Kaima to be resumed after a certain period of time (Meggitt 1973:21). The
history of the Kaima is difficult trace; even though its performances are mentioned in early historical narratives, no descriptions of cult procedures are given.
Although many clans have their own sinister myths (concerning cannibalism and
the origin of leprosy) to explain its beginnings, none that we collected further
elucidated beliefs about the aggressive bird represented by the bark painting or
about the logic of cult rites.

The impression we received is that the Kaima is a composite cult incorporating
several overlaid systems of belief imported from surrounding areas at different
periods in history, as is so typical for Enga cults. These systems include beliefs
surrounding the Kaima spirit, the sun, sky people, and the spirits of the ancestors,
all of whom are summoned in the cult's spells. The component of feeding the
sacred pools has parallels to the south: the Huli, for example, feed river pools

believed to contain spirits of the ancestors as a part of their *gebe* ritual (Chris Ballard, personal communication, 1991). Some of the other features of the Kaima fit neither Enga cosmology of the twentieth century nor that of surrounding groups to the south. For instance, Enga have only a vague sense of what the Kaima spirit is, of the significance of the "dance" of the bark painting, and of the greeting of the sun. The fear that the "beings" in the pools, thought to be the spirits of the ancestors, will rise up like snakes and try to devour those who feed them is incongruous with the concept of the snake as a symbol of long life and regeneration in the Enga Kepele ancestral cult. Some of these features may have come from the north prior to the introduction of the sweet potato.

The Kaima cult of western Enga and the Yainanda cult of eastern and central Enga thus have little in common. To contrast the two: the Yainanda, a festive, positive, and open cult, was held for a general pool of ancestors with the goal of communicating with them to establish balance. Fertility of gardens, pandanus trees, pigs, and humans was the desired outcome. The Kaima combined rites for the Kaima spirit with propitiation of both individually named male ancestors and pools of water containing anonymous male and female ancestors. Inwardly oriented and permeated with mystery and fear, it was aimed more at appeasement than at balance and communication, offering a sacrifice of pork in place of another human victim. Whereas the Yainanda was a ritual of sedentism, with cult stones buried in the center of clan territory, the Kaima was suited to mobility, the ancestral pools mysteriously appearing in the forest near new areas of settlement. The Yainanda was male oriented, in keeping with the stronger patrilineal organization of eastern Enga; the Kaima incorporated male and female components and expressed bilateral kinship and residence. Primary ritual foods of the Yainanda and Kaima varied inversely with subsistence base: in the east, where pigs were more plentiful, marsupials were required for sacred rites, and in the west, where hunting contributed regularly to the diet, pork was the major ritual food. Finally, ritual experts were required for the Kaima but not for the Yainanda. In short, the Yainanda and the Kaima shared the underlying belief that the spirits of the dead could affect the fate of their living descendants, and both were communal responses to pressing problems. Beyond that, the two were molded by separate histories and cosmologies and tailored to the different systems of production of east and west.

THE DINDI GAMU CULT   The Dindi Gamu cycle had its heart among the Huli people, but its network of sites penetrated into the territory of the western Enga, Ipili, Duna, and groups on the Papuan plateau.[18] Its ideology was embedded in the Huli doctrine of entropy — that the cosmos is unstable and follows a general trajectory of decline. Therefore, regular ritual intervention was required to restore vitality and fertility to both the natural environment and the social order (Goldman 1983; Frankel 1986; Ballard 1995). An excellent description of the Dindi Gamu cycle and its place in Huli sacred geography has been given by Stephen Frankel (1986:19-23):

The geographical dimension of the Dindi Gamu cycle concerns the flow of the ritual power broadly from south-west to north-east, from the Papuan plateau to the central highlands. Key sacred sites are said to be joined by the "root of the earth," which has the physical form of a thick liane entwined by a python and provides the channel through which flows water and, during performances of the Dindi Gamu, smoke. The muffled roar of an underground stream is said to mark the passage of the root of the earth. It is conceived of as a pathway of power for Dindi Gamu and as the physical support of the earth. Active points along this pathway are marked by the major sacred sites. Such places are referred to as, literally, "the knots of the earth" (dindi pongone), where the key strands of the earth's fabric interweave, and so gain strength. The root of the earth is said to be accessible to ritual manipulation at these points. . . .

The source of ritual power is said to lie in the lowlands of the Papuan plateau. The major Dindi Gamu cycle capable of summoning mbingi is said to be initiated by ritual activity on the Plateau.

Frankel then goes on to name the major Huli sites—Hari Hibira (on the slopes of Mount Sisa at the southwestern boundary of Huli country), Gelote, and Bebenete (map 12)—and to describe the Dindi Gamu cycle in the south and its extension north into Enga.

Beyond the restoration of fertility in the Dindi Gamu cult lay a much greater undertaking: bringing about the return of the mbingi ashfall and the "time of darkness" (Goldman 1983; Frankel 1986; Ballard 1995). Should these efforts fail, the world could end in a fiery apocalypse (Ballard 1995), a fate that was also widely feared in western Enga. The inability of ritual to achieve a return of the mbingi ash fall so far is attributed by some to an error in a performance of the ritual three to ten generations ago, when a boy named Bayebaye was killed in an excess of ritual enthusiasm. His Duna mother, in her mourning lament, cursed future generations of Huli, and as a result Huli believe that the world will come to an end in the fifteenth generation from the beginning of their genealogies (Frankel 1986:24). (The 1980s were in the thirteenth Huli generation.) In Enga the end of the world is generally expected in the thirteenth generation, which for the Enga is still to come. In the Porgera valley of western Enga, where much credence is still put in this prediction, old men are able to conjure up ever more signs of impending disaster as bulldozers level mountains for gold—and with them, Enga tradition.

Enga readily acknowledge the extension of the Dindi Gamu network north-

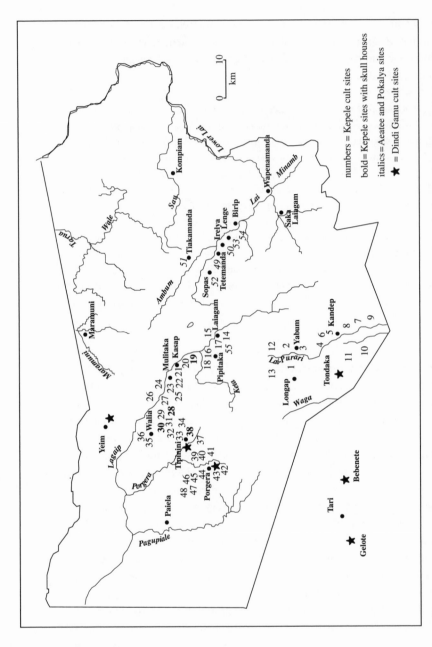

Map 12. Tribal cult houses in the Kepele, Aeatee, and Pokalya cult network. (Names following "of" are those of tribes and sometimes clans. Many of these houses have several names.)

ward in a series of sites that skirt the boundaries between the Enga and the Huli (map 12). Contrary to Frankel's views that the Dindi Gamu was a post-sweet potato cult, the evidence we collected points to an older origin. Of several Dindi Gamu sites in Enga, the scene of by far the largest and most important performances was Tondaka (Tuandaga), a site in southwestern Kandep on land of the Yamape, a tribe that straddles the Enga-Huli linguistic boundary. As the myth goes, Tondaka was established long ago when one of the sons of the mythical tribal founder, Yamape, turned into a beast in the form of a snake that devoured nine sons of the neighboring Timitopa tribal founder. The last son, searching for his missing brothers, encountered an old woman who advised him on how to defeat the beast. Following her directives, he dropped a hot stone into the creature's mouth. Writhing in agony, it crawled away and disappeared into a tunnel at the Tondaka site. From that time on, men of Yamape and surrounding tribes held the Dindi Gamu to appease the beast.

At Tondaka, the Dindi Gamu branched off in two or three different directions. One branch went into the Porgera valley and on to Yeim in the northeast corner of Enga, where the cult was called Awalo by some, although in Enga the Dindi Gamu is most commonly referred to as Tondaka after the largest site. Another is said to go northwest into the Paiela region, but because we did not work in this area, we have no further information about it.[19]

The origin legend for the Dindi Gamu, or Awalo, cult in the Porgera valley is the well-known Papaiyakali legend. It has many versions (see also Gibbs 1975:158). Long ago, the "hero," Papaiyakali, leaves his home at Tipinini to attend a pig feast near Yeim in the north, filling bamboo containers with water, putting them in the house, and warning his wife not to leave the house while he is away. Papaiyakali's wife, Tapu, does as he says and remains in the house, but when he stays away longer than planned, the supply of water runs out and she is forced to go out to seek water during a dry spell. She finds his secret spring at the base of a pandanus tree and unplugs it; the water gushes out, flooding the valley.[20] Try as she might, she cannot stop the flow and sends a message of despair to Papaiyakali via a *kutubu* beetle.

He hurries home to try to stave off disaster. In most versions, finding his house deserted, he follows a trail left by his wife, climbs Mount Tongopipi and ascends to the sky, meeting her in a world beyond. In the version concerned with the Dindi Gamu-Awalo, he tells his wife, Tapu, and sister, Lakeame, that they will ascend to the sky, but while cutting branches to protect his house before they leave, he tumbles to his death. When his wife and sister try to lift his corpse, they realize that he is pinned to the ground by a thick strand of cane wrapped around his neck, part of the root of the earth that links the Dindi Gamu sites. They leave the corpse there, and on that spot the cult house is built. The wife and sister then travel southward, spending one night at Suyan and another at Pauatete, a site west of the Waga river between Karekare and Tari, where the sister disappears into a cave. Papaiyakali's wife continues on and vanishes in the cave at Tondaka.

Following this myth, a ritual called the *awalo* was held at Tipinini, involving sixteen clans but still smaller than and subsidiary to that at the Tondaka site. At Yeim, to where Papaiyakali brought a brown pig, a smaller Awalo cult site was established near a whirlpool of light mud produced by thermal activity. Minor Awalo performances were also held at Pauatete and Suyan to mark the travels of the two women. Enga branches of Tondaka-Awalo cults were linked, with representatives from Yeim and Porgera participating in the Tondaka. The Tondaka site, in turn, was associated with Huli sites via the emergence of smoke from the Huli Bebenete ceremony at a location near Tondaka and the participation of ritual experts from Bebenete (Chris Ballard, personal communication, 1991).

Research on the Dindi Gamu posed more problems for us than any other single topic in Enga history, with discussion curtailed by fear that the world would end if any sacred information was disclosed. The unparalleled sense of fear associated with the Tondaka-Awalo cult, combined with concepts of fiery destruction, suggested that some natural phenomenon might underlie the cult. After a fortuitous series of events,[21] it became evident that the ritual power that emanated from the Papuan plateau and flowed through the root of the earth, described as "smoke," "wind," or "fire," was related to the many natural gas leaks in the region. Our first empirical test was made by Akii's throwing a lighted match into the hole near the Tondaka site where the "smoke" from Bebenete was said to emerge. The result was explosive, and after the initial accumulation of gas had burned away, a small blue flame remained hovering in the center of the hole like the eye of the beast. With this knowledge, it was not difficult to get Tondaka participants to discuss the role of the gas outlets. Ballard (1995) has come to similar conclusions for the Huli. That natural gas played a role on the Papuan plateau is also evident from the work of Edward Schieffelin and Robert Crittenden (1991:55-56).[22]

The testimonies of the few people who had participated in the last performances held at Tondaka during the 1940s to mid-1960s and who were willing to talk are fascinating, though couched in veiled speech. Here we give but a sketch of the cult—to do more would require the consent of the majority of owners of the cult, something that will probably never be obtained. Impressive and mysterious performances were held at the Tondaka site, organized by the Kokati clan resident at the site and by other Yamape clans. The celebrants included men from Yamape clans and some men born of Yamape women living elsewhere. Many clans living west of the Lai-Purari river also contributed,[23] bringing pigs and other foods to the borders of the site. A representative from Yeim came to "open the door" with a donation of a dried leg of pork, sugarcane, and taro. The food was stacked by the Sasa creek, the women departing immediately, and then heaved across the creek and brought to the ritual site to be fed to the "creature" within. Food placed on a stone said to be the "jaw of the snake" disappeared without leaving a trace, while the rest was cooked by mysterious means for senior participants to partake.[24]

Afterward, ritual experts and other celebrants went through myriad strenuous journeys of mind, body, or both within the cave at Tondaka, to which a scenery of stalactites, stalagmites, iron pyrite, and other natural features apparently lent an aura of mystery.[25] The journeys elicited visions from which predictions were made: if a pig was seen getting up and leaving, it would mean that people would have plenty of pigs; if a woman appeared as an old person, it meant that girls would be unhealthy; and so on.[26] The ritual experts emerged from the cave without looking back and remained mute for a week, subsequently revealing their predictions to their own people and to representatives from other tribes of western Enga who had come to listen. Participants and spectators then dispersed, except for keepers of the site who remained year-round.

The Dindi Gamu never penetrated Enga deeply, because, among other things, Huli beliefs in entropy or decline were not widely shared in Enga. Furthermore, many features of the cult departed significantly from Enga ritual: its centralized organization with Tondaka as the key site, its expenditure of huge amounts of food to be consumed or disposed of in a nonsocial context, and the pronounced authority of its ritual experts. As a result, only the prediction that the world would end in the thirteenth generation, either in fire or, following the Porgera origin myth, in flood, and other subsidiary ones proclaimed after each performance reached the tribes of western Enga not directly involved. Nonetheless, participation in the Dindi Gamu on this limited scale lent much mystery and power to concepts of the spirit world in western Enga and made people there conversant with the beliefs of groups to the southwest.

THE KEPELE CULT   The Kepele cult, undoubtedly the largest and most influential cult of Enga within the span of historical traditions, had its roots in mythical time among the "hunter-gatherer" tribes of the high country south of the Lagaip river. Though many tribes have local traditions for the beginnings of their own Kepele cult that tie it to specific places, one myth is generally acknowledged as the charter for its ultimate origin.[27] It has at least three major parts, told separately in some versions and joined in others. The first gives the origin myth of the Bipi tribe (map 12:1) and its split from its brother tribe, Kuu. The second, given in full in Appendix 7, concerns the lifestyle of the forefathers of Bipi and their ambiguous relationship with agriculturalists of southern Kandep. The third, which appears later in this chapter, tells of the settlement of Bipi clans and the spread of the Kepele cult to surrounding agriculturalists. Here we summarize the second part.

An agriculturalist from the Maulu tribe of southern Kandep travels north into the high country seeking somebody to help him clear a new garden. There he encounters a snake-man, Molopai (rainbow python), the founding ancestor of the Bipi tribe, sitting alone in a clearing. Molopai invites him to stay for the night and Maulu accepts, wondering where he will sleep, for there is no shelter. As evening falls, Molopai's sons converge on the clearing from all directions, singing and bearing bundles of food from the forest. In a flash they assemble a house from their own bodies, some becoming the walls, others the beams and posts. Molopai hosts Maulu with a lavish meal of forest products and sends his favorite son back with him to clear the garden. Molopai's son hunts along the way, killing far more game than Maulu can carry. The next day he skillfully helps with the garden.

Following the father's one demand, Maulu lets Molopai's son sleep alone in the men's house. After three days Maulu's curiosity overcomes him and he goes to the house at night. There he finds a large python encircling the house. The next night he and his fellow clansmen club the snake and put him in the oven pit with hot stones. Molopai's son wakes up, manages to crawl out of the pit, bind his wounds, and make his way home. The father turns himself into a forest demon and takes revenge.

This part of the Molopai myth lays down key themes around which Kepele cult ideology and rites revolve. The first of these is the contribution of each to the creation of a whole: Molopai's sons return from the forest in the evening, singing and bearing parcels of food, to assemble a house from their own bodies. It provides the model for the building of Kepele cult houses — the clans or subclans of a tribe converge singing and dancing on the ritual site, each bearing essential materials for building the cult house and provisioning the feast. Each gives something of himself for the completion of the whole that will "shelter" the group.

The second pivotal theme is that of transformation and regeneration. Molopai's son exhibits superhuman energy on the trip with Maulu, transforms himself from human to snake and back to human, escapes the earth oven, binds his wounds, recovers his strength, and journeys home. The ability of the python to survive and regenerate is in keeping with more general Enga serpentine symbolism. Snakes in general, and the rainbow python in particular, are symbols of survival and long life through a complex chain of associations. That is, the rainbow and the python are thought to be one, because when the sun's rays strike snake scales a rainbow of color is reflected and because the ring of rainbow that is sometimes seen around the sun is thought to be the python.[28] The rainbow, in turn, is the neighbor of the sun, the life-giver.[29] Accordingly, the interiors of

Kepele houses were adorned with drawings on bark plaques of the rainbow or python, the sun, and other figures. In some, a long, woven figure of a python, called the *malinu,* encircled the ceiling. The python symbol thus embodied the aim of the Kepele cult—to overcome misfortune and bring about regeneration of humans and the environment.[30]

The first part of the Molopai myth, so far as we can determine, also refers to earlier Kepele cult performances. These consisted of at least two core Kepele rites that persisted into the post-sweet potato era: (1) the building of a cult house, with all tribal members contributing complementary materials, and (2) the initiation of young men into the secrets and authority of the spirit world in the *mote* initiation rites during which the "water of life" was given to the novices and sacred plaques were revealed to them. Both rites evoked forest life: many of the materials used to construct the cult house were found only in the high forest, and all of the sacred plaques revealed to the boys during the initiation pertained exclusively to the forest, not to agriculture. Neither of these two rites had an equivalent in the early cults of eastern Enga or in those of other surrounding groups. So far as we know, the *mote* initiation of young men into ritual secrets within the context of ancestral cults had no counterpart among the Mai and Layapo Enga, the Kakoli, Melpa, Mendi, or Wola. The Huli conducted initiation rites as part of their Tege cult, but apparently these were adopted sometime around the end of the nineteenth century from groups of the Papuan plateau (Chris Ballard, personal communication, 1991).

The *mote* boys' initiation appears to have been directed at the *molopai* python and the sky people (*yalyakali*). For example, the sacred plaques revealed to the initiates depicted sun, moon, snake, rainbow, and specific sky people, and the water of life (*yalipa*) partaken to confer health and long life stemmed from the sky people. The woven image of the snake encircling the ceiling of the cult house directed attention toward the sky. Whether the pre-sweet potato Kepele cult also solicited the assistance of the ancestors or other deities is no longer known, for much of the early history of the Kepele is buried in the layers of tradition added after the introduction of the sweet potato.

Summary

Pre-sweet potato religious rituals indicate a marked separation between east and west in the past, the eastern Enga being ritually associated with the Melpa, Mendi, and Kakoli, and the western Enga having closer ritual ties with the Huli and perhaps groups to the north.[31] The Dindi Gamu cult that skirted Enga's westernmost boundary created links, though indirect ones, beyond Huli to groups on the Papuan plateau and to the Duna. Rituals of eastern Enga were pragmatic and direct, involving feasting with the ancestors to elicit their goodwill and cooperation. In the west, a wider range of cult rituals was performed, both for the ancestors and for other supernatural beings. These were permeated with mystery, fear, and goals of appeasement. Cults of the east were in the hands of elders, whereas those of the west required ritual experts who held specialized knowledge, procedures, and spells. Initiation ceremonies that gathered the tribe and introduced young men to the secrets of ritual life appear to have been absent in tribes that primarily practiced agriculture, whether in the east or west, but to have been powerful in "hunter-gatherer" groups of the high altitudes.

From the reconstruction of pre-sweet potato cults, it is apparent that ritual for the spirit world occupied a much larger sector of life in the west than it did in the east. Accordingly, masters of cult rites were more influential in the west. For this reason, when new problems and possibilities arose after the introduction of the sweet potato, leaders in the east and center of Enga initially turned to economic strategies while those of the west turned to the spirit world. We say "initially" because it was not long before leaders of the center and east realized that economic solutions alone did not suffice.

The Post-Sweet Potato Transmission of Cults

The history of post-sweet potato cults is one of innovation and the importing and exporting of rituals across boundaries, and so it is appropriate to begin this section with a brief discussion of principles underlying their transmission.[32] First, following Enga logic that "name" and prosperity stem from distribution rather than from retention, cults or elements of them were exchanged widely throughout Enga and with neighbors from different linguistic groups, even though they were directed at in-group affairs: identity, welfare, and unity. Both importers and exporters stood to benefit: those exporting a cult or elements of it established points in common with recipients, opening the way for further interaction. Importers gained confidence in enhanced group fortune and benefited from shared tradition and equal footing with donors.

Cults were readily transmitted across linguistic boundaries when (1) donors and recipients faced comparable problems, so that underlying beliefs and overt procedures were meaningful, and (2) the owners of the cult were perceived as being successful. Societies that met these conditions within the span of Enga historical traditions were largely highland groups—the Melpa, Kakoli, Mendi, Wola, Huli, and Ipili (see map 1). Much less exchange of ritual took place between Enga and groups to the north living at lower altitudes.[33] New cults were often obtained from higher areas with harsher climates because these were the areas that formed natural boundaries between linguistic groups and because people of these areas sought ever new ways to overcome their environmental problems. As Boyope Kangie Didi (1982a, 1982b) pointed out for the Tambul region, such groups acquired a reservoir of cults and a reputation as ritual masters (as distinct from ritual brokers), something that made them attractive exchange partners as well.

Second, the importation and exportation of cults provided big-men with the potential to steer the course of change, for it was the cults that set values, ideals, and meanings. Cults were imported in order to acquire new and more effective ways to communicate with the spirit world, as well as to emulate those who appeared more successful. The triggering incident leading to the purchase of a cult was often an unusual event interpreted by clan leaders as a sign from the supernatural.[34] The purchase was usually organized and financed by clan leaders who consulted with and received contributions from other clan members, because clan leaders had the broadest intra- and interregional ties with which to locate and negotiate the transfer of cults that might be beneficial to their groups. They were also the ones with the wealth, influence, and organizational abilities to arrange initial performances. They did so by going to the group that possessed the cult, discussing the matter with an influential relative or exchange partner there, and summoning one or more ritual experts to provide the purchasing group with rites, spells, sacred objects, training for local experts, and supervision of the performance.

Third, the importation and exportation of cults formed loose networks across boundaries—networks that were neither centrally nor hierarchically organized. Cults were purchased with wealth such as pigs, salt, axes, and oil, according to the belief that if sacred objects and incantations were given freely, their power would be transmitted to the receiver and lost to the giver, but that if they were sold, it would be retained by both parties. The sale of a cult was a one-time transaction that necessitated no further interaction between the groups once procedures were well established among the recipients. The donors presided over initial performances. Later, the recipients became the true owners, performing or altering the cult as they pleased and reselling its sacred spells and objects to another group if so desired. Alterations might include giving a cult another name or local origin tradition or adapting procedures to the buyers' own context or needs. With the transfer of cults, information such as origin myths, certain rites, and their meanings was often lost. Sometimes an entire cult was accepted and added to the clan's or tribe's repertoire, whereas at other times only certain rites were retained and integrated into a preexisting cult, creating a very complex ritual map. In oral traditions prior to the fifth generation, the exchange of cults is usually phrased in mythical or metaphorical terms: for instance, cults are said to have been spread by wandering women or during the travels of a mythical rainbow python.[35] Their actual exchange is likely to have followed procedures similar to those of later times.

Fourth, although many groups had their own ritual experts, it was the convention to invite those from other cult houses to participate, paying them lavishly. For the Kaima cult, only one or two ritual experts were invited, whereas for the Kepele, experts from many different cult houses in the network would participate, each with his own subarea of expertise. Ritual experts had a continual incentive to innovate in order to enhance their reputations. The upshot of circulating ritual experts was the formation of cult networks in which common beliefs, themes, and procedures were maintained, on one hand, but in which innovations spread rapidly, on the other. Cult networks were organized following "egalitarian" principles, no cult house having authority over the performances of others. Nonetheless, ritual experts from what were considered to be originating groups or the owners of powerful performances or both were invited most frequently. The acceptance of an innovation thus depended on its intrinsic appeal and the success of the group holding the cult, not seniority in adopting it.

Ritual experts, as the "holders" of spells and rites, enjoyed relative autonomy and could pass them on to other groups as they pleased. Although cult purchase usually also involved communication between the big-men of the clans involved, ritual experts were the ones who received payment for the transactions (see also Bulmer 1965; A. Strathern 1979b). No historical traditions that we collected describe interactions among ritual experts or between ritual experts and big-men. When asked, elders said that ritual experts and clan or tribal leaders cooperated and that there was little overt competition between ritual experts simply because they were so few.

Given the tradition of importing and exporting cults, the nonhierarchical structure of cult networks, the circulation of ritual experts, and the far-ranging traffic of Enga to attend cult performances hosted by relatives in other groups, it is probably fair to say that knowledge of the rituals of surrounding regions was considerable, as was the potential for acquiring them. In view of this, what is perhaps most important to understand is why leaders sought certain cults or elements of them at certain points in history, and why the members of their group accepted or rejected them. Two principal reasons for importing a cult were common, the one for migrants to maintain contact with their groups of origin, and the other to ameliorate clan fortunes and set the pace of change. Examples of the former, which created a virtual soup of cults in border areas, are given in Appendix 8. For the latter, we have chosen three examples of imported cults that had significant effects on Enga history: the Kepele cult, the subject of this chapter and part of chapter 11, the Sangai bachelors' cult, presented in chapter 8, and the Female Spirit cult, discussed in chapter 11.

Post-Sweet Potato Developments in the Kepele Cult

Kepele traditions held by Enga groups of the high country took quite a different turn after the introduction of the sweet potato. Whereas some versions of the Molopai myth given earlier end with the son's return home, other renditions describe his homeward journey in more detail, linking his travels to the establishment of a Kepele cult network throughout Kandep and, in some cases, the Lagaip and Porgera valleys:

The snake woke up in the earth oven, crawled out, and escaped. The young man was severely wounded on his head. On his way home he took some *take* leaves and bound his wounds. He spent many nights along the way on his journey home, and each place where he stopped became a Kepele cult site. He arrived at Bipi Kama, which was the origin place of the Kepele cult, and rested there. The young man had crossed the Lai-Purari river many times before reaching home, and so all the people in this area performed the Kepele except for the [Kamani] clan at Kepe, which has its own cult. (Peter Yomo, Tatali Sai clan, Mutipa, Kandep)[36]

When the myth is told by clans of Bipi origin in the Lagaip and Porgera valleys, the location is changed so that the young man journeys down the Lagaip to Porgera, stopping at what are to be Kepele cult grounds in these valleys. After the son arrives home, the father warns his other sons to disperse and settle, so that they will not meet with the same fate. Subsequent historical narratives describe just that—the dispersal and settlement of numerous clans from the Bipi and Kuu tribes, some at higher altitudes and some in the Lagaip and Porgera valleys and Tari region. So far as we can determine, when groups of the high country settled in the lower valleys, distinctions between hunter-gatherers and horticulturists broke down, and horticultural groups adopted the Kepele as a ritual of harmony, integration, and identity. Some created their own local origin myths to fit it to tribal identity, introducing great complexity into Kepele history. Nonetheless, these groups still accept the Molopai myth as the authoritative one for the origin of the cult network.[37]

With more permanent settlement, several new layers of tradition were added to the Kepele; here we attempt to trace the history of each. The first was the adoption of the sacred stones associated with wandering "fertility" women who brought the sweet potato, as discussed in chapter 4, together with rites for feeding, mating, and burying the sacred stones to promote agricultural fertility and prosperity.[38] Focus was then shifted from forest, sky, and sky people to earth, soil, and ancestors. The cooperative building of the cult house was altered to mark a fixed tribal center rather than temporary aggregation, and agricultural produce was substituted for the packages of forest foods brought by Molopai's sons. Throughout all these changes, former *mote* initiation rites persisted, subjecting boys to the authority of elders and the spirit world.

Where the first sacred stones were obtained from remains an open question. There is absolutely no historical tradition that we recorded which describes pre-sweet potato rituals involving sacred stones in western Enga,[39] though ancestral stones were used throughout Mai and Layapo areas and probably by the Mendi, Wola, and Huli as well. Interaction between western Enga and all of these other areas was high, owing to the salt trade at the Keta river, so the western Enga must have known of ancestral stones for a long time, adopting them when they were perceived as appropriate. Wherever they came from, their inclusion in the Kepele cult established a view consistent with that of the Yainanda cult of eastern and central Enga—that the spirit and human worlds did not work at cross-purposes. With proper ritual, the two could cooperate to bring about prosperity. Sights were set beyond mere alleviation of misfortune, as in the Kaima cult, to prosperity and production. From then on, eastern and western Enga had a common orientation in their ancestral cults.

Not long after sacred stones were introduced to the Kepele, and with them a significant female component, a powerful new male symbol was added via basketwork figures (*yupini*) that were tangible representations of male tribal founders and the ancestors. Tribal members could rally behind these. Though very similar to Sepik basketwork figures and most likely of Sepik influence or origin,[40] the first *yupini* figures manufactured in the Lagaip were said to be made by a man named Tauni of the Konemane tribe at Mulitaka (map 12:25), who lived during the sixth to seventh generation. The male *yupini* was woven in a human form and dressed in ceremonial clothing. In the seclusion of the cult house, he was made to copulate with the female, either a flat, round basket that represented female reproductive organs, a stone mortar, or other stones that had features reminiscent of breasts or vaginas. Afterward, both the *yupini* figure and the sacred stones were symbolically fed with pork fat and laid to rest. As the social component of Kepele performances expanded, the popularity of the *yupini* basketwork figure grew throughout the Lagaip and Porgera valleys, where it was paraded in public before crowds of spectators. Only between the fifth and third generations, however, was it incorporated into many Kandep Kepele performances, where male ancestors had previously been represented by phallic-shaped sacred stones.

The Kepele cult continued to be altered with changing times, for the generations after the introduction of the sweet potato saw new-found wealth and accompanying problems. With the redistribution of people over the landscape, social complexity increased and intratribal wars became endemic. Perhaps as a result of the more permanent settlement of people, sickness, particularly leprosy, became a severe and chronic problem that persisted well into the colonial era. In the west as in the east, one solution was the mediation of tension through pig exchange and communal feasting. It was in this context that the Kepele took new directions. Most prominently, the building of the cult house was expanded to formally express the relations of different tribal segments to the whole. Their oppositions and tensions were acted out in the drama of house construction, where clans or subclans converged on the house site in full ceremonial dress, each bringing its own contribution. Resolution occurred in the successful completion of the house for the good of all. Such spectacles drew large crowds, and virtually every phase of the Kepele was elaborated into a social event that culminated in the consumption of ritually prepared pork within the sacred area and widespread sharing of nonritually prepared food outside. In some performances, the spirit of ritualized competition was revived at the end of the ceremony when different segments of a tribe vied to pull down or burn the cult house, signaling the completion of a successful ceremony.

In some Kepele cult performances of larger Lagaip tribes, broad-scale measures to combat sickness were integrated via the rites of "skull" houses built at Kepele sites (map 12:19, 28, 30, 38, and perhaps more in the Porgera valley). There, skulls of all recently deceased tribesmen—and with them their ghosts, who formerly were believed to have lingered near homesteads or around rock shelters in the high country—were consolidated.[41] The harmful power of the dead was first dampened through private rituals for the ghost of every deceased tribesman, and when the house was full, the entire lot was banished to the realm of the ancestors through ceremonial cremation. Although skull house rites were aimed at the alleviation of sickness, their social and political impact as rituals of centralization must have been very significant at a time when groups were being redistributed over the landscape.

Origin myths for skull houses are sinister, telling of fiends who cannibalized children. They contain little historical information, and so the development of skull house rites remains a gray area in our research. Why skull house rites were instituted only by a few major tribes of the Lagaip and Porgera valleys is an interesting question. Our best guess is that skull houses were considered to be highly dangerous, and few were willing to import rites bearing such risks.

The Kepele Cult Network

The appeal of the Kepele cult as an expression of tribal unity, as a means of dealing with environmental problems, and as an outstanding social occasion must have been great, for it spread widely. Unlike other Enga cults, which were not interconnected, the Kepele was regarded as a loosely knit ritual network—

metaphorically, as a python whose head lay in Kandep, its tail in Porgera. Map 12 delimits what is usually considered to be the extent of the network, plotting Kepele cult houses reported to us. Our data are not complete but should cover approximately 90 percent of Kepele houses in the Lagaip, 80 percent of those in Kandep, and 70 percent of those in Porgera. Within this network, there was a great deal of variation in cult procedures, making it difficult to pinpoint where the network ended—that is, what should be called Kepele and what were related but different cults to which some Kepele rites had been imported. Enga ritual experts share our difficulty in defining the borders of the network.

Three major branches of the Kepele can be delimited. The first, the southern branch that extended from Kandep to Laiagam (map 12:2–14), was most frequently called Aiamane and was linked to the travels of Molopai's son. No Aiamane cult sites had skull houses, some used the *mote* initiation primarily for the training of ritual experts, and in most, the *yupini* figure was adopted only between the fifth and third generations, if at all. The second was the core branch that included the original Kepele site of Bipi at Telyatesa (map 12:1) and Kepele sites down the Lagaip stretching from Kanake of Sambe (15) to Kumbate of Kundiki (38). Cult practitioners at most of these sites recognized the Molopai myth as the general origin myth but also had specific traditions of their own linked to the wandering women bearing sweet potatoes or to tribal settlement. The third branch wound its way through the Porgera valley (39–48) and continued on to the Paiela area sites (not shown on map 12). Some Porgera cult houses are said to have been established after the famine and subsequent introduction of the sweet potato, when clans settled in the lower valleys. Others are said to have been founded during the travels of Molopai's son, and still others by groups who migrated from the Lagaip to Porgera and established "daughter" houses in their new areas of settlement. Porgera Kepele performances had most of the features of Lagaip ones, but owing to the small size of their hosting groups, they were smaller in scale.

The "snake" of Kepele was kept intact by shared underlying beliefs and ideology, by incantations naming the major cult houses, by the initiation of boys in Kepele performances of other tribes where they had close relatives, by the widespread attendance of relatives from outside the tribe, and by the circulation of ritual experts. How the Kepele network was woven together by the exchange of ritual experts is illustrated by a list of Kepele cult performances over which Aniki Wee, a Kepele specialist from the Kamani tribe of Yapumi in northern Kandep, presided before his career was cut short by the arrival of the missionaries. These included performances at seventeen major houses: four in the Lagaip, three in northern Kandep, four in southern Kandep, two in southwestern Kandep near Margarima, two in the Tari area, and two in the Mendi area. The last four would not have been true Kepele performances.

The Kepele Cult in Central Enga

Once established in the Laiagam region, the Kepele cult was imported by some groups of central Enga, who called it by the term that western tribes used for it in song, Aeatee. In central Enga it was substantially revised to organize the Tee cycle and work out problems brought about by the growing ceremonial exchange network. Its importation and diffusion are described in two different waves of tradition. The first, an exceedingly complex tale of marriages between sky people (*yalyakali*), hunters, and agriculturalists, stretches back into mythical time.[42] In the end, marital strife, misunderstandings around the giving of a *kundu* drum, and the drum's subsequent theft result in a fight during which the opponents turn into rainbow pythons (*molopai*). From the Laiagam region, one of these pythons journeys down the upper Lai valley and into the Ambum, stopping at a number of points, only to be driven on repeatedly by the noise and bustle of human communities. It finally settles at Tiakamanda on the northern ridge of the middle Ambum valley (map 12:51). At or near the places where the python stopped, variants of Kepele-Aeatee cult performances were held.[43] Although the snake is not specifically linked to that in the Molopai myth, many of its actions are reminiscent of the former.

The arrival of the rainbow python at Tiakamanda, on the land of the Potealini tribe, is recorded in the popular myth of a girl who swallows an egg, gets pregnant, and gives birth to a son. While working in a garden, she hangs the baby in a net bag on a tree. When it cries, her brother goes to comfort it, and upon finding the python in the bag, beats it. The snake flees up the mountainside singing a song very similar to the one sung by Molopai's son in some versions of the Kepele origin myth. It disappears into the men's house at Tiakamanda, later making its home in a small pond nearby. For cult performances, the snake is represented by a stone mortar shaped like the *kundu* drum, the object of the original conflict. The story then continues: when two Potealini clans migrate into the Sau valley, the snake is believed to follow them and settle near Paipa.[44]

Just when the Kepele was first brought into central Enga is impossible to determine, for the myth of its arrival is not placed within a specific generation. It is also unknown whether certain elements of the early Kepele were imported and fused with the Yainanda cult or whether the entire cult was performed and later certain rites such as the *mote* initiation were dropped. Possibly the Potealini tribe brought the cult with it when it migrated into the Ambum valley in the fifth to sixth generation or imported it at the beginning of the Great Ceremonial Wars to strengthen tribal organization. Certainly the elements that were retained were relevant for this purpose — elaborate rites for building a tribal cult house, with each clan or subclan contributing specified materials; the assembling of skulls in the cult house (for some cult houses, not all); and the ritualized destruction of the cult house, involving formal sportive competition between different segments of the tribe.

A second wave of Kepele tradition came into central Enga in approximately the sixth generation (see also Lacey 1975:126), but its rituals were first performed on a large scale—by the entire Yanaitini and Apulini tribes—during the fourth to fifth generation in conjunction with the expansion of the Tee cycle. The origin myth is an extension of that mentioned earlier telling of the journey of two women from Kasap up the Lagaip river valley (map 12:21) to establish Kepele sites at Keokungusa (16) and Kanake (15). From the Kanake area the mother and daughter travel to the Lai valley during a period of famine. The daughter goes to the men's house at Tetemanda to get fire while the mother waits in the bushes. The daughter, seduced by a Yanaitini Kia man (49), never returns, so the mother goes on to Irelya and marries a man named Ikipale from the Kapeali subclan of the Apulini tribe (50). Both turn into Aeatee stones. In the Apulini version (Lacey 1975: 120-21) it is the mother who stays at Tetemanda, the daughter who goes on to Irelya. There she meets Kapeali, a son of Talyulu, teaches him protective magic spells for sexual intercourse in which all the names of the food crops are called, and has sexual intercourse with him.[45] Kapeali builds her a house at the head of the Talyulu ceremonial grounds at Irelya, where she settles, turning into the sacred Aeatee stone. Her house becomes the cult house for the Aeatee. Because she brought the magic spells to Irelya, a cult expert from Irelya presided over the feeding of the sacred stones at Tetemanda.[46]

A similar tradition exists in the Yakani and Depe tribes (map 12:53-54), telling how two women left the Laiagam region, the daughter staying at Lenge and the mother moving on to the Birip area, where she turned into the sacred stones used in the Pokalya, a cult related to the Aeatee and Kepele. In Depe, the Pokalya is attributed to both the rainbow python and the wandering women. Further discussion of the Aeatee and Pokalya cults is taken up in chapter 11, when it will be possible to put them in their broader socioeconomic context.

Kepele Performances of the 1920s to 1950s

By the twentieth century, the Kepele cult network exhibited considerable variation, although most performances had at their core the rites of house building, male initiation, and feeding and mating of sacred stones. Here we describe performances of this century, drawing on material in eyewitness testimonies from the Lagaip valley and northern Kandep, supplemented by the research of Lacey (1975) and Gibbs (1978).[47]

PREPARATIONS AND THE CONSTRUCTION OF CULT HOUSES   The Kepele was called when environmental conditions deteriorated and the performance of smaller rituals determined that it was warranted, one of these being the *aina pungi toko,* the bridge of the sweet potato vines, discussed earlier. Tribal leaders then met to make plans and launch the intensive campaign necessary to organize such a large-scale performance. Once a moratorium on warfare within the tribe had been achieved, word was sent out to all clans and subclans urging people to plant gardens and raise pigs for the upcoming occasion. Leaders called a traditional dance to gather people, put them in the right frame of mind, and plan for the first stage of the Kepele: construction of the cult house or houses. After the dance, tribal leaders and ritual experts delegated each subclan of the tribe to bring specified building materials.

For large Kepele performances, ritual experts from other cult houses were summoned. The best known of these had designated seats in cult houses to which they were regularly invited. Ritual experts for the Kepele were some of the few specialists in Enga, carefully chosen from among the sons of former ritual experts.[48] They were usually eccentrics who, having experienced altered states of consciousness, dreams, and visions, felt that they were directed by the power of the ancestors. Because they were feared and respected for their contacts with the spirit world, people, especially women and children, fled and hid upon their approach. Young men accompanied their fathers to learn the secrets of the trade, but once fully trained they enjoyed considerable autonomy in conducting sacred rites and received generous payments after each performance. Yet because they were feared and constantly on the move, they could not apply their wealth and influence to become clan leaders in everyday affairs. Inherited position, wide travels, vast knowledge of the Kepele cult network, lavish payments, and a narrowly defined realm of influence thus characterized Kepele ritual experts as well as ritual experts in most other ancestral cults. As men apart, Kepele ritual experts were given unique burials: the corpse was woven into a basketwork frame to resemble a large *yupini* figure, decorated with a cassowary feather headdress and pearl shells around the neck, buried upright like the *yupini,* and covered over to rest with the ancestral spirits.[49]

When ritual experts had assembled on the appointed day, the required materials were brought to the cult site with great ceremony and festivity. All subclans, singing and dancing, converged on the site from different directions and presented their contributions. The king post for the Kepele house was rubbed with oil, wrapped in ferns, and brought in a special procession:

When it was time to build new houses for the Kepele, each clan was delegated to bring certain materials. Tiangane and Malataini cut *ipiliaka* logs in the high forest, greased them with cosmetic oil (*mamba*), and carried them to the ceremonial grounds in a parade, the celebrants singing, dancing, and adorned in ceremonial attire. Malataini was helped by Laemasa and some Temanga men who live up in the high country. Other Tiangane subclans collected posts for the cult houses and round stones for the earth ovens. Malataini clans usually brought *aepa* (cedar) bark, collected other bush materials, and came singing and dancing down to Papyuka. . . . Maliwane gave the stone ax to cut the [previously mentioned] wood. The members of Maliwane who lived high in the forested mountains provided *lyau* wood. They put on their ceremonial dress and danced as they came down from the mountains. . . . Together they built several different houses including one with a tall pinnacle. (Councilor Amu, Sambe Tiangane clan, Papyuka [Laiagam])

The sacred area of the cult site was fenced off, and under the direction of the ritual experts the construction of the Kepele house began. The Kepele house was given a variety of names including *kepele anda, nee nape anda, aiyamane anda,* and *aeatee anda* and was the most sacred of all the cult houses, for it was in this house that the ancestral stones and basketwork figures were fed and made to copulate by the ritual experts. First, the king post to constitute the tall central spire was erected, and then the perimeter posts for the circular walls were inserted, each post contributed by and representative of a subclan, following the model laid down in the Kepele origin myth when the house for Molopai was formed by the bodies of his sons. Ritual experts recited spells for each stage of construction.

After the Kepele house was complete, a similar house was built for the *mote* boys' initiation; it was called *mote anda, mupa anda,* and *anda mange katenge,* among other names. We were told of no other houses that were common to all Kepele sites other than the Kepele house, *mote* house, and houses to accommodate initiates and ritual experts. Some Kepele sites had special houses to be torn down or burned at the end of the ceremony; others had houses where predictions were made, war rituals performed, and the sacred water for the boys' initiation prepared; and still others had structures where food was ritually prepared or sacred objects were kept (see also Lacey 1975; Gibbs 1978).[50] Celebrants then feasted and went home, leaving the houses to deteriorate for months or even several years until the preparations for the major phase of the ceremony, *anda lakenge,* had been made.

As the time for the main ceremony drew near, word went out to celebrants and guests to assemble the young men to be initiated and prepare the necessary foodstuffs and materials for the ceremony. The Kepele and *mote* houses were repaired and decorated, and shelters were constructed to house the hundreds, or in some cases thousands, of people who would attend. Chosen ritual experts then painted the bark plaques and filled the gourd with "the water of life" (*yalipa,* or sky water) for the *mote* initiation, laboriously blowing on a cool stone ax over a period of some days and allowing the liquid condensed from the warm breath to drip into the bespelled gourd.[51] This formula was supplemented with sugar-cane juice, pork fat, and opossum fat.

On the appointed day, all members of the host tribe converged on the Kepele cult site, including the descendants of former tribal members who had moved to their wives' clans. One pig, and only one, was provided by each male family member, whether adult or child, along with other foods to provision the feast. All men, as equals, were to contribute similarly. Guests from all over the region brought specialties from their own areas, their travel being more or less unrestricted: ambush of voyagers to and from Kepele performances was considered taboo. Some men engaged in hunting to provision the feast with marsupial meat, but pork was the essential sacred and secular food. Outside the fenced-off sacred area began the feasting and dances that would continue for the duration of the cult performance — the Kepele offered a rare opportunity for people to gather, escape the grudges and drudgery of everyday life, socialize, engage in exchange, and arrange marriages in a peaceful, festive atmosphere.

The next morning, the pigs were staked out and clubbed. Some of the meat was reserved for rites to be performed within the sacred area, and the rest was distributed freely and generously to all present with no obligations for repayment. Throughout, the pork prepared by elaborate ritual procedures for the different categories of celebrants (the initiates, initiated adult males, ritual experts, and very old men who would soon join the ancestors) was carefully separated from that given to women, children, uninitiated men, and spectators. The large pig kill marked the beginning of the Kepele rites that would take place within the enclosed sacred area.

THE MOTE INITIATION   Between the ages of approximately eight and sixteen, all young men of western Enga were expected to attend at least one *mote* initiation. In it they were symbolically separated from their mothers and the impurities of breast milk, given the sacred "water of life" to confer longevity, and introduced to the secrets of the spirit world. It was said that young men who attended the *mote* initiation would become strong, hardworking, responsible men who would be able to replace their fathers, raise many pigs, speak in public, father many children, and live long and productive lives. Once having been through the *mote* initiation, they could partake of ritually prepared pork and no longer be "like women" who had to stay home during the sacred phases of the Kepele rites.

A boy could be initiated in the *mote* of his father's tribe or that of others in which he had immediate relatives, for the secrets of the Kepele cult were not specific to individual tribes. Initiates were brought by their fathers to special *mote* shelters built within the sacred enclosure and were not permitted to go out during the three-day initiation, even to urinate or defecate, a restriction that probably connoted an infantile state. Their diet was limited to sugarcane juice for liquid and the few sweet potatoes given to them by their mothers beforehand.

When all the preparations had been made, the *mote* boys assembled for the initiation rites and were lined up by clan and tribe and by height and age. Age groups were indicated by features of dress. A ritual expert then appeared on the scene to lead them to the initiation house, his face concealed by a mask fashioned from a dried gourd with two holes cut for the eyes and one for the mouth, his head covered by a foul, disheveled wig, and his neck bedecked with strings of dried bones. As he flicked his tongue in and out of the mouth hole of his mask, the young men were separated from the little boys: quite a few candidates fled in terror, returning to attend another *mote* initiation only when they were considerably older. Cane belts were then tied around the waists of the initiates while the ritual experts recited spells.

The next steps of the *mote* differed from tribe to tribe, though a common core of ritual concerned with symbolic separation from mother, revelation of cult secrets, and rites to assure future health and productivity was a part of most performances. Initiates were led to the cult house in the evening. Before entering the house or once seated within it, they were given the "water of life" from the gourd prepared by the ritual experts.[52] The water of life symbolized the breast milk of two sky women, Yongalume (dawn) and Kulume (evening), who in Enga cosmology appear as the evening and morning stars, respectively. Their point of contact with the earth was the sacred mountain Tongopipi behind Tumundan. Once a boy had partaken of this liquid, he was cleansed from the impurities in breast milk and the close contact with women that had characterized his early years of life and could hamper his physical growth, abilities, and mental acuity. The spell recited while the boys drank from the gourd is intriguing in that it mentions different body fluids — blood, menstrual blood, and sperm — recalling themes from initiations of many highland fringe societies.[53]

Inside the ritual house, the initiates sat in total darkness, fearfully anticipating the formidable events ahead, when they would come into contact with the spirit world. Outside the cult house, experts whistled to signal the presence of ghosts and augment the boys' fear. Ten to twelve men dressed as *yupini* figures concealed themselves in the rafters to frighten the boys. A man crouching in the corner imitated a *tekea* (spiny anteater).[54] After some time, two men dressed as the spirit women, Yongalume and Kulume, in ceremonial attire entered the cult house and, by the light of their torches, briefly revealed to the young men the sacred bark paintings (for example, sun, moon, man, woman, rainbow, cassowary, dog, specific sky beings, and two stars, Yongalume and Kulume), the *yupini* basketwork figure, and the *malinu*, the woven image of a rainbow python coiled around the ceiling of the *mote* house. The hearts of the boys were said to leap in fear, for never in their lives had they seen drawings of any kind.

In some performances, the boys exited by a back door where they passed by a man of wisdom and knowledge holding the following symbols (Lacey 1975: 133-34): a piece of ginger (*alamo* or *kokali*) so that their enemies would taste them like ginger and suffer a long time before they died; a green plant (*ema*) so that the young men would own the most fertile part of the land; a piece of pork liver (*mena pungi*) so that they would be rich men; and a piece of opossum meat (*saa wapisa*) so that they would be skillful hunters. They were to take a deep breath and smell each object. In other performances, similar objects were shown upon entry, and after the revelation of the sacred plaques, the "women" bade the boys to come home, at which point the boys were instructed to break through the house walls and flee, not to stay and listen to women.

Some ritual experts allowed all initiates to witness the feeding and mating of the sacred stones, and others, only those who had attended *mote* initiations several times and were preparing to become ritual experts themselves. Boys were sworn to secrecy concerning everything they had seen and done during the ceremony. After the initiates emerged from the *mote* initiation, their cane belts were cut off by the ritual expert and either tied around the roots of a pandanus tree or planted beneath the roots of other trees, so that as the roots grew they would be fastened firmly in the ground. Such measures were believed to protect the boys from untimely death from illness, "since trees usually die only when chopped down or uprooted, not from disease." When the *mote* initiation was complete, the young men, elated by the power of the Kepele, danced on tree branches and performed stunts for the spectators. After attending *mote* initiations twice, they could eat ritually prepared pork from cult houses where they were initiated.

When the rites were complete, the initiates returned to the men's house to observe a period of strict food taboos. A tree was ringbarked and a stand of pitpit cut to the ground to keep track of time. At the beginning, the boys were permitted to eat only sweet potatoes steamed together with ritually prepared pork to flavor them; the pork was not for consumption. All food received from women was taboo. Stringy foods, such as various kinds of pitpit, were avoided because of their association with worms. Similar taboos existed for marsupials, which were known to be worm infested. Over the months and years that followed, the taboos were lifted one by one. For example, when the leaves of the ringbarked tree fell, they could eat certain greens and ferns steamed with pork. When the top broke off, they could start eating *tanakae* opossums, and when the tree fell, they could eat *komaipa* opossums. The end of the food restrictions was marked by the consumption of taro in which pork was inserted. From then on the consumption of snake meat was permitted and believed to confer good luck.[55]

THE RITES OF ANCESTRAL STONES Rites to communicate with ancestral spirits were among the most sacred of the entire cult. In most performances they were open only to ritual experts, elder men of wisdom, and experienced *mote* initiates who were armed with the appropriate ritual knowledge and spells to withstand the concentrated power of the ancestors. Of all the sacred objects, the *yupini* basketwork figure was the only one that would be witnessed and celebrated by the public: in some Kepele houses, spectators were allowed to peek through the fenced enclosure to witness the *yupini* as it was made to "dance" around the sacred site. In the Sambe tribe's Kepele at Papyuka near Laiagam, the *yupini* figure was paraded from the men's house to the cult house through throngs of spectators:

> The skeletal remains of the children of Sambe were collected and preserved as a part of the Kepele ritual. The woven image (*yupini*) of Sambe was the point of contact with the deceased forefathers. During the rites, it was decorated like a real human. Two ritual experts, one from the Malipi clan and the other from the Temanga clan, held the woven figure, supporting it so that it stood on its feet as they carried it along in the procession and made it dance to the ceremonial grounds together with the parade of participants and spectators. The two ritual experts wore special armbands, and a woven cassowary headdress was placed on the head of the Kepele figure. It was made to look like Sambe—its arms, ears, nose, legs, and torso were made in the image of Sambe. (Councilor Amu, Tiangane, Laemasa subclan, Papyuka)

Once the *yupini* figure had danced and was brought to the Kepele house, the public was strictly excluded. Inside the cult house, pig fat, prepared with elaborate ceremony, was rubbed on or inserted between its lips to symbolically feed it. Then a vulva-shaped female stone or female *yupini* figure was uncovered and the male *yupini* made to have sexual intercourse with it while spells were recited. Afterward, the stone was wrapped in pork fat and leaves and buried, the *yupini* figure being placed on a platform where it would "sleep" accompanied by one or more ritual experts who also slept in the cult house.[56] The performance was repeated on three or four consecutive evenings. Gibbs (1978:442–47) gives an excellent detailed description of this part of the ceremony as performed by the Pulumani clan at Porgera, including accompanying spells.[57]

When the stones and the *yupini* had been laid to rest for the final time on the fourth or fifth day of the cult performance, the ritual experts, accompanied by *mote* initiates, dramatically destroyed one of the cult houses. For example, during the Sambe Kepele at Papyuka, ropes were tied to the pinnacle of the *mote* house by the ritual experts, and with the help of many men the house was pulled down, torn to pieces, and burned. At Kasap and Tumundan, the Kepele house itself was burned by ritual experts who climbed onto the roof, mysteriously escaped death, and reappeared unharmed from amid the flames. Often, ritualized competition within the tribe was expressed just before or during the destruction of the house. In some performances, for example, an opossum in a bag was thrown back and forth over the roof of the cult house from men of one segment of the tribe to the other—those who dropped it were proclaimed the losers. In others, men divided by tribal segment competed to tear or burn down the house. The ceremonial destruction of one of the cult houses was a festive occasion, carried out in sportive spirit accompanied by dancing, singing, and a large pork feast to mark the end of a successful ceremony.

THE RITES OF THE SKULL HOUSE   Kepele performances held jointly by some large tribes or "brother" tribes could be performed at either a male or female Kepele site. Male sites included a tribal skull house in which the skulls of all deceased male tribal members were deposited and an accompanying private ritual was performed to protect the family from the ghost.[58] People traveled considerable distances to deposit skulls. Members of the "brother" tribes Sakate and Yambanima who had migrated to Maramuni, for instance, brought skulls of the deceased back to the tribal skull house in their original homeland, Ipakatupya near the Keta-Lagaip river junction (map 12:19).

Kepele cults aimed primarily at achieving fertility were held at female sites, but when severe misfortune struck in the form of epidemics (particularly leprosy) and the skull house filled rapidly, the Kepele was performed at the male site following the usual procedures plus the ritual cremation of the skulls. For this event, a pyre was constructed within a circular fenced enclosure well away from the house. On top of the pyre were placed layers of fat, vegetable foods, all species of plants used by humans, and a layer of skulls covered by another layer of fat, plants, and firewood. Every species had to be represented so that it would grow well in the years to follow. The stones were removed from the skull house and buried nearby, and people were warned to stay in their houses so as to avoid the smell of burning skulls.

In the middle of the night, numerous ritual experts from the participant tribes assumed posts around the outside of the enclosure, holding long sticks.[59] The huge bonfire had to be lit by surprise, else it was believed that the skulls would have time to escape. As the explosion of the fat hurled the skulls into the air, the ritual experts struck them back down into the fire. It was said that if enemy skulls were in the same pyre, they would rise up, fight each other, and escape. Other skulls that did not want to be burned might pop up or roll out of the fire and down to the swamp by the Lagaip river. They were not collected because they themselves had escaped the fire. When the skulls had burned to ash, the ritual experts went home satisfied that the harmful ghosts of the deceased had been banished to the general pool of ancestors.

Upon completion of the Kepele performance, the ritual experts were paid and began their journey home, heavily laden. Only a few from the host group remained to take care of the premises and conduct a number of smaller rituals on the cult grounds during the years between the large *anda lakenge* phases of the cults. These smaller rituals were for war, healing, and the depositing of skulls.

Summary

The Kepele of the twentieth century was at once the most encompassing cult of western Enga and the major ceremonial exchange network. Its original basis was a cult in which mobile tribes of the high country gathered to initiate boys into the secrets of the spirit world. After the introduction of the sweet potato, new elements were imported from surrounding areas including eastern Enga, the Huli area, and the Sepik that turned the Kepele into a ritual of tribal unity and regional integration with a large social component, solving problems that resulted from the redistribution of population relative to resources by ritual means rather than by economic ones as in eastern Enga.

In a sense, the Kepele became a "cult for all seasons" of Enga life. Within the realm of the sacred, boys were initiated and sent on their way to become men, dangerous spirits of the dead were banished, the ancestors were appeased, and confidence in the future was restored. Ceremonies for building the cult house and assembling skulls pulled together highly dispersed tribes, expressed divisions, reduced tensions, and reaffirmed cooperation between clans of a tribe. The Kepele underwrote each of the two dimensions of Enga kinship by rallying agnatic relatives in rites of cooperation, on one hand, while, on the other, including people with a wide range of affinal ties from other tribes to help finance and support the ceremonies. Social activities outside the sacred area enabled contacts to be renewed, marriages to be contracted, and trade to be transacted, lifting spirits and relieving the monotony of daily life.

Finally, the Kepele affected the social order: for its performance to take place, hostilities had to be put aside, particularly the vicious wars between neighboring clans or subclans that were so frequent in Lagaip history. Although the truces called for in the Kepele could hardly solve serious underlying problems, its cooperative and joyous activities broke the vicious circle of anger and revenge that often characterized resurgent Enga warfare. The collective goodwill and generosity of participants were believed to please the ancestors, while the vitality of a large crowd working toward the welfare and prosperity of the group conveyed a spiritual experience to everyone involved. Together, the awe of the sacred and the power of community effort created a unique atmosphere.

In a broader historical context, the post-sweet potato Kepele was both the mainstay of traditional social values—equality, sharing, and cooperation—and a forerunner of change. It revised political organization by drawing dispersed groups into a center, articulating tribal structure, and channeling competition. The Kepele network established homogeneity over a vast area that had previously encompassed diverse populations of "agriculturalists" and "hunters." Amid all these changes, it remained the mainstay of egalitarian values, with all celebrants contributing and benefiting more or less equally. As a cult that celebrated the pig by putting forth pork for virtually every important rite and demanding a contribution of one pig per male celebrant, the Kepele conferred new social and symbolic value on pigs, and with it, incentives for production. Its elaborate organizational requirements shaped big-men who were competent in intertribal relations. Finally, the broad net cast by the Kepele cult over western Enga and into the Huli, Ipili, Wola, and Mai-Yandapo areas gave formerly diverse groups many common denominators for exchange.

Ancestral Cults and History

The map of Enga ancestral cults at the time of contact was a veritable collage that cannot be understood outside of a historical perspective. Classifications made at any point in time produce a complex and confusing picture owing to variation introduced by two sources. One, stemming from the pre-sweet potato era, was the marked differences that existed between east and west, corresponding to different local ecologies and spheres of interaction. The second was complexity added in later generations by the exchange of cults within and across boundaries. The importation of single rites of cults, as well as entire cults, and their integration into existing rituals further complicated the picture.

Just as Enga religion and ritual cannot be understood without a historical perspective, Enga history cannot be understood without a sound knowledge of cosmology and cults, for these were built upon to set new directions and solve problems that arose. In western Enga, for example, where many aspects of life were entwined with rituals for the spirit world and where ritual experts had considerable influence, much of the surplus production was invested in communal exchange with the ancestors. This trend curtailed competition. By contrast, in the east and center a greater proportion of surplus production was invested in economic exchange, setting off a spiral of accelerating competition and production to meet its demands.

In closing, so as not to lose sight of the major thrust of ancestral cults in the maze of their transmission, we return to the opening quote from the Pulumani Kepele *nemongo:* "You give, I give, all must give." Whereas developments in warfare and ceremonial exchange presented in the chapters to come paint a picture of individuals and groups engaging in never-ending competitive struggles, the cults provided a counterpoint of opposing ideals—ones of equality, sharing, and cooperation within and across boundaries that limited or structured the growing competition. They rewove the fabric of society when it was torn by competition, in order to reestablish continuity and balance in relation to the past, for the present, and to lead into the future. And lead into the future it did, for these developments meant that while the Tee cycle was forming in the east, quite a different system of ceremonial exchange was taking shape in the west. It would not be long before the two met.

8

Bachelors' Cults
Purity, Prosperity, and Politics

... ongo endame pyu injapae ongonya endakali lu sili. Ongome endakali wasia ongonya baa endakali enda ongome wasia ongonyana endakali koopi epepi ongo kalyakumao au pyo wamba wasiamopa kateamupya, lepe ongo mambele.

... so [the sacred objects of the] Sangai originated from a woman, and therefore they are regarded as persons. Because the [spirit] woman made men, they [the sacred objects] always helped all men, the ugly and the handsome alike, so that they would be healthy and good-looking.[1]

Origin myth for the Sangai bachelors' cult, Malipini Kombane-Komaini clan

As the bachelors emerge from the seclusion of the cult house in the slow, measured strides of their majestic parade, it is clear that both nature and culture have left their marks. At the front of the line come tall, mature men, their proportions magnified by layers of full-length aprons and broad wigs, their oiled skin glistening, their bodies adorned with ornaments of value. They emanate power, discipline, competence, and self-assurance. As the parade files by, men give way to boys and the image falters. The last in line are but skinny, awkward lads behind facades of finery, striving to catch up with their older "brothers." Surely the transformation of

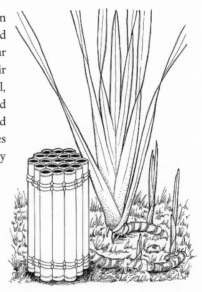

215

boys to men over the years, both physically and intellectually, is such that one can readily believe the supernatural had a hand in it, as the origin myth maintains.

The chapters to come will take us through three to four generations of complex developments in ceremonial exchange that were played out following a set of ground rules and values laid down in the bachelors' cults. Because such rules shaped the options and choices of the actors, many historical events can be better understood against their background. To this end, we have chosen to explore the history of bachelors' cults first—their origins, central themes, and diffusion, and the way innovations in them were used to steer the direction of change—and only later the corresponding developments in ceremonial exchange. This requires "jumping the gun" from time to time and mentioning developments that are not discussed in detail until chapters 10 and 11.

What emerges from Sangai cult history is a view of the role of bachelors' cults in Enga society quite different from that given by Meggitt (1964a). He suggested that tension between the sexes, expressed most strongly in sexual contamination beliefs, stemmed from the fact that men often married women from enemy clans, and enduring political tensions were carried over into male-female relations. Bachelors' cults, according to Meggitt, were part of this complex. There may indeed be some truth to this argument, but the history of bachelors' cults illustrates a somewhat different role: they were manipulated to set new goals and values, regulate relations between men of different generations, overcome problems between the sexes, and standardize associated beliefs from one area to the next, thereby facilitating marriages across boundaries and permitting exchange to flow freely.

Sangai-Sandalu Bachelors' Cults

Enga recognize that the distribution of physical and mental abilities at birth is not equal. They believe that as a rule of thumb, those who come from successful families will have a better chance of being endowed with superior qualities. A number of adages express this view—for example, poor or unhealthy trees do not bear good fruit; it is the good or healthy ones that bear well. This notion, however, is imbued with neither determinism nor rigid valuation: it is well accepted that the sons of capable men are often "losers," just as sons of the less capable can rise to the top. Furthermore, although the qualities of a big-man— skills in oratory, mediation, and management of wealth—are held in the highest esteem, every man who works to the best of abilities is appreciated. This concept is expressed in the simple proverb, "you need a person" (*endakali yangingi*), voicing an underlying respect for the positive attributes of each and every individual:

A man who has many pigs is often regarded as a leader, because he uses his pigs to help others in the clan, if need be. Another person may be needed because he is a good fighter and can defend the clan in case of an enemy attack. One may be a good builder or another a good gardener. Another may be a good fence maker. One person may be good at one thing and another at something else, all being needed for their respective abilities. A person may possess many ornaments for ceremonial dress, if he has the ability to gather and hold on to them. Now suppose that good fence maker might want to go to a traditional dance. The person having many ornaments would then lend these things to him free of charge so that he could take part, because he had received or would receive help from him. So you see, people are needed by the others for their abilities. (Kyakas Sapu, Yanaitini Lanekepa clan, Lupamanda Wabag)

A fundamental ideology is expressed here: potential equality (within the sexes) and respect for individual attributes. In the past it was through the bachelors' cults that each man received an opportunity to transcend the inequalities of birth or background and to mature, develop his abilities, and contribute to clan fortune. Today bachelors' cult performances are held infrequently and by only a few clans. Still, some of the associated beliefs and values persist.

The Enga bachelors' cults called Sangai, "that which is hidden" (Meggitt 1964a:210), centered on the symbolic marriage of the bachelors to a spirit woman believed to be one of the mythical sky people. Should young men participate in the Sangai, remaining faithful to the spirit woman from the onset of puberty until marriage, they would be transformed into mature, handsome, socially competent men, their inner worth reflected in outward appearance. The concept of first marriage to the spirit woman can best be understood within the context of prevalent beliefs concerning male-female contamination.[2] These were based on the idea that menstruation or contact with menstrual blood, which bestowed beauty and fertility on a woman, severely endangered a man's health, appearance, and, above all, social effectiveness. It was this complex of beliefs, among others, that excluded women from public realms and equal jural status. If proper precautions were taken and menstrual magic practiced, however, a husband's health and success in all realms of life could be enhanced (Gray 1973; Kyakas and Wiessner 1992). Added to this notion in western and central Enga, but generally not in the east, was the idea that a woman's vagina was a "fire," burning out a man's strength and causing him to age prematurely if certain precautions were not taken.[3] Similar beliefs were (and still are) found throughout highland New Guinea with varying degrees of specificity and rigidity (e.g., Meggitt 1964a; Strathern and Strathern 1971; Sillitoe 1979; Hage 1981; Biersack 1982; Goldman 1983; Frankel 1986),[4] running along a continuum from relaxed in the east to tense in the west.[5]

In Enga, it was through marriage to the spirit woman that young men were formally separated from women, transformed, and given the power to withstand the dangers of close contact with the opposite sex in adult life. The spirit woman was represented by one or, in some clans, two sacred objects: the *lepe* plant (bog iris, *Acorus calamus,* among other species) and the *penge,* bamboo containers filled with sacred fluid said to originate from the blood of the spirit woman. Before coming into close contact with her via the sacred objects, young men of the appropriate age in a clan or large subclan retired to a secret place in the forest where a cult house had been built. There rites were performed to purge their bodies and senses of all that was considered impure – prior contact with women, female fluids such as breast milk and menstrual blood, and sights of pig feces or human feces.[6] These rites included lying open-eyed under a waterfall to cleanse the eyes. Only then were the young men permitted to enter the cult house, where they were disciplined by a strict dietary and behavioral regime and required to speak in measured, symbolic language. Senior bachelors presided over all events.

During the next four days, the young men tended their plots of *lepe* plants and conducted rites for the communally owned sacred fluid, including transferring the liquid into new containers when the old ones had deteriorated. Mental capacities were sharpened by a number of exercises. For example, evening sessions to comprehend and memorize the *sangai titi pingi,* a lengthy praise poem for the sacred objects told in obscure metaphors, taxed the keenest of minds. Nights were spent by lapsing into short periods of sleep followed by discussion and dream interpretation. Most dreams were read as having implications for warfare or *tee* exchange, and the process of putting the products of the imagination or subconscious into a political frame instructed young men to reflect on the broader positions of their clans. Verbal skills were trained by turning dream interpretations to metaphor and song. During the day, attention turned to physical transformation: cleansing of the body with the aid of leaves from the sacred *lepe* plant, wig making, and preparation of ceremonial attire for emergence. The young men of a clan or subclan who endured the rites, hardships, and dreams together emerged from the cult with bonds of brotherhood and solidarity that would last throughout their lifetimes.

Formerly when the bachelors came out of seclusion they were greeted by their elders and judged ready or unready for marriage.[7] They were then sent to the men's house, where they stayed for a few days before taking off their ceremonial attire and returning to everyday life. Around the end of the nineteenth century, the bachelors' emergence was made public – the young men left the cult house and paraded in full dress to the ceremonial grounds to perform a dignified traditional dance in which the predictions made from dreams were revealed. Age divisions were distinguished by styles of dress.[8] Emergence festivals gave the Sangai wider public appeal, and subsequently it was imported throughout eastern Enga, where it was called Sandalu and was closely tied to the planning of the Tee cycle. Just prior to the colonial era, overt courtship became integrated into bachelors' cult performances in the form of boisterous female competition — the *enda akoko nyingi* that disrupted the end of the festival.

Young men attended bachelor's cult rituals at one- to two-year intervals from the onset of puberty until they reached their mid-twenties and were considered marriageable. Senior bachelors (*isingi akali*), the custodians of the sacred objects, carefully selected and trained their successors, handing over cult objects, spells, and knowledge upon marriage and going on to lead normal lives. Some senior bachelors attained the status of big-men, but because the skills required of the two were different and senior bachelors married late, they were not on a direct path to bigmanship. A number of good descriptions and discussions of the Sangai-Sandalu exist in the literature on Enga (Gibbs 1975; Gray 1973; Lacey 1975; Kyakas and Wiessner 1992; Meggitt 1964a; Schwab 1995). To avoid projecting themes and rites of more recent bachelors' cults back in time, we now turn to their history.

Sangai Oral Traditions

Oral traditions concerning the Sangai can be divided into three general categories. The first consists of origin myths for the cult itself, which also embrace its philosophy and objectives. Because the myths are fictive, narrators freely add details to bring them up to date, to entertain, or to fit them into the mythical landscape of the area. One cannot, therefore, regard origin myths as historical descriptions of past performances, though comparison of origin myths from different clans and regions can elucidate shared fundamental themes. That is the sole purpose for which we used such myths.

The second category is a body of poetry and spells recited during different stages of the Sangai. For historical purposes, the most informative of these is the *sangai titi pingi*, a lengthy poem telling of the power of the sacred objects, where they were obtained, when, and by whom. Although few men can recite the poem in its entirety, most can give a synopsis of the history of the clan's sacred objects. We used this information to trace the spread of the Sangai cult, taking care to distinguish traditions concerning when the clan first adopted it from those describing the purchase of the sacred objects used in the most recent performances. The remaining spells, which largely concern purification, physical enhancement, or love magic, contain little specifically historical information, although they give some idea of aims of the cult in recent generations.[9]

Eyewitness accounts of Sangai performances comprise the third source. These are easily obtained because the Sangai, as one of the few cults that not all missionaries discouraged, persisted well into the colonial period and is still held by some subclans today.

Oral traditions concerning the Sangai constitute an enormous body of material, because each clan or subclan has its own history telling when, where, and how it received the sacred objects. The material is not only vast but also complex—translating spells from the Sangai, particularly the poetry for the sacred objects, is a long and painstaking job that can be done only with the sustained help of senior bachelors. We thus collected the following information: (1) myths concerning the origin of the Sangai itself, (2) information on where and when a clan first obtained its sacred objects for the Sangai (if time did not permit, we did not pursue the matter further); and (3) a few examples of *sangai titi pingi* from different areas, if we found men who could recite and interpret them. The history of the Sangai presented here provides only an initial sketch—we hope a more thorough study will follow before it is too late.

The Origin of Bachelors' Cults: Where, When, and Why

So far as we could determine, prior to the origin or acquisition of the Sangai two different ceremonies for young men were performed in Enga: the *mote* boys' initiation in the Kepele cult and the *sauipu* (literally, "hair come"), *yomondi* ("hair"), or similar, smaller-scale rituals for growth.[10] The *sauipu* involved periodic sojourns of young men in the forest to dream and interpret dreams and to perform rites of growth for hair, skin, and body with the help of individually owned *lepe* plants. The *sauipu* was still held by some clans of eastern Enga, Kandep, and the Lagaip within the lifetimes of elders or their fathers, but in most clans it was subsumed by the Sangai or Sandalu prior to first contact. Separation from women in order for young men to grow and mature was a shared theme of both the *mote* initiation and the *sauipu*.

The origin of the Sangai remains something of an enigma. All clans or subclans that held the Sangai have traditions telling where they first obtained their sacred objects, poetry, and spells, but traditions that explain how the cult itself came to be are known by few and are always mythical. Our studies revealed only three "centers" with Sangai origin myths for the Enga or their immediate neighbors—among the Mai and Yandapo dialect speakers of central Enga, the Ipili of the Porgera valley (Gibbs 1975), and the Huli of the Tari area (Goldman 1983; Frankel 1986) (map 13).[11] That there are no Sangai origin traditions among the Layapo of eastern Enga was confirmed by our investigations and by those of Roderic Lacey (1975) and Fr. John Schwab (1995:3).[12] The latter stated: "The ultimate origin of the Sandalu ceremony is somewhere in the unknown past. Individual clans trace their Sandalu back a few 'steps,' but then there is nothing further."

Although these areas are widely separated in space and their inhabitants speak different dialects or languages,[13] bachelors' cults from all three have the same essential beliefs and practices and share certain themes in their origin myths. A young bachelor encounters a beautiful woman who seduces him and, through her power as a supernatural being, transforms him into an attractive, socially competent, mature man. He then unintentionally betrays her or does her harm, resulting in her death. Upon or after her death, he is instructed either to fill a bamboo container (*penge*) with her blood or to pluck the bog iris plant (*lepe*) on her grave to pass on with the appropriate spells — or to do both — so that all young men in future generations can be similarly transformed.

Origin myths from central Enga and the Porgera valley (Gibbs 1975) depict the woman as one of the mythical sky beings to whom human origins are traced in Enga cosmology, who are believed to protect people so long as they obey certain standards of conduct. This detaches the Sangai from specific tribal ancestry and issues concerning land, in stark contrast to ancestral cults. Huli oral traditions collected by Stephen Frankel (1986:99-100) and Laurence Goldman (1983:325-26) also attribute the origin of bachelors' cults to a spirit woman with supernatural powers but do not specify her relationship to Huli deities or ancestors.

What is most puzzling about these origin traditions is that we could find no direct links between those of the central Enga and the Ipili. Though sharing the common theme of transformation via a relationship with a spirit woman and the objects representing her, origin myths from central Enga differ considerably from those of the Porgera and Paiela areas (see Gibbs 1975). The history of bachelors' cult diffusion also confirms this division: Enga clans east of Tumundan trace their Sangai cult and its sacred objects to central Enga, not to the Ipili, and no traditions that we collected (and we did ask widely) link the Sangai of central Enga to that of the Ipili, despite the fact that there was considerable migration from the Keta river area to Porgera in the past. Conversely, no Enga or Ipili interviewed in the Porgera valley said that his clan's sacred objects and spells for the Sangai came from central Enga.[14] The Huli of the Tari area attribute the origin of the sacred *lepe* plant and containers of sacred fluid used in their Ibagiya bachelors' cult to the Ipili or, in some cases, to the Laiagam Enga (Chris Ballard, personal communication, 1991). Correspondingly, we found no Enga clan that claimed to have received them from the Huli.

On the basis of these patterns of distribution and diffusion, it seems most likely that the core ideas of the Sangai concerning a spirit woman who transforms men did not originate in Enga but came from the south, reaching the

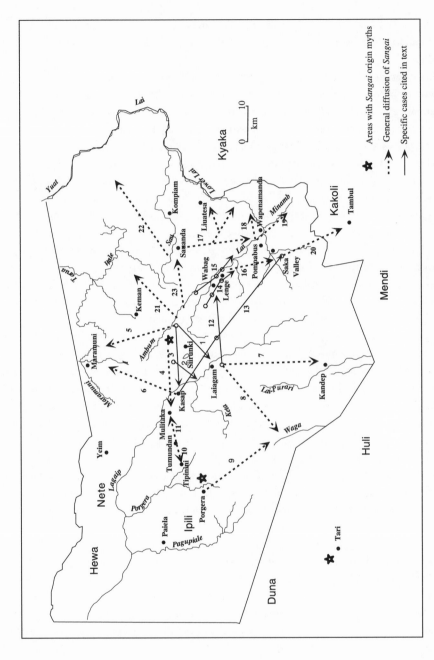

Map 13. General patterns and specific cases of diffusion of the Sangai bachelors' cult. Unless specified otherwise, diffusion is of the entire cult.

1. From Sakalini Titi clan to Sambe clans at Papyuka.

2. From Sirunki area via intermediaries to Sakate Yandapakini clan.

3. *Penge* from middle Ambum valley via Mulapini Andamane clan of Sirunki to Monaini Lakini clan.

4. From Sirunki or Ambum valley to numerous clans between Kasap and Mulitaka.

5-6. From Mai-Yandapo clans (5) or from clans of origin in Lagaip valley (6) to migrants living around Maramuni.

7. From Laiagam area to Atone clans of eastern Kandep between sixth and second generations.

8-9. Complex diffusion of Sangai to Katinja Enga from central Enga (8) and the Ipili (9).

10-11. *Lepe* from Pumane Kelyanyo at Tumundan to clans of Tipinini and Mulitaka.

12. *Lepe* from Sambe Pupu clan to Apulini Talyulu clan.

13. *Penge* from Monaini clans to Yambatane Yana clan (Lacey 1975:218).

14. From Itapuni Nenaini clan to Apulini Sikita Netuli subclan to Lyipini Wiokini clan (Lacey 1975:219).

15. *Lepe* from Yanaitini Kalepatae clan to Yakani Timali clan to Yakani Waimalae clan.

16. Diffusion along western Tee route from Depe and Lyipini clans to Sikini clans.

17. From upper Sau valley into middle and lower Lai.

18. From Pompabus area to lower Lai valley.

19. From Saka or Wapenamanda clans along Kulanga route to Minamb valley clans in second to third generation.

20. From Saka valley to Tambul clans in third generation.

21-23. Diffusion with migrants out of Ambum valley in sixth to seventh generation.

Yandap area of central Enga and the Ipili over different pathways, most likely routes for the salt trade.[15] Interaction with the Hewa may also have occurred during the cult's diffusion to the Ipili, for Sangai origin myths from Paiela all involve Hewa women (Gibbs 1975). Until extensive research on the Sangai has been carried out in the Kutubu area and among the Huli, Ipili, Duna, and Hewa, the last word will not have been said on this matter — and perhaps not even then, for the spread of the Sangai was undoubtedly a complex process taking place through several different channels. What does appear to have been an Enga innovation, however, is the idea of communal bachelors' cult performances held in a cult house with seniors presiding. Both the Huli and Duna bachelor's cults, though similar to those of Enga in underlying concepts, involve primarily individual apprenticeships. The Huli do have a final group phase in the cult house after a year or more of individual isolation, but they claim that this was imported from Enga.

When the Sangai first began to be practiced by the central Enga is also difficult to discern. On one hand, Mai and Yandapo clans generally do not see the Sangai as something they have had for time immemorial like the Yainanda and Kaima cults and the *yalyu* feast. On the other, they cannot place its overall "origin" in a particular generation, suggesting only that it began around the generation of subclan founders. Lagaip clans east of Mulitaka claim to have acquired it between the seventh and fifth generations; Kandep clans received it between the sixth and third, though some never adopted it; and clans of eastern Enga received it largely between the fourth and second. The great majority of these clans trace its origin to central Enga. Its limited distribution in the early generations and subsequent well-documented spread indicate that it was indeed acquired after the introduction of the sweet potato.[16] More we cannot say.

Perhaps even more intriguing than the questions of when and from where is that of why the Sangai was imported (or initiated) at a certain time. We have little information for the Ipili, but for the central Enga it is possible to make some suggestions. One advantage would have been to assist in reorganizing groups to form larger fighting forces prior to and during the large wars in the Ambum valley discussed in chapter 5. That is, by placing the young men of a clan firmly in the grips of their elders for education, discipline, and time of first marriage, young men attending the Sangai could be restrained from causing trouble within alliances and bonded into a unified fighting force. Another might be the Sangai's potential to standardize attitudes regarding relations between the sexes, which ran from relaxed and cooperative in eastern Enga to anxious and tense in the west. The common and "safe" road to marriage that it prescribed could have facilitated (1) intermarriage, and with it, integration of groups from the high country with those in the valleys, and (2) construction of trade alliances between east, center, and west along lines of affinal kinship. In the latter context, it is pertinent that the Yambatane clans of the Saka valley at the hub of the salt-stone ax trade alliance imported the Sangai two to three generations earlier than most other Layapo clans. We return to this point later.

Sangai Origin Traditions

In what follows, we summarize two Sangai origin traditions from central Enga. Those for the Ipili can be found in Gibbs (1975, 1978), and those for the Huli, in Frankel (1986:99-100) and Goldman (1983:325-26). The first is our synopsis of a lengthy tradition narrated by Isingi Tembe of the Malipini Kombane clan in the middle Ambum valley, who updated the myth with details of the modern Sangai to entertain.[17]

A despised, ugly bachelor is scorned by his peers who are going to perform bachelors' rites. When he arrives home dejected and sad, an elder in the clan advises him to go to a certain place in the forest. During his journey he comes across a perfectly kept house and, realizing that nobody is home, goes in, sits down, and waits to see what will come. As he sits there, he suddenly feels something like an earthquake and hears footsteps of somebody walking around at the back of the house. He remains very still with eyes wide, wondering what will happen next. When he glances at the door, he sees the most beautiful woman he has ever seen standing in the doorway and looking straight into his eyes. Clues such as the quake of the earth at her footsteps and flashes of lightning with her smile indicate that she is a sky being (yalyakali). She goes to the courtyard, cuts a cluster of pandanus nuts,[18] steams them for him together with sweet potato, and tries to seduce him, a scene described graphically. Overcoming his contamination anxieties, he gives in with pleasure. In the morning she is gone. The same thing happens the next two nights, except that this time she remains in the morning, dresses him in the finest paraphernalia, and transforms him into a being as magnificent as she. He then joins his clan brothers, who marvel. From this time on he is named Lyaiakali Lelya, a name commonly given to sky beings who are protagonists in myths.

Meanwhile, another miserable, rejected bachelor with a long neck and ugly face notes Lelya's transformation and follows him day and night to learn his secret. Overcome with pity, Lelya tells him to follow the same bush track. The same thing happens, but this bachelor refuses the woman, saying that he has come to be transformed via the bachelors' cult, not to be seduced. She runs out of the house and stays away all night. The next night the same thing happens, and on the third, angered by her advances, the bachelor shoots the spirit woman. The drama sets off a violent storm, and Lyaiakali Lelya realizes that something is wrong.

He rushes to her house and weeps in despair over her body. She instructs him to cut some bamboo containers and arrange them in two clusters of four separated by a cluster of two. When this is done, she tells him to pull out the arrow and fill the containers with her blood, plug them with clay and leaves, and bury them in a swampy area. Then she instructs him to bury her and return later to harvest *lepe* plants from her grave, one of which will grow by her head and the other by her feet. She then teaches him the procedures and spells for caring for these sacred objects and for passing them on, so that future generations of young men can be similarly transformed. With a faint smile, she dies.

Isingi went on to add the following comments, unlocking the door to much of the lore behind the Sangai—namely, that the bachelors are considered to be symbolically married to the spirit woman, and it is through this "first marriage" that they are transformed if they remain faithful to her.

All the things I have talked about for the Sangai have been created or brought to us by a [spirit] woman. It is believed that she is always there, represented by the *lepe* plant and the fluid in the bamboo containers [*penge*]. When young unmarried men have sexual contact with [human] women, their Sangai *lepe* plants wither and die.[19] The sacred liquid shrinks down to the bottom of the container or dries up.[20] But if young unmarried men observe the taboos and keep themselves away from women, then nothing affects the *penge* and *lepe*. They remain well and healthy. Since the spirit woman is alive and represented by the *lepe* and the *penge*, all care is taken to avoid human women so as not to arouse her jealousy and kill the *lepe* plants. So in the past young men avoided seeing women, and women avoided them.

If the senior bachelors who looked after the *lepe* plants and sacred fluid have sexual contact with women, on the very same day the fluid goes bad, the liquid turns white, and the *lepe* plants wither and die. This indicates that the [spirit] woman was jealous and left. But if the men who look after the *lepe* plants and containers of sacred fluid have taken care and avoided women, the next time they go to see the *lepe* plants they throw a stick toward them [to signal their coming].[21] The *lepe* plants sway backward and then forward to greet the man or see who is approaching. So the Sangai [*lepe* and *penge*] originated from a woman, and therefore they are regarded as persons. Because the woman made men, they [*lepe* and *penge*] always helped all men, the ugly and the handsome alike, so that they would be healthy and good-looking.

The transformation described here is not just a matter of individual physical features. With faces blackened beyond recognition, bodies enlarged with full-length aprons and majestic wigs, and skin glistening beneath a film of oil, natural features are disguised. It is posture, movement, and assurance—what might be

described as aura or charisma—that are judged. A good aura signals physical
health, inner worth, and social effectiveness (see also A. Strathern 1975; Biersack
1982) and is believed to have a direct impact on the generosity and cooperation
of others. Through participation in the Sangai, all young men are given the
chance to develop such an aura and the qualities underlying it.

What Isingi and others clarified later is that half of the Sangai *penge*, the
bamboo containers with sacred fluid, were female, for the spirit woman, and the
other half male, for the bachelors. Female and male containers were buried in
discrete clusters linked by a single male-female pair as described in the preceding
myth (see also Kelly n.d. as cited in Lacey 1975:214). This arrangement expresses
the paradox in Enga life of the necessary separation and opposition of male and
female for the fraternity of men who jointly defend land, among other things,
and yet the fundamental interdependency of the sexes for production, exchange,
and reproduction. Each is legitimated in the cosmological scheme through the
Sangai, and each is given its proper time and place.[22]

Isingi went on to explain that when approaching the female containers, the
bachelors act out the duties of marriage, bringing bespelled *lioko* leaves (*Evodia*
sp.) and placing them in the containers, just as a married Enga man brings *lioko*
leaves to his wife on the fifth day of her menstrual period. If her period is over,
she chews them and spits them out, marking the end of menstrual prohibitions.
The spirit woman does likewise:

The men [senior bachelors] said magic spells over the *lioko* leaves and put them in the
containers of sacred fluid [*penge*]. Later, if they found foam where they had left the
leaves, this was taken as an indication that she [the spirit woman] had accepted them,
chewed them, and spat them out just as human wives do. This was also a sign that it
was safe to approach the *penge* and the *lepe* plant—that the woman had promised to
help them.[23] So all attempts were made to stay well away from [human] women before
marriage. You see, the *lepe* plants and *penge* were not bad things at all.

When a senior bachelor wanted to marry, in order for the *lepe* and *penge* to stay
healthy he had to teach a younger bachelor the procedures involved in looking after
them. When he got married, he paid bridewealth with items such as pigs, stone axes,
kina shells, woven shell headbands, and brown cassowary plume headdresses. If the
proper measures were taken, a long and enduring positive association with the *lepe*
plant and *penge* was secured for the other young men. The *lepe* and *penge* would not be
affected in any way.[24]

Gray (1973) collected a very similar origin myth from the Lyaini Wapane
Menge clan of Laiagam. Its opening is fascinating because, like all other Sangai
origin myths from central Enga (though not those from Porgera), it implies the
existence of former smaller-scale bachelors' rites in which young men went to

the bush and performed rites to promote growth. It begins: "Long ago, when the founding father of the clan, Waepan [Wapane], was still alive, even then men had the ritual known as Sanggai but of a very inferior form, which did little to help boys in their struggle to grow into men" (Gray 1973:108).[25]

The myth then goes on to tell of Wapane's son, who is left behind and so decides to hold growth rites by himself. He goes to the bush, cleanses himself, builds a small lean-to, and falls asleep at dark. The next morning, a beautiful woman appears outside his hut and offers him pandanus. She then takes some nuts, lines them up on her outstretched leg, and asks him to eat them off her leg without using his hands. He does so and, overcome with desire, makes love to her. In the morning he finds himself transformed into a mature, handsome man. She dresses him magnificently, changes his name to Italikali ("real man"), and sends him home.

The other young men marvel at his transformation and ask him to reveal his secret. He tells them what to do and they follow his instructions, but when she tries to seduce them they are outraged, kill her, cut her into bits, and depart, leaving her corpse to rot. Italikali seeks and finds her dismembered body and weeps bitterly over it. Her spirit appears, instructing him to cut off her breasts and bury them. The sacred *lepe* plant for the Sangai grows out of the earth where the breasts were buried.

Another Sangai origin myth that we collected lays out similar themes, although transmitted through a very different plot. It was narrated at Laiagam by Makia Kupini of the Tia Waneposa clan (a brother clan of Lyaini, where Gray collected the foregoing tradition). We purposely selected it because it differs so greatly from Isingi's myth while transmitting the similar core messages. The following is a summary.

A young man who lives alone in his men's house goes to perform bachelors' rites. Along the way he comes to a cliff, starts to climb, and sights a *kepa* opossum. He shoots it, loses his balance, and falls into a lake to emerge transformed. He sees an exquisitely beautiful *lepe* plant by the lake and thinks that it is this plant that transformed him. Then he looks across the lake and sees a perfect men's house, goes there, and finds that the sweet potatoes he had brought with him are mysteriously steamed together with marsupial meat and bush foods. He sleeps in the house and the next morning finds magnificent ceremonial attire prepared for him. He puts it on, walks out in the courtyard, and finds himself at home.

Some days later while he is out hunting, his dog barks at a woman up a tree who is collecting bark fibers. He convinces her that she is the woman he has been looking for his whole life and brings her home. She tries to seduce him but he protests that he has just returned from bachelors' rites and must go once again. He tells her that he has procured a *lepe* plant called "Pulukulu-Yungula Alualu-Kutepa" that he will keep for his descendants, and that if they make love, it might die.

She replies, "This 'man' you are talking about, 'Pulukulu-Yungula Alualu-Kutepa,' is it your father's Sangai plant? Alualu-Kutepa, is it your father's Sangai plant? Woman, Mama's sweet potato leaves Mambeamo transformed you. Woman, Mama's house-front-*kunai*-grass tops, Mambeamo, transformed you. Today we must make love. Where is your Sangai plant from? Your transformation was possible with my [female] Sangai plant, not yours [male plant]. Was that pearl shell yours? The aprons and all the other attire, were they yours? I decorated you so that you could marry me." And she won.

The last passage requires explanation. Pulukulu-Yungula and Alualu-Kutepa refer to male plants from a previous form of bachelors' cult. *Lepe* plants in Enga symbolism can represent a variety of mythical characters, and thus when the woman asks, "This 'man' you are talking about, 'Pulukulu-Yungula Alualu-Kutepa,' is it your father's Sangai plant?" she is implying that his plants, derived from men, have not succeeded in transforming him. Mambeamo refers to the *lepe* plant that represents her, which he found when climbing out of the lake. She makes it clear that her female plant brought about his transformation. Thus, both myths describe the addition of a female principle to former bachelors' rites and explain the origin of sacred objects representing the spirit woman. The themes of seduction and symbolic marriage to the spirit woman, complementarity of the sexes, transformation, and, with transformation, potential equality for all men enter into most Sangai, Huli Ibagiya, and Ipili Umaritsia origin myths, regardless of local area or linguistic group. They define its core principles, even though the plots of the myths and the styles and emphases of the narrators differ.

Transformation: New Directions

With the introduction of the Sangai cult, whether from without or within Enga, the concept of transformation via marriage to the spirit woman, the communally owned sacred objects that represented her, and the senior custodians who procured them, cared for them, and initiated bachelors into their secrets were added to former smaller-scale rites of growth for boys. The Sangai's age-based hierarchy offered new potential for the education of young men, and very importantly, the concept of transformation offered leaders much leeway for defining the ideal end product within the context of their aspirations and the clan's position in time and space. In the hands of clan leaders, the Sangai was thus a powerful tool for setting new directions.

Among the Ipili, transformation appears to have remained directed largely at physical growth (and something more), as Aletta Biersack writes (1982:253-54):

Physical growth affects the fatty underlayer of the skin, the "inner" rather than the "outer" skin. But there is a kind of *social* growth the Paiela recognise. This pertains to a person's face, his or her renown. . . . Social (and not purely physical) stature rests on a variety of things: how many houses and gardens, how many pigs, how many wives and children a man has. . . .

Houses, gardens, pigs and children are the products of the adult conjugal relationship and not of the adolescent conjugal relationship. Now, all of these assets that augment a man's renown and make him "big" in the social sense are said to "come to his skin." . . . But, then, it is a man's outer skin that is the particular transactional product of adult conjugality. The ritual's competence pertains to the *inner* skin instead, which is the sole transactional product of adolescent conjugality.

Biersack does not say so explicitly, but she implies that the adolescent conjugal relationship—that is, the marriage of the bachelors to the spirit woman—is indeed believed to confer something more than mere physical growth: the potential to develop the "outer" skin. This point is clarified by Gibbs (1975:90-1):

Not only does the *Umaritsia* ritual act as magic to enhance a young man's personal appearance and growth, but it is also a form of wealth magic. In the myth the woman not only helped Kaunala Tape and Kimale to grow. She gave them pigs and pearlshells. There is a close association between personal appearance and possessions. The *Umaritsia* rites help a man become rich and successful.

True wealth magic, however, called *takia* or *take,* was performed apart from the Umaritsia, the Ipili bachelors' cult, on an individual basis during instruction sessions for small groups of young men.

Comparison of poetry for the sacred objects (*sangai titi pingi*) of different areas gives some insight into directions added to fit bachelors' cults to the needs of the time and social landscape. Take for example, the *sangai titi pingi* of Yomondaka,[26] an Enga clan of Tipinini and Karekare who live at the periphery of major exchange networks but are nonetheless important middlemen in the trade. The major portion of the poem gives the history of the sacred objects and cites their effects on each body part. It does not stop there, however, but goes on to call young men of clans in central, eastern, and southern Enga to come to the Sangai, giving the bachelors the sense that they belong to a broader society.[27] Like the Ipili praise poems for the sacred objects, that from Yomondaka does not pertain directly to wealth acquisition, although rites to attract wealth (*take*) were included in the Sangai.

For central Enga, in contrast, poetry for the sacred objects concentrates heavily on what Ipili describe as the "outer skin" in the passage quoted earlier—the ability to manage wealth and attain renown. This trend can be traced back through some poems from central Enga as far as the fourth to fifth generation, a time of intense competition in central Enga as leaders tried to channel or absorb some of the mounting tension via ritualized warfare and massive exchange in the Great Ceremonial Wars. The values for emulation laid down in this poetry go beyond physical growth, encouraging hard work in agriculture, development of mental capacities, and the achievement of name through the distribution of wealth.

Appendix 9 gives as an example the *sangai titi pingi* from the Potealini Anae Taanda subclan of Tiakamanda (Kundis) in the middle Ambum valley. It traces the history of the sacred objects as they were transferred from clan to clan and pays tribute to their power to physically transform young men. These points are characteristic of most poems for the sacred objects. This poem goes one step further, however, to include a roll call of the big-men (*kamongo*) of the area whom the sacred objects had transformed in the past (within both the clan and surrounding ones) accompanied by a formalized description of their accomplishments. The most successful in the area were thus put forward as models for emulation—as, for example, in verse eleven, which describes the transformation of Ameane, the senior bachelor who acquired the sacred objects for his subclan:

> Ameane's physical and mental capabilities were always there,
> His influence and renown were always there,
> People keep saying the long horizontally laid fencing is Ameane's,
> People keep saying the long picket fencing is also Ameane's,
> The long-leafed pandanus palm is also Ameane's,
> The sweet potato garden ready to harvest is also Ameane's,
> What makes Ameane as popular as he is?
> That huge, untamed, and slit-eared pig is also Ameane's,
> He keeps saying that he has been alone at a funeral feast,
> He keeps saying that he has been a major force in organizing the distribution
>   of live pigs and butchered pork,
> What makes Ameane as renowned as he is?

The meaning of this verse, which details Ameane's accomplishments, is generally clear. Note that importance is placed on agricultural production as well as exchange. Slitting the ear of a pig (line 8) designates it for ceremonial exchange, usually war reparations. Line 9 implies that Ameane was wealthy enough to host a funeral feast alone.

The Potealini poem for the sacred objects thus looks back into history with great pomp and glory to set a course for the bachelors: emulation of the leaders of the past and achievement of success parallel to that of the best who went before them.[28] Success is gauged in terms of self-presentation on ceremonial occasions, agricultural production, intellect, and managing wealth in Tee exchange — but interestingly, not in terms of skill in warfare. Other examples from central Enga, such as that from the Kombane clan in the Ambum valley,[29] elaborate on the Enga concept of a wealthy, influential man as one who not only produces and receives prolifically but also gives generously. One verse tells of two men going to a Tee festival where the power and teachings of the Sangai are fulfilled. They receive large quantities of wealth from a network extending south to Kandep and west to Porgera, given with "open heart and sincere words." They eat their fill but then return home to give what they received without keeping a scrap for themselves. Here, as in the Potealini poetry, the ideal is framed in more than just physical appearance and details of dress but also in terms of pig production, mental capabilities, and success in exchange (see Lacey 1975:199 for a similar example). All of these were important skills in the context of the Great Ceremonial Wars.

The foregoing provide but a few examples of how the concept of transformation was tuned to the needs of time and place. Note that this was done by addition and not by substitution: although young men of central Enga were challenged to emulate big-men and excel in production and exchange, verses giving the history of the sacred objects and their effects on physical transformation were not eliminated.

Diffusion of the Sangai: The Transactions

Following the Enga tenet that success comes from distribution, the sacred objects were widely exchanged. We do not know the prices paid in earlier times, but around the third to fourth generation, payments were similar in composition and amount to those of bridewealth. There are suggestions in Sangai oral traditions that the purchasing of *lepe* plants and sacred fluid was seen as paying symbolic bridewealth for the spirit woman.

Plans were made to purchase the *lepe* plant and sacred fluid when a clan or subclan wanted to adopt the cult for the first time, when the *lepe* plant and sacred fluid that they already owned had dried up because of inappropriate sexual behavior on the part of the bachelors, or when they were judged to be less effective than those of other clans. The purchase was a clan or subclan affair, and so all interested clansmen met to discuss the economic and political statuses of surrounding clans. On the assumption that the Sangai contributed to a group's success, they decided which clan to approach. They considered criteria such as appearance of the owners in a dance, whether the clan's bachelors were well built, its success in production, exchange, and defense of clan land, and whether the clan had some young men of prominence (*kamongo*). The clans or subclans chosen were often neighboring ones, but not always, for long journeys to obtain sacred objects are described in some Sangai traditions. Sacred objects could even be purchased from enemy clans, but the price was high.

When the arrangements had been made, senior bachelors took a secret journey via obscure forest paths to the clan of the owners, bringing with them pigs, axes, oil, shells, or other valuables for the purchase. This wealth was contributed by the bachelors and other clan members. There they either attended a Sangai performance of the owners to learn the rites and spells or asked the senior bachelors of the owners' clan to come and teach during one of their, the purchasers', performances. The owners seem not to have been reluctant to sell cuttings of their *lepe* plants, portions of their sacred fluid, and accompanying spells if the purchasers and price were right. Exchange neither reduced the strength of the "parent" objects nor necessarily conferred the secret to success on another group—that a human element was involved was clearly recognized. The sacred objects would be ineffective unless treated properly in the hands of disciplined and capable bachelors.

When the transaction was complete, the *lepe* plant and sacred fluid were brought back under the cover of night to shield them from the view of women and married men who had sexual relations with women. The transaction was a one-time deal that remained secret and involved no further financial or ritual dealings between buyer and seller. Nonetheless, sharing the same sacred objects, knowledge, and prescriptions created a sense of common heritage that facilitated other interactions. This fact constituted part of the logic behind the "trade" of cults. The recipient bachelors slaughtered the pig and distributed the pork to all bachelors or, in some cases, to all households in the clan or subclan. The valuables received in payment for the sacred objects were put in the custody of one of the senior bachelors and lent out to others to wear or use when need arose.

Some clans or subclans of Enga purchased *lepe* plants, others sacred fluid, and many both.[30] A few clans claim independent discovery of Sangai *lepe* plants. The sacred fluid in bamboo containers was most common among eastern clans who held the Sandalu cult and in some areas of central Enga. Most of these had both *lepe* plants and sacred fluid, as did Porgera clans and some clans in the Lagaip and Kandep. Possession of the *lepe* alone was more prevalent in the Lagaip. Both *lepe* plants and sacred fluid were used in Huli bachelor cults and in the Ipili Umaritsia. The choice of sacred objects thus appears to have been a matter of clan preference, though it is fair to say that the *lepe* plant, used in a variety of

Enga private rituals, represents a more conservative choice than the sacred fluid, which was believed to contain female blood. In Enga (though not among the Ipili), possession of *lepe* plants alone is more often associated with clans who hold stronger pollution beliefs, but notable exceptions do occur.[31]

The Westward Spread of the Sangai

The diffusion of the Sangai cult from the Mai-Yandapo area to western tribes "long ago" (that is, within the span of historical traditions but before approximately the fifth generation) is remembered in the oral traditions of some Lagaip clans up to Mulitaka (map 13:1-5). For Enga clans between Mulitaka and the Porgera valley we found no true origin traditions for the Sangai cult itself or poems tracing it to the Mai-Yandapo Enga or the Ipili. Poems for the sacred objects telling how the objects were purchased from other clans are not prevalent in this area; the majority of Sangai cults there own offshoots of a *lepe* plant that was discovered and exported widely by the Pumane Kelyanyo clan near Tumundan.

The account of Pumane's discovery is particularly interesting when told together with two other historical traditions that put it into context. The first concerns Pumane Kelyanyo's first large ceremonial pig kill (*mena yae*) in the sixth generation, hosted by Kupa and Kandalu, "grandsons" of the tribal founder. It describes how new public wealth distribution was for them and how awkwardly they handled it. The second is a short account of how Topepione, a Pumane clansman of the fifth generation, discovered a *lepe* plant for attracting wealth and, thinking it was a Sangai *lepe*, planted it near the Sangai cult house to bring "wealth magic" into the Sangai. The third, also from the fifth generation, tells of Kupa's son's discovering *take*, or wealth magic, on his way to the Sangai.[32] The last narrative may reflect a transition in the subsistence base of the Pumane tribe from emphasis on hunting to horticulture: Lelya climbs the pandanus tree, killing one opossum, then two more, and finally finding the pig rope at the top, a charm for attracting wealth based on agricultural production. The planting of the *lepe* to attract wealth, together with the other Sangai *lepe*, indicates the growing importance of ceremonial exchange and the incorporation into the Sangai of magic to attract wealth.

As news of the Kelyanyo clan's discovery and success spread, others sought to purchase their secret. Virtually all clans that we interviewed in the Tumundan and Mulitaka area, as well as some clans of the Porgera valley, claimed to have acquired cuttings of the sacred *lepe* plant and spells from Pumane (map 13:10-11). Lacey's studies (1975:220) also record the trade of Topepione's *lepe* plants eastward through Mulapini at Yoko to Monaini Kipula near Mulitaka. Why Pumane was so successful is not known—elders give explanations to the effect that they happened to have a number of clever, innovative men at that time.[33] From that time on, the Sangai cults of the Tayato Enga and Ipili were oriented toward the management of wealth as well as toward physical transformation.

The Sangai in Eastern Enga

Although bachelors' cults flourished throughout central Enga and had spread to most parts of western Enga by the fifth generation, they seem to have caught the interest of few Layapo-Saka clans in the east. There, the *sauipu* was practiced to promote the growth of boys, and magic to acquire skill in warfare or attract wealth could be purchased from experts.[34] The Sangai was adopted only by a very few clans of eastern Enga in the fifth to sixth generation, those who were focal clans in the early Tee cycle. For instance, the Apulini Talyulu clan has an oral tradition telling how it obtained Sangai *lepe* plants from the Sambe Pupu clan at Papyuka near Laiagam in the sixth generation via a spirit woman (map 13:12). Farther down the Tee and trade route, the Yambatane Yana clan of the Saka valley (map 13:13) purchased containers of sacred fluid from the Monaini at Kasap (Lagaip) through the Sakalini Kalopea clan near the salt springs in the fifth to sixth generation (Lacey 1975:218). The Yambatane Yandamau clan also claims to have procured its bachelors' cult items from the Mai of central Enga around the same time, and soon afterward sold them to the Waimini Nene subclan. Interestingly, however, the Yanuni Kasimu clan of Tambul at the eastern terminus of the Tee route did not acquire the Sandalu cult until the third generation. We encountered no other Layapo Enga clans outside of Yambatane and Waimini clans in the Saka valley who claimed to have adopted the Sangai by the fifth generation.[35]

We can make some suggestions as to why the Sangai made few inroads into Layapo clans prior to the third to fourth generation. The Sangai of earlier periods was a secret, private cult that lacked the widespread appeal it assumed later, when public emergence festivals were added. Because of its secretiveness, it may simply have failed to catch the interest of the Layapo. Additionally, with relations between the sexes more relaxed among the Layapo, the Sangai may have seemed "foreign" and potentially disruptive to exchange networks based on female links. Ambone Mati, whose clan in central Enga joined the Tee cycle in the third to fourth generation, elaborated at some length on lessons learned from clans to the east regarding attitudes toward women and Tee exchange:[36]

My mother gave birth to five sons. They all grew up to be men; three married and two didn't. They were afraid of a woman's vagina. They were told that if they did marry they would become poor, for a woman's vagina was a fire that would burn out the strength of a man, so that they would never possess masculinity, the pride of men. They believed these things and did not marry. I was told these things too.

People in the east had a different view on the matter. The older generation told their young men that woman was the source of life, that women created man. It was said in those parts [the east] that it is a woman who keeps the house warm, breeds the pigs, and looks after the children. Men in the east looked after and protected women. (Ambone Mati, Itapuni Nemani clan, Kopena [Wabag])

Ambone then went on to give examples of how women facilitate Tee relations, why it is necessary to consider women's friends and relatives in distributing meat at a feast, and how women can be sensitive to the feelings of others, helping their husbands make decisions concerning the distribution of food and wealth. He then discussed marriage in clans that, unlike his clan, had long been involved in the Tee cycle:

The Yanaitini Kia clan [the pivotal clan at the western terminus of the Tee cycle] was very wise and thoughtful about women. When a person from Kia married a woman, he took care of her. For example, Pupanga, a big-man from the Kia clan, married many wives and had children with these women. He told his servants to build houses for them and attend to their needs. His male servants had to build houses, make gardens, and do all sorts of things that contributed to the well-being of his wives and children. Pupanga also told his sisters to bring their children to Tetemanda. This sort of family structure was designed by the Kia clan.[37]

I also heard some words of wisdom from Pangali, the well-known leader of the Timali clan. He said to me, "Ambone of the Nemani clan, at Lenge I have many wives. You are a man who has one wife only. Whenever there was to be a feast at Lenge, I would tell each of my wives to kill a pig at her house and steam it. If possible each wife should kill and steam more than one pig, depending on how many friends and relatives would come. I would tell each one that the pork was for her only, and that she could cut it into pieces and give them away to anybody that she felt she should give it to, particularly her relatives. I would tell the same thing to all of my wives; then I would kill and steam a pig for myself. On the afternoon when the feast was to be held, I gathered all the people of my household so that we could meet and go to the ceremonial grounds together. All of my wives and their supporters would come carrying pork, and I would lead them to the ceremonial grounds. As our procession arrived, people did not look at my wives. They looked at me and how many pigs I had killed for the feast. In this way I gained prestige and became famous. What I am trying to tell you is this: women do all the work and you have to depend heavily on women to prosper."

This man from Lenge did something that not everybody had the nerve to do. He married many wives who helped him look after pigs, among many other things. With the help of his wives, he became a wealthy man. The poor men from the Itapuni clans suffered, having lost sight of the value of women. Pangali of the Yakani tribe saw the value of women and made use of it.

Ambone's remarks recall the Tia Sangai origin legend: the bachelor refuses the spirit woman on the grounds that he has more bachelors' rites to perform, but she convinces him to marry her immediately because it is only through relations with women that men become truly transformed. The Sangai can easily be understood from the outside as a cult concerned primarily with contamination and purification, and so it is possible that Layapo Enga interpreted it as a cult that might complicate relations between the sexes and, with them, the paths to prosperity.

Layapo interest in the Sangai increased in the fourth generation, a time of great change as the Tee cycle and Great Ceremonial Wars became coordinated. Both exchange networks boomed, resulting in the intensification of pig production, ever-thickening politics, and denser ties between east and west. In association with these events, a number of clans involved in coordinating the two systems imported the Sangai. It had much to offer during this period of complex politics. First, as mentioned earlier, it gave the older generation more power to steer the younger one. Second, it strengthened bonds of brotherhood and, with them, the potential for growing clans to reach consensus in matters concerning warfare, ritual, or exchange. Finally, though some of the cult's beliefs concerning relations between the sexes were problematic for the Layapo, it standardized the road to marriage between east and center, facilitating the intermarriages pivotal for coordination of the Tee cycle and Great Ceremonial Wars.

The beginning of the eastward spread of the Sangai is widely documented in the histories of Layapo clans. Lacey (1975:217-20), who conducted more than one hundred interviews on the Sangai-Sandalu, gives some interesting examples of the initial acquisition of the Sandalu by Layapo groups near the Mai border. In one case (map 13:14), the Lyipini Wiokini clan of the middle Lai valley acquired its Sangai from the Apulini Sikita Netuli subclan near Wabag in the fourth generation after Wiokini men attended a traditional dance held by the Netuli and were impressed by their performance (Lacey 1975:219). The Netuli had obtained *lepe* plants from the Itapuni Nemani clan near Wabag. The Depe Lyalakini clan of the middle Lai and Aiyele valleys then bought the Sangai from Wiokini. In another instance (map 13:15), the Yakani Waimalae clan in the third to fourth generation obtained *lepe* plants from the Yakani Timali at Lenge; it then sold them to the Lyipini Kepeo clan during the third generation. The Timali clan claimed to have obtained *lepe* from the Yanaitini Kalepatae clan in the Ambum valley. All the clans mentioned were heavily involved in the Tee cycle.

Emergence Festivals

It was during the fourth generation, a time of great flourishing of ceremonial exchange, that the secrecy of the Sangai was inverted by two additions in central Enga. The one was public emergence festivals during which the bachelors left the cult house in a formal parade, proceeding to the ceremonial grounds majestically and in full ceremonial dress to present the predictions derived from dreams in a public dance. These performances held political import, drawing spectators from many surrounding clans who wished to evaluate the strength of the upcoming generation and to glean information and hints of political intentions from the predictions. Although emergence festivals structurally transformed the Sangai by juxtaposing the private and the public, they were but a logical progression of the Sangai: the formal presentation of the results of cult activities. The other addition was the performance of love magic by the older bachelors in the cult house to attract girlfriends the night before the emergence ceremony. Meanwhile, young women visited the parents of boyfriends, who gave them food. On the morning of the bachelors' emergence, young women made visits to the outer gate of the bachelors' cult house to express interest in particular young men. Favored women were received cordially but briefly and asked to go home relaying a request that certain items of dress be sent for the emergence festival.

These two developments appealed to different segments of society. Ordinary clan members could reassert equality at a time when the Great Ceremonial Wars and Tee cycle had consolidated considerable power in the hands of a few key families: every young man was given a public debut and stood a chance to make a name for himself regardless of family background. Courtship and love magic, formalized though they were, brought marriage and adulthood within reach, allowing the bachelors to express marriage preferences within a community of peers. Bachelors who completed the Sangai would be assisted financially by clan members in procuring a bride. Last but not least, public events provided big-men with occasions to demonstrate the strength of the upcoming generation and assemble a "captive audience" to plan *tee* exchanges.

Enhanced by emergence festivals, the Sangai's eastward diffusion accelerated in the third generation to reach all the Layapo clans, who called the cult by the term *Sandalu*. Though Sandalu rites were similar to those of the Sangai proper, some outstanding differences did exist (see also Lacey 1975:204). Sandalu cult houses were more elaborate and less secluded than the forest huts of the Sangai. The recitation of poems for the sacred objects was either omitted or greatly abbreviated,[38] and origin traditions were transmitted rarely, if at all. The concept of marriage to a spirit woman thus faded, and with it, some of the original meaning of the rites. Emergence festivals became closely tied to the planning of the Tee cycle, and accordingly, dream interpretation, so relevant to political events, received great attention. Despite these changes, fundamental themes persisted: the potential equality of male clansmen and the paradox of the separation of the sexes and their essential interdependence, each with its own time and place.

The diffusion of the Sangai in the third to fourth generation followed a number of routes shown on map 13 (16-20).[39] It reached easternmost Enga by the second to third generation. Kepa Pupu of the Yoponda clan in the upper Minamb valley (which borders on the Kola area) mentioned briefly that the Sandalu had come to his area within his lifetime, bringing with it new ideas concerning relations between the sexes. Prior to that time, eastern Layapo Enga had held beliefs concerning menstrual contamination and had observed related taboos but were unfamiliar with ideas concerning the dangers of contamination from sexual intercourse and accompanying protective magic (see also Meggitt 1964a:221n16). According to Kepa:

The Sandalu came from that part of the area [central Enga]; it must have come from the Kala, Aipiyape, Yakale, and Kayalu clans [near Wabag]. Women [of central Enga] in those days were told to live in separate quarters. The men, old and young, lived in separate houses, and even after a man married a woman he would stay away from his wife for some time. . . . In the Kola and Timbai areas [of Western Highlands Province], men and woman slept together; there were no strict taboos. Then the influence of the Sandalu reached the Saka valley and eventually came to my area. That happened in my lifetime. (Kepa Pupu, Yoponda Ipupa clan, Walia)

Interestingly, the few clans of the Saka valley who had acquired the Sangai in the fifth to sixth generation also purchased the Sandalu in the third, holding both Sangai and Sandalu rituals well into the colonial period and recognizing a distinction between the two.[40] Though rites were similar, the Sangai was performed primarily for physical growth and dream interpretation in houses far removed from settlements, with no emergence festivals and no link to the Tee cycle. The Sandalu was held nearer to settlements and had elaborate emergence festivals that gathered people to discuss the Tee.

The pattern for the Kompiam area, as depicted in the sketchy information that we obtained, shows a similar diffusion of Sangai-Sandalu from central Enga to the north and east. Clans north of the Sau river, who had been driven out of the Ambum valley in the sixth to seventh generation, obtained the sacred objects from central Enga shortly after they settled in their new areas (map 13:21-23). They added to them exotic species of *lepe* plants from the low country, becoming known as masters in Sangai lore. Their performances were without emergence festivals until the onset of the colonial period. Clans south of the Sau river who had originated in the Lai and Saka valleys obtained the Sandalu along pathways similar to those by which it had reached the Layapo of the central valleys, and at around the same time.

The Sandalu and the Tee Cycle

Once established in eastern Enga, Sandalu performances were increasingly used by big-men for gathering people to plan upcoming events of broader political significance such as the Tee cycle (see also Waddell 1972; Schwab 1995):[41]

There were times when we were not sure at what time the Tee cycle would come to our area, or when we were expecting it to arrive in a month or so. At these times the elders who were eager to discuss plans for the Tee told the bachelors to go for the Sandalu. (Iki Pilisa, Yandamani, Yalesa)

Sometimes the reason for holding a Sandalu is associated with fighting, because the dreams can tell us who, where, and how to kill. However, it was also held to gather a large crowd to talk about the Tee cycle. (Lupa Yanda, Yandamani Yokoenda clan, Pompabus)

And that [the Sandalu] was done for the purpose of holding meetings in relation to the Tee cycle. The Tee leaders of the clan who put on the Sandalu monitored the meeting, listening to the debates of the great Tee leaders who had gathered on the ceremonial grounds. (Lopao, Sikini Lyonai clan, Lauwanda, Aiyele valley–middle Lai)

The reason that we were sent for the Sandalu was so that they [the older men] could assemble people to discuss the Tee. Men gathered on our ceremonial grounds and discussed the upcoming Tee cycle while we were in seclusion. When we emerged, we presented ourselves to the public and traveled for the next four to five days to the ceremonial grounds of Waimini, Itokone, Waiminakuni, and others to sing songs asking for the Tee to begin. (Pakea Yakani, Yakumane Waetesa clan, Wapenamanda)

In central Enga as well, the political advantages of emergence festivals as optimal occasions for political oratory did not go unexploited, to the lament of the bachelors, who felt that their elders stole the show (Meggitt 1964a). Eventually, the political value of emergence festival was appreciated in the west, and within the lifetimes of elders interviewed at Mulitaka, Tumundan, and Tipinini

they were included in the Sangai performances of most but not all clans of the
Lagaip and Porgera valleys.

Enda Akoko Nyingi: Female Courtship at Emergence Festivals

Many of the ideas regarding relations between the sexes exported with the Sangai
were antithetical to the relaxed attitudes of eastern Enga and the relatively
independent stance of Layapo women. A few Layapo women, though very few,
even participated in the Tee on their own behalf and reached the status of Tee
organizers and big-men (*kamongo*) (Kyakas and Wiessner 1992). Apparently, such
women were not content with the attitudes instilled during the Sangai, for they
took advantage of a spontaneous incident to introduce a tradition of direct and
rowdy courtship that reversed the traditional roles of men and women.

It began around 1910-20 at an emergence festival near Pompabus (map 13)
when two Layapo women, Pyasowana of the Kaekini clan and Luatae of
Waiminakuni, overcome by jealousy, pulled an Itokone man named Tuingi out
of the dance line and fought ferociously over him. Poor Tuingi was obliged to
marry both. The news spread fast, other Layapo women followed suit, and before
long there was born a new tradition of women's disruptive courtship during
emergence festivals called *enda akoko nyingi*. In it, young women attending emergence *sing-sings* courteously respected the performance—up to a point. When
they felt that the bachelors had had sufficient time to present themselves and
their dreams in song, they rushed forward, shattering the sanctity of the dance,
dragging their boyfriends out of the line, stripping them of some of their
finery—and sometimes far more (which the young men were to reclaim privately
at a later date, if interested)—encircling them with a group of supportive
girlfriends, and singing bawdy songs. Popular themes included expressions of
pride that the boyfriends had attended the Sandalu, followed by verses pointing
out that the Sandalu or Sangai was just a formality, for they had slept together
long before the bachelors went into seclusion (Meggitt 1964a; Kyakas and Wiessner 1992). Young men thrived on the attention of their suitors, elders frowned
on such unruly protest action, and the crowds were enthralled. Recognizing its
potential to draw great throngs, clan leaders, who could have put an end to the
scene, accepted it with grudging tolerance.

The *enda akoko nyingi* entertained, and so its popularity grew rapidly. Intrepid
women of central and western Enga initiated it in their own clans, removing
barriers between the sexes. Even today the names of these women are recalled.
To give one example, the *enda akoko nyingi* in the middle Ambum valley is said

to have been started by Nongome of the Piao Kumbini clan and Laleme of the
Piao Maipilai clan in roughly the 1920s. The songs that Nongome sang are
remembered, including this one:

> Aipiawane Lumbuwanakini, liakapapu tipisaka setao palenge
> Kalepyala pato lapiasa maokalo.

> Lyumbuwana from Aipinimanda, I make love to her son at the back of the
> house,
> I released him to attend the Sangai.

Wohlt (1978) reported that the *enda akoko nyingi* became part of the Sangai of
the Bipi Kapii clan at Yumbis (Karekare) in northern Kandep in the 1960s. Men
of the Lagaip and Porgera valleys who are in their sixties today say that it was
first practiced when they were bachelors, giving a date similar to Wohlt's for its
acceptance in the west. The work of Gibbs (1975) in the Porgera valley, however,
and testimonies that we collected from some clans of northern Kompiam indicate that emergence festivals interrupted by women's courtship were not accepted in all areas.

As human women assumed a greater role in the Sangai, the spirit woman
withdrew, and only fragments of the original concept remained in Sandalu lore
of eastern clans. For example, Schwab (1995:27), drawing on interviews conducted in the 1950s and 1960s in clans of the middle Lai (Waiminakuni, Itokone,
and Sikini), cites a number of vague statements by elders that the Sangai had
originated from a woman. He also quotes part of a magic formula (*nemongo*) that
he considers "unusual" only because he was unfamiliar with the Sangai origin
myth, as were his informants, who could not explain the meaning of the formula
to Schwab. It refers back to the instructions given by the spirit woman in the
origin myth to cut the bamboo (container) evenly: "Not this knife but the one
from 'heaven' is cutting [the bamboo]. You spotless, powerful woman [above the
clouds] told me how to cut it evenly. As mouth and lips and nose say it now: I
cut it."[42] Similarly, the concept of marriage to a spirit woman remains in a
fragment of a formula used in a Waiminakuni Sandalu performance recorded by
Schwab (1995:40).

The establishment of the *enda akoko nyingi* thus came about through processes
quite different from other developments in the Sangai—through the spontaneous
protest action of women. It had unintended consequences in its western rebound
by relaxing relations between the sexes and thereby facilitating interregional
marriage just as the Tee cycle began to supplant the Great Ceremonial Wars and
as the economies of eastern and central Enga became inextricably tied to one
another. Although the intrusion of courtship into the Sangai-Sandalu seemed

inappropriate to older men, it did not alter the original meaning of the Sangai as radically as it appeared to. The fundamental idea that in the bachelors' cults all young men would be transformed into handsome, socially competent equals through complementary relations with women remained. The major alteration was that the "first" marriage with the spirit woman was retracted and the "second" marriage with human women brought to the fore — and appropriately so, in the face of the economic developments taking place.

Summary

The origins and history of the Sangai cult are complex, and many questions about them will certainly never be answered.[43] Although investigations into Sangai origins yield little more than general suggestions about the areas and time periods in which it arose, the wealth of information from later generations clarifies its role in Enga history — one that differs considerably from the roles posited in other analyses (Meggitt 1964a; Schwab 1995). The Sangai-Sandalu was used as a forum in which to instill new ideas, values, and goals in the upcoming generation, thereby steering the course of change. Sacred objects and accompanying incantations were purchased in the hope of setting new directions and improving clan fortunes. They were sold following the logic that distribution leads to prosperity. In this respect, the Sangai-Sandalu was quite successful, for it homogenized ideas on relations between the sexes in eastern, western, and central Enga, facilitating the expansion of exchange networks based on marriage ties. In most cases it was clan leaders — that is, senior bachelors and big-men — who manipulated the cult to meet the needs of time and place, though they were not the sole authors of change; in the case of the *enda akoko nyingi,* women did the job.

The consequences of innovation and transfer in the bachelors' cults, whether intended or unintended, were that within the span of historical traditions they underwent structural alterations that closely corresponded to the developments they mediated. The first set of alterations was the incorporation of a female principle into bachelors' cults through marriage to the spirit woman, the institution of an age hierarchy with senior bachelors on top, and prescription of a standard and safe road to marriage. These innovations were initiated or adopted at a time when people of central Enga were changing subsistence and settlement patterns, reorganizing for larger-scale military campaigns, and attempting to devise new ways to absorb mounting competition within and between groups through ceremonial exchange. Then, during the third to fourth generation, in conjunction with the complex politics involved in coordinating the Great Ceremonial Wars with the Tee cycle, a public emergence phase was added, modifying the strictly private nature of the cult. This turned the Sangai into an occasion that drew crowds to discuss a wide range of other events, including the Tee cycle. Finally, just prior to contact, when the Tee cycle subsumed the Great Ceremonial Wars and the economies of eastern and central Enga become fused, principles of separation of the sexes were reversed by assertive courtship during the *enda akoko nyingi.*

The bachelors' cults, like the bachelors themselves, were thus transformed. Despite these changes, the development of the Sangai was guided throughout by certain principles that remained constant. The association of outward appearance with inner worth persisted, and at all points in history young men went to the Sangai to become mature, handsome, charismatic men inside and out. Young men who went through the Sangai, whether well off or poor, were guaranteed that fellow clan members would assist them in procuring brides. The Sangai continued to be aimed at resolving the contradiction inherent in Enga society — the periodic separation of the sexes necessary to achieve male solidarity within the clan, on one hand, and fundamental dependency between the sexes for production, reproduction, and the gaining of support from affinal kin, on the other. The latter took on more importance as networks of ceremonial exchange built on marriage ties expanded. The principle of potential equality of all male clan members stood fast and was passed on from generation to generation, even though the Sangai challenged the bachelors to break with it, excel, and follow in the footsteps of the greatest leaders of the past.

9

War Reparations and Leadership

Mena lenge ongo katao londenge,
Endakali yati lenge ongo katao londala naenge.

You live long if you plan the death of a pig,
But not if you plan the death of a person.

While the Tee cycle was expanding in the east, developments were taking place in other forms of ceremonial exchange throughout Enga. One of the most significant of these was the extension of war reparations, formerly given only to allies, to enemies as a means of restoring
peaceful relations and reestablishing the
balance of power in the face of problems
aggravated by a steadily growing population.[1] The place of war reparations both
to allies and to enemies is a central one in
Enga oral history. They were the only
forms of secular exchange in Enga that
were organized by the clan as a whole
outside the sphere of the Tee cycle and
Great Ceremonial Wars.[2] They furnished
incentive and fuel for the growth of the
Tee cycle of eastern Enga and laid the
foundation for the Great Ceremonial
Wars that arose in central Enga. Practiced
by all clans, they were a common denominator of exchange throughout Enga.

Enga concepts of war reparations did not conform closely either to the idea of "blood money" or to the substitution of wealth for human life that prevailed in some other New Guinea highland societies (Modjeska 1982; Lemonnier 1993). Wealth paid in property could not acquit the loss of human life, for a one-time payment could never replace a lifetime of love and labor lost.[3] Unless revenged in a payback murder, the imbalance was carried over into future generations. War reparations were, rather, a means of restoring active communication and exchange so that lives lost could be compensated for on a sustained basis. That is, warm sentiments engendered through renewed exchange mitigated emotional losses; the opening or reopening of relationships of mutual assistance and finance that would continue for years made up for labor lost over the longer term. Even for those less closely attached to the deceased, renewal of ties was of paramount concern, for each armed conflict damaged one of the most valuable assets—relations with in-laws and maternal kin (see also Brown 1964).

If skillfully executed, the process of mediation and paying reparations laid grievances to rest and reactivated pathways of exchange through which peace could be maintained in the future. Or, seen in the perspective presented in chapter 3, the payment of war reparations to enemies marked the end of physical defense of the perimeters of clan land and opened the possibility for social boundary maintenance, a much less costly means of maintaining clan property and rights. Furthermore, as the land filled and dispersal became no longer a desirable option, war reparations allowed clans to stay put after fighting. So significant were the social and political accomplishments of war reparations for both group welfare and the careers of big-men that such payments occasionally became the goals of warfare in and of themselves (Sillitoe 1978)—in some cases, semiritualized battles were provoked and fought primarily for the exchange to follow.

Unfortunately, early historical traditions offer little detailed information on procedures for war reparations, even though the fact of their payment receives regular mention. Here, we first piece together a sketch of their early history and briefly discuss their impact on symbolic communication and leadership. Then we present testimonies from elderly big-men that give a deeper understanding of the fine art of paying reparations.

The History of War Reparations: Regional Differences

As we discussed earlier, war reparations to allies are cited in the very earliest of Enga historical traditions, and there is no reason to believe they had not already been carried out for centuries. War reparations to enemies, however, receive no mention until approximately the fifth to sixth generation. There are some grounds to propose that the history of war reparations to allies may have varied with local geographic position and pre-sweet potato ecology, a topic we take up briefly even though the evidence is sparse.

In eastern and central Enga, war reparations to allies, composed of food for feasting, land won, and other spoils of war, are a part of historical narratives from the founding generations. In contrast, early historical narratives from Lagaip clans west of the Keta river and those of northern Kandep describe dispersal after serious tribal wars but do not cite the payment of war reparations to either allies or enemies. Whether or not this is due to local bias in transmitting such information is uncertain; even though war reparations receive no mention in the early historical narratives we collected in these areas, elders had not been told of a time when there were none. There is, however, at least one historical narrative suggesting that *tee* exchange involving numerous pigs may indeed have begun later among groups living at higher elevations. It concerns what is said to have been the "first" large pork distribution of the Pumane Kelyanyo clan of Tumundan. The incompetence of the inexperienced participants is relayed with amusement.[4]

Lagaip historical traditions are thus insufficient to enable us to draw conclusions concerning whether, how, and to whom war reparations were paid prior to the fifth generation. Whatever the case, a widely known metaphorical legend from the fourth to fifth generation, the *yambilia* ("hanging wealth"), heralds a time when larger-scale ceremonial exchange took hold, including war reparations, and when pearl shells entered the exchange networks. The narrators insist that it is history told in veiled speech, not myth.

A woman came from Kandep with pearl shells and stayed near Mamale [Laiagam]. A large crowd gathered as people from all over the area came to try to get shells from her, but she left Mamale and went to lake Kitapame near Yakenda [see map 12:20]. The crowd of people followed her, singing and shouting, and tried to get the shells at Yakenda. She continued on to Kasap, and the gathering followed her, trying to get her pearl shells. She went on to Ipi Yambalia [Mulitaka] with the throng of people following her and built her house there. She hung the shells on a *yowaipa* tree. People came in from all directions to try and get the shells. They could not reach them, because she had hung them on the branches of the tree and protected them with a thicket of stinging nettles below and bees and snakes in the branches above. The people dug tunnels to try to reach the wealth but went home for the night when darkness fell.

The next day a man came from the lower side (*kyoa*)[5] and secretly dug a tunnel to the tree, pulled down a shell, and ran away with it. The woman then left and hung her shells at Yoko (map 12:27) with the crowd still following her, singing and shouting. She left Yoko and went to Walesia, stopped to rest there, and then took her shells on down to Pumakopau near Walia [possibly map 12:35 or another Walia in Hewa country], accompanied by the singing and shouting throng. From there she went to Kopiago and did not return. These people sent us the amount of shells we wanted, and we gave them an equal amount of pigs or shells in return. (Kambu Matuia, Monaini Kipula clan, Mulitaka)[6]

There is no good reason to dispute claims that this legend represents developments that took place in the fourth to fifth generation. That the woman with her display of shells comes from southern Kandep indicates the south-north expansion of at least some forms of ceremonial exchange. Probably it pertains to war reparation exchanges, for in parts of the Kandep region the pearl shells distributed in such exchanges were hung on the skeleton of a tree planted in a small mound in the center of the ceremonial grounds (Meggitt 1956:132). The scrambling of people for wealth may point to a change in the social climate as competition increased — certainly it transmits an air of striving, competition, and frustration. That it is a woman who brings the display of shells follows a general trend in the oral traditions of highland New Guinea in which major innovations are spread by wandering women, possibly reflecting diffusion through marriage links. Her route from Kandep through Laiagam and down the Lagaip follows the Kepele cult network, with the displays of shells held near major cult sites where people from different regions convened for ritual performances. The westward movement of the shells in some versions follows trade routes into Hewa country, from where pigs and other goods were exchanged for wealth, mainly shells that were sent back eastward. In short, the *yambilia* appears to mark changing times during which Lagaip clans began to be drawn into the expanding exchange networks of surrounding regions and, as a result, intensified their own.

In contrast to the situation in the Lagaip and northern Kandep, war reparations to allies occupy an important place in the early historical narratives of the Atone Enga of southern Kandep, despite the region's remote location, harsh climate, and sparse population. Most likely this is due to frequent interaction with the Mendi and other groups in lower valleys to the south. As in the east, war reparations in the early generations were composed of land and food for feasting, including pork. After the fifth to sixth generation, pearl shells are said to have been incorporated in both bridewealth payments and war reparations. Their arrival is recorded in an oral tradition from the Kupa and Yakumba tribes of north Mendi, major middlemen in the trade between Tambul and areas to the south (see Appendix 10). It begins with a Kupa man named Gulu marrying a woman from the Aimbatepa tribe of southern Kandep, though they speak mutually unintelligible languages.[7] After a series of adventures and close calls as a "wanted man," he settles in her place not far from Kandep station and sets off to the south in search of the tree on which pearl shells grow. Giving out salt to solicit help during this long journey, he is finally given some shells and told that "the pig is the source of shells. When you have pigs to exchange, the shells will come." Versions of this tradition are told elsewhere in the area around Mount Giluwe (Andrew Strathern, personal communication, 1990). Though certainly a mix of fact and fiction, the Gulu tradition does coincide with the beginning of a more intensive trade in pearl shells through Kandep and northward into the Lagaip, a trend taken up in the *yambilia* legend given earlier. One of their principal uses was in war reparation distributions.

Extension of War Reparations to Enemies

The most significant development in war reparations described in historical traditions is the extension of them to enemies to reestablish peace and allow both winners and losers to remain on their land. Though we cannot rule out the possibility that such payments were made in earlier generations for special cases, they appear to have become a more regular practice around the fifth generation. The reason why war reparations were not paid to enemies before that, unless there was a strong incentive to do so, is explained as follows:

A long time ago much pork was given to the clans of allies killed in a war, but only one or two pigs were slaughtered to compensate the enemy clan. They were usually given by people closely related to the victim. But as I said earlier, even if the victim in the enemy clan had relatives on the other side, not many pigs were slaughtered to pay reparations for his death. The reason was simple: the death of an ally deserved to be compensated, because he came to help fight off the enemy. It was argued that there were no grounds to pay reparations for the death of an enemy — after all, he had come to kill them. (Kopio Toe Lambu, Yakani Timali clan, Lenge [Wabag])

Recall from chapter 5 that after wars of the early generations, one party usually dislodged the other, whether to a new settlement site a kilometer away or to another region, without paying reparations for enemies killed. Through time, such strategies of dispersal became less easy, effective, and desirable ways of solving problems. Former tribal "bush lands" were filling up, and much of the fertile land in fringe areas was already claimed. Furthermore, migration meant leaving homelands in the rich valleys at the center of social, ritual, and economic life and striking out into little-known country to be faced with the laborious task of clearing land in rugged terrain, building a new community, and linking it to existing social, ritual, and trade networks.

Not only was dispersal difficult but in many cases it was also undesirable, particularly when expanding "brother" groups fought to establish their independence and redefine social and physical boundaries within the tribe.[8] The fissioning of clans was usually a painful process accompanied by warfare, but once it was accomplished, "brother" clans sought to restore peaceful relations. To have friendly neighbors and allies for wars with major enemies was the overriding concern. Ambivalent feelings between clans who had to hold their own against each other's quarrelsomeness and encroachments yet maintain an alliance in the face of threats from outside form a common theme. To give two examples, a metaphorical legend from the Kambitipa Laka clan of southern Kandep underscores dependence between "brothers," and one from the Waiminakuni clan of the middle Lai valley, the trials of such relationships:

One day Kinupa and Katati went out to slaughter a pig for a ritual. When they reached the ritual site, there lay a pig rope and a bamboo-tipped arrow. Katati snatched up the bamboo-tipped arrow while his brother looked on. Kinupa was surprised because he thought that his brother would take the pig rope instead. However, seeing that his brother already had the arrow, he took the rope. From that time on they made a good pair—the descendants of Katati have been fierce warriors and a menace to surrounding clans, and the descendants of Kinupa, who are very successful in breeding pigs, are able to provide the reparations for the men killed in the wars of their "brother" clan. (Yamala Kuniapa, Kambitipa Laka clan, Lakalapa, southern Kandep)

This is how the tribal war broke out between the Yakumau and Waiminakuni clans [of the Aluni tribe]. One day two brothers built a men's house at Pokatisa and went out to collect sugarcane husks to put on the floor. When they brought them back to the house, they could not agree on how to divide the house between them. Their disagreement escalated and they fought. Since that time it happens that when there is a problem between them, they become bitter enemies and fight. But one might find that the next day the fight unexpectedly quiets down again, and they become friends once more, licking each other with their tongues. (Lato Tambaiya of Aluni, Sambakamanda [Pumakosa])

Those who chose not to disperse after tribal fighting were faced with the problem of reestablishing peace and the balance of power. To do this, old solutions were adapted to meet the changing situation—namely, war reparations were extended to enemies. This was not an entirely new concept, for small-scale exchanges had previously been made between closely related families in enemy clans after hostilities had died down. Because warring clans were usually linked by a multiplicity of kinship ties, extending reparations to enemies involved reopening ties with the intent of using them to work for peace. Because this had to be done while anger and suspicion were at their peak, not after they had died down, reparations to enemies required more mediation and diplomacy than did those to allies. Until the postcolonial period they remained merely an option dependent on circumstances:

> If words of reconciliation were exchanged, then war reparations were paid for the death of the enemy. However, if such an intention was not manifested by either party, war reparations were not paid for enemy deaths. Each clan thought that it might as well forget about war reparations, because the enemy would probably take revenge anyway. That sort of feeling prevailed between clans when words of reconciliation were not exchanged. The payment of war reparations to enemies depended very much on the circumstance that existed around a particular war. (Kepa Pupu, Yoponda Ipupa clan, Walia, Minamb valley)

One of the most important factors influencing the choice of peace over revenge was whether or not the enemy was a "brother clan" and thus a potential ally in the future. For instance, Meggitt (1977:137), in his study of war reparations paid to enemies for men killed in wars between about 1900 and 1955, found that only 3 out of 28 enemy deaths (11 percent) in wars between "brother" clans were not compensated for, in contrast to 16 out of 36 (44 percent) for deaths of enemies from other tribes.

The growing trend to fight, stay put, and pay reparations to enemies had reverberations for payments to allies as well. In the earlier generations, the spoils of war, particularly land, made up a significant component of war reparations. But when wars ended without the substantial displacement of one group, gifts of land to allies had to be replaced by gifts of pigs and other forms of wealth.[9] After serious wars, families were left with little to give and had to ask relatives outside the clan for finance. Assistance was then delivered just prior to or during the war reparation ceremonies in the framework of obligations to affinal and maternal kin, belated bridewealth, or payments for children's growth or injuries:

> If you go to a pandanus tree, you will see the *angabana* leaves that cover the nut cluster. So it is with these small payments; these things actually make up a larger *tee*. . . .
>
> Initiatory gifts were given first in anticipation of these smaller payments and precipitated their performance. The payments were made on a day set by the receivers of the initiatory gifts, who were in most cases in-laws or maternal relatives. Quite often they were carried out just before or within a major war reparation ceremony or during a campaign for the Tee cycle.[10] When the time came for war reparations or Tee, they asked the parents of children [born to women who had married out of their clan] to make child-growth payments. The asking was done by word of mouth. *Tee* literally means "to ask," and from this the term *tee* was borrowed to refer to the actual giving of pigs. (Minalyo Katape, Yakani Kalia clan, Wakumale [Wabag])

When wars produced fewer spoils to give to allies and reparations were paid more frequently to enemies, the increased demand for pigs and other forms of wealth filtered down to the smaller exchanges with affinal and maternal kin that financed the larger reparations. Whereas early historical narratives describe affinal and maternal kin sharing food, providing allies with places of refuge, exchanging small gifts, and helping with various tasks, from the fourth to fifth generation onward provision of wealth becomes one of the central obligations of such relationships.

To summarize, the sparse information available on regional patterns indicates that in eastern Enga, central Enga, and southern Kandep, war reparations were paid to allies from the beginning of historical traditions and most likely long before. For Lagaip clans west of Kasap and for northern Kandep, they are first cited with some regularity in narratives from the fourth to fifth generation, though the possibility that they were practiced earlier cannot be ruled out. Land made up a major part of the war reparations in earlier times, because one of the warring parties was usually dislodged or chose to move. As the land filled up, pigs and in some regions pearl shells came to compose the greater part of war reparation payments. During the fifth generation, war reparations began to be more frequently extended to enemies, putting greater demands on agricultural production. The destructive spiral set off by choosing a solution to conflicts that accentuated an important source of strife — competition for pigs and the labor and land with which to raise them — has yet to be resolved.

War Reparations and the Growing Influence of Big-Men

Most Enga say that the power of big-men (*kamongo*) grew hand in hand with ceremonial exchange (*tee*). Why this was so becomes evident if one considers Enga views of how men reach the status of *kamongo*. In response to the question of how a man became a big-man, Apanyo Maua replied:

It was like the political system today, men had to campaign to become leaders and the people cast their ballots, but not in the same way that they do today. Men campaigned by giving pigs or other things to those who needed them. They paid bridewealth for others. They became spokesmen for their clans during confrontations with other clans. They offered hospitality to strangers. Anything done to benefit or promote the clan would be regarded as part of their campaign for leadership. The people recognized men who did these things as big-men. (Apanyo Maua, Yambatane Watenge clan, Saka Laiagam)

In addition to these sorts of actions, the commonly cited attributes of men who attracted followers included their ability to mobilize work parties; settle internal disputes; distribute food appropriately at events such as funerals; provision group members with items of dress and ornaments for ceremonial occasions; host traditional dances that gathered people to plan events or negotiate marriages; conduct peace negotiations successfully and orate elegantly in public; help finance bridewealth and other payments for clan or subclan members; mobilize the clan to go out and get pigs for *tee* exchange and organize their distribution; and manage and distribute wealth in *tee* exchange.

Of these, the intragroup activities offered a limited career. It was skill in intergroup relations and *tee* exchange that promised ever-higher rungs on the ladder of influence. Men who could mediate effectively in tense intergroup affairs drew more followers to the security they provided. Furthermore, *tee* exchange gave big-men more tangible influence over others because they could preferentially withhold or provide finance. While war reparations to allies and enemies held roughly equal advantages for aspiring men in terms of *tee* exchange, managing the payment of war reparations to enemies required much greater mediation skills. Men who could master these came to represent the clan as a whole.[11]

The opportunities offered by war reparations were great but not unbounded, for they did not guarantee peace. As will become apparent in testimonies given later, failures of war reparations to bring about peace, and the accompanying loss of investments, inhibited rapid inflation of payments and the corresponding development of longer chains of finance; people invested cautiously in efforts that could fail. For western Enga, where war reparations remained the largest form of ceremonial exchange outside of ancestral cults, the economic and political power of big-men was thus curbed,[12] remaining at levels similar to that portrayed in Wohlt's (1978:97–98) superb description of big-men in a remote community of northwestern Kandep:

A bigman at Yumbisa is described in the following way. He has six to ten female pigs, two or three gold-lip shells and several wives. If his "brothers" kill someone, he himself will arrange to line up five to ten big pigs and six small ones (not all his "own" pigs) and direct the *tee*. When his clan receives pigs, he distributes them. He also organizes wars because he can give the *tee* (can get lots of pigs), and if he is killed, his clan stops fighting because they could not give *tee* if somebody else is killed. He directs fence construction, settles quarrels, and shares the food of his garden which all his female relatives work. He is an eloquent orator, and all fear him. . . .

The foremost arena of their endeavors is the exchange system. . . . [T]he bigman manipulates both the multiplicity of interpersonal relationships in any exchange situation and the ambiguities surrounding who proper receivers are for his own and his group's advantage. He is nothing if he is not a genius at devising intricate plans which seem to benefit everyone, including the persons who do not receive pigs, and then convincing people to implement them.

For the fertile valleys of eastern and central Enga, the situation was otherwise. There, as we shall see, opportunities offered by different systems of *tee* exchange that did not carry the risks of war reparations to enemies, such as the Tee cycle and Great Ceremonial War exchanges, permitted big-men to integrate ever more people from outside the clan into their networks of finance and support. The competition set off by such possibilities launched ceremonial exchange and the "bigmanship" that went with it into an accelerating spiral, generating ever more powerful leaders whose influence was felt far outside the boundaries of their own clans. We return to this point in subsequent chapters.

Developments in Song

The intergroup politics of Enga during the generations prior to contact were punctuated with song. Songs, heavily couched in symbolic speech, were used to challenge, insult, gently convey intentions without committal, feel out others' responses, share information with some while withholding it from others, or deliver a devastating two-line coup. They could make or break negotiations for war reparations. Despite the sophistication and widespread use of political songs within living memory, Enga from all parts of the province almost invariably say that songs were first used in the context of intergroup political communication in the fifth generation. These are not mere stereotyped statements. Men and women are indeed able to chant the jingles of previous generations, even though the meanings are sometimes incomprehensible to them,[13] and to give examples of songs sung in the context of certain events in the last five generations, demonstrating how songs have increased in complexity through time.[14] Their development is often attributed to a growing population and the ever-thickening soup of political relations that accompanied it.

The following testimony is fairly representative of the Enga view of the history of political song. It was given by the late Lao Tai of the Lungupini clan, who was just short of stone deaf, and was elicited by his grandson's shouting "SONG!" into his ear. No further questioning or discussion was possible.

The first songs were sung by Lungupini and others of his generation; before that, people did not sing songs.[15] The first songs were short and simple and were sung about the things that people did while they were doing them. One early song was

> Ipa lipa pyo ae,
> Sanga lipa pyo ae.
> Eteteneo pangi lipu pyo ae.
> So kulimbao, ita sumbao.[16]

Such old songs are still sung today, but it is difficult to know what they mean. Songs sung later by people in my father's generation and in mine had more underlying meaning and were sung to send messages. Early songs were not used to convey people's thoughts and intentions [that is, in a political context], because people before my father's and grandfather's generations lived isolated and far apart from one another. As the population increased, there were more people to deal with and a greater need for people to be able to communicate well. During these times our cultural traditions were enhanced. Our language developed and songs were composed with underlying meanings to tell others of our thoughts, feelings, and intentions. As people took part in more activities with others, the kinds of songs sung became more diverse. There were lots of things to sing about and lots of opportunities to communicate through songs— for instance, during bridge building, at wars, during the Tee, and so on. (Lao Tai, Lungupini Yakau clan, Imalemanda [Yalisa])

The earliest songs with political messages that we collected were sung in the context of the Great Ceremonial Wars. Because people from all corners of the province were so consistent in their claims that songs bearing political significance were first sung around the fifth generation, and because the influence of the Great Ceremonial Wars spilled over into the east and west alike, our best guess is that they began in this context. Once in vogue, they were adopted into a wide variety of other public events associated with war reparations, the Tee cycle, the emergence festivals of bachelors' cults, and the public phases of major cults.

War Reparations in the Second to Third Generation

As oral traditions move toward the present, the organization and spirit of Enga war reparations come into focus. Most instructive are the testimonies of leaders of the second generation telling how peace was negotiated and war reparations carried out in their lifetimes and those of their fathers.[17] The understandings they provide clarify both the road to peace and the pressures that shaped the big-men of the twentieth century. To this end, we focus on the accounts of two big-men who were already influential by the colonial period. Although war reparations as described in what follows cannot be projected back indefinitely in time, they appear to have been similar from approximately the fourth generation on. Beyond that we cannot say, though many of their basic features must have been well established long before.

The basic procedures of war reparations were as follows: Reparations were paid first to allies and only later to enemies, if peace was desired.[18] When men were killed on both sides, reparations to enemies were reciprocal. Reparations to allies of enemies, standard practices today, were usually made only in the interest of future exchange (see also Meggitt 1977:137). The high cost of war reparations when there were several allied deaths, together with fear that the wealth would be spread too thinly to satisfy anybody, provided a strong incentive to cease hostilities before many lives were lost.

Reparations to both allies and enemies followed a set sequence after initial peace overtures were made, war reparations were requested, and a desire to pay them was expressed.[19]

1. *Saandi pingi*. Optional, informal, initiatory gifts given in private by bereaved allies or by families in the clan of the victim to request reparations. This step was unnecessary in the case of allies to whom reparations would be given automatically, but it could be important to indicate to the enemy a desire to receive reparations rather than take revenge. Acceptance of *saandi pingi* gifts committed a clan to paying reparations. If reparations to allies could not be paid immediately, sometimes a small promissory payment of cooked pork was given by the liable clan. This payment was called *poketapange* in easternmost Enga, *wanepaelyoko* in eastern and central Enga, and *sapya* in western Enga.

2. *Kepa singi*. The first payment of war reparations in the form of steamed pork distributed formally in public on the clan's ceremonial grounds by the "owners of the fight" to bereaved allies or, in the case of enemies, to the clan of the victim. Much of the meat went to the family of the deceased.

3. *Saandi pingi* or *yangenge*. Initiatory gifts of pigs or piglets, axes, salt, and other goods and valuables given in private by bereaved allies to owners of the fight or by the clan of the victim to the clan of the killer to oblige the payment of live pigs, *akali buingi*.

4. *Akali buingi*.[20] Formal payment in public on the clan's ceremonial grounds of live pigs, live cassowaries, axes, salt, or other goods and valuables by owners of the fight to families in the allied clan or enemy clan who had given initiatory gifts.

In most areas of Enga, after the *akali buingi* was delivered war reparations were considered complete, and regular exchanges between related families or newly formed exchange partnerships continued, making up for lives lost over the longer run. Essentially, this was the transition point between physical and social boundary maintenance, and both clans involved ceased to be on guard. For all deaths, the subclan of the victim had to give pigs to maternal kin as funerary prestations (*laita pingi*). This was done whenever they could raise the wealth—before, during,

or after reparations. All families tried to do well in contributing to war reparations, and those who did gained respect. In this sense they were competitive,
though overt competition between clan members was discouraged.

A testimony given by Kyakas of the Yanaitini Lanekepa clan near Wabag
explains with great sensitivity and acuity the spirit and process of war reparations, their corporate aspects, and the importance of time in mending wounds.

When a war was over, plans were made to carry out reparations. First, the killer's clan
slaughtered pigs and gave the sides of steamed pork to the clan of the deceased [*kepa
singi*]. Much of the pork was given "to the grave" — in other words, to the immediate
family of the victim. If the number of pigs killed was not large, then all of the sides of
pork went to the grave. The recipient family then cut it into small pieces and gave it to
other members of the clan. However, if many pigs were killed, then everybody in the
clan of the deceased was also given pork. After these war reparations were paid, the
killer's clan did not ask for anything in return, but the victim's clan took the initiative
by giving gifts to the killer's clan [*saandi pingi*]. Then a spokesman from the killer's clan
would say that they should not have done that, for they would have continued the war
reparations anyway without the initiatory gifts. The killer's clan tried to be very
friendly and diplomatic, for they respected the victim's clan with a certain sense of fear
[of a payback murder]. In such situations the value of pigs was not regarded highly —
the life of a person was more important.

For two years, members of the clan of the deceased would periodically give initiatory gifts to families in the clan of the killer. The men from the killer's clan would
then say that their pigs were growing old and it was time they held war reparations. Before they even thought of holding the ceremony [*akali buingi*], they must have additional pigs to give away; that is, they not only had to settle the debt from the initiatory
gifts, but each person who received initiatory gifts was expected to reciprocate these
and give an extra pig on top of that. A person who had received a number of initiatory
gifts was expected to give two or three additional pigs.

After war reparations were paid with live pigs, people lived in peace. However, if
debts remained outstanding, or if a person had received only a small pig in return for
initiatory gifts, he would think of avenging the death of his clansman who had been
killed in the tribal war. So war would erupt again, many people would be killed, homesteads destroyed, and allies killed. Further death and destruction would take place on
both sides. . . .

You see, a pig would have been initially raised and kept alive specifically for the occasion when the owner in the killer's clan would tie it to a stake on the ceremonial
ground and give it formally to somebody in the victim's clan during *akali buingi*. Over
two years the clan of the victim would give initiatory gifts to the clan of the killer.
When the killer's clan decided that all the debts could be paid because the pigs raised
for *akali buingi* had grown big and fat, only then would the killer's clan think of holding *akali buingi*. The pigs told us to hold *akali buingi*; in other words, the timing of *akali
buingi* was heavily dependent on the growth of pigs. The pigs that were specifically

bred and raised for the occasion had their ears slit. Meanwhile, the men from the victim's clan [who expected to receive these pigs] kept on maintaining the social relationship with the continual offer of all kinds of gifts. Of course, the most important things given were live pigs and cooked pork.

War reparations carried out in this manner were regarded as fulfilling or satisfying by the clan of the victim and others in the area. The men from the victim's clan would comment that indeed they wanted to live in peace and harmony. It is said that in some cases they were so happy that they went over and embraced the men from the killer's clan.

You see, one of the fundamental features of war reparations was the additional or "profit" pigs given to individuals in the victim's clan. Additional pigs must be given at the time of *akali buingi* if the reparations were to be considered well done and correct. When the killer's clan met to plan *akali buingi*, if one man boasted that he had enough pigs to give to a person in the victim's clan [in reciprocation for the initiatory gifts] but no additional pigs, they sneered at and ridiculed him. He was sent home to look for an additional pig, his fellow clansmen saying that otherwise he should stay away from the ceremonial grounds [out of shame] and let his wife stake out the pigs. Every aspect of *akali buingi* was discussed and considered very carefully and every man had to indicate that he had an additional pig to stake out on the ceremonial grounds and give away. If this were the case and everyone had one or two additional pigs to contribute, then they all rose to their feet and sang songs. However, if even one man said that he could pay back the initiatory gifts but could give no more, they would postpone *akali buingi* for another month while he looked for another pig to give. And so the payment of war reparations was the collective responsibility of the clan as a whole, not just a matter for one or several clan members.

Kyakas then departed from his discussion of formalities to show the role that emotion played in keeping the situation volatile even after reparations were paid. It was here that big-men with skills far greater than those of manipulating wealth and organizing the clan were required:[21]

When a person was killed, he was gone forever. You would miss him always. His bed would be empty and his fellow clansmen, upon seeing the empty bed, would be overcome by emotion and feel like going out to avenge his death. It was said that men from the killer's clan should be careful of such a situation, for it could well be that a person from the victim's clan could come and chop off someone's head.

To prevent such feelings, one [of the victim's relatives] had to go and remove his bed from sight, get rid of his pipe, and dispose of his net bag and anything else that would remind people of him. Quite often these things were removed after the war reparations were completed, both *kepa singi* and *akali buingi*. You see, the victim would not be seen around his house, and his wife and children would miss him. Only when his clan was paid war reparations would they slowly forget the death of the person killed in the war. Sometimes they had to give *mongalo* stone axes to the victim's clan to prevent "payback" killing; in many instances shells were given away after war reparations for the same purpose.

If a person from the victim's clan said he would kill somebody from the killer's clan [while reparations were being paid or afterward], then another would tell him that he would be doing exactly the same thing that the killer's clan did. The reasons for such feelings [desire for revenge] were many, for example that a person from the victim's clan was always quarreling with his wife who was from the killer's clan. Another reason might be that a pig belonging to somebody in the killer's clan destroyed a garden of someone in the victim's clan. These were the things that made somebody think of committing a payback killing. Then somebody in the victim's clan who did not want further conflict would tell him to overcome such feelings, saying that the conflict was dead and buried and therefore he should not bring it to life again. In this way the situation was kept under control. The same problem also cropped up when somebody from the victim's clan did not give initiatory gifts to the killer's clan, and as a result he was not given a pig or anything when war reparation ceremonies were held. It was always possible that such a person would try to revive the conflict. In order to prevent this, a person who had received many pigs as war reparations would give one to the poor fellow who did not receive anything. In most cases it was the clan's big-man who did this to prevent him from committing a payback murder, for if war broke out again the big-man would have to return the pigs that he had received in the war reparations [that is, by paying further war reparations].

You see, not all people in the victim's clan would be satisfied with the war reparations, and a poor person in the clan was most likely to miss out, receiving no pigs at all for such purposes as paying bridewealth for his wife. A wise man from his own clan would give a pig to such a person; it required wisdom to do such a thing. The big-man of a clan had to make sure that no dissatisfied person would think of taking revenge, for he did not want to see chaos come to his place and did not want the houses and gardens to be destroyed. For such reasons the big-man had to give a pig, preferably one that he had decided to keep for himself, to the person who was most likely to cause trouble. (Kyakas Sapu, Yanaitini Lanekepa clan, Lupamanda, Wabag)

Outstanding in Kyakas's testimony is the description of how the process of paying war reparations played on the healing hands of time. Through the promise of concrete profit, the bereaved were encouraged to foster good relations for a period of about two years while the earmarked pigs were being raised and memories of the deceased faded. It was well recognized that peace involved far more than the absence of conflict. It required active communication and exchange. Meeting after meeting was held to assure that the reparations would satisfy everyone in the victim's clan, and big-men, who had the most to lose, played a critical role in this process. Just as pressure was put on every man to fight for his clan, it was also exerted on every family to contribute adequately to the reparations, activating as many exchange ties as possible to deter future aggression. There is no word for peace in Enga, only terms to describe the cessation of hostilities: *yanda konjingi*, "to cut off the fight," *yanda tambuingi*, "to terminate the fight," and *yandate lakenge*, "to break the spear." For peace to prevail, the spear of every clan member had to be broken.

A final and critical point in understanding the nature of Enga war reparations is the role of persuasive speech in dealing with both the ultimate causes of warfare—political struggles, homicide, and land disputes—and the proximate ones—anger and desire for revenge. Death in warfare left both a feeling of deep personal loss among the bereaved clan members and a sense of imbalance between the clans involved. If feelings could not be soothed and a sense of balance reestablished through conciliatory speech, war reparations had no chance of getting off the ground:

All things happened because of the tongue, the uncontrollable tongue that ought not to have said certain things that were said. This instigated tribal wars. My father said that just as one soothes a cut in cold water, one must say such soothing words to the ones in the victim's clan whom you thought would be most likely to cause trouble. He said that with your heart you must decide not to say bad things, but to keep the good things in the right side of your heart and the bad things in the left side. After you had comforted the victim's clan with words, you must give them food at any opportunity. Then finally you offer food to them in the form of *kepa singi*. After that, if the clan was inclined to do so, they would come to you and offer initiatory gifts. He said to let them do this on their own initiative. After that you were expected to pay reparations with live pigs [*akali buingi*].

The tongue was the thing that in most cases brought trouble to a clan. Wars started from the tongue. It was the tongue which said things that could provoke somebody who already had ill feelings, and those who did not want to fight had to go and fight, all because of the tongue. If you use the tongue to make peace, then you will have peace in the clan. (Ambone Mati, Itapuni Nemani clan, Kopena [Wabag])

A variety of oratorical strategies was used in the service of peacemaking. One strategem was to restore balance by avoiding implications of superiority or promises that could not be kept. For example, an orator might indicate in metaphor or song that the clan was wealthy enough to pay only limited reparations and then pleasantly surprise the recipients by giving generously. Another was to attribute the death to fate, not to the strength or weakness of either side:

At the time that men from the victim's clan went to see those from the killer's clan to negotiate war reparations, the killer's clan was prepared to meet them, having steamed sweet potatoes and cut sugarcane. When the men from the victim's clan had arrived and were seated on the ceremonial grounds, men from the killer's clan spoke on behalf of their clan. The most important thing said on such an occasion by the killer's clan was this: you must tell the clan of the victim that it was unfortunate that he was killed, but that it was fate . . . and that you will not let the death of this person go uncompensated. After making such a speech, you should offer them steamed sweet potatoes and sugarcane.

The word of peace from the killer's clan was of utmost importance. However, if the clan of the victim was met in a different way, such behavior did not go unheeded. For instance, the killer's clan might say that they didn't want the victim's clan to come and ask for reparations and might ridicule them by saying that they did not invite the victim to come and fight, that the poor man brought on his own fate and deserved to die. Such words were very provocative. Even if they were said not in front of the victim's clan but in private and leaked out, the victim's clansmen would become furious. They should not say anything like that, for if the victim's clan heard of it, they would think of avenging the death of their man even if the liable clan was an ally. Many tribal wars were set off in this way. (Kyakas Sapu, Yanaitini Lanekepa clan, Lupamanda, Wabag)

The primary tool of Enga oration was rich but often obscure metaphor that left the better part of the audience pondering the meaning. Reasons given for the widespread use of such veiled speech or song included the intent to share information with a circle of close associates while shutting others out and the desire to hint at intentions without making definite commitments to certain actions, thereby facilitating the give and take of negotiations. For example, through song clansmen could express a desire to pay war reparations and feel out the response of their opponents without committing themselves. Another reason was to demonstrate power: big-men deployed metaphor to predict events to come, and if they were able to bring these about, their effectiveness was demonstrated; they were shown to be "men of their metaphors," so to speak. It also left them a way out—should their plans not eventuate, their precise intentions would never have been directly announced. Additionally, clever and soothing words were used as "verbal gifts."[22] Examples given of the strategic use of veiled speech in the past four generations were many. The subject is vast and complex; more thorough discussion of Enga symbolic speech must be relegated to an entire study in and of itself (see Goldman 1983 and Eibl-Eibesfeldt, Schiefenhövel, and Heeschen 1989 for such studies in other highland New Guinea societies).

In short, the major points of war reparations emphasized by Enga leaders were as follows: First, long-standing exchange relationships with kin outside the clan were essential for the negotiation of war reparations. Second, skill in oration on the part of big-men to quell anger and reestablish a balance of power could make or break peace negotiations. Third, war reparations followed a set routine during which the clan of the victim was encouraged to keep the peace through anticipation of financial gain. The protracted process of earmarking and raising pigs for the occasion allowed time to heal emotional wounds. Fourth, although the amount of reparations to be paid was not stipulated, some measure was set for expected return: a full-grown pig in exchange for every initiatory gift, plus one or more "profit pigs," depending on the number of initiatory gifts given. A clan gained "name" from paying generous reparations, but the amount given was kept within certain limits with the intent of establishing balance rather than provocative superiority. Fifth, war reparations, though made up of the sum of the gifts of individuals to their own exchange partners in the clan of the victim, were the corporate responsibility of the clan. Clan members met repeatedly to make sure that the reparations were generous and were distributed with sensitivity to the bereaved. Finally, war reparations were precarious, working toward peace but not assuring it. Should they fail to establish good relationships, hostilities could be resumed.[23] It should be added that women, who had withdrawn with the children and pigs during the fighting and thus had been removed from the emotional heat, returned to play an important role in arranging reparations. They privately discouraged the outbreak of new hostilities and obtained pigs from their relatives to finance the reparations (Kyakas and Wiessner 1992).

War Reparations, Marriage Ties, and the *Kauma Pingi*

Marriage ties and their accompanying lifelong exchanges constituted both the channels through which peace was negotiated and one of the reasons why peace was desired. Thus, the greater the number of marriage ties between clans, the greater the chance for peaceful relations to be reestablished and prevail. And so when peace was truly desired but relations were tenuous, efforts were made to strengthen ties between groups through events such as the *kauma pingi,* a formalized dance during which marriages between formerly hostile groups were arranged.[24]

Although the *kauma pingi* could be held at any time, it was usually staged when warfare had left an imbalance in deaths and when the clan of the victim, perceiving itself as weaker or not wanting to be responsible for more allied deaths, preferred reparations over revenge. The clan of the killer, which was to pay the reparations, sent a message to the clan of the victim announcing the event and requesting that it send its young women to attend, particularly those who had boyfriends in the clan of the killer. The girls were to be accompanied by a few young men from the victim's subclan who were shaved and dressed as women as an indication that they were not interested in revenge but would wait submissively, like women, for proposals from the killer's clan to pay reparations.

On the appointed day, men in the killer's clan initiated the dance (*sing-sing* or *mali*). Young women from the victim's clan sought out boyfriends or potential boyfriends from the subclan of those who had initiated the trouble and danced beside them. The young men clothed as women embraced the same men and danced on the other side of them. Throughout the dance, spectators from both clans observed and made predictions on the basis of appearance and movements about whether the young men and women would be suitable marriage partners. In this relaxed context, clan leaders began war reparation negotiations.

The purpose of the *kauma pingi* as spelled out by elders was twofold: to begin peace negotiations and to contract marriages that would help assure that peace be maintained. However, if all subclans from the clan of the victim did not send girls and young men in female dress, then the clan of the killer knew that not all desired to submit and that the fight would probably flare up again before long. In response, the clan of the killer would withdraw the men from one of its subclans or not participate at all.

Summary

To end our discussion of Enga war reparations, it should be reemphasized that fighting in Enga was inseparable from exchange, because the two constituted alternative strategies for boundary maintenance. In the earlier generations, enemies were widely spaced across the landscape, and reparations paid to allies consisted of land gained and food for feasting—pigs, marsupials, and desirable vegetable produce. Problems were solved or political goals reached by spacing and displacing. Around the fifth generation, when land was no longer so abundant, significant changes began to take place. Land gained no longer sufficed to compensate allied losses, and so pigs were substituted for land. Likewise, problems with enemies could no longer be resolved by resettlement after warfare. Either armed hostilities had to continue indefinitely until one side was evicted and dispersed or reparations had to be paid to allow boundaries to once again be maintained through social means. Consequently, war reparations were extended to enemies to "break the spear" and restore the support of affinal and maternal kin in opposing clans. By "eating the food of war reparations," peace was reestablished—not merely peace as the absence of war but peace as active communication, exchange, and intermarriage. It was the benefits of these relations as much as the reparations themselves that made up for the loss of an individual over time. Because virtually all wars in which someone was killed involved subsequent reparations, clans going to war did so in the full realization that wealth would be required for conflict resolution—that they would have to produce pigs for the purpose and draw on networks of finance outside the clan.[25] Moreover, the close association between warfare and exchange meant that warfare offered the potential to pursue not only aggressive goals—taking land or eliminating competitors—but also affiliative ones, creating exchange ties. As we will see in the next chapter, wars could be triggered and fought primarily for the exchange that would ensue.

10

Yanda Andake

The Great Ceremonial Wars

Yanda andake dupa nee dii pyo pingi.

The Great Wars were fought for the sole purpose of producing food. In other words, they were planned or planted like a garden to produce a harvest.
Ambone Mati, Itapuni Nemani clan, Kopena (Wabag)

By the fifth generation before the present, the early Tee cycle linked Kakoli clans of Tambul with Saka-Layapo clans of eastern Enga, groups who claim a common origin and a long-standing history of intermarriage, exchange, and ritual despite linguistic differences. Owing to the mi-gration of a Layapo tribe, Yanaitini, to Tetemanda, Tee cycle alliances were ex-tended into the eastern portion of cen-tral Enga, the home of Mai and Yandapo speakers. There they ended abruptly, abutting on an entirely different system of exchange in the making: the Great Ceremonial Wars, *yanda andake*. These spectacular, semiritualized "tournament" wars between two tribes or pairs of tribes were fought repeatedly over generations to forge alliances, formally display strength, and set in motion the exchange festivals that followed.[1]

At least three factors were significant in keeping the development of these two

265

very different ceremonial exchange networks separate. First, substantial cultural differences existed between the Saka-Layapo and Mai-Yandapo Enga that inhibited the spread of the Tee cycle. Among other things, the Mai-Yandapo were more mobile, more dependent on hunting, and less strictly patrilineal in descent. They maintained different women's traditions (Kyakas and Wiessner 1992), procedures of bridewealth exchange, and relations between the sexes. The last were of particular significance, for the Tee was constructed along lines of marriage ties. Second, in its initial stages the Tee cycle had a low profile, its benefits not immediately apparent to people of surrounding areas. It was a system maintained by big-men who had much greater access to wealth through trade than did the average Layapo family. For central Enga, there is little evidence of big-men with similar influence in the early generations, outside of one or two clans involved in the early Tee cycle. Third, and perhaps most important, the population of central Enga was embroiled in its own problems for which the thin web of Tee could do little. The large and vicious wars of central Enga after the introduction of the sweet potato had disrupted relations to land, balance of power, and trade routes. Broader coalitions backed by displays of force were necessary to hold land and resources, reestablish balance, and craft new pathways of exchange, particularly for those who had been driven into the upper Sau, Wale, and Tarua valleys.

In principle, the Great Ceremonial Wars (from here on, the Great Wars) were nothing new, for their roots lay in the dual nature of Enga warfare — fighting to oppose the enemy and space or displace them, followed by exchanges with allies. What was new were the scale and priorities: much larger forces were mobilized, emphasis was put on display of force rather than on ousting opponents, and exchange took precedence over fighting. In other words, the Great Wars were planned and fought primarily for the "harvest" from exchanges that followed, as was expressed in the opening quotation.

The development of the Great Wars from original conflicts is not well documented in oral traditions, the spectacular events of recent generations eclipsing earlier ones. Many narrators jump directly from the incident that gave birth to a Great War long ago to episodes of the war fought during their lifetimes, greatly telescoping the war's history. Nonetheless, the information that is available leaves little doubt that (1) the Great Wars originated in areas where there was serious contention over resources — both the salt springs of the Yandap, where trade routes converged, and the fertile land of the Ambum valley; (2) they were a response to the need for larger coalitions to hold resources; (3) the social events accompanying the Great Wars and the ensuing exchanges, which facilitated the flow of goods between the Lai, Ambum, Lagaip, and upper Sau valleys, were important from the beginning and became more important than the fighting in later generations; and (4) Great Wars were not fought in any other part of Enga at any time within the span of oral history.[2]

The Great Wars are said to have commenced in approximately the fifth to sixth generation; certainly that is when they become prominent in historical traditions. Four Great Wars between different tribes of central Enga were fought in repeated episodes at ten- to thirty-year intervals from the fifth generation until the early twentieth century. Each episode was a complete event in and of itself, consisting of formal arrangements, battles lasting for weeks or months, and subsequent exchanges. Some say that prior to the sixth generation there were no Great Wars because the population was too sparse and dispersed to support them. Smaller-scale, semiritualized fighting followed by exchange may have occurred earlier, however: a number of early oral traditions briefly mention tribes of the Laiagam-Sirunki-Keta area periodically provoking one another, putting on ceremonial dress, and going to battle.[3]

In this chapter we present the history of each of the Great Wars fought from roughly the fifth generation, when they first enter historical narratives, until the late 1930s, when they died a natural death or were supplanted by the Tee cycle.[4] First, however, we outline the features common to all Great Wars.

The Great Wars

Though each Great War stemmed from a different set of circumstances, they all shared certain features. Episodes of Great Wars were carefully arranged and fought to display military strength, form alliances, and cultivate exchange. They were, in effect, tournaments that established and maintained both social and political territory, making it clear who supported and exchanged with whom. To continue from the opening quotation:

The Great Wars were fought for the sole purpose of producing food. In other words, the Great Wars were planned or planted like a garden to produce a harvest. They were arranged when goods and valuables were plentiful and there were so many pigs that women complained about their work loads. Everybody knew what they were in for, how war reparations would be paid for deaths, and what the overall results would be. They were designed to open up new areas, further existing exchange relations, foster tribal unity, and provide a competitive but structured environment in which young men could strive for leadership. These qualities of the Great Wars made them differ from conventional wars, which disrupted relationships of trade and exchange, causing havoc and sometimes irreparable damage. The distributions of wealth that took place after the Great Wars brought trade goods from outlying areas into the Wabag area on the trade paths initially established by the salt trade. (Ambone Mati, Itapuni Nemani clan, Kopena [Wabag])

The Great Wars also displayed strength, numbers, and solidarity as a deterrent to future aggression:

A long time ago, there were fewer people; they were widely scattered and lived relatively isolated from one another. Now the question is, why did people living at that time engage in the Great Wars? The main reason was the following: they did not fight for the sake of fighting. The Great Wars were not serious ones, but they were not mock wars either. Warriors received arrow and spear wounds and some of them died from their wounds. The underlying purpose of these wars was to bring people together—they were formal and ceremonial. They were fought to show the numerical strength and solidarity of a tribe and the physical build and wealth of the warriors; figuratively it is said that in the wars, "they exposed themselves to the sun." The Great Wars were events for socializing [between warriors and their allies and hosts, not with opponents]. After getting to know each other, they would kill many pigs and hold feasts [Great War exchanges]. (Depoane, Yakani Timali tribe, Lenge [Wabag])

The Great Wars involved not just single clans and their allies, as did conventional wars, but all members of a tribe or of two "brother" tribes and their allies. This meant that "brother" clans, who periodically fought each other in bitter conventional wars, had to call a halt to existing hostilities and unite for the Great Wars and their subsequent exchanges.

The "owners of the fight"—the principle opponents—and their allies were hosted by intermediary tribes. That is, when a Great War was to be fought, the opposing sides asked other tribes to host them. For the duration of the fight they would not be living on their own land and fighting at their own borders but living with hosts and fighting in a designated zone on land of the hosting clans. Each side had its own hosts who provided the food, water, housing, and front-line warriors. Though most clans in a hosting tribe contributed in some way, two to three usually assumed the principal responsibility. That the Great Wars were hosted provides the key to understanding them. First, it meant that the Great Wars served to forge close personal relationships between hosts, owners of the fight, and allies. Second, because battles were fought not near the borders between enemy clans but in designated areas of the land of hosting tribes, no land could be gained or lost even if one side was greatly superior.[5]

Each clan and household enjoyed considerable autonomy in its degree of participation. When the war commenced, warriors would meet with one to three men from the hosting clan, usually those with whom they had some kinship tie, who offered to provide them with food and accommodation for its duration.

Warriors lived in the men's houses of their hosts or, if they were too numerous, in men's houses built specially for the occasion. Aside from additional housing, no special structures were built for the Great Wars. Each night the warriors ate together, chewed sugarcane, rehashed the events of the battle, and engaged in courtship parties with young women from hosting and allied clans. The many days spent fighting for a common cause and nights together in the warmth of the host's houses forged bonds between hosts and hosted; subsequent marriages turned these into concrete kinship relations. This is what is meant when it is said that people fought to socialize.

Allies joined for a number of reasons — young men participated to make names as brave warriors or to meet young women during the accompanying festivities; others fought to work out old grudges in a formal tournament that would not bring havoc to their own clans; and still others came to support kin or simply to enjoy the event.

Strict rules forbade exchanges between enemies, particularly between hosts and the enemy. It was believed that the hosting clan or clans opened their central men's houses to the sky people (*yalya* or *yalyakali*) so that they would stay by them in battle.[6] Should a host be disloyal by partaking of food from the enemy side during the war or subsequent exchanges, the *yalya* would desert that person, laying him or her open to death. Through these conventions, marriage across enemy lines was hindered and exchange alliances were channeled along clear lines between hosts, the hosted, and their allies.

Great War episodes were organized and led by big-men called *watenge* — organizers, orators, and showmen who had the political ties and savvy to coordinate their followers for the battles and subsequent distributions of wealth. In most cases these were also men with good knowledge of military strategy, though they did not need to be outstanding warriors. Each side had five to ten *watenge*, at least one from every clan of the owners of the fight. Some of these rose to extraordinary prominence, their names and deeds being passed on in historical traditions. It was considered foul play for enemies to kill *watenge*, who were highly respected by all parties involved and who would organize the Great War exchanges. The goal, rather, was to capture or otherwise humiliate them.

Great War episodes lasted for weeks or months. With strict rules forbidding violence outside the limits of the battlefield, warriors and spectators came and went freely to visit their families or attend to matters at home. During periodic breaks, feasts were held to plan the course of the war and the exchanges to follow.

Great War episodes could be provoked by prearranged aggressive acts or initiated by formal challenges, but once they were agreed upon, certain procedures were followed. Despite some variation in the degree of ritualization of different Great Wars, the opening and closing episodes of all battles were highly formalized and executed with much fanfare. Hundreds of warriors adorned in full ceremonial attire converged on the battlefield on the appointed day while spectators from near and far gathered to watch. Fight leaders met, greeted one another, voiced challenges, embraced or exchanged axes, and called a beginning to battle.

The actual fighting followed the procedures of conventional wars (see Meggitt 1977:19–20). Since so many people from different clans fought in ceremonial dress with blackened faces, it was often hard for warriors to identify allies, and sometimes warriors unintentionally shot and killed men from their own side. The corpses of men killed in battle were not physically mutilated and could be retrieved by their clansmen without interference, though they were defaced verbally in gruesome and gleeful songs of victory.[7]

Death tolls in the Great Wars were not high in proportion to their sheer size and duration. For example, during the last Great War episode, fought in the late 1930s, one Malipini warrior and two allies were killed on the Malipini-Potealini side, and on the Itapuni-Awaini side, three Itapuni-Awaini warriors and one ally. These figures may be below average, for this war was very closely linked to the Tee cycle and highly ritualized. The dead were mourned by their fellow tribesmen and allies as men who had died for a "good and worthy cause." Ideally, the Great Wars were "without anger," and only in the event of foul play were deaths avenged.

After months of intermittent fighting, leaders decided to call a formal end to battle, lining up shields and weapons and casting them into the river. Large pork or marsupial-meat feasts were then held on both sides. The death toll was announced and the side with fewer losses was considered the winner, though little significance was placed on this measure of winning or losing. It was display, numbers, fighting prowess, and organization and size of exchanges that drew pride and praise. When the war came to an end, older men looked forward to the exchanges that would follow, when the bonds engendered during the Great War would be solidified into partnerships of trade and exchange. Young men lamented the end of the excitement, returning home crying, "Yandao" (the fight), as if mourning the end of the war.

The Great Wars were like a game for young people that everybody enjoyed playing. After the Great War ended, our hosts provided us with a final feast. They killed many pigs, steamed all kinds of food in earth ovens, and distributed so much food to warriors of Malipini and Potealini clans that we could eat some and bring the rest home. On our way back home, we wiped the tears from our eyes, saying, "The days in which we entertained ourselves in the Great War are gone and now it will be a sad day through and through." With these words, we cried and cried as we walked slowly home. (Waingia Lyambi, Malipini Sakatawane clan, Sopasa)

All episodes of Great Wars were followed by an extended period of exchanges that conformed more or less to those following a conventional war, except that they were much larger, more elaborate, and very festive. The following is an outline of the standard exchanges that took place; greater detail is given later for specific episodes.

1. *Endaki kamungi* (fetching water). Initiatory gifts of cooked pork, marsupial meat, cassowaries, goods, and valuables were given to the owners of the fight by the hosts during a feast held shortly after a formal end was called to battle. The name refers to the fact that the hosts had fetched water for the owners — in other words, provided for them during the fighting. This distribution was dramatized by a procession of hosts bearing pork decorated with red, yellow, and black stripes, led by two men carrying decorated bamboo poles with pigs' hearts implanted on the ends. These were presented by the hosts to two representatives from the owners of the fight in a ceremony called *akali maingi*, "to give the man," or *mena mona naloa pingi*, "the sharing of the pig's heart." Since the hosts had given their men to fight as allies, it signaled that they now expected payment or reparations.

2. *Kepa singi* and *akali buingi*. These war reparation exchanges for allied men killed were paid soon after the end of the war by the hosting clans, not by the owners of the fight. They were not paid for enemy deaths, because exchanges between the two sides were strictly forbidden, or for men from among the owners of the fight, who were said simply to have died for a worthy cause.

3. *Yanda andake kepa singi (saka sapya)*. An extraordinarily large payment of raw, butchered pork supplemented by marsupial meat was distributed to the host clans by the owners of the fight for hosting them and fighting with them as allies. For some Great Wars, these wealth distributions were so large that they had to be organized individually by the donor clans, with individual clan festivals being coordinated and held on appointed days. Families from hosting clans attended the clan distributions of the individual men they had hosted to receive their due.

4. *Akaipu tee* (or *yuku pingi*). Initiatory gifts for the final payments given by the hosts to the owners of the fight were composed of cooked pork, goods, and valuables.[8] *Akaipu pingi* means "to put on cordyline leaves to clothe the buttocks" — in other words, the hosts had taken care of all the owners' needs, even fetching

cordyline for them when all their time was occupied with events
of the Great War.

5. *Lome nyingi*. This was the large final payment of live pigs, cassowaries, marsupials, goods, and valuables given by the owners of
the fight to the hosts. *Lome nyingi* means to build a fortress or
stronghold, implying that the hosts had built and opened their fortress to the owners of the fight.

As in reparations for conventional wars, everybody tried to give generously in
the Great War and gained status by doing so, although overt competition disruptive to group unity was discouraged. Great War exchanges were initially based
on home production with little finance from outside, because most families in
the area participated and there was little left to give to finance others. Men who
married more wives and raised more pigs, however, could enter into exchanges
with more families in the hosting clans, and vice versa, thereby increasing their
spheres of influence. As we shall see, this situation changed in approximately the
fourth generation when big-men in clans spanning the two exchange systems
sought to finance the Great Wars via the Tee cycle.

Great War episodes, as events requiring enormous amounts of resources that
established longer-term exchange relationships, were fought infrequently. Episodes of any given Great War were separated by some ten to thirty years, with
no more than five episodes held in the lifetime of a single individual and usually
only two or three. Because they drew the participation of the population of
much of central Enga, episodes of different Great Wars were never fought
simultaneously.

The Great Wars were competitive on two levels. First, and by far the most
prominent, was the contest between the opposing tribes in numbers, display,
fighting prowess, organization, and wealth exchanged. The second was interindividual competition, which we discuss at the end of this chapter. The enthusiasm and excitement generated by the intergroup competition—the common
cause, danger, and spectacle—drew gatherings of unprecedented size. Every
participant and some spectators brought pigs for the exchanges, and more wealth
was exchanged at one place and time than had ever been exchanged before in
Enga history. For the *yanda andake kepa singi* of the last episode fought between
Itapuni-Awaini and Malipini-Potealini, more than twenty clans killed pigs on one
day. With each family contributing a minimum of one pig, some one thousand
to two thousand pigs must have been slaughtered and distributed, and more
likely double that. The majority of pigs killed were raised at home, putting heavy
demands on agricultural production. In view of this situation, it is not surprising
that the big-men of clans who took part in both the Great Wars and the Tee cycle

constructed ever longer chains of finance via the Tee to tap into wealth outside of central Enga and fuel the Great Wars as they grew.

The Four Great Wars: History and Politics

So far as we could determine, only four Great Wars were fought between the sixth generation and first contact with Europeans, and all but one of them had been discontinued in the first two decades of the twentieth century.[9] Here we present each individually, try to place it in its social and political context, and give descriptions drawn from the testimonies of elders who had witnessed an episode firsthand or received secondhand information about past episodes from their fathers or grandfathers. It should be noted that the Great Wars were embedded in the context of many smaller conventional wars and other events that occurred between episodes, which affected who hosted the next episode, when it was called, where it was fought, and so on. We are unable to place each episode within its specific sociopolitical context.

Yanaitini versus Monaini

Among the earliest of the Great Wars reported in historical traditions was that between the Yanaitini tribe of Tetemanda, near Wabag, and the Monaini tribe of Kasap in the Lagaip valley (map 14:1). When the first episode was fought is no longer known, but in the majority of historical traditions it is said to have begun early, within a few generations after Yanaitini moved to Tetemanda (probably around the sixth generation). Its origins are described in a tradition that indicates deep-seated competition over the salt trade, though the politics are not directly spelled out. Shortly after the arrival of the sweet potato, Yanaitini and Itokone went to make salt in the Yandap, caching some sweet potatoes at Tetemanda for their return journey. While they were gone, a Monaini man stole them. Furious, Yanaitini pursued the Monaini man clan by clan, following a major trade route up to Laiagam until he reached Sambe Pupu. Sambe Pupu, aware of the theft, helped Yanaitini find and kill the culprit. Afterward, Yanaitini was said to put on ceremonial dress to fight Monaini, hosted by Sambe Pupu, and so the Great War began. Leme Poul of the Kandawalini Kaekini clan, who gave a detailed narrative describing this event, said that even recently he had heard a song at a traditional dance commemorating the event:

> *Talo piyamo Sanda pote mendai kolao neo. Pote yako lao katenge pyaa.*
>
> Being hungry, took out a Sanda sweet potato. You never stop crying over the sweet potato.
> [Sanda is the term used in song to refer to the Yanaitini Kia clan.]

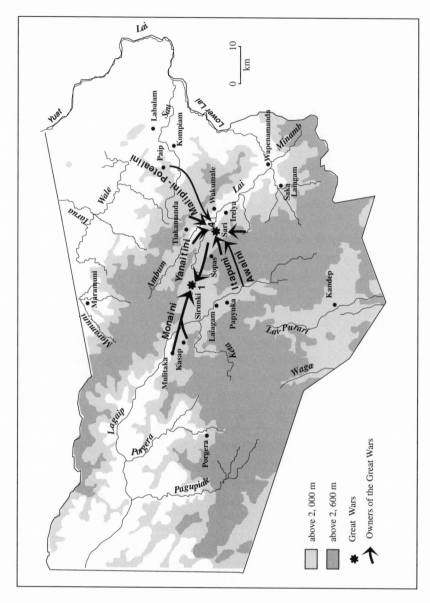

Map 14. The Yanaitini versus Monaini and Malipini-Potealini versus Itapuni-Awaini Great Ceremonial Wars. Arrows indicate the areas from which the owners of the fights came to participate.

Though phrased in metaphorical terms, the politics that sparked the Yanaitini-Monaini Great Wars are not hard to grasp: Monaini had clans who were closer to the salt springs than Yanaitini and who could have profited greatly by directing the salt trade westward. Were Yanaitini to lose its hold on the salt springs of the Yandap, it would forfeit its winning card in the Lai trade.

The battles between Yanaitini and Monaini were fought at Lyamala Pau, Angalende (near what is now the high-altitude agricultural station of Taluma). Yanaitini was hosted by Sambe clans near Papyuka, particularly Sambe Pupu, whose members provided food, shelter, and allies for Yanaitini warriors. At least in the early episodes, Itokone warriors came all the way from the middle Lai to help Yanaitini. Monaini warriors, who also lived far from the battlefront, were hosted by Lyaini and Kunalini clans at Sirunki.

Episodes of the Yanaitini-Monaini Great War were held periodically from its onset until the early 1900s. Pisoto Pisini, who was probably the oldest surviving Yanaitini man at the time of our research, participated in the last episode when he was in his teens, and two other Yanaitini men were named Monaini because their fathers were away fighting Monaini when they were born. The ages of these men place the last round of the war between about 1915 and 1920. Though too young to understand the political context of the war, Pisoto recalled his stay of approximately six months with hosting families, the excitement of the battles, their glamour and spectacle, and the courtship parties at night.[10]

The costs of this formidable display of wealth and power must have been enormous, particularly in terms of manpower, since the men fought so far from home. Nonetheless, the investments appear to have paid off: Yanaitini strengthened bonds with Sambe, securing an ally on the western side of the salt springs and at the crossroads of the trade coming from Kandep and the Lagaip valley. Gains were also significant for Monaini and Lyaini: Monaini channeled goods from the Lagaip to Lyaini and Kunalini, both of whom had access to trade routes coming from the east via the Ambum valley. Lyaini, furthermore, owned land on which some of the salt springs were located.

The last episode of the Monaini-Yanaitini Great War, fought in the beginning of the twentieth century, became very taxing in terms of time, manpower, and wealth for some Yanaitini clans who were involved in other Great Wars and the Tee cycle. Strapped for wealth with which to pay reparations to Sambe, around 1915–20 Yanaitini gave its hosts land in the Yandap that included the Nakatima salt pools, calling an end to the Great Wars with Monaini once and for all. By that time Sambe clans had already become feeder groups into the Tee cycle, and Yanaitini then obtained salt indirectly through them.

Lyaini-Sakalini versus Pumane-Aiyele

The roots of the Lyaini-Sakalini versus Pumane-Aiyele Great War lay in the devastating Ambum valley wars of the sixth to seventh generation (see chapter 5). During them the Lyaini and Sakalini tribes, together with allies from Yanaitini and Malipini, expelled the Pumane and Aiyele from virtually all of their land in Sirunki and the upper Ambum valley. The war was sparked by a quarrel over the theft of a stalk of sugarcane, though it is generally acknowledged that the underlying aim was to take the fertile Ambum land. The refugee clans of Pumane and Aiyele then fled into the upper Sau valley, from where they later challenged their victors to a Great War. We could not determine from historical legends whether or not the first episode of this war was fought shortly after the Ambum valley wars or whether it had to do with testing the strength of the victors. What we do know is that by the fourth generation it had become a true tournament war.

Although the precise location of this Great War shifted from episode to episode, it was always fought in the middle Ambum valley, the last episode occurring early in the twentieth century at Waipu swamp near Yampu. Potealini clans at Kundis, particularly Anae, and four Malipini clans on the north side of the Ambum (Bia, Kombane, Angaleane, and Maiome) hosted Pumane and Aiyele. Malipini Kamaniwane and at least some families in Yanaitini Lanekepa and Kumbini hosted Lyaini and Sakalini. Because Lyaini and Sakalini land stretched west to Laiagam and north to Maramuni, and Pumane-Aiyele land well into the Sau, Wale, and Tarua valleys, the exchange networks created were truly vast (map 15:2).

On the Lyaini and Sakalini side, the pig killing [at the end of the Great Wars] would start way back behind the land of Wambili and Kombatao [upper Lai-Sirunki] and sweep down through every clan in the valley until it reached the battlefront. At the northern end, people from as far away as Maramuni would take part; pigs were also killed in places like Londol [upper Ambum]. When it was time for the Aiyele and Pumane clans to kill pigs, the *yae* would begin in the land of the Pumane Yaupu clan [upper Sau]. All the clans that lived between Yaupu and the battlefront killed pigs. Virtually everybody, even those who came to watch the Great War, killed a pig. (Yakapusa Mioko, Malipini Kamaniwane clan, Kaeyapa, Lai-Ambum ridge)

Some elders who are still alive today witnessed the exchanges from the last episode in their childhoods and were able to describe them firsthand. Outstanding in these exchanges, and consistent with Lyaini and Sakalini's reputations as great hunters, is the large number of cassowaries and marsupials distributed:

Lyaini and Sakalini are big tribes. The tribal land of Lyaini extends as far as Laiagam. It is the same with Sakalini — its territory stretches all the way to Maramuni. In the Great Wars

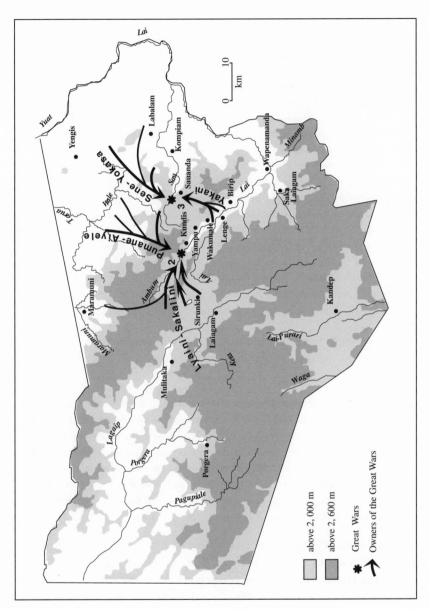

Map 15. The Lyaini-Sakalini versus Pumane-Aiyele and Sene-Yokasa versus Yakani Great Ceremonial Wars. Arrows indicate the areas from which the owners of the fights came to participate.

all the people from Sakalini would come and give pork to the clans of Malipini, especially Kamaniwane, and to some clans of Yanaitini as well. We would slaughter pigs and give pork to these clans for hosting our Great War, and later we would give the same clans live pigs. During the latter exchanges, many cassowaries were also given, for Sakalini was renowned for its ability to capture cassowaries. Along my ridge [the ridge separating the upper Lai and Ambum valleys], one would find many ponds made to water cassowaries [for the distribution]. There is also a stretch of Kamaniwane land where ponds can still be found, and at Lakuia there are three such ponds. We would give not only cassowaries but all kinds of marsupials—for example, *lyamano, andeape,* and many more. Malipini and Yanaitini clans would come up to receive these large quantities of food. . . . As I said, some time after the pig killing festival, the Sakalini clans would give live pigs followed by cassowaries, marsupials, and other items of value.

You know it was a great social event. They [the Kamaniwane] were our friends and hosts, and to express their friendship they first gave sides of pork and later live pigs, cassowaries, and other things [as initiatory gifts]. You see, they were like a stronghold for us against the enemy, and during the times when the fighting took place they hosted the war. The distribution of live pigs was called *yuku pingi*. You see these paths? Well, it was through these paths that Sakalini used to give cassowaries to those who hosted the Great War. (Pyakole Pakena, Lyaini Malyee clan, Lakui [Lai-Ambum ridge])

Later during the interview in which he gave this description, in response to a question about whether or not men from Sambe clans participated as allies, Pyakole said:

These wars were Great Wars. Clan after clan would ally with either side. Every capable warrior from far and wide who heard of the war came to take part. How then could the Sambe men have stayed home? Surely they must have come to the war, for it was a great event. All of the warriors would put on full ceremonial attire. They wore neck- or headbands of shells embroidered on opossum tails, planted bird-of-paradise plumes in their wigs, and painted their faces with red clay and ashes from burnt wood. So you see, they were Great Wars, not small wars that they should stay at home. They came to watch and to fight.

Others said that women were also given to hosting clans as part of reparations with no bridewealth expected, in the interest of future exchange ties.

The last episode of this Great War was fought in the early decades of the twentieth century. By this time, Pumane and Aiyele had joined the Tee cycle and lost interest in the Great Wars, and Lyaini and Sakalini had become major allies of Malipini and Potealini in their Great War against Itapuni and Awaini.

Sene-Yokasa (Kungu-Tiaka) versus Yakani

Shortly after Lyaini and Sakalini, together with allies from Yanaitini and Malipini, drove Pumane and Aiyele clans from the upper Ambum valley into the upper

Sau, Yakani clans did the same to Sene and Yokasa of the lower Ambum valley, the "cousin" tribes of Pumane and Aiyele (chapter 5). Unlike Pumane-Aiyele, Sene-Yokasa clans did not muster up forces from their new locations and initiate Great Wars with the victors soon after their defeat, but rather expanded throughout the northern Kompiam area. Only in the fourth generation, when they were well installed in their new homeland, did they revive their struggles of the past and, following the trend of the times, engage in a series of Great Wars with Yakani. These were some of the most highly ritualized of the Great Wars. They were fought primarily to construct social networks that would put the Sene and Yokasa tribes back in contact with the mainstream of exchange of central Enga while giving Yakani access to the large pig herds of the Sau valley at a time when the Tee cycle was expanding.

We know for certain that two episodes of this Great War were fought in the fourth generation, and most likely there were three. The first episode was fought at Samalemanda and Kutaipaka near Sauanda in the upper Sau valley, and the chief instigators were the Yakani Timali of Lenge and Yokasa Yokotini clans near Sauanda (map 15:3). Aiyele Tiakai, Pumane Yaupa, and Pumane Sane clans hosted Yakani, while some Sene-Yokasa clans fought from their own land and others were hosted by Aiyele near Wapai. Because Sene-Yokasa clans were already so widely dispersed, participants came from the entire northern Kompiam area. For example, Sene and Yokasa men interviewed at Labalama said that their fathers had traveled all the way from Labalama and Yengis to fight in this Great War or contribute to the war reparations, despite their fear of being subjected to witchcraft in unknown areas so far from home. On the southern side, warriors from all Yakani clans participated. Although no men who fought in these Great Wars were still alive at the time our research, Yakani historical traditions vividly recall scenes from the episode fought in the Sau valley. They portray the pomp and ceremony as well as the brutality:

Here is a description of what it was like on the battlefront at the time of [the Great War leaders] Piuku and Pendaine. Most of the [enemy] Yokotini [Sene-Yokasa] clans lived down the Sau valley and still do.[11] That is to the east. The Kambi and Lapai subclans of Yokotini are neighbors of the Aiyele clan,[12] and so the territories of these three groups became the battlefront on the Yokotini side. These groups supplied the warriors who came to fight for Sene-Yokasa with food, water, and weapons. All the Sene-Yokasa living farther to the east were hosted by and allied with Kambi, Lapai, and Aiyele. The Aiyele were not only suppliers of provisions but also frontline warriors in battle. The Sau river was the buffer zone—it was no-man's-land. On our side of the river, the clans of Aiyele Tiakai and Pumane Sane and Yaupa joined forces, hosting and supplying the provisions for the Yakani warriors. Their land was also used as a battlefront. On this side the warriors gathered at Kutaipaka, an area bordering on the territories of our hosting clans, namely, Aiyele Tiakai and Pumane Sane. The two forces met by the banks of the river. When the Yokotini warriors gained ground, they crossed the river and invaded Kutaipaka; conversely, when the Yakani warriors made their main thrust, they also crossed the river and invaded Samalemanda [the gathering place for Sene-Yokasa].

It was told that in the Great Wars the men were decorated. They put on all kinds of feathers except the plumes of the King of Saxony bird of paradise, *mioko* feathers, feathers of all kinds of birds, you name them, they were all put on. Cut shells of pearl were worn around their necks, and they were fully armed with spears, bows, and arrows when they went to fight. Piuku [from the Sene-Yokasa Yokotini clan] and Pendaine [from the Yakani Timali clan] were rival Great War leaders. Really they were figureheads to represent the tribe. Talking of valor, victory, and fame, they kept the spirits of the warriors high.

On one occasion, the Yakani warriors were gathered on this side of the Sau river, and on the other the Yokotini warriors were mobilizing themselves for action. Pendaine, my grandfather, was there among the Yakani warriors who were at the battlefront. He shouted to the other side of the river asking the Yokotini warriors to tell his rival Piuku to come forward and show himself. Piuku appeared in the front line. When one of the Yokotini warriors shouted back saying that Piuku was there, Pendaine demanded that he reveal his son. Piuku did not say anything because he did not have a son. It was told that he just roamed around the front line without saying a word. However, warriors on this side presented Ima Waiona, Pendaine's nephew, in the front line, a giant man and very heavily built. A young man with such a gigantic build was indeed a fearful sight for the enemy. Pendaine said that this was his son, the heir to his leadership. He told them how sad it was to see that Piuku did not even have a son, and his words made Piuku very envious. By the way, Ima Waiona was not Pendaine's real son, but he presented him as such because at that time his real son, Lambu, was still a toddler.

Another day, the Great War had started early in the morning. The Yokotini warriors had managed to come over to this side of the river and were advancing toward Kutaipaka. The Great War leader Piuku led his men. He was described as being of average height. He wore a wig on his head and on top of it two bright yellow plumes of the *kaiwae* bird of paradise, the yellow plumes bright like the color of *amboko* fruits. He was a heavily built man and showed no signs of fear. He stood there looking really cool and calm, but then who really wanted to kill him anyway? He was the leader of the Yokotini, and the Yakani wanted him but not to kill. They just wanted to capture him and pluck the two plumes from his wig, so when the main forces met and were fighting, a few Yakani warriors went after the Yokotini leader with wooden clubs, trying to capture him. Piuku moved from one place to another, darting swiftly here and there. He zigzagged and dodged, always keeping out of reach of the Yakani warriors who were trying to grab him. They could not get the plumes from his wig. With the plumes swaying to the left and to the right, the proud man went home with his warriors in the afternoon.

On the same day, Pendaine wore two long black plumes of the *mioko* bird of paradise. Pendaine said that he went up to the battlefront and talked to his rival, Piuku. Then both of them exchanged the challenging and insulting songs I told you earlier:

Kingikini Talua nyo naepelyamo pyao, galane nao alu pilyamo pya.

Kingi's son, if he does not bring the Talua men to war, he probably has disappeared chasing lizards for food.
[Sung by Yakani to degrade Sene Yokasa by making fun of the rubbish food they ate. Kingi's son is Piuku, and Talua is the song term for Yokotini.]

Kepakini Tipili nyo naepelyamo pya, ayomba nyo alu pilyamo pya.

Kepa's son, if he does not bring the Timali men to war, he probably has disappeared with the previous heads.
[Sung by Sene-Yokasa to say that even if Kepa's son, Pendaine, does not bring Timali men to war, it is because he already has enough deaths on his hands to pay reparations for. In other words, it boasts of the number of enemy men they have killed and derides their opponents for being too poor to pay the reparations for all of them. Tipili is the song term for the Timali clan.]

Pendaine said that he led the Yakani warriors down to the bank of the Sau river. Actually they went into some bush by the river and hid themselves there. The main force followed shortly after, and thinking that the Yakani warriors were still on the way, the enemy eagerly crossed the river and headed toward Kutaipaka. They were mistaken. Suddenly, out of the bush came the Yakani warriors and attacked the men. It was a fierce battle. They fought, killed two men, and then retreated to join the approaching main force, which was not far away. One of their men by the name of Lapulapu did not realize that they had retreated and remained hidden after the ambush. As the enemy warriors moved forward, Lapulapu realized that it was too late to come out of hiding, for he would be spotted and killed by enemy warriors. He crouched down on all fours and hid there. The Yokotini warriors soon discovered the place where the Yakani men had been hiding for the ambush and some of them searched the thicket, parting the bush with their hands to take a close look at each spot where an enemy warrior had been hiding. By sheer chance, one of them came across the spot where Lapulapu was hiding. The enemy warrior was quick to see him and yelled, "There is someone hiding here." Many more warriors came and identified him as being from the other side. They showed no mercy. An enemy warrior lifted his *watae* spear and pierced the poor man, who had hidden his face in his hands. He died from the spear wounds and the Yokotini warriors shouted victory cries: "Au!"

Upon hearing the cries, the Yakani warriors looked at each other wondering whom they had left behind. They discovered that Lapulapu was not with them and knew that it was he who was being killed. It is said that after the Great War the reparations for his death were paid by the Yokotini.[13]

The primary motive for starting these wars was not to kill men. The underlying reason was to do *tee* exchange and hold big feasts. That is not to say that the Great Wars were mock wars. No, they were real wars. There were people who were mortally wounded and lay there on the battlefield to die. The Great Wars were more or less an excuse to slaughter pigs. Of course, the pigs were used to pay war reparations for those killed on both sides.

The Europeans did not stop the Great Wars; they ended before that. (Kopio Toya Lambu, Yakani Timali clan, Lenge [Wabag])

The second or third episode of this Great War was moved to Wakumale, near the junction of the Ambum and Lai rivers, bringing Sene-Yokasa directly into the exchange networks of central Enga. It was strategically arranged: the Sene and Yokasa were hosted by Malipini and Potealini clans in the Ambum and allied with Pumane and Aiyele. Some Yakani clans fought from their own land and others were hosted by Apulini near Irelya; Depe and Lyipini of the middle Lai were major allies. The result was the establishment of a far-flung exchange network that linked major valley systems (map 15:3). For reasons that will be discussed in the next chapter, the Yakani versus Sene-Yokasa Great War was the first of the Great Wars to be supplanted by the Tee cycle, the last episode being fought around the turn of the century.

Malipini-Potealini versus Itapuni-Awaini

The Malipini-Potealini versus Itapuni-Awaini Great War was the longest-lived of all the Great Wars, capturing the attention of central Enga for at least three generations (map 14:4). Its origin is attributed to a war that broke out over a "Peeping Tom" incident in the fifth to sixth generation: a young Malipini Kamaniwane man went to peek at Takoname, an extraordinarily beautiful woman from the Itapuni Nemani clan, as she went naked into a pond to cut reeds for grass skirts. While he ogled her, the branch on which he was perched broke and he crashed to the ground. Terrified, she ran home screaming, "Rape!" The incident stirred up grudges between tribes who had been neighbors and competitors in the upper Lai valley for generations, and the challenge for a Great War was sent to Kamaniwane.

Ambone Mati of the Itapuni Nemani clan said that one and perhaps several episodes of this Great War were fought in the generation of his grandfather (fourth to fifth generation), five during the life of his father, and two in his lifetime. The first six or more episodes were fought at Kopena and Sari, a few kilometers up the Lai valley from Wabag. Clans of the Yanaitini tribe living on the ridge that separates the Lai and Ambum valleys hosted Malipini and Potealini.[14] During the episodes of the twentieth century, the Yanaitini Kia clan of Tetemanda, at the western terminus of the Tee cycle, remained neutral, assisting both sides in a variety of ways. It is said by most that Itapuni and Awaini fought from their own land and only held exchanges with allies, but some suggest that in earlier episodes, Kia may have hosted Itapuni.

Whatever the case, early in the second decade of the twentieth century, when Malipini and Potealini warriors marched down to begin another episode at Sari, Kia men turned them away for reasons not clearly understood today.[15] Perhaps it was too close to home for the Kia clan, which was heavily involved in the politics of the expanding Tee cycle. The battle site was then moved down to Wakumale, where Apulini hosted Itapuni and Awaini and where the Yanaitini clan of Piao Lakiamanda and the Yakani Laita clan were the principal hosting clans for Malipini and Potealini.

A number of the older men in the area at the time of our research had witnessed this Great War as children or teenagers, recalling some of the events in considerable detail. The description by Yamu Yakia given in Appendix 11, based on what he saw as a child and learned in discussions over the years that followed, gives a good idea of the preparations, gathering of the warriors, weeks of prewar festivities, sessions to compose songs, dances for their rehearsal, and food taboos polarizing the two sides. From this testimony, it becomes clear just how much time, effort, enthusiasm, and spirit was involved in the "brewing of the war." He also touches on extensive prewar exchanges carried out to procure the necessary materials for weapons and items of ceremonial dress. In the end, Yamu briefly describes how the elaborate exchanges following this Great War were integrated into the Tee cycle, a topic we leave for the next chapter.[16] Certainly by the early 1900s the Great Wars were highly ceremonial.

The last episode of the Malipini-Potealini versus Itapuni-Awaini Great War was moved back to Kopena and fought for the last time after 1934 and before 1939.[17] Itapuni-Awaini fought from its own land, assisted by allies from a number of other clans, and Malipini-Potealini warriors were hosted by the Yanaitini clans mentioned earlier. This episode must have involved between one thousand and two thousand warriors, some of whom were still alive in the late 1980s and early 1990s. It is nevertheless difficult to get a thorough, step-by-step description of Great War episodes from any single informant, because the wars were so large that each participant witnessed only a small portion of the action. For the Kopena episode, we have chosen a testimony from a viewpoint rather different from that held by Yamu in Appendix 11 — that of Yopo Yakena, a daring and bold young warrior who later became a key figure in drawing the Kamaniwane clan into the Tee cycle. In his testimony, Yopo described his exploits in battle, the social life by night, and the exchanges that ensued. The testimony given in the following passages consists of excerpts from three interviews. It begins with Yopo's recollection of how the last Great War episode was initiated:

After the war [at Wakumale] in which Kombeakali's father was killed, Malipini and Potealini put on a dance at Aipinimanda to initiate the next Great War episode. That was when I was a young man. In order to brew a Great War, they would hold a traditional dance to gather allied forces, hosts, and enemies. It was called *yanda andake ia minao mali lyingi,* "the dance for breeding the Great War." Everybody dressed in such a way as to indicate his intentions, songs of provocation and rivalry were exchanged, and Great War leaders from both sides made speeches. They boasted of the bravery of their warriors and how well their hosts would look after them, and they mocked the enemy for how little they had given away in the exchanges after the last episode [years earlier]. The tension between the two sides mounted, but the actual war did not start there. First the Malipini and Potealini warriors would go to the land of the host clans and spend days on end talking about the upcoming event.

It was not necessary to kill a man to start the Great War—one day when we were making a garden at Laowale [in the middle Ambum], some Malipini and Potealini men came and gave a spear to someone from one of the hosting Yanaitini clans. The handing over of the spear was an indication that Malipini and Potealini wanted an episode of the Great War to begin. The Yanaitini man then went over to the Lai valley, found an Itapuni man and hurled a spear at him, missing intentionally. The Itapuni man ran off screaming that he had been speared, and the Great War was launched.

Warriors then gathered on either side and moved toward the battlefront. Many of them had donned full ceremonial dress—their best full-length aprons and wigs topped with *kaiwae* feathers—and smeared their bodies with tree oil. Dressed in such a way for the war, they met on the battlefield uttering war cries. The battles were fought in much same way as conventional wars, with many wounded on both sides and some killed. (Yopo Yakena, Malipini Kamaniwane clan, Kaeyape, Ambum-Lai ridge)

In response to a question, Yopo then went on to tell of the social life by night. Particularly important here was courtship and resulting marriage ties, not only for young men but also for older men seeking second or third wives.

Akii: What happened to the Malipini and Potealini warriors who lived farther away? Did they go home after a day of fighting to return the next morning?

Yopo: Look, they stayed and spent the nights in the houses of Yanaitini clans or in Malipini and Potealini houses that were near the battlefront. For instance, men from some distance away gathered at Tole [Piao Kumbini clan], where food was steamed for them. After they ate, they spent the night in the houses at Tole. Another place where food was prepared for the warriors was at Injinja. Many warriors spent the nights there. So they did not go home after a day's fight, they only returned home when the Great War was over. When they first arrived they would bring food for a few days, but after that they were fed by people of the hosting clans. It was a great occasion—many of the girls from the surrounding communities would come and entertain us. Of course, that meant that some of us would eventually end up marrying them. In the evenings we would dance with the girls, and that was the situation in every household where the warriors slept. For example, many would dance at Aipinimanda, and others would stay at Mukatisa on the land of the Kokope clan. You know Andamale's wife? When she was a young woman we stayed at Mukutisa. We had courtship parties with these girls, and we did these things while the Great War was still on; many of the warriors were still in full ceremonial dress from the day's fight. As I said, many of these girls eventually married the warriors. Here is a song sung by Andamale's wife [at one of these parties] when she was a young woman:

> Takapia kote tii sepa nae mendenya tii sio, Pauli balu yana pyao pititu lao tii sio.

> I was too young for sex with this man from Pauli [Potealini], but I did knowing that I would marry him after all.

You know Yama's wife? She was a pretty girl at that time, and she was with us. I courted her. She married her husband while the Great War was still going on.

Akii: So you spent the nights courting girls and dancing with them. And in the morning, did you go to fight?

Yopo: All nights were social nights; we had lots of fun with the girls. We courted them by night and went to fight during the day. It was exciting and fun. All the men, dressed for war, converged on the battlefield in the morning. The young men from the Kumbini clan fought in the front lines; that was why a Kumbini warrior was always killed in the Great War. That was how it was when the war was fought at Kopena — one of them was always killed, it was inevitable.

At this point Yopo went into battle exploits and one particularly interesting case in which the enthusiasm of the young men got out of hand and he and fellow warriors ambushed and killed a Great War leader (*watenge*) named Tima on his way to battle. Their rational was that it was a justified payback for the death of one of their men whom they considered to have been killed in foul play. Such revenge, particularly when taken out on a Great War leader, was frowned upon by their seniors, though all the young women gathered, danced, and sang victory songs in support of their young heroes.

The next part of Yopo's testimony turned to the Great War exchanges. First he described the casting of the shields into the river to formally mark the end of the battles, *yanda andake konambi ipaka pyandenge*. Then he turned to the *endaki kamungi* in which the hosting clans of Yanaitini gave initiatory gifts to Malipini and Potealini clans they had supported in order to kick off the Great War exchanges. *Endaki kamungi*, the fetching of water, indicated that the hosts had taken good care of their guests and now expected reciprocation. It was rich in symbolism, particularly since hosting clans had not only provided for the hosted but also offered their men as frontline warriors. All clans involved on one side gathered for the event:

For this ceremony the Yanaitini host clans killed many pigs which they steamed in large earth ovens. The heads, sides, and hearts of the pork were decorated with red, white, yellow, and black stripes using charcoal, clay, and ochre as paints. The heads were then impaled on sticks so that they could be dramatically presented. A striped heart was taken and pierced onto the end of a long bamboo stick that was painted in the same fashion and adorned with flowers, *metae* ferns, and other decorative leaves. All of the Yanaitini men from the host clans then dressed as they would for a traditional dance, except that in addition they applied ochres to their bodies in the same manner that they had painted the pork. The men from Malipini and Potealini did the same.

When all of the necessary preparations had been made, the Yanaitini men went to Tole, gathering some distance away from the ceremonial grounds to organize for their formal entrance. They lined up in two rows, bearing all of the pork and other foodstuffs to be presented. The two men who led the lines were each given one of the decorated bamboo poles with the pigs' hearts impaled on the ends, and the procession began to dance and sing, slowly making its way to meet the men from Malipini and Potealini at the ceremonial grounds.

Upon hearing their songs, the Malipini and Potealini men formed two long rows, one for each tribe, and advanced singing and dancing to meet their hosts. On this occasion they chose me to head one of the lines and a Potealini man to head the other. We were to snatch the hearts off the bamboo sticks borne by the leading men of the Yanaitini procession.

The two lines of men met face to face on the ceremonial grounds, and the two Yanaitini men bearing the stakes with the hearts of pigs made a gesture to offer them to the two of us who led the Malipini and Potealini lines. As we grabbed for them, they pulled them back, continuing these teasing gestures while slowly moving backward as our lines approached. All the while the men in both lines were singing and dancing. Eventually they allowed us to pluck the hearts from the sticks. We tossed them backward down the line, those who caught them doing the same until the two men at the very end of the line caught and ate the raw hearts. In our case it was a Malipini Mangelonde man named Pyole who ate the heart. The act of giving the raw hearts was called *akali dingi* by Malipini and Potealini and *akali maingi* by the Yanaitini.

After this event, the pork and other food was distributed to those from Malipini and Potealini. Each of the Yanaitini men gave the striped heads and sides of pork to those they had hosted during the Great War as initiatory gifts for payments to come. When the food had been distributed, the ceremony ended.

No people from the Itapuni or Awaini clans could eat any of this pork or come anywhere near the ceremony. If they did, they would die. For instance, Peange's mother and her sister from Awaini died. Why? Because they ate from this pork. So we would not eat pork treated in this manner given to us by the enemy.

Akali dingi and *akali maingi* mean literally "to give the man." Yopo explained that because the Yanaitini clans had "given their men" to Malipini and Potealini as frontline warriors in the Great War, they now expected reparations for hosting and helping them and for their men lost in battle. He suggested that the tossing of the hearts may have symbolized the flow of wealth out of Great War exchanges, noting that the wealth would have been widely distributed, much of it going east in the Tee cycle.

After initiatory gifts were given, dances and marsupial feasts were held by different clans of the owners of the fight to plan the great pig kill and first payment to hosts (*yanda andake kepa singi*). Yopo described the organization of the pig kill this way:

The Great War pig kill would begin on the land of Potealini Kombatao and Wambili clans of the upper Lai valley. It began very early; before the break of dawn the Wambili clan killed pigs, and then at daybreak the Kombatao clan killed theirs. The Sakatawane clan [at Sopas] killed pigs about the time that we usually open our house doors in the morning. The pork was then brought to the ceremonial grounds, that is, to one ceremonial ground after the other. . . . There was so much pork that they had to give away the meat uncooked. Additional meat was left on the sides of pork so that those who received them could cut it off, cook it, and eat it on their way back before they passed the sides on to people [Tee cycle partners] farther down the Lai.

In the meantime, Yanaitini men got ready to attend these festivals, putting on their wigs of human hair, chest plates, and, on top of their wigs, woven cassowary feather headdresses. Dressed in this way, they went to the ceremonial grounds, sat down, and waited for the men from the donor clans to bring in the pork and distribute it. The donors entered, bringing some steamed sides of pork and many that were raw. Others came carrying the chests and intestines. The heads of pigs were neither steamed nor carried to the ceremonial grounds but put away for each family to eat at home. All the men from the hosting or assisting Yanaitini clans, namely, Lanekepa, Piao clans, Kia, and so on, received sides of pork, and they in turn gave them to men in the Kalia and Timali clans [who sent them eastward in the Tee cycle].

In the Ambum valley, the Kamaniwane clan killed pigs at sunrise. When the sun was just above the horizon the men from Potealini at Tiakamanda killed pigs. In the middle of the day, men from the Kombane, Angaleane, and Wailuni clans killed pigs, and just after midday, men from the Itapu area [that is, Malipini and Potealini clans on north side of the Sau valley near Paipa] killed theirs. All this was done on the same day, and as I said earlier, all of the pork except for the pigs' heads was brought to the ceremonial grounds.

During these festivals, Yanaitini men who had hosted warriors went around from ceremonial ground to ceremonial ground in full attire to receive sides of pork and other portions of meat. Many open fires could be seen along the paths where people stopped to roast pork. In the evening they went home and straight to bed, not feeling hungry at all.

Akii: The pigs from all of the clans were killed on the same day. If I have got it straight, what happened then was that the hosts or supporters went to the respective ceremonial grounds of those they had hosted to receive sides of pork and other portions of meat.

Yopo: Yes, that is what happened. In the Great War, the Lanekepa, Piao, Kia, and other Yanaitini men who had hosted or provided food and water for our warriors attended these festivals. It was these hosts who were given sides of pork and other portions of meat by the individual warriors they hosted. The relatives and friends of these men would also come to the festivals, and they in turn would bring their own friends and relatives. Because of this, many, many people attended the *yae* festivals. To prevent the pork from going bad, much of it was cooked again the next morning. One cannot say that anybody really ate up the pork from these festivals—there was just too much to consume it all.

Then we put on dances again to plan the next phase of the reparations—the distribution of live pigs, *lome nyingi*. First the pigs had to be bred and raised, and when they were large enough we slit their ears to mark them for the distribution of live pigs. Before their ears healed, we gave them away.

Even though these distributions were held on a massive scale, with food distributed to all participants and spectators, debts were also paid on an individual basis. Families from among the owners of the fight gave to the particular families who had hosted them, striking up enduring exchange relationships. The *lome nyingi*, the final grand distribution of live pigs, food, and valuables to hosts, was organized similarly. Clan members and allies distributed to those who had hosted them large numbers of live pigs and cassowaries whose eyes were encircled decoratively with red ochre, together with other goods and valuables. The donors were adorned in full ceremonial dress, their bodies glistening with *mamba* oil and their wigs decked with bird-of-paradise feathers. Recipients were in ordinary attire. Because of the sheer size of this distribution and the fact that the animals had to be cared for and taken home by the recipients, the *lome nyingi* festivals of different clans were held on consecutive days. The *lome nyingi* that Yopo described swept through more than twenty clans, beginning in the upper Lai valley, moving down the Lai and over into the Ambum, and continuing on into the upper Sau.[18] The Yanaitini clans received far more wealth than they could absorb, and so they reinvested some of it by sending it east as initiatory gifts for the next Tee cycle.[19] Finally, it should be noted that whereas important components of the *lome nyingi* of earlier Great Wars were cassowaries and marsupials, these had largely been replaced by pigs by the time of the final episode of the Malipini-Potealini versus Itapuni-Awaini Great Wars.

The Relationship of the Great Wars to Conventional Wars

All the descriptions just given of the four major Great Wars came from their more recent episodes. We will not speculate on the priorities of earlier Great

War episodes, but it is probably fair to say that display of force to impress and intimidate opponents was secondary to exchange interests in the episodes of the twentieth century. Nonetheless, the spirit of opposition remained crucial for a number of reasons: to rally enthusiasm, to unite allies on each side, and to demonstrate a military force capable of defending land and the exchange networks formed through the Great Wars. Furthermore, intra- and interclan wars had to be terminated and peace had to prevail within each opposing side before a Great War could be called, in order to establish a unified fighting force and permit the free flow of goods and valuables during the Great War exchanges. Although internal peace brought about by the Great Wars could do little to solve deep-seated political problems, it could halt runaway aggression — the senseless igniting of intra- and interclan wars to take revenge for deaths in former ones.[20]

It should be noted, however, that the Great Wars had no close link to smaller, conventional wars. Aside from the initial incidents that were said to have led to Great Wars, elders claimed that there were no cases in which subsequent episodes grew out of smaller wars or in which Great Wars were called to put order to the chaos caused by local conflicts, as appears to have been the case for the ritualized interalliance wars of the Dani of Irian Jaya (Larson 1987).[21] Conversely, we were given no examples of Great Wars deteriorating into all-out vicious wars in which one of the opponents suffered great losses or was expelled from its land. Between episodes of Great Wars, single clans frequently fought smaller conventional wars, continually altering the political setting of each Great War episode. The Enga Great Wars, as wars that were fought to organize and maintain pathways of exchange but left population distribution unaffected, appear to have had no parallels in other parts of the New Guinea highlands. Though superficially similar in some respects to the ritualized wars of the Dani, the latter were fought to alleviate internal conflicts and redistribute population, not for the purpose of exchange (Larson 1987).[22]

Watenge: Great War Leaders

With the Great Wars, a new category of leader emerged: *watenge,* Great War leaders from clans of the owners of the fight, whose names fill the roll calls of central Enga history.[23] Great War leaders were proclaimed "wanted men" who were to be chased and trailed until the enemy finally got them — though only figuratively. They were to be captured or otherwise humiliated on the battlefield but not killed, for they were esteemed by both sides as public figures behind whom people could rally and as symbolic targets for the enemy. They were the men who could organize the wars, direct their course, call an episode to an end, arrange Great War exchanges, and plan the next episode. The deaths of Great War leaders, whether by violent causes or natural ones, were mourned by followers, allies, and enemies alike. When their end came, however, *watenge* and big-men were given the same burial as ordinary men, with no grave goods added to indicate their status, although many people attended their funerals and participated in the exchanges surrounding their deaths.

Great War leaders assumed all the roles and had all the qualities discussed earlier for big-men (*kamongo*), plus a flair for showmanship. Between episodes of Great Wars they were the big-men of a clan who organized feasts and cults, negotiated peace, and arranged war reparations. They were chosen not only by their own clansmen but also by the enemy, for it was the enemy who challenged certain big men of the opposing side to present themselves as representatives during battle. Unlike ordinary big-men, whose power base was seated in their fellow clansmen, the status of Great War leader required more — maternal and affinal ties in the leading families of hosting and allied groups, through which *watenge* could wield regional influence.

The position of Great War leader was inherited, provided that the accomplishments of the young men in line for inheritance were sufficient. Whereas any gifted man could become a big-man, most people interviewed insisted that the public looked to the sons or nephews of Great War leaders to replace them, and that the sons of poor or ordinary men could not become Great War leaders. This was the significance of the event described earlier when the Yakani Great War leader Pendaine presented his nephew, a giant of a young man, as his son and heir to humiliate his rival, Piuku, who had no son. A further testimony describing the rise of Satutu, one of the Great War leaders of the most recent episode, which underlines the roles of both public expectation and personal competence, is given in Appendix 12.

The principle that the title *watenge* be passed down in a family line if a Great War leader had capable sons or nephews was adhered to whenever possible, because such men had the family connections necessary to arrange a Great War episode. Such connections could be built only over time. Of seven Great War leaders for whom we have genealogical information, five were indeed the sons of *watenge,* and two of these had both fathers and grandfathers in that role; information on the status of the fathers of the other two was unavailable. All seven were either married into the hosting clan or had mothers or sisters in it. Inheritance of the title of Great War leader had a second advantage in that it narrowed the arena for internal competition and focused rivalry on Great War leaders from different sides, since only a limited number of men in each clan were eligible.

What one sees, then, in the context of the Great Wars is the development of inherited social inequalities in response to demands from the people that consistent leadership be instituted in order to provide predictable, established figures behind whom large groups could rally. There is no indication that such inherited status had deeper historical roots; it appears to have developed within the context of the Great Wars. By contrast, in the east the position of big-man who organized the Tee cycle was based on, among other things, the efforts of individuals to attain and maintain their positions in controlling the flow of wealth along Tee and trade routes, rather than on appointment by the group. There, sons of big-men were in a better position to follow their fathers, owing to established connections, but very capable sons of low-status men became big-men nonetheless.

The Tee Cycle and the Great Wars

Between approximately the eighth and fourth generations the Tee cycle of eastern Enga and the Great Wars of central Enga developed separately, despite some common features in organization and problems addressed. The big-men of the east constructed Tee alliances to keep control of the trade in the face of immigration from the south and east. A subtle threat, one of newcomers usurping control of the trade, was thus met by a discreet response—the formation of private alliances to counter their moves. For the first generations of its existence, the Tee cycle remained small in scale and somewhat out of the limelight, with only a limited number of families in a clan stepping up production in order to participate. Its subtlety was deceiving, however, for beneath it lay a powerful innovation—the creation of chains of finance that exceeded the bounds of direct kinship. These chains made it possible to tap into the wealth of a much broader segment of the population.

The Great Wars of central Enga also grew out of the need for coalitions, but coalitions between clans of a tribe or entire tribes, not private alliances between families or lineages. The vicious wars of the preceding generations had left the population uprooted and shaken, and leaders sought a means to forge alliances and display their power in a way that would deter future aggression while simultaneously expanding exchange ties. There were few innovations in their strategies. They merely built on existing options—namely, fighting and the payment of war reparations—and made them bigger, better, and more entertaining through drama and ritual. Owing to the sheer number of participants, the Great Wars constructed vast exchange networks fueled by intensified home production within a broad segment of the population. The glamour, excitement, group spirit, and ceremony of these great tournaments lent much greater social and symbolic value to pigs, mobilizing each and every household to step up production for the exchanges. This gradual shift from an exchange economy based on wild game and nonagricultural trade goods to one with a heavy emphasis on pigs can be detected in descriptions of Great War exchanges: earlier ones dwell heavily on the distribution of cassowaries and marsupials, and later ones on pigs.

For quite some time the Tee cycle and the Great Wars ran parallel to each other, the Great Wars being by far the more prominent. As the Great Wars expanded, the big-men who played a role in both exploited the potential of the Tee chains to finance the wars and then reinvested the wealth they received, dramatically altering the course of Enga history.

11

Later Developments in the Tee
The Completion of the Exchange Cycle

> **The Tee is like a great river which flows out of the past through the lives of Enga.**
> Maua Pakiala, Yambatane Watenge clan, Saka Laiagam, quoted in Roderic Lacey,
> "Holders of the Way"

In the fifth generation before the present, the Tee cycle encompassed but a sparse network of clans along four trade routes radiating out from the Saka valley. Three generations later, it was like a flooding river of wealth that swept through virtually every clan of eastern and central Enga. Could families from the fifth generation have journeyed through time to attend a Tee festival held by their great-grand-

children in the mid-twentieth century, they would have been astounded by what they saw. Rather than the expected thirty to fifty pigs, as many as a thousand would have stood tethered to stakes on the ceremonial grounds. Previously scarce pearl shells would have been distributed in numbers inconceivable to them. Standing amid thousands of participants and spectators from clans who in their time had been far removed from the Tee cycle, they would have marveled at the wealth and display of the great *kamongo* (big-men).

During the span of three generations, the Tee cycle had expanded in almost every dimension. In space (map 16), the eastern routes extended well into the Nebilyer,

Kaugel, and north Mendi areas (Western and Southern Highlands Provinces). The northern routes branched out as far north as Yengis and as far east as the Baiyer river area. The once-narrow western path from the Saka valley to Tetemanda had broadened to draw in all clans of the middle and upper Lai valley. Upon reaching central Enga, the Tee cycle no longer abutted the Great Wars but had supplanted them, replacing their spheres of exchange with routes west into the Yandap-Laiagam area and north into the Sau, Wale, and Tarua valleys. According to our calculations, the number of clans directly involved in the Tee cycle had soared from an estimated 30–50 in the fifth generation to 375–85 or more in the second.[1] Not only did the number of participant clans increase, but so did the number of Tee-makers within a clan. Whereas in the early Tee, only wealthy or well-connected members took part, as the benefits of the Tee became more perceptible, ever more families joined. From the mid-1950s on, when new wealth from Europeans was in circulation, every family, no matter how poor, gave out some wealth in the Tee as a matter of pride and an expression of independence.

Parallel to the Tee cycle's expansion in space ran developments in its organization. Although sequences of giving in the early Tee were short, involving five to fifteen clans at most, those of the mid-twentieth century ideally linked all Tee-making clans or subclans into a stepwise sequence of festivals. These began in either the southeast or northwest and proceeded to the opposite end of the network.[2] The incorporation of new clans transformed the linear pattern of the early Tee cycle, which had clung closely to trade routes, into a meandering one incorporating all clans in a valley (Meggitt 1974:173). Chains of allied big-men formed, crosscutting clan boundaries and in some cases extending more or less from one end of the network to the other. Men on these chains jointly planned a Tee cycle and then returned home to persuade fellow clansmen to comply.

By the twentieth century, gone too was the ad hoc nature of earlier cycles, which had been arranged to finance specific needs of a participant group, such as war reparations. The three-phase cycle of the Tee left so many outstanding debts and credits that the completion of one cycle compelled the beginning of the next. The Tee cycle thus became a general system of finance with its own momentum once a cycle was launched. War reparations, funerary gifts, child growth payments, and bridewealth were timed to fit into the Tee cycles that financed them, rather than vice versa, though the most powerful big-men still strove to time Tee cycles to suit their needs and those of their clans.

The cycles of the twentieth-century Tee began with a first phase that involved the distribution of initiatory gifts, or *saandi*, consisting of small pigs, tree kangaroos, shells, axes, salt, tree oil, and other valuables, which were given to partners on a private basis. Initiatory gifts could also be received during other distributions such as war reparations, but there were no formal festivals in this phase. *Saandi*

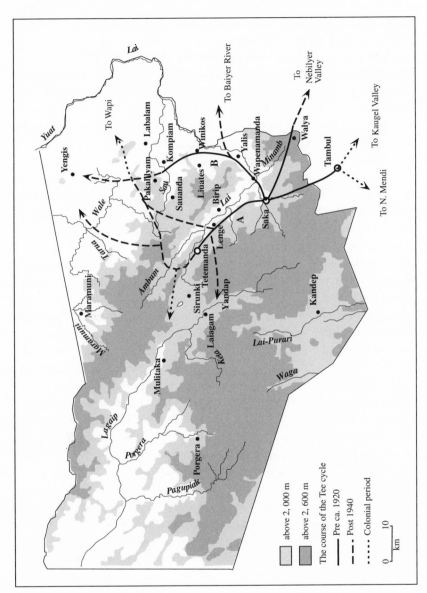

Map 16. The course of the Tee cycle before 1920, after 1940, and during the colonial period. The years from 1920 to 1940, a period of great change, are not shown.

gifts flowed in one direction and were intended to "pull" the *tee pingi*, the phase of the main gifts (Meggitt 1974:171).[3]

When a sufficient number of initiatory gifts had been sent up-valley or down-valley, depending on where the cycle began, big-men made efforts to launch the phase of the main gifts, *tee pingi*. They often disagreed about the timing and course of this phase as they vied to make arrangements that suited their needs and those of supporting clansmen. The *tee pingi*, an event of unsurpassed excitement, suspense, pomp, and ceremony, began either in the east or the west, wherever the *saandi* phase had ended, and proceeded through the Tee network clan by clan in the direction opposite that of the *saandi* gifts. Suspense and anticipation were high throughout, for to give and receive large numbers of pigs, pearl shells, axes, and other goods indicated political victory in controlling the flow of wealth.[4] Success conferred great prestige in addition to providing wealth to finance family and clan enterprises.

First in the *tee pingi* came the distribution of pigs, followed by that of cassowaries. Then the procession and prestation of pearl shells was held, an event that carried much more weight in eastern than in central Enga (Meggitt 1974). Finally, the distribution of remaining gifts—axes, salt, oil, shell ornaments, and other goods and valuables—assured the wide circulation of trade goods. Recipients were people in a number of different clans down the line from the hosting one, mostly but not exclusively within the three or four clans who would be the next to hold festivals. Families who received too many pigs to care for passed some of them on immediately to partners. The latter brought them back to be given formally in public during the Tee festival of the donor's clan. The event ended abruptly as participants and spectators dispersed, hastening home before dark. Tee cycle organizers remained and discussed the progress of the Tee. A few days later, the next clan in the sequence held its festival.

When the phase of the main gifts had worked its way through the network to the last clan involved, efforts were made to launch the reciprocal phase, *mena yae pingi*, or *yae*, the distribution of butchered, cooked pork that moved in the opposite direction of the main gifts, retracing their steps. This phase was usually launched promptly, because houses were crowded with pigs, and executed swiftly, so the pork would not rot. Approximately half of the pigs received in the *tee pingi* phase were slaughtered and butchered, the meat steamed in earth ovens and brought to the ceremonial grounds for distribution. The butchering of pigs into *mena sapya*, sides of pork with forelegs and hindlegs attached, left much extra meat for home consumption. Donors in the previous *tee pingi* received approximately one side of pork for each pig given. Some of these sides passed through many hands before reaching their final destination in a state of advanced deterioration. Nonetheless, the spirit of the *yae* was one of joy and festivity as everybody feasted. Pork received in the *yae* was used to pay a variety of debts and establish credit with which to initiate the next Tee cycle.

The *yae* completed a three-phase cycle that spanned approximately four years (Meggitt 1974:68). It left the Tee hovering in a state of imbalance, compelling a new cycle that would send the main gifts in the opposite direction. Such was the ideal; in reality, the Tee changed so rapidly throughout its history that no single cycle can be taken as representative of the system. In some cycles, several waves of initiatory gifts might be required to "pull" the main gifts. In others, particularly more recent ones, the main gifts might be delivered in two phases, and so on (Meggitt 1972, 1973; Feil 1984).

The increasing number of feeder routes into the mainstream and the growing number of participants within clans posed additional difficulties in organization. New routes had to be coordinated with the mainstream, and the course and timing of the flow of wealth along them was not equally advantageous for all. As a result, two or more chains of allied partners formed along each major route. Men on these chains competed with one another to maximize the amount of wealth that would arrive in the hands of their members at one time, a situation that could pit two big-men in one clan against each other. For instance, men along one Tee chain might prefer to hasten the course of a Tee cycle coming from the Sau valley, while those on another might wish to delay it until a Tee coming from the Yandap had arrived. Such planning and politics eventually engulfed the Tee cycle, so that the festivals themselves became public testimonies to the success of some alliances and the failure of others.

Throughout all these developments, fundamental features remained the same, for the Tee cycle was indeed a river that flowed out of the past. Chains of finance, constructed primarily along lines of marriage ties, continued to provide the infrastructure for the Tee. Even at its height, when the Tee cycle incorporated some 375 clans or more, organizational tactics had not changed greatly from the time of Kitalini, the legendary founder of the Tee. Men traveled over hill and vale to the houses of their partners, reached agreements with them during night-long discussions, and then journeyed on together to persuade other relatives along their Tee chains to comply with the plans. Big-men who were most active in organizing a Tee cycle could be absent from home for over a year while making their way from one end of the network to the other.[5] Although the boasting displays of big-men during Tee festivals appeared to steal the show, the primary goals of the Tee cycle remained virtually unchanged from the fifth generation on. At the clan level, it provided finance for exchanges that lay at the core of social and political relationships, particularly war reparations, as Enga strove to manage the opportunities and problems of a growing population. For individual men, it furnished wealth that could be used to procure more wives, to influence others by being withheld or extended, and to attain prestige, which was significant in eliciting active support of many kinds (Bourdieu 1977).

The Tee cycle of the 1950s through the 1970s has been described in a number of excellent publications (Bus 1951; Elkin 1953; Kleinig 1955; Meggitt 1972, 1974; Feil 1984). G. A. M. Bus gives a vivid description of the Itokone Tee at Tilyaposa in 1949–50, and I. E. Kleinig describes the Tee cycle of the middle Lai during the 1950s and its relation to Christian missions. A. P. Elkin's account of the Tee in the Wabag area adds facts, figures, and a perspective from central Enga. Meggitt's comprehensive paper "Pigs Are Our Hearts" looks at almost every aspect of the system, drawing a particularly astute picture of its role in the broader politics of Enga. Feil's work portrays the Tee cycle from the perspective of a remote corner of Enga at a unique point in Enga history: that of pacification imposed by the colonial regime. It analyzes the structure and nature of Tee partnerships in great depth, capturing their warm and supportive nature. It illuminates the finer workings of the system and provides the only account in the literature documenting the competition between chains of allied partners. We did not look further into the Tee cycle of recent decades, and so, after this brief foray into the colonial period, we turn back to the Tee cycle of the fifth generation and try to trace its development as big-men crafted it from three major exchange systems: the Tee cycle of the east, the Great Wars of the center, and the Kepele cult of the west.

Lengthening the Tee Chains

The Tee chains of the fifth generation that radiated out from the Saka valley might have remained short, like those of the Melpa Moka, had it not been for events taking place in central Enga. By the fourth generation, the popularity of the Great Wars was rapidly mounting, drawing participants from far and wide and placing enormous economic demands on the "owners of the fight" and their hosts. Big-men in three tribes of central Enga involved in both the Great Wars and the Tee cycle—Yanaitini, Yakani, and Apulini—realized that if they could organize the Tee into longer coordinated sequences of giving, they would greatly increase the amount of wealth received at one time. With it they could finance the Great Wars and use the wealth that flowed out of them to pay back their creditors.

A number of historical narratives recall the journeys of big-men of central Enga to organize and campaign for longer Tee cycles. Had we worked one or two generations earlier, we might have obtained step-by-step documentation of the lengthening and sequencing of the Tee. Unfortunately, this was no longer possible by 1991. Too few former Tee organizers who could put specific events into a broader regional picture were still alive. It is possible, however, to give excellent single examples of Tee tactics used in the fourth generation that illustrate the politics involved.

What was perhaps the most widely recognized milestone in the development of the Tee comes from the history of the Yakani Timali clan. It tells how the great Tee organizer and Great War leader Yakani Pendaine met with big-men while on a journey to Liuates (near Winikos) in the Kopona area and persuaded them to take a short Tee that was heading for the Saka valley (map 16:B) and channel it into the western route from the Saka to Lenge (map 16:A), rather than letting it return to Kopona in the *yae* phase as was originally planned.[6] The arrangements were first made in words and then realized in deeds: when Pendaine returned home, he persuaded his fellow clansmen and Tee partners in neighboring clans to send initiatory gifts east to the Saka valley in order to "pull" the Kopona Tee on to central Enga once it had arrived there. The result of Pendaine's Tee campaign was to join exchanges along two major branches of the Tee into one long Tee cycle (map 16:A and B).

The first long Tee cycle took place in the lifetime of Pendaine, the son of Kepa and his wife Lai Kete. Recall that Lai Kete was from the Anjini clan of Liuates in the Kopona area. This is how the first major Tee cycle began. There was a big Tee being held in the Kopona area that was heading toward the Saka valley. Pendaine called together some men from here [Lenge] and went with them to Liuates during the Kopona Tee. When they arrived at the house of his [mother's] kin, they saw that there were some guests from the Saka valley. The guests were eating ginger seasoned with traditional salt and pitpit [*Setaria palmaefolia*] provided by the women of the household. The men of the Saka and the group brought by my grandfather sat together in the house and had a brief discussion about the Tee. They proposed that Pendaine and his men should bring to Liuates a parcel of cooked salt from the west [Yandap salt springs] and that they would send up stone axes in return. Note that they held this meeting at a time when a big Tee was about to head in the direction of the Saka valley. They all agreed on this plan. The Kopona Tee did in fact go to the Saka valley. When it arrived there my grandfather and his men solicited the Tee, and as a result it changed its course and headed westward [rather than returning directly to Kopona in the *yae* phase]. That was how the Tee began to be done over a long distance. My father continued to do this kind of Tee until fairly recently in our time. . . .

The men from the Saka valley were the big-men Kiua and Makaenge.[7] When Pendaine went down to Liuates, he brought salt, and Kiua and Makaenge had received the ginger from their hosts. Pendaine gave them the salt that they put on their ginger. Kiua and Makaenge ate it and said it tasted good. It was then that Pendaine said that he would "cook" salt for them if they wanted. This was symbolic speech; in plain language what they meant was that if Pendaine "cooked salt" or sent initiatory Tee gifts first, they in turn would take the Tee coming from Kopona and send it westward as they had planned during their meeting at Liuates. This is how they started the Tee cycle that covered long distances and included many people. After this Tee cycle was held, other branches were added and these remained a part of the Tee. (Kopio Toya Lambu, Yakani Timali clan, Lenge)

It was common practice for the names of principal organizers of a certain Tee cycle to become associated with it. This specific Tee, known as the first of the long cycles, is generally attributed to Pendaine, though others were involved, too. For Kiua and Makaenge, who were in the middle of the network and could efficiently manipulate the shorter chains that converged on the Saka, longer chains would be harder to organize and would bring little more in return. Nonetheless, they had reason to comply with Pendaine's plans in order to gain access to the wealth that flowed out of the Great Wars — and if longer chains were to exist, they wanted to make sure that these would pass through the Saka valley.

Another key example of the efforts of the big-men of central Enga to draw more clans into the western route comes from the histories of the Kandawalini Kaekini clan near Yaibosa in the middle Lai valley and the Yanaitini tribe of Tetemanda. It took place in the fourth to fifth generation when Yanaitini was involved in two costly Great Wars. The big-men of Yanaitini knew that there were numerous north-bank Lai valley clans, particularly those of the Kandawalini tribe, who were rich in pigs but not directly involved in the Tee cycle. Recall from chapter 6 that their exclusion was a matter not of isolation or chance but of past politics, namely, the efforts of Yambatane clans to prevent new trade routes from developing down the Lai that would bypass the Saka valley. Although Yambatane and Itokone did not desire the direct participation of Kandawalini clans in the Tee, they did desire their pigs and wealth. Accordingly, Itokone had engaged Kandawalini Kaekini in a series of semiceremonial wars beginning in the fifth generation and apparently continuing for some time after Kaekini joined the Tee cycle. Though similar to the Great Wars of central Enga in that they were fought primarily for the exchange that followed, they were much smaller in scale and shorter in duration, and they were not hosted but fought in the area bordering the two clans. Subsequent exchanges were both with allies and between enemies, not only between hosts and allies as was the case in the Great Wars. Leme Poul described the Kaekini-Itokone conflict and subsequent exchanges:

Yes, the two clans used to fight. During their wars they exchanged insults to make each other angry. For example, Itokone would say, "You are nothing but a burner of *luti* grass and a wearer of *ambano akaipu* leaves over your anus. You will never be able to put on *yuku akaipu* leaves. You are of nothing but low status."[8]

I [the Kaekini clan] would answer, "You are nothing but a loner and a good-for-nothing simpleton. You do nothing but kill female *wale* lizards and mourn over them." After these insults, we used to laugh, saying, "Ka ka ka ka a a ll." You know what I mean.

If we fought in the evening, then on the morning of the next day we stopped fighting and that was all we did, we did not continue. The battle we fought was the first and last [of that episode].

[Some time later] Itokone would come over to this side and burn away the grass. Then I would accuse him of unrightfully crossing the border. Then after the grass grew back again, it was my turn to burn away the grass and he would accuse me of causing troubles. That is how another episode of the war started.

During the conflict, I would compose songs to humiliate him.

[The songs he gives concern ties to Yanaitini. While Itokone boasted of its strong ties with the Yanaitini Kia clan through the Tee cycle, Kaekini boasted of its connection to Kia's brother clan, Yanaitini Kalepatae.] . . .

The underlying motive for the fighting was that we wanted to have an excuse to hold feasts and get to know each other. After the fighting was over, we made plans to pay war reparations, that is, if there were people who were killed in the war. Later, when the wind blew from the east, Itokone gave us food to eat ["wind" refers to the Tee, and "food" to pork, pigs, or other forms of wealth.] When the wind blew from the west, I gave them food. If he gave me live pigs, then I gave him cooked pork.
(Leme Poul, Kandawalini Kaekini clan, Yaibosa, middle Lai valley)

Owing to the exchanges following these wars, Kaekini and other Kandawalini clans were well poised to join the Tee. Noting this, the Yanaitini Kia clan responded with a series of strategic moves to draw Kaekini and other Lai clans into the Tee cycle. They took advantage of trouble that started over a Yanaitini woman who left her husband in the Sikini Mangalya clan for a man from the Kaekini clan (near Pina), provoking a tribal war between Mangalya and Kaekini in which a man from the Sikini Mangalya clan was killed.[9] Yanaitini big-men then persuaded the neighboring Itokone clans to go to the Saka, ask people there to initiate a Tee, and give some of the wealth to Kaekini to finance its war reparations to Mangalya. Itokone agreed, the phase of initiatory gifts was launched, and Kaekini was drawn directly into the Tee cycle for the first time. Kaekini paid war reparations to Mangalya, and Mangalya gave part of the wealth received to the Depe Kumba clan one step farther up the Lai valley as funerary payments to maternal kin. Depe Kumba was thereby drawn into the Tee cycle as well. Yanaitini then asked Apulini clans and others in the area to campaign to bring the Tee phase of initiatory gifts, which had reached Kumba, up to Tetemanda. The campaign succeeded, and when this phase of the Tee reached Tetemanda, Yanaitini launched the reciprocal phase of main gifts, which swept through all the clans in the middle Lai valley for the first time.[10] Through its secret dealings,

Yanaitini thus accomplished its goal—to directly involve more clans of the middle Lai in the Tee cycle and thereby obtain more finance for the Great Wars.

Pearl Shells in the Tee Cycle: A Pull from the East?

The flow of pigs, goods, and valuables via the Tee cycle into the Great Wars was not one-way, for debts were paid back with wealth from the Great War exchanges. During the fourth generation, as ever-increasing wealth was received from central Enga, some of it was invested in pearl shell crescents. Pearl shells were not unknown to Enga, but their incorporation into major exchange systems is said to have occurred during the fifth generation in the Kandep area for bridewealth distributions and war reparations and during the fourth generation for the Tee cycle of eastern Enga. In Western Highlands Province there is also some evidence for their recency: Andrew Strathern (1971:235–36) quotes one informant as saying that the arrival of pearl shells was in the time of his father, a claim Strathern believes foreshortens the time scale. Ian Hughes (1977:193) was told by old men from the Waghi that pearl shells were unknown to them when they were children in the 1920s.[11] A number of testimonies from eastern Enga describe how connections to obtain pearl shells for the Tee were established by big-men of the fourth generation. The following one, for example, comes from the Saka valley:

Pakiala, the father of Maua, went over to the *kyoa* [foreign, unknown, or strange people] in the vicinity of Ialibu, which is within the general area of Mendi. The people of this area gave him pearl shells, and he brought them to the Saka valley. Some particular pearl shells were preferred and were given special names. After they were introduced into the Tee cycle they became very precious. In those days, pearl shells were rare, the supply increasing greatly only with the pearl shells brought by the white men. Probably all the pearl shells came via Kerema. I think the people of Kerema gave pearl shells to the *kyoa* and Mendi people, who in turn gave pearl shells to the Kola people, and my grandfathers received them through trade from the Kola people. . . .

In this area, it was Pakiala who saw pearl shells for the first time. At first he was given only one pearl shell, and after a lengthy period of time, two more. In his time if a person possessed one or two pearl shells he was regarded as extremely rich; pearl shells were rare and precious. In those days it was said that men from the Watenge clan went up to the Kola area to get pearl shells, and when Watenge gave pigs to the people in the Kola [Tambul] direction, they gave them pearl shells in return. The Tee was enriched by the giving of pearl shells. Up there [in central Enga] people gave shell-embroidered headbands and necklaces [*mako, angata tenge*]; pearl shells served the same purpose at this end of the Tee cycle. Pearl shells also went up into the western area and later returned to the

Saka valley through Tee routes. Originally, pearl shells were first brought in through the Saka valley. (Apanyo Maua, Yambatane Watenge clan, Saka valley)

Other Enga also said that before the arrival of Europeans, pearl shells were highly valued and so rare that they were the property of only the most influential big-men. Since they were almost exclusively in the hands of those with the appropriate exchange connections, it is possible that big-men of eastern Enga tried to use them to help consolidate their power, as Melpa big-men did in the Moka (A. Strathern 1979b:533). Unfortunately, the window of time from their introduction until the market was flooded with pearl shells brought in by Europeans was too narrow for their effect to be well noted in historical traditions. What is certain, however, is that big-men exerted considerable effort to enhance their worth. Among other things, they imported the Female Spirit cult from the southeast, with its dramatic parade of pearl shells that placed the new valuables in the center of attention and conferred upon them both economic and sacred value.

In central Enga the situation was quite different. There, pearl shells were less highly prized than pigs and other valuables, such as stone axes, that constituted essential components of bridewealth. Had pearl shells been integrated into the Tee cycle for a longer period before contact or after the Female Spirit cult had time to move westward, perhaps standards of value in central Enga would have changed. As it happened, they did not, and the power of pearl shells in the Tee cycle was constrained by their lower value at the western (and northern) end. Big-men in the east, finding it inexpedient to send the best pearl shells westward in the Tee cycle, sent them back into Western Highlands Province:

My clan is situated near the Timbai [Melpa] and Kola area, where they love pearl shells. There are all kinds of pearl shells, and some are valued much more highly than others. They are given to us by people from these areas, and we give them to the people of the Saka valley. Some of the pearl shells were regarded as so precious that people could even start a tribal war over them. Women fall in love at the very sight of a pearl shell of this kind. Several pigs could be given in exchange for one of them. Such pearl shells would go to the Saka valley but that is as far as they would go, the reason being that people farther up the valley do not like pearl shells so much, even those pearl shells that were so highly valued by people from Timbai and Kola. Therefore I would return the pearl shells to Timbai and Kola and send westward via the Saka things that were desired by people farther to the west—for example, stone axes used for both ceremonial and practical purposes. Kundina, Kombomoka, and Gayamu stone axes were desired by people in the west. They also liked bailer shells, necklaces, and headbands of opossum tails embroidered with shells. In the past these were the things that were sent westward through the Saka valley.

[In response to a question about whether people in the west preferred work axes or ceremonial ones:] Both types of axes were sent up-valley—people liked both types. They were given away in bridewealth payments. People liked them so much that they just grabbed them when they saw them, so highly desired were they by people in the west. You see, people of my age liked these things very much. (Kepa Pupu, Yoponda clan, Walia, Minamb valley)

Because information on pearl shells is sparse in Enga historical traditions, we can conclude only the following:[12] First, pearl shells became integrated into the Tee cycle beginning in the fourth generation. Second, their high value in Western Highlands was shared only in easternmost Enga, not in northern or central Enga. There, people put greater value on pigs and large stone axes, the latter of which facilitated forest clearance and formed an essential component of bridewealth. What is certain, however, is that pearl shells served as important valuables that big-men of eastern Enga were able to exchange profitably for stone axes with the peoples of the Kola and Timbai areas. Thus, in the fourth generation, when big-men of the west sought wealth from the east to fuel the Great Wars, men in the east may in turn have required more pigs, salt, and valuables from the west with which to purchase pearl shells. Their reciprocal needs may have exerted a two-way pull to expand the Tee. Exactly how strong the pull from the east was and what effect it had on the Tee is difficult to ascertain.

Coordination of the Tee Cycle and Great War Exchanges

The longer Tee cycles brought more wealth to central Enga for financing the Great Wars and provided pathways for reinvesting the wealth that flowed out of them, but not without complications. The Great Wars were fought along a north-south axis bisecting the Tee route that ran from the Saka valley to Tetemanda and drawing the wealth from the Tee in different directions (map 17). For example, a Tee cycle coming from the Saka organized to supply the Great War exchanges of Yakani could pull a significant amount of wealth north into the Sau valley rather than sending it on to Tetemanda. When it came time for a return phase to be sent back east, it was unclear where, when, and with whom it should start. Thus, beginning in the fourth generation and continuing into the third, historical traditions describe agreements reached by big-men of major clans linking the Tee cycle to the Great Wars to "straighten" the main route of the Tee in central Enga, so that it would flow parallel to the Lai river and keep its traditional western terminus with the Yanaitini Kia clan at Tetemanda. The Tee cycle then ran a set course from Tambul to the Saka valley to Tetemanda, and the networks formed by the Great War exchanges became feeder routes into the mainstream linked through Yanaitini at Tetemanda, Apulini at Irelya, and Yakani Timali at Lenge.

For at least some decades, and in the case of Yanaitini even longer, big-men of three focal tribes succeeded in steering the course of the Tee along the western route and keeping the Tee and Great Wars apart, so that those three tribes would be the only major links between the two exchange systems. Such a monopoly put them in a position to strategically invest the wealth from one into the other. Though knowledge of the Great Wars could not be kept from Tee organizers in the east, Yakani, Apulini, and Yanaitini did their best to convince them that it was dangerous to venture directly into these areas. By contrast, knowledge of the Tee, which at the time was a relatively low-profile stream of finance, could be kept from most clans that took part in the Great Wars. Discussing why Yanaitini big-men told Tee cycle organizers from clans to the east not to go north of Tetemanda, one Yanaitini man gave this explanation:

We did not want these people to see our source of pigs. Those places [where the Great Wars were held] were our source of pigs and were referred to as our "Tee tree" in figurative speech. I am talking about places like the land of Malipini Kamaniwane, Bia, Maioma, and all the others directly to our north. We told them that these places were the lands of savages. We did so because we did not want them to see these places; if they did it would have weakened our position. (Kyakas Sapu, Yanaitini Lanekepa clan, Lupamanda [near Wabag])

It appears to have been through such strategies—forging close ties with Layapo clans for the Tee cycle and keeping Mai clans who participated in the Great Wars somewhat apart—that the Kaina dialect group, comprising Yanaitini, Apulini, and Yakani, came to be. Certainly the Kaina (meaning middle) are not mentioned in historical traditions before the coordination of the Tee cycle and Great Wars began. Later, when Itapuni and Awaini were pulled into the Tee, they too became part of the Kaina.[13]

While the Tee cycle could be arranged in part to finance the Great War exchanges, the Great Wars had their own momentum, and their exchanges could not always be timed to fit the Tee cycle. As a result, the channeling of wealth from the Tee cycle to and from the Great Wars did not follow a fixed plan but was opportunistic, varying with the direction and conditions of each cycle. Great War kepa singi could be sent east as initiatory gifts for the first phase of Tee cycle, or as part of the yae (fig. 1). When hosts were the ones involved in the Tee cycle, the Great War akaipu pingi could be financed by either initiatory or main gifts coming up from the east. The lome nyingi—the large, final payment to hosts in live pigs, cassowaries, and valuables—was usually sent east in the phase of the

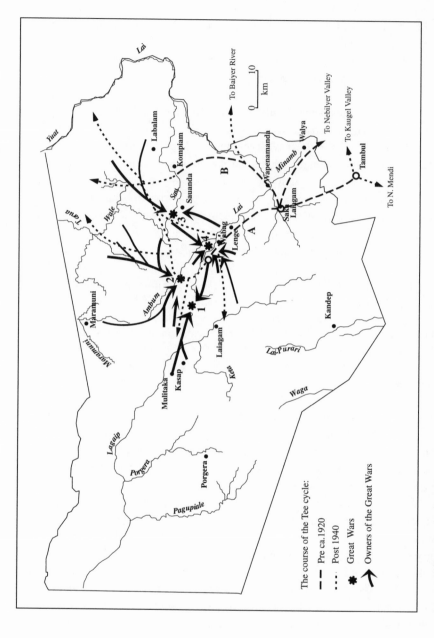

The course of the Tee cycle:
Pre ca.1920
Post 1940
Great Wars
Owners of the Great Wars

Map 17. Great War networks subsumed by the Tee cycle. 1, Yanaitini versus Monaini; 2, Lyaini-Sakalini versus Pumane-Aiyele; 3, Sene-Yokasa versus Yakani; 4, Malipini-Potealini versus Itapuni-Awaini.

Tee cycle   Great War exchanges

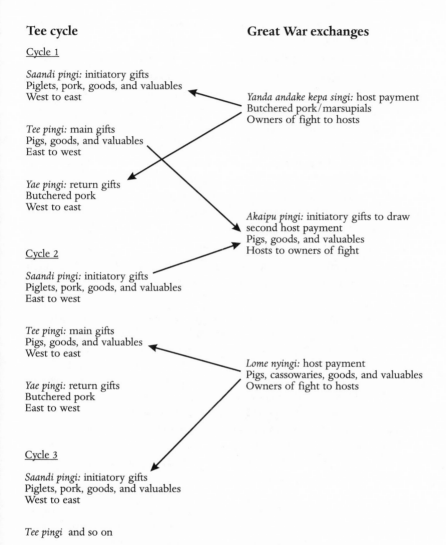

Cycle 1

Saandi pingi: initiatory gifts
Piglets, pork, goods, and valuables
West to east

Tee pingi: main gifts
Pigs, goods, and valuables
East to west

Yae pingi: return gifts
Butchered pork
West to east

Yanda andake kepa singi: host payment
Butchered pork/marsupials
Owners of fight to hosts

Akaipu pingi: initiatory gifts to draw
second host payment
Pigs, goods, and valuables
Hosts to owners of fight

Cycle 2

Saandi pingi: initiatory gifts
Piglets, pork, goods, and valuables
East to west

Tee pingi: main gifts
Pigs, goods, and valuables
West to east

Yae pingi: return gifts
Butchered pork
East to west

Lome nyingi: host payment
Pigs, cassowaries, goods, and valuables
Owners of fight to hosts

Cycle 3

Saandi pingi: initiatory gifts
Piglets, pork, goods, and valuables
West to east

Tee pingi and so on

Figure 1. Flow of wealth between the Great Wars and Tee cycle.

main gifts, but the wealth could also be used for initiatory gifts. Further flexibility
was afforded by the possibility that the main gifts could be delivered in two waves
of Tee festivals, one containing wealth from the Great Wars, before a return
phase was initiated. Conversely, when it was the owners of the fight who were
involved in the Tee (not shown in fig. 1), as in the case of Yakani and Sene-Yokasa,
the *tee pingi* phase could be used to finance the *lome nyingi* and so on.

So far as we could determine, regular transfers of wealth between the two systems began in the fourth generation, making it unlikely that large amounts of wealth from the Tee reached the Pumane-Aiyele versus Lyaini-Sakalini Great Wars. Certainly, historical traditions make no mention of it. For the Monaini versus Yanaitini Great Wars, it is very probable that Yanaitini used some wealth from the Tee to finance payments to its hosts in Sambe, but we found no one who could give any details. That the Yakani versus Sene-Yokasa and Itapuni-Awaini versus Malipini-Potealini Great Wars were linked to the Tee is widely reported, though many clans participating in the Great Wars were unaware that wealth was channeled between the two systems. This lack of awareness is explained in the following two testimonies. The first pertains to the Yakani versus Sene-Yokasa Great War (map 17:3). It describes how the Sene-Yokasa side was financed by the northern Tee route (map 17:B) and how Yakani was financed by the western Tee route from Tambul to Tetemanda (map 17:A). Clans in the Ambum valley gave pigs to relatives involved in the Great Wars and Tee cycle without knowing that they would be sent eastward in the Tee:

Our friends and relatives came from clans involved in the Tee cycle to get pigs, but we thought we were giving them for purely social purposes [traditional payments to maternal and affinal kin]. Actually they came to get pigs to send down to Kola [in the Tee]. Then the people in Kola [Tambul] initiated the Tee cycle that came up through Winikos. We did not know this; we were deaf to what took place between the two peoples. Not even my father had seen or heard of the Tee cycle. You know, it was like somebody telling a small boy to go and get some *mondai* leaves with which to spice food. The boy would not know why he was being sent to fetch them; so it was with us. We gave pigs but we did not know for what. It was only in more recent years that we came to know what the Tee cycle was and how it was carried out. (Auaka Taliu Waliu, Malipini Wailuni clan, Meriamanda-Ambum)

The second testimony, by Yopo Yakena, makes it clear that knowledge of the Tee cycle was kept from participants in the Great Wars not by chance but by strategy. After finishing his description of the *lome nyingi* exchanges of the Great Wars—the major Great War payments given by the owners of the fight to the hosts—Yopo went on to explain what happened to the wealth that flowed out of these exchanges. The hosting clans then held their own public distributions called *lome nyingi Tee* to send the wealth eastward in the Tee cycle, because they could not absorb all the wealth received and wanted to reinvest it. The distributions described in the following passage were thus at once the end of the Great War payments and the beginning of a new phase of the Tee cycle.

After all the Malipini and Potealini clans had done their *lome nyingi*, then the [Yanaitini] host clans took the wealth received and held the *lome nyingi Tee,* beginning with Kumbini at Tole. Kumbini gave it to people in the Yanaitini clans on the [Lai-Ambum] ridge, Kaimanguni, Kokopa, Yapakone, Kalepatae, Lanekepa, and Neneo, as well as other clans down the valley. After all the Yanaitini clans on the ridge [who had hosted the Great Wars] held their wealth distributions, Kia was the final Yanaitini clan to hold the *lome nyingi tee* at Tetemanda, though by this time it was really not the *lome nyingi* Great War Tee but the normal Tee cycle. . . .

Akii: After pigs were given away by Kia at Tetemanda, the final Yanaitini clan, did this Tee continue farther down the Lai to tribes like Yakani, Apulini, Lyipini, and Depe, or did it stop with Kia?

Yopo: Yes, it continued farther down the Lai. The Tee cycle as we know it today came to us just recently in my lifetime. Before that, we [Malipini and Potealini] had only Great War exchanges. The Tee cycle organizers from the east who came to Tetemanda were told not go beyond Tetemanda, that people on the ridge, including Malipini and Potealini, were hostile, and that if anyone ventured farther away from Tetemanda they would be killed. [Yopo smiles.] This was a pack of lies that Kia told Tee cycle organizers from the east because they wanted to be the focal point at this end of the Tee cycle. They wanted nobody but the Yanaitini Kalinatae clans [Kia, Kalepatae, and Yapakone] to have a monopoly on Tee negotiations and to prevent others from having direct access to the wealth from the Great War exchanges to channel into the Tee cycle. The Tee cycle came only to the Kalinatae group and went back. It expanded and spread to us only within my lifetime. . . .

Akii: Does this mean that you did not know what Yanaitini did with what you gave them in the Great War exchanges, or that you simply were not concerned?

Yopo: No, we did not really know what they did with the wealth that we gave them in the Great War exchanges. You see, at that time we did not quite understand the Tee cycle and how it functioned, and so Yanaitini used what we gave them for their Tee cycle and took what they received from it to use during the Great War exchanges. I told you earlier that Yanaitini prevented Tee cycle organizers from the east from venturing past Tetemanda. . . . So you see, we did not have much contact with these people who were directly involved in the Tee cycle and so could not get a good view of how it worked. . . .

Kia lied to us so that the Yanaitini Kalinatae clans would be the only ones who could tap into wealth flowing from the Great War exchanges—so that the wealth coming from the east and that from the north or west could be exchanged only by them. Eventually, when the Tee cycle did come to Kaeyapa, Tole, and into other Malipini-Potealini areas, Tee organizers from the east told us that they then realized that Kia had told them lies and why they had done so. (Yopo Yakena, Malipini Kamaniwane clan, Kaeapa)

Yopo's testimony gives some measure of the sophistication of Tee politics—of how wealth received in Great War exchanges was further distributed in the Tee festivals of Yanaitini host clans and blended into the Tee cycle by Kia at

Tetemanda. The blueprints for exchange were drawn by a limited, but not closed, circle of powerful big-men who preserved the secrecy of their plans through private meetings and exclusive metaphorical speech. Since marriage ties were the avenues over which they exerted their influence, families of big-men from different clans and tribes intermarried to the extent that an open circle of elites formed that had a strong hold on the flow of information.[14] Not only men were active but also wives, sisters, mothers, and daughters. As trusted emissaries and diplomats, women were given an increasing share of the responsibility to work toward certain goals via private ties. Some women of eastern Enga, though very few, even became active Tee cycle participants and organizers in their own rights (Kyakas and Wiessner 1992). And so a distinction developed between minor big-men, traditional clan leaders, and major big-men who worked widely outside the clan to organize the Great Wars and Tee cycle (Pupu 1988). Once decisions had been made within a small circle of leaders, however, the task of persuading fellow clan members and others to lend support required extensive politicking and persuasion—few plans succeeded without the consent and joint efforts of a broad base of supporters.

The Tee Cycle and the Aeatee Ancestral Cult: The Western End

The Great War exchanges grew with wealth received from the east, and in turn the Tee cycle was flooded with wealth flowing out of the Great Wars. As rewards of the Tee became evident and more people joined, organizational problems arose that could not be resolved within the limited circle of Tee leaders. First, Yakani, Yanaitini, and Apulini each encompassed some clans who were involved in the Great Wars and others who were involved in the Tee; close cooperation between them was necessary to organize a Tee cycle. Second, the Tee cycle, unlike the Great Wars, was not structured by formal battles that defined sides, gathered people, and coordinated them in the spirit of opposition. Therefore, it did not begin by its own momentum but required assertive campaigning to succeed. Given the number of clans involved, the way communities were dispersed over a rugged landscape, the difficulties of communication, and the conflicting interests of egotistical big-men, this task was formidable. And third, social inequalities had become accentuated, causing tensions and competition within clans. Nonetheless, big-men still had no decisive authority but had to elicit the energy and goodwill of their fellow clan and tribal members as equals to coordinate a Tee cycle.

To overcome these problems, Tee organizers turned to the most powerful traditions in their heritage that gathered people and inspired cooperation through the charisma of communal and spiritual action: the cults. In the fourth to fifth generation, an array of cults was available in central Enga and surrounding areas. Both prominent and appropriate for the problems at hand was the Kepele-Aeatee cult of the Lagaip, which, unlike most cults of central Enga, was for entire tribes, not single clans.[15] It articulated relations of different tribal segments to one another and thus could be used to coordinate tribes divided between the Great Wars and Tee cycle. Its large gatherings provided excellent opportunities for communication. As a cult of the west in which conservative, egalitarian values were strongly expressed, it restored a sense of equality among celebrants, giving each family the feeling that it had a hand in determining the future. Finally, the cult's formidable organizational requirements and display of wealth provided one of the key elements for successfully launching a Tee cycle — convincing the celebrants themselves that if they cooperated they would be on a winning team, and convincing the spectators from the east that clans at the western end were wealthy, well organized, and ready for the Tee. In these respects the Kepele was a made-to-order cult that could be imported in the name and intent of improving tribal fortunes and yet mediate the organizational problems of the Tee cycle.

Recall that the Kepele was not new to central Enga but had been imported earlier in two waves of tradition, first with the journeys of the mythical python and later by the wandering women. By the fifth to sixth generation, the Aeatee cult was performed on a small scale by Apulini and Yanaitini (see also Lacey 1975:126). Only around the fourth generation, however, did the Aeatee flourish, after it was recrafted to meet the needs of the Tee cycle by the big-men who sponsored it and performed it on an ever-larger scale. The phases of building and destroying the cult house that expressed complementarity between different segments of the tribe became elaborated to the point that they and their corresponding feasts dominated the performance. The *yupini* basketwork figure was not used to represent male ancestors, but rites for the sacred stones representing the Aeatee woman and her family were performed. The *mote* boys' initiation was either never imported or dropped; initiation to introduce young men into the secrets of the spirit world was foreign to central Enga. The wandering women replaced the rainbow python, but the central theme laid down in the Kepele origin myth — that all tribal members must give something of themselves for the welfare of the whole — not only persisted but was strengthened.

Organizational changes also took place in the cult. With the reduction of the *mote* initiation and other sacred rites, the ensemble of ritual experts was diminished to the few who could conduct the ceremonies for the house building and caring for the sacred stones. The need for big-men to orchestrate the various building phases was enhanced, and organizing big-men became directors of the Aeatee to a much greater extent than in the Kepele of western Enga.

In what follows, we give a brief description of the Aeatee based on a very detailed eyewitness account of the last performances at Tetemanda in the 1930s and 1940s. A similar description of Apulini Aeatee cult procedures can be found in Lacey (1975:123-25). The Aeatee was a cult with six distinct stages separated from one another by months or years. From start to finish it could take four years or longer to complete. In preparation for all stages of the Aeatee, peace was established within household, clan, and tribe, and Yanaitini men were discouraged from participating in the wars of other tribes. In this sense the Aeatee, like the Kepele, was a ritual of peace. All attention was to be centered on the Aeatee. Gardens were planted and pigs raised for the feasts. Only when these conditions were met could each stage be initiated.

The first stage of the Aeatee involved a marsupial feast to gather people for the collection of building materials. At this time each subclan was delegated the task of collecting specific logs and building materials for the cult house. These were wrapped in ferns, brought quietly to the building site, deposited, and covered with grass. A small marsupial feast followed.

The second stage was held a few months later and culminated in a marsupial feast. First, a major hunt was launched and requests sent out for different kinds of foods to be brought in from all directions. Relatives from other tribes and Tee cycle organizers from eastern Enga came to participate in the hunt, bringing contributions for the feast. Just after midnight, Yanaitini divided into two groups—the descendants of Yanaitini's son Kepa and those of his other son, Paule. With faces and bodies blackened, they donned cassowary feather headdresses and descended to the cult grounds, an eerie sight. Hand-in-hand they marched forward and backward throughout the night, stamping the ground flat. A line divided the site in half, the respective tribal segments keeping to their sides. At dawn the two groups marched separately back to the ceremonial grounds to dance—the entire area was packed with dancing men. When the ceremony was over, the big-men who had come up from the east discussed the Tee cycle in the quiet of men's houses. If an agreement was reached, they might be given initiatory gifts for the next Tee cycle. Women were excluded from all house construction, sacred rites, and Aeatee feasts, though they were given food that was not ritually prepared to take and steam in their own homes.

The third stage was held for the construction of the Aeatee house followed by a large pork feast. At daybreak, men of Yanaitini gathered by subclan to clear the site of debris, insert the posts, and build the scaffold for erecting the king post. Afterward, Yanaitini men went to the forest, fetched the king post, and carried it to the building site to the music of bamboo flutes and marching feet. Two women in ceremonial dress representing the Aeatee women led the procession. Hoards of spectators from other clans, including men from the east, accompanied the festive procession, the king post being sheltered from view by layers of ferns and the throngs of Yanaitini men surrounding it. A hole was dug for the king post, and gourds of tree oil were poured into it, one provided by each Yanaitini subclan. It was lined with red pigment and leaves from all the food crops. After a spell requesting fertility was chanted, the king post was mounted with ropes and fixed in place. The rest of the house was completed and thatched, the descendants of Kepa responsible for one half and those of Paule for the other.

Every male in Yanaitini provided one pig for the feast to celebrate the completion of the house. The pigs were slaughtered, their blood collected in breadfruit leaves, and their kidneys, livers, and hearts steamed and eaten by very old men who resided in the cult house. These elders then daubed the walls with blood and decorated the house with leaves and ferns. The remaining pork was steamed and distributed freely and generously in a great feast. Once again, big-men from the east lingered after the feast, discussed the Tee, and received initiatory gifts.

In the fourth stage, about one month after the construction of the Aeatee house, a marsupial feast was held to clean up the ceremonial area and decorate the house once more. At this time a live *kepa* opossum was put in a basket with sweet potato leaves, thrown back and fourth over the cult house from the descendants of Kepa on one side to those of Paule on the other, and buried alive in a nearby swampy area to bring fertility to the soil.

In the fifth stage, the rites for the sacred ancestral stones were held, together with a large pork feast. To open this stage, the ladders used to thatch the cult house roof were taken down and torn into pieces, each Yanaitini subclan being given a piece as a symbol that it would kill pigs specially raised for the feeding and burying of the sacred stones and the accompanying feast. A ritual expert was summoned from the Apulini tribe at Irelya to conduct the sacred part of the ritual, along with a very few old men from Yanaitini. The sacred stones were composed of a female stone representing the Aeatee woman, a male one for the man she married, and smaller ones, their offspring, expressing both male and female principles and their essential interdependence for fertility. These were cleaned, covered in large chunks of lard, wrapped in the leaves of food crops, and buried, the hole fenced to keep out pigs. A pork feast involving all celebrants and spectators followed, after which big-men of Tetemanda set off for the east to campaign for the phase of the main gifts of the Tee cycle. In the year or two that followed, the stones were periodically unearthed, rewrapped in fat, and buried with a pig kidney during a small ceremony called *poketa yuli*. Traditional dances were held upon these occasions to keep the spirit of the Aeatee cult alive.

The sixth stage saw the dramatic competition to burn the Aeatee cult house and the biggest pork feast of all. This occurred about two years after the rites for feeding the sacred stones. It attracted spectators from Tambul, the Saka valley, the Lai valley, Kandep, and the Lagaip valley. Once again the grass was ceremonially trampled by night in preparation. It was not Yanaitini who burned the house but the "owners" of the Malipini versus Itapuni Great War who competed to set it aflame. This was the first event of the Aeatee in which they actively took part, for they had been excluded from the other feasts by the food taboos of the Great Wars.[16] Winning or losing in the Great Wars, as measured by numbers of warriors lost, was considered secondary to success in burning the house, a competition that was said to be "over the lap" (for the favor) of the Yanaitini Kia clan, the center of exchange at the western terminus of the Tee.[17] Contenders woke just before dawn, approached the house stealthily, set fire to it, and slipped quietly away. Kia men pursued the "culprits," shooting arrows here and there and engaging in mock battle. Those who burned the house returned for the great feast the next day. The burning of the Aeatee cult house and subsequent feast marked the beginning of pig kills for the *yae* phase of the Tee. However, the pork from this feast was distributed freely and more or less equally to participants and spectators, not as a part of the Tee gifts.

All elders present the Aeatee first and foremost as a massive ritual of exchange designed to contact the spirit world and thereby improve the future of all celebrants. Through the Aeatee, rifts within the Yanaitini tribe were mended and tensions between clansmen caused by growing social inequalities mollified. Its performance evoked the goodwill of the ancestors and the spirit of group unity before individuals went out to pursue their own interests in the Tee. Celebrants were reminded that their successes would not only promote their own names but also provide for the needs of their fellow group members. Once unity was established, broader-scale economic plans could be realized.

The association between the Aeatee and the Tee was constructed with such care that the general public saw Yanaitini's fertility and prosperity as the sole goal of the cult. For example, exchange within the Aeatee was not directly related to other economic ventures: pork from pigs raised for the various stages by Yanaitini households was distributed freely to celebrants and guests without incurring or discharging debts for the Tee cycle. The atmosphere of solidarity was not ruptured by big-men's displays or political speeches. Meanwhile, other strategies unfolded in the shadow of the cult. Yanaitini demonstrated to Tee cycle organizers from the east that they had the wealth, unity, and power to launch a Tee cycle and then drew up plans in the seclusion of men's houses. The various stages of the Aeatee, spread out over years, kept the cooperative spirit alive within Yanaitini throughout one entire Tee cycle and fixed times for the different phases of the Tee cycle to begin and end. In short, although the Aeatee cult and the Tee cycle were not directly intertwined either ritually or economically, the development of one depended on the other.

Descriptions of the most recent Apulini Aeatee (also called Aeatee *anda* after the ritual house), performed between 1925 and 1945 at Irelya, suggest that it had a similar relationship to the Tee, except that it was the big-men of Apulini clans on competing Tee chains who assembled their Tee collaborators and competed to burn the house (see Lacey 1975:120-31). In a testimony collected by Lacey from a middle-aged man named Kepai, who based his ideas on childhood experience, accounts of his father's, and what he had reasoned out himself, Kepai clearly delineated the role of the Aeatee in the Tee:

The making of an Aeatee *anda* takes ten years altogether to ensure that the pigs and their offerings are big enough for use in the ritual. The Aeatee *anda* begins and makes the Tee possible. When the clan decides that it is going to burn its Aeatee *anda,* clansmen call in their pigs. Yama traveled from dancing ground to dancing ground telling his allies that he was ready to call in and kill his pigs. He gathered in the pigs owed to him at each dancing ground. But when he had all his pigs from farther down the Lai, he did not burn his Aeatee *anda* until his relatives at Tetemanda had killed their pigs and burnt their Aeatee. (Lacey 1975:127-28, quoting Kepai, Apulini Talyulu-Talene subclan, Irelya)

When we interviewed Kepai in 1991, he projected the burning of Aeatee houses to every clan down the Lai, based on personal speculation rather than on historical tradition. Careful interviewing revealed that not all clans down to the Saka constructed Aeatee houses, but only those at the western terminus of the Tee where the Tee cycle and Great Wars merged—at Irelya and Tetemanda.

The association of Aeatee and Tee in central Enga is also recorded in the oral history of eastern clans, such as that of the Yambatane Watenge clan of the Saka valley:

We did not have the Aeatee cult, but we have something similar to it. . . . The Aeatee cult was practiced by people of the far west. It was not performed here. No one else ate the food prepared during the Aeatee at Irelya—only I, the Watenge clan, would go up to take part in the cult and eat the food prepared throughout the performance.[18] We would also take part in cults held at Lenge by Nandi and Pendaine (Yakani Timali clan), and of course we also ate the food prepared for the Aeatee cult at Tetemanda. Not everybody was invited; we were the only special guests in these ritual houses; by "we" I mean the Watenge clan. At Tetemanda we would even go to the bush and hunt marsupials [for the cult] together. It was during the performances of these cults that people planned strategies for the Tee with us. They would say that in such and such a month or year we will hold the *tee pingi* and at such and such a time we will begin the *yae.* If a Tee cycle was to begin in the west, they would tell Yanaitini to get a pig from the Yandap area. After passing on the word, they would go and sleep at Lenge. Their next stop was at Birip. From there their next stop was Puakale. They also slept at the place of the [Sikini] Muitapa and Wapai clans, and then via the Sambaka route they would reach their homes in the Saka valley. . . . You see, all was arranged ahead. They would tell people farther up the valley when they would arrive at their place and which route they would take. Such things were arranged beforehand, and then they made the tour campaigning for the Tee. (Apanyo Maua, Yambatane Watenge clan, Saka Laiagam)

Developments in the Aeatee of central Enga did not go unnoticed in the Laiagam area, from where the Aeatee was originally imported. As Tee routes extended to Laiagam tribes, the public events of their Kepele performances were also accentuated. House building was elaborated, the *mote* initiation was redirected to the few young men who were candidates to become ritual experts, and the *yupini* figure representing the male ancestors was paraded before the public in great ceremony outside the sacred area to attract crowds for planning exchanges.[19]

The Tee Cycle and the Male and Female Spirit Cults: The Eastern End

The use of ancestral cults to sequence and organize the Tee cycle in the west was mirrored at its eastern terminus in Tambul. There, the Yanuni tribe held performances of a cult called the Polaoanda or Yae-Poloanda, a cult said to be a version of the Kope, which (we think) is the Male Spirit cult, or Kor Wop (A. Strathern 1970; Strauss and Tischner 1962).[20] Kepa Pupu, one of the key Tee organizers of his generation, recalled going to Pakapuanda to burn the Yae-Polaoanda cult house in the late 1940s or early 1950s:

Akii [after describing the Aeatee cult in the east]: In the Kola area, for instance, did Yanuni have an Aeatee house or anything resembling one?

Kepa: Yes, there was an Aeatee-like house at Pakapuanda, the village of the Yanuni clan. People came from the west through the Yalu route, through the Sambe route, and then into the Saka valley [see map 11]. Then they traveled on the Walepa route, came to Kola, and burned the "Aeatee" house. They came down with cassowaries, pigs, and salt to burn what was usually called the *yae* house. The village was well known for this activity; the "Aeatee" house was called the *yae* house. It was a long [rectangular] house. My forefathers brought men from the west to Kola to burn the house. What a great occasion—people would dress in full costume and bring cassowaries and pigs. The pigs were tied to stakes and then all the men would dance and march onto the ceremonial grounds to burn the house. The house at the ceremonial grounds was called the *yae-polaoanda*. It was first demolished by hand—people pulled off the thatch, broke up the rafters, and so on, and then all the materials were set on fire. The group of people that made it to the place in time to burn the house was the winner.

Akii: Who burned the "Aeatee" house at Kola? Were there people who competed to burn it?

Kepa: Yes, there were people who competed to burn down the house. I was in the forefront. I would send word to the Sau valley to bring pigs so that I could take them down to Kola for the burning of the house. I was the man in the forefront of the competition. I would send word to people [Tee collaborators] from the west, particularly to men from the Yakani and Yanaitini tribes. The word could even travel as far as the Yandap and Laiagam areas. They would gather pigs, salt, and cassowaries, saying that Kepa wanted to burn down the *yae* house. After the Tee, word reached the Kola area that Kepa would come to burn down the *yae* house. I was well known for this. My forefathers did the same thing—they would go to Kola through the two famous routes and burn the *yae* house.

Akii: Who were the people who burned the *yae-polaoanda*?

Kepa: All my Tee collaborators from all areas. I was the man who led the group, went ahead, and burned the house first. If I reached the house first with my group and burned the house, then we were the winners. If we arrived late, the others were the winners.

Akii: Where was the *yae-polaoanda* actually situated?

Kepa: It was located on the land of the Yanuni clan. There are two paths to it. They are called Pukumba and Paua. Paua is my road; it is connected to the Kulanga route. That is the route that I travel when I go there. The other is linked with the Kunja route. That leads [more directly] to the Saka valley. If I go through the route that I have just mentioned and burn the house, then I am the winner. If the other group goes through the Kunja route and burns the house, then the other group is the winner. The house is called *polaoanda*.

Akii: When you go to burn down the house, it is a competition, isn't it?

Kepa: Yes, there is competition. The same competition that exists in the Tee cycle is expressed in the burning of the house. Here in Kola the *polaoanda* is burned. In the west, the Aeatee house is burned. (Kepa Pupu, Yoponda Ipupa clan, Walia)

Thus, when a Tee cycle was to begin in the east, the *yae-polaoanda* was built and feasts held. Big-men from the west attended and afterward remained to discuss plans for the Tee cycle, returning home with initiatory gifts. After a sufficient number of initiatory gifts had been received, clans of the west sent the phase of the main gifts eastward in a long series of festivals moving from clan to clan. When the main phase reached Tambul, men along two major routes that converged there competed to burn the *yae-polaoanda*, an event that launched the *yae* phase of the Tee cycle. The competitive burning of the cult houses in the east, as in the west, thus marked a transition from the solidarity and cooperation of the cults to the interindividual and clan competition of the Tee cycle.

Clans in the middle of the Tee cycle had less say about when phases of Tee cycles should be initiated than did those at the end points in the network. As Apanyo Maua put it, other clans along the Tee routes were "like ferns in the middle of a folded side of pork." Nonetheless, they all had bachelors' and ancestral cults, and some used these occasions for uniting the clan or tribe for planning the Tee cycle. In the Saka valley, where many Tee routes converged, a new cult was imported for this purpose, among other reasons, in the fourth generation: the Female Spirit cult.

The Female Spirit cult—Amb Kor in Melpa and Enda Yainanda in Enga—originated in the Mendi area and spread widely (see A. Strathern 1970, 1979a; Strauss and Tischner 1962). It was directed not at the ancestors but at a mythical "sky woman" who came to men as a bride but remained a virgin with a closed vagina, giving men protection against the menstrual fluids of human females and bringing fertility to them and their families. The underlying concept was similar in some respects to that of the Enga Sangai cult, except that the Female Spirit came to married men and not bachelors, was asexual, and brought fertility rather than transformation into adulthood. The Female Spirit cult departed from the traditional Yanainda-Kepaka ancestral cults described earlier not only in details of ritual procedure but also in a number of fundamental respects.

The first of these departures was that two cult houses, one male and one female, were constructed and fenced in, and adult male celebrants were divided into two opposing but complementary moieties, one representing males and the other females. The cult's central theme, that "male and female must be both separated and indissolubly linked" (A. Strathern 1970:49), was present in both the Aeatee-Kepele and the Sangai bachelors' cults but not in the major ancestral cults of the east such as the Yainanda and Kepaka. Second, authoritative ritual experts were required, generally one from a place considered to be near the point of origin of the cult and another from a group nearby. These men were paid handsomely. And third, the cult involved lavish display at its climax. When the ritual procedures were completed within the fenced sacred area, the male participants emerged in a dramatic parade, holding pearl shells in front of them and dancing with stamping movements, to the great excitement of the crowd. Entering the cult houses once again, they reemerged carrying net bags of pork for the grand distribution.

The earliest historical narrative concerning the importation of the Female Spirit cult that we recorded was from a ritual expert, Pingini Yalyanda of the Pauakaka tribe (Saka valley), who said that the magic spells for the cult were brought by a woman from the Mendi area named Kangala who had married his great-grandfather Manali.[21] The cult's rituals were first performed later when the sacred cult stones were imported (in about the fourth to fifth generation). The magic formulas were passed word for word from father to son, and though Pingini could recite them, he was not certain what language they were in. Shortly after Pauakaka had secured the cult, it was purchased by the Yambatane Watenge clan under the initiative of Pakiala, the father of the great Tee cycle organizer Maua, in the third generation:

Man, this was a great event! Before the performance began, word was sent to all the areas. The Yambatane tribe would announce that on the next day the slitting of the pigs' ears would take place. After the news reached all the areas, people would come to the Saka valley from all directions. They would arrive in full dress and take part in the pork feast, bringing net bags with them to carry home the remaining pork, for many sides of pork were given to guests at the feast. Many came from the *kyoa* region [Mendi-Ialibu], the Yandap area, and Kola, among other places. [Later he mentions that a ritual expert was summoned from the Kola area to preside over the ceremonies.] Here is how it happened. Yambatane's neighbors would tell clans up the valley that the cult feast was to be held. The news even reached the clans in the far west, that is to say, the news would arrive at the Apulini clan and the people of Apulini would relay word on to Yanaitini at Tetemanda. Then all the people from the west would come down. During the feast, when a person was given pork, he would share it with a friend—sometimes pork would be given to a person one had never met before. In this way pork circulated to all those who attended the feast. They carried home the pork that they had received directly from relatives.

[In response to a question concerning whether the Tee cycle was discussed at this time:] Yes, that is what we do. One person from each clan would be present in the men's house—say, for instance, one man from the Sikini Muitape clan, one from Sikini Lyonai, another from Depe Liala, Yakani, Yanaitini, and so on. Itokone was also represented. When all were present, one person would ask on behalf of all of the guests why the Watenge clan had performed its cult. They would ask about their pigs. Were they fully grown? When were they going to hold *tee pingi*? When would they kill pigs for the *yae*? Such questions would be asked by the guests and Watenge men would answer. They held long discussions on the subject of the Tee cycle and finally agreed on a time to start the *tee pingi* or *yae*, whichever it might be. (Apanyo Maua, Yambatane Watenge clan, Saka Laiagam, Saka valley)

The Female Spirit cult was somewhat simplified in the Saka valley, and most Enga appear not to have assimilated its origin myth and ideology, regarding it as a powerful cult for the ancestors that would bring fertility. Two good descriptions of Saka performances have been published—a general one by Paul Brennan (1977) based on a performance staged for demonstration in the 1970s and a patrol report describing the cult's purchase and first performance by the Waimini clan in the 1940s (Lacey 1975). The latter is a fascinating document. Aspects of the cult that seem to have had greatest appeal in eastern Enga were (1) the lavish display of wealth that could signal to those who came to organize the Tee that the hosting clan or tribe was wealthy, powerful, and organized for the Tee, and (2) the parade of the pearl shells, a feature entirely exotic to other Enga cults. The Female Spirit cult was imported just as big-men were first incorporating pearl shells into the Tee cycle, which would have helped establish them as coveted valuables with a sacred dimension. The interdependency of male and female principles expressed in the cult was also timely, corresponding to the needs of the Tee cycle.

So intense was the desire for cults that might confer an advantage in the context of the expanding Tee cycle that some groups resorted to dire solutions. Men from a Yakumani clan at Wapenamanda, for example, in the late 1950s or early 1960s made a night journey to steal the sacred stones of a nearby Waimini clan. They then proclaimed that the stones had mysteriously appeared at their place and, pretending to take their appearance as a sign from the spirit world, paid ritual experts from Kola to orchestrate their first performance of the Female Spirit cult. Because it was common belief that such stones could wander, nobody suspected theft.

The integration of cults into the planning of the Tee cycle continued along the western route from the Saka. Notable performances were held at Birip and Lenge, where the Pokalya, a cult that had its roots in the Kepele, was enacted.[22] For other clans of eastern Enga and Kompiam, where ancestral cults were generally less prominent, the emergence festivals of the Sangai-Sandalu bachelors' cult were used as occasions to gather people to discuss the Tee. Whether it was the Aeatee, Pokalya, Female Spirit, or Sangai-Sandalu, cults associated with the large ceremonial exchange systems brought the female principle to the fore, symbolically recognizing the role of women as producers of pigs, bearers of children, and quiet diplomats who formed ties between groups. Male and female principles were then united during the sacred rites in order for fertility and prosperity to be realized.

In short, the problems that arose from coordinating the Tee cycle with the Great Wars, and from the enormous expansion of the Tee that ensued, were mediated by the bachelors' and ancestral cults. In a very real sense, Kepai's statement that the ancestral cults made the Tee possible was true, at least during a critical period of its development. After the arrival of the missions in the late 1940s, the large cults of eastern and central Enga vanished rapidly, stripping the Tee of significant social and ideological underpinnings and laying it open to less restrained expressions of individual economic interest and competition.

The Conclusion of the Great Wars

The Great Wars, as the centerpiece of interest and exchange for central Enga, sowed the seeds of their own demise. Their popularity grew until a majority of able-bodied men in a tribe were fighting for months, together with hosts and hundreds of allies, some from far afield. The costs were high in terms of time expended, wealth exchanged, and, to a lesser extent, lives lost. The Tee, by contrast, with its chains of finance, held the promise of managing even more wealth without comparable costs. Accordingly, as the Tee took on an even higher profile with the inflow of wealth from the Great Wars, Great War leaders and others in their clans began to see it as a more efficient system of ceremonial exchange and made efforts to join. Simultaneously, some big-men involved in the Tee realized that it would be to their advantage to replace the Great War networks with Tee routes. The first to be affected were the Yakani versus Sene-Yokasa Great Wars (map 17:3).

People like Pendaine wanted to maintain the social excitement but without the Great Wars. They thought it would be possible to stop the Great Wars and instead take part in the Tee cycle. One of the main reasons people wanted to stop the Great Wars was that they saw that many people were being killed, so instead they took part in the Tee.[23] They did that, however, only when the Tee cycle became large and provided a lot of food and additional social benefits. Only when they were convinced that they could get the same things they were getting in the Great Wars did they give them up for the Tee. (Kambao Toya Lambu, Yakani Timali clan, Lenge)

For the Yakani and Sene-Yokasa to replace the Great War network with the Tee cycle was a relatively straightforward matter. Owners of the fight from both sides were already in the mainstream of the Tee, Yakani on the western route and Sene-Yokasa on the northern one. Only the hosts, Aiyele and Pumane clans in the upper Sau valley, stood in the middle. Having seen how much wealth flowed in the Tee cycle, they realized that it could bring benefits similar to those of the Great Wars without the costs. Consequently, after the episode fought at Wakumale around the turn of the century, they discontinued this Great War and became fully integrated into the Tee cycle.

The other Great Wars did not give way to the Tee so easily, but gradually came to an end in the fourth and third generations. Reasons for this reluctance have been voiced earlier: the Great Wars provided unparalleled social excitement and interaction for men, women, and children alike. They broke up the drudgery of everyday life, brought together people separated by steep mountains and valleys, channeled and ritualized aggression, and stimulated the flow of wealth between different areas. Many of their participants, removed from Tee routes and only vaguely aware of the Tee cycle, had to be convinced that it would provide benefits equal to those of the Great Wars.

Approximately a decade after the Tee cycle had supplanted the Yakani versus Sene-Yokasa Great War, the last Great War between Lyaini-Sakalini and Pumane-Aiyele was fought (map 17:2). Some men still remember seeing the Great War exchanges and can list the men who were killed. The reasons for the termination of this Great War are not stated directly in the testimonies we collected, but presumably costs were high and similar benefits could be gained by joining other Great Wars as allies.

The conditions for the termination of the Yanaitini versus Monaini Great Wars are clearer (map 17:1). In the early 1900s, Yanaitini was faced with numerous other demands from both the Tee cycle and the Malipini-Potealini versus Itapuni-Awaini Great War. The Great War with Monaini was particularly taxing in terms of manpower, since men from all Yanaitini clans fought far from home, to the neglect of household needs and Tee cycle negotiations. After an episode around 1915–20, Yanaitini paid its hosts in Sambe with the land in the Yandap that contained the renowned Nakatima salt pools, putting an end to this Great War once and for all. The Great War exchange network between Yanaitini and Sambe, well developed by this time, allowed Yanaitini to take salt and other wealth from Sambe clans and integrate it into the Tee.

The "diehard" of the Great Wars was that between Malipini-Potealini and Itapuni-Awaini (map 17:4). As the other Great Wars were phased out, it drew more attention and participants. Because it was fought near the terminus of the Tee cycle, wealth coming from the east could be used to finance the hosts on both sides, and that flowing out of Great War exchanges could easily be reinvested. With few limits to growth, it escalated to the point where its organization was complex and conflict-ridden. In the second-to-last episode, some of the Yanaitini clans who had previously hosted Malipini-Potealini refused to do so, and the location was moved to Wakumale. After the Wakumale episode, the Itapuni Nemani Great War leader, Satutu, among others, made arrangements for Itapuni and Awaini clans to participate directly in the Tee.

Yanaitini later agreed to host another episode at Kopena, near Tetemanda, in the late 1930s or early 1940s, which was to be the last. After that, Yanaitini clans who had hosted the Great Wars became full-fledged participants in the Tee cycle. Next, Mioko, the Malipini Kamaniwane Great War leader, integrated his clan into the Tee on the basis of his maternal ties with the Kia clan, and other Malipini-Potealini clans followed suit. A new route was formed through clans on the ridge separating the Lai and Ambum valleys, following the footsteps of exchange networks established in the Great Wars (map 17). Interviews with big-men of the second or third generation in Yanaitini, Itapuni, Malipini, and some clans of Potealini all concur: the concluding episode of the Great Wars was fought at Kopena, after which they gave way to the Tee.

In these parts, the people were involved in the [Malipini-Potealini versus Itapuni-Awaini] Great Wars.[24] It was because of the Tee cycle coming up from the east that the

Great Wars were eventually stopped. Those who took part in the Great Wars saw the large number of pigs that came in Tee cycles held by people from the east. They thought it was a good idea to join the Tee cycle, so they stopped fighting and took part in the Tee. The trend to stop fighting and join the Tee cycle was a fairly recent one; it took place in our time. In other words, I was the first to participate in the Tee cycle in the Ambum valley. However, down there along the Winikos route it had been in existence for some time. Tee cycles had gone through this route but we, the people of the Ambum valley, did not know this. You see, during the Great Wars, people saw the large number of pigs coming through the Tee, stopped fighting, and began to participate in the Tee. . . . In this way the two Tee routes joined [that is, the western and northern routes from the Saka]. (Auaka Taliu Waliu, Malipini Wailuni clan, Meriamanda-Ambum)

The replacement of the Malipini-Potealini versus Itapuni-Awaini Great War exchange network with the Tee cycle joined western and northern routes to complete the circle of the Tee. Still, these connections did not change the flow of the Tee from a linear to circular one. The main axis continued to be south-east-northwest from Tambul to Tetemanda, with clans to the east of Pakalilyam in the Sau valley and the Kopona area feeding into the northern Tee route to and from the Saka (map 16:B) and those west of Pakalilyam connecting with the mainstream of the Tee at Tetemanda or Lenge (map 16:A).

One motive for the Great Wars — creating pathways of exchange — was more than satisfied by the Tee. The Great Wars had a second dimension, however, that bore no relation to the Tee whatsoever — providing a formal setting in which antagonism between groups could be fought out. Because competition in the Tee cycle was structured differently from that in the Great Wars, the Tee did not provide an alternative form of competition. Furthermore, although the Great Wars had never substituted for smaller conventional wars, they did require peace within sides and offer an outlet for other enmities: young men hankering to try their hand in warfare were told to wait for the Great Wars, and those who bore grudges could fight them out in a contained context. Even though people thought that supplanting the Great Wars with the Tee would avoid loss of life, some elders believe that fewer lives were lost when there was a formal outlet for such aggression.

Summary

The Tee cycle as we know it today was crafted over a period of two to three generations from the major exchange systems of eastern, central, and western Enga. The early Tee, with its ingenious chains of finance, provided the means for almost unlimited growth; the Great Wars, with their dramatic intergroup competition and display, furnished both the demand for and the bulk of wealth; and the cults held the social techniques for the Tee's organization and the ideology for its mediation. The major thrust for the expansion of the early Tee cycle came when big-men in clans that spanned the east and center campaigned to lengthen Tee chains as a means of finance for the Great Wars. Working through personal ties and the medium of the cults imported from the west, they succeeded. A similar but weaker pull to expand the Tee cycle may have been exerted as big-men of eastern Enga sought more wealth to invest in pearl shells, the ultimate valuable of exchange systems to their south and east. Between these two forces, the Tee cycle flourished. Participants and hosts in the Great Wars of central Enga then saw the large amounts of wealth that circulated in the Tee, weighed the costs and benefits of the Great Wars, and were gradually convinced to discontinue the latter in favor of the former, adding new routes and many clans to the network. By approximately a decade before the colonial administration and missions became established in Enga, the river of Tee, with its many tributaries, had flooded.

12

Competition and Cooperation
A Family History of Leadership and Tee

To compile the developments of the last three to five generations in Enga, it has been necessary to forfeit much of the spirit and detail of the past as presented in historical traditions. This is a significant loss, for it does not allow the reader to appreciate how historical traditions were used in the service of change: for instance, to inspire, direct, or challenge the young. Furthermore, the absence of personal narratives leaves the Tee described only from the outside and obscures just how different the cycles of the rapidly developing Tee were in each generation. To recover some of what has been lost, in this chapter we present excerpts from a family history that extends from the eighth generation until contact, becoming increasingly vivid as it moves into the struggles and victories of family members in the twentieth century.

Our intent is threefold: first, to offer a personal history of the Tee that complements more standardized clan histories, shows how the actions of specific individuals affected the system, and gives a sense of the power of oral history for inspiring social action; second, to follow the rise in power of big-men hand in hand with *tee* exchange; and third, to shed light on issues of anthropological debate. Depictions of the Tee cycles of the 1950s and 1960s by Meggitt (1972, 1974) and portrayals of cycles of the 1970s by Feil (1984) give

such different views of the Tee that it has been difficult for readers to know whether to regard the Tee of the central Enga and that of the Tombema as somewhat different institutions or to attribute the differences described to the theoretical standpoints of the two authors. To sort out these differences is essential, for such studies will provide the primary documentation of the Tee cycle for the generations to come.

The core of the differences between Feil's and Meggitt's analyses of the Tee lies in the purpose of the Tee cycle and the locus of competition. Meggitt (1972, 1974), in keeping with his hypothesis that the Enga experienced constant land shortages, sees the Tee cycle as a form of competition between clans and corporate groups whose aim was to acquire and defend land. That is, the display of wealth in the Tee provided regular opportunities for expanding clans to discover which of their neighbors was likely to be too weak to defend its territories (1974:170-71, 179n27). These ideas rest on the assumption, which we questioned earlier, that it was land rather than labor that limited production, so that clans were forever poised to take the land of their neighbors. They do not recognize that because of the limits of household labor forces, neighboring clans with cooperative partners who could provide pigs and valuables for *tee* exchanges were more valuable than the land they inhabited.

Feil (1984:156-60), going to the other extreme, sees the Tee as strictly an individual enterprise. He argues that individual men cooperated with others outside the clan with whom they were linked by female ties and with whom they had warm complementary relationships and alternating inequality in exchange. Conversely, they competed with those linked through males—that is, fellow clansmen—with whom they maintained relationships of equality and keep strict accounting in exchange. The fiercest competition was thus between subclan and clan members. Tee, he argues, was "the ultimate cultural value," and the purpose of the Tee was prestige for prestige's sake (Feil 1984:195-96): "The Tee is an individual's statement about his financial ability and the value he places on his Tee partners. . . . The rewards of a successful Tee accrue only to the individual making it."

Surprising in both arguments is the neglect of what virtually every Enga whom we interviewed stated and what history confirms: that the Tee was a system of finance. Though it had many other benefits, such as the formation of strong ties across clan boundaries, its primary purpose was to provide finance for both individual and clan enterprises. Pigs do not live forever; they are a form of wealth that must be spent. The phase of the main gifts in the Tee brings a mass of wealth, particularly pigs, into the clan, and in the *yae* phase about half the pigs received as main gifts are slaughtered and the meat distributed to donors. The other half of the pigs circulating in the Tee were used to finance individual and clan needs—needs that varied by generation. So closely was the Tee cycle tied to the ventures it financed that pigs received in a Tee festival were often staked out then and there by the recipients and immediately redistributed to pay other obligations. As elders emphasized, it is finance that ultimately counts, not display, for many words are spent in Enga, and what is important is that they are backed by action.[1] In the pages to follow we discuss what the Tee was called on to finance at different points in history and the corresponding nature of competition as portrayed in the struggles of big-men in Tee politics, descriptions of their appearance and movements, and the contents of their speeches.

The Lambu family, whose history we present, is an extraordinary one because its members played a pivotal role in the Tee cycle over generations.[2] Its history was narrated by Kambao Toya Lambu, the son of Lambu, the great Tee *kamongo* (big-man) of the 1930s through 1960s, and by Lambu's nephew and adopted son, Kopio Toya Lambu. It was collected and translated by Nitze Pupu, a grandson of Lambu's, as part of a series of interviews with Kambao and Kopio. The question "Tell us about leadership and Tee exchange in the past" elicited the family saga presented here. Although this history was imparted to Nitze as part of his family heritage, it was told with generous explanation, for the narrators were well aware of the circumstances of our project—that the history was intended for future generations of Enga and for people from other cultures who might know nothing of the Tee cycle.

A few words must be said about the gloss of words decribing social position. To preserve the flow of the text, we retain the Enga term for big-man, *kamongo*. Direct partners in the Tee cycle, called *kaita miningi*—literally, "holders of the way"—are glossed as "Tee partners." Others further down an individual's Tee chain are called "Tee associates." Low-status men who are termed *kendemane* ("roped men") in Enga and *"rabisman"* ("rubbish man") in Melanesian Pidgin are here called "servants," for indeed the majority of them attached themselves to the households of big-men and worked more or less exclusively in their service for the duration of their tenure.

The Early Generations of the Lambu Family

Kopio began with a brief sketch of the early generations, for he was eager to move on to the part of the history that he knew so well:

My name is Kopio Toya Lambu of Lenge village. My grandfather Pendaine told me this history. Our forefather was Ipawape, founder of the Yakani Timali clan.[3] It is said that he lived in Kilyadisa. He had many pigs, but there is no story that tells of him participating in the Tee cycle. According to the oral history told by my grandfather Pen-

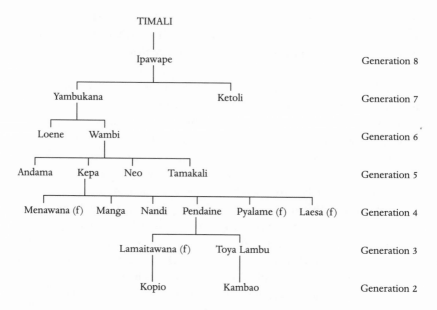

Figure 2. Genealogy of members of the Lambu family, Yakani Timali clan.

daine, Ipawape and his generation did not perform any Tee pig exchange ceremonies.[4] That does not mean that they did not give away pigs. For example, he paid bridewealth for his sons and gave pigs to his friends and kinsmen.[5]

Ipawape and the people of his time traveled a lot without fear of attack. They took trips to the east and to the west. One day Ipawape took such a trip to the west and arrived at Yambipaisa, the land of the Kunalini tribe [near Laiagam]. There he married a Kunalini woman and had two sons, Ketoli and Yambukana [fig. 2]. They more or less followed the footsteps of their father. In other words, they owned pigs but did not have the Tee cycle. Let us forget about Ketoli and Yambukana and talk about their descendants, because it is said that the first [Timali] *kamongo* came from the descendants of Yambukana.

Yambukana, the son of Ipawape, had two sons, Loene and Wambi. Wambi was destined to have success in life; he was born to be a leader.

It was for Wambi's lifetime that Kopio was first able to speak in some detail about leadership and exchange. After presenting some details of Wambi's life, he told how Wambi emerged as clan *kamongo*. The example he gave reflected the beginning of a trend discussed earlier, the extension of war reparations to enemies to reestablish peace rather than driving away the losing party. In this incident, following the cold-blooded murder of Wambi's brother by men from the neighboring Sane clan, a war broke out. The fighting was short-lived, and then confusion reigned, for the "brother" clans, Timali and Sane, had never fought before and both wanted peace. Wambi stepped forth and arranged for what are said to have been Timali's first war reparations paid to enemies and the first public distribution of wealth on its ceremonial grounds.

Wambi's first public distribution of wealth was during this war reparation exchange. All other members of the Timali clan also gave away pigs, but Wambi gave away more than the others. His row of pig stakes was longer than all the rest. There was nothing exciting or dramatic about our first *tee.* For example, Wambi and his men did not sing any songs, he did not wear any intricately woven bird-of-paradise feathers on his wig, and he did not make eloquent speeches. When I say that he did not sing any songs, I mean songs boasting of their wealth, but it is said that he and his men sang a song concerning the war. This war song was probably one of the first public songs sung by the Timali clan. The songs were simple and straightforward. . . . Although Wambi was the first leader of our clan, according to what my grandfather said, his leadership was fairly weak. He did not have strong influence but merely made comments and suggestions.

There was no pig exchange on a large scale in the time of Ipawape, Yambukana, and his son Wambi. There were pork feasts, but only with neighboring clans. During the lifetime of Wambi, the pig exchange called *tee* involved only the exchange of goods between neighboring clans for war reparations.[6] . . . The great pig exchange, the Tee cycle that we know today, began in the lifetime of Kepa, the son of Wambi.[7]

Kopio then turned to events in the lifetime of Wambi's son, Kepa, when the Tee cycle had already become prominent in the Timali clan. Tee cycles at this time were short and were called to supply specific clan enterprises such as war reparations. This lent the corporate aspect stressed by Meggitt (1974) to a system of finance that had been instituted by *kamongo* to serve their interests in the trade. The primary locus of competition at this time was in the events financed by the small stream of Tee, such as trade and war reparations, rather than in the Tee cycle itself. It may be for this reason that this narrative from the fifth generation describes social activities and the condition of pigs, in contrast to the physical appearances and speeches of Tee *kamongo* that fill the oral record of later generations.

Kopio's testimony on the life of Kepa began with genealogy, listing Kepa's six children and two wives. He then moved directly into a Tee cycle that must have taken place in the 1870s or 1880s.

In Kepa's lifetime, Tee cycles were held, but they were short ones. In other words, in Kepa's time the Tee [from Lenge; map 18] did not reach the Yandap, Sau, Kopona, and Saka regions. The Tee cycles in Kepa's time extended from Wabag [Yanaitini at Tetemanda] to the land of the Itokone tribe [Pompabus]. Here is an account of how the short Tee cycles were conducted. The clans of the Awaini tribe [Wabag] — Kayalu,

Yakale, Sapipi, and Aiyape—did not participate in the Tee. Rather, they gave pigs to the Yanaitini Kia clan [at Tetemanda], and Kia gave them in Tee to the neighboring Yanaitini Yapakone clan. Yapakone gave pigs to Kia in exchange, and Kia took these pigs and held their Tee festival. They gave pigs to Apulini [Irelya] and Yakani [Lenge], and then pigs went down the Lai valley and stopped in the land of Itokone.[8] From there the Tee returned to Tetemanda. This is how the Tee was done before the major Tee cycle existed.

What is told of Kepa's participation in the Tee begins when the phase of the main gifts [which Kopio referred to as Tee] was already complete and the *mena yae* phase involving large pig kills and the distribution of pork was about to follow. These events took place when Kepa was living in his house at Kilyadisa where Naepea now lives. Kepa owned a lot of large pigs, some of which were too fat to enter the doorway of his house. He left them roaming around the courtyard of his house and fed them there.

The great *yae* phase of the Tee began and soon it was Timali's turn to slaughter pigs at Lenge. Many pigs were killed on this occasion, and as expected, many potential recipients turned up that day. All the necessary preparations had been made, but the number of pigs to be steamed in the rectangular earth oven was so great that they ran out of leaves, stones, and firewood. Therefore the sides of pork were left raw, and only the chests and intestines were steamed. Most of the people who came that day were from the west [Irelya and Tetemanda], some of whom were Kepa's Tee partners or associates.

Toward the end of the evening, the earth oven was uncovered and the pork and other foods were laid out for the feast. The sides of pork were so heavy that they were hung from poles that had to be carried by two men. Each side of pig was carried in that manner. Because of their weight, they were not brought to the ceremonial grounds but were given out near the spot where they were killed. There was so much pork to eat! Kepa himself killed about twenty pigs, and some of the meat rotted before it was consumed and had to be thrown into the Lai river. One of his sons was born while the pigs were being killed, and therefore he was named Yaesa after the great pig killing ceremony.

In the Tee cycle that followed that *yae*, Kepa planted his stakes on the ceremonial grounds in a single line. His row of pigs was the longest. In this Tee, Kepa counted his pigs. The counting system went like this: two, four, six, eight, ten, twelve, and so on. Kepa was the first Timali *kamongo* to have participated in a real Tee cycle and the first [Timali] *kamongo* to apply the counting system.[9] After all the pigs were counted, casuarina trees were planted at each end of the line to mark its length. The trees grew and became very old; only recently were they cut down for firewood. Many people came to watch the Tee; among them were the recipients of his pigs. It is said that some of these men were from the Potealini Anae and Pumane Sane clans of the Ambum and Sau valleys, and that they came to see the Tee when a war was going on in that part of the region.

It is said that my great-grandfather Kepa did not wear a headdress of bird-of-paradise feathers, nor did he boast. Kepa did not sing any songs about how wealthy he was. He wanted to be friends with everybody and was very cautious not to create bad feelings among his people and especially with his Tee partners. It is said that in this Tee cycle, Kepa gave away about sixty pigs.[10]

It was in the time of Kepa that stronger leaders began to emerge. Toward the end of his lifetime, when Kepa was an old man [that is, in the time of his son Pendaine], competition began to appear in the Tee cycle, and along with it, Tee politics.[11] All of these things happened following one important event: the introduction of the counting system. Before its introduction, nobody really knew for sure who was the real *kamongo*. When the counting system was introduced, people were able to tell who was the real *kamongo*. The Tee and strong leadership grew together and reinforced each other. This did not happen overnight.

Noteworthy in this part of Kopio's testimony is his discussion of the counting system. Kopio's logic of causality here is probably inverted: it was not the counting system that introduced competition into the Tee cycle, but the reverse. So far as we could ascertain, the counting system used in the Tee cycle was imported into central Enga from the east. In keeping with the fact that the Tee originated out of the efforts of *kamongo* to control the trade, the counting system focused attention on individual distributions. Lines of pigs given by individuals were counted and compared, not the contributions of clans as corporate units, although the counting system could have accommodated the latter. Thus, the emphasis on individual competition in the Tee noted by Feil (1984) was there from the beginning and was never removed from the system, even though the Tee increasingly took on corporate aspects as the wealth that flowed in it was applied to a wide variety of clan needs.

The Life of Pendaine

With the lifetime of Kepa's son Pendaine one enters a new era of Enga history. It was a time of great change as the Tee cycle began to be used to finance the Great Wars and to reinvest the wealth that flowed out of them, flooding the Tee with pigs and increasing its prominence. Pendaine is not a new figure to this text: his pivotal role as a Great War leader and Tee organizer who first constructed longer Tee cycles and coordinated them with the Great Wars was discussed extensively in chapters 10 and 11. Pendaine's life history begins with his domestic arrangements, documenting the intensification of production in the households of *kamongo* to meet the needs of the Tee. Here are Kopio's words:

Now I will tell you about my grandfather Pendaine, the son of Kepa. Pendaine married a woman from the Pumalini Kandano clan [middle Lai]. All of his forefathers had married more than one woman, but he married only one, for his wife did not approve of

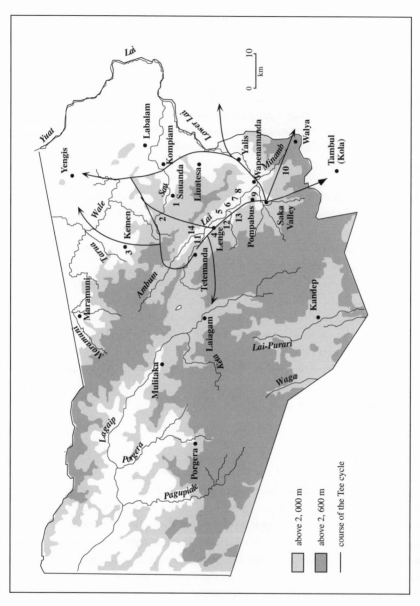

Map 18. Tribes and clans mentioned in the history of the Lambu family. 1, Aiyele Tyakai clan; 2, Pumane Yaupa clan; 3, Aiyele Neowali clan; 4, Yakani Timali clan; 5, Pumalini Kandano clan; 6, Kandawalini Ambulyini clan; 7, Lungupini Sau clan; 8, Kandawalini Anjo clan; 9, Itokone tribe; 10, Yatapaki tribe; 11, Yanaitini Piao clan; 12, Yakani Sane clan; 13, Sikini tribe; 14, Yakani Kalia clan.

his intention to take a second wife. She said that unless he was too sexually passionate to be content with one wife, there was no need to marry a second woman. She assured him that she could do all of the necessary work for him and that his pigs would not go hungry. As time passed, Pendaine saw that his wife was indeed a hardworking woman, so he gave up the idea of seeking a second wife. His wife looked after all of his gardens. As for his pigs, there were so many that one woman could not feed them all, so Pendaine gave away some of the female pigs in his herd to people in neighboring clans, except for the Kainabotepa clan. These people merely took care of his pigs, they did not own them.[12] The female pigs were bred and raised until they grew big. All these pigs, plus the ones that were raised in his own house, made up his large pig herd. It was said that his pigs were [numerous] like the leaves on trees. It was necessary to keep an eye on them because many became wild. Their caretakers had to make sure that the pigs did not roam too far or trespass into the bush of another clan. Pendaine was the *kamongo* of the land.[13]

Because of his high standing, no ordinary man could talk to him face-to-face. If anybody wanted to talk to him, the word was passed through members of his household. He spoke little, but his words carried much weight and had a sense of authority. Indeed, Pendaine was a man of high social status and prestige, and therefore he was a focal person in the Tee. People of the west and east hung upon his words, and Lenge became well known because of him. Even today it is spoken of as "the place with the house for the pig killing phase of the Tee cycle called the *yae*." His fame reached far and wide and it grew during his married lifetime.

Kopio then went on to tell of Pendaine's four children: a girl who was put to death after birth upon his orders because he had wanted a son;[14] a son, Pendaine's pride and joy, who died of an injury received during play; Toya Lambu; and Lamaitawana, Kopio's mother. He continued by describing Pendaine's exploits in the Great Wars and his journeys to construct longer Tee chains (see chapters 10 and 11). Although Pendaine was said to have participated in two or three Tee cycles earlier in his lifetime, the one that Kopio described took place later in his life (ca. 1910), after the Yakani versus Sene-Yokasa Great War had been discontinued and replaced by the Tee. By this time, Tee chains were already long, involving most clans of eastern Enga. War reparations to enemies were regular events that required wealth, and the Malipini-Potealini versus Itapuni-Awaini Great Wars were in full swing, adding further demands to the Tee. Whereas Tee cycles in Kepa's time were organized to meet the needs of a single clan, when the Tee became a means of finance for the Great Wars, many different parties participated whose plans did not always coincide. It was in the context of these events that more complex "Tee politics" evolved, including extensive campaigns necessary to coordinate and launch a Tee cycle. *Kamongo* such as Pendaine who were renowned Tee organizers worked out a plan with fellow clansmen and Tee associates and then went on extended journeys to organize the Tee. Meanwhile, independent households in his clan campaigned similarly, though on a more limited scale, with their own relatives toward the same end.

The following excerpt from a narrative by Kopio Toya Lambu describes one of Pendaine's journeys to organize a Tee cycle that took place around 1905–10; Kopio uses "Tee" to refer to the phase of the main gifts and *yae* for that of butchered pork. It gives a superb portrayal of the close cooperation between Tee partners and associates, which Feil (1984) noted, as they traveled along their Tee chains to be received with warm hospitality at each stopover. We chose this long passage because it illustrates the way in which strong bonds were formed between partners along one Tee chain. By the end of Pendaine's lifetime, these chains were to become powerful new units of competition in the Tee.

Before his death, my father [Pendaine's daughter's husband] was a key link to the Sau region in many of Pendaine's Tee exploits. In one Tee cycle, Pendaine went to the Sau region campaigning for the start of the phase of the main gifts. Pendaine, the great *kamongo*, came to the house of his son-in-law [of the Aiyele Tyakai clan near Sauanda (map 18:1)], who was, of course, my father. My father welcomed him and extended to him the hospitality that was fitting to a man of Pendaine's status—my father killed a pig for him and they slept in the men's house together that night. In the morning the two went to the house of Yakapyakape, who had two brothers named Yaka and Kanopato. They were *kamongo* of the Pumane Yaupa clan [map 18:2]. When the two arrived at their place, the brothers gave them a warm welcome. They spent the night at their house and were entertained and given food. In the men's house Ipalyone told them why they had come and Pendaine explained his plan for the next Tee. The brothers listened to him intently, and the next day they set off together for the house of Neowali Yakani. The small group made its way over the mountainous terrain, arriving at Neowali's house [near Keman, map 18:3] on the evening of the same day.[15] He received them and gave them food and water. When they were in the house together, Yakapyakape told them of the purpose of their visit and they talked about the Tee. Neowali listened very carefully, and at the end of the discussions, he agreed to their proposals.

Neowali Yakani was the one who was to begin the Tee cycle. For weeks Pendaine stayed in the Sau region with these men, and led by Neowali they campaigned for the Tee. They went from house to house, village to village, and clan to clan. Occasionally they went back to the house of Neowali to sleep, but most of the time they stayed with the people they visited. In this way the word was spread to every clan about the possibility of doing Tee. The *kamongo* of each clan then gathered his men on the ceremonial grounds and discussed the plans for the Tee. The issues at hand were who was the *kamongo* advocating this Tee, its course, the *yae* phase to follow, and so on. Then a day was fixed on which one clan would actually begin the phase of the main gifts. In the meanwhile, preparations were made: stakes were planted on the ceremonial grounds of the clan that was to begin the Tee and those of other clans in the region that would participate.

On the planned day, the Tee began on the designated ceremonial grounds. Many Tee organizers from different regions arrived for the event, including Pendaine and his associates. On the first ceremonial grounds Neowali Yakani received many pigs, as he did in the Tee festivals of other clans that followed. He also received valuable stone axes.

When some months had passed, the day came for Neowali Yakani and his clan to hold their Tee festival. On this day, all of the pigs were brought to the ceremonial grounds and tied to stakes. There were a number of pigs that were desired by everyone because they were particularly large and fat. These were passed from *kamongo* to *kamongo* and so became particularly well known. They were named Pai Kotao, Waputali, and Andolo. They ended up in the house of Neowali; that is, they were given to him. Why? Because Neowali Yakani was a *kamongo*, of course. Before the crowd of spectators, Neowali gave the famous pigs to Yakapyakape, the *kamongo* of the Pumane Yaupa clan. The Yaupa *kamongo* came forward from the crowd and ran around the entire ceremonial grounds boasting, "I campaigned for this Tee cycle, therefore all the pigs moving in it are mine! All must come to me! The Tee is mine!"

After the Tee distribution, Yakapyakape took the pigs home. The named pigs were among the many that had been given to him. Pendaine, the great *kamongo*, followed the Tee all this time, for he knew that these pigs, in particular the famous ones, would be given to him. Many people in the crowd had also guessed that they would go to none other than the Yakani *kamongo*.

The testimony goes on to describe the Tee festivals of the Pumani Yaupa and Aiyele Tyakai clans, with a remark at the end indicating that at this time rivalries between big-men on different Tee chains were beginning. Nonetheless, in other discussions Kopio pointed out that influential Tee organizers were few at this time and Pendaine was not faced with serious challenges.

At the Sauanda ceremonial grounds, Pendaine was given many pigs, among them the named ones. He was given twenty altogether, in addition to three cassowaries and five stone axes. Pendaine was highly esteemed for his ability to mastermind the Tee cycle and outmaneuver other *kamongo*; it was therefore that he received so many pigs. His name was known as far as the Saka valley. . . . Pendaine became so extremely wealthy during this Tee cycle that people from distant places called him Yakani Pendaine.[16]

The Tee cycle then moved down the Ambum to reach Pendaine's own Timali clan at Lenge (map 18:4). The following passage describes the events there— meetings, preparations, and challenges from Pendaine's ambitious brother, Nandi. One can feel in this testimony the growing focus on the individual. Unlike in Kepa's time, great attention is put on contents of speeches, movements, and outward appearances as leaders increasingly become public representatives of their clans and magnets for wealth that will be applied to clan needs.[17] An old principle is extended: that outward appearance reflects inner integrity and social competence. Blackened faces and formal apparel also confer a certain anonymity, substituting for the individual a cultural ideal. It is in this context of group representation that powerful leaders solicit public support.

A week before the Tee was to take place at Lenge, Pendaine held meetings on the [Timali] ceremonial grounds. He explained to the crowd how he had carried out the campaign for the Tee and told his Tee associates from the east what he would like them to do with the Tee when it reached their clans. Endless debates were held from morning to evening. His Tee associates more or less approved of his plans, but his jealous rivals sat in the midst of the crowd listening carefully to catch any flaws in his speeches. Only his talkative brother, Nandi, would sneer at him and tell him to shut up when he wanted to speak. Nandi was also a *kamongo*, but not a Tee politician. Pendaine always complained that Nandi tried to monopolize the debates. Pendaine spoke low and little, yet the crowd held its breath when he opened his mouth to speak. He was an awesome figure with a towering build that naturally attracted attention. It is said that his leg muscles stood out like the trunk of a *waima* tree.

The meetings went on for a week. During this time, people from distant places were accommodated at Lenge. Pendaine's Tee partners stayed in his men's house, and those who lived nearby went home for the night.

As I said earlier, Pendaine married a Pumalini Kandano woman [map 18:5] whose mother was from the Kandawalini Ambulyini clan [6]. Somehow his wife's parents were related to Kalepo of the Lungupini Sau clan [7]. Sau Kalepo was a Tee partner of Lawai of the Kandawalini Anjo clan [8]. Lawai was a Tee partner of Lendeane of the Itokone tribe [9], and this Tee link continued as far as the Yatapaki tribe [10] of the Minamb valley.[18] What I have described was one of Pendaine's many Tee links that built his vast Tee network and brought him fame. Such links extended to the Saka valley in the east, as far west as Tetemanda, and from the Sau region into the Wale-Tarua.

One week passed and it was time for the Yakani Timali clan to hold its Tee festival. Kinsmen, Tee partners, associates, and friends had come to watch. Many arrived early and spent several nights at Lenge, among them Pendaine's Tee associates from the Saka, Minamb, and lower Lai valleys to the east. All members of the Timali clan went about making preparations for the great occasion. The great Yakani Pendaine had already sent word to friends in the Saka valley to bring bird-of-paradise feathers to Lenge. These were no ordinary plumes but were woven into intricate patterns like the ones you find [in the Saka valley] today.

On the morning when the event was to take place, the recipients were told to bring the pigs to the ceremonial grounds and tie them to the stakes. As had been the tradition for some time, they were also supposed to decorate the pigs with white clay to make them look handsome for the crowd of spectators. All of these things were done upon the instructions of Pendaine. All wives in the Timali clan were told to bring ornaments to their husbands at their respective men's houses, where they dressed in ceremonial attire.

Pendaine was in his men's house located near the ceremonial grounds, and all the necessary items of dress had been brought there. His wife brought the following basic items to him in her ordinary net bag: long, woven frontal aprons, belts, armlets, neck-laces, plume headdresses, and so on. As planned during the previous days, male friends brought cordyline leaves (*yuku akaipu*) to cover his buttocks. A number of these men were from his household. With the help of others, Pendaine dressed; each item and or-nament was arranged with great care. His nose and eyelids were painted white with clay and then the rest of his face blackened with charcoal. A wig of human hair was placed on his head and blackened with a mixture of powdered charcoal and lard. On top of the wig his friends placed the plumes of birds of paradise. Leg bands were worn on each leg with opossum testicles attached, and pig ropes were tied around his wrists. In the right side of his belt, Pendaine tucked a valuable stone ax called *gayamu*. Finally, his torso was completely rubbed with tree oil (*mamba*).

The great Pendaine was dressed to perfection from head to toe. It was midday and his body glistened under the sun's rays. Because of his tall stature, his plumes seemed to touch the sky. It was a dazzling, spectacular sight, as the colors of his ornaments and plumes reflected the bright sunlight. On one hand, his appearance was awesome, pow-erful, and glorious; on the other, he made a savage and fierce impression.

Yakani Pendaine rose and stood tall. Then he took a step forward and said to the small crowd that had gathered to watch him being decorated, "Have all of the pigs been brought to the ceremonial grounds? All the pigs that I received in the Tee must be tied to the stakes toward the end of the line. All of the pigs that have been bred for this purpose must be tied to the stakes in the front of the row. People must see that not only have I received many pigs in the Tee, but also I have raised many pigs at home. This will be a time of fulfillment. I have waited for this moment."

With the greased black spear in his right hand, Pendaine stepped forward and made his way to the ceremonial grounds. The small crowd followed. People parted to his left and right as he moved forward. When the procession reached the edge of the ceremo-nial grounds, it dispersed, leaving Pendaine to proceed to the center alone. Most of his clansmen were dressed in a similar fashion, and many had already tied the pigs to the stakes in their own rows. A great crowd gathered all around the edge of the ceremo-nial grounds, and people milled around looking for a better standing or sitting place from which to watch the Tee.

The great Yakani *kamongo* appeared on the scene. As he walked through the rows of stakes toward the center of the grounds, he said in a loud voice, "Auu!"[19] All eyes were fixed upon him, and as the expression goes, even the frogs down by the Lai river stopped croaking. There was complete silence. It was broken by a sudden commotion in the back of the crowd at the eastern end and by the sound of marching feet. The noise became louder as a group approached; the squealing of pigs drowned out every-thing else. The crowd backed off as the group of men and women burst onto the grounds, driving forward the pigs that they held on rope leashes. Pendaine's father-in-law led them, holding the rope of one of the named pigs, Waputali. Pendaine stood right next to the first stake and signaled to his father-in-law to tie the pig to it. Then he gave similar instructions to the others until every pig was tied. His line of stakes, which was the longest of all, was soon filled with pigs.

The crowd looked on as Timali men dressed in full ceremonial attire went to and fro through the lines of tied pigs. The pigs, which were smeared with white clay, did not make a sound but rooted in the ground around their stakes, their tails wagging. The three named pigs from the Sau region were tied to the first three stakes in the row.

Pendaine moved over to the first stake after he saw that everything was going well. "I have campaigned for this Tee cycle," he said. "People of the east, please listen to what I have to say. I have gone to the Sau and to the upper Lai to get this Tee. I have followed your word. I have done this so that you can hold the *yae* [return phase] for me and the people of the west." Then, pointing to Waputali with the tip of his spear, he said, "Look, I received Waputali from the Sau region. Take this pig with you and hold the *yae* with it." He addressed the public, but his words were aimed at his father-in-law and Tee associates. After the speech Pendaine signaled to one of his fellow clansmen to count his pigs.

Pendaine, the counter, and several others made their way down to the end of his row of stakes. Young Lambu followed at their heels. When they reached the end, they started counting the pigs. Every Timali participant in the Tee did the same: each made a short speech and each counted his pigs.[20] Pendaine's team kept counting on, since his row was the longest. They went on and on counting the pigs until finally they came to the beginning of the row, where the pig Waputali was tied. Pendaine stood next to Waputali and called out the last number in a loud voice: "One hundred pigs in all," the counter said. Everybody listened; many in the crowd murmured with applause. As soon as the final count was announced, the great Yakani *kamongo* moved closer to the first stake. He raised his spear, positioned it to throw, and jumped up and down. Then very slowly he leapt forward, jumping and bounding through his row of pigs, careful not to trip and fall on the stakes. Young Lambu, who was dressed colorfully, followed his famous father. When the two reached the end of the line, they were completely exhausted and stopped to rest.

A bundle of dry twigs and grass was piled near the last stake. One of Pendaine's servants brought fire and set it alight. The fire gave out a lot of smoke, and when the crowd saw the smoke [so far away], they were amazed. Some asked how on earth a man could become so wealthy. Then another man brought a cordyline plant [*akaipu*] and a casuarina seedling to the spot and planted them a short distance from the fire.[21] The casuarina tree grew and became very old, and was only recently cut down. The cordyline tree also grew but was recently plowed away by a bulldozer during road construction.

After this was done, the recipients untied the pigs and led them off the ceremonial grounds. Those from neighboring clans who received many pigs [too many to care for] then planted their stakes in the ground, tied the pigs to them, and gave them away on the spot. For example, all of the pigs received by the neighboring Yakani Sane clan were given away then and there.[22] Those who were from distant places took their pigs and made their way home before evening drew near. Those who expected to receive more stayed on.

After some time the pigs were out of sight, and Timali clansmen gathered on the ceremonial grounds once again. This time they gave away cassowaries, stone axes, and minor items of wealth like beads and shell-embroidered headbands.[23] Pendaine gave away many cassowaries and about ten stone axes. The great Tee festival was finally over at Lenge.

And so the Tee cycle carrying the wealth of Pendaine and others moved on from Lenge and made its way to the Saka and Tambul. Though Pendaine followed it for some clans down the line, he then went home and tended to his duties as household head and *kamongo,* for the Tee was flowing downstream from Timali and he would receive no more until the return *yae* phase.

From here the testimony goes on to describe the *yae* at length (see Appendix 13 for the full text). It tells how Neowali, Yakapyakape, and others come from the Sau valley to Lenge upon receiving news that the *yae* phase of the Tee cycle is to begin, and how together they journey up the Lai and into the Minamb. They gather ever more Tee associates along the way and have to follow broader paths. They go as far as the Yatapaki clan in the Minamb valley, where the sides of the largest pig slaughtered are sent westward with the message, "Send word that this side of pork is from a pig that was raised by a woman named Lyalame," reflecting women's important but private roles as producers. As the *yae* moves up the valley and approaches Lenge, Kopio describes the bustle of activity as each household makes its own preparations. When the day of the Timali *yae* arrives, Pendaine and Nandi put aside their rivalry and display their sides of pork in one row as an expression of clan unity. Nandi speaks first, boasting of his own success and that of his clan and praising their ceremonial grounds. Pendaine then makes a speech pointing out that he is a man of his word and that people should listen to him in planning the next cycle. Everybody participates, everybody gives, and everybody receives in this joyous event.

Pendaine and Nandi's display of unity was common for this period, unless a clan was on the verge of splitting. Other testimonies that we collected from the Saka valley even tell of meetings in which plans were made to step up rivalry between the *kamongo* of a clan in order to brew interest and investment. Then, in the final hour, the competing *kamongo* changed course and took a united stand for clan interest. To say that success accrued only to the *kamongo* with the longest lines of pigs is tantamount to saying that credit for winning a football match goes only to those who score goals. A successful Tee could be engineered only by strong leaders; people knew that and supported them by their own smaller campaigns.

Kopio then went on to reflect on Pendaine's status and character:

Pendaine gave away more pigs in this Tee than any other. He had the longest line of stakes [in Timali], the last one being planted where the bush path leads to your [Nitze

Pupu's] uncle's house. It is there that Pendaine planted the trees. Pendaine did not have any strong rivals in any of the Tee cycles held during his lifetime.[24] Rivalry emerged during the lifetime of Lambu. Pendaine was sort of a modest man; he was friendly and diplomatic, did not want to offend anyone, and treated the members of his household fairly. . . .

A while ago I said that Pendaine had no strong rivals. That is not true, for in the Great War that was fought at Wakumale, Pendaine was a war leader and there was intense competition between Pendaine and Piuku of the Yokotini tribe. It was in the Tee cycle that Pendaine had no major rivals.

Pendaine's life story reveals an extraordinary man, a man of few words but a man of his word, who possessed acute skill and foresight in politics. We encountered no clan in the Tee network in which his name was unknown. Unlike so many other *kamongo*, he was quiet, loyal to his one wife, and tolerant of rivals. In a sense, the peak of leadership can be said to have been reached during Pendaine's generation in conjunction with the flourishing of the Tee cycle and Great Wars. By this time a new category of leader had come into being, *kamongo andake*, who had influence far beyond the boundaries of his own clan and tribe. These men were highly esteemed, widely supported, and could execute their plans with solid campaigns. In the next generation, big-men were able to construct larger networks and assemble more wealth, but the bitter struggles and devious tactics required to do so began to erode their positions.

The Life of Lambu

Quite a different character and context emerges in the life history of Pendaine's son, Lambu, which covers a period of even greater changes than those of Pendaine's lifetime. Born around 1900, Lambu never experienced the Great Wars of his own tribe but witnessed those of tribes to the west. He first participated in the Tee when it contained massive amounts of wealth from the Great Wars. When the Malipini-Potealini versus Itapuni-Awaini Great War was supplanted by the Tee in the late 1930s, many participants and new feeder routes were added to the Tee cycle, greatly complicating its course and timing. Clans had grown and participants within a clan were many, and so opposing Tee chains formed along major routes, crosscutting clan boundaries and adding a new and sometimes ruthless level of competition. Later in Lambu's lifetime, the colonial administration and missions were to set new directions again.

It is in this context that the events of the following testimony by Kambao Toya Lambu take place. Lambu's life history begins with the circumstances of his birth and events of his childhood and goes on to tell of his exploits in battle as a young adult. It becomes clear in this part of the testimony how display of prowess in battle and willingness to sacrifice one's life for the clan were first steps to fame, and how allied participation in warfare was used strategically for the formation of Tee ties. Two examples of Lambu's war exploits are given in Appendix 14.

When Lambu reached maturity, his father arranged for him to marry three wives at once, an unprecedented event. In years to come he married another nine women in the process of building his "Tee empire."[25] Jealousy and tragedy in his domestic life left some women childless, though he fathered fourteen children who survived to maturity and had children of their own. Lambu's polygyny, which contrasted sharply with his father's monogamy, may have been due in part to Lambu's flamboyant nature, but it was largely planned to try to keep abreast of the growing complexity of the Tee cycle. Because his wives required men to clear gardens and carry out chores, his roll call of servants was long:

Before I go further, recall that my father had many wives; well, he also had many servants. They did a wide range of jobs for him, including looking after his pigs, fencing, making gardens, and building houses. When the time came to build a new house for his family or to accommodate his pigs, Lambu instructed his servants to collect materials for the houses. Some went deep into the bush to find vines suitable for ropes; others went to the forest, selected a large tree, felled it, and chopped it into pieces of appropriate size. Should Lambu want to talk to a Tee associate, he would send a message via a servant. When he ran out of his salt, he sent one of his servants to the Yandap where the salt pools are with a pig to pay for the salt; sometimes the salt was processed by his servants, other times it was prepared and delivered by the owners of the pools. Lambu's servants also made ropes for his many pigs, rain shields, and so on. During the Tee, one of his servants would leap down his row of pigs to express his elation and success, because Lambu was too heavy to run and leap for that distance without becoming physically exhausted. When it was time for a Sangai bachelors' initiation or a cult for the ancestors to make the gardens grow, he sent his servants to the bush to hunt marsupials for the feast.

In return for their labor, Lambu looked after his servants. Most of them came from neighboring clans, but some were married and came from far away. He allotted them plots of land so that they could support their families, and gave them pigs. When their children married, he provided bridewealth. Most servants stayed for their entire lifetimes; others went back to their own clans after some time. Lambu gave them what they wanted, and they were generally satisfied and liked the great *kamongo*. If I am not mistaken, he had about thirty servants, all men.[26] [Here he names fourteen, all from other clans]. It is said that there were about thirty, but I do not recall the names of the rest.[27]

Lambu also gave his servants sweet potato vines, sugarcane tops, and seeds of other crops to plant. So you see, one of the reasons his servants stayed on was to get food. He gave them food and killed and steamed pigs for them. On top of that he gave them live pigs, female ones, so that they could breed them. Of all that he gave them, pigs were the main attraction. Lambu had plenty of pigs, for he was the *kamongo* of the clan. He also had a large supply of salt, for which he had bartered pigs, and grew plenty of ginger, the two things that made food tasty. Many people worked for him on a periodic basis in return for salt.

The recruitment of servants into the households of big-men appears to have a long history in Enga society. Since the number of servants attached to a household varied with wealth, households of Tee cycle organizers had by far the most. Because fellow clansmen were equals, servants were almost always men from other clans who could not set up households on their own land—for instance, war refugees or the handicapped from within or outside the clan who could not stand on their own. Blatant exploitation of one's own clansmen, who were by definition equals, would eventually lead to loss of support.

After this introduction, Kambao went on to tell of Lambu's exploits in a Tee cycle of the late 1930s or early 1940s, around or shortly after the end of last Great War, when many new routes were added at the western end. The most intense competition was between powerful *kamongo* from different clans on different Tee chains as representatives of their clans, Tee chains, and, to a certain extent, tribes. It was neither between fellow clansmen, as Feil (1984) observed for the 1970s, nor between clans as corporate units, as Meggitt (1974) advocates. The following excerpt describes the bitter struggles between Lambu and his greatest opponent, Peke, from the Sikini clan. Unlike in Pendaine's time, contests filled with hard words and humiliation were carried out in the public eye:

Now I will tell you how my father brought up and did the Kola Tee [ca. 1935–40]. The politics around this Tee were complex: many from the east and west did not want to do this Tee, but Lambu and his Tee associates wanted it to succeed. In his campaign, Lambu went down to Tilyaposa, the land of his Itokone in-laws [map 18:9], and told them to do the Tee. Before the Tee actually started, my maternal uncles gave him pigs in anticipation of the Tee to come. Samanga, Tipitapu, Yama, Tindi, and Mioko were the names of the pigs given to him by his in-laws.[28] . . .

The controversial Tee was about to take place, and the *kamongo* from the east and west who were in favor of it allied with Lambu. Those who wanted it to take place at another time campaigned against them. Peke of the Sikini tribe [map 18:13] and Yalona of the Yanaitini Piao clan [11] were two of Lambu's rivals who vehemently opposed this Tee cycle. The great debate for and against it began, and a large meeting was held at Tilyaposa. Orators from the region dominated the discussions while spectators from the west sat and listened, among them my father, Lambu, and his Tee associates. It was in this meeting that Tuingi, my uncle from Itokone, made a speech from which a quotation is still remembered. My father quoted him as saying, "I want to hold the Tee and the *yae,* but there are some people who are trying to block it. We must stop them. So far as I am concerned, they are but a bunch of 'witches' skipping over my *sakae* rope."[29]

At this time the Tee had already begun at Kola [Tambul], and after some time elapsed, it began to move westward [because the chain of associates to which Lambu belonged had prevailed in their campaign over Peke and Yalona]. It swept through the clans in the Minamb valley, through the famous Kulanga bush track, and into the Saka valley [see map 11]. The Tee moved through the Saka and into the Lai valley. Itokone clans held the Tee, and then it swung westward, on and on through each clan in the Lai valley until it reached Rakamanda. At Rakamanda, the Sane clan [map 18:12] was prepared to do the Lyunguna Tee, which had finally reached its area.[30] For the Rakamanda Tee, my father dressed in full ceremonial regalia. He put on his wig of human hair, layers of newly woven, ground-length aprons, and fresh cordyline leaves to cover his buttocks. He tucked the handle of his stone ax, a prestigious *gayamu* ax, unmistakable by its dark, dull green color, into the right side of his waist belt. A feather of the *sapale* bird was planted on top of his wig. The great *kamongo* was in high spirits as he led a party of spectators from the west to the ceremonial grounds just before midday.

During this Tee, Lambu was given many pigs, which he assembled and tied to stakes for counting.[31] The *kamongo*, my father, moved up to the first stake to begin the count—the spectators held their breath, for they knew that as was customary, a short speech would follow. Lambu proudly held his head high and looked around to make sure the crowd was watching him. He spotted Peke of the Sikini tribe in the crowd, sitting on a raised hump of ground. Peke, one of his greatest rivals, had been in the forefront of the opposition to this particular Tee cycle. For some minutes he just fixed his eyes on Peke and did not utter a word. The message hit home, the battle was won, and the bitter rivalry ended. Peek's face drooped; he gave a smile that slowly turned into a grimace as he sat swallowing his defeat, which must have tasted like ginger gone sour. He was dressed as would be expected for a *kamongo*, with a wig of human hair trimmed with *yumbi mata* leaves just above his forehead that stood out vividly against the black background. He crossed his arms, putting his right hand on his left shoulder and the other on his right. In this position, the *kamongo* sat motionlessly.[32]

This particular Tee took place when I was a young boy, say, about the size of your son but a bit older [that is, 10–15 years]. I was there when my father stood beside the first stake. I held a leafy *kapano* branch and the top of a piece of *kola* grass. Then my father began his speech, saying, "People of the Mai [central Enga] want to do the Tee, but there are certain elements who are trying to discourage people from taking part. They are in effect dismantling our united stand in this matter. I would like to say this before the crowd: this person is like a witch who dances to and fro on a *sakae* rope. Be it known to you that the Mai are going to hold the Tee as you are already witnessing here today. Spread the word that the Mai will hold the Tee and the *yae* to follow. Tell everyone that Lambu has said this."

Then he took the *kapano* branch and *kola* grass from me with such force that it almost knocked me over.[33] He took a step toward his greatest rival and threw the leaves at him, saying, "Close your eyes forever. You will walk around no more." The great Sikini *kamongo* sat there humiliated in front of the entire crowd.

From here, Kambao goes on to tell how Sikini Peke, boiling with hatred, took what he felt would be the most vicious form of revenge possible against Lambu and his clan. While Yakani men were busy preparing for their *yae* festival, Peke slipped into their Pokalya site, the sacred home of the Yakani ancestors, and cut a stem of *kyoo* bamboo to anger the ancestors and bring disaster to Lambu and his supporters. Peke's decision to violate the Yakani ancestral site underscores the close association between the cults and the Tee discussed earlier and noted by Kleinig (1955). It is said that blood dripped from the severed stem, and upon its discovery, Lambu and his men pursued Peke but turned back when he crossed their clan boundary. To take revenge on the land of another was strictly forbidden. Some months later, Peke was "mistakenly" shot by a man while tending his pigs in a zone of land vacated after warfare. Possibly the murderer was a hired assassin, but Kambao and Kopio attributed his death to the wrath of the ancestors and Lambu's prophetic words: "Close your eyes forever. You will walk around no more!"

Tee Cycles of the Colonial Era

The next cycle was small, for Lambu's rivals, including those within his clan, prevailed in blocking widespread participation. Kambao glossed over these events and continued to a Tee cycle of the mid-1950s that marked the pinnacle of Lambu's career. It occurred after the colonial administration was well established in eastern and central Enga, bringing new wealth. Administrators were ambivalent about the Tee, feeling on the one hand that it interfered with their development plans but on the other that it encouraged initiative, pride, and leadership among the Enga. The compromise was to be a "quick" Tee:

Now let's go on to another of Lambu's Tee exploits, those in the Atiapa Tee [from the Melanesian Pidgin *hariapa*, "hurry up!"]. It was given this name because the colonial police constables were ordered to hurry up the Tee by the colonial administration, which needed the local labor force to open up the area.[34] The white men had come to Wabag a year before, and the master wanted us to build roads and bridges and clean up the area. So you see, the white men took plenty of our time. We could give them the time that we had for other things, but not the time that we needed for the Tee cycle. We just could not give up the Tee to do what the white men told us; it was out of the question. This particular Tee was on when the colonial administration wanted us to build the portion of the highway that extended from Wapenamanda to Wabag. However, it was the Tee [not the road] that was the center of interest for the people of the Lai valley. Lambu and his Tee associates were in the forefront of the campaign. His rivals were also interested in the Tee, that is, interested in stopping it. Seeing that the Tee took precedence among the local population and that it would be impossible to stop people from taking part in it, the kiap at that time called all *kamongo* to Wabag to discuss the matter.[35] He appointed *tultul* in their respective clans, and Lambu was appointed *tultul* of the Yakani tribe.[36] The kiap told them to hurry up the Tee and gave them approximately a week to do it. The *kamongo* and the kiap, on behalf of the administration, came to that agreement.

The first Kola Lyunguna Tee was over, five years had passed, and the next Tee cycle was to begin. In order to initiate the Tee, people from the east came to the west and asked the Mai to kill pigs and give them sides of pork as initiatory gifts (*saandi*). Lambu and his Tee associates were in favor of the Tee; Yalona of the Yanaitini Piao clan from Lakiamanda village [map 18:11] and his gang were against it. My father strongly supported the Tee, and Yalona was his greatest rival.[37] They exchanged bitter words, and a heated debate took place at a planning meeting at Wakumale hosted by the Yakani Kalia clan [map 18:14]. Early in the morning of that day, Kalia clansmen and clanswomen steamed sweet potatoes, yams, bananas, beans, and spinach and cut sugarcane. While the food was in the earth ovens, the members of the Kalia clan gathered on the ceremonial grounds, which were already crowded with people from all over the region.

This was the scene: Kalia men grouped themselves and sat in the middle of the ceremonial grounds. The members of other clans sat facing them in such a way that their backs were turned in the direction of their own territories. Yalona with his Yanaitini Piao clansmen sat in the front at the western end of the ground, those from Apulini at the southern end, and Lambu and his men at the eastern end. Most of these men were wearing ceremonial dress fitting for the occasion. The debate was already on when the Kalia men came in and sat in the middle of the ceremonial grounds. As soon as they were seated, the other orators stopped talking. All of the spectators then sat quietly, waiting for the Kalia men to formally open the meeting. Then the Kalia *kamongo* stood up to speak, saying, "I have steamed food to host this meeting. Lately there has been a lot of talk about the Tee, and I have a pig here which I do not wish to give out until I am certain of public opinion.[38] Whether we should be for or against this Tee is the great issue for us to debate. Now I will give the floor to anyone who wishes to speak. Before the rain spoils everything, those who wish to speak should stand up and talk."

The Kalia *kamongo* sat down after having made his opening speech. There was a brief pause, and then somebody who was sitting in the front line of the western contingent stood to speak. He was Yalona, a short sturdy man wearing a wig of human hair and a small *tamenge* shell around his neck. In a loud voice he said, "Listen everybody. There is no Tee in the east. The Kola Tee has already been done. There is no Tee down there. Now I want to do my Tee. I have many pigs, and they are so big and fat that they can be killed only by a white man's musket. I am very strongly against doing this Tee." Yalona sat down after he finished speaking.

Immediately my father took to his feet and stood up. He turned his head to the left and to the right. The crowd was well balanced; all regions—the Yandap, the Sau, the north, the south, and east—were represented, and he was satisfied. Clearing his throat, my father raised his voice and said, "My brother, you are right in saying that you have a lot of pigs. However, regarding the Tee, you do not have the slightest clue how a Tee begins and ends. You are the son of a poor man and only just a beginner in the Tee.[39] There are a few clans in the Kola [Tambul] region that did not take part in the last Tee. I am going to get this Tee and I will do it, with or without you!"

While he was still talking, Yalona got up and rebutted his speech, saying, "How will you get the Tee when I say no? This Tee shall not be done!" He was very resolute. Yalona removed the cut shell around his neck, turned it over, and then put it around his neck again to emphasize to the crowd that his rivals would not get the Tee.

He did this in front of the crowd, and my father was provoked by his action. This time, even louder, my father said, "Son of a poor man, if you stop me, your name will live!"

Their verbal battle went on for a while, and then they ran out of words, stopped talking, and sat down. Other speakers then took sides with the rival leaders, many supporting my father and many supporting Yalona as the opposing factions developed.

The meeting then came to an end and the steamed food was brought to the ceremonial grounds and distributed to all people present. They ate, continued to discuss the Tee, and went home later in the evening.

To succeed in this Tee, Lambu had turned to deceptive tactics. He killed and steamed two pigs and gave them to *kamongo* in clans to the west of him, claiming that these were gifts that had already arrived from clans to the east and proof that the Tee he was advocating was already under way. In fact it was not. He told them that it made no sense to comply with the plan of his rival, Yalona, and his supporters to launch a Tee in the other direction, when the Tee planned by his Tee chain was already moving up from the east. The word spread; people of the west were convinced that Lambu had won and no longer supported Yalona's attempts to launch a Tee in the opposite direction. And so his plan succeeded, though it could easily have failed. Such a coup could be carried out only by a renowned *kamongo* leading a powerful Tee chain.

All of the things that I have just said took place while we were building the road under the supervision of the local men appointed by the kiap. The Tee coming from Kola was now on, and the kiap gave the order that it should be done in a week. He told them that if it were not done in a week, he would come and stop it and then he would be the winner. If, however, the Tee were done in a week, they would be the winners. The *tultul* told the people to do the Tee quickly: to put it in the common phrase [of the time], "they hurried up the Tee." There were two *tultul* who were well known for carrying out the orders of the kiap—Tipitapu of the Itokone clan and Kipoenge of the Pumane clan. They hurried up the Tee, and that it is how it got its name. It is still remembered as the Ariapa Tee.

As expected, the Ariapa Tee was soon hurried along. It reached the Saka valley and stayed there for two weeks. Meanwhile, the *tultul* were constantly supplying the kiap with information on the progress of the Tee. When the kiap heard that it was taking an additional week, he sent a contingent of policemen to speed it on. Yalona and his men took advantage of this and sent word to the kiap via the *tultul* that the Tee was taking too long and should be stopped. Probably Yalona offered bribes to the *tultul* and policemen. Then he spread the word in public that Lambu would never get the Tee done.

My father was very angry about this. The police were on their tails as they did the Tee day and night. At Taimasa, the Sikini Yopo clan was getting ready to do the Ariapa Tee. Because the Tee had taken two weeks in the Saka valley, the *tultul* and police were very disappointed. At Taimasa, Kipoenge with his "hurry-up stick" broke the pearl shell that was worn around the neck of Nyio from the Sikini Palinau clan. The shell shattered and fell to the ground in fragments. My father, Lambu, and I were there when the incident took place. When we saw it happen, we were very angry at the sight of this noble man being treated like an ordinary man. We approached Kipoenge and said, "We are doing exactly as you say. Why then are you breaking this shell?"

Then we retaliated. We said that the Tee would not be done for a week, and during this week the Tee was not done. Seeing that we meant business, the *tultul* and police became more relaxed about carrying out the orders of the kiap. So the Tee stopped for a week, the kiap eased up on his order, and the Tee slowly moved up the Lai valley.

The battle of words between rival *kamongo* continued as the Tee proceeded westward. Now my maternal uncles [from Itokone] did the Tee at Tilyaposa. We, my father and I, received many pigs from them. All the clans in the neighborhood held their Tee festivals. When it arrived at Pumalini Kandano, our associates gave us many pigs, and I defeated Imbini of the Talyulu clan, who was one of the men against this Tee cycle.[40]

While the Tee was still on, Yalona died. Our greatest rival was dead. We felt very sorry for him and even though he had been our opponent, we gave many pigs to his brother Pyalumana as a token of our sympathy for his brother's death. Not only we but many others expressed their condolences to the Yalona family by giving pigs. Pyalumana received many, oh, so many pigs!

Eventually the Tee reached Lenge. Now I did the Tee at my father's place. He became so rich that his line of stakes surpassed all other lines, including the *akaipu* trees that he had planted in previous Tee cycles. This time his row of stakes reached Sangurapa — it was the longest line in the history of the Tee [at Lenge]. My line of stakes reached my father's previous mark. It was one of the greatest Tee cycles ever done in history, and it happened like this: the rivalry among *kamongo* had reached the highest point ever, and so a huge crowd gathered to see the Tee, including rival *kamongo* from nearly all of the regions involved in the Tee. Because the entire ceremonial grounds were covered with stakes, the crowd packed in around the edges. The pigs were tied to the stakes of the owner by the men who would receive them. Wives and daughters helped with the tying, and not a single stake was left standing without a pig tied to it. Timali men walked to and fro along their respective lines of pigs to make sure that the pigs did not bite each other.

All were fully dressed for the occasion. Lambu, being the clan's greatest *kamongo*, was adorned in all magnificence. The huge, towering man in his late middle age seemed much taller than he actually was with his horned wig and bird-of-paradise plumes. His body glistened as the sun hit his oiled body. The brightly colored plumes were so vivid that they seemed to have been plucked from live birds that very day. The *sapale* feather swayed back and forth gracefully from the top of the wig as the *kamongo* gently walked around the ceremonial grounds. His famous *gayamu* stone ax was tucked into his waist belt on the right side. The noble and awesome figure was a spectacular sight. I was dressed in a similar way. Eyes opened wide, eyebrows were raised, and murmurs of applause came from all sides and from both men and women. The image of our decorations still remained vivid in their minds when they returned home after the Tee.

During this Tee Lambu said, "Nobody will do a Tee like this again. I have carried out this Tee following in the footsteps of my grandfather and father. To do the Tee I breed pigs. When it is time to do the *yae*, I do the *yae*. Nobody will ever do it in the way that I have done. Many have been against this Tee. In spite of the opposition, I have campaigned for this Tee and I have brought it here. You people of the west, when you do the *yae*, make sure that you kill and steam even the dogs."

At this point in the testimony, Kopio contributed to describe how the big-man Kutai of the Kamaniwane clan came to tie a pig in Lambu's line and was astounded by its length:

Lambu then returned to the ceremonial grounds. He went over to the first stake and stood there. Walosa, his servant, was with him. He was of short build and dressed in the same way as Lambu. On his small wig, plumes of birds of paradise were planted, and tree oil was poured over his body. He stood beside the great *kamongo* as Lambu made a brief speech: "This is the Tee I have been waiting for. All men of the west in this Tee cycle, it is for you to do the *yae*. All houses must kill pigs, not a single one must be left out." When he had finished talking, he told his servant to leap along his row of stakes. The excited Walosa jumped up and down, the plumes on his wig swaying back and forth. His foamy sweat and oil ran down the trunk of his body and collected at his waist belt. Then he stopped jumping and surged forward. Skipping through the pig ropes, Walosa ran up the row of stakes that belonged to the great *kamongo*. When he had passed a few stakes, Lambu joined him. The *kamongo* followed his servant, and so Walosa was the first to reach the end of the line. The jubilant servant jumped up and down again, breathing very heavily. Then, completely exhausted, he stood there resting. Not long after that Lambu himself reached the end of the line carrying the top of an *akaipu* [cordyline] tree. He planted it at the end of the row, and the few who watched him from close by clenched their fists in applause and deep admiration for the great *kamongo*. After he made the short speech that Kambao talked of earlier, one of the Timali men counted his pigs. Of course all the other Timali men did the same. Then the recipients untied the pigs from the stakes and gave them away to their Tee associates and friends. The great Tee at the Lenge ceremonial grounds was over.[41]

After Kombio had finished, Kambao resumed his narrative:

Before the coming of the white man, all the people in this part of the region paid close attention to my grandfather. People from the Yandap, Kandep, and Sau came to Lenge to hear what Pendaine had to say. They also did that in the time of my father. People also paid respect to me. That was the situation until just recently. Many leaders have arisen in the last two decades. My father then became a Seventh-Day Adventist and gave up the Tee and pigs altogether.[42]

Although Lambu's accomplishments were greater than the accomplishments of those who had gone before, their foundation was less solid. By the early 1950s, with so many participants and divergent interests, obstructive strategies including deceit, murder, and instigation of tribal fights to block Tee cycles were standard practice. Even the most powerful *kamongo* had great difficulty executing their plans, and so even though they may have commanded more wealth than in the previous generation, their positions were more tenuous:

Have you ever heard of Nandi and Pendaine? Have you ever heard of Toya Lambu? Well, Toya Lambu was the man who took pigs from here and went down to Kola to exchange them for pigs and other items of value [that is, he gave *saandi* gifts]. Brown pigs then came up [in the Tee] through the Sambe route, and he took them and gave them to the people of central Enga. That was the Tee route that existed in former times. In a way the Tee was secretive, because not many people [in this region] knew about it. In recent times we came to know what the Tee is, and now it is something for almost everybody. All people in Yanaitini clans know what the Tee is. When this happened, Lambu saw that his position was being threatened. For many years he had been an unrivaled Tee leader, but when many new routes were opened his reputation began to decline. For this reason he gave up the Tee altogether and became a Seventh-Day Adventist. (Auaka Taliu Waliu, Malipini Wailuni clan, Meriamanda-Ambum)

The arrival of Europeans further complicated the situation. The missions put an end to the cults for the ancestors, the major expressions of group interest and unity associated with the Tee cycle. Individual interest was then afforded greater expression. This trend was reinforced by the ban on warfare in the 1960s, which temporarily removed the need for defense, one of the fundamental reasons for the existence of clans as corporate groups. It also meant that clans no longer had to raise war reparations, the most important clanwide event financed by the Tee cycle. New forms of wealth (first steel axes and pearl shells, and later cash and the things it could buy) made it possible for more individuals to reach the status of *kamongo*. Their positions could then be formalized with appointments as *luluai* and *tultul* by the colonial administration. The delivery of payments from the administration to the clan via *luluai* and *tultul* (Meggitt 1974:84) further freed *kamongo* from continual pressures to measure up to the qualities of traditional leaders.

Nonetheless, for two decades after contact the Tee cycle flourished and expanded rapidly as new wealth flowed into the system and the peace imposed by the colonial administration permitted greater freedom of movement. In the east it extended from Tambul along two routes, one running down the Kaugel valley and the other into the north Mendi valley (see map 16). From Walia it moved into the Yangupini and Komakai tribes of the Nebilyer valley.[43] In the north it went on into the Wapi region "until there is no longer people, only bush" (Feil 1984:64). At its western end, the Tee incorporated most of the clans of the upper Lai. The Yandap branch swung through clans in the Laiagam area and into Sirunki and even reached some of the Monaini tribe on the north side of the Lagaip. When Meggitt (1956) visited Kandep in the 1950s, he reported that clans on the eastern side of the swamps were expecting to join the Tee before long.

The expansive spiral of the Tee was cut short by the sheer size of the network, by accompanying organizational difficulties, and to some extent by increasing individualism. We did not have the time or resources to cover the history of the colonial period, but Feil's (1984) detailed study of the Tee cycle in the Kopona region in the 1970s gives some idea of these trends and where they led. By the 1970s the cults for the ancestors were something of the past, warfare had been dormant since the late 1950s, and, consequently, the need for finance for group projects was greatly reduced. The population had increased to the point that the Tee was held by subclans. Perhaps owing to the large number of participants in the network and the great amounts of wealth that flowed in it, there was no longer a limited circle of powerful *kamongo* from Kopona who traveled widely to organize the Tee cycle. The individual spheres of influence of Kopona men of the 1970s extended a mere two or three clans in either Tee-making direction from a man's own (Feil 1984:65).[44] The Tee no longer conformed to the standard cycle, but often several rounds of gifts were sent in one direction before they drew a return. Tee was a more individualistic activity, with the boycotting of a Tee cycle launched by one chain the rule rather than the exception. Individual *kamongo*, such as Kepa of the Lyongeni Mamagakini clan studied by Feil, even held Tee festivals alone:

With the help of some partners, Kepa successfully made Tee Lyunguna when other clansmen could not. Or, so he could claim. In his Tee speech, Kepa directed remarks to his intra-clan opponents. "If they had any pigs," he said, "they were obviously too wild to tie to sticks." Kepa alone was making the Tee, only he had tamed the pigs of others. Kepa made each payment with a specific, personal objective in mind. He represented only himself, and the "political" impact of his Tee increased his prestige within his clan and elevated his name above his rivals. A Tee is a man's individual statement about his financial ability and the value he places on his Tee partners. (Feil 1984:195-96)

What a contrast to the communal efforts and group festivities of the Timali clan in the Tee cycles of Pendaine's lifetime!

Summary

Understanding the Tee cycle as a system of finance rather than as an "ultimate cultural value" or a "vehicle of display" clarifies many issues, since the character of the Tee, the locus of competition, and the influence of leaders developed hand in hand with the ventures it financed. Family histories are effective for tracking these changes because their vivid portrayal of the actions of individuals—their styles of leadership, struggles, and public presentations—permits finer interpretation of more general trends given in clan or tribal histories. They were, moreover, powerful tools for bringing about change by laying down models for the younger generation.

The Tee began as a discrete system of finance manipulated by individuals who sought to control the trade and thereby gain access to wealth, influence, and prestige. Interindividual competition for these rewards continued to be a significant force in the Tee throughout its history, as Feil (1984) has emphasized. As its purpose broadened to include the financing of clan enterprises, particularly war reparations to enemies, the corporate group aspect stressed by Meggitt (1974) was added, although at this stage intergroup competition was more intense in the activities it financed than in the Tee itself. Great complexity was added to the Tee network in the fourth to fifth generation, when it transferred wealth to and from the Great Wars and eventually subsumed them. At this time a new locus of competition became prominent, that between competing chains of Tee partners as expressed in contests between the leading *kamongo* on each chain. Needs for finance for clan interests were many at the time, and so the corporate dimension noted by Meggitt (1974) held strong. By the 1970s, toward the end of the colonial era, the Tee had grown so complex that it began to fragment. Pacification and the abolishment of ancestral cults removed some major demands for finance by corporate groups, allowing the individual dimension of the Tee to be accentuated in some contexts, as was witnessed by Feil (1984).

After numerous false starts, a major Tee cycle was launched in 1978-79 that swept through most of the network. Since then the Tee has continued to show fragmentary tendencies: small cycles have been initiated along feeder routes but have not caught on.[45] The reasons for this are many: other interests occupy the young, and the Tee is no longer the sole path to leadership—success in government or business can accomplish the same thing. Finance may be obtained through other means, such as through business or the use and abuse of government funds. As influential Tee organizers of the past grow old and pass away, it is questionable whether the interest, knowledge, and contacts will remain to successfully organize and carry out another major cycle in such a vast network. Whatever happens, if there is a Tee of the twenty-first century, it will have its own character, just as most Tee cycles have had since the generation of Kepa.

13

Yandaita
Wrapping Up

Toward the end of our research, a trip in pursuit of answers to our "last questions" took us from the Porgera Mine site clear through Enga to Walia at the easternmost border. Between these two points there was hardly a place that had not taken on new significance: Kutepa rock shelter, from where Papui Mamuni had unwittingly set out to distribute the sweet potato to clans of the high country; Mount

Tongopipi, the towering peak that Lemeane Papaiakali ascended in desperate pursuit of his wife; Kasape and Ipakatupya, the sites of the most magnificent of Kepele performances; the high, open country of Sirunki where Monaini men donned ceremonial dress to fight Yanaitini in the Great Ceremonial Wars; Tetemanda and Irelya, where Aeatee cult houses were set aflame; the trees on the old ceremonial grounds at Lenge, planted to mark the success of the great Tee *kamongo;* Kamongo Creek at Lamandaimanda, the source of precious Sambe stone axes; Wapenamanda, where Mona Sepena staked out pigs to attract his Mendi brides; and Walia, an entry point for migrants seeking a better future and fortune in the salt trade. Landscapes that upon first view were striking exclusively for their physical features and natural beauty had been transformed by

historical overlays that gave them a new dimension, one that could be conferred only by time depth. Enga have marked out their countryside in these measures for centuries. Permeating all impressions was a sense of the people, wealth, and ideas that had circulated so widely on the paths of Enga since the distribution of sweet potato vines long ago.

There are many ways in which oral history can be written, and reading a final draft of a book like this one brings mixed feelings. On one hand, single pages present with ease conclusions that took months or years to work out from historical traditions. On the other, there is a sense of incompletion because of the numerous testimonies and sources that have been omitted or dryly summarized. By looking at change, for example, we have only touched upon a rich body of tribal origin traditions. By choosing synthesis, we have not compared views of history held by those who stood in different vantage points. Fortunately, however, the writing of an oral history in one way does not preclude using the same material to look at history from quite another perspective.

In these final pages we offer an overview of the changes that led to the formation of Enga's large networks of exchange: what set those changes off; what propelled them onward; how the social structure and cultural orientations that existed at the onset guided the course of events; how individuals altered these original conditions; and what role unintended consequences played in historical processes. We then return to one of our original questions: What was fundamentally altered by cumulative social action across the span of historical traditions, and what remained intact? We then relate the Enga case to problems in highland New Guinea ethnography and to broader anthropological issues. Finally, we consider the advantages of looking at history through the lens of theory centered on social action in its cultural context, to complement the materialist approaches previously applied to New Guinea highland societies.

The Roots of Change

Population shifts and migrations that disrupted people's relations to the land, resources, or surrounding groups were the most prominent catalysts for the changes described in Enga historical traditions. Certainly there were other factors as well, but these are not voiced with any regularity in the oral record. Population shifts, in turn, appear ultimately to have been set off by new opportunities after the introduction of the sweet potato. Unfortunately, without a solid date for its arrival, we can neither relate early developments more precisely to the new crop nor determine how much time elapsed before people in different niches exploited its potential for different ends. It is possible to say only that the redistribution of groups over the landscape began at least four to five generations before the sweet potato began to be used by a large segment of the population to intensify pig production for ceremonial exchange.

Reactions to population shifts that took place after the introduction of the sweet potato are, by contrast, well within the scope of Enga historical traditions. Some of these were militant, solving new problems by an old formula: aggressively spacing and displacing competitors to maintain boundaries by physical means. They continue to be so into the present. Others built on preexisting institutions of ritual and exchange to channel, divert, or contain competition and cooperation through a variety of methods: employing social and economic techniques to control the flow of wealth, as in the Tee cycle; ritualizing aggression to hold land and define spheres of exchange, as in the Great Wars; resolving conflict and permitting continuation of social boundary maintenance through verbal and material reparations; and integrating groups and mediating problems through the cults. All of these "peaceful solutions" contributed to the formation of regional networks of exchange. All were constructed against a background of, or in response to, recurrent hostilities (see also Lemonnier 1990). The course of each was at least partly intertwined with the continuation of armed aggression.

Population Growth

Once set into motion by shifting relations between people and resources, change was further propelled by a steadily growing population. Population growth has been hotly debated as a prime mover of agricultural intensification worldwide (Brookfield 1968; Cowgill 1975; Boserup 1981; Lee 1986) and as a force behind increasing political complexity (among many others, Naroll 1956; Flannery 1972; Spooner 1972; Johnson 1982; Johnson and Earle 1987; Upham 1987, 1990). The implications of the population factor in Enga for intensification of agricultural methods has been examined by Waddell (1972:219), who concludes that a more complex explanation than population growth alone is warranted. Unfortunately, historical traditions do not contain enough information on agricultural developments to give further insights.

As a mover behind social change, however, population growth must be counted as highly significant, though more for the opportunities it opened than as a driving force that incited competition over essential natural resources.[1] Our best estimate is that the population increased from ten or twenty thousand to over a hundred thousand within some 220 years. After the earliest generations, gone are remarks in the oral traditions about the difficulty of finding spouses or the great distances traveled to attend public gatherings, for a denser population brought opportunities closer to people's homesteads. Clans grew and split more rapidly than in former times, often resettling side by side and seeking new ways to reestablish peace after conflict broke out. The dynamics of intergroup relations then became more complex but were also filled with new possibilities for finance and alliance. The larger the regional economy, the greater were economic prospects. Fortunately, the environment could support expansion. Only around the time of European contact did population pressure on land begin to limit opportunities in some areas.

Steady population growth had a second effect that should not be underestimated: it rendered strategies and solutions established in the early generations, contingent on a sparse population, less effective or more problematic in later generations. Society and economy were thereby kept in a state of imbalance. A good example of this can be seen in chains of finance for the Tee cycle. Originally such chains took each household down its own separate path in pursuit of wealth, enabling it to avoid competition and enhancing the clan's ability to finance essential payments. As Tee chains lengthened and carried more wealth, the optimal timing and course for the flow of goods along one chain often ran at odds with optima along another. Serious conflicts of interest were then generated between clan members on different chains, obstructing the flow of the Tee.

Similarly, warfare had effectively solved problems in earlier generations by spacing groups over the landscape. As the land filled, pigs were increasingly used as a currency with which to mediate and repair ties, making it possible to reestablish peace without the displacement of one party. The use of pigs as a currency for social and political mediation was initially effective, for land was plentiful. Later, human and pig populations grew and the sizes of payments became inflated, putting pressure on household labor and, to a lesser extent, land. Pigs then became both the cause of and the solution to the same problems.

Guiding Change and Changing the Guidelines

The foregoing factors—population movements that disrupted relations of people to land, resulting competition, and population growth—were prevalent forces in most highland New Guinea societies after the introduction of the sweet potato. There were, however, cultural structures and orientations more specific to Enga that constrained, channeled, or broadened actors' choices. Important among these were (1) the very different patterns of cooperation and competition existent in eastern, central, and western Enga, which stemmed from regional economic differences and historical affiliations before the introduction of the new crop, and

(2) principles of kinship and exchange that structured interaction. These principles were based on affinal and maternal kinship, on one hand, which opened groups up by forging ties outside the clan, and on agnatic kinship, on the other, which defined clan membership and acted to close social groups. The many unintended outcomes of individual and collective action were also significant for introducing ever new problems and possibilities.

Competition and Cooperation: Regional Patterns

Competition has been named as a ubiquitous force in most New Guinea highland societies; an insightful analysis of its various forms and outcomes has been made by Pierre Lemonnier (1990). Throughout the period considered in this book, competition generally appeared in one of two closely linked expressions: warfare and ceremonial exchange. Ceremonial exchange took different forms and underwent great growth and development. Warfare, in contrast, was unrelenting, and although its causes and outcomes changed through time, its scale, organizational strategies, and degree of destructiveness seem to have depended on the goals of specific wars, not on the generation in which it occurred. From the data available, we can say nothing definitive about changes in the frequency of warfare; however, historical traditions give no impression of a great increase on a per capita basis.[2] This is in part because many forms of ceremonial exchange were instituted to absorb the mounting competition and permit social boundary maintenance throughout the time span considered.

Despite its prevalence, competition should not be seen as a uniform "natural current" unleashed by the potential for surplus production after the introduction of the sweet potato. Though certainly a tendency for competition exists in all cultures (Wiessner and Schiefenhövel 1996), it can be radically curtailed or accentuated by specific cultural factors including structures of kinship, cooperation, and norms of reciprocity. Within Enga alone, competition occurred at different levels of social organization—between families, chains of exchange partners, clans and tribes, or alliances of tribes. It could be over essential natural resources, objects of cultural value, or prestige, which brought both emotional satisfaction and attracted support of many kinds. It could be aimed at specific opponents or could merely be expressed in an effort to "put on a good show" (Lemonnier 1996). Finally, it could be overt and punctuated with colorful boasting displays, or it could be repressed, running only as a current beneath the surface. The nature, level, extent, and focus of competition and cooperation, all of which differed substantially between eastern, central, and western Enga in the pre-sweet potato era, determined to a significant extent the choices available to people in exploiting new opportunities and solving problems in the post-sweet potato era.

For eastern Enga, it appears that long-standing competition between *kamongo* of renown revolved around control of nonagricultural goods and valuables in the trade. Trade alliances created well-organized chains of partners crosscutting clan boundaries from Tambul to the salt springs of central Enga. At the group level, cooperative clan and tribal structures were well developed, and clans or alliances of clans periodically spaced or displaced one another through warfare. Fertile land was plentiful, however, and appears not to have been an object of competition. With these axes of cooperation and competition already in place, when control of the trade was challenged by immigrants the scene was set for individual *kamongo* to take action and construct an ingenious system of finance on the basis of existing trade alliances: the Tee cycle. Once in motion, the purpose of the Tee was broadened to include the financing of needs resulting from intergroup competition, namely, war reparations.

In central Enga, the subsistence base, the layout of the land, and corresponding patterns of cooperation and competition presented quite different choices. There appear to have been no formal trade alliances permitting significant inequalities to develop between individuals as they did in eastern Enga. Instead, high repute was gained through hunting, a pursuit that had natural limits. At the group level, clan and tribal structure was well developed, and intergroup rivalries were played out through warfare. The land of central Enga was highly differentiated, with very fertile agricultural land limited largely to the Ambum valley. Consequently, when the sweet potato made sedentary agriculture a more desirable mode of subsistence, tribes of the higher regions who sought to take over lower-altitude agricultural land drew on existing structures of cooperation within tribes, rallying their members into unified fighting forces for what were probably the largest-scale wars in the history of Enga.

After population redistribution had been achieved militarily, intertribal competition continued to be played out at the group level via the Great Ceremonial Wars. These involved grandiose shows of force, numbers, and wealth that deterred aggression, defined fields of competition and cooperation, entertained extravagantly, and brewed the massive exchanges that opened equal opportunities for all. Such dramatic and ritualized intergroup rivalry spurred the expansion of the Great Wars to enormous proportions over just a few generations, in contrast to the slower progression of the Tee cycle. The outstanding achievements of some men as heroes, organizers, and group representatives in the Great Wars gradually created a new leadership.

People of western Enga faced quite different options. Life was precarious in pre-sweet potato times, the population sparse, and settlements temporary, owing to the subsistence base of hunting, gathering, and shifting horticulture. Problems were addressed through private ritual and through a repertoire of public cults that periodically assembled clan or tribal members. In the face of widespread sharing and mobility to meet subsistence needs, economic competition between individuals appears to have been discouraged. Clan and tribal structure was weakly developed, with intergroup competition taking place more frequently through skirmishes or feuds than through organized wars. Important, though tense, relations of cooperation and economic dependence existed on a family basis between "hunter-gatherers" of the high country and shifting horticulturists of the lower valleys.

After the introduction of the sweet potato, when groups in the western high country sought to settle in the valleys, they had — unlike groups in central Enga — neither the numbers nor the structure with which to organize offensives to take land. Land was acquired on an individual basis through marriage ties. Surplus production was channeled into cults such as the Kepele whose intent was integrative and cooperative, in contrast to the competitive atmosphere of the Great Wars and Tee cycle. Participants in the Kepele cult strove to put on as good a show as possible, their display reassuring the performers and the ancestors of their own strength, numbers, and unity and of the value of cooperation. Big-men gained respect because of their organizational roles, while ritual experts won lavish payment and reverence within their profession. Otherwise, interindividual economic competition was curtailed. The greatest system of ceremonial exchange that arose in western Enga, the Kepele cult, was without defined competitors and overt competition, in keeping with norms and structures established in generations past.

The upshot of these differences was that by the fourth to fifth generation before the present, eastern, central, and western Enga offered diverse economic and ritual institutions that can all be counted as networks of ceremonial exchange. For some generations the growth of these networks remained geared to the problems, pressures, and potentials of the different areas, developing somewhat independently. Because change draws on diversity, the diversity among the three areas offered great opportunity. Nonetheless, competition and the need for cooperation, together with the new potential for producing a surplus on the hoof, yielded two unforeseen but common outcomes. First, the greatest economic expansion took place via the currency of pigs, whose social and symbolic value was elevated through dramatic presentation in the Tee cycle, the Great Wars, and the cults. Pigs had some noteworthy attributes absent in nonagricultural products: anyone owning land could raise pigs and enter into the competition; supplementary feeding permitted rapid intensification of production; and because pigs do not live forever, after numerous exchanges they had eventually to be slaughtered, cooked, and shared. The definition of something with these natural qualities as the prime currency of inter- and intragroup competition and mediation—in contrast to valuables that could not be produced by all, divided, or shared, and which could be kept for longer than a lifetime—was, paradoxically, amenable to egalitarian concerns while facilitating intensive production that provided greater potential to rupture the egalitarianism itself.[3] Second, competition in the Tee cycle, Great Wars, and Kepele cult produced leaders with organizational abilities, group backing, and proficiencies in regional politics that were not shared by the average clan member.

Principles of Kinship and Exchange

Openness: A Dimension of Affinal and Maternal Kinship

The openness of Enga society to innovation, experimentation, import, and export—an attribute not shared by all New Guinea societies—was one of the orientations most critical in shaping Enga history.[4] Openness is closely related to patterns of marriage, kinship, and exchange, as Godelier (1991, 1995a, 1995b) has proposed. For example, sister exchange within a group, such as that practiced by the Anga of the eastern New Guinea highlands, tends to close the group, whereas payment of wealth to procure brides from outside the group tends to open it. The latter is the case in Enga. Openness there stems from relationships with in-laws and maternal kin outside the clan, relationships initiated by bridewealth exchanges. Hand in hand with openness in the marriage system comes a parallel logic of exchange: success comes from distribution rather than from retention. Had this principle not prevailed from the onset throughout Enga, but had bigmen instead been preoccupied with accumulating wealth, then post-sweet potato history would have taken quite a different course. Herein one sees the strong effect that cultural orientations have on individual motivations and the corresponding course of economic developments.

From the early generations onward, Enga was a society of long-distance travelers, traders, importers, exporters, innovators, and experimenters venturing out along paths formed by marriage ties.[5] New crops, cultivation techniques, goods, valuables, cults, and even styles of leadership were given and taken readily, as in the initial distribution of sweet potato vines—but experimentally so. They were accepted into the current repertoire, placed side by side with existing heritage, and left to settle into their own niches over time. For example, historical traditions were not erased or revised with each generation but became situated deeper into the chapter and farther from the conclusion as each new tradition was added. Although the sweet potato gradually became the staple crop of Enga, taro and yams continued to be produced regularly, not only for food but also to uphold social and ritual traditions. As pigs became the greater part of wealth distributed in ceremonial exchange networks, ornaments, axes, and other goods retained their value as wealth and as markers of social status, among other things.

Such openness also extended into the realm of ritual. New cults were readily purchased and added to the existing repertoire. For clans that had eight to twelve cults or healing rituals, the solution to competing possibilities was not to narrow the field by discarding some but to perform rites to determine which was appropriate for the problem at hand. The same even held true for styles of leadership. The often flamboyant performers and orators who organized the Tee cycle and Great Wars did not replace local clan leaders, though their roles overlapped. The value of both was recognized, the one to represent their clans in a larger political arena and the other to provide stability in internal affairs. And so the old continued to reproduce the cultural heritage of the past and provide continuity while the new kept abreast of change.

In a broader perspective, it was the openness of Enga society and its common basis in affinal and maternal ties that furnished the opportunity for big-men to draw on diverse competitive and cooperative elements of the exchange systems of eastern, central, and western Enga to craft the full-blown Tee cycle. This was possible only once the pig had become a common currency of exchange. Specifically, the thin web of the early Tee, with its cooperative chains of finance, was extended along lines of marriage ties to fuel the Great Wars, removing the limitation of finance by home production (A. Strathern 1969). As the Great Wars in central Enga expanded under the forces of dramatic intergroup competition, big-men constructed longer Tee chains to tap into the wealth of the east and to reinvest the great mass of wealth that flowed out of the Great War exchanges. The Tee network was thereby transformed from a relatively discreet stream of finance into a river flooded with wealth. The spheres of exchange carved out by competition in the Great Wars later provided the pathways along which the Tee cycle expanded. The cost, conflicts, and complexity of organization of the Tee cycle then became formidable. To counteract these disruptive forces, big-men at the critical junctures imported either the Kepele cult of the west, the Female Spirit cult of the east, or other cults to organize the vast exchange networks and realign the sentiments and goals of tribal members.

From the foregoing vantage point it is possible to come to grips with one of the more puzzling aspects of the Tee cycle: why it took on its unique linear configuration and developed much longer chains of finance than did similar ceremonial exchange systems of the Mendi, Wola, Huli, and even the Melpa, all of whom share many features of Enga kinship and exchange and inhabit similarly favorable environments.

Closure: A Dimension of Agnatic Kinship

Recall from earlier chapters that Enga metaphor describes the relationship between individual and clan in terms of birds who roost in the same nest or tree. When dawn breaks they go different ways, seemingly pursuing their own interests, but eventually they return with their harvests to the same nest. So it was with individuals and families—their innovations, ideas, and achievements had to be woven into the clan nest. Those who successfully did so won "name," which they could convert into active assistance and support when need arose. In this sense the "openness" of Enga society was not unbounded but was contained by obligations of clan membership ideally defined by descent through the male line.

The introduction of the sweet potato brought both new problems and new opportunities, affording greater potential for social inequalities to develop. Because the protective umbrella of clan membership was crucial for existence, any personal projects that were initiated had to be integrated into those of the clan. Materially, the successful returned a good part of the products of their efforts to the group by contributing to bridewealth and war reparations, among other things. They also used subtler tactics to quell problems at the source by altering ideals and expectations. At the grass roots level, leading households worked to bring about change by employing young people as "helpers" for a few months or years in exchange for "education" and contribution to bridewealth.[6] Household production was thereby augmented and recognition won for assisting young people. The risk of creating future competitors was mitigated by two factors: first, such an education produced clan members who accepted their benefactors' goals and standards, and second, it ensured that there would be more productive members to share the burden of clan payments.

Influence that could be exerted through such personal means was limited—in the competitive atmosphere of Enga society, the moves of households were carefully scrutinized. Bachelors' and ancestral cults offered a much broader forum in which to bring about change, ostensibly transcending individual interests and appealing to supernatural forces for the prosperity of the entire group. Cults were obtained from those who appeared to be more successful and were introduced with the intent of enabling the clan to compete with the strongest in the region. In this context they were used to set the parameters for competition: they stipulated which things were of value through display and ritual, such as the dramatic presentation of pigs in the Kepele cult or of pearl shells in the Female Spirit cult. The worth of cooperative male-female relations was conveyed symbolically through the elaborate rites for the sacred objects during bachelors' cults. The formal praise poems of the bachelors' cults laid down ideal models for ambitious young men. Finally, ancestral cults reinforced tribal structure, formally expressed cooperation and competition within the tribe, and gave an objective for competitive efforts: that a good portion of the returns be contributed to group welfare.

Anybody could import a cult, but it was usually big-men or aspiring big-men who did so. Together with ritual experts they had the authority to interpret dreams, visions, and other signs from the spirit world indicating that the group should adopt a cult. They also held the broadest perspective on the relative success of other groups and on what would be important for the future, as well as the financial and organizational abilities to carry out the transaction. Clan or tribal members could then exert their own influence by contributing to the cult's purchase, accepting it enthusiastically, encouraging modification, or showing little desire to participate. Finally, senior bachelors, ritual experts, and, in the case of the *enda akoko nyingi* (disruptive courtship during bachelors' cult performances), women made their own innovations and revisions.

Though the course of ritual development was influenced by those occupying different positions within the clan, big-men managed to play on both progressive and conservative elements of cults to meet their own interests. For one example, the importation of Sangai bachelors' cults to central Enga (or their origination there) at the onset of the Great Wars gave influential elders more control over the younger generation. The goal of physical transformation was superimposed by the ideal of transformation into producers and managers of wealth, a model that made the ideals laid down for bachelors compatible with the aspirations of big-men. For a second example, as the organization of the Tee cycle grew more burdensome and conflict-ridden, big-men used the phases of the Aeatee cult that expressed community and equality to assuage the concerns of others while they quietly pursued their own goals. And for a third, big-men imported the Female Spirit cult with the intent of improving group fertility at a time when pearl shells were entering the Tee cycle. Its dramatic parade of pearl shells boosted the symbolic worth of the new valuables, to the advantage of big-men who had a virtual monopoly over their acquisition. In these ways symbols were manipulated in the service of personal and group projects.

The "cult trade" had repercussions far beyond the immediate plans of the transactors. When buying and selling cults, those in charge were aware that such transfers would provide common orientations and thereby facilitate interaction with donor clans. Only with such integration could economic undertakings proceed smoothly. The broader regional and interregional homogeneity that resulted from the import and export of cults, however, was to a large extent fortuitous. Most significant in this respect were bachelors' cults, whose intentional import and export by men and spontaneous alteration by women helped standardize norms and relations between the sexes at the time when the Tee cycle, so heavily dependent on male-female cooperation, was spreading throughout central Enga.

In view of such trends, it is no paradox that cult rites and sacred objects securing prosperity, production, and reproduction for the clan or tribe were exchanged and not hoarded, for success came not only from turning back to the ancestors and inward to group members but also from opening up to new opportunities. Intended and unintended consequences of ritual innovation and exchange in turn sowed the seeds for further economic development. This is the converse of the situation today, in which economic change from outside sets the pace, and the social and ideological stumble along behind.

In summary, big-men invested economically to set ritual trends that would direct their group and themselves toward prosperity and fame while simultaneously legitimating their own goals. On one hand, conservative forces exerted by the group on leaders slowed the pace of change and put a lid on the development of social hierarchy. On the other, while integrating personal advances with clan interests, leaders brought others along with them, coalescing their interests into group interests. It was for this reason, among others, that development was not uniformly distributed but was concentrated in clans where big-men were skillful integrators; these became "boiling points" for change. The broader the participation in new trends, the more expansive were the economic networks. The organization of larger networks in turn required stronger leadership. It was through such processes of alternation between initiatives and responses by those holding different positions in the social order that change unfolded.

The preceding discussion underlines the importance of structures of marriage, kinship, and exchange for understanding some of the historical processes that created diversity in highland New Guinea societies. Although studies so far have concentrated on comparing societies practicing sister exchange with those practicing bridewealth exchange (Godelier 1982; Godelier and Strathern 1991), such models can be productively expanded and thereby contribute to our understanding of the great range of variation found in big-man societies. Take, for example, contrasts between the Enga and their southern neighbors. For the Enga, exogamous marriage, the payment of bridewealth, and recurrent obligations between in-laws after marriage provided an extraordinary openness. At the same time, clan or tribal membership based on patrilineal descent exerted closure by compelling leaders to integrate their innovations and winnings into the clan. Those who could successfully do this established a strong, unified power base.

In southern highland societies such as the Mendi, Wola, Huli, and Duna, kinship systems and accompanying exchange operated differently (Lederman 1990, 1991). Marriage obligations acted to open groups up as they did in Enga, but groups based on patrilineal descent were weakly developed and did little to counteract openness. The successful were those who coordinated collective action, but they did not have to pay the same heed or fees to group needs as did

Enga big-men. In turn, they did not build a consolidated power base within the clan or rise to the same levels of influence as did Enga who had strong local backing. These differences in structures of kinship and exchange and accompanying openness and closure may in part account for why southern highland societies never developed systems of enchained intergroup exchange as complex as the Enga Tee or Melpa Moka.

The Extent of Change

Accepting that cultural orientations guided actors, whether individuals or groups, and that actors in turn were able to bring about change, we now turn to some related questions. How *much* change could be brought about by social action? What was indeed changed in the face of rapid quantitative growth? And what remained unchanged?

Subsistence Base, Settlement Patterns, and Relations of Production
Within the span of oral traditions, the landscape of Enga was reshaped by the growth, dispersal, and adaptation of human and pig populations. Whereas in the early generations there was ample land to reserve certain zones for gardening, pig forage, and hunting, over time settlement patterns became altered. Homesteads were established higher and higher up the valley slopes and into the hinterland. Gardens were fenced or ditched to keep out pigs, and with less land on which pigs could forage, their diet had to be heavily supplemented with garden produce. This required still more land to be cleared. By the beginning of the twentieth century most of the inhabitants of the central valleys were no longer horticulturist-hunters but sedentary agriculturalists. Hunting then made but a minor contribution to the diet. Still, pigs were too precious as social and political currency to be consumed on a regular basis to fill the protein gap.

Gender relations of production were likewise altered.[7] Much of the burden of sweet potato gardening was placed on the backs of women, for at the time the sweet potato was introduced men already had a heavy load: hunting, house building, forest clearance, and defense. Some writers have proposed for other areas of the highlands that this involved a marked shift to male exploitation of female labor in men's pursuit of prestige (Modjeska 1982, 1991; Jorgensen 1991). To evaluate this proposal, one must first separate pre- and post-sweet potato relations of production. Although it is difficult to get a good handle on male-female relations in a male-centered history, certainly male superiority and dominance in the public realm was laid down long before our starting point in time. As Ray Kelly (1993) demonstrated for the Etoro of the Papuan plateau, inequality between the sexes can be cosmologically stipulated. This appears to have been the case for male-female relations in Enga as well. Recall that the foundation of this inequality lay in myths of the sky people that attributed mortality to breast milk and told of fiery vaginas that cooked food and burned out the power of men. How, when, and why Enga ideology subordinating women was "cooked up" is beyond our reach, but it must have deep roots, for it is prevalent throughout the highlands. It leaves women without adult jural status or public voice and with no recourse other than "protest action" (M. Strathern 1972) to exert direct influence. The latter often elicits physical violence (Kyakas and Wiessner 1992).

After the introduction of the sweet potato, women were burdened with heavier work loads to fuel what appears to have been men's quest for renown in *tee* exchange. But was increased exploitation indeed the case? On the male side, "name" brought a more active public role, psychological satisfaction, influence, support of many kinds, more frequent pork consumption, and the surplus resources required to finance polygynous marriages. It also had its costs in terms of time and energy investment in political efforts, including extensive travel, and a high risk of death from intergroup hostilities: about 25 percent of men in central Enga clans died in warfare in the first half of the twentieth century (Meggitt 1977). Only after a man had reached the top did the status of big-man afford some protection.

On the female side, though name, fame, and political influence were publicly attributed to men, their benefits accrued to the family. "Wealthy" families attracted more investment and could more easily find suitable marriage partners for their children, among other things. Interviews with women indicate that they fully shared men's preoccupation with success in *tee* exchange in order to obtain a good name and wealth for the family, and they felt corresponding satisfaction with their achievements (Kyakas and Wiessner 1992). Moreover, women received a fair share of pork at feasts, including those of ancestral cults, and could give a large portion of the pigs they raised to their own relatives. By assuming private roles, they avoided becoming targets for aggression and experienced approximately one tenth the likelihood of dying in intergroup conflict.[8]

Women's work loads at the height of the Great Wars and Tee cycle did increase, although they were mitigated to some extent by the rise in women's status as essential producers and private envoys who negotiated exchange with their own kin outside the clan. This change is both documented in historical traditions and mirrored in representations of women during the Aeatee, Female Spirit, and bachelors' cults. A very few women from eastern Enga even obtained the status of Tee *kamongo* just prior to contact (Kyakas and Wiessner 1992).[9] The greatest burden on women was an increase in the frequency of polygynous marriages by big-men who sought to augment the size of their household labor forces and create broader networks for *tee* exchange. For wives, polygynous marriage meant having to share the husband's labor, attention, garden land, and pigs to be given away in exchange. And so the final tally of the ledger for exploitation after the introduction of the sweet potato remains unclear.

What is evident is that with the expansion of the large ceremonial exchange networks, women, as principal producers, did increase their active roles in exchange (albeit largely in the private realm), and with that increase their status rose as well. In central and western Enga, inroads were made in the severity of contamination beliefs that assigned women a lower status than men—inroads achieved in part through women's active role in courtship during bachelors' cult performances. This trend might have led to greater structural change in male-female relations had the process not been disrupted by the arrival of Europeans.

Female labor could only partially meet increasing demands for production. Polygynists recruited additional male labor for house building, garden clearance, and fencing by eliciting the help of young people and employing men who were unable to support a household, such as war refugees or those who suffered mental or physical disabilities. Additionally, pigs were given to young people within the clan or to relatives outside it who raised and bred them in exchange for various forms of support. Although individuals who could not make it on their own had always attached themselves to more productive households, the consolidation of twenty to thirty such individuals in a few leading households occurred only at the height of the Tee cycle and Great Wars.

The Exchange Economy

The exchange economy of Enga underwent transformation as well as growth within the span of historical traditions. From a heavy basis in nonagricultural production—products of the hunt and the forest, along with trade goods such as stone axes, salt, cosmetic oil, and net bags—it shifted to a basis in which pigs quantitatively made up an equal or greater part. This was not the result of new agricultural opportunities alone but also of the manipulation of public events to assign value and meaning to material goods. For example, in the early generations, large traditional dances where cosmetic oil, shell ornaments, plumes, net cloth, and ceremonial axes were displayed before the eyes of the public were perhaps the most significant social events reported. Gradually, sacred and secular wealth distributions engineered by big-men, involving massive pork feasts and the presentation and distribution of live pigs, came abreast of and overtook the dances in importance.[10] Traditional dances were then used to gather people in order to plan the wealth distributions. By approximately the fourth to fifth generation, pigs had acquired sufficient economic and social value through labor input and dramatic display that their transfer could compensate for enemy deaths in warfare and reopen ties of kinship and exchange.[11]

Developments also occurred in the organization and finance of exchange, although these were surprisingly few given the rapid expansion of the networks. Marriage ties remained the only significant basis for external finance for all wealth distributions other than the Tee cycle. A true innovation was made in the Tee cycle through the quiet, persuasive tactics of Tee cycle organizers: the concatenation of kinship relationships along trade routes into chains of finance that gave participants access to the resources of those who would not be linked by ordinary kinship.

Nonetheless, Tee chains remained heavily embedded in kinship, each step built on a close affinal or maternal kinship link. Chains of finance never brought about what might be called a "transitive" restructuring of kinship in which, for example, family A on a Tee chain redefined family D or E as direct relatives or exchange partners, jumping over B and C. Even when the Tee cycle reached its height, the greatest of the big-men worked down their own female-linked Tee chains over vast distances, negotiating each step in the warmth and congenial atmosphere of the men's house with good food and good company. They let their wills be known at each step but left most of the private persuasion to immediate kin and public speech to the big-men of the clan visited. Apparently the trust, persuasive power, and goodwill that existed between close kin were not easy to replace. The single great alteration, then, was that kinship relations devised to handle exchanges between single families or clans were enchained to organize the very large networks that developed within Enga.

The Cults

Bachelors' and ancestral cults, as strongholds of tradition and mediators of change, incorporated both conservative and progressive forces that were at work in Enga society. One thus sees in them both continuity and transformation through time. Sangai-Sandalu bachelors' cults, closest to the pulse of change in that they educated protagonists of the future, were transformed to keep pace with or lead economic developments. First came the introduction of a female principle into formerly individual male rites of growth; accompanying it was the institution of an age hierarchy for instruction. This put young men firmly in the grips of elders and laid out a prescribed course for marriage at a time when larger fighting forces were being assembled in central Enga and exchange networks based on marriage ties were expanding. Second, emergence festivals turned a private ritual into one with a public phase. The potential of the upcoming generation was thereby displayed and crowds gathered to discuss politics and exchange, just at the time when the Great Wars were being linked to the Tee cycle. Finally, when the Sangai bachelors' cult was adopted by eastern clans, the invention of the *enda akoko nyingi* courtship phase by women reversed principles of separation of the sexes. This dealt a further blow to ideological barriers between eastern, central, and western Enga, facilitating the flow of ceremonial exchange that was heavily dependent on male-female cooperation. With each addition of new rites, former ones were retained but were qualified or placed in a different context.

Cults for the ancestors, as expressions of group interest, were more resistant to change. Equality, reaffirmation of group structure, and improvement of group fortunes remained at their core, counteracting the inequalities and individualism fostered by growing exchange networks. As ancestral cults became linked to networks of exchange, however, tribal leaders did restructure them from inwardly oriented rituals to events that had bearing on issues of broad regional significance. Sacred rites for an exclusive circle of men were then reduced in proportion to public celebration, and the interdependence of male and female principles were more overtly expressed. Overall, though bachelors' and ancestral cults did much to alter values and structure group relations, they never ruptured the ethics of potential equality of male clan members or the principles of symmetrical reciprocity between those who engaged in exchange.

Social and Political Organization: Intraclan Relations

The existing social and political structure of Enga was pushed to its limits as the population and economy grew. Numerous experiments in reorganization were attempted, but few took root. At the base of resistance to change was the refusal of individuals or households to relinquish certain prerogatives linked to kinship, including (1) land rights passed down within the family; (2) the rights of every young man to procure a bride with financial support from clan members and to develop his own network of affinal and maternal ties; (3) the autonomy of households as units of production and distribution; (4) the potential equality between male clan members or households; (5) the rights of each clan member to be supported, defended, and revenged, right or wrong, by fellow clan members; and (6) the recognition of social status for those who furthered group interests and distributed rather than retained wealth.

These rights were upheld by a number of checks and balances present since the beginning of historical traditions that prevented big-men from undermining the autonomy of other households within the clan. First and foremost was the segmentary lineage system of the Enga, which had at each level — lineage, sub-clan, and clan — big-men of varying degrees of influence seeking to move into positions of clanwide influence (Meggitt 1964b). Actions on the part of any big-man that threatened to exploit followers or enhance individual profit at group expense provoked followers to switch allegiance to a contender. Second was the separation of secular and ritual power. Big-men could and did manipulate ritual by importing and exporting cults and summoning certain ritual experts from outside, but direct ritual knowledge, power, and innovation remained in the hands of experts occupying inherited positions. Big-men had little control over ritual experts. Conversely, ritual experts held little influence over the social hierarchy—that is, they never achieved the authority to promote others or to stigmatize and demote them through means such as sorcery accusations that are used in other New Guinea societies (Knauft 1987; Kelly 1993).

As a result, the ever greater amounts of wealth managed by the households of big-men came from outstanding individuals and their families who played their cards of kinship well, bent the rules as far as possible, and devised means of indirect influence such as the importation and exportation of cults. They were not based on structural changes in the social order. However, the big-men of each generation were expected to exceed the accomplishments of their predecessors and in doing so raised tolerance for inequalities in wealth and social status. During the sixth generation, a man who could distribute fifteen to thirty pigs was a man of high status; by the third generation, this figure had increased tenfold.

Yet because political and economic gains were based on pushing the structure to the limits rather than altering it, the power of big-men remained "power to" accomplish something rather than "power over" others. Even at the height of their careers, big-men had on average no more land than their fellow clansmen (Meggitt 1974:191n43) and could not appropriate the labor of fellow clanspeople without reciprocation. The principle that name and prosperity came from distribution rather than retention held fast: no item of value was moved into the category of something to be accumulated and retained indefinitely as a marker of social position, though axes, shells, plumes, and other ornaments continued to be used widely as indicators of wealth and prestige. No formal hierarchy or centralization of production and redistribution was instituted that could be passed on to the next generation; each household kept hold of its own pig ropes, so to speak. Even the sons of Great War leaders, who were offered the privilege of inherited position, had to prove themselves worthy. Essentially, each generation had to start anew, for the "empire" of even the most powerful of big-men was as transient as the pigs, personality, and oratory on which it was built. In the end, equality was restored, and the graves of the "rich" and influential contained no more than those of ordinary men.

There is one notable exception to the foregoing: inequality in access to information. Information was an intangible asset to which male clan members could not demand equal access (see also A. Strathern 1989:301). Knowledge of the

politics of exchange became increasingly consolidated in the hands of the managers of large exchange networks. Crucial information was transferred between
such big-men, passed on from parents to children, and imparted to young relatives on the rise. It was communicated in the secrecy of men's houses, couched
in obscure metaphorical speech, and contained by the intermarriage of families
or lineages in control. Elders say that by the time of European contact, differential access to information was so great that the average clansman had little idea
of the planning and politics of a Tee cycle. This foot in the door of political
inequality might have brought about much greater erosion of egalitarianism had
the colonial era not intervened.

Interclan Relations

Intergroup relations underwent a profound restructuring in the course of historical traditions as population growth rendered warfare ineffective as a means of
solving problems through the spacing of groups over the land. Formerly, after
one party had been displaced or expelled, reparations were paid to allies in the
form of land gained and food for feasting. This process replaced hostile neighbors
with friendly ones and permitting boundaries to be maintained by social rather
than military means. As tribal land filled and much of the territory in fringe areas
was claimed, spacing after warfare ceased to be an easy or desirable solution,
particularly when fights were between "brother" clans who would be valuable
allies in the future. War reparations were then extended to enemies in the form
of pigs, goods, and valuables in an attempt to reestablish exchange and good
relations. Allies, too, had to be compensated with such items, because land
gained was minimal. The resulting need for pigs had great repercussions throughout virtually all systems of production and forms of exchange.

Other than in war reparations, few alterations occurred in interclan relations.
In the Kepele cult and Great Wars, efforts were made to integrate clans of a tribe
or allied tribes into larger, centralized cooperative units, but for a number of
reasons these efforts never permanently congealed. First and perhaps foremost
was the reluctance of clans to give up their autonomy and become enmeshed in
larger groups. Within the clan, many checks and balances prevented clan "brothers" from exploiting one another, but this was not the case between clans, where
traditionally the only form of defense was aggression. The costs of forfeiting
autonomy and risking domination apparently were perceived as overriding the
benefits of longer-term cooperation.

Second, communication posed a problem throughout Enga. Rumor, suspicion,
and misunderstanding are reported frequently in historical traditions and remain
a problem today. Rumor was and is manipulated skillfully to equalize the control
of information: it can be constructed by anybody and believed by those who

wish to take it as a basis for action. As a result, most communication had to be interpersonal and backed by action to be credited (see also Biersack 1980, 1981, 1982:240), a costly system for large-scale organization. Some formalized means of communication—metaphorical song, styles of dress, and public oration— were elaborated to more efficiently brew group spirit and disseminate information, but communication costs remained high.

Third, enormous amounts of energy and resources went into staging the spectacular events that united entire tribes or pairs of tribes. Only with great and sustained benefits could such alliances be worthwhile on a permanent basis. Great they were, but sustained they were not. For the Kepele, goals of integration were achieved during cult performances, and for the Great Wars, objectives of defining fields of cooperation and competition were reaffirmed during each episode. The alliances that promised returns on a more regular basis were those of the Tee cycle, but their structure was linear, not localized in space, and therefore not conducive to the formation of larger groups. As it was, substantial changes in group structure would have required lasting mutual dependencies that were not easily kindled in the rich and rugged landscape of Enga.[12]

The Persistence of Equality

On first glance, the brilliant performances of the big-men of the twentieth century obscure to some extent what they could not change: that fundamental alterations in Enga social and political structure lagged behind economic and ritual developments. Individual and collective action restructured the economic base, ritual repertoire, and even aspects of cosmology, but rights that were essential for prosperity and reproduction were staunchly defended: rights to land, the products of labor, equal status, and symmetrical reciprocity. Inequalities between the sexes that had existed for many generations were maintained. It appears that only sustained quantitative growth, both demographic and economic, might have tipped the balance toward more enduring social inequalities by making the social rules and orientations of generations past no longer compatible with existing conditions. At such a point, actors might have found an opening to institute more formalized inequalities either by coercion or by providing greater benefits through their representational and organizational skills than followers could reap from equality. Or, under the pressure of unrestrained growth and competition, it might have been the people who instituted more formalized, inherited positions of leadership to reduce interindividual competition, as they did in the Great Ceremonial Wars when leaders (watenge) were chosen by public acclaim from among the sons or nephews of former Great War leaders.

Studies from many other areas of the world indicate that the Enga case is not unique. They suggest, first, that egalitarian systems show a strong tendency to "defeat the formation of hierarchy," as William Mitchell (1988) puts it. Second, members of such systems are apparently reluctant to forfeit checks and balances based on the familiarity and trust of close kinship for fear of becoming enmeshed in groups composed of distant relatives or nonrelatives who might exploit and repress more readily (Eibl-Eibesfeldt 1995, 1996). And third, comparative studies suggest that the limits of group size based on face-to-face communication is around five hundred. Beyond that size, errors in information transmission increase, causing conflict (Johnson 1982; Kosse 1990, 1994). So powerful are these pressures that it seems likely that centralized, stratified societies developed independently only rarely in history out of combinations of unusual circumstances, while others formed out of competition with or domination by more complex societies (see, among others, Fried 1975; Gailey and Patterson 1987; Bender 1990).

Change in a Comparative Perspective

By the time of contact, Enga society was the product of forces prevalent throughout the highlands, of local and regional orientations, and of specific historical circumstances, actions, and events. The first two should be comparable across the highlands, and the third gives Enga a character of its own. Unfortunately, too few comprehensive historical studies exist to enable meaningful comparisons, a situation that may change as more attention is focused on history in the highlands (Burton 1984, 1989; Stürzenhofecker 1993, 1995; Heeschen 1994; Ballard 1995). At the moment it is possible to use our understanding of historical processes in Enga only to make some observations on comparative frameworks proposed by others and to discuss the advantages of using elements of practice theory for collecting, organizing, and analyzing historical material.

Since James Watson (1965a, 1965b) recognized that the cultures of central highland New Guinea did not represent a long-established situation, either ecologically or socially, but had been "remade within the last three centuries through the introduction of a new food plant, sweet potatoes" (1965b:302-3), numerous models of change have been proposed. First were Watson's own, which enumerated four possibilities along a continuum. At one end was a model in which nomadic or seminomadic foraging bands who practiced seasonal, intermittent, or supplementary horticulture were radically transformed by the introduction of the sweet potato. At the other end was a model in which groups of already well-established horticulturalists made a gradual transition to dependence on the sweet potato (1965b:302-3). Watson's view of transformation was comprehensive, including subsistence, demography, work patterns, sexual division of labor, and warfare. The prime movers he specified included social tension resulting from the growth of human and pig populations and the "Jones effect" — "competitive escalation of production resulting from competition among pig producers for limited goods and benefits" (Watson 1977:64), or, simply put, "keeping up with the neighbors." Based on his knowledge of the eastern highlands, Watson favored the first model and proposed an "Ipomoean revolution," after the scientific name for sweet potato, *Ipomoea batatas.*

Watson's proposition was challenged by Harold Brookfield and Peter White (1968:49), who advocated a model of gradual evolutionary change based on pure energetics: "Sweet potatoes may simply have become dominant in those areas where they offered a notably higher return for comparable inputs of land and labor." In retort, Watson wrote his classic "pig fodder addendum," criticizing Brookfield and White's approach as "a simple materialist frame" (Watson 1977:59).[13] Drawing on suggestions he had made earlier, he argued that "the domestic pig was a main force of Ipomoean conversion and that a principal, initial attraction and use of the new crop was as fodder" (1977:61). The "use value" of pigs was measured in pigs as a source of animal protein in the face of a decline in hunting (see also Morren 1977), and in the "prestige" syndrome as "an essential coin for procuring brides and the support of affines, partners and allies" (Watson 1977:64).

Later, Nicholas Modjeska (1982), taking up the social aspects of Watson's proposition, argued that the key to understanding production lay in the historical transformation of human needs and motivations. He proposed that the value of pigs was socially constructed and based not only on their use value as hunting declined but also on their serving as a "mediative substance for lost human life and a valuable that could be exchanged for rights in humans through marriage." Pig production thus permitted the development of a new and more "economic version of social control and social order" (Modjeska 1982:55-57). Increasingly complex social relations were mediated by exchange in which the substitution of pigs for human lives was a solution alternative to warfare. The pig then became an all-purpose coin for social strategies. In Modjeska's approach, social factors thus replaced the energetics and demographics that others had proposed as the causes of agricultural intensification and the transformation of exchange systems. In other words, transformation of human production systems began with human intervention (see also Kelly 1988).

Daryl Feil (1987), taking off from the work of Watson, Morren, Modjeska, and others, has looked comparatively at highland New Guinea societies from an evolutionary approach. Drawing on interpretations of archaeological evidence by Jack Golson (1977, 1981, 1982), he argues that western highland societies practiced intensive agriculture and the surplus production of pigs at a very early date. They were thus able to capitalize on the introduction of the sweet potato "to accentuate a well-established pattern: pig production and linked exchange on an intensified agricultural base" (Feil 1987:31). Production in eastern highland societies, by contrast, was for a long time domestically oriented, constraining, inward-looking, narrow, and limited in objectives (1987:31). There, the coming of the sweet potato, which occurred later than in western areas, was less readily appreciated. It is to these prehistoric differences in production intensity and time of introduction of the sweet potato that Feil relates economic and organizational configurations of contemporary highland New Guinea societies along an east-west continuum, with an impressive and stimulating synthesis of ethnographic data.

How much applicability do these models have for Enga history? To review briefly, it is probably fair to say that all four of Watson's possibilities—from revolutionary change to gradual change after the introduction of the sweet potato—occurred in parts of Enga, depending on local ecology. The impact of the sweet potato appears to have been felt in two waves: the first with the redistribution of people over the landscape as households moved into new niches, and the second at least four to five generations later with the boom in pig production in response to new opportunities, competition, and new ways of regulating intergroup affairs. Increasing pig production and exchange in all areas further transcended local ecologies to bring greater unity to Enga economics. What Enga history fails to support is the hypothesis concerning the use value of pigs to fill the protein gap. By the time hunting declined, pigs apparently had already gained too much social and political significance to be slaughtered regularly as a dietary supplement.

Modjeska's proposition that the value of pigs was socially and historically constructed applies to Enga with qualifications. One is that the use of valuables or property as a "mediative substance for lost human life and a valuable that could be exchanged for rights in humans through marriage"—in other words, for war reparations and bridewealth—seems to have been a long-established concept in Enga history. However, it was not specific to the pig. In the early generations of Enga oral history, trade goods and valuables, land, and the products of the hunt filled this need. Pigs began as a supplementary component and gradually moved into a prominent position. The replacement of other goods with pigs had great implications for competition—pigs could be produced by all, and when properly fed, pigs, unlike land and valuables, reproduced rapidly, allowing competition to escalate indefinitely (see Lemonnier 1996 for an excellent discussion of this point).

Modjeska's model for the causes behind agricultural intensification departs from Watson's in regarding the "achievement of pig production as the achievement of new forms of social integration, rather than the consequence of some universal law" such as Watson's competition over limited goods and benefits:

brides, rights over children, personal prestige seeking, and tokens of status (Mod-jeska 1982:57). Both Watson's and Modjeska's models are insightful and have considerable explanatory value, and they are neither contradictory nor mutually exclusive. Certainly, intensification of production in Enga began with the trans-formation of needs and motivations and with the new forms of social integration devised to fill these needs. Watson's "Jones effect," however, is an equally strong current that runs through Enga history propelling these developments further.

Finally, the Enga data do not directly endorse Feil's thesis that western high-land groups engaged in intensive pig production prior to the introduction of the sweet potato and were thus in a more advantageous position to use the new crop. Historical traditions do lend indirect support in that clans of eastern Enga, with more intensive pre-sweet potato agriculture, had developed exchange alliances to channel the flow of nonagricultural products in the trade. They were thus better positioned to integrate pigs into the repertoire of things that could be used as all-purpose social and political currencies. Although Feil's scheme has certainly been valuable for synthesis and comparison, such exceptions represent more than minor departures. They point out the weakness of models that lay down a set developmental path steered by a single cause: in this case, the intensity of agri-cultural production.

The limitations of Watson's, Modjeska's, and Feil's models for the Enga case lie not so much in what has been proposed—for they make sound contribu-tions—as in the aspects that materialist approaches fail to uncover. First, materi-alist approaches tend to ignore how change is brought about—they rarely look beyond the general force of competition and the need for conflict resolution that it brings. Competition is not a unitary force with a single dimension but one with many parameters that are culturally set: who competes with whom over what, when, how, and to what outcome. The most fundamental change is brought about by altering these parameters, for they are what steer the course of com-petition—Watson's Jones effect.

Second, materialist approaches applied so far have ignored some of the most significant problems that emerge as a result of competitive escalation of produc-tion in societies with strong egalitarian structures and sentiments, and what is required to solve them. The models of Watson, Feil, and Modjeska all identify increasing complexity as a generator of conflict and see its solution in pig ex-change. There is, however, another set of tasks that arise when unbridled socio-economic competition collides with egalitarian ideals: altering social and sym-bolic values, setting new directions and standards, bringing about their acceptance, establishing objectives of competition, and mediating the conse-quences. Until ideological integration is achieved between neighbors, in-laws, and groups, new forms of intergroup social integration via exchange cannot come about, nor can competition accelerate or find common points of orientation. The acceleration of social competition cannot occur if egalitarian structures and sentiments prevail. It depends on agreement to compete rather than to squelch, and on accepted social definitions of what is desirable. Some of the hardest work to be done in an "egalitarian" society during a period of economic expansion is that which is closest to home. And it cannot be achieved through the exchange of pigs.

Because of the limitations of the materialist theories applied to the evolution of highland societies, the equation of change has omitted a critical agent: the cults. (Certainly their omission stems from no lack of prominence: performances that drew hundreds of participants and expended huge amounts of wealth are well documented in the literature of the highlands.) Only with an understanding of the role of the cults can one fully understand the processes of change in Enga. They were used in the first run to set the parameters for competition by imbuing certain objects or relationships with value, by laying out new ideals, and by defining competitors and the objectives of competition. Then they were called on to solve ensuing problems of social harmony by means subtler than pig exchange or punishment—means that transcended everyday dealings, appealed to higher supernatural forces, and left deep impressions. The cults' link to systems of production is evident in terms of motivation imbued, ideals rewritten, and resources expended.

The widespread import, export, and innovation in cults as instruments of change place in another perspective a point made by Godelier (1982, 1991): that for highland societies with big-man leadership, economic exchange replaced myth and ritual in establishing the social order. To briefly reiterate the argument, Godelier identified two "logics" of New Guinea societies based on configurations of marriage, kinship, exchange, and power. "Great-man" societies were those in which equivalent exchange prevailed—a woman given in marriage for another woman, a warrior killed to avenge the death of another warrior. Because competition was severely constrained by equivalent exchange, it was initiation in great-man societies that established and reproduced social relations, defining some men and lineages as dominant over others and subordinating women. Big-man societies, predominantly those in the richer valleys of the western central highlands, were, in contrast, characterized by nonequivalent exchange: the exchange of women for bridewealth or the life of a warrior for material reparations. Initiation was not needed to establish relations of dominance, because men constructed their kinship relations and social position through production and exchange. Transfer of bridewealth rather than initiation provided adult status, and social position was achieved thereafter through the competitive distribution of wealth, not through command of the sacred.[14]

That competitive exchange produces and reproduces kinship relations and social position in big-man societies such as Enga is undeniable. Yet ritual, too, remains important for hierarchical relations by setting the parameters for competitive exchange and reinforcing the kinship structures that guide it. What we see, then, is an interesting reversal: in great-man societies, where production and manipulation of surplus do not lead to hierarchy, ritual establishes dominance, and in big-man societies, where differential success in production and exchange creates status differences, ritual defends initial equality by putting everyone at the same starting line and thereafter laying down the rules for the race.

Our findings also run at odds with Modjeska's (1991) interpretation of Duna history: that men were formerly bound together by initiation rituals in which the chief metaphors (the use of sperm and menstrual blood) related to the human body, but that after the introduction of the sweet potato, social relations were increasingly defined by production and exchange of wealth with a corresponding decline in the centrality of ritual. In Modjeska's words (1991:253), the "enchanted" great-men of a more heroic age were displaced by political and economic entrepreneurs (perhaps enchanted great-men as opposed to enchained big-men?). But rather than postulating a decline in ritual with expanding competitive exchange, is it not more accurate to interpret the situation as a shift from a form of ritual that defined hierarchical relations to one that stipulated the rules and the objectives of competition? Was not the shift from emphasis on the human body as a metaphor for society to the pig body that is decorated, cut, cooked, and presented with such rich symbolism in highland cults to mediate social relationships? Certainly this case study points to an accentuated importance of ritual in the face of rapid economic growth, as well as to the fact that the public finds purely political entrepreneurship disenchanting.

And it does not appear that the Enga case is an exception. There is growing evidence that cults and their trade flourished with the growth of competitive exchange in other areas of the highlands. Take, for three examples, the interweaving of ritual, ecology, exchange, and warfare during the Maring *kaiko* festival so superbly documented by Roy Rappaport (1968); the initiation, massive exchange, and other events that took place within the framework of the Huli Tege cult for the ancestors (Glasse 1965; Ballard 1995); and the incorporation of final funeral proceedings, initiation of boys, and marriages in the Dani *ebe akho* pig feast (Heider 1970, 1972). All of these require huge numbers of pigs that could hardly have been raised prior to the introduction of the sweet potato and involve the integration of ritual and ceremonial exchange. In these cases, as in the Enga case, it seems likely that the two are intertwined, the former providing direction and integration for the latter (see also Nihil n.d.).

Further support comes from Andrew Strathern's (1994) insightful work on the

cult trade, in which he discusses five mythical/ritual traditions that crossed re-
gional boundaries in parts of the western and southern highlands. Groups that
appear to have been active in such cult trade are many, including the Melpa, Wiru,
Kakoli, Mendi, Kewa, Wola, Enga, Duna, Ipili, Huli, and possibly some Mountain
Ok (Poole 1994; Stürzenhofecker 1994). Strathern, taking off from an insight of
Didi's (1982a, 1982b), suggests that the lines of power of the cults were also vectors
for other exchanges of wealth, a point that is certainly borne out by our material.
But that is not all they were. As Strathern (1970, 1979) demonstrates for the Female
Spirit cult, cults did not spread just at the whim of ritual experts. They were
purchased and performed at great cost, usually under the initiative of big-men,
and tailored to local tradition and needs. Surely purchasers in other linguistic
groups, like those in Enga, aimed for more than just another attempt to address
the spirit world but sought cults that would set new directions, legitimate changes
that were under way, and bring about ideological unity at a time when growing
exchange networks were straining the seams of equality.

Historical Ethnography and Anthropological History

The various theoretical perspectives we brought to our precolonial history of
Enga might, at first glance, seem odd partners. Our intent in juxtaposing them
was to write both a historical ethnography and an anthropological history. In
working toward a historical ethnography, we tried to identify some of the
broader forces behind change, whether they were internally or externally generated. First we looked at the effects of changing population size and ecology
within the period considered, for all cultural orientations and individual actions
are continually explored within the potential and constraints of the external
world. Next we sought sources of change stemming from conflict or competition
in internal relations—between individuals, the sexes, generations, and political
groups—that led to new forms of social integration and alliance. By applying
ethological concepts, it was possible to situate some of the strategies employed
within an encompassing repertoire of behavior shared by most human societies,
beyond the particularism of specific cultural orientations. Together these approaches provided a framework within which to write a political and economic
history of Enga and to identify forces and processes of change subject to comparison with those operating in other societies.
    Turning to the second goal, to write an anthropological history, recent decades
have seen the rise of theoretical approaches designed to further the rapproche-
ment of history and anthropology. One such approach, often termed "political
economy," looks at the articulation between a society and the larger social,

political, and economic order in which it has been embedded in its history, especially colonial influence and the expansion of Western economic systems. Studies in political economy may emphasize economic and political domination or may concentrate on local societies' reactions to and interactions with the goals, economics, values, institutions, or individuals coming from Western economic systems (see Carrier 1992 for a collection of excellent studies on these topics in Melanesia). A second approach comes from practice theory, which puts cultural concepts into the equation of change by looking at how cultural categories, rules, values, or meanings guide people's perceptions and actions, and in turn at how actions work to reproduce or alter those cultural features. In doing so, it makes a truly anthropological history possible (Sahlins 1985; Douglas 1992; Kirch and Sahlins 1992).

Practice theory as we used it was not a "soft" approach but required the most rigorous and systematic work of the study. The first task was to establish a baseline for cultural orientations that was sensitive to local variations and from which change could be measured. The next was to evaluate whether Enga historical traditions could indeed be used as a record of change. By painstakingly analyzing historical traditions and other oral sources collected from over a hundred tribes, it was possible to gain an understanding of the structure of the Enga oral record and to identify principal cultural orientations present from the onset, their effects on actors, and their susceptibility to being altered. These should be amenable to cross-cultural comparison.

Methodologically, the most difficult step came with the "how" questions—how actors brought about change. Some narratives told it straight, as in the testimony describing how Yakani Pendaine constructed the first long Tee sequences. In most instances, however, leads for answers to "how" questions lay in details of actions: the words said in the Yatapaki Tee distribution of Pendaine's time, requesting that the name of the woman who raised the pig be passed along with the pork; the stance of Lambu as he stared down his rival Peke; or Pendaine's presentation of his "son" during the Great Wars to humiliate his rival, who was without an heir. From such leads it was possible to work back and understand the changing power relations or ideologies that they encapsulated: the increasing influence of women with the Tee cycle, new strategies for manipulating networks, and tendencies toward inherited leadership, respectively. It is because a long series of political actions culminate in these moments that such detailed scenes often intrigue Enga readers more than the general plot of events and that they are so precious to their history.

Answers to "how" questions, though by no means always possible to obtain, were also the most rewarding because of the dimensions they uncovered that must be included in the equation of change: cultural values, rules, motivations, and meanings that had to be altered before economic and political goals could be realized. And it was through the efforts of actors to alter them that some of the finest cultural achievements of Enga came to be—a rich and factual oral history, elaborate public speech and song, dramatic modes of self-presentation, and a wealth of ritual innovations. Nonetheless, just as materialist models have failed to uncover the roles of these cultural factors in the process of change, the application of concepts from practice theory alone would not have sufficed. Existing cultural rules, meanings, values, and principles, and the innovations made in them, are continually tested against an external world of environment, economy, society, and politics.

As a final note, we realized that in choosing to draw our finish line with the onset of the colonial period, our work would not follow the trend of the time— studying the articulation of Enga society with expanding Western economic systems. This decision, however, had advantages on theoretical as well as practical grounds. Looking at change introduced or imposed by a dominant culture is not the same thing as looking at change that occurs in the absence of powerful outside influence. For the former, the outcome is partly predetermined: change will occur, new values and meanings will be introduced from outside, and in most cases the result will be a galloping history. In the precolonial context the outcome is not predetermined: the actions of individuals or groups may not bring about change; new values and meanings may be generated from within or borrowed from long-time neighbors; and change may only plod, as the archaeological record attests. Furthermore, history is told with respect to the contents of its last chapter, although history itself proceeds without a knowledge of the end. If elders believe the last chapter is the colonial period, they will eclipse precolonial events and attempt to synthesize past and present. Quite a different history is told when the narrator knows the end point is first contact. In view of these facts, we hope that our decision to omit the colonial period has enabled us to provide a sound understanding of processes of change in the absence of interaction with a dominant culture that can be compared with processes dating to the colonial period. It is from juxtaposition of the two that the greatest insights will come.

Enga on the Edge of Contact

Competition such as that played out via the Great Wars and Tee cycle cannot accelerate forever without something giving way. By the time of European contact we see numerous indications that the fabric of Enga society was being strained by contradictions from within. These included the growing incongruity between the principle of potential equality of men and the achievements of the renowned Tee *kamongo* and Great War leaders; the desire for accelerated pig production versus the limited labor force of the household; the inefficiency of kin-based, face-to-face organization for managing large exchange networks; conflicts of loyalty within households torn between fellow clansmen, who jointly defended resources, and affinal and maternal relatives, often in enemy clans, who provided finance; and the fact that pig exchange—the solution to many conflicts—put pressure on labor and land and thus exacerbated some of the very problems it sought to solve.

By the time of contact, further changes were imminent, in the form of either reorganization or collapse. The Great Wars, having expanded rapidly with the influx of wealth from the Tee cycle, crumbled under their own weight. Their networks were then subsumed by the Tee cycle. Although lives would no longer be sacrificed in spectacular battles, a formal context in which to vent hostilities and establish a balance of power was lost. Some of the competition and opposition was shunted into other areas of Enga life, including the Tee cycle.

Though the Tee cycle was in full swing in the late 1930s, there were already signs that it was beginning to labor under the weight of its competing factions after it subsumed the exchange networks of the Great Wars. The rate of Tee acceleration during the colonial period was runaway. In each cycle big-men exceeded not only the victories of their forefathers but also their own former achievements. So complex were Tee cycle politics that Tee organizers of this period find it difficult to say whether its net effect was to bring about peace or warfare: historical traditions are filled with examples of both. By the 1970s many attempts to launch new Tee cycles were failing (Feil 1984), and the Tee was beginning to fragment. Since the late 1970s, no Tee cycle has succeeded. Whereas some attribute the younger generation's lack of interest in the Tee to the cash economy, elders who walked from Tambul to Tetemanda to organize past cycles feel that the Tee simply had grown too large to survive.

Within the fertile environment of eastern and central Enga, the expansion of exchange networks was hampered only by conflicts of interest and organizational problems. The situation in the west was quite different. There, the population had experienced equal or even greater disruption after the introduction of the sweet potato. Like people in surrounding areas, the western Enga devised means to solve problems through ritual and ceremonial exchange. In doing so, they became drawn as suppliers into the expanding exchange networks of others—the Great Wars, the Tee cycle, and the Mena Yae, or Mok Ink, of the Mendi. These new developments required accelerated pig production, an extremely labor-intensive activity in the poorer environment of the west. By the twentieth century the stress that had been mounting during the previous generations was evident in persistent warfare and the prevalence of nutritionally related diseases such as leprosy. Some elders voiced dismay about demands to produce large numbers of pigs for ritual, social, and political occasions that in turn incited conflict over pigs and good garden land, setting off a spiral of rampant and destructive warfare. So severe was this violence, they said, that the lives of young men appeared to have little more value than the lives of pigs.

These conditions, together with epidemics of the early 1940s and rumors of European intrusion, were interpreted according to the prediction of the Tondaka, or Dindi Gamu, cult—that the end of the world was imminent. This prediction was expressed in a popular song from a cult known as Ain's cult:

> Paina mende pitamo ongopa taukopo tato lelya palita,
> Nakandapya kukuaka pyu katapu nakandapya?
> Nakandapya tataloaka pyu katapu nakandapya?

> On a fine sunny day the taukopa beech trees will catch on fire,
> Don't you see us drying up for the day?
> Don't you see us preparing for the bush fire day?[15]

Ain's cult, or the Mata Katenge, was initiated by the four sons of Ain, whose family came from a long line of ritual experts in the branch of the Dindi Gamu held at Yeim. The cult's aim was to stave off this fiery disaster through ritual intervention. It quickly swept through western Enga (Meggitt 1973; Gibbs 1977; Feil 1983; Wiessner and Tumu 1985). The history of Ain's cult is complex and beyond the scope of this book, but a brief summary of it indicates how troubled western Enga was at the time of contact.

Ain's cult demanded abolishing many of the "old ways," among them the Kepele cult, Sangai bachelors' rites, sexual contamination beliefs, and warfare. Massive numbers of pigs should be ritually sacrificed as offerings to the sun. Essentially the cult was designed to turn back the clock, erase many of the developments since the introduction of the sweet potato, reduce the need for pigs, and redirect the course of change. When it reached Tumandane, transformed through a dream of a man named Aipa, it took on a new focus: if cult prescriptions were followed, then giant pigs would appear in women's houses, pearl shells would be found in pools, and new crops would sprout in gardens. Wealth would come to all, and overnight people would possess what others in richer surrounding areas had and even more. Conflict and decline would cease. With this new impetus, the cult spready rapidly to the south and east, bringing about dramatic reductions in pig populations. After roughly two years, it met its end through rejection by powerful big-men of central Enga, measures taken by the Australian administration, and its own inability to fulfill its promises.

The end point of this book falls at a curious time, one in which growth over the preceding two hundred to three hundred years was bringing about significant internal imbalance in the structure of Enga society. Enga who had experienced precontact years as adults described them as a time when people sought ever new ways to keep abreast of change, maintaining equilibrium and harmony through exchange and ritual. Balance was tenuous, however, for ever-accelerating production for exchange depended on a generous environment. Should exchange or ritual fail, warfare was by no means muted but alive and well-practiced as an alternative solution. And the environment could not be infinitely generous. In the face of growing pig and human populations, a time would come when resources would be insufficient for all. Choices then would be more severely constrained by the natural environment. As it happened, Australian patrols marched into Enga in 1939 to set off on an entirely different trajectory of developments, rich and fascinating in their own right. But one is tempted to ask, had the patrols not marched into Enga, what then?

The Structure of Enga Genealogies

To determine the cutoff point between the formalized sectors of Enga genealogies, which lay out tribal structure and in which individuals represent groups, and the sectors that appear to record real persons born into the clan, we analyzed 166 personal genealogies collected from 86 tribes.[1] For each genealogy, we calculated the number of sons born to each male in each generation. From this count we could see whether, at a certain point in the genealogies, the average number of sons born to men became comparable to known figures for the twentieth century and thus was likely to record real people born into the clan. Judging from figures in the 1980 census and Wohlt's (1986) fertility survey, the average woman who was between approximately 50 and 65 years of age in 1980 had between 1.5 and 2.0 surviving sons. The average number of sons born to men would have been slightly higher, perhaps 2.0-2.3, for several reasons. First, some 20-25 percent of men had more than one wife (Meggitt 1977:4; Waddell 1972:24), and so the number of sons per man would be higher than the number of sons per woman. Second, in collecting personal genealogies that link an individual to the tribal founder through the male line, one does not record families who left no descendants or those who had only daughters who all married out of the clan.

For the analysis, we aligned genealogies by generation: the earliest generation was by definition made up of founding ancestors; the following one, of tribal founders; the next, of clan founders; the next, of subclan founders; and so on.[2] The average number of sons fathered by men in each generation was then calculated for all genealogies.

As can be seen in Table 8, founding ancestors, according to Enga tradition, gave birth to the first humans, and so their sons were few — 1.5 per founding ancestor. Tribal founders, in contrast, had an average of 5.0 sons each, most of whom were clan founders. Clan founders in turn had an average of 3.5 sons. Compared with known reproductive rates in the twentieth century, those of tribal and clan founders were extremely high, and so these personages are likely to be representatives of groups. With the generation of subclan founders, the average number of sons per father drops to 2.4, and for generations thereafter it varies between 1.8 and 2.2. On the basis of this shift from an unrealistically high

Table 8

Average Number of Sons Fathered by Men in Each Enga Generation

Generation	Average No. of Sons	No. Genealogies Considered[a]
Founding ancestors	1.5	56
Tribal founders	5.0	86
Clan founders	3.5	166
Subclan founders	2.4	162
Generation 7	2.2	115
Generation 6	2.1	73
Generation 5	2.0	41
Generation 4	2.0	22
Generation 3	2.1	14
Generation 2	1.8	12

Note: Generation 1 is currently under about 45 years of age and has not yet completed its reproductive years.

[a]This column gives the number of individuals in each generation for whom information on number of sons was available. Since we interviewed several people in each tribe, the number of sons for the tribal founder of each tribe is counted only once. The same applies to clan and subclan founders. Number of genealogies counted decreases rapidly after the fifth generation because at this point many men went over to the short form of their genealogies. Looking back, we should always have recorded the complete genealogies.

reproductive rate to one that approximates known rates, we surmise that the break between the formalized sectors of genealogies and the portions that record actual males born into the clan falls around the generation of subclan founders. Wohlt (1978) reached a similar conclusion in his in-depth study of the Bipi Kapii clan.

A modern analogy can be drawn to illustrate how a genealogy might shift from a formalized scheme to one that keeps track of individuals in a group. For example, if the PNG National Assembly began a group genealogy for its members, it might choose the bird of paradise as the founding ancestor, the prime minister as his "son" (tribal founder), and the names of political parties or their leaders as "sons" of the prime minister (clan founders). The names of actual assembly members would be recorded as "sons" of political party leaders, and from that point on the genealogy would be composed of the real sons and daughters of the members.

Estimating Enga Population Size

As discussed in Appendix 1, we divided Enga genealogy into two periods: one of fictive founding ancestors and tribal and clan founders, who represent groups, and another of presumably real clan members that begins in or just after the generation of subclan founders.[1] Thus, population could first be estimated for the generation of subclan founders. The method we used to do this is as follows.

Assuming that subclan founders were real people and heads of households, we calculated clan size as the number of subclan founders in a clan times average household size (Table 9). Since we did not collect numbers of subclan founders for every clan in Enga, we had to estimate this figure on the basis of the average number of subclan founders in our 166 genealogies for 86 tribes. Average household size was set at 5.4 according to 1980 census figures (Lea and Gray 1982:47) and the studies of Wohlt (1986:45), because there is no suggestion in historical traditions that households were either larger or smaller than they are today. Thus, if a clan had four subclans and the average household had 5.4 members, then in the generation of subclan founders the clan would have had approximately 21.6 members. If the clan belonged to a tribe with five other clans, then the tribe would have 108 members, and so on.[2]

Certainly, some men would have been omitted in the genealogies of this early period, mainly those who left no male descendants and those who emigrated out of a clan. We cannot, however, assume too many omissions, because all male clan members can be traced to these subclan founders without invoking an unreasonably high birth rate in each generation (see clan genealogies published by Meggitt 1958a; Wohlt 1978; Talyaga 1984). Let us propose, then, that the maximum average would be no more than the double, or 30-46 persons per clan. This would accord with the Enga claim that clans at this time were composed of but a few men's houses (see Appendix 5). Note that clans in western Enga are smaller, with fewer subclans than those in central and eastern Enga. This is predictable from their history, which suggests greater mobility.

Table 9

Estimated Minimum Enga Population in the Generation of
Subclan Founders

Area	No. Clans[a]	Average No. Subclans per Clan[b]	Est. Average Clan Size[c]	Est. Total Population[d]
Saka	56	3.9	21.0	1,179
Layapo	72	4.0	21.6	1,555
Mai-Yandapo	76	3.8	20.5	1,560
Upper Lagaip	48	3.7	20.0	959
Tayato	127	3.3	17.8	2,263
Atone	62	2.5	13.5	837
Katinja	34	2.8	15.1	514
Total	475	3.5	18.7	8,860
Immigrants				
To Kandep	21	3.1	16.7	351
To Saka and Minamb	36	3.4	18.4	661

[a]The number of clans present in Enga approximately seven to eight generations ago was systematically collected during the study. However, it cannot be used as a figure for the number of Enga clans today, because more than 10 percent of those reported in the founding generations have died out or migrated out of Enga. Additionally, many subclans have grown rapidly and become independent clans, and there have been numerous migrations into Enga. The current number of clans will be two to three times the figure given here.

[b]Based on 166 genealogies for 86 tribes.

[c]Calculated as average number of subclans per clan times average household size of 5.4 persons.

[d]Calculated as number of clans times average clan size.

APPENDIX 3

The Introduction of the Sweet Potato

Alo Peter, Pumane Kelyano clan, Tumundane

I, Alo Peter, will tell the story of how food [sweet potato] came to be.

Probably they were children of a man [that is, they were human, not mythical figures], but there lived two sisters and a brother in the Sepik at a place called [or near] Naiya, which is supposed to be somewhere around Yangoru.[1] After their parents died, they found that their people rejected them, and so they decided to move. They assembled their belongings, including seeds for crops and seedlings, and moved from the east Sepik westward toward our direction.

Of all the things that they brought with them when they moved, the most important were sweet potato vines, which they planted where they settled at some place in the *wapi yuu* in the direction in which the Lagaip river flows. [*Wapi yuu* refers to the altitudinal zone in the north of Enga that lies at about 1,000 meters and is well into the malaria belt.]

While they were living in this new place, the two sisters found that their brother hardly did any work to help them, and so they went and found him a wife. After he married his attention was centered completely on his wife and not on them, so they decided to move on. They assembled their possessions, including sweet potato vines, and headed up this way more or less following the Lagaip river.

They stopped at a place called Leaku Maulu Kakandoka [in Hewa territory] and decided that this was where they wanted to settle next.[2] They built fires at the bases of trees and under uprooted trunks. They stayed there, cleared gardens, and grew lots of sweet potatoes, supplying those up valley with vines.

While the two sisters were down there, a man from up here, who may have been from Pumane, Yandap, or Kundiki clans from below [that is, segments of these clans settled north of the Lagaip] or from Porgera, went down the Lagaip into the *wapi yuu* in search of lowland foodstuffs such as eggs and *nitupa* [*Pandanus conoideus*] and to hunt opossums with his hunting dog. He arrived at a certain place and noticed that the trees were dead. For the first time saw sweet potato vines growing. They grew in one big mass that resembled a lake ["a sea of sweet potato vines"]. He also saw bananas and sugarcane thriving in the same garden. Surprised to see all of these things in a place where he did not expect them, he just stood there not quite knowing what to do. Then he stepped on a twig that snapped, and the two sisters looked up and saw the man coming toward them. They thought that he was their brother, but when he came closer they realized that he was a stranger. They could not talk to him because they did not speak his language and were a bit frightened because they did not know where he came from. Still, they gestured with their hands for him to follow them, and he did.

After arriving at the place where the two sisters lived, the man started to eat some of the bananas and a piece of yam that he had brought with him, but the two sisters gestured to him to eat the sweet potato that they had roasted instead. The man ate the sweet potato and found that it tasted good, and that he liked it.

The man then went back there two or three times and brought sweet potatoes back with him each time he went. Finally he brought the two sisters back to his place, and it was at this time that they brought the sweet potato vines up to our area. From here they spread to most parts of Enga. Before the sweet potato came to Enga, they grew only bananas, taro, and yams and hunted marsupials. It was at this time that these sisters brought the sweet potato vines from the east Sepik. While they were here, the older sister gave birth to a baby boy. Of the two sisters who brought up the sweet potato vines, the older one went back with her child, while the younger one stayed here.[3] This is the story of how the sweet potato came here.

The History of the Lungupini Yakau Clan

Lao Tae, Lungupini Yakau clan, Imalemanda

The following testimony tells how a branch of the Lungupini Yakau clan gradually settled land further and further up the mountainside and into the hinterland, moves made possible by the productivity of the sweet potato at high altitudes. The point of departure is not far from Pompabus (1,700–1,800 meters) in the Lai valley, where Lungupini land borders on that of Itokone; the final settlement, Imalemanda (2,100 meters), is approximately 10 kilometers to the east on the high plateau above Yalis (see map 8:21).

The interview with Lao during which we obtained this information was a memorable one. At the time, Lao was said to be one of the oldest living men in the area. His land and the surrounding area had been devastated by warfare. During our two- to three-hour walk to find him, we crossed through what appeared to be abandoned grassland broken here and there by large wooden structures set up to send signals to allies and by ditches dug so that warriors could pass through high points unseen. Only on the return trip did we become aware that the zone was still "hot" and that we had been watched constantly by sentries with homemade shotguns.

We arrived at Lao's homestead to find only him, his wife, and his family there—all others had moved out for fear of continuing conflict. The first sight of the shriveled figure crouched outside his house assured us that Lao was indeed one of the oldest surviving Enga elders, but when we approached and tried to talk to him, we realized with disappointment that he was totally deaf and could no longer be reached. His great-grandson persisted. He leaned over and shouted directly in his ear, "Kaua-oo" (grandfather), "Lungupini tee pia" (Lungupini origin story), several times, loudly and clearly. With those three words, a light came into Lao's eyes and he began to tell the Lungupini story with perfect clarity. When his story came to an end, his great-grandson did the same for other subjects, shouting only one or two key words into his ear. No further questions were possible; some months later Lao passed away, taking with him a wealth of knowledge.

Beyond this mountain [to the west] there is a piece of land called Pinakama. On this land lived a man named Pinalima. He married and had a son named Lungupini. When Lungupini grew up, he married and had many sons. Their names were Sau, Yakau, Yambalekini, and Taekini. The descendants of Sau and Yakau live to the west and those of Yambalekini and Taekini to the east. I will give you the genealogy of Yakau. Yakau gave birth to Mena and Paui. Mena gave birth to Tina, Waekini, and Koleala. Paui married and had many sons, named Aepe, Yapena, Kiua, and Kepakepa. Kepakepa gave birth to Tambuaka, Yapu, Kuala, and Waiyo. Kuala gave birth to Tambuaka. Yapu gave birth to Katea and Kome. Waiyo gave birth to Saui and Kangupae.

Waiyo [sixth to seventh generation before the present] had an old garden site at Pukale. Waiyo also had a daughter who was named Yukuli. She was married to an Itokone man named Kelyakali, a man of considerable wealth. Waiyo gave the old garden at Pukale to Yukuli, which meant that it would belong to her Itokone husband, Kelyakali. Waiyo's sons, who normally would have inherited the land, were discontent with the transfer of the garden to their sister, because it would then become a part of Itokone tribal land.[1] They complained to their father, who replied that he had given the land to their sister and would not change his mind. He pointed out to them that the relationship established by the marriage of their sister to a wealthy Itokone man would create potential ties for *tee* exchange.

So there was a dispute between Waiyo and his sons, Saui and Kangupae. For some time afterward, the two sons lived apart from their father. As time passed, Kangupae married a woman named Andae Winima, the daughter of Talinana from the Apitili clan. Winima saw that her husband, Kangupae, had not been given land. She went to her father's house and said to her relatives, "I was not given garden land by my husband's father."

Her father was working on a new garden when she arrived, and after she explained why she had come he said, "It is good that you came now. I have been busy clearing land to make a new garden, and I will give a portion of it to you and your husband. Go and get your husband and tell him to come and help me make the garden fence."

Winima did as her father told her, and her husband, Kangupae, together with his younger brother, Saui, came to live on the land of their in-laws. Winima's father gave an entire hillside to Kangupae and his brother. For some time they worked on clearing the land, and then they gathered and cut materials to build their house. Clearing the land was a hard and time-consuming job, so Winima returned to her husband's place and said to his relatives, "I have come to ask you to help me and my husband build our house and finish clearing our new garden." Kangupae's kinsmen agreed to come and help, so Winima went back the way she came. When she arrived home, Kangupae and Saui were working in the garden. She told them the news, and she and her relatives prepared food for the helpers who would come the next day. With the help of all the men, they cut down a large casuarina tree and chopped it up. They stacked the big logs on the spot where the house would stand and laid the small pieces nearby to build the fence. They worked until late in the evening and then went home for the night.

In the morning the men came to complete the work. Meanwhile, Kangupae had said to his wife, "Winima, will you go to your place and ask all the women you can find to bring food. Also we will need some young women to help carry the *kunai* grass for the roof."

Winima went out and gathered women to help. Yandamani women and women from other clans brought bananas and taro. Before long the garden had already been completed and the house was nearly finished. Then the roof had to be put on, and a large group assembled for the event. Men, women, and children of all ages participated; almost the entire Lungupini Yakau clan was there. They finished up the hard work and then sat and ate together. Everybody enjoyed such events.

In this way the sons of Waiyo settled on their new land. When some years had passed, Saui had grown up and it was time for him to marry. He married a girl from the Yandamani Kyakae clan.

Saui and his wife moved to Lyambikama. At Lyambikama Saui built a house and cleared new gardens as his brother had done. Kangupae remained at Ipianda where he and Winima had first settled on the land given to them by her father. One day, for some reason Kangupae killed a man named Sina Muni. Kangupae and all of his relatives living at Ipianda packed up their possessions and left the area in fear of a revenge attack. Kangupae and the others came up this mountain. At that time, all the land was thick forest, and there was only an infrequently used bush track up the mountainside. He followed the track until he came to the house of a man from the Yandamani Kiungukini clan who was a cousin of Kangupae's father. Kangupae said to him, "I have killed Sina Muni and his men are after me. They have raided my house and are destroying my gardens and stealing my pigs. What can I do? Do you know anyplace where I can hide?"

"Come, I will show you a place," said the Kiungukini man after he heard these words. He motioned for Kangupae to follow. He led him up into the forest and showed him an area called Lepai. Kangupae stayed there with his relatives and hid from his enemies, planning to return to his own home when things had settled down. He built a hideout, dug a trench around it, and fortified it.

While Kangupae was in hiding he heard news of the war. Sina Muni's clansmen had come from the east to take part in the war. After some time it ended, but the son of Waiyo did not return home. He remained at Lepai and settled there permanently. He and his relatives cut down the trees in the forest, burnt off the grass, and made gardens. They also built a men's and a women's house and then named the place Imalemanda. This included the entire area where the houses and gardens were built. While they were living there, Andae Wimina, Kangupae's wife, gave birth to Pyati, Kyakae, and Pangali. Pangali later returned to the land where his parents had settled before, but his parents remained at Imalemanda. Kyakae married a Waiminakuni woman whose name was Leme and had a son named Tae and two other sons, Kuli and Kopa. Tae was my father.

Later Tae had another son, Mulae, who was the youngest. When he was a teenager he went to a garden at Yapekama and secretly dug up sweet potatoes with a wooden stick. The owner of the garden found out about the theft and drove the young man away. He fled to the land of the Lungupini Yambalekini clan, where he stayed with a man named Kolo, who adopted him. When Mulae grew up he married a woman named Koma from the Yandamani Kyakae clan and had a son, Lomeane. He married a second wife, Makimi from the Walena clan, and she gave birth to Waluni and Ambone. The descendants of Mulae became part of the Lungupini Yambalekini clan. Now I have told you something about the history of Lungupini.

The Migration of the Yatapaki Tribe

Lete Ayaka, Yatapaki Palyamuni clan, Yatamanda

Yatapaki originated near Wialukana near Paikona [upper Nebilyer valley, Western Highlands Province, some 40 kilometers from their current location; see map 8:10]. Ayaka was the father of Muiputae, and Muiputae was my father; it was he who told us the story of our origin. The founder of our tribe came up from Wialukana and settled at Tomba [their former hunting grounds]. At Tomba was the house site of our tribal founder. From there the founder of our tribe came up, up, up, and up through Walia.[1] That is the land of the Yoponda tribe today. In what is now the land of Yoponda Kepa [a well-known Yoponda leader], there was a portion of land that used to belong to Yatapaki. This land near Walia was once the home of wild cassowaries, and Yatapaki settled there. From there some of the descendants of Yatapaki went to Pelemanda [in the Minamb valley], where they built a cult house that became the home of our ancestors. Later, all the Yatapaki families moved to Pelemanda. That is what my father told me. Then the founder of his subclan came down to Pakumanda and settled there. The land of Pakumanda was all grassland. They cleared that place and built houses. Then they held a traditional dance where people dressed up and danced, to gather people so that they could see how many people they had in their group. When they saw that there were enough people, they built a men's house with a roof of *sambai* grass where all the men lived. Then they cleared a taro garden—I mean the kind of gardens that are made today for mixed cropping [slash-and-burn]. The taro did well because the soil was fertile.[2]

When they saw that the taro was ready to harvest, they decided to hold another feast called *maa yae* [to steam taro]. This was the time that Yatapaki were given their clan identities. It happened like this. When all the people had gathered, my grandfather's grandfather put the taro into net bags and gave one to the Pelemanda men's house and another to the Palumanda men's house. He himself was from the Palyamuni men's house. After that, the three Yatapaki groups took on their own identities. In those times there were not so many people, about ten in each men's house, that's all. . . .

My forefathers later went down to Wialukana to recruit another group from their tribe of origin to come up and live with them, attracting them with a parcel of salt from the

Yandap [an indicator of opportunities in the salt trade]. They did this because they felt that there were too few of them in their new settlements. Today the descendants of these people are part of Laikini and Pamanda.

Some time later [when other migrant families had joined Yatapaki in the Minamb valley], Yatapaki men suggested that they should hold another traditional dance [*mali*]. The others thought it was a good idea, because then they could see how many people there were in the area. Such traditional dances were already customary in the Nebilyer valley. And so the Yatapaki men at Pelemanda held theirs, and those who lived at the grassy land of Pamanda did the same. The founders of my subclan at Palumanda organized their own dance. . . . That was how we came to live here.

Other testimonies tell how Yatapaki later recruited new members, such as members of the Yoponda clans (map 8:12) who were facing problems in the Tambul area because of a war that began over a stolen pig (see chapter 3 for a description of this war and its outcome). Hearing what a perilous situation Yoponda was in, a Yatapaki man named Kulupai went to get the members of his wife's lineage, who in turn brought many others from Yoponda. Before long they had taken much of Yatapaki land and the two fought; Yoponda forced Yatapaki further down the Minamb, beginning a long-lasting enmity.

The Legend of Tiane's *Kingi*

Anjo Nakandalu, Yanaitini Kia clan, Tetemanda

I will tell you the story of how Tiane's *kingi* was given to Yanaitini who lived at Tetemanda.[1] The story begins with Yanaitini, who was by no means a small man but a formidable figure. One day during a dry spell he went to hunt in the thick bush, leaving his provisions in a small forest hut where he stayed during hunting trips. He killed some marsupials and brought them back to the hut. The weather was fine and dry, so in the evening when a full moon rose, Yanaitini set out with his ax and bow and arrows to hunt for more marsupials in the moonlight. He wore bespelled rope slings around his neck.[2]

He went quite a distance from the hut into the bush but did not come across any marsupials, so he continued on until he reached a pandanus tree upon which he could see two large nut clusters hanging. He heard the noise of two ring-tailed opossums [*kepa*] chasing each other in the tree, and he went closer. The noise continued, and he paused to listen once more. Sure enough, the sound coming from the tree was that of two opossums playfully fighting in the branches. He wanted to shoot them with his bow and arrow, but the leaves of the pandanus were thick, and it was impossible to take accurate aim. He decided to climb the tree instead, so he took off his rope slings, put the bow under his armpit, and secured it with his arm. He tucked his ax in one side of his belt and stuck two arrows in the opposite side. Cautiously he stepped onto the trunk of the pandanus, put the rope slings around his feet, and began to climb. When he reached the crotch of the tree he secured himself and rested. From there he scanned the leaves above, searching for the opossums. Try as he would, he couldn't see them — he looked up, down, left, and right, but the foliage of the upper branches was so thick that he could see nothing. Finally he caught sight of a paw. Fully alert, he wasted no time and quickly reached out to grab the leg. The opossum was preoccupied and did not seem to feel Yanaitini's grip; perhaps it thought that the other [opossum] was holding its leg. When Yanaitini began to tug on its leg, it responded for the first time by trying to free itself with full force. Yanaitini did not let go, the opossum held its ground, and so the battle began. Yanaitini tugged and tugged until he was exhausted and drenched in sweat, but, determined not to let go, he regained his balance and rested. This is what he did next: he leaned his back against one of the branches, braced his knees against the other, and with both hands free, he pulled as hard as he could on the leg. In response, the opossum mustered all of its strength and resisted with such force that Yanaitini was pulled off balance and almost fell out of the tree.

"What can I do now?" Yanaitini wondered. Thinking that the opossum would die if he cut off the thumb of its paw, Yanaitini took out his ax, placed the thumb against the tree, and struck it with his ax, all the while keeping hold of the paw. To this day *kepa* opossums do not have this digit on their paws. Then, certain that the opossum was dead, he searched the leaves with his hands for the body, but could not feel it anywhere. With the thumb in his hand he stood up, removed the dry pandanus leaves, and thoroughly searched the upper leaves. The opossum was nowhere to be found. It was simply gone.

Yanaitini gave up his search and climbed down the tree. He brought the opossum's thumb with him and placed it in his hut. In the morning he was astonished to find that the opossum's thumb was not an opossum thumb at all but a human thumb. He was completely bewildered, and many thoughts crossed his mind as he tried to figure out what had happened. Baffled, he loaded the marsupials he had killed earlier onto his back, wrapped up the thumb with care, and set off for Tetemanda. On the way home he gathered different kinds of leaves from trees in the forest.

When he got home he laid out some marsupial fur and placed the thumb on it. He took the leaves he had gathered from *titakai, kaiyama, tindakope,* and other trees and used them to wrap up the thumb. Then he went to the Tetemanda men's house, slaughtered some of his pigs, and prepared to steam the pigs and marsupials in an earth oven to perform a ritual out of respect for the thumb and the strange event in the forest. He decided to host a traditional dance to accompany this ritual, and so after he had roasted the food he sent out word of his intention to hold a dance at Tetemanda.

It should be understood that in Yanaitini's lifetime there were other people in the neighborhood, namely, there were Yakani, Itapuni, Malipini, Potealini, Lyaini, Sakalini, and others. He sent word to the people of these tribes, and they came to the traditional dance at Tetemanda. When Yanaitini came to dance, unknown to the others he wore the thumb, Tiane's *kingi,* as a charm. People did not notice it, but they did know that something had happened, for Yanaitini was not the man they knew. He was completely different in his appearance, decoration, and movements. The spectators watched him closely and whispered to each other, for he was an awesome figure with an air of charisma about him. By the end of the day, people from the Yakani, Itapuni, Awaini, Apulini, Depe, and Lyipini tribes left for home talking of his greatness.

Some days before the traditional dance was to end, Yanaitini began to give public speeches. He announced that he was going to hold a pig feast [*yaeanda*]. The dancing and speeches continued, and the next day Yanaitini found two women in the crowd of dancers. It was not told where these women were from, only that Yanaitini took them home. He had a wife already but thought that he would marry two more, since he had many pigs and so many visitors that he needed other wives to receive and welcome them. He did not, however, tell his first wife of his intentions. Meanwhile his first wife had found it quite natural that he should have so many visitors and graciously entertained them.

Yanaitini's wife was not at all pleased when he brought home the two other women. She removed Tiane's *kingi* from the secret place where she kept it, so that when Yanaitini went to dance, he had to go without it. People watched him carefully, but this time he did not stand out. He was described by the spectators as a man who had come out of the ashes in the hearth or, even worse, as a man who had emerged from the grave. They said that surely he would die. It was late in the afternoon when the crowd dispersed; Yanaitini went home feeling very downhearted. He knew what had become of Tiane's *kingi* — that his wife had removed it from its secret place. He said to her, "I know that you have taken away the thumb. You have done it because I have taken two other women as wives. If you return it, I will send the two women home. In addition, I will let you give away the pigs that you rear to anybody you please."

As I told you earlier, Itokone was related to Yanaitini, and so many people from Itokone came to the dance. Itokone was married to the daughter of Yambatane, so Yambatane along with another man accompanied Itokone to Tetemanda. They had heard many stories about Yanaitini, and while watching him dance wondered what it was that gave him so much charisma and success. Yambatane went over to the first wife of Yanaitini and asked if she knew anything about the source of his greatness. His question was posed at a time when Yanaitini's wife was not on good terms with her husband. He placed a bundle of two hundred sticks at her feet to represent the number of pigs he would give her if she would disclose Yanaitini's secret. She replied, "I put a human thumb on his forehead beneath his headband when he goes to dance and then he dances well, but yesterday I took it away and he danced poorly." She told him to watch Yanaitini the next day, because she would return his charm.

The next day Yanaitini came to dance after donning his ceremonial attire. The charm, Tiane's *kingi*, was concealed on his forehead under his headband. Once again his decoration, stature, and dance movements blended harmoniously, distinguishing him from the others. His splendid appearance radiated charisma and power. His fame spread far and wide. During the dance he stopped from time to time to rest, smoke, or eat, as all dancers must, and immediately his wife removed Tiane's *kingi*, for to do so was said to be necessary. The men from the east observed all of this very carefully, noting that Yanaitini wore Tiane's *kingi* only while he was dancing and that his wife removed it as soon as he stopped, even during breaks. Yambatane had planned secretly to snatch Tiane's *kingi* from Yanaitini's wife when she removed it from his forehead and had posted men at intervals along the way between Tetemanda and Sangurapa in the Saka valley to pass on the charm by relay once it was acquired. The place where Tiane's *kingi* actually ended up was at Pakapuanda of the Yanuni tribe [in the Tambul area], which is today one of the centers of the Tee ceremonial exchange cycle and accompanying *yae* pig feasts. Thus a couple of men from Pakapuanda came with Yambatane, and others were stationed along the way.

As usual, Yanaitini left the dance line to take a break and walked through the crowd on the sidelines. His wife rushed up and took the charm out of his headband. As she tried to put it into her net bag, Yambatane closed in on her and snatched it out of her hand. She tried to resist but was taken off guard and overpowered. The onlookers minded their own business and did nothing, for they thought it was only a matter of some friends or relatives trying to settle a dispute. Everybody was taken by surprise when Yambatane overpowered Yanaitini's wife, snatched Tiane's *kingi,* and passed it on to the first man in the relay. The first man ran a stretch and passed it on to the second, the second man ran and passed it on to the third, and before long Tiane's *kingi* had been passed by relay to the Saka valley and on to Pakapuanda in Tambul.

When people realized what had happened, Yanaitini and some of his men pursued Yambatane. They came to Yalumanda only to find that the path was blocked by a contingent of men who had been stationed there. This is the place where *wapename* pandanus trees now grow. They had cut some trees to block the path. A similar barricade was built at Sambakamanda to prevent Yanaitini and his men from catching up with Yambatane.[3] To this day you will see a forest of trees growing there. While Yanaitini was still in pursuit of Yambatane, Yambatane arrived at his home, where he had made a conspiracy with Yanuni of Sangurapa [Tambul] to take Tiane's *kingi* to Sangurapa and hide it there. Everything was arranged secretly. The place where they kept Tiane's *kingi* later became known as Pakapuanda, which means "guarded house." So Tiane's *kingi* ended up in the men's house at Pakapuanda. Yambatane gave it to Yanuni hoping that he would get it back later. Then he prepared to fight against Yanaitini.

The man who took away Tiane's *kingi* was called Yambatane. *Yambe yaki* means parcel of good fortune, and that is where Yambatane got his name. As you have heard, the bundle did not originate down there; it was Tiane's *kingi* that was taken down from Yanaitini at Tetemanda by Yambatane and brought over to the Sangurapa in the Tambul area via the Kunja route. Now, Pakapuanda is one of the central points for the Tee cycle. Since Tiane's *kingi* was carried off by Yambatane, Saka Laiagam is the center for the Tee cycle today. Because of the link created in the past when Yambatane and Yanuni stole Tiane's *kingi,* the Tee is never started at the request of other tribes like Itapuni and Awaini [of Wabag]; it is done only at the request of Yanaitini. It is done only when the Yanaitini Kia clan goes down and says, "I want to begin pig exchange in this month, on this day, and at this time." All other Yanaitini clans hang on these words and listen to the Kia clan, which mobilizes people for the Tee, because they know that Tiane's *kingi* was of our blood, and they listen to the same blood from generation to generation.

Had Tiane's *kingi* remained here [in Tetemanda], then the mother of *kina* shells and pigs would be here at Tetemanda, but when Yambatane stole Tiane's *kingi* these things left here. Because Yanuni could not constantly stay in his house to guard Tiane's *kingi,* he invented black magic, *tomokai,* to guard it so that Yanaitini could never come and get it back. He told Yanaitini not to come for it because the *tomokai* would kill him. Yanuni was then left alone with Tiane's *kingi* and thus became rich in pigs, stone axes, *kina* shells, and other shells. Here we have traditional salt, shell headbands, rope, *itatu* [*Pangium edule*] fruit, cassowaries, oil, and a male and female pig. We gave all of these things to people in the Saka and Tambul during the Tee, and when we went down to get returns for these things, they gave us stone axes, shells, and pigs. We took all of these things and gave them on to our "fathers" and "brothers" who contributed to the wealth that we sent to the east.

The Kepele Cult Origin Myth

Painda Kaimane, Kuu Wapinyo clan, Taitengesa, Longap

This tradition is part of the origin myth of the Bipi and Kuu tribes (see map 5:74–75). The first part tells of a quarrel between Bipi and Kuu that led the two tribes to separate. The second part, given here, begins after they have separated. A third section, given in chapter 7, links this tradition to the post–sweet potato spread of the Kepele cult.

One day after Kuu and Molopai [the Bipi tribe's founding ancestor] had separated, a Maulu man [map 5:78] came into the area following the river. Molopai was at home at Bipi Kama when he arrived. The Maulu man had made a long journey and was very tired, for it was already late afternoon.

"From where did you come?" Molopai asked him.

"I came from Maulu Pausa and am just passing through this area," he answered.[1] "Before I tell you any more, let me light my pipe and heat up the sweet potato I brought with me."

By this time it was getting dark and Maulu wondered where he could spend the night. There was no house in sight, and Molopai was just sitting in a clearing.

As they sat there in the forest clearing, they could hear a chorus of voices singing. The voices, which were coming from all directions, came closer and closer. In the darkness the Maulu man could only make out some figures approaching, many figures carrying small, wrapped bundles. They approached Molopai and dropped the bundles at his feet, making a large heap. Then, as if by magic, they made a houselike formation and turned into a house, some of them becoming the rafters, others beams and posts, and still others thatch on the roof.

There before him stood a house where he could sleep. The Maulu man was amazed and could not in any way understand what had happened. Maulu went into the house with Molopai. The inside was comfortable and spacious. They brought all of the parcels into the house, and Molopai gave some of them to the Maulu man. They opened the parcels and to Maulu's surprise they contained all the foods his heart could desire — cassowary meat, *kepa* and *tanakae* opossums, mushrooms, and other bush foods. Molopai and Maulu ate their fill and went to sleep.

A *tinalupi* bird made its call to signal daybreak. Molopai woke from his sleep and sat there wide awake. Then he said to the figures who made up the house, "Do not sleep soundly, but wake up because I have something to tell you. We must ask this man who is staying with us why he came here. Nobody must leave until we find out."

The figures who made up the house were Molopai's children, and they did not want to ask the man why he had come. Only one agreed to do so. When Maulu awoke, he asked why he had come.

"I have come from Maulu Pausa to ask if there was somebody who could help me cut down the trees in my newly made garden," he replied.

"I'll come and help you," replied Molopai's son. By this time Molopai's other sons had left for the bush, and Molopai gave this son permission to accompany the Maulu man. The young man and the Maulu man prepared for their trip back, taking with them some leftovers from the previous night.

They set off on their journey, and not too far from Bipi Kama the young man decided that he would hunt along the way. Maulu told the young man to take another route and go hunting, and they would meet farther down the valley.

They met down the valley as they had agreed to, and there the young man gave Maulu some of the opossums he had killed. The Maulu man stuffed them into his net bag. They went down into a steep gorge and climbed the next ridge. The young man carried a heavy load but showed no signs of weariness. He went ahead and kept hunting, leaving some of the opossums on the next ridge for the Maulu man to carry. The Maulu man, who was tired by this time, stuffed them in his net bag and continued. The young man kept hunting until he reached another rocky ridge near the place that is called Titip today and left some more opossums there for the Maulu man to carry. When the Maulu man reached this spot and loaded the additional opossums in his net bag, it was so heavy that he could hardly lift it. He managed to load it on his back but could barely get up. He staggered on to the next rocky ridge, where the young man had left the last load of opossums.

"If I try to carry all of this, it will kill me. My lungs and ribs will burst and my bones will pop out of joint," he gasped when he saw all the food.

The young man, seeing how tired the Maulu man was, picked up the heavy load and carried it for him. Finally they reached the Maulu men's house. From there they could see the new garden that he had talked about. It was at a place called Lyakipau. The garden was almost complete—only the branches of the trees needed to be cut off. The Maulu man took some dry wood he had stacked nearby, made a fire, and roasted sweet potatoes. They supplemented these with the forest foods the young man had gotten along the way. Maulu remembered what the boy's father had told him before they left—that they should eat and work together but not sleep close to each other, so he told the young man to go and sleep alone in the men's house, which was nearby.

With the first call of the *tinalupi* bird at dawn, they set out to work in the new garden. The young man worked hard and diligently, and they spent the whole day cutting branches. At night they roasted *teke* and *tanakai* opossums, and the young man went to sleep in the men's house as he had done the night before. The Maulu man slept in the women's house. The next day the young man worked so hard that by evening the garden was nearly completed.[2] On the third day, the young man went to sleep in the men's house as he had done the night before.

By this time the Maulu man was really curious. There was one thing that he just had to find out about. After the young man had gone to bed, he gathered some stems of tall grass, brought them to the women's house, tied them in a bundle, and lit them. Using this as a torch, he left the women's house and had not gone far when he ran into something. In the torchlight he saw that something was encircling the men's house and the stack of firewood. Taking a closer look, he saw that it was a python. He went on to the men's house and saw that the young man was not there. He was suspicious but went back to the women's house to sleep.

In the morning, he called all of his brothers and clansmen together and told them to chop firewood, collect stones and leaves, and prepare for a feast. When all the preparations had been made, he said, "We will roast *tanakae* opossums."

The men waited for the evening, went with the Maulu man to the place where the snake was lying, and clubbed it. He struck the python's head with his ax to knock it unconscious, heated stones for the oven pit, and laid it in the pit. They decided that the python would not be well cooked until the morning, so they went off to sleep. And they noticed that the young man was not sleeping in the men's house that night.

At daybreak, the young snake-man woke up from his sleep and found himself in a most unlikely situation. He realized that he was in an oven pit; the steam from the hot stones was uncomfortable. His head felt burning hot. Somehow he managed to crawl out of the oven and fled. When Maulu woke up and came out to uncover the roasted food, to his amazement he found that the oven had already been opened and was empty. The snake had barely escaped death.

Meanwhile the snake had changed himself back into a young man and was making his way home. His wounds ached and he felt dizzy, so he bound his wounds with *take* leaves and fastened them with gum from a tree. He continued until he reached Kepa, where he changed the dressing on his wounds. He did the same at Kokolo, and finally he arrived at Bipi Kama, his home. He dressed his wounds at Bipi Kama while his father sat watching.

"You are in bad shape, my son," he said. "What happened to you?"

"I was beaten and roasted by the man you sent me with. He wanted to eat me, but I escaped and came home," the young man answered quietly.

Molopai welcomed his son home.

The narrator then went on to tell how Molopai turned himself into a forest demon and took revenge on the agriculturalist.

Minor Post-Sweet Potato Cults Imported into Enga

Border areas between Enga and other linguistic groups feature a veritable soup of cults, because migrant groups who settled in Enga, after reaching a critical size, often returned to their places of origin asking ritual experts to bring the necessary spells and paraphernalia to establish branches of former cults in their new homelands. For example, Yoponda clans of the Minamb valley, who are former immigrants from Kola (map 8:12), held a fertility ritual that they called *yainanda imbu*, which had some of the features of the Eimb cult as described by Strauss and Tischner (1990) for the Nengka of the Temboka area (Tambul-lower Kaugel valley). A ritual expert from a Lyomoi clan in the Tambul area was summoned to preside at its performance. Pyapini clans of the Minamb and lower Lai valleys held their own versions of the Munja cult from their area of origin near Yangini in Western Highlands Province (map 8:8). Tokopetani history (map 3:21) includes a narrative telling of a woman from the Wisini tribe in Western Highlands who left her Tokopetani husband in the lower Lai after he had harmed their child, stealing one of the ancestral stones as she fled to her homeland. From that time on, Tokopetani men periodically visited Wisini, where the stone was kept, to participate in their ancestral cults. Cult performances and the exchange of ritual experts thus provided one means by which migrant tribes remained in contact with groups in their areas of origin.

For southwestern Kandep, the situation is even more complex. Virtually every cult described in Mawe's (1985) monograph on Mendi cults was imported into Kandep at some point in history by groups who straddled the linguistic boundaries. For larger performances, clans of the Marient returned to their places of origin in the north Mendi valley. The same was true for groups who straddled the Enga-Huli linguistic boundary. As a result, most tribes in the Kandep area held a common core of cults, but few had exactly the same repertoire. Interestingly, cults imported by migrants as conservative efforts to retain the traditions of their parent groups rarely caught on among other groups in their new areas of residence, in part because the migrants who brought them were more often perceived as unsuccessful for having had to leave their homelands than as successful groups to be emulated.

The *Sangai Titi Pingi* of the Potealini Anae Taanda Subclan

The Anae Taanda subclan bought its sacred objects for the Sangai cult (*lepe* plant and *penge* sacred fluid in bamboo containers) in the second generation before the present (ca. 1940-50) from a man named Ameane, a senior bachelor in another Potealini subclan at Tiakamanda. Ameane had purchased them from Pakili and Kepoli of the neighboring Malipini Bia clan. We interviewed Pakili, who told us that his clan's sacred objects were originally purchased with a red-haired pig and other valuables in about the fourth generation by two Bia men named Tulyangane and Opone. They were brought back secretly in the cover of night and planted or buried near Talemanda on Bia land. Pakili was not sure where Tulyangane and Opone had purchased them. The sacred objects and accompanying spells and rites were then passed down to him through three generations of senior bachelors in his clan: from Opone and Tulyangane to Milya and Nale, from Milya and Nale to Luikane, and from Luikane to Pakili and Kepoli.

Wae Wangatoto of the Potealini Anae Taanda subclan at Tiakamanda in the Ambum valley gave us a recitation of thirteen "verses" of his subclan's *sangai titi pingi*, the praise poem for the sacred objects. Verses 1-6 praise the power of the sacred objects, describing how they transformed the original owners. Verses 7 and 8 tell how they were transferred to Ameane of Potealini Anae. Verse 9 tells of the effects of the sacred objects on Ameane's body and attire (in lines virtually identical to those of verse 2) when he brought them from Yakangemai to the Potealini Sangai site. Verses 10 and 11 then detail the transformation of Ameane and the bachelors of his subclan to make them as well known as the Bia men from whom they acquired the sacred objects. Verse 12 tells of Wae's purchase and the effect on himself. We reproduce verses 1-4, 8, 11, and 12; the others have been omitted because they are highly repetitive.

The basic Bia *sangai titi pingi* is updated with each transaction by adding the names of the purchasers, descriptions of their journeys to purchase the *lepe* plant and *penge*, and descriptions of how the Sangai in turn transformed them. There is much repetition and little change in the form throughout.[1] Because this poetry, recited in highly symbolic language, is extremely difficult to interpret, the translation was made by Akii Tumu with Wae's help. Presentation is problematic. On one hand, a word-for-word translation would be difficult to comprehend, but on the other, to do justice to poetic qualities would require greater freedom than should be imposed on Wae's explanations. The following is a compromise, using enough of Wae's explanation to make it comprehensible but without taking the liberties that would be required to produce a more artistic rendition.

Potealini Anae Taanda *Sangai Titi Pingi*

Verse 1

> *Yakangenya Kuka lata Aa laita pilyamo*
> *Yopone lata Kakepone lata pilyamo.*
> *Dutupa kalyamo akipaeme kelyapeaka leamosa?*
> *Dutupa lelyamo akipaeme lelyapeaka leamosa?*
> *Yopeao, Yaoaleao, Panoao, Lipanoao*
> *Ange mambele lengena.*
> *Dutupa Kepoli akali mendepa katambu lamo lao*
> *Pakili akali mendepa katambu lamo lao.*

> They say there are the men named Kuka and Aa
> Yopene and Kakepone from Yakangemai.
> What makes them who they are?
> What makes them as renowned as they are?
> Yopeao, Yoaleao, Panoao, Lipanoao
> It is this thing that makes them who they are.
> They, Kepoli is the man that I have been staying with
> And Pakili is the man that I have been staying with.

Kuka, Aa, Yopene, and Kakepone are the names of well-known deceased Bia clan leaders of the past. Their high status is attributed to the power of the sacred objects of the Sangai. Yopeao, Yoaleao, Panoao, and Lipanoao are the names given to the Sangai *lepe*. Kepoli and Pakili, who are twins, are former Bia senior bachelors and clan leaders from whom the Potealini purchased their *lepe*. In 1990 they were in their early seventies. Yakangemai is a central place name for the Bia clan.

Verse 2

> *Yakangenya Petau lata, Kakapone lata, Yopene lata pilyamo*
> *Dutupanya utu balulyaka ipao pikipokomai lao minamameamo lapolapo*
> *Timu waelyaka pikipokomai lao minakameamo lapolapo*
> *Yongo wangimilyaka pikipokomai lao minakameamo lapolapo*
> *Kiitolelyaka pikipokomai lao minakameamo lapolapo*

Moko tuakapelyaka pikipokomai lao minakameamo lapolapo
Yambale maimailyaka pikipokomai lao minakameamo lapolapo
Timi matapulyaka pikipokomai lao minakameamo lapolapo.

They say that there are the men named Petau, Kakepone, and Yopene from Yakangemai
The power of the Sangai took hold of their wigs in a swift and flowing manner
The power of the Sangai took hold of their beards in a swift and flowing manner
The power of the Sangai took hold of their bodies in a swift and flowing manner
The power of the Sangai took hold of their armbands in a swift and flowing manner
The power of the Sangai took hold of their calf muscles in a swift and flowing manner
The power of the Sangai took hold of their aprons in a swift and flowing manner
The power of the Sangai took hold of their belts in a swift and flowing manner.

Once again the names given in the first line are those of clan leaders of the past. Sangai refers to the Sangai *lepe* plant. This verse describes how the power of the Sangai *lepe* takes over and transforms the bachelors, carrying them forward to success; it refers not only to their physical transformation but also to charisma and the capabilities believed to underlie it.

Verse 3

Dutupa Kepoli akali mendepa katambu lamo lao
Pakili akali mendepa katambu lamo lao.
Kopele, kepele, ambole pia kandapa
Sikimina takimina pia kandapa
Dutupanya utubalulyaka pikipokomai lao minakameamo lapolapo.
Dutupa kalyamo akipaeme lelyapeaka leamo?
Dutupa lelyamo akipaeme lelyapeaka leamo?
Yopeao, Yoaleao, Panaoa, Lipanoao,
Ange mambele lengena.

They, Kepoli is the man I have been staying with
Pakili is the man I have been staying with.
It fit, it rotted, it decayed when seen
Supported like a vine, but falls when seen
The power of the Sangai took hold of their wigs in a swift and flowing manner.
What makes them who they are?
What makes them as renowned as they are?
Yopeao, Yoaleao, Panoao, Lipanoao,
It is this thing that makes them who they are.

Line 3 refers to the Sangai *penge,* which are suitable for holding the sacred liquid when new, but which decay as time goes by and must be replaced. Line 4 describes one of the *lepe* plants. In both of these lines, the dangers of sightings of the sacred objects by those other than bachelors who have been through purification rites are described: the *penge* decays and the vine withers and dries. Bia had two kinds of *lepe:* one called *wau* that is a vine and climbs trees and another called *kombatau,* which is bog iris or sweet flag (*Acorus calamus*). The "thing" mentioned in the last line is the Sangai *lepe* and *penge;* though in fact two separate things, they are referred to as one.

Verse 4

> *Dutupame yae sakaleaka lapo mende iki anguo pyapelyoaka leamosa*
> *Kumanda aiyena lapo mende iki anguo pitipelyoaka leamosa*
> *Lipu pyape londe dama dutupanyaka leamosa*
> *Katala pyape londe dama dutupanyaka leamosa*
> *Dutupa kalyamo akipaeme kalyapeaka leamosa?*

> These men keep saying that they have been the major force in organizing the exchange
>   of live pigs and butchered pork [in *tee*]
> These men keep saying that they have been the only ones at a funeral feast
> People keep saying that the long horizontally laid fencing is theirs
> People keep saying that the long picket fencing is theirs
> What makes them who they are?

Line 2 means that these men had the resources to organize and host a funeral feast by themselves. Lines 3 and 4 describe their extensive gardens fenced by two different techniques to keep out pigs—the first type is made by attaching boards horizontally to posts, and the second is a picket-style fence.

Verse 8

> *Ameanenya Kaenepai dokonya pitu lao kandele piamo*
> *Paliua lao kandele piamo*
> *Nee napenge lapo mende nala kaeao nasiapya*
> *Kindi pyakindi lapo mende nala kaeao nasiapya*
> *Dutupame baa sambao pao maele piapya*
> *Maipao pao maele piapya.*
> *Dutupa Kepoli akali mendepa katambu lama lao*
> *Pakili akali mendepa katambu lamo lao.*
> *Endaki kuka pyalamo yaneki dupa kandakuia lao peteapya*
> *Endaki kotaka pyalamo yaneki dupa kandakuia lao peteapya*
> *Endaki kenge Poka lata Pokalitu lata pilyamo*
> *Elyo lata Eylope lata pilyamo*
> *Yongaipa lata Temo lata pilyamo*
> *Dutupanya kuka pyalamo yaneki dupa kandakuia lao peteapya*
> *Kotaka pyalamo kandakuia lao peteapya.*

> Ameane from his Kaenepai sat and saw
> Ameane from his Kaenepai slept and saw
> There was not any food left
> There was not any food left even for private consumption

It was all given away in purchasing
It was all taken over to purchase.
They, Kepoli was the kind of man I have been staying with
Pakili was the kind of man I have been staying with.
Night bridges over rivers were checked, and darkness longed for and waited for
Day bridges over rivers were checked, and darkness longed for and waited for
Rivers Poka and Pokalitu say they
Elyo and Elyope say they
Yongaipa and Temo say they
Their night bridges over rivers were checked, and darkness longed for and waited for
Their day bridges over rivers were checked, and darkness longed for and waited for.

This verse tells of Ameane's voyage to purchase the Sangai *lepe* from Bia men. It names the rivers and creeks that were crossed as Ameane brought the *lepe* plant from Yakangemai to the Potealini Sangai cult house, where it was planted. This was done at night to avoid being seen by women and married men.

Verse 11

Ameanenya kisakisa waina doko katalanyaka kateamo
Lipu pyape londe dama Ameanenyaka leamo
Katala piape londe dama Ameanenyaka leamo
Yoko londe peange dama Ameanenyaka leamo
Pingipingi ambonge dama Ameanenyaka leamo
Ameane lelyamo akipaeme lelyapeaka leamo?
Alu kumbalo kale pyalo lapae dama Ameanenyaka leamo,
Kumanda aiyena lapo mende iki anguo pitipilyoaka leamo
Yae sakale lapo mende iki anguo pyapelyoaka leamo
Ameane lelyamo akipaeme lelyapeaka leamo?

Ameane's physical and mental capabilities were always there
His influence and renown were always there
People keep saying the long horizontally laid fencing is Ameane's
People keep saying the long picket fencing is also Ameane's
The long-leafed pandanus palm is also Ameane's
The sweet potato garden ready to harvest is also Ameane's
What makes Ameane as popular as he is?
That huge, untamed, and slit-eared pig is also Ameane's
He keeps saying that he has been alone at a funeral feast
He keeps saying that he has been a major force in organizing the distribution of live
    pigs and butchered pork
What makes Ameane as renowned as he is?

The meaning of this verse, which details Ameane's accomplishments, is generally clear. Note that importance is placed on agricultural production as well as on exchange. Slitting the ear of a pig (line 8) designates it for ceremonial exchange, usually war reparations.

Verse 12

Nambame nambanya kaenepai kisakako dokonya pitu lao kandele pipuni
Paliu lao kandele pipuni
Ameane kalyamo akipaeme kalyapeaka lapusa?
Ameane lelyamo akipaeme lelyapeaka lapusa?
Kisakisa waina doko kalyanyaka katapumosa
Lolo waina doko kalyanyaka katapumosa
Nambanya nee napenge lapo mende nalakaeao nasalame lamo
Kindi pyakindi lapo mende nala kaeao nasalame lamo
Yati yambali lapo mende sala kaeao nasalame lamo
Dutupanya baa sambao pao amele pipuni
Maipao pao maele pipuni.
Dutupanya kisakisa waina doko katalanyaka katapumu
Nambanya utubalulyaka pikipokomai lao minakapumu lapolapo
Timu waelyaka pikipokomai lao minakapumu lapolapo
Yongo wangimilyaka pikipokomai lao minakameamo lapolapo
Moko tuakapelyaka pikipokomai lao minakapumu lapolapo
Yae sakale lapo mende iki anguo pyapelyoaka lapusa
Kumanda aiyena lapo mende iki anguo pitipelyoka lapusa
Namba kalyeno akipaeme kalyepeaka lamusa
Namba lelyamo akipaeme lelyapeaka lamusa
Yopeao, Yaoaleao, Panoao, Lipanoao
Dakepeame lelyamoaka lamusa.
Nambanya kisakisa waina doko kalyanyaka katamusa
Lolo waina doko kalyanyaka katamusa
Kumanda aiyena lapo mende iki anguo pitipilyoaka lapusa
Yae sakale lapo mende iki anguo pyapelyoaka lapusa.

I from the upper limits of my Kaenepai sat and saw
I from the upper limits of my Kaenepai slept and saw
And asked, "What makes Ameane as renowned as he is?
What makes him who he is?"
My physical and mental abilities are seen to be there always
My influence and renown are also there
I have no food left
I have no food left even for private consumption
No personal attire left
These I have given to him in purchase
I have taken these over to him
These have made it possible for
The power of the Sangai to take hold of my wig in a swift and flowing manner
The power of the Sangai takes hold of my wig in a swift and flowing manner
The power of the Sangai takes hold of my body in a swift and flowing manner
The power of the Sangai takes hold of my beard in a swift and flowing manner
The power of the Sangai takes hold of my calf muscles in a swift and flowing manner.
I keep saying that I have been a major force in organizing the distribution of live pigs

and that of butchered pork [in *tee* exchange]
I keep saying that I have been alone at a funeral feast.
People keep asking, what makes me who I am?
People keep asking, what makes me as renowned as I am?
Yopeao, Yoaleao, Panoao, Lipanoao
It is this thing that makes me who I am.
My physical and mental abilities are always there
My influence and renown are always there
I keep saying that I have been alone at a funeral feast
I keep saying that I have been a major force in organizing the distribution of live pigs
and butchered pork.

Here, in the final verse, Wae Wangatoto tells how he bought the Sangai *lepe* from Ameane, and how it transformed him.

Excerpt from the Adventures of Gulu

Apa Pimbia, Aimbatepa Pao clan, Dikitesa, Kandep

Gulu was satisfied that his grassland [in Kandep] was suitable for raising pigs. Now he wanted to discover the source of pearl shells, so this man from Kandep took a long journey. He brought with him two bags of salt from the springs of the Yandap. One was large and the other small. He came to Birip, where he met some people who asked him, "What are you looking for?" He told them that he was looking for the tree on which pearl shells grew, giving them some of the salt that he had brought with him. They tasted it and, pleased by its taste, showed him the way to the tree of pearl shells.

When the man from Kandep arrived at Komo, he asked the inhabitants where he might find the tree that bore pearl shells. They said that the tree did not grow there and asked where he had come from. He told them that he was from Kandep and gave them some salt. They found it so delicious that they said, "The tree that you are looking for does not grow here. It is in the land of Dima."

"Where is the land of Dima?" he asked.

They told him that this place was beyond the clouds and horizon and that one had to pass two large bodies of water, Kutuma [Kutubu] and Takali, before reaching a third in the land of Dima.[1] They explained that the homeland of the shells was in Dima but that they had no idea how they got here. So the people of Komo said, "It is a waste of time for you to come down here," and, having said this, gave him five pearl shells. Then they brought him to their house and took the shoulder bone of a pig that they kept in the house, saying, "Take this with you. You have lots of pigs up there at your house. Well, you will see that the pig is the source of shells. When you have pigs, the shells will come."

He put the bone into his net bag. After saying farewell to them he returned to Kandep. Along the way he gave salt to people whom he met, so that they would show him the way back. He brought with him the first shells to Kandep. Later, many more people from Kandep went down to get shells in exchange for pigs. . . . In that way the shell trade to Kandep via the Mendi was established. Because of this trade, there are now many shells in Kandep.

An Episode of the Malipini-Potealini versus Itapuni-Awaini Great War, 1910-1920

Yamu Yakia, Yakani Kalia clan, Wakumale (Wabag)

The Itapuni-Awaini versus Malipini-Potealini Great War was fought on the Wakumale grassland when I was a boy living with my parents at Irelya where Reverend Burce's house used to be.[1] At that time this plot was the Apulini ceremonial grounds made specifically for the purpose of assembling Itapuni and Awaini warriors whom Apulini hosted for the Great War at Wakumale. They built men's houses to accommodate the warriors, planted gardens to provide food for them, and made weapons for them with materials brought in from distant places [e.g., black palm wood]. Pigs were also bred and the piglets raised for the occasion. After all these preparations were made, the Great War began.

For the Great War, Itapuni and Awaini warriors gathered on the ceremonial ground, many of them arriving in full ceremonial dress with colorful headdresses, and others bringing their decorations with them to dress at Irelya. Warriors continued to swarm in from near and distant places. They stayed in the men's houses at Irelya for a week [before the Great War], their food and water supplied by Apulini clans. At night, Great War leaders would gather their warriors and discuss the upcoming war. They talked of the war leaders on the enemy side, engaged in endless discussions about how to make sudden attacks on the enemy, and composed songs to be sung on the battlefield, particularly songs of victory for enemy deaths. By day, some warriors decorated themselves, quite a number of them smearing their bodies with tree oil, and lined up on the ceremonial grounds to dance, while others worked on their weapons. In the meantime a group of Apulini men went down to the Lai river and made a bridge that the warriors could cross when going to battle. It was a busy week, and everybody had something to do.

At the beginning of that week, the word went around in the neighboring tribes that a Great War was imminent. It did not stop there but spread far and wide. Some of the people from distant places who heard about it brought materials to make weapons.[2] Of course, these things were brought to us only by people on our side. Food was also supplied by the hosts of the Itapuni and Awaini warriors, but no food could come from the enemy camp. People who had links with the enemy were not allowed to enter men's houses on our side, and knowing that the Great War would start that week, the public also did not travel much between Irelya and Lakiamanda.[3] That was how things were the week before the Great War.

The [Yakani] Kalia clan was not involved in the Great War. It was the [Yakani] Laita clan that hosted the Malipini and Potealini warriors and supplied food and water for them. The Yakani clans to the west, Sambeoko, Mulyao, Lilyai, Takikini, and Laita, also supported Malipini and Potealini. Those of us from the Kalia clan who had social ties with Apulini were told not to accept food offered by Malipini and Potealini warriors, hosts, or anybody who had ties with the enemy side.

On the first day of the week when the Great War began, the warriors decorated themselves and put on bird-of-paradise plumes as they would for a traditional dance. The warriors spent the first half of the day dancing and singing war songs that they had composed and sung during the past week. At about midday men holding shields crossed the bridge, followed by the warriors. The Itapuni and Awaini warriors climbed the hill at Apipasa and assembled at the men's house, from where they could see the enemy getting ready to cross the Ambum river. They sang songs boasting of their bravery and their upcoming victory while the scouts went out to see what was ahead and to trample the grass on the battlefield.

On the other side of the Ambum river, the Malipini and Potealini warriors were preparing similarly for the battle. They were also in full ceremonial dress, a magnificent sight. Most striking were the warriors from the north [Sau valley] who wore bright yellow *kaiwae* bird-of-paradise feathers in their wigs. Others wore woven cassowary feather headdresses, while some were not decorated at all. They also wore newly woven frontal aprons.

The events proceeded much like a traditional dance. Led by Great War leaders, they went down to the Ambum river and crossed the bridge to Ikiale. The scouts returned to tell our side what was going on, how the enemy were dividing up and preparing for battle. At the same time the men carrying shields, on guard for sudden attack, trampled the *sambai* grass on their side of the no-man's-land that formed the border between them, working their way closer and closer to the battlefront. The event gained momentum and tension built up as the two forces approached the battlefront.

Along the Sau valley there are more Malipini and Potealini than in the Ambum valley, and they were the driving force on that side.[4] They came in great numbers and stood out for the *kambi* [hawk] and bright yellow *kaiwae* feathers they wore, bringing many feathers with them for their fellow warriors. The latecomers assembled at the men's house, from where they moved down the ceremonial ground and sang songs about the war while those who had come earlier went to battle. The area where Kilyo's house now stands and that adjacent to it was all covered by thick *sambai* grass that both sides trampled flat. There the two sides met and fought. Epelya, a Timali man, was killed there, and so was a man from the Kia clan.

It was noon when they met at the battlefront, for the first half of the day had been spent decorating the warriors and making other preparations for the Great War. Those of us who were on the side of the Apulini tribe went to Irelya and stood at the top of the hill to watch the men as they went to battle. . . .

At noon of the first day the two forces fought. Warriors from both sides gathered in masses on the small stretch of land. It was told that it was a war of rivalry and valor. The war became so hot on the battlefield that it is said that the plumes of the birds of paradise found their way into the leafy branches of *mandi* trees and then fell into the Ambum and Lai rivers. In other words, the Malipini and Potealini chased the men down to the Lai river. In the same way, the Itapuni and Awaini warriors chased the northern groups off to the Ambum river. People said that was the way the war was fought. I saw the men in full ceremonial dress, but I did not see the actual fighting.

Basically the Great Wars were fought with the same strategies as conventional wars. One side would advance, driving the other back, and vice versa. They also tried to ambush the enemy—for example, the Timali man was killed in an ambush.

The Great Wars went on for weeks. When an end to the fighting was called, the warriors brought the shields and stood them against posts they had placed in the ground. The same was done on the other side. Then the men of both sides took their shields, cast them into the river, and the Great War came to an end. Afterward, the hearts of pigs were taken out, wrapped in *palyo* leaves, and given to the Malipini and Potealini warriors. I do not know why they ate the raw hearts of pigs, but I know it was tradition in the Great Wars.[5] It is said that those who brought bloody hearts painted their faces with red ochre and danced. Only the old men in the Laita clan ate the meat that was left over. No pieces of pork intended for the northern [enemy] warriors should reach our premises, and we told the Laita clan not to even bring the steamed leaves to scatter around our area. It was strictly forbidden. We were also told not to sleep in the houses of those who supported Malipini and Potealini warriors. Most importantly, they must not enter the men's house of the Kepa subclan of Apulini.[6]

Then both sides prepared to kill pigs. The pork was to be given to the hosting clans who had provided for the warriors and had paid reparations for the deaths of allies killed in the Great War. The Sakatawane clan was the first clan to kill pigs, and from there down the line, every clan in the Potealini and Malipini clans killed pigs. In the Ambum valley, the Potealini Anae clan also planned to kill pigs. It was a marathon pig killing festival. Day and night they steamed pigs until at last it stopped by Yanga Creek. Side of pork after side of pork was carried down [to hosting Yakani clans], and along with them the backbones of pigs as well. Throughout the night people roasted the ribs over open fires along the way. The sides of pigs were carried to homes to be heated through in the morning, and then they were brought to the ceremonial grounds and cut into pieces. The pieces of pork were distributed to those in the host clans as well as those who came to watch the feast. The same pig killing festivals took place on the southern side.

Some time after these festivals were over, the Apulini clans killed and steamed pigs and gave the sides of pork to the clans they had hosted, what was called the *akaipu tee* [initiatory gifts]. Then the Laita clan did the same [for those they had hosted]. When that was over, clans to the west on both sides reciprocated and gave away live pigs to their hosts. This was the beginning of a Tee cycle that went far to the east and returned as the *tee pingi* [the phase of the main gifts of the Tee cycle]. Then it was time for the return *yae* phase of the Tee cycle [distribution of cooked pork]. This Great War episode came to an end with these exchanges. Malipini and Potealini never fought again against Itapuni and Awaini at Wakumale.

APPENDIX 12

The Making of a Great War Leader

Ambone Mati, Itapuni Nemani clan, Kopena (Wabag)

In this testimony, Ambone Mati gives a brief life history of Satutu, a popular fight leader from the last Great Ceremonial War. Two points here are particularly noteworthy. The first is how the public watched the sons or nephews of great fight leaders and chose one, whom they would like to see replace his father, and made him popular. The second is the importance of marriages between leading families for keeping the peace within a side or arranging the Great Wars.

It is said that bad and unproductive fruit trees do not bear good fruits, but that only good and healthy trees do. As such, it was always the sons of *watenge*, Great War leaders, who became *watenge*. A man could have many pigs, be a wealthy *kamongo* [big-man], could dress up and look good in the Great Wars, but these things would not win him the title of *watenge*. There was nothing a man could do to rise to this position. It was always the son of a *watenge* who became a *watenge*. . . .

We insisted that it is the son of a *watenge* who becomes a *watenge*, because he would be from a reputable family and therefore well brought up and exposed to the leadership qualities of his father and grandfather, that is, if both had been *watenge* as in the case of Satutu. Satutu's grandfather and father were both *watenge*.

At the time of Walosa, Satutu's father, there were very bitter wars between the Yanaitini Kia clan and Itapuni Nemani, even before Satutu was born. The Kia clan, in an effort to make peace, sent a woman from the Kia Andati subclan named Yaupiwana to marry an Itapuni man. Their efforts were unsuccessful and the fighting continued. The next move that the Kia clan made was this: they sent another Andati woman, Pangilya, the sister of a Kia big-man and Tee cycle organizer, Yomo, to marry Satutu's father, Walosa. Actually Pangilya was married to a Yakani man, but they took her away from her husband and sent her to the Nemani clan in a second effort to make peace. After this the fighting stopped instantly and completely, until about three months ago when they had a war over the rape of a Kia woman. While taking Pangilya away from her Yakani husband to give to Walosa, they used this metaphor: "I have built a one-log bridge, and it is weak and shaky. I need

416 • APPENDIX 12

another log to place beside the first to strengthen the bridge." Another sister of Yomo's was married to Mioko, the Malipini *watenge*.

Pangilya was the mother of Satutu. His father, Walosa, was burned to death in a bush fire when Satutu was in his early teens. He built a fire while working in his garden, and it got out of control, turning into a raging bush fire. When Walosa tried to put out the fire, he became enveloped in the flames and smoke and was burned to death. When Malipini men, his enemies in the Great War, heard how he died, they came to mourn his death, saying that they had lost a fine *watenge*. They lamented his death with the following song:

> *Epalekini akali lao watao katapu tatapumbu nyo kalyamo lelyaimipi?*

> The son of Epale was hailed, trailed, and chased by many, bush fire ashes had he collected, are they saying?

They meant that Epale's son Walosa was hailed, followed, and trailed by many warriors. They could not believe that his end came in a bush fire. A more appropriate death for him would have been a warrior's death in battle, but that chance was now lost to both sides. Now there was one less Great War leader for us.

After his father's death, Satutu was taken to Tetemanda, his mother's place, and lived there. Several years later, when he was a young man, he dressed himself in his best traditional dress to take part in a traditional dance at Laiagam [the local place name for the area where the Wabag community school now stands]. When he made his first appearance there in public at the traditional dance, people were awed and said, "That is Satutu, the son of the *watenge* Walosa." His appearance was similarly praised in the Sangai bachelors' cult and smaller wars; thereafter he was hailed as a *watenge* himself.

Satutu, aware of his possible future role, sang this song when he appeared in the traditional dance at Laiagam [Wabag]:

> *Akalimi Laipi lao pyuku pyuku lelyamona kungu mende tuu pita aipape?*

> So many people are talking about my clan, that my clan land is shaking.

In this song he was referring to his family history, about his father's and grandfather's status as *watenge*. *Watenge*, in the context of fighting, means one who is chased after or trailed, and that in due course his enemies will get him. The public knew that his father and grandfather were dead and gone, and in this song he laid open to the public the question of whether he, too, would become a *watenge*. Satutu knew that it was one's people who make a *watenge*, and no one man could do it by himself.

Itapuni was not yet in the Tee cycle in the lifetime of my father. As the Great Wars ended, it was Satutu Walosa and Mioko [the great *watenge* from the Malipini Kamaniwane clan who married Satutu's mother's sister] who were key figures in getting the Tee cycle to spread to their areas. The Yanaitini Kia clan used their direct links as maternal kin of Satutu and Mioko to integrate Itapuni and Malipini into the Tee cycle.

The *Yae* Phase of the Tee Cycle in the Lifetime of Pendaine (ca. 1910)

Kopio Toya Lambu, Yakani Timali clan, Lenge

This testimony continues from the point where Kopio's testimony in chapter 12 left off.

One year had passed since the Tee was held [by the Timali clan] at Lenge [map 18:4]. During this time Pendaine stayed home looking after the pigs that he had reserved for the *yae*. He received news from time to time from his Tee associates about how the Tee was proceeding. When the message reached him that the Tee had finally arrived at the easternmost end, he sent word that the great *yae* pig-killing phase of the Tee should begin. At his word the *yae* began,[1] and those involved in the Tee from the west, men from the upper Lai and Sau valleys, went down to see it. They traveled from house to house, village to village, and ridge to ridge. For example, having received news of the *yae*, Neowali Yakani [map 18:3] set out in the morning for the house of Yakapyakapa and his brothers [2]. After a long trip, he reached their house and stayed for the night. He told them of the reason for his visit and they made plans to go to the east. On the morning of the next day, Neowali Yakani, Yakapyakapa, and his brothers traveled on to the house of Ipalyone at Sauanda [1]. The group spent the night there and were refreshed with food and water. The *yae* was the topic of their discussions. On the morning of the next day, they left for Lenge via the bush tracks that crossed the mountain range. It was a long journey, and they did not arrive until the evening.

At Lenge they went directly to the house of Pendaine. The great Pendaine, who had been expecting them, greeted them and asked them into his house. He sent word to his servants to prepare food for the visitors; they did as they were told by the great *kamongo*. One of the servants brought a bundle of sugarcane, the first thing required by a visitor who had arrived from a long journey. Others brought all kinds of food to the house including pork from a fat pig that was slaughtered and roasted for the occasion. At night, as the men sat in the house and ate and drank, they quite naturally became involved in an intense discussion of the Tee and *yae*. Pendaine knew that these men had carried out the main phase of the Tee cycle according to his wishes and that he must return their favors. He must take them to the *yae* phase; if he did not, they would not regard him as trustworthy.

In the middle of the night Pendaine took them to the men's house to sleep and the next morning they prepared for the trip. Pendaine dressed: he put on his wig and woven aprons that were reserved for special occasions and tucked a stone ax into his waist belt. They did not bring any sweet potatoes for the trip, because Pendaine had friends and Tee associates who would provide for them if they were hungry along the way. Just before midday they set out and made their way to the village of his in-laws. Accompanied by his in-laws, they traveled on to the Ambulyini clan (map 18:6), where many other people from clans down the valley joined them. Soon they reached the natal clan of Pendaine's wife's mother, and after having picked up her relatives, they went on to the house of Sau Kalepo [7]. The group grew larger as more and more men joined. Indeed it was big, and so they stuck to the main trail down the valley. However, Pendaine and his men made a detour via the house of Lendeane of the Itokone tribe [9].

In this way, they traveled east to see the *yae* festivals. Pendaine and his men ended up in the land of the Yatapaki tribe [10], where Yatapaki men gave them pork and other food and then took them to the *yae* festivals of their neighbors. Sides of pork were passed from one person to another and then given to the men from clans to their west, who carried them home. It was a long journey and so they had to spend the night along the way.

Now it was time for the *yae* of the Yatapaki clan. In the morning, all of the Yatapaki men participated in the slaughtering and steaming of pigs. By the afternoon a large crowd had gathered on the ceremonial ground, and before long it was packed with spectators. Then Yatapaki men, women, and children entered the ceremonial grounds, the men lining up the sides of pork for distribution. The women and children stood in back and the men in front while the clan's wealthiest *kamongo* made a speech. He said that the *yae* was for the men of the west who had sent down the Tee a couple of years ago, and that they should eat the sides of pork and make plans for the next Tee cycle. Kiua was the man who made the speech. He had killed a very fat pig whose side was by far the largest on the ceremonial grounds. He lifted it up and called out the name of a man, who came forward to receive it. He was one of the middlemen in Pendaine's Tee chain. As he received it, the *kamongo*'s wife Lyalame said, "Send word that this side of pork is from a pig that was looked after by a woman named Lyalame." Like her husband, she knew that it would eventually reach the house of Pendaine. The side of pork was passed on to Lendeane of the Itokone tribe, the Itokone man gave it to a man from the Kandawalini Kaekini clan, and that man gave it to Sau Kalepo. Sau Kalepo in turn passed it on to a relative of Pendaine's wife's mother, who gave it to his brother-in-law in the Kandano clan, Pendaine's wife's father, who in turn gave it to Pendaine.

Pendaine then stayed home. The great *yae* did not stop; it swept down the Minamb valley. Another branch of the *yae* that had moved into the Saka valley continued on. It swept through every clan; not a single ceremonial ground was left out. Every recognizable clan took part in the *yae*, and side after side of pork continued to come up from the east.

Pendaine built a small hut for preserving the pork that he received, and while the *yae* was on, it was always full. Some sides of pork were given away to Tee associates and other pieces steamed again in earth ovens and eaten in his household, especially by those who had looked after his pigs.

The *yae* continued to move west, and more and more sides of pork were brought to the house of the great Yakani *kamongo*. It is said that there was so much pork that some rotted and had to be thrown into the river. As time passed, the *yae* came closer and closer to Lenge, and when it was but a few clans away, Pendaine told the men and women in his household to give more food to the pigs that had been earmarked to be killed for the *yae*. That was the final attempt to fatten the pigs. Pendaine also told the men of his household to chop firewood and store it in the houses to dry, and to collect stones [for the earth ovens] and store them in a dry place. All other necessary preparations were made in advance. Other households made similar arrangements for the great occasion.

The *yae*, which had begun along two routes,[2] came together as it moved into the Lai valley. When the *yae* reached the Itokone tribe [9], the number of spectators increased as people came from the Sau, Ambum, and upper Lai valleys. Most of them were from Yakani, Yanaitini, or Apulini. Pendaine had little time for himself—many people ended up at his house on the way down the valley, because he was a great *kamongo* and a key link between the east and the west. More and more sides of pork were brought to his house at Lenge.

The *yae* was only a few clans away from Yakani Timali when Pendaine told his male and female servants to make further preparations. All kinds of edible leaves were then collected for steaming the pork. In compliance with instructions given by Pendaine, every able-bodied man and woman in his household went about doing the work assigned to them. Several men were told to split firewood and bring it to the ceremonial ground. Pendaine appointed one or two men to find *kinjone* trees from which to make the clubs for killing the pigs and bamboo to make knives to slice the pork. Two men were sent out to cut two long poles and bring them to the ceremonial grounds, where they would be laid across the tops of posts to make a framework on which the sides of pork could be tied in display. Others provided ropes for tying them. The boys were told to help the older men, if they had nothing else to do, or to fetch water in bamboo containers. Such were the preparatory chores of the men in his household.

The women [of the household] were by no means left out but were told to do their part. Their major task was to bring stones for the earth oven. They also had to provide food to steam with the pork. The women divided themselves into work groups supervised by Pendaine's wife. One group went to collect edible leaves in the bush and gardens; another peeled bananas, taro, yams, and sweet potatoes. Girls helped their mothers. All of these activities took place about two days before the *yae* was to be held. The days of preparation, as well as the actual feast day, were lively ones filled with excitement.

Pendaine had nothing in particular to do on these days. He remained more or less an overseer, going here and there to make sure that everybody was doing his or her job. Most of his time was spent with visitors on the ceremonial grounds talking about matters pertaining to the *yae*. As I said, many of the visitors were his Tee associates, and if one of them had some personal complaint about what he was to receive in the *yae*, he was free to bring it up with Pendaine. If a large crowd were present, Pendaine might make a speech or brief them on the *yae*.

The Sane clan killed pigs and held its *yae* festival on the day before the *yae* was to take place at Lenge. That morning a big crowd gathered on the ceremonial grounds at Lenge and discussed the *yae* and the next Tee cycle that would follow. In the afternoon, when they thought that the Sane clan was ready, the crowd made its way to the Sane ceremonial ground at Rakamanda [12], Pendaine and other Timali men taking the lead. When they arrived, the sides of pork were already lined up on the ceremonial ground for distribution; they were large and fat, as expected. The crowd led by Pendaine sat on the ceremonial grounds with their backs turned toward Lenge. The Sane *kamongo* made an opening speech that was implicitly directed toward Pendaine, the Timali *kamongo*.

Then Pendaine got up to speak and the crowd held its breath. He said, "This *yae* was done as the result of the Tee that I did some years ago. It takes a man to plan a Tee and *yae* like this one. A good Tee and *yae* are ones in which almost every single man, woman, and child takes part in one way or the other. Only I can plan such a Tee and *yae*. I assured my men of the west that I would do the *yae* after the Tee. Well, this is it. You can see for yourselves. All must know that I am a man of truth and a man of his word." After making the speech, Pendaine sat down to watch as the Sane men gave away their sides of pork. As the *kamongo* of the clan next to Sane, Pendaine received more than any other person. Another reason that he received so much was that he had a sister married to a Sane man named Kepao. Everyone had plenty of pork to eat, for the recipients passed on some of the pork they had received to their own Tee partners, associates, and friends. As was the trend in the *yae* phase, the pork moved westward, because the Tee phase some years before had begun in the west. In the evening, the crowd dispersed. The next day would bring the *yae* festival at Lenge. For this reason Timali men did not give away any of the sides of pork that they received at Rakamanda but carried them home with the help of the potential recipients from near and far. All the other men carried their own pork home. At home, Pendaine's pigs that were to be killed the next day were tied, some being kept in the pig stalls of his house and many more in the courtyard.

In the evening people went to their houses, which were crowded with Tee associates and visitors, many of who had come straight from the Sane *yae* at Rakamanda. Pendaine's men's house was full of guests including Ipalyone, Yakapyakapa, and Neowali Yakani. Only men stayed in the men's house, for in every family women and children slept in the women's house. *Yae* fever affected men, women, and children alike: the children in particular could not sleep, wishing the night were over. The women chattered throughout the night. The men sat up in the men's house and talked continuously — the topic, of course, was the Tee and the *yae*. Pendaine and his men were no exception, and only in the middle of the night did they finally go to sleep.

Early in the morning before the first birds began to sing, the Timali clan began its great *yae* festival. Pendaine and several other *kamongo* went up to the ceremonial grounds, where they would club their pigs. Men and women from their households followed, leading the pigs. Men who had no more than one or two pigs to kill did not go to the ceremonial grounds but clubbed and steamed them at home. Pendaine waited on the ceremonial grounds for the men of his household. They soon arrived and made preparations to club the pigs, laying breadfruit and banana leaves on the ground to catch the blood. The smaller pigs were clubbed on their foreheads with *kinjone* clubs, while the large and heavy ones were tied to stakes and clubbed while rooting in the ground. All of the pigs were killed in this manner, one after the other. So many pigs were killed for the *yae!*

After their bristles were singed off, the pigs were carried to the bed of leaves by their legs and lined up in a row. Women and children who had come to watch were told to sit in an orderly fashion on one part of the ceremonial grounds and guests on another part so that they could all see well. Pendaine then told some of the men, many of whom were potential receivers of the pork, to remove the intestines. While the pigs were being butchered, Pendaine told one of the men to count all of the people present, including women and children. The number was given to the men butchering the pork, who busily cut it into pieces, leaving only the sides and vertebrae. They wrapped each piece in leaves, and the pieces were given to each and every person, first to the distinguished guests such as Ipalyone, Yakapyakapa, and Neowali Yakani, and last to the women and children. After receiving their portions, people gathered into small groups composed largely of families and close relatives. The members of each group kindled a fire, using firewood from the great piles stacked on the ceremonial grounds during the preceding days. Some pieces of meat were skewered on sticks, and the rest was wrapped in leaves and steamed in small earth ovens, using the smaller stones from the main pile. These were later uncovered and the contents eaten. Everybody present took part in the feast with great joy.

The women sat around gossiping, giggling, and talking, the children ran about play-fully, but the men had to work on. After the pork was cut into sides, these were bound with ropes and hung from the framework that had been constructed for the purpose. The bowels, vertebrae, and heads were put into net bags, the women lending a hand. The poles, called *yoleta*, stretched from one end of the ceremonial grounds to the other. Nandi, Pendaine's brother, who was also a *kamongo*, hung his pork sides from the *yoleta* so that all of the pork belonging to the two brothers was displayed together. The other pieces of pork that had been put in the net bags were carried to the back of the *yoleta* under the watchful eyes of the women, for those pieces were to be steamed on the next day. There was no time to steam them that day!

It was about noon when the spectators arrived and found a place to sit. Pieces of pork that had been set aside for the latecomers were then distributed. In the afternoon, other Timali men arrived with their families, friends, and Tee associates carrying in their steamed pork. All pork other than the sides was carried in by the women. The Timali men stood in front of the row of pork sides; the women and children sat behind. Most of the spectators were crowded together at the western end of the ceremonial ground. They were the people who had held the previous Tee [phase of main gifts].

Nandi was the first to give a speech to the crowd; he told them how great he was, praised his family and his clan, and boasted of his ceremonial grounds. The next man to speak was his brother, Pendaine. He made a similar speech, assuring the crowd that the *yae* phase was done to repay the people of the west, because they had held the Tee phase and given pigs to him a few years ago. He told them that they should remember that he was a man who kept his word and listen to him in planning the next Tee and *yae*. Then the *kamongo* of the west responded to the speeches; your [Nitzi Pupu's] grandfather Tukiapa, the *kamongo* of the Kalia clan, was one of these men.

After the speeches, the Timali men gave away the sides of pork and then distributed food and small pieces of meat to be eaten on the spot. The raw pieces of pork such as the heads, tails, and so forth were given to very close friends, Tee partners, associates, and relatives. Among the men who received a lot of meat from Pendaine were Ipalyone and your grandfather. In terms of clans as a whole, Yakani Kalia clan received more sides of pork than any other neighboring clans. There was so much meat to eat that some of it was cast into the river, as the saying goes.[3] Every adult took home more than his or her share.

Lambu was in the forefront of the event. He followed his father, Pendaine, and helped him in the distribution of pork sides and pieces. His father told him not to hide himself and to be swift in his actions. Some men in the crowd were quoted as having said that some day Lambu would take the place of his father. . . .

On the following day, all the bowels, vertebrae, and other pieces of pork were roasted in a long earth oven. Many people also came for this event, even though nobody felt like eating any more pork. Those who had looked after Pendaine's pigs were given plenty of pork, which was preserved in water, especially running water, so that they could go on eating it for almost three weeks. And so during the next three weeks Pendaine's storehouse was full. The *yae* continued to move west until it reached the point where the Tee had started. Neowali Yakani was one of the last *kamongo* to hold the *yae*.

Lambu's Exploits in Warfare

Kambao Toya Lambu, Yakani Timali clan, Lenge

The following passages describe how Lambu organized and participated in parties of allies to as-sist other clans in warfare. In the first case, that of Pumalini, he came to the aid of his mother's kin; in the second, the motive was to form Tee ties through the reparation exchanges that would ensue, for Depe Liala, the clan assisted, was a key clan in the Tee cycle. The situation that Lambu encountered in the second case, in which he met a relative and good friend face-to-face on the enemy side, is not uncommon. Enga often marry women from enemy clans and encounter in-laws in battle, at which point one or both withdraw from the fighting or move to other positions on the battlefront. The ritualized cannibalism described at the end of the narrative is the only case of its kind that we were told of. It was not common Enga practice, though the mutilation of corpses in the heat of battle occurred frequently.

Lambu was physically a very large man and most people thought of him as slow on his feet and unable run and move about with agility; nonetheless, he proved to be a good fighter. Here is another account of how he led his men to fight in an intratribal war between the clan of his maternal uncles [Pumalini Kandano] and another clan of the Pumalini tribe. In this war a number of his relatives had been killed, and so word was sent that Lambu should gather some men and come to help. The message arrived when he was attending a funeral feast at Rakamanda where a large crowd had gathered; as soon as he received the news, he decided to go. This is what he did: he took the many sides of pork that he had received from his Sane relatives who hosted the feast, piled them on the ceremonial grounds, gathered all of the men, and told them come with him. He asked some of them to carry the pork and other food to his house at Lenge; the others followed. He led them to the ceremonial grounds at Apomanda, where he took the pork, cut it into pieces, and distributed it. As they sat eating, he explained to them why he had invited them to come—that he wanted them to help his relatives in the war. Most of those who came were young men from the neighborhood who knew of his reputation as a *kamongo*. They were ready to follow him, for they knew that if one of them were killed he would be in a position to pay reparations for the death. Again he emphasized his point, "There is a poor man who is taking the lives of my relatives," he said, referring to the Pumalini [throughout this narrative Kambao calls the enemy clan by the tribal name, Pumalini]. "I have gathered you here so that we can go and help the clan of my uncles and cousins. If you are killed in the war, I shall be most willing to compensate your death. Tomorrow early in the morning we will start down valley."

As planned, Lambu led his men to Wee, the land of his mother. They arrived at the ceremonial grounds, where there was no sign of women or children—they had sought refuge from the fighting in neighboring allied clans. Many of the Kandano warriors had gathered on the ceremonial grounds, and there the two forces joined. One warrior, who spoke on behalf of his clansmen, told Lambu and his men how happy they were to see that they had come to help. Lambu then told of his plans for a small party of men to sneak over onto the enemy's side and lie in ambush. The others readily agreed. The major force of warriors then took the main path to the battlefront as the enemy would expect. Meanwhile, a small group led by Lambu followed a deep ravine and penetrated enemy territory. Under the cover of trees and tall grass they hid and waited. The main party of warriors then sent two scouts ahead to see how the enemy was preparing for attack. The scout's report, as anticipated, was that they had gathered on a certain small stretch of open land.

Just before midday, when the sun was overhead, the two forces moved forward. When they were but a short distance apart, the scouts from each side charged ahead, uttering battle cries. With their shields to protect them, the men were able to get within easy reach of each other. The warriors on both sides followed their war leaders, armed with arrows and spears. Meanwhile, Lambu and his men were at the edge of the buffer zone, crouched behind bush and hidden from the enemy. The warriors from both sides moved onto the open ground, ready for battle. The war began: arrows and spears flew back and forth. Bearing in mind their battle plans, the Kandano warriors pretended to be pushed back. The Pumalini warriors took that as a sign of weakness and charged in a sudden onslaught. The Kandano warriors retreated as if overwhelmed and fearful, while the enemy pursued them. They crossed the buffer zone and entered Kandano territory. From their ambush, Lambu and his men followed the movements of enemy warriors with their eyes to assess the situation developing on the main battlefront. Seeing that the enemy had already crossed the strip of no-man's-land, Lambu signaled to his men to carry out the surprise attack. With a shield in one hand and a spear in the other, Lambu came out of the bush shouting a battle cry. His men followed and attacked. It took the Pumalini warriors by surprise—they turned and fled for their lives. In their consternation, those in the front line were completely cut off from the rest of their men, who were rapidly abandoning them. As Lambu and his men attacked from the rear, the main party of Kandano warriors, who had feigned flight, turned and made a counterattack. Certain of victory, the Kandano warriors fought bravely.

A few Pumalini warriors were tightly cornered in the crossfire of arrows from both parties of Kandano, trapped with little hope of escape. As they made one last attempt to flee, Lambu aimed and hurled a spear at one of the men. It pierced him directly in his back. He staggered and fell. Lambu then grabbed another spear from one of his men and raised it to inflict a final blow on the fallen enemy. Just then an arrow shot by a fleeing enemy penetrated his hand. It was barbed like a fish hook, so that it could not be pulled out again. Lambu kept that arrow in his house—I have seen it with my own eyes. The man whom Lambu had speared died instantly, but all the others somehow managed to escape. The Kandano warriors swept through the enemy's land, cutting down small trees, ringbarking large ones, burning houses, and destroying gardens.[1] The entire Pumalini clan was driven off their land and fled to Liuates by the Tapili trail, where they stayed for some time until they returned and resettled on their land.

Here is another account of how Lambu assembled warriors from this area and went down to Birip [middle Lai valley] to help the Depe Liala clan in its war against the Kandawalini Wapukini clan. Lambu was at Lenge when a message reached him asking that he come down and help in the war. The message was sent to him because he was a *kamongo* of the Yakani tribe, and it requested that men, in particular those from Yakani clans, come to help. Lambu then sent word throughout his clan and neighboring ones asking for all men who were capable of fighting to come to Lenge. By evening most of the men from Timali had gathered, and big-men [*kamongo*] like Pangali, Toepa, and Kitapena were present. *Kamongo* from neighboring clans also came with parties of young warriors from their own clans. Lambu gathered this sizable group of men on the ceremonial grounds and briefed them on the plan to go and help Liala in the war. He told everyone to be armed with spears, bows, and arrows. He added that since they would be fighting in a land where they had never been, they should stick together or they might be mistaken for the enemy.[2]

Most of the men slept at Lenge that night; only a few went home and returned on the morning of the next day. Lambu took them to his men's house, where he had had many kinds of food prepared for them and a pig slaughtered and steamed. After they ate, they talked of nothing but the war in which they would take part. They spent the night there and the next morning set out fully armed, led by Lambu and Pangali. They arrived at Birip and proceeded to the battlefront, where the *kamongo* of the Liala clan greeted them and expressed his appreciation for their coming. The warriors divided themselves into small groups and prepared for battle.

Since the war had begun, the Wapukini clan had always been victorious and was overconfident. They were so confident that their women and children remained in their homesteads and did not move their pigs and belongings to a safer place for the duration of the war. That day the war proceeded as usual, and they continued fighting all day. In the evening, Liala warriors and their allies killed three Wapukini men and swept through the entire territory of the Wapukini clan, slaughtering pigs and burning houses. The women and children fled in terror, leaving everything behind while Liala warriors destroyed the entire community.

One of the three victims had been speared and lay on the battlefield unknown to anybody but his killer, who was none other than Lambu. Lambu hid the corpse and kept the death a secret. When the battle was over, the warriors milled around the battlefield discussing the war and how it had been won. Of course, there were many Liala men there, among them the Liala *kamongo* Tumanga and Andeape. Lambu shouted to them from afar, calling them by name and telling them to come. The two men heard the call and shouted back, asking the caller to identify himself. Lambu answered that he was a man of the west. The two men asked what on earth a man from the west was doing there and wanted to know why he had called them. Lambu answered assertively that he, a man of the west, was calling. Tumanga and Andeapa came to him, and when they appeared out of the bush, he signaled for them to approach by lowering his shield. As the two men made their way toward him, one warrior from the Diuapini clan asked Lambu why he had called. Lambu cut him short by saying, "I, Yakani Lambu, am telling them to come. I am the man who is telling them to come." They knew who he was, the Yakani *kamongo*.

"You are not one of us, so why are you calling for us?" the two Liala men asked. When they came near he told them of his secret. He said that there was an enemy lying out there to be taken away for burial. The men smiled. They asked him where the corpse was, and he took them to the place where he had hidden it. The two men were more than happy [when they saw who it was], cut off the head, and broke the skull open. Then one of them—I think it was said that Tumanga was the one—said, "Let me eat the brain. He was my man." He was the man wanted by the entire Liala clan as the fiercest Wapukini warrior and a notorious killer. He had slain many Liala men and their craving for revenge was at last fulfilled. So strong was their feeling that they ate his brain.

Lambu told me of an encounter with his brother-in-law on the battlefield during the same war. The name of this man was Tipitapu; he is from the Itokone clan and still lives at Puakale. My father said that while he was in the fighting zone ready for battle, there was a certain warrior standing a short distance away in front of the enemy's main line. Lambu did not recognize him, because he was wearing war regalia and was partially covered by his shield. He was tall, heavily built, and wore a headdress of woven cassowary feathers. His face was smeared with charcoal. In one hand he held a shield and in the other a spear. He moved back and forth with agility, jumping up and down, fully vigilant, and "on the war path," so to speak. "This man sure has guts," Lambu said from the hiding place where he was totally concealed. The young man approached, every sense alert to the danger of a sniper's arrow. He "danced" forward slowly but surely as the main body of warriors advanced. On the other side, the Liala warriors were doing the same, soon to meet the enemy. The young, brave, and bold enemy warrior showed no signs of fear and danced forward, his eyes fixed on the Liala warriors coming to meet them. They were within the range of a spear throw now, and instantly flying arrows filled the air. War cries drowned out the moaning of wounded men. Like a skillful dancer, the young warrior dodged the spears and arrows that came his way.

Suddenly, when he moved his shield aside for a brief moment, he came face-to-face with a man poised to spear him. Tipitapu gave a ghostly smile waiting for the spear to pierce, but Lambu recognized the familiar face, cursed, and lowered his spear. Then he quickly moved away, for the man was Tipitapu of the Itokone clan, the brother of his Itokone wife. He said that had Tipitapu not removed his shield for that brief moment, he would have instantly killed him at such close range. Tipitapu, having narrowly escaped death, withdrew from the battlefield.

I told you that Lambu was a *kamongo* from the Timali clan—well, he was also a leader of the Yakani tribe. When he spoke at a gathering, no one moved, even the women and children. They paid very close attention to him—you know how in the colonial days we all listened to the government because we feared it? Well, it was like that when Lambu spoke. He had great influence throughout the region, and people responded when he gave the word to do something. For example, when he called together young men for one of his war ventures, many young men volunteered. You know how in the colonial days people went up to Wabag to get information and disseminate it? In the same way people from all over the region came to hear what Lambu had to say. They listened to him carefully and nobody spoke until he had finished. People came from the Sau, Kopona, Saka, and Yandap to hear him. Now things have totally changed and everybody is going their own way. In the days of Lambu people paid a lot of respect to *kamongo*.

Notes

Introduction

1. Our use of the term "tribe" for the largest Enga political unit, an aggregate of clans united by a common origin tradition and genealogy that links members to a common ancestor, is discussed in chapter 1.

2. The *ee* in Tee is pronounced as the long *a* in *say* or *they*, not as the vowel sound in English *tea* or *tee*. All wealth distributions that involve giving out pigs and valuables in public, except bridewealth prestations, fall under the general category *tee*. The Tee ceremonial exchange cycle that developed in eastern Enga is distinguished from other forms of *tee* exchange by a number of Enga terms. To standardize, we use *tee* to refer to pig exchange in general, and Tee to refer to exchange in the Tee cycle.

3. A thorough and responsible history of the colonial period should receive high priority for future research.

4. We also tried sending out grade ten graduates or university students on holiday to collect information, but the results were generally inadequate and had to be followed up. On such short-term assignments, interviewers did not have enough knowledge and experience to pick up on leads, ask appropriate questions, or make the necessary cross-checks.

5. A survey of the history of the Kyaka Enga living in Western Highlands Province was canceled because of frequent armed holdups in the Baiyer region at the time.

6. This style of interview departs from guidelines set down for oral historians by Jan Vansina (1985:61–62). We found his recommendations to be of value for distinguishing different kinds of oral traditions by their form, intent, circumstance of original production, and means of transmission. Those that concern relations with people, however, are far off the mark for areas like the PNG Highlands that had but a short period of colonial domination and in which there are no "official"

tribal histories. For an excellent critique of Vansina's approach that is also appropriate for PNG societies, see Rosaldo (1980).

Chapter 1. The Enga, Their Historical Traditions, and Our Approach

1. Echoes of the presence of European traders along the coast probably reached Enga from the seventeenth century onward (Waiko 1993), for awareness of people with European appearance and technology is reported to have existed long before first contact and was sometimes integrated into Enga myth and ritual. Northern Enga traders encountered Europeans in the headwaters of the Sepik prior to the 1930s. For instance, Kirschbaum (1938) published a counting system that he recorded from Maramuni Enga visiting the Sepik in the late 1920s.

2. The term "phratry," as used by Meggitt (1965a), is perhaps the most accurate anthropological term for the *tata andake* of Enga. We do not use it here, however, as it is unfamiliar to Enga and cannot be found in standard dictionaries. Good definitions are absent even from most anthropological textbooks. Though the term "tribe" is notorious for being an imprecise notion (Fried 1975), it is the gloss Enga most commonly use for *tata andake,* and so we use it throughout the text. It has also been criticized by some anthropologists as having derogatory implications, as in "tribalism" or "tribal mentality," and as indicating an evolutionary stage. Our usage is purely descriptive, for want of a better familiar term, and none of these implications is intended.

3. For the Kompiam region, where clans are highly dispersed, and for clans of eastern Enga that are very large, the Tee cycle distributions are organized and held by subclans. Bachelors' cults are also held by large subclans throughout Enga.

4. Since the sweet potato was one of the foods distributed, this tradition may also pertain to its spread, though there is no supporting evidence for this.

5. Though easternmost Enga feel affinity with the Mount Giluwe myth, and western Enga with Hela Obena, the two myths are used only to explain affiliation with Kakoli and Huli, respectively, and do not express opposition between eastern and western Enga. Many central Enga have heard that the Saka-Layapo came from the Mount Giluwe region and are familiar with the Hela Obena myth, but they do not identify with either.

6. Meggitt (1965a:107) wrote that the sky people were believed to be organized into patrilineal descent groups with each sky phratry (tribe) sending a member to found a terrestrial phratry (tribe) homologous to his own. Although we asked among knowledgeable elders, we did not find that this was a clear or widespread belief. There is indeed a general belief that people descended from sky people, but this is not projected down to the phratry level. No origin traditions that we collected directly traced specific founding ancestors to sky people, though many traced them to nonhuman ancestors—birds, animals, or plants.

7. For example, many myths of western Enga have been revised or reinterpreted in the last five years to explain the discovery of gold and oil in Enga and Southern Highlands Province.
8. This refers to clans that existed around the time of first contact; since then, many of these clans have split into two or more independent clans.
9. We collected genealogies from two to ten men in each tribe, depending on its size and complexity, recording the shorter or longer form according to their preferences. If we received different versions in the early generations (usually owing to unintentional omissions), we continued to collect genealogies until we could establish one to three versions for the tribal and clan founders on which many men agreed.
10. Rapid population growth starting in the colonial period has led to the establishment of numerous independent clans. In more complex tribes today, men who are well informed on other topics of history have a poor overview of tribal structure and will readily admit this when presented with a genealogy given by those considered to be authoritative in historical matters. Care must be taken not to confuse inconsistencies owing to lack of knowledge on the part of informants with inconsistencies in views of tribal structure.
11. Although we questioned people about it, nobody confirmed the corresponding scheme of "usual events" that should take place in the different months, from planting to ceremonies and tribal fighting (Meggitt 1958c:76). Meggitt himself now feels these "usual events" may have been a scheme fabricated by one informant (Chris Ballard, personal communication 1995).
12. Lacey (1975) attaches dates to genealogical chronologies back to the eighth generation; he may well be correct in doing so, but we prefer not to.
13. We use three terms here: myth, legend, and historical narrative. Myths are fictive; legends are believed to have a historical basis but are not verifiable; and historical narratives are renditions of historical events that can often be verified via the histories of other clans. This terminology is applied to oral traditions from the generation of tribal founders only, because traditions from this period are hard to verify. After the generation of subclan founders we use the terms myth and historical narrative only.
14. Many people today have confidence in the power of *nemongo,* and even though men were willing to talk openly about ancestral cult procedures, some preferred to withhold the accompanying *nemongo* just in case they should invite misfortune by doing so.
15. The history of the development of songs is a topic that urgently awaits further research. It is particularly promising because at least some songs of the last five generations can be ordered by generation and placed in context. See Talyaga (1975) for an excellent presentation of modern Enga songs.
16. Of course, the passages we reproduce are but a small fraction of the material recorded and translated.
17. It might be noted that human ethology, though following the paradigm of evolution by natural selection, departs from other approaches such as sociobiology in that it

does not assume that the behaviors it identifies as having a biological basis are necessarily aimed at maximizing reproductive success at any single point in time. It assumes only that certain behavioral tendencies have been advantageous over the course of our evolution and thus have become part of our biological heritage.

Chapter 2. Environment, Population, and Subsistence in the Early Generations of Oral History

1. Because virtually all oral traditions used in this chapter are from the "founding generations," between approximately the seventh and perhaps tenth or eleventh generation before present, readers should be aware that we are drawing on different kinds of historical sources: myths used to transmit historical information, historical narratives, and genealogies.
2. Parkinson (1974) has shown that around the time of first contact the population of PNG was concentrated either above 1,300 meters or below 600 meters. The former zone was malaria free, and in the latter, malaria was endemic and adults had developed some resistance owing to constant exposure. The middle zone was hazardous, for malaria was epidemic, causing the heaviest mortality. Today the heavy traffic to and from the coast constantly brings malaria into higher areas—the parasite cannot complete its life cycle at high altitudes and must be constantly reintroduced (Cattani 1992).
3. Only two Enga tribes, Lakani and Waitini (32 and 33 on map 5), claim origins in the upper Sau area of the Kompiam district adjacent to the Ambum valley. Two other small tribes, Ingi and Nenge, who today live near Labalama, may also have been in the upper Sau.
4. Enga and Ipili populations of the Porgera valley blend into each other, and most people there are fluent in both languages. The question of where the border lay the past was apparently meaningless, for it drew blank responses. We encountered no traditions that separated or opposed Ipili and Tayato Enga. Mixed Enga-Ipili groups that claim origins in the Porgera valley are not shown on map 5.
5. Saka and Layapo Enga do not constitute separate dialect groups today, though they may have in the past.
6. Meggitt (1973:3) refers to them as the Paroko Enga. We asked about this term in several parts of Enga but found that it referred to the areas around Karekare south of the Lagaip and did not include people of the Laiagam region.
7. From 1980 census figures, excluding areas with predominantly non-Enga population (Lea and Gray 1982). Though population growth from 19,000 to 150,000 seems enormous, it requires only about a 1 percent population increase per year, compared with an annual increase of more than 2.3 percent in recent decades.
8. Elders say that only in the early decades of the twentieth century did game populations seriously decline as more land was cleared.
9. As Golson also recognizes, natural factors including frost, drought, fire, and intru-

sion of pollen from lower valleys within 10 kilometers of lake Ipea may have influenced pollen profiles.

10. Since most younger Enga today are unfamiliar with the crop, it is possible that in a few instances *kotena* was mistranslated as a variety of sweet potato or a kind of yam.

11. Hunting dogs were highly valued, but there is no mention of trade in dogs.

12. Carbohydrate values are not available in Rose's analysis of the mesocarp, so we cannot determine whether the opinion expressed by some Enga, that it could be used as a substitute for root crops for short periods of time, is correct.

13. An important topic for future research, for understanding both past and current nutrition of children, would be a systematic study of wild foods.

14. There is no mention of hunting wild pigs in early oral traditions. Enga claim that wild pigs are rarely found in areas above 1,200–1,500 meters, except for domestic pigs that have gone wild.

15. Kelly's data apply to lower altitudes, but a recent example from Enga similarly attests to the feasibility of pigs' surviving on forage at very high altitudes. When frost destroyed the sweet potato crop in 1972, the Bipi Kapii clan at Yumbis (2,550 meters) turned its pigs loose to forage for months without their showing any signs of suffering (Wohlt 1978:170).

16. Deaths during periods of frost were most numerous when clans had been at war and left too late for lower valleys out of fear of enemy attack along the way.

17. Though such statements imply a change in male-female productive relations through time, we have no grounds on which to specify what these meant for relative male-female status. It appears that women never had public influence within the time span considered.

18. Though we inquired again and again, nobody we asked knew historical traditions explaining why the sweet potato became a female crop.

19. Note that in the Lyipini origin tradition presented at the opening of this chapter, it is said that "hunters" and "gardeners" were distinguished by dress styles.

20. This myth was told to us by Paul Tamupae, Malipini Sakatawane clan, Sopas, upper Lai valley.

21. The "pandanus" language of the high forest replaced important words with indirect descriptions. For example, an arrow was called "a pointed thing"; a hand, "a holder"; a pig, "snort"; an opossum, "the night"; and a cassowary, "the owner of the land."

Chapter 3. Social Organization, Leadership, and Trade in the Early Generations of Oral History

1. The time of darkness occurred too early to be used as a reference point in Enga historical traditions, unlike the situation among the Huli (Ballard 1995).

2. Interestingly, Mawe's study (1987) and our brief investigations among the Kupa-Yakumba tribes of northern Mendi indicate that the Mendi, whose patrilineal de-

scent groups are much less cohesive than those of Enga, do have legends recording the exploits of heroes. These extend into the southeastern part of the Kandep region.

3. A few Enga expressed the opinion that people of the founding generation were very primitive and lived without fire, speech, and song. Since this idea is not widespread, not grounded in myth, and evaporates with further questioning, it is possible that it is not a traditional Enga concept but a distortion of evolutionary theory circulated after contact.

4. Marriage was clan exogamous in recent generations and appears to have been tribe exogamous in the founding generations, at least for smaller tribes.

5. The reason given for this war is a commonly used stereotype for a dispute over property. The context of Aimbatepa and Yamape history and the outcome of the war suggest that this large and vicious war was over Yamape's desire to gain land in the fertile Kaumbo valley. As in many historical narratives, tribes are personified by the names of their founders.

6. Further interviews that we conducted revealed that this war was part of a long series of conflicts in the area. Sassipakuni, a clan of the Yatapaki tribe, did not welcome all Yoponda clans but invited families to whom they were related in marriage. These in turn brought their relatives to the Saka, burdening Sassipakuni with many more immigrants than they had originally invited

7. Mawe (1987), in his brief study of north Mendi history, obtained strikingly similar results: that land was plentiful, that wars were over possessions and women, not land, and that large tracts of land were given as war reparations to allies.

8. The Enga word for trade, *aloa pingi*, "to alternate" or "to substitute," implies direct exchange or barter. It is distinguished from *tee pingi*, ceremonial exchange, in which wealth is distributed in public and reciprocated at a later date—preferably, but not necessarily, with "interest" added.

9. Origin traditions of the following tribes include some mention of the trade in salt for ax stone: Itokone, Yanaitini, Yambatane, Sambe, Pyapini, Malipini, Sakalini, Pumane-Wau, Aimbatepa, Depe, Ima, Limbini, Itapuni-Awaini, Ingi-Nenge, and Kupa-Yakumba.

10. An origin myth for the Yandap salt pools goes like this: a pig is said to have come from somewhere, perhaps Kandep, and dug out the depressions that form the salt pools while rooting for worms. When it urinated, the depressions were transformed into saltwater pools. A man came by, dipped some leaves into the pig urine, and ate them. Discovering that they tasted good, he began the salt trade. There is no way to judge whether this is an old myth or one composed within the past four to five generations.

11. These include Sakalini, Lyaini, Malipini, Yanaitini-Itokone, and Itapuni. Sambe is the only Lagaip tribe that has claims to the Yandap salt springs, and most of its claims were established three to four generations ago when the Yanaitini gave some of their land in the Yandap to Sambe as payment for hosting them in their Great War with Monaini.

12. Even today Yandap residents keep alternate houses in the upper Lai or Ambum valley where they reside for part of the year.

13. Itokone elders say that excavation of Sambe stone began long ago, before the span of historical traditions.

14. Other goods traded in later generations that are not specifically named in early oral traditions are black palm wood for bows, bamboo for knives and arrows, and cane for making belts, all of which came from low-altitude regions.

15. We have given names to routes for ease of reference, but it should be noted that some routes have several names, others have different names for different segments, and so on. To make more than a schematic map, one would have to travel all the major routes. Many routes existed from Kandep southward and from Porgera southward and westward. We do not have good information on the names of these.

16. The two major routes from Mulitaka to Maramuni are the Embele and the Masa (the latter not shown on map 6).

17. The Yanuni and Yambatane claim to be descended from siblings (see the Mount Giluwe myth in chapter 1); Yambatane and Itokone identify marriage ties between children or grandchildren of their tribal founders.

18. Oral traditions simplify. It could be that Saka tribes had a number of trade alliances with other tribes but that they receive no mention. The Yanuni-Yambatane-Itokone-Yanaitini alliance, however, is generally acknowledged to have formed the main axis of the trade.

19. Since then, the Pumane tribe has migrated to Porgera, where it is called Pulumani, and so much conflict has taken place near the Keta-Lagaip junction (and still does) that it is difficult to get further information.

Chapter 4. The Introduction of the Sweet Potato

1. Interestingly, Robert Lowie (1917) found that the Canadian Assiniboine Indians did not remember the introduction of the horse in their oral traditions, though it arrived in the eighteenth century and transformed their way of life.

2. An excellent and thorough discussion of the archaeological evidence and the influence of anthropological approaches on archaeological interpretation of the New Guinea evidence can be found in Ballard (1995).

3. Groups hosting the *aina pungi toko* at Walia include Yolo, Kundiki, Pandame, Yolene, Wanjepe, and Maeyango.

4. It should be noted that all foods harvested in abundance, whether taro, pandanus, or sweet potatoes, are sometimes distributed in large gatherings that include visitors from outside the clan.

5. Recent archaeological excavations have shown that this site has been occupied on a seasonal basis for at least ten thousand years (Jo Mangi, personal communication 1991).

6. This may refer either to famine foods or to root crops that were so scrawny that they resembled earthworms. In the reciprocal version they are scrawny roots.
7. Note that in the origin myth for Sangai bachelors' cults (chapter 8), the sacred plants also grew out of a woman's sexual organs.
8. The myth of Anda Kopa's distribution on Mount Giluwe (chapter 1; Didi 1982a, 1982b) possibly also relates to the distribution of the sweet potato.
9. *Moro* is still one of the terms used in central Enga for sweet potato. Waddell (1972:136) says that it is also used to describe the planting of sweet potato vines concentrically around the top of a mound.
10. The first concerns the migration of Yanaitini to Tetemanda (chapter 6), and the second, the migration of a branch of Yanaitini to Saka (meaning "fertile") in the upper Ambum valley near Anditale.
11. Some Enga oral traditions, like Huli traditions (Ballard 1995), claim that people had sweet potatoes before the eruption of Long Island and the "time of darkness" that occurred in the mid-1600s (Blong 1982).
12. Figures on taro yields are not available for Enga, but Clarke's (1977:163, Table 1) dryland trials for taro in the Mount Hagen district yielded between 5.0 and 5.3 metric tons per hectare for good soils after twelve months and less than 1 metric ton for poor soils after thirteen months. In contrast, Clarke's dryland trials for sweet potato yielded 18.4 metric tons per hectare for good soils and 9.3 metric tons for poor soils, both after eight months.
13. Such symbiotic relationships between hunter-gatherers and agriculturalists are common in both Asia and Africa.
14. The small mounds, (*yukusi*) are about 0.45 meters in diameter and 0.23 meters high, in contrast to the large mounds (*mondo*), with dimensions of some 3.8 meters in diameter and 0.6 meters high (Waddell 1972:42). The initial yield of a *mondo* is no greater than that of a *yukusi*, but multiple harvests are possible.
15. In addition, Waddell (1972:134–36) noted that the Enga of the middle Lai valley also recognize that the compost put into mounds fertilizes the soil and promotes the growth of sweet potatoes, and Sirunki residents are aware that the elevation of the vines on mounds protects them from light frost.
16. Sweet potatoes are a suitable food for small children, but as with most carbohydrates, young children do not consume sufficient amounts for adequate nutrition before they feel "full." Prolonged breast-feeding is thus important. Prior to contact, Enga women maintained a birth interval of at least three years. Today, store-bought foods rich in fat and protein have alleviated this problem, allowing for narrower birth spacing.

Chapter 5. Tribal Migrations and Warfare

1. One note of caution: when asked about migrations, people often gave subclans or lineages in other tribes founded by one of their members who moved to his wife's

or mother's clan. Such subclans and lineages are frequently named after the man's tribe or clan and can be distinguished from clan migrations only by careful questioning.

2. For instance, approximately 10 percent of clans given in genealogies are disbanded today.

3. Not included here is a small group, Kumbi, that came with Yatapaki (map 8:10). Whether or not they were an independent group at the time, and how large they were, is uncertain.

4. Bowers (1968) found that settlement of the upper Kaugel valley occurred within the last 200 to 250 years. If this is the case, then at least some of these groups did not stay long in Kola. A more precise date for the introduction of the sweet potato will shed light on the temporal dimensions of all post-sweet potato migrations discussed in this chapter.

5. This is a minimal estimate; it is possible that the rate of immigration into eastern Enga was considerably higher, for we recorded only immigrants who established independent clans or tribes, not individual families that left their own groups to become integrated into clans of eastern Enga. For a good example of what sort of impact the migration of individual families can have on the growth of clans, see Wohlt (1978).

6. We were told of some twenty to thirty clans that entered Enga from Kola, tried to settle in the Minamb or lower Lai valley, and were driven out or moved on into the Baiyer river area. This finding agrees with Bulmer's (1965) observation that most Baiyer clans trace their origins to the south or southwest. Since histories of transient groups are poorly remembered, there were probably more.

7. We have no reason to doubt these claims, because Enga readily admit that regions north of the Sau were inhabited. Certainly, though, this area had been inhabited some time in the past, for Enga immigrants report finding mortars and pestles while clearing gardens made by unknown previous inhabitants. The smaller of these were used as sacred stones for fertility rituals, and the larger mortars, which can be 80 centimeters or more in diameter and weigh some 40 kilograms, were filled with water and used as mirrors.

8. Exceptions include subclans of Depe and Sikini who established the independent groups of Waipalini, Lyakani, and Matea in the lower Lai (map 3).

9. The origin tradition for Lakani and Waitini places them at Laialam in the upper Sau, but they are said to have come originally from the Ambum.

10. The Sene-Yokasa were generally called Kungu-Tiaka after they left the Ambum valley.

11. Estimates of land areas taken are based on figures in Lea and Gray (1982).

12. The distinction between the southern part of the Kompiam district settled by Layapo migrants and the northern part settled by Mai from central Enga is still clear today.

13. For instance, "clans" called Putini, Kunjaini, and Matalini, presumably Wapi speakers, were encountered at Labalama; they intermarried with and lived side by side

with Enga immigrants. Most of these, and many Enga as well, perished in a severe epidemic during the fourth to fifth generation before the present. The description given by Councilor Laima Lalyo of Labalama indicates that it may have been small-pox. Encounters with people of different linguistic groups in areas to the north were not so peaceful.

14. There were, in addition, many wars that resulted in local dispersal of groups.

15. Migration to and from the Porgera valley is not included here, for we did not sys-tematically collect data from Ipili-speaking clans. Our brief study and the work of others indicates a continual flow of people to and from the Tari area and regions to the north.

16. For example, in some genealogies that we collected for new communities, up to 30-40 percent of clans, subclans, or lineages were formed by descendants of clan daughters whose husbands moved to their places of residence.

17. Of these, four cases involving similar misunderstandings are included in Table 6, because they are likely to have involved armed aggression, even though physical ag-gression is not directly mentioned. They are the only cases included in Table 6 for which the presence of organized armed conflict is not described in the narrative.

18. Murdering somebody on the land of another clan had severe consequences. Thus, an aspiring murderer had either to trespass on the land of the enemy clan to com-mit the murder, wait some years until an unsuspecting person from the enemy clan attended an event in the prospective murderer's clan, or hire a killer from an-other clan.

19. For instance, we were told of instances in which big-men hired murderers of rela-tively high status in other clans and paid them with land, wealth, and a wife, thereby establishing a long-term exchange tie. Then, after the murder was exe-cuted, they called a quick end to the conflict and used the war reparations to estab-lish further exchange ties with families in the enemy clan.

20. See Young (1986) for a sensitive discussion of this last point, and Allen and Giddings (1982) on the complexities of Enga warfare. Furthermore, some Enga say that if one does not want to participate in tribal fighting, then one must never start, for after one's first fight the spirit gets in the blood and men thereafter seek out wars in which they can participate. Certainly this does not apply to everyone, but it makes the point that the excitement and spirit of brotherhood "addicts" some men to fighting.

21. Both Bill Wormsley (Wormlsey and Toke 1985; personal communication 1985) and Doug Young (1995; personal communication 1995), who have studied Enga war-fare, also feel uneasy with Meggitt's thesis. The causes of warfare among the Enga are far more complex than land alone.

22. To quote Meggitt (1977:9) on this point: "The basic pre-occupation of the Mae is with the possession and defense of clan land. Participation in the Te, as in other prestations, is but a means to this end."

23. Lakau (1994) writes that he could not identify the six groups that Meggitt claimed were totally ousted from their land between 1950 and 1955. Try as we did, we

could identify the subclan but not the five clans, even though wars of this period are very well remembered. The tribal genealogies we collected for central Enga include the same clans as those published by Meggitt (1956); many of the narrators are the same. The information we obtained on the Great Wars of this period is much more comprehensive than Meggitt's, and both Akii and Lakau come from tribes in Meggitt's sample. Why we could not replicate Meggitt's result is puzzling. Early in our study we wrote Meggitt about this question, but he replied that he could no longer recall the names or extract them from his field notes. Without such information it is impossible to explore these cases further.

24. The Pumalini tribe of the middle Lai, who were totally dispersed at the time of the study, provides the best example.

Chapter 6. The Early Stages of the Tee Ceremonial Exchange Cycle

1. The Tee ceremonial exchange cycle that developed in eastern Enga is sometimes distinguished from other forms of *tee* by a number of terms: *yae tee* (*yae* refers to the phase of the Tee cycle when pigs are slaughtered and steamed pork distributed), *mena tee* (pig *tee*), and *mamaku tee* (pearl-shell *tee*). Because there is no fixed term for the Tee ceremonial exchange cycle, we stick to the terminology used by other authors (Meggitt 1974; Feil 1984) and call it simply "the Tee" or "the Tee cycle," using more specific terms to refer to other distributions: war reparations, payments to maternal kin, and so on.

2. There are some indications in historical traditions that the Apulini may also have spanned the division between eastern and central Enga, but their precise role in the early trade is not clear.

3. Itokone and Yanaitini had the only significant ax-stone quarry in Enga on their land, although historical traditions give no idea of how important these locally produced axes were in the early trade.

4. Another oral tradition describing this event tells of the marriage of Mama's only daughter, Kuwame, to Itokone. Whether the death of Mama's sons refers to a real event or is representative of a disaster that struck the Yambatane tribe in the past is not known. *Yama* is a disease believed to stem from social tension surrounding giving and sharing (Kyakas and Wiessner 1992).

5. Kitalini's isolation in the forest probably represents the *sauipi*, growth rites for boys practiced before the Sangai and Sandalu bachelors' cults spread to the Saka valley. During the *sauipu*, boys would periodically go to the forest, live in seclusion, and perform small rituals accompanied by the recitation of magic spells to make them mature and grow strong.

6. Alumanda was one of Yambatane's ceremonial grounds, and a traditional dance held there would have drawn people from the immediate area. Kitalini's leaving the women of Alumanda to go to a traditional dance held by Yandamani expresses

his desire to establish affinal relations in clans of another region, presumably because they would give him an advantage over new competitors in the trade.

7. The word *tee* comes from *tee lenge*, "to ask for," and most appropriately so, because in this distribution Kitalini reciprocated the wealth he had asked for.

8. At the time of the interview, the late Saiyakali, one of the oldest and most authoritative leaders in the Saka, was in his eighties and tired very quickly.

9. The Kandawalini Kaekini clan built a bridge over the Lai river that accidentally collapsed when an Itokone man crossed it. The man drowned, and Itokone used this as an excuse to fight Kandawalini.

10. *Tee ipae apae kende yakane ongonya piti ongo mee petala kepengena kepatana patapata lao pyo katape.*

11. In another version of the Kitalini legend given by Apanyo Mauwa of the Yambatane Watenge clan, Apanyo clearly states that Kitalini's was the first public distribution of wealth on the clan's ceremonial grounds.

12. Mupa means eldest or firstborn, so here Nenae is saying that he is not like his elder brother. The Gote cult is said by some to have come from Tambul via the Saka valley, and so in making this statement he is indicating that unlike his brother, he is following new trends coming from the east.

13. This is not always true for later generations, when some entire clans joined the Tee by phasing their death compensations into the wealth distributions of a Tee cycle.

14. From the testimony given by Palane Yakenalu, Itokone Nenae clan, Tilyaposa.

15. The information in this paragraph was given by the following individuals: for Yanuni, Katimbi Tumanga, a well-known Tee organizer; for Itokone Nenae, Palane Yakenalu, Waeyambu Teame, and Yambatane Saiyakali Patao Yaki; for Aluni Waiminakuni, Kamanjo Lyapoko; for Yakani Timali, Kambao Lambu and Itokone Palane Yakenalu; and for Lyipini Kepeo, Ambulya Yalao. Informants name only specific marriages that drew forefathers from their lineages or subclans into the Tee. Consequently, other clan members may name different marriages.

16. Since the legendary origin of the Tee dates to the founding generations, one cannot rule out the possibility that it actually originated earlier, though this seems unlikely.

17. This testimony is excerpted from a long discussion of the western routes of the Tee cycle. Additions in brackets are clarifications that came from Leme's earlier or later comments. The last statement, that the Tee "belonged to you, Yanaitini," was addressed to Akii Tumu, who is from the Yanaitini Kalepatae clan.

18. Apakasa, though an important Tee cycle organizer from the 1950s on, was almost a generation younger than most of our other informants. Interviews with older men make it clear that the events that "flooded" the Tee with wealth and participants happened in the four decades before contact with Europeans and laid the groundwork for its postcontact boom.

19. We are also grateful to Lopao of the Sikini Lyonai clan for fruitful discussion on this matter.

20. Different versions of the same historical accounts indicate that numerical figures vary greatly and are not passed on accurately from generation to generation. These figures should not be taken at face value. However, since trees were planted to mark the ends of lines of pigs distributed in the Tee, the observation that the number of pigs given in Tee cycle distributions increased from generation to generation can be taken with confidence.

21. The dynamics here closely mirror Watson's (1965a, 1965b, 1977) "Jones" effect: the desire or necessity to keep up with the neighbors.

22. See Meggitt (1965a:93) for a list of these prohibitions, which are most effective in distributing the marriage ties of subclan and clan members widely.

23. Though Lete knew little of the Great Ceremonial Wars of central Enga, here he unknowingly describes the flow of pigs from the Great War exchanges into the Tee cycle.

24. It is difficult even to estimate population density at this time, but certainly it was not high. Historical traditions indicate that these moves were not due to pressure on garden land but rather to conflict or the search for better land or ample hunting land near settlements. Population densities today in this region are between 20 and 30 persons per square kilometer of usable land (Lea and Gray 1982).

25. Statements that the Tee cycle originated in Tambul often refer to the fact that the east-west phase of a single Tee cycle starts in Tambul and then proceeds westward. The beginning or origin of one Tee cycle should not be confused with the historical origin of the Tee.

26. There is no reason to believe that the Moka developed earlier than the Tee. One Melpa big-man and ritual expert told Andrew Strathern (1971:235–36) that the Moka developed in the time of his father. His time estimate may be foreshortened, as Strathern proposes, but nonetheless it indicates that the origin of the Moka is also within the span of Melpa historical traditions.

27. In other words, they went as far as Paikona in the Nebilyer valley, approximately 40 kilometers by road from Walia.

Chapter 7. Cults for the Ancestors

1. *Koroka* (*karuka*) is the Melanesian Pidgin word for pandanus; *puli* wood is a symbol of strength.

2. Brennan (1977) and Gibbs (1975) made important contributions to the understanding of ancestral cult symbolism and underlying beliefs; Lacey (1975) made an initial attempt to place cults in their historical context.

3. Our discussion is restricted to cults held by entire clans or tribes. Elders could list some six to twelve cults and rituals formerly performed in their areas, the majority being smaller healing or fertility rituals held by individuals, families, or lineages. Descriptions of some of these can be found in Brennan (1977) and Meggitt (1965b). In addition to healing rituals and cults for the ancestors, spells (*nemongo*) were recited

and certain actions performed to accompany most personal enterprises of any importance, from planting gardens or making net bags to dressing for traditional dances (Kyakas and Wiessner 1992). Some spells conferred the desired outcome by unspecified magical powers, and others by invoking the sky people or ancestors.

4. Enga also believe that there were a number of forest demons, the protagonists in some Enga myths.

5. Enga find it hard to articulate the role of the sky people. This may be because beliefs concerning the sky people are older and are overlaid with those of more recent cults and the influence of Christian missionaries, some of whom drew parallels between the concepts of Aitawe and God, in contrast to the ancestors, whom they dismissed as evil forces.

6. A more elaborate form of the *yalyu* feast, similar to the *Ogla-morn* described by Strauss and Tischner (1962:283) for the people of the Mount Hagen area, was held in eastern Enga.

7. Opinions differ on whether the spirits of deceased females were included among the ancestors.

8. Neither we nor others (Meggitt 1965b; Lacey 1975; Brennan 1977), however, have found any indication that ancestors of one clan or tribe affected the affairs of others. For instance, they were not believed to harm aggressors who took a portion of their former land, as is stated by Lakau (1994), but rather resettled in new locations with their descendants.

9. The variation in terms used for the Yainanda cult is considerable. It was called Kepaka in the lower Lai valley; Ipalema in the Saka valley and some parts of the middle Lai; Yainanda or Kepakanda among the Mai Enga; and Talosa, Uaa Ende Yalo Pingi, Nuli Yaowenge, and Yanai Pingi in various parts of the Kompiam district. The general term *yainanda*—literally, "house of sickness"—is understood in all regions.

10. Our findings diverge from Brennan's (1977), owing to different methodologies. Brennan categorized cults on the basis of their features in the twentieth century, and his investigations apply only to eastern and central Enga. Our historical investigations indicate that the basic Yainanda cult was originally practiced throughout most of eastern and central Enga and was later overlaid by two more elaborate cults with similar aims: (1) the Amb Kor, or Female Spirit, cult that was brought into eastern Enga from Western Highlands Province, where it was called Enda (female) Yainanda, and (2) the Kepele cult, which was adopted into central Enga from the west and called by its "song" term, Aeatee. What Brennan describes as the Yainanda cult appears to be the Enda Yainanda, and what he described as the Aeatee, a version of the Kepele. Unlike Brennan, we found that the term *imbu* was commonly used for the Yainanda ritual not among the Mai but rather among the eastern Enga (see also Bulmer 1965:147), though it was sometimes applied to smaller ceremonies held before larger ones. Brennan glosses the term *imbu* as "anger," but with a different tone *imbu* also means "to sprout," a more likely meaning in this context.

11. Ancestral stones could be any oddly shaped stones found on clan land: prehistoric stone club heads, mortars (female stones), pestles (male stones), fossils, iron pyrite, and figurines of unknown origin. They were regarded both as skeletal remains of the ancestors—as such they were called *kuli* (literally, bones)—and as anonymous "persons" who wandered around clan land. Female stones were believed to reproduce and bear offspring. The collection of clan stones increased steadily with new finds, but sacred male and female stones were not mated as they were in the Kepele cult of the west. Some clans had as many as ten to twenty sacred stones. Though central to clan ritual, the sacred stones, as representatives of or repositories for the spirits of the ancestors, were not strictly inalienable possessions. Historical narratives tell of sacred stones being stolen to be used by the clan of the thieves and of clans being driven off their land, abandoning their stones, and finding new ones in their area of resettlement.

12. During later generations, when features of the Kepele or other cults were incorporated into Yainanda cults, ritual experts were summoned.

13. Only some Layapo-speaking clans on the north side of the Lai river did not hold the Yainanda cult.

14. In the Porgera region, the cult ritual is called *ipa nee* (to feed the water or pools) or *ekekaima*. A good description of the Ipili *ekekaima* can be found in Gibbs (1975: 52–55).

15. Dress for the *kaima* ritual was unlike that for any other ritual we know of. The bodies of celebrants were striped with red, white, and yellow ochre and then stamped with star or flower designs. Skirts of *pitpit* flowers were worn around the waist, and gourd masks covered the face, topped by cassowary feather headdresses.

16. Most elders had trouble specifying what the Kaima spirit was, though the term *kaima* means "bat" or "flying fox." At Tumundane in the Lagaip valley we were told that the Kaima spirit was a giant bird, *yumboto waipa,* believed to devour everything. For the Porgera valley, Philip Gibbs (personal communication 1997) says that an important element in the ritual is *utu koima,* a parrot with a strong beak that attacks when wounded. Gibbs feels that there may be a connection between a bird that attacks people when wounded and ancestral spirits coming back to "bite" people.

17. One explanation for this was that the women did it so that they could marry soon and bring bridewealth to their parents. Some men and women who played these roles report being haunted by the spirit of the Kaima throughout their lifetimes.

18. Dindi Gamu is the Huli name for the cult; the Enga name is Tondaka (meaning blood), taken from the major Dindi Gamu site in Enga territory. A name used frequently in the Porgera valley is Awalo.

19. A third branch, mentioned by Frankel, is said to continue from Tondaka northeastward to Bipipaite, from where the Huli believe the root of the earth ascends to the sky (Frankel 1986:23). Enga who participated in the Dindi Gamu at Porgera and Tondaka say that this is incorrect, that there is no Dindi Gamu site called Bipipaite in this region. Frankel proposes that this site is one described by Raich (1967) in his article on the *yupini* basketwork figure of the Kamani clan. Raich's work, however,

describes the figurines used in the Kepele, a cult that has little, if anything, to do with Dindi Gamu. The Huli say that Bipipaite is in the Paiela area (Chris Ballard, personal communication 1997).

20. The notion of a flood is inconsistent with the geography of the Porgera valley and no doubt stems from Tari, where floods are of serious concern (see Ballard 1995).
21. During a visit to Chris Ballard at Tari in 1991, Akii Tumu put several sources of information together to support the "natural phenomenon" hypothesis, which was then further supported by Ballard's work, our research, and references in the literature.
22. Christian concepts of the fiery end of the world further enforced these beliefs.
23. People from the following places, among others, were said to contribute: Longap, Karekare, Yumbis, Pauandaka, Liualiua, Puliape, Imapiaka, Aitiaka, Umbiatepa, Yanakali, Bioko, Wau, Kanyaka, Pelyap, and Winja.
24. Possibly "cooking with gas."
25. A Tondaka participant, upon seeing an article in *National Geographic* on the caves of Kentucky, indicated that the inside of the Tondaka cave was similar.
26. There are some suggestions presented in metaphorical speech that in the past, if it were judged that pigs did not suffice, humans may have been sacrificed, as they were at some Huli sites.
27. We encountered a few Enga in clans near Tumundane who thought that the Kepele might have originated from the Dindi Gamu, but men from clans who participated in both cults disagreed, pointing to their separate histories, underlying beliefs, and ritual procedures.
28. See also Gibbs (1978:440) on Kepele cult bark paintings: "The snake is said to be the same as the rainbow."
29. While undergoing purification rituals for having killed, a warrior is given a preparation of snake scales and ginger to eat, so that when the sun sees the rainbow colors that encircle him, it will consider him to be his neighbor, shield him from harm, and confer long life.
30. Like many symbols, that of the rainbow python, or *molopai,* can also take on the reverse significance and become the agent of death, as it is in the myth of Molopai's revenge. Its negative significance does not seem to have played a role in Kepele and other rituals until missionaries introduced the association of snake with evil in a biblical context. Among the Huli, snakes are a symbol of regeneration and immortality, peeling off their dead skins and living on (Goldman 1983:96).
31. In the past, western Enga had burial practices that were attributed to the Huli: removing skulls from the grave and placing them in rock shelters.
32. These principles do not apply to the Dindi Gamu cult.
33. This may not have been true for western Enga prior to the introduction of the sweet potato, when interaction with peoples to the north was said to have been more intense.
34. These signs could be the appearance of an oddly shaped stone, the sprouting of vegetation from cult sites in a nonsacred area, a strange vision or dream, and so on.

35. The prevalence of Enga "wandering woman" traditions is shared with other highland societies and probably relates to the transfer of cults along lines formed by marriage, among other things. Note that mythical men rarely transfer cults, possibly because this would imply domination by men of another group. We cannot definitively say that transfer followed the same principles in earlier generations as in later ones, but it is likely, because the exchange of everything involving supernatural power in Enga was carried out through "purchase." There is nothing that suggests this is a recent practice.

36. Other versions that we recorded, and the version collected by Wohlt (1978), say that Molopai's son bound his wounds with *take* leaves (a variety of pandanus) and cut a walking stick of *pai* (chestnut) to help him hobble home. Wherever he stopped he planted *pai* and *take,* and so these two trees mark the Kepele sites he founded.

37. The Molopai myth can be distinguished from those that fit it to local place in the fact that the latter, unlike many versions of the former, have little relation to cult rites.

38. For tribes that did not incorporate the "wandering women" theme in their Kepele cult traditions, settlement and agriculture are still dominant themes associated with the adoption of the cult and cult stones. Examples include the Molopai myth given earlier (see also Wohlt 1978:41–42) and the history of the Sambe, Pyaini, and Tekepaini tribes, in which it is stated that Kepele sites were established where tribal founders permanently settled, the Kepele stones representing their skeletal remains. The tribal and Kepele origin tradition of the Ima tribe tells of a woman, previously a gatherer and hunter of bush rats, who domesticates the first pig. Shortly afterward, she finds a human baby in a hawk's nest, takes him home, and raises him on pork fat. The child grows up to be the founder of the Aiyamane people of southeastern Kandep. The Payame origin myth for the Kepele ritual at Porgera is intertwined with a description of severe famine followed by the introduction of the sweet potato, which prompted Payame to settle more permanently in the Porgera valley. Several other Kepele origin traditions from the Porgera valley describe the same famine, the acquisition of land through marriage ties, settlement, the discovery of sacred stones, and the establishment of Kepele sites. Kepele origin myths such as those of Sakate, Tiwini, and Yambanima have to do with the defeat of forest demons who caused devastation to the tribe, clearance of forest, and the founding of Kepele sites.

39. Western groups that did not hold Kepele rites, such as those settled north of the Lagaip, never adopted cults centering on sacred stones, indicating again that ancestral stones were not formerly part of western Enga tradition.

40. The figure shown in the Air Niugini flight magazine of 1991 (no. 86, p. 30) displays a Sepik basketwork figure virtually identical to those used in the Kepele.

41. The past practice of placing skeletal remains in rock shelters is said to have come from the Huli. Rock shelters in the high country of Enga are said to abound with skeletal remains as a result of different burial practices in the past. Men of more recent generations used these remains in private rituals to attract wealth (*take*).

42. The most detailed version of this myth that we collected was narrated by Paul Tamupae of the Malipini Sakatawane clan. The same tradition is widely known in the Pyaini tribe of Mamale.

43. These places included Yakananda, Nandi, Sakalipa, and Sopas (map 12:52) in the Lai valley and Tiakamanda (51) in the Ambum.

44. Themes from the Molopai tradition also are found in legends of the Depe tribe of the middle Lai valley, which has two ritual sites associated with the python—one near Birip crater lake and another at Waimalemanda (map 12:54). The tradition is also reflected in an origin-related myth of the Amaini tribe near Wapenamanda and in one from the Aluni tribe, which occupies the ridge separating the middle Lai valley from the Saka valley. These last two tribes did not perform a variant of the Kepele cult.

45. Here, as in the Kepele of the Lagaip, the concept of women marrying in and bringing fertility to the tribes of their husbands is celebrated.

46. The reciprocal version is told in the Sambe Pupu clan, a story of a mother and daughter who leave that clan in a time of famine carrying sacred stones and bring them to Tetemanda and Irelya.

47. Owing to turmoil and tension in the Lagaip valley at the time of our study, our research on the Kepele was not as thorough as that on other subjects such as the Tee cycle and the Great Ceremonial Wars. Much remains to be done.

48. All five Kepele ritual experts with whom we conducted more extensive interviews had been trained by their fathers.

49. This was the case for parts of the Lagaip; we do not know whether it also applies to Kandep ritual experts.

50. Shelters for housing participants, initiates, and ritual experts and some of the other subsidiary houses were built not in this phase but just before the large performance.

51. Although the connection is not explicitly stated in testimonies, the rites involving the sacred gourd recall the famous myth from Mulitaka of how humans became mortal (see chapter 1).

52. The names used in the *mote* house at Kasap to describe the stages of filling the gourd and drinking from it depict symbolic weaning from the mother. The filling was called *wane manjanya pilyamo,* "the pregnant woman is expecting," the completion of this process, *wane mandipalamo,* "the baby is born," and the drinking of the sacred liquid by the initiates, *wane andu tuu nelyamo,* "the mother's breast milk is drying up."

53. Most Enga ritual experts prefer that spells accompanying the Kepele cult not be made public, in case their revelation should bring misfortune. That is why we cite none here.

54. The spiny ant eater (*tekea*) is an animal that is rooted to the ground because when frightened does not flee, but goes into the ground. It is used in metaphor to indicate that one should value the land, be tied to it, and not be moved.

55. A few remarks need to be made with regard to the work of D. Gray (1973). Al-

though her work on Enga puberty rites contains much valuable information, that on the *mote* rites of the Kepele cult (the Morea cult in Gray) is inaccurate, probably because the group with whom she worked did not hold the *mote*. To try to set the record straight: (1) The *mote* is part of the Kepele cult, not of the Kaima cult as Gray writes (1973:177). (2) Participants in the *mote* ritual were not called "warriors" (1973:133), nor was the purpose of the *mote* the training of warriors and admission into an inner circle of trusted warriors (1973:118). It was an initiation into the secrets of the spirit world. (3) Informants who had been through the *mote* said that in contrast to the Sangai, it was not a time of inculcating moral values (1973:179) and not one of direct instruction. The boys learned of the spirit world by experience. (4) Houses, gardens, and sweet potatoes and other domestic foods were not shown on the sacred plaques (1973:177). (5) The informants we talked to said that there were no taboos on food sharing for five months (1973:118), though indeed they were warned that if they shared information by revealing the secrets of the Kepele and *mote* to others, they would die. (5) Adolescents were not burned to death when the Kepele house was set aflame (1973:135). (A ritual expert stood on the roof of the burning house and mysteriously escaped the flames – Gray's interpreter probably mistranslated this event.) (6) *Tato*, southern beech, is a strong symbol of masculinity in Enga, not of femininity (1973:135).

56. Some tribes had smaller stones as well, usually river pebbles, representing the ancestors of each subclan. These were similarly fed and buried.

57. Pulumani (map 12:45) is an Ipili clan that had its origins near the Keta-Lagaip river junction and migrated to Porgera approximately six generations ago.

58. Procedures were as follows: the deceased was buried in a sitting position within a wooden structure, so that the head could later be easily separated from the body. About a year later, the head was removed from the grave and brought to the skull house by the son or brother of the deceased. The skull house was divided into at least two rooms – a front room with a hearth where private rituals for the deceased were carried out, and a back room where the skulls were deposited. The sacred stones were also kept in the skull house. If the skull house was shared by brother tribes, it was further subdivided into tribal skull rooms. The person who brought the skull to the house killed and steamed a pig outside, held a small ritual to protect the family from its ghost (together with a ritual expert), rubbed the skull in pork fat, and deposited it in the skull room.

59. For the skull house rites at Ipakatupya, eight ritual experts from the Sakate tribe and eight from the Yambanima tribe participated.

Chapter 8. Bachelors' Cults

1. This quote, freely translated, is taken from a long passage. While the term Sangai can refer to the cult as a whole, to the period of seclusion, and to the sacred objects (see also Meggitt 1964a:210), here it indicates the sacred objects. The second

occurrence of *endakali* has been glossed "men" rather than "people," for when the quote is placed in context it clearly does not refer to both men and women.

2. The idea that contact with menstruating females and menstrual blood is harmful to men is widespread throughout the highlands. Often this complex of beliefs is called pollution, a term we avoid because the central concept is one of harm rather than one of filth.

3. Contamination is reciprocal. Male semen can also be harmful and damage a fetus during the last months of pregnancy; the male gaze can inflict harm on a newborn (Gray 1973; Kyakas and Wiessner 1992).

4. Contamination beliefs appear to be very old, for in all myths and the earliest of historical narratives it is taken for granted that men and women have always lived in separate houses and women have observed menstrual taboos. Note that unlike in some societies along the fringes of the highlands of Papua New Guinea (Herdt 1984), the eastern highlands, and other parts of Oceania, Enga do not practice ritualized homosexuality in their bachelor' cults or in any other cults.

5. A myth with many variations explains this east-west continuum: Originally, a woman and her daughter cooked food by squatting over it and broiling it with vaginal fire (see also Frankel 1986:97–98). Men who partook of this either died or were stricken ill. A man took the matter into his own hands and decided to undermine a bridge that the two crossed regularly. The bridge collapsed under their weight, and both were carried down the current. The mother was rescued first, only partially cooled. The daughter, fished out downstream, was well cooled. The "hot" mother migrated west and the "cool" daughter east, and so men who marry western women must take strict precautions for sexual intercourse. East and west have no fixed border; the central Enga regard Tayato and Ipili women as more dangerous, and the Enga of the Porgera valley regard Huli women as such.

6. The Sangai was not exclusively for clan or subclan members; in certain cases, young men attended performances of clans or subclans where they had close kinship ties, such as the clan of mother's brother.

7. Following Meggitt (1964a), we have called the Sangai a bachelors' cult, although its status as such can be debated. It can also be seen as a rite of passage into manhood, because the relationship with the spirit woman ends only upon payment of bridewealth for a human bride.

8. For central Enga, first-year bachelors wore aprons to just above their knees and four tapa-cloth caps with flaps hanging just below the eyeline, lifted with two small sticks inserted into the hair or behind the ear. Second-year bachelors wore aprons to the knee and three tapa caps, and third-year bachelors, aprons below the knee and two tapa caps. Fourth-year bachelors had ankle-length aprons and round *kangala* wigs. From the fourth year on, bachelors wore the full ceremonial dress of men, with *balu* wigs. Juniors carried spears; seniors, bows and arrows; and seniors attending for the last time, long, solid sticks and small net bags over their shoulders (see also Schwab 1995: 32), indicating their entry into a life of hard work.

9. Comparison of the poetic structure and content of such traditions from area to

area, as suggested by Lacey (1975) in his excellent discussion of Sangai poetic traditions, would undoubtedly yield insights into patterns of diffusion.

10. Girls also practiced such rites of growth (Kyakas and Wiessner 1992), although these did not involve extended seclusion.

11. We did not look into this for the Nete, Penale, Hewa, or Duna.

12. Lacey (1975:213–14) collected one Sangai origin myth from the Saka valley that attributed Sangai origins to Mount Giluwe. We followed this up carefully but could find nobody in the Saka valley who traced Sangai origins to this region, even in the Winau clan where Lacey recorded the myth. All of Lacey's other interviews place Sangai origins in central Enga. It appears that this myth was adapted by a Winau senior bachelor to the pervasive belief in the Saka valley that all cultural traditions originated from Mount Giluwe. Such personal interpretations occur occasionally and underscore the importance of verifying claims at both ends and looking for regional trends.

13. Ipili bachelors' cults are called Umaritsia, and those of the Huli, Ibagiya. Eastern and southeastern neighbors of the Enga, such as the Mendi and Melpa, do have rites to promote the growth of boys but not true bachelors' cults (Strauss and Tischner 1962).

14. Exchanges of other cults between the Lagaip, Kandep, and Porgera were readily acknowledged.

15. Supporting evidence for this idea comes from the fact that the Female Spirit cult, which also centers on a spirit woman who assists men, came into Enga from the south.

16. Note in this context that the sweet potato was the only food brought to the Sangai cult house, in contrast to other cults and ceremonial occasions, for which taro was an important ritual food.

17. The recording was made by Danny Kili Nembo, a colleague in our project and a fellow clansman of Isingi's. Isingi, a former senior bachelor, is well known for being one of the masters of Sangai lore. Pesone Munini made a preliminary translation of the myth, and Akii Tumu transcribed and retranslated a number of critical passages to capture finer shades of meaning.

18. Consumption of pandanus is a widely used image associated with sexual relations in highland New Guinea.

19. Though unaware of the concept of first marriage to a spirit woman, most other researchers have given indirect evidence of this. For example, Lacey (1975:215n30) noted that human qualities were attributed to the sacred objects and that *lepe* plants were often given female names. Lacey (1975), Meggitt (1964a), Gibbs (1975), and Schwab (1995) have all noted that the *lepe* and *penge* respond to the behavior of the bachelors, withering or retracting if they have had sexual contact with women.

20. The culprit must then provide the wealth to purchase new sacred objects.

21. Bamboo flutes were played when approaching the *lepe* and *penge.*

22. See A. Strathern (1979a) for a discussion of this theme in the Female Spirit cult.

23. Gibbs (1975:182) gives a spell from the Porgera valley concerning the menstruation of the mythical woman which was recited upon the plugging of the bamboo containers with *makua* leaves. Biersack's (1982) description of this part of the Paiela Sangai is similar to that given by Isingi, though there are many substantial differences between beliefs and rites of the Enga and Ipili bachelors' cults. These are in part related to the fact that separation between the sexes and reinforcing pollution beliefs are much stronger among the Ipili than among the central Enga.

24. It was through their symbolic marriage to the mythical woman that the bachelors were believed to acquire the wealth needed to pay bridewealth for a human wife, just as men were supposed to seek the approval of their first wives for polygamous marriages and ask them to raise pigs for the bridewealth. If these procedures were followed, the spirit woman was believed to be content with the second marriage of the bachelor, this time to a human wife.

25. Whether this bachelors' cult was called Sangai or whether the narrator chose Sangai for want of another term is uncertain.

26. Recited by Tindiwi Loape of the Yomondaka clan at Porgera.

27. Clan and tribe names called include Sambe of Laiagam; Kunalini of northern Kandep, Sirunki, and Ambum; Itapuni Kala near Wabag; Ima and Alitipa near Kandep station; Awaini Sapipi and Yanaitini Lanekepa and Kia near Wabag; Sakate of the Lagaip; and so on.

28. When peeling off the leaves of the sacred *lepe* plant to rub on their bodies, the bachelors also recited the names of big-men.

29. Recorded by Danny Nembo Kili; recited by Namuni Pyapala, Kombane Komaini clan, Awalemanda, Ambum valley.

30. Lacey (1975:213), in plotting the distribution of the *lepe* plant and sacred fluid in bamboo containers (*penge*), found the *penge* to be limited to clans in eastern Enga and parts of central Enga and the *lepe* plant to be used throughout Enga. Our investigations did not completely confirm these results.

31. A more thorough study of the Sangai and the trade of sacred objects may well reveal other patterns and provide better explanations.

32. Narrated by Pastor Alo Peter, Pumane Kelyanyo, Waimalama (Tumundan), Lagaip valley, and by Sakatao Waso, Yandape Konowai, Tumundan, Lagaip valley.

33. It appears that Kelyanyo big-men or senior bachelors at this time were extremely enterprising, creating their own line of sacred objects rather than importing them and portraying them as so powerful that all clans in the area sought cuttings from these prized *lepe* plants.

34. Throughout Enga, wealth magic, *take,* was purchased individually from experts or transmitted to small groups of young men who retired to a men's house or forest hut for three to seven days of instruction. Dreaming and dream interpretation were important parts of these sessions. Experts who imparted the magic and spells were well paid.

35. Systematic interviewing of senior bachelors in every Layapo subclan, particularly those along the route of the early Tee, might reveal more.

36. The discussion here began in response to our question about whether and why attitudes toward women were different between eastern and central/western Enga. No doubt Ambone's views have been strengthened in recent decades by the efforts of missionaries to foster cooperation between the sexes; nonetheless, his ideas on east-west differences in the past and on the correlation between gender relations and success in ceremonial exchange are shared by others.

37. A family consisting of a man, several wives, and male servants was typical for big-men in the Tee cycle from at least the fourth generation on. Ambone attributes it to Yanaitini Kia simply because it was the closest clan to his that was focal in the Tee cycle.

38. This removed an important source of historical information.

39. A study of the spread of the Sangai-Sandalu that included every Layapo subclan would undoubtedly uncover fascinating connections between clans and identify nodes of power and influence in the last three to four generations.

40. It is interesting in this context that during our study of women's traditions (Kyakas and Wiessner 1992) we found few Layapo women who knew protective spells concerning sexual intercourse and menstruation, except for some Yambatane and Waimini women in the Saka valley. It seems likely that these spells were imported with the Sangai in the fifth to sixth generation.

41. Waddell (1972:108) reports that a Sandalu emergence festival held by the Yakumani clan at Kumbasakama in 1966 attracted some twenty-five people.

42. Schwab did not punctuate this, so we have added the two periods for clarity. The words in brackets are his.

43. We have, in addition, bypassed many fascinating areas of investigation: purification, concepts of physical attractiveness, dreams, and dream interpretation, among others.

Chapter 9. War Reparations and Leadership

1. Homicide and other damage payments following warfare are generally called compensation in the literature on Enga. We use the term "war reparations," however, because they are precisely that: a way of repairing ties. For the Melpa, A. Strathern (1971:90) correctly distinguished war reparations to allies from compensation to enemies, but since the Enga use the same terms and follow the same procedures for both kinds of payments, we do not make this distinction.

2. Funerary payments, bridewealth, and child growth payments were relegated to lineages or subclans (see Meggitt 1971).

3. In a sense, the same principle holds true for bridewealth as for war reparations. Payments of bridewealth cannot replace the labor and reproductive potential of, and the love of the family for, a woman who marries out of her clan. Thus payments made in a social context were given to the woman's family periodically throughout her lifetime in the form of child growth payments, payments for in-

jury to the woman or her children, and payments upon their deaths (see also Godelier 1995a:17–18 for an interesting discussion of debts that cannot easily be acquitted).

4. Narrated by Alo Peter, Pumane Kelyanyo clan, Tumundan.

5. *Kyoa* is the word for somebody truly foreign and is sometimes used to denote a cannibal. The lower side is the north side and probably refers to the Hewa.

6. In another version, the woman goes to Yoko and hangs her shells on a *tai* tree; from there she goes to Pusa Yape, where she hangs them on a *lioko* tree. Then she moves on to Pumakopau and finally to Walesia in Nete territory, where people are dwarfs and strange things are said to occur. The narrative ends as she travels west to a place surrounded by water, perhaps lake Kopiago.

7. The Gulu "legend" is a form of oral tradition concerning the exploits of a "folk hero" that is common in the Mendi area (Mawe 1987), but not in Enga.

8. Though such growth and fission of clans within a tribe is an old theme, it appears to have accelerated between five and six generations ago as a result of population increase. For example, Lacey (1979), in his study of the foundation of ceremonial grounds of the Yakani tribe, found that prior to five generations ago Yakani had five ceremonial grounds. During the fourth and fifth generations, nine new ceremonial grounds were built, and during the second and third generations, another four, as more independent clans within Yakani were established.

9. Meggitt (1977) has shown that Enga tribal wars between about 1900 and 1950 frequently led to the loss of some land, but the plots vacated were often too small to be split with allies.

10. War reparations were almost always phased into the Tee cycle in eastern Enga, and whenever convenient in central Enga.

11. Lineages and subclans each had their leaders (Meggitt 1967), but if any of these were to become clan leaders, they had to play a significant role in organizing war reparations, among other things.

12. There are some exceptional Kandep big-men, particularly those within the sphere of the Mendi ceremonial exchange system, called Mok Ink in Mendi and Mena Yae in Enga, who gained extraordinary influence by marrying ten to twenty wives. Tindiwi of the Yomondaka clan near Karekare, the father of the former premier, is one example, and Nenge Pasul of the Aimbatepa tribe near Kandep station is another. Pasul, Nenge Pasul's father, married nineteen wives and had twenty-five sons. It is said that each of his wives looked after twenty to thirty pigs. Nenge Pasul himself, a member of the national parliament who died in 1989, had twenty wives.

13. A Western equivalent might be the old English song "Ring Around the Rosy," whose meaning is no longer known to most people who sing it today.

14. We could get no information on the history of courtship songs.

15. Lungupini was the tribal founder (tenth generation). The idea that prior to the time of tribal founders people were very primitive and might not even have had speech is not uncommon but certainly is not a stereotype shared by all.

16. Though it is not possible actually to translate this song, a number of the words in-

dicate that it is a jingle about clearing a garden, fencing, harvesting, and leaving the garden to lie fallow.

17. We are grateful to Nitze Pupu and Minalyo Katape of the Yakani Kalia clan for productive discussions on this topic.

18. It should be noted that after the murder of a man, rape of a woman, or some other incident of violence, reparations could be paid immediately to avoid warfare.

19. War reparation procedures differed from region to region in the twentieth century, much of the variation resulting from their links to larger ceremonial exchange systems such as the Tee cycle, the Melpa Moka, or the Mendi-Wola Mok Ink. Clans of easternmost Enga, whose big-men imported and exported shells from the Melpa Moka, and those of Kandep, who participated in the Mendi Mok Ink (Lederman 1986:162–65) added a final round of prestations to the war reparations made to allies, involving the distribution of pearl shells. Among clans of northern Kandep and the Lagaip that did not participate directly in larger exchange systems, war reparation distributions were more centralized, with payments given to a big-man in the lineage who then distributed them.

20. If a woman or child died a violent death, this payment was called *enda buingi* or *wane buingi*, respectively.

21. The work of Ploeg (1969) on peacemaking among the Dani provides many interesting parallels.

22. The reasons given here are based on interviews with Kepa Pupu, Yoponda clan, Walya, Minamb valley.

23. Misunderstandings over reparations paid by Melpa to Enga today indicate a true divergence of concepts, the former expecting the transfer of wealth to extinguish the debt for a human life lost. It is perhaps for this reason that Melpa reparation exchanges could escalate into competitive exchanges between giver and receiver (A. Strathern 1971). By contrast, in Enga, where reparations did not erase the debt but initiated ties that compensated for the loss of a person over a lifetime, cooperation rather than competition prevailed between giver and receiver. Exchange then could become a way to peace but not a form of competition alternative to warfare between two clans, as it could be for the Melpa.

24. The *kauma pingi* was practiced in central Enga but not in other areas, so far as we could determine.

25. Similarly, today, when tribal fighters must pay to receive medical care for wounds received in battle, the hat is passed and funds gathered at the beginning of a war.

Chapter 10. *Yanda Andake*

1. *Yanda andake* means literally "great war" or "big war."

2. Small-scale battles were held between the Kandawalini Kaekini clan and Itokoni clans in the middle Lai valley, primarily for purposes of the exchange that ensued, but these did not resemble the Great Wars in scale and organization. Some elders

said that in the Kopona area near Luma, a Great War was fought between Yanjini-Pakaini and Lakani. Although this had some features of a Great War, the few descriptions we could obtain depicted it as a large, conventional war.

3. Part of the difficulty in determining whether or not the Great Wars existed prior to the fifth generation is posed by the fact that the term for them, *yanda andake,* can also be applied to unusually large conventional wars.

4. Because the Great Wars were largely discontinued before European contact, they occupy but a few pages in the ethnographic record (Meggitt 1977).

5. Conventional wars were also hosted if opponents did not occupy adjacent land, though such cases were exceptions. In conventional wars, however, land could be gained and given to hosts, while in the Great Wars it could not.

6. Beliefs about *yalya* (*yalyakali*) are somewhat inconsistent. The *yalya* protect all people—there are no clan- or tribe-specific *yalya.* Nonetheless, people often talk of their own *yalya,* just as Christians say "my" God or "our God."

7. For example, in one episode of the Itapuni-Awaini versus Malipini-Potealini Great War, a Great War leader from the Awaini Kaealu clan named Mumu was shot in the eye but did not die. The enemy sang:

   Yanakini tambuaka pyao lyaa nyeteno kambi lenge palyomoli pyapomo.

   Son of a dog [Mumu's father was named Yana, meaning dog], if you kill a brown pig in a healing ritual, your beautiful eye will reappear in its place.

   In a Great War battle between Sene-Yokasa and Yakani, the former gloated over the death of a Yakani man:

   Pangalikini amenyaka kingi palyolo lape, enda apinya yangi mandenge lape.

   Pangali's son was fat where my hand went in, wondered who was the woman who fed him?

8. In the Lyaini-Sakalini versus Pumani-Aiele war, this was also called *yuku pingi.*

9. Additionally, in the Sambe versus Kunalini war discussed in chapter 5, Kunalini appears to have continually tried to turn the vicious struggle into a Great War, but Sambe would accept no less than totally ousting them from the area.

10. Pisoto's is the only eyewitness testimony of the Yanaitini-Monaini Great Wars that we were able to collect, but it is not detailed or vivid enough to add further insights. Other, secondhand accounts recorded in clans of Monaini, Sambe, Lyaini, Kunalini, and Yanaitini outline some features. The political, economic, and logistical contexts of the battles and subsequent exchanges are internally consistent concerning the main points, but the accounts give no good descriptions.

11. In the highly dispersed communities of the Kompiam area, the concept of tribe is weak and clans are usually spoken of as the highest level of organization. Sene-Yokasa clans (also called Kungu-Tiaka) have little sense of tribal identity. In this pas-

sage, Kopio alternately uses Yokotini, the Sene-Yokasa clan nearest the site of the war, and Sene-Yokasa to refer to the enemy side.

12. Aiyele is the name of both a large tribe and one of its constituent clans.

13. War reparations to enemies were not, as a rule, paid in the Great Wars. This exception may be due to the fact that the clans involved were becoming linked through the Tee cycle.

14. The Yanaitini clans of Piao Kumbini, Piao Kaimanguni, Piao Maipilai, Kokope, Neneo, Kalepatae, and Yapakone hosted Malipini-Potealini, Piao clans assuming the major responsibility. Some families from the Yanaitini Lanekepa clans also hosted warriors.

15. This is because organization of the Tee cycle and Great Wars was in the hands of a few big-men only, men who are now deceased.

16. This integration was also confirmed in a testimony by Yakopya Yangomina of Apulini Talyulu.

17. Apparently it was fought after the Leahy brothers made their disastrous journey into central Enga in 1934 (Connolly and Anderson 1987), and before Taylor's Hagen-Sepik patrol in 1938-39. So far as we could determine, neither arrived during a Great War or subsequent festivities.

18. The distributions occurred in this order: upper Lai valley: Potealini Wambili, Kombatau, and Langape; Malipini Sakatawane, Maia, Nate, Metaene, and Kamaniwane. Ambum valley: Malipini Sakatawane at Kasi; Potealini Awape, Anae, Bia, Maiome, Angaleane, Kombane, and Wailuni. Sau valley: Malipini and Potealini clans near Paip.

19. In the last Great War episode, Yanaitini reciprocated the *lome nyingi* by a final large pig kill, something that seems not to have been customary for the other Great Wars.

20. Meggitt's (1977) studies of warfare between 1900 and 1955 were carried out largely among the tribes involved in the Malipini-Potealini versus Itapuni-Awaini Great Wars and thus give an idea of the frequency and nature of the smaller, intra- or interclan wars that took place between episodes of the Great Wars.

21. We asked about this directly and indirectly many times in many different ways.

22. Anton Ploeg (personal communication 1995), who has firsthand experience among the Dani, also finds little similarity between the Great Wars of the Enga and the Dani.

23. The term *watenge* can also be applied to fight leaders in smaller, conventional wars.

Chapter 11. Later Developments in the Tee

1. Figures for the fifth generation are based on information given in historical narratives. These were independently confirmed by informants in several clans. Those for the second generation (1945-75) were calculated from several sources. For clans in Enga Province, censuses of current clans and their locations within the sphere of the Tee cycle in the 1950s yielded a total 296 clans. Big-men interviewed at

Tambul listed another 15 clans in the Kaugel valley and 14 in the north Mendi valley who took part in the Tee. The number of participant clans in the Baiyer river area was estimated from Bulmer (1965:134) to be 39, giving a total of 364. We do not have figures for the Nebilyer valley or for routes connecting it to Tambul, but certainly 10 to 20 clans of this area were involved. It should be recognized that in most of the Kompiam-Kopona area (Feil 1984:26) and among some tribes of eastern Enga (Waddell 1972:108), Tee festivals were organized and hosted by subclans. Since clans in the Kompiam area have an average of 3.8 subclans each, and those of eastern Enga, 4.0 (Feil 1984: 22, Table 2), in the largest Tee cycles as many as 500-600 Tee festivals could have been held by the time the Tee had swept through all clans in the network.

2. The starting points for Tee cycles were recognized to be at Tambul, Saka Laiagam, and Tetemanda until approximately the 1920s. With the addition of feeder routes in the twentieth century extending far beyond these places—for example, into the valleys of Western Highlands Province, northern Kompiam, and the Yandap—the starting points became less clearly defined. It is probably fair to say, however, that once a Tee cycle beginning along a feeder route reached Tetemanda, Saka Laiagam, or Tambul, it was recognized that a new phase of the cycle had been successfully launched. The work of Feil (1984) indicates that numerous attempts to initiate a new cycle might begin in more remote areas but fail to catch on.

3. Here we use the Enga terms or those applied by Meggitt: "initiatory gifts" for *saandi* and "main gifts" for *tee pingi*. We use the Enga term *yae* (from *mena yae*, cooked pork) for the distribution of cooked pork that Meggitt glossed as "return gifts." Feil (1984:39) glossed *saandi* as "the debt incurring payment," an appropriate term but awkward to use in discussion. His gloss for *tee pingi*, "debt requiting payment," seems less appropriate, because the main gifts do far more than requite *saandi* gifts.

4. The vast majority of the wealth was promised or given to partners privately in advance, on the understanding that it would be returned later for formal, public distribution during the clan's Tee festival. The suspense came from the fact that few knew the totality of private dealings of others until their success was revealed in public. (See Foster 1993 for an interesting discussion of the role of "revelation in exchange.)

5. A song sung in the third to fourth generation by the wife of Yomo, a Tee organizer from the Yanaitini Kia clan, recalls the domestic problems such voyages could incite. Yomo returned home to hear his wife, frustrated that one of the pigs was destroying the house, singing the following song:

> *Talemakini yae lyokao katapu lao yapa ipa naenge, yaepete tanao pua tao tanao.*

> Talemakini's son [Yomo], away for the Tee, does not return quickly. I wish I could urinate in his Tee pool.

He crept sheepishly into the men's house and waited until she cooled down.

6. Liuates, though a mere thirty kilometers northeast of Lenge as the crow flies, is a three-day journey over rugged terrain. It falls outside the normal sphere of interaction of people of central Enga.

7. In another recording, Kopio says the men were Kiua and Matimba, Matimba probably being another name for Makaenge.

8. Both kinds of leaves are cordyline—*ambano* are used to line earth ovens, *yuku* are worn to cover men's buttocks. *Yuku* are often used in symbolic speech to represent men; hence, in this metaphor, not being able to put on *yuku* leaves means that they were unable to recruit allies in warfare because of their low status and "poverty."

9. Whether or not Kipame's family encouraged her to leave her husband to spark the conflict is not stated. Certainly such plots were well within the range of strategies employed in Tee politics.

10. That most of the clans on the north side of the middle Lai (that is, all Kandawalini clans, Tinilapini, Lungupini clans in the Lai, and some Depe and Yakani clans) were not included in the Tee until the fourth generation is confirmed in their own histories. Thus, even though Leme's statement that all northside clans were drawn into this specific Tee is an exaggeration, it does hold true for the majority.

11. See Clark (1991) for an excellent discussion of the history and symbolism of pearl shells in the highlands in general and among the Wiru in particular.

12. Feil (1984:ch. 3) discusses the effect of pearl shells on the Tee and the Moka. We do not have enough information to add to his ideas except to mention that before the colonial period, salt, stone axes, and other trade goods played a very significant role in the Tee cycle.

13. If this was indeed the case (and certainly more research is needed), it gives some interesting insights into the processes of dialect group formation.

14. An Enga proverb describes the wisdom of marriages between active influential families:

> *Itate tenge mendalapo maki petatenopa itaita pingina pita, mendai iki ongome kapa napenge.*

> When two pieces of burning wood are brought together, they generate a great heat; one alone does not.

To give some examples of how the Tee cycle was engineered through strategically placed marriages: in the fourth generation, when Yakani Pendaine campaigned to lengthen Tee chains, he did so through affinal ties, and when he sought to fix the course of the Tee cycle at the western end with the cooperation of Apulini and Yanaitini, he called on maternal ties. The leading big-men in Apulini, Yanaitini Kia, and Kalepatae with whom he negotiated were all sons of Yakani Timali women. The eventual integration of the "owners of the fight" in the Great Wars into the Tee cycle was similarly achieved: the Itapuni and Malipini Great War leaders Satutu and Mioko, born of Yanaitini Kia women, used their maternal ties to draw their clans into the Tee cycle.

15. Recall that Aeatee is the term used for the Kepele in song in parts of western Enga.

16. These taboos forbade Itapuni-Awaini clans from eating food prepared by Yanaitini clans who hosted Malipini and Potealini, and the latter from eating food prepared by Yanaitini Kia.

17. From the testimony of Pyaene Pyaso of the Yanaitini Kia clan. Others expressed similar opinions.

18. Here the speaker means ritually prepared food, not merely that provided for the general public. Later he acknowledged that key Tee organizers from other clans also participated.

19. Additionally, some cults that had originated in the Lagaip, been exported to the Lai, and been altered to fit the needs of growing ceremonial exchange systems there were later reimported in their new form by Lagaip tribes as Tee routes moved westward. For instance, the Pyaini tribe of Mamale (Laiagam) traces its Pokalya cult to Yakani Timali, who had adopted some elements of the Kepele at an earlier date, transformed it into the Pokalya, and exported it back to Laiagam.

20. At the time we collected information on the cults discussed in this section, serious tribal fighting was taking place in Tambul, there were armed holdups along the highway, and a devastating tribal war was going on in the Saka with the use of fire-arms. Consequently, we were unable to return to Tambul, and people in the Saka were tense and less forthcoming than usual. Our information is thus not as com-plete as we would have liked.

21. Katimbi Tumanga of the Yanuni Kisimu clan of Tambul told us that a Kisimu man named Melene purchased the cult with pigs, pearl shells, cowrie shells, stone axes, and *kaleta* shells at a place called Kambetepa in the Mendi area in the fifth to sixth generation.

22. A testimony by Apakasa of the Depe Liala clan at Birip specified how that clan's Pokalya was used to gather people for planning the Tee cycle.

23. How great a concern loss of life was in the Great Wars is difficult to determine. Certainly for Pendaine personally it was, for he is said to have been deeply shaken when he killed one of his own clansmen in battle, mistaking him for an enemy.

24. Later in the interview, the speaker, Taliu, described his participation in the Great Wars.

Chapter 12. Competition and Cooperation

1. Surprisingly, the idea that display in the Tee was important for deterring aggres-sion was strongly rejected by all elders with whom we discussed the matter. They stressed that display incited jealousy and that it was the act of giving that deterred aggression, whether a clan was weak or strong.

2. Such a family history is the result of an unusual combination of circumstances: at least one skilled narrator in each generation who kept the tradition alive and intact and the presence of a man in each tier of the genealogy whose accomplishments were considered noteworthy.

3. In most cases Kopio and Kambao speak of clans, not tribes. For clarity, we have added the tribal name before the clan name the first time each clan is mentioned in a section. After that we use the clan name for ease of reading.

4. In using the term Tee, he is referring to the Tee cycle only.

5. These are commonly expressed views of exchange prior to the seventh generation.

6. Here Kopio has taken for granted that smaller exchanges such as bridewealth exchanges and exchanges with maternal kin had been held since Ipawape's time, as mentioned earlier.

7. That Timali was the first Yakani clan to join the Tee cycle in the fifth generation is supported by a study conducted by Lacey (1979) on the founding of Yakani ceremonial grounds and the entrance of Yakani clans into the Tee cycle. Clans of the east and Yanaitini at Tetemanda, however, joined at an earlier date.

8. According to other testimonies, Tee cycles at this time began in the Saka valley, although men in Timali may not have been aware of this.

9. The former counting system in western and central Enga was based on body parts, starting with the tips of the fingers and moving up the arm, over the head to the nose, and back down the other side to reach twenty-seven. The counting system used in the Tee cycle went by twos up to forty and then continued with one bundle of forty and two, four, six, and so on. Theoretically, it could go as far as forty bundles of forty or further.

10. Numbers of pigs given in historical traditions do not appear to be accurately remembered—for any single event, they sometimes vary greatly from testimony to testimony. The figure of sixty pigs is certainly a guess and probably just a way of saying "many" for the time.

11. Other testimonies agree with this observation for the western route, although in eastern Enga rivalries are said to have begun earlier.

12. Families, particularly wealthy ones, loaned out pigs to others to care for, giving the caretaker a fee for his or her efforts—for example, a piglet born to the pig, contributions to bridewealth, or support in disputes. Whether this was a new practice or a long-standing one is uncertain. *Kamongo* sometimes used "concern for their pigs" as an excuse to interfere and try to make peace when war broke out in these clans.

13. The status of Pendaine as an extraordinarily skilled and influential organizer of the Tee is acknowledged independently in historical traditions of clans throughout the Tee network. Such boasting statements, however, rarely occur outside of histories told within the family.

14. Infanticide is extremely rare in Enga, and boys are not necessarily preferred over girls, for marriages of the latter form essential exchange ties. Kambao later agreed that there might have been more behind this incident than was recorded in oral tradition—for instance, the child might have been deformed. According to Enga belief, deformed children can be the result of broken sexual taboos, particularly those that apply during performances of ancestral cults. A deformed newborn would thus be an embarrassment to the family.

15. From the clan identification attached to his name, Neowali Yakani was from the

Aiyele Neowali clan, which is located around Keman in the Wale-Tarua district to
the north of the Sau valley.

16. *Kamongo* of great renown were usually referred to first by the name of their clan
or tribe, followed by their personal name, enhancing both personal and group reputation.

17. This is not purely a matter of detail having been lost, because other details are remembered for earlier generations.

18. This gives a good idea of just how much Tee mileage could be gained from one
kinship tie.

19. *Auu* can be translated as "good," "great," or "well done."

20. Here and throughout the narrative, Kopio makes it clear that each family participated as a self-sufficient unit in the Tee cycle, their individual distributions carefully coordinated with those of their fellow clanspeople.

21. The fire was built because the line of pigs was so long that spectators at one end
did not know where it ended until they saw the smoke rising. The trees were
planted to keep a permanent record of where the line ended. In subsequent Tees,
kamongo would try to surpass this mark.

22. It was common practice for recipients to give pigs to the next man along their
chain immediately after they had received them or to distribute them to cover
debts such as war reparations. However, recipients would bring the pigs back for
the donor's Tee festival so that they could be given out in public on the donor's ceremonial grounds.

23. Note that pearl shells, which were just beginning to enter the Tee in very small
numbers during the fourth generation, are not even mentioned.

24. What Kopio means here is that in central Enga, rivalry was not yet strong between
men on different Tee chains. Within the Timali clan, Pendaine competed with his
brother, Nandi.

25. Few men manage marrying three women at once, and Lambu was no exception.
Shortly after the wedding, one of the three wives murdered another out of jealousy and fled home, leaving him with one wife only.

26. Women worked as servants, but usually only prior to marriage. Their services
were repaid by the employer's contributions to their bridewealth. Presumably
Lambu did not need female helpers because he had enough wives to tend his pigs
and gardens.

27. Servants were usually people who were not backed by their own kin, as is indicated in the following passage from Kambao's testimony: "Most of the time
Lambu was satisfied with what his servants did, but once in a while he would go
mad when he found out that one of the servants had done him wrong. For example, one day Diua of the Yandap went into Lambu's garden and stole a stalk of sugarcane. The great *kamongo* was very angry when he found about the theft. In a
rage he went straight to the men's house, where the man was sleeping on a raised
platform used as a bed, lifted him up by the piece of wood that he used as a head-
rest, took him around the waist, and carried him out of the men's house. He car-

ried him all the way down to the Lai, out onto the middle of the bridge, and dropped him into the river. The poor man drowned and was carried away by the current so that no trace of him was left. He met his fate. Nobody worried about him and nobody from his clan came to look for him, though the people in the Timali clan and Lambu's household knew about his death."

28. These were not *saandi*, or initiatory gifts, but *punggisa* pigs, pigs given in advance to important Tee partners to assure them that they would receive the best pigs in the Tee. A stake for each *punggisa* pig was planted in the donor's ceremonial grounds to which the pig would be tied when it was returned for formal presentation in public (see also Meggitt 1974:68).

29. This metaphor was explained as follows: the *sakae* rope represents Tuingi's chain of Tee partners. The term "witch" is a rough translation for a lowly and inferior creature, usually female, who causes mischief, harm, or misfortune. Presumably this concept comes from outlying areas, as central Enga generally do not hold sorcery beliefs.

30. Sane, Timali's eastern neighbor, holds its Tee just before or after Timali's, depending on the direction of a particular Tee.

31. Prestige is gained both by giving out more than others on one's own ceremonial grounds and by receiving more in the distributions of other clans. As mentioned earlier, when a person received more pigs than his household could care for, they were immediately staked out and given to Tee partners down the line, on the condition that they would be later returned for formal distribution. Lambu took advantage of this secondary distribution to put down his rival Peke.

32. Note the great detail with which the "body language" is remembered for this encounter.

33. The significance of the *kola* and *kapano* was explained by Kambao as follows: in Enga tradition, when someone has done another wrong, such as stealing from gardens or trespassing, the offended person plants the top of a piece of *kola* grass in the ground to mark the spot where the damage was done. The first two letters of *kola*, "ko," mean bad. The person who plants the grass communicates symbolically that the wrongdoer is of low status. *Kapano* wood is used in the following context: sickness is sometimes attributed to the ill feelings of somebody toward the afflicted, though the former does not intend to do harm to the latter. The latter then calls for a ritual expert, who strikes the walls of the house with a *kapano* stick while uttering magic words to banish the "spirit" of the one with the ill feelings. In taking the *kola* and *kapano* from his son, Lambu indicated that Kambao would inherit his wealth and continue his Tee chains and rivalries. He was also communicating symbolically to Peke that he, Peke, was a man of low status and that his campaign against the Tee was wrong.

34. According to our estimates and those of Feil (1984:246), the Atiapa Tee took place around 1955.

35. Kiaps were field officers of the Australian Colonial Administration. At the time of the "Hurry-Up Tee," all of Enga was manned by one assistant district officer, three

patrol officers, one cadet patrol officer, and a small detachment of the Royal Papua New Guinea Police constabulary (Gordon and Meggitt 1985:42).

36. The colonial administration gave local leaders (*kamongo*) official recognition first under the title of *bosbio* (boss boy), a title later changed to *luluai*. Since most *luluai* were illiterate and could not speak Melanesian Pidgin, younger men, *tultul*, were appointed to help them (Gordon and Meggitt 1985:37). Possibly Kambao has confused the terms here, for Lambu, as a powerful *kamongo*, would probably have held the position of *luluai*.

37. Here, as in the case of Sikini Peke, Lambu's greatest rivals were not other *kamongo* of his own clan but the most powerful *kamongo* from other clans on competing chains (contrast with Feil 1984:198).

38. This is a typical understatement meant to express his desire to hold the Tee.

39. In calling Yalona the son of a poor man, Lambu is emphasizing that he, Lambu, comes from a long line of leaders and Yalona does not. It may have another meaning as well: while the Yanaitini Kia and Kalepatae clans were initiators of the Tee, most other Yanaitini clans became involved in the twentieth century upon the termination of the Great Wars. Thus, not only Yalona himself but also his clan might be considered beginners in the Tee.

40. In other words, he defeated him by receiving more pigs.

41. Lambu is said to have distributed six bundles of forty, or 240, pigs in this phase of the Tee cycle.

42. The Seventh-Day Adventist Church forbids the consumption of pork, so becoming an SDA removed Lambu from the greater part of traditional exchange.

43. Kaugel clans said to have joined the Tee after contact included Komolatepa, Upulatepa, Takepoka, Panyimbu, Ekakanyimba, Gulga, Walomati, Kaakuni, Wenda, Koelya, and Petai. These clans formed an extension of a route formerly made up of the Kaugel clans Kuluminyu, Yapukini, Kepa, and Kipioko. The first two are Enga speakers. Those originally along the route into the north Mendi valley included Kainyambatepa, Lyotepa, Angiwale, Kondilya, and Kaulga. Kainyambatepa, Angiwale, and Kaulga are primarily Enga speakers. Those who joined this route after contact were Munjini, Petetepa, Kaiakuni, Anamuli, Nokopa, Motopange, Dauka, Laima, and Alya.

44. This was not the case for the Tee in the main valleys.

45. In 1986 we witnessed an attempted to begin a major Tee cycle in the north Mendi area. Some middle Lai tribes, anticipating its arrival, set out pig stakes. It did not succeed.

Chapter 13. *Yandaita*

1. Population growth can be counted not only as an independent variable but also as a dependent one. That is, as ceremonial exchange grew, desire for large families appears to have increased, and with it, protective measures for women and children.

2. Some elders feel that the frequency of warfare increased through time, although they, like us, can base their opinions only on impressions, not figures. A sense of increase could be conveyed if warfare grew proportionately with population, simply because it would then become a more frequent event.

3. For contrast, see Wiener's (1992) discussion of the use of "inalienable possessions" — things not to be given away — as objects legitimizing status.

4. Ploeg (1969:195) has noted the same open orientation among the Dani.

5. The openness of the Enga is manifested in numerous ways today: for example, in the constant circulation of people riding in the three hundred to four hundred public motor vehicles that currently operate on the roads of Enga, and in the success of Enga businessmen outside of the province.

6. When collecting life histories of women, it was surprising to discover how many women had spent a few years living with maternal kin or in-laws during their teenage years.

7. Even greater changes in relations of production must have occurred when former "hunting-gathering" groups of the high country of western Enga shifted to horticulture, though oral history does not record these.

8. Interestingly, few writers, if any, have suggested that women exploited men for defense.

9. Increase in status appears to have applied largely to women from the households of big-men who had far-flung exchange networks. It was slower to filter down to the wives, sisters, and daughters of ordinary men.

10. See Hayden (1990, 1995) for an interesting discussion of the role of feasting in political strategies.

11. Enga gauge the value of pigs in terms of labor investment. It is for this reason that prices of locally sold pigs today are two to three times commercial prices.

12. Bruce Trigger's work on the Iroquois (1976, 1990) provides a fascinating example of how hereditary hierarchical organization can exist without undermining equality. Had Enga social structure undergone reorganization within the sphere of the Tee cycle, a similar course is conceivable, for powerful Tee cycle organizers were gaining influence far beyond the boundaries of their own clans and were often succeeded by one of their sons.

13. Brookfield (1984; Brookfield and Allen 1989) has subsequently broadened his argumentation, acknowledging the effects of both social and technological innovations.

14. Both Lemonnier (1991) and Godelier (1991), the latter in response to prodding from Modjeska, have attempted to construct models for the transformation of great-man to big-man societies. We do not regard these models as evolutionary or prehistoric ones, because they are aimed at demonstrating theoretically how such a transformation could be made and at elucidating how great-man societies have recently been transformed into big-man societies after colonial intervention. There is no reason, however, to postulate that big-man societies grew out of great-man societies in the precolonial past. Big-man societies prevail in the highlands, and oral evidence suggests that areas where great-man societies are found were more likely to

have been settled by groups that migrated out of the central valleys than the reverse. One might then expect that big-man and great-man societies represent divergent paths of development from an open orientation in the distant past. Great-man societies developed a much greater degree of closure than their counterparts, perhaps as leveling responses to competition and developing social inequalities, although this is mere speculation (see Poole 1994:192 for echoes of this).

15. In other songs from Ain's cult, *taukopa* is used to describe a "wind." So far as we could determine, it refers to the natural gas outlets that play a major role in the Dindi Gamu cult.

Appendix 1. The Structure of Enga Genealogies

1. Mention of men who joined a tribe through a female link, adopted children, or men with several wives each of whose tribe of origin was known indicates that genealogies were well remembered.

2. In other words, if there was a generation between tribal and clan founders, as there were in fifteen out of eighty-six genealogies, it was necessary to omit this generation in order to make figures from different tribes comparable.

Appendix 2. Estimating Enga Population Size

1. The lengths of genealogies from subclan founders to the present varies somewhat from tribe to tribe and region to region. For Layapo, Saka, Mai, and Yandapo genealogies, there are usually 7.5 to 8.5 generations from subclan founders to the present; for Laiagam, Atone, and Katinja, seven to eight generations; and for Tayato genealogies, 6.5 to 7.5. The average number of generations from the present to subclan founders for all Enga is 7.3. We do not know precisely how many years this period covers but estimate that it is between 200 and 250 years.

2. Enga political units are dynamic, constantly growing and splitting into new segments (Meggitt 1965a). Therefore a clan of the founding generations would be more like a lineage today. There is no easy terminological way to indicate this, for we do not want to begin by describing a unit as a lineage and later call it a clan or tribe. We have, therefore, retained the same terms throughout, but readers should realize that these units encompass ever more members through time.

Appendix 3. The Introduction of the Sweet Potato

1. "At Naiya near Yangoru" is either Alo's speculation or hearsay, not part of the narrative. Because it is the home of former Prime Minister Somare, it may be the only place in the eastern Sepik known by most Tumundan residents.

2. Alo Peter, who was a pastor among the Hewa for some years, said that the local place names in the area where the sisters settled were Mandopa, Taipoko, Wapelyakale, Alumu, and Totali.
3. The older sister is said to have gone north to attend a ritual called the *yama yae* at Londena Mandaka in Nete country. She was killed when a hot stone for an earth oven exploded, and her son, Alepea, was said to have been brought up by a forest spirit. His descendants are characterized by a birthmark that looks like a bite mark on their shoulders.

Appendix 4. The History of the Lungupini Yakau Clan

1. This garden must have been at the border between Yakau and Itokone; otherwise, it would not have become Itokone land under these circumstances.

Appendix 5. The Migration of the Yatapaki Tribe

1. Other testimonies say that this was during a time of frost and famine.
2. Lete said that they also brought sweet potatoes in their initial migration.

Appendix 6. The Legend of Tiane's *Kingi*

1. Tiane's *kingi* is one name for a bundle of charms believed to have power to attract wealth if the appropriate spells are recited over them. *Kingi* means thumb; we could not find out who or what Tiane was. Among the Mai and Kaina Enga of recent generations, such bundles consisted of the dried head of a *muio* opossum, a tooth from a *lapai* opossum, and the hip bone of a flying fox, all dusted in red ochre and wrapped in *lakanda,* a clothlike web spun by a species of caterpillar found in the lowlands of the Sau, Lai, Wali, and Tarua valleys. Other small, unusual objects could be also added (see also Lacey 1975:178). Yanaitini represents the Yanaitini Kalinatae clans (Kia, Yapakone, and Kalepatae), the only Yanaitini clans who took part in the Tee cycle during its early stages.
2. The slings were bespelled to give hunting success.
3. Sambakamanda and Yalumanda are the major mountain passes or ridges over which the Tee route between the Saka and Tetemanda crosses.

Appendix 7. The Kepele Cult Origin Myth

1. Different versions of this myth name men from different "agricultural" tribes in

southern Kandep as the visitor, including Aimbatepa and Timitopa. In complement, most southern Kandep tribes claim that it was one of their members who
came to Bipi Kama seeking help.

2. In other versions it is noted that through the young man's labor, the agriculturalist
became prosperous.

Appendix 9. The *Sangai Titi Pingi* of the Potealini Anae Taanda Subclan

1. Akii Tumu collected another *sangai titi pingi* from the Yanaitini Kumbini clan,
which had also obtained its Sangai from Potealini at Tiakamanda. The format,
structure, and content are almost identical to those in the verses given here, except
for the circumstances of recent transactions.

Appendix 10. Excerpt from the Adventures of Gulu

1. Interesting here is the vague knowledge that pearl shells come from the sea, the
third large body of water in the land of Dima.

Appendix 11. An Episode of the Malipini-Potealini versus Itapuni-Awaini Great War

1. This account, recorded by Nitze Pupu, has been edited for repetition; if additional
facts were recalled at the end, they were placed where they belong.

2. This would have been black palm wood for bows and spears and binding materials
for axes, both of which were obtained from low-lying areas in the Kompiam and
Maramuni areas or via traders in the Kandep area who in turn procured them
from the Lake Kutubu region. The same is true for the tree oil worn for traditional dances.

3. Irelya was the center for Apulini, Itapuni, and Awaini's hosts, and Lakiamanda for
Piao Lakiamanda, a host for Malipini and Potealini.

4. In fact, it is not true that there are more Malipini and Potealini in the Sau valley
than in the Ambum—this is only Yamu's impression. However, there were several
large clans of both tribes who had migrated to the Sau valley and had a vested interest in participating in the Great Wars to become integrated into major trade networks of the central valleys.

5. What he is describing here is *endaki kambungi*, a ceremony held just after the end
of the Great Wars (see chapter 10).

6. Kepa was a major subclan hosting this episode.

Appendix 13. The *Yae* Phase of the Tee Cycle in the Lifetime of Pendaine

1. This is from the Yakani perspective — in another region other *kamongo* would take credit for mobilizing the *yae*.
2. Probably the route coming up the lower Lai valley from the Kopona area into the Saka and that from Tambul down the Minamb and into the Saka valley.
3. This is not literal; it means that far more pork was given away than necessary for satisfying the recipients.

Appendix 14. Lambu's Exploits in Warfare

1. In principle, pillaging the territory of the loser was reserved for intertribal wars, not intratribal wars like this one; Enga frowned upon inflicting such damage on "brother" clans. Such incidents did happen, however, in the heat of battle, if the death toll were high and tempers raging.
2. This could be a real problem in wars where allies came from afar to help. It is curious that no conventions of dress were developed that allowed opposing sides to be easily distinguished from each another.

References Cited

Allen, B., and R. Giddings, 1982. Land disputes and violence in Enga. In *Enga: Foundations for Development*, eds. B. Carrad, D. Lea, and K. Talyaga, pp. 179–97. Enga Yaaka Lasemana, vol. 3. Armidale, Australia: Department of Geography, University of New England.

Ballard, C., 1995. The death of a great land: Ritual, history and subsistence revolution in the southern highlands of Papua New Guinea. Unpublished Ph.D. thesis, Australian National University.

Bellwood, P., 1987. *The Polynesians: Prehistory of an Island People*. London: Thames and Hudson.

Bender, B., 1990. The dynamics of non-hierarchical societies. In *The Evolution of Political Systems: Sociopolitics in Small-Scale Societies*, ed. S. Upham, pp. 247–63. Cambridge: Cambridge University Press.

Berndt, R., 1971. Political structure in the eastern central highlands. In *Politics in New Guinea*, eds. R. Berndt and P. Lawrence, pp. 381–423. Nedlands: University of Western Australia Press.

Biersack, A., 1980. The hidden god: Communication, cosmology and cybernetics among a Melanesian people. Ph.D. diss., University of Michigan. Ann Arbor: University Microfilms.

———, 1981. "To die laughing": Paiela games and the organization of behaviour as communication. In *Play as Paradox*, ed. J. Loy. West Point: Leisure Press.

———, 1982. Ginger gardens for the ginger woman: Rites and passages in a Melanesian society. *Man* 17:239–58.

Blong, R., 1982. *The Time of Darkness: Local Legends and Volcanic Reality in Papua New Guinea*. Seattle: University of Washington Press.

Bonnemère, P., 1993. *Pangium edule*: A food for the social body among the Ankave-Anga of Papua New Guinea. In *Tropical Forests, People and Foods: Biocultural Interactions and*

467

Applications to Development, eds. C. Hladik, A. Hladik, O. Linares, H. Pagezy, A. Semple, and M. Hadley, pp. 661-72. Paris: UNESCO/Parthenon Publishing Group.

Boserup, E., 1981. *Population and Technological Change: A Study of Long-Term Trends*. Chicago: University of Chicago Press.

Bourdieu, P., 1977. *Outline of a Theory of Practice*. Cambridge: Cambridge University Press.

————, 1990. *The Logic of Practice*. Stanford, California: Stanford Unversity Press.

Bourke, M., and D. Lea, 1982. Subsistence horticulture. In *Enga: Foundations for Development*, eds. B. Carrad, D. Lea, and K. Talyaga, pp. 76-92. Enga Yaaka Lasemana, vol. 3. Armidale, Australia: Department of Geography, University of New England.

Bowers, N., 1968. The ascending grasslands: An anthropological study of succession in a high mountain valley of New Guinea. Ph.D. diss., Columbia University. Ann Arbor: University Microfilms.

Brennan, P., 1977. *Let Sleeping Snakes Lie: Central Enga Religious Belief and Ritual*, Adelaide: Australian Association for the Study of Religions.

————, 1982. Communication. In *Enga: Foundations for Development*, eds. B. Carrad, D. Lea, and K. Talyaga, pp. 198-216. Enga Yaaka Lasemana, vol. 3. Armidale, Australia: Department of Geography, University of New England.

Brookfield, H., 1968. New directions in the study of agricultural systems in tropical areas. In *Evolution and Environment*, ed. E. Drake, pp. 413-39. New Haven, Connecticut: Yale University Press.

————, 1984. Intensification revisited. *Pacific Viewpoint* 25:15-44.

Brookfield, H., and B. Allen, 1989. High-altitude occupation and environment. *Mountain Research and Development* 9(3):201-9.

Brookfield, H., and P. White, 1968. Revolution or evolution in the prehistory of the New Guinea highlands: A seminar report. *Ethnology* 7:43-52.

Brown, P., 1964. Enemies and affines. *Ethnology* 3:335-56.

————, 1990a. Big men: Afterthoughts. *Ethnology* 29:275-78.

————, 1990b. Big men, past and present: Model, person, hero, legend. *Ethnology* 29:97-116.

Bulmer, R., 1960. Political aspects of the Moka ceremonial exchange system among the Kyaka people of the western highlands of New Guinea. *Oceania* 31:1-13.

————, 1965. The Kyaka of the western highlands. In *Gods, Ghosts and Men in Melanesia*, eds. P. Lawrence and M. Meggitt, pp. 132-61. Melbourne: Oxford University Press.

Burton, J., 1984. Axe makers of the Waghi: Pre-colonial industrialists of the Papua New Guinea highlands. Unpublished Ph.D. thesis, Australian National University.

————, 1989. Repeng and the salt-makers: Ecological trade and stone axe production in the Papua New Guinea highlands. *Man* 24:255-72.

Bus, G., 1951. The Te festival or gift exchange in Enga (central highlands of New Guinea). *Anthropos* 46:813-24.

Carrier, J. (ed.), 1992. *History and Tradition in Melanesian Anthropology*. Berkeley: University of California Press.

Cattani, J., 1992. The epidemiology of malaria in Papua New Guinea. In *Human Biology in Papua New Guinea: The Small Cosmos*, eds. R. Attenborough and M. Alpers, pp. 302-12. Oxford: Clarendon.

Clark, J., 1991. Pearlshell symbolism in highland Papua New Guinea, with particular reference to the Wiru people of Southern Highlands Province. *Oceania* 61:309-39.

Clarke, W., 1977. A change of subsistence staple in prehistoric New Guinea. In *Proceedings of the Third Symposium of the International Society for Tropical Root Crops*, ed. C.L.A. Leakey, pp. 159-63. Ibadan, Nigeria.

Connolly, B., and R. Anderson, 1987. *First Contact: New Guinea's Highlanders Encounter the Outside World*. New York: Viking Penguin.

Cowgill, G., 1975. On causes and consequences of ancient and modern population changes. *American Anthropologist* 77:505-25.

Didi, B., 1982a. Kuru Kopiaka: Goddess cult in the lower Kaugel valley of the Tambul sub-district, Western Highlands Province. *Oral History* 10:5-43.

———, 1982b. An overview of the traditional cults in the lower Kaugel valley of the Tambul sub-district, Western Highlands Province. *Oral History* 10:44-87.

Dornstreich, M., 1973. An ecological study of Gadio Enga subsistence. Unpublished Ph.D. diss., Columbia University.

Douglas, B., 1992. Doing ethnographic history: The case of fighting in New Caledonia. In *History and Tradition in Melanesian Anthropology*, ed. J. Carrier, pp. 86-115. Berkeley: University of California Press.

Dwyer, P., 1985. The contribution of non-domesticated animals to the diet of Etolo, Southern Highlands Province, Papua New Guinea. *Ecology of Food and Nutrition* 15:101-15.

Eibl-Eibesfeldt, I., 1975. *The Biology of War and Peace*. Viking Press: New York.

———, 1989. *Human Ethology*. New York: Aldine.

———, 1995. *Die Biologie des Menschlichen Verhaltens*. München: Piper.

———, 1996. The evolution of nurturant dominance. In *Food and the Status Quest: Interdisciplinary Perspectives*, eds. P. Wiessner and W. Schiefenhövel, pp. 33-38. Oxford: Berghahn Books.

Eibl-Eibesfeldt, I., W. Schiefenhövel, and V. Heeschen, 1989. *Kommunication bei den Eipo: Eine Humanethologische Bestandsaufnahme*. Berlin: Dietrich Verlag.

Elkin, A., 1953. Delayed exchange in Wabag sub-district, central highlands of New Guinea, with notes on social organization. *Oceania* 3:161-201.

Feachem, R., 1973. The Raiapu Enga pig herd. *Mankind* 9:25-31.

———, 1975. Pigs, people and pollution: Interactions between man and environment in the highlands of New Guinea. *South Pacific Bulletin* 25:41-45.

Feil, D., 1978a. Straightening the way: An Enga kinship conundrum. *Man* 13:380-401.

———, 1978b. Women and men in the Enga *tee*. *American Ethnologist* 5:263-79.

———, 1983. A world without exchange. *Anthropos* 78:89-106.

———, 1984. *Ways of Exchange: The Enga Tee of Papua New Guinea*. St. Lucia, Australia: University of Queensland Press.

————, 1987. *The Evolution of Highland Papua New Guinea Societies.* Cambridge: Cambridge University Press.

Flannery, K., 1972. The cultural evolution of civilization. *Annual Review of Ecology and Systematics* 3:399–426.

Foster, R., 1993. Dangerous circulation and revelatory display: Exchange practices in a New Ireland society. In *Exchanging Products: Producing Exchange,* ed. J. Fajans, pp. 15–31. Oceania Monograph 43. Sydney: University of Sydney.

Frankel, S., 1986. *The Huli Response to Illness.* Cambridge: Cambridge University Press.

Franklin, K., 1972. A ritual pandanus language of New Guinea. *Oceania* 43:61–76.

Fried, M., 1975. *The Notion of Tribe.* Menlo Park, California: Cummings Publishing.

Friedman, J., 1974. Marxism, structuralism and vulgar materialism. *Man* 9:444–69.

Gailey, C., and T. Patterson, 1987. Power relations and state formation. In *Power Relations and State Formation,* eds. T. Patterson and C. Gailey, pp. 1–25. Washington, D.C.: American Anthropological Association.

Gibbs, P., 1975. Ipili religion past and present. Unpublished diploma thesis, University of Sydney.

————, 1977. The cult from Lyeimi and the Ipili. *Oceania* 48:1–25.

————, 1978. The *Kepele* ritual of the western highlands, Papua New Guinea. *Anthropos* 73:434–47.

Giddens, A., 1979. *Central Problems in Modern Social Theory.* Berkeley: University of California Press.

————, 1984. *The Constitution of Society: Outline of a Theory of Structuration.* Berkeley: University of California Press.

Glasse, R., 1965. The Huli of the Southern highlands. In *Gods, Ghosts and Men in Melanesia,* eds. P. Lawrence and M. Meggitt, pp. 27–49. Melbourne: Oxford University Press.

Godelier, M., 1977. *Perspectives in Marxist Anthropology.* Cambridge: Cambridge University Press.

————, 1982. *La production des grands hommes.* Paris: Fayard.

————, 1991. An unfinished attempt at reconstructing the social processes which may have prompted the transformation of great-men societies into big-men societies. In *Big Men and Great Men: Personifications of Power in Melanesia,* eds. M. Godelier and M. Strathern, pp. 275–304. Cambridge: Cambridge University Press.

————, 1995a. L'Enigme du Don. Part 1. *Social Anthropology* 3:15–47.

————, 1995b. L'Enigme du Don. Part 2. *Social Anthropology* 3:95–114.

Godelier, M., and M. Strathern (eds.), 1991. *Big Men and Great Men: Personifications of Power in Melanesia.* Cambridge: Cambridge University Press.

Goldman, L., 1983. *Talk Never Dies: The Language of Huli Disputes.* London: Tavistock.

Golson, J., 1977. No room at the top: Agricultural intensification in the New Guinea highlands. In *Sunda and Sahul: Prehistoric Studies in Southwest Asia, Melanesia and Australia,* eds. J. Allen, J. Golson, and R. Jones, pp. 601–38. London: Academic Press.

————, 1981. New Guinea agricultural history: A case study. In *A Time to Plant and a Time to Uproot: A History of Agriculture in Papua New Guinea,* eds. D. Denoon and C. Snowden, pp. 55–64. Boroko, Indonesia: Institute of Papua New Guinea Studies.

————, 1982. The Ipomoean revolution revisited: Society and the sweet potato in the upper Waghi valley. In *Inequality in New Guinea Highlands Societies,* ed. A. Strathern, pp. 109-36. Cambridge: Cambridge University Press.

Golson, J., and D. Gardner, 1990. Agriculture and sociopolitical organization in New Guinea highlands prehistory. *Annual Reviews in Anthropology* 19:395-417.

Gordon, R., and M. Meggitt, 1985. *Law and Order in the New Guinea Highlands.* Hanover, New Hampshire: University Press of New England.

Gray, D., 1973. The logic of Yandapu Enga puberty rites and the separation of the sexes: Responses to ecological and biological pressures in New Guinea. Unpublished M.A. thesis, University of Sydney.

Groube, L., J. Chappell, J. Muke, and D. Price, 1986. A forty-thousand-year-old occupation site at Huon peninsula, Papua New Guinea. *Nature* 324:453-55.

Hage, P., 1981. Pollution beliefs in highland New Guinea. *Man* 16:367-75.

Hather, J., and P. Kirch, 1991. Prehistoric sweet potato (*Ipomoea batatas*) from Mangaia Island, central Polynesia. *Antiquity* 65:887-93.

Hayden, B., 1990. Nimrods, piscators, pluckers, and planters: The emergence of food production. *Journal of Anthropological Archaeology* 9:31-69.

————, 1996. Feasting in prehistoric and traditional societies. In *Food and the Status Quest: Interdisciplinary Perspectives,* eds. P. Wiessner and W. Schiefenhövel, pp. 127-48. Oxford: Berghahn Books.

Healey, C., 1990. *Maring Hunters and Traders: Production and Exchange in the Papua New Guinea Highlands.* Berkeley: University of California Press.

Heeschen, V., 1994. Mythen und Wandergeschichten der Mek-Leute im Bergland von West-New Guinea (Irian-Jaya, Indonesien). In *Geschichte und mündliche Überlieferung in Ozeanien,* ed. B. Hauser-Schäublin, pp. 161-84. Basel: Wepf & Co.

Heider, K., 1970. *The Dugum Dani: A Papuan Culture in the Highlands of West New Guinea.* New York: Aldine.

————, 1972. The Grand Valley Dani pig feast: A ritual of passage and intensification. *Oceania* 42:169-97.

Herdt, G., 1984. *Ritualized Homosexuality in Melanesia.* Berkeley: University of California Press.

Hughes, I., 1977. *New Guinea Stone Age Trade.* Canberra: Department of Prehistory, Research School of Pacific Studies, Australian National University.

Hyndman, D., 1984. Hunting and the classification of game animals among the Wopkaimin. *Oceania* 54:289-309.

Hyndman, D., and G. Morren, 1990. The human ecology of the Mountain-Ok of central New Guinea: A regional and inter-regional approach. In *Children of Afek: Tradition and Change among the Mountain-Ok of Central New Guinea,* eds. B. Craig and D. Hyndman, pp. 9-26. Oceania Monograph 40. Sydney: University of Sydney.

Johnson, G., 1982. Organization structure and scalar stress. In *Theory and Explanation in Archaeology: The Southampton Conference,* eds. C. Renfrew, M. Rowlands, and B. Segraves, pp. 389-421. New York: Academic Press.

Johnson, G., and T. Earle, 1987. *The Evolution of Human Societies: From Foraging Group to Agrarian State.* Stanford, California: Stanford University Press.

Jorgensen, D., 1991. Big men, great men and women: Alternative logics of gender difference. In *Big Men and Great Men: Personifications of Power in Melanesia*, eds. M. Godelier and M. Strathern, pp. 256-71. Cambridge: Cambridge University Press.

Kelly, R., 1977. *Etoro Social Structure: A Study in Social Contradiction*. Ann Arbor: University of Michigan Press.

————, 1988. Etoro suidology: A reassessment of the pig's role in the prehistory and comparative ethnography of New Guinea. In *Mountain Papuans: Historical and Comparative Perspectives from New Guinea Fringe Highlands Societies*, ed. J. F. Weiner, pp. 111-86. Ann Arbor: University of Michigan Press.

————, 1993. *Constructing Inequality: The Fabrication of a Hierarchy of Virtue among the Etoro*. Ann Arbor: University of Michigan Press.

Kirschbaum, P., SVD, 1938. Über Zahlensysteme im Zentral Gebirge von Neuguinea. *Anthropos* 33:278-79.

Kirsh, P., and M. Sahlins, 1992. *Anahulu: The Anthropology of the History of the Kingdom of Hawaii*. Chicago: University of Chicago Press.

Kleinig, I. E., 1955. The significance of the *Te* in Enga culture. New Guinea Lutheran Mission Papers. Unpublished.

Knauft, B., 1987. *Good Company and Violence: Sorcery and Social Action in a Lowland New Guinea Society*. Berkeley: University of California Press.

————, 1993. *South Coast New Guinea Cultures*. Cambridge: Cambridge University Press.

Koch, G., 1984. *Malingdam. Ethnographische Notizen über einen Siedlungsbereiche im oberen Eipomek-Tal, Zentrales Bergland von Irian Jaya (West-Neuguinea), Indonesien*. Berlin: Dietrich Reime Verlag.

Kosse, K., 1990. Group size and societal complexity: Thresholds in the long-term memory. *Journal of Anthropological Archaeology* 9:275-303.

————, 1994. The evolution of large, complex groups: A hypothesis. *Journal of Anthropological Archaeology* 13:35-50.

Kyakas, A., and P. Wiessner, 1992. *From Inside the Women's House: Enga Women's Lives and Traditions*. Brisbane: Robert Brown.

Lacey, R., 1975. Oral traditions as history: An exploration of oral sources among the Enga of the New Guinea highlands. Unpublished Ph.D. diss., University of Wisconsin.

————, 1979. Holders of the way: A study of precolonial socio-economic history in Papua New Guinea. *Journal of the Polynesian Society* 88:277-325.

————, 1980. Coming to know Kepai: Conversational narratives and the use of oral sources in Papua New Guinea. *Social Analysis* 4:74-88.

————, 1981. Traditions of origin and migration: Some Enga evidence. In *Oral Tradition in Melanesia*, eds. D. Denoon and R. Lacey, pp. 45-56. Weigani: University of Papua New Guinea.

————, 1982. History. In *Enga: Foundations for Development*, eds. B. Carrad, D. Lea, and K. Talyaga, pp. 8-22. Enga Yaaka Lasemana, vol. 3. Armidale, Australia: Department of Geography, University of New England.

Lakau, A., 1994. Customary land tenure and alienation of customary land rights among the Kaina, Enga Province, Papua New Guinea. Unpublished Ph.D. thesis, University of Queensland.

Lang, A., 1973. *Enga Dictionary.* Canberra: Research School of Pacific Studies, Australian National University.

Larson, G. F., 1987. The structure and demography of the cycle of warfare among the Ilaga Dani of Irian Jaya. Ph.D. diss., University of Michigan. Ann Arbor: University Microfilms.

Lea, D., and N. Gray, 1982. Enga Demography. In *Enga: Foundations for Development,* eds. B. Carrad, D. Lea, and K. Talyaga, pp. 41-58. Enga Yaaka Lasemana, vol. 3. Armidale, Australia: Department of Geography, University of New England.

Lederman, R., 1986. *What Gifts Engender: Social Relations and Politics in Mendi, Highlands Papua New Guinea.* Cambridge: Cambridge University Press.

―――, 1990. Big men large and small? Towards a Comparative Perspective. *Ethnology* 29:3-15.

―――, 1991. "Interests" in exchange: Increment, equivalence and the limits of bigmanship. In *Big Men and Great Men: Personifications of Power in Melanesia,* eds. M. Godelier and M. Strathern, pp. 215-33. Cambridge: Cambridge University Press.

Lee, R., 1986. Malthus and Boserup: A dynamic synthesis. In *The State of Population Theory,* eds. D. Coleman and R. Schofield, pp. 96-130. Oxford: Basil Blackwell.

Lemonnier, P., 1990. *Guerres et festins: Paix, échanges et compétition dans les Highlands de Nouvelle-Guinée.* Paris: Maison des Sciences de L'Homme.

―――, 1991. From great men to big men: Peace, substitution and competition in the highlands of New Guinea. In *Big Men and Great Men: Personifications of Power in Melanesia,* eds. M Godelier and M. Strathern, pp. 7-27. Cambridge: Cambridge University Press.

―――, 1993. Le porc comme substitut de vie: Formes de conpensation et échanges en Nouvelle-Guinée. *Social Anthropology* 1:33-55.

―――, 1996. Food, competition and status in New Guinea. In *Food and the Status Quest: An Interdisciplinary Perspective,* eds. P. Wiessner and W. Schiefenhövel, pp. 219-34. Oxford: Berghahn Books.

Lindstrom, L., 1981. "Big man": A short terminological history. *American Anthropologist* 83:900-905.

―――, 1984. Doctor, lawyer, wiseman, priest: Big-men and knowledge in Melanesia. *Man* 19:291-309.

Lowie, R., 1917. Oral tradition and history. *Journal of American Folklore* 30:161-67.

Mackenzie, M., 1991. *Androgynous Objects: String Bags and Gender in Central New Guinea.* Chur, Switzerland: Harwood Academic Publishers.

Mai, P., 1981. The "time of darkness," or *yuu kuia.* In *Oral Tradition in Melanesia,* eds. D. Denoon and R. Lacey, pp. 125-40. Waigani: University of Papua New Guinea.

Malinowski, B., 1922. *Argonauts of the Western Pacific.* London: Routledge and Kegan Paul.

Mangi, J., 1988. Yole: A study of traditional Huli trade. Unpublished M.A. thesis, University of Papua New Guinea.

Mawe, T., 1985. *Mendi Culture and Tradition: A Recent Survey.* Papua New Guinea National Museum.

———, 1987. The Mendpo: An account of a Mendi tribe's origin, dispersal and settlement history in conjunction with the Kup and Yakumb tribe's oral history as regards their origin and settlement. Unpublished paper prepared for Oral History Fieldwork seminar, University of Papua New Guinea.

May, R., 1984. *Kaikai Aniani: A Guide to Bush Foods, Markets and Culinary Arts of Papua New Guinea.* Brisbane: Robert Brown.

Meggitt, M., 1956. The valleys of the upper Wage and Lai rivers. *Oceania* 27:90–135.

———, 1957. The Ipili of the Porgera valley. *Oceania* 28:31–55.

———, 1958a. The Enga of the New Guinea highlands: Some preliminary observations. *Oceania* 28:253–330.

———, 1958b. Salt manufacture and trading in the western highlands of New Guinea. *Australian Museum Magazine* 12:309–13.

———, 1958c. Mae Enga time-reckoning and calendar. *Man* 58:74–77.

———, 1964a. Male-female relationships in the highlands of Australian New Guinea. *American Anthropologist* 66:204–24.

———, 1964b. The kinship terminology of the Mae Enga of New Guinea. *Oceania* 34:191–200.

———, 1965a. *The Lineage System of the Mae-Enga of New Guinea.* New York: Barnes and Noble.

———, 1965b. The Mae Enga of the western highlands. In *Gods, Ghosts and Men in Melanesia,* eds. P. Lawrence and M. Meggitt, pp. 105–31. Melbourne: Oxford University Press.

———, 1967. The pattern of leadership among the Mae Enga of New Guinea. *Anthropological Forum* 2:20–35.

———, 1971. From tribesmen to peasants: The case of the Mae Enga of New Guinea. In *Anthropology in Oceania,* eds. L. Hiatt and C. Jayawardena, pp. 191–209. Sydney: Angus and Robertson.

———, 1972. System and sub-system: The "Te" exchange cycle among the Mae Enga. *Human Ecology* 1:111–23.

———, 1973. The sun and the shakers: A millenarian cult and its transformation in the New Guinea highlands. *Oceania* 44:1–37, 109–26.

———, 1974. "Pigs are our hearts!" The Te exchange cycle among the Mae Enga of New Guinea. *Oceania* 44:165–203.

———, 1976. A duplicity of demons: Sexual and familial roles expressed in western Enga stories. In *Man and Woman in the New Guinea Highlands,* eds. P. Brown and G. Buchbinder, pp. 63–85. Washington, D.C.: American Anthropological Association.

———, 1977. *Blood Is Their Argument.* Palo Alto, California: Mayfield Publishing.

Mitchell, W., 1988. The defeat of hierarchy: Gambling as exchange in a Sepik society. *American Ethnologist* 15:638–57.

Modjeska, N., 1982. Production and inequality: Perspectives from central New Guinea.

In *Inequality in New Guinea Highland Societies,* ed. A. Strathern, pp. 50–108. Cambridge: Cambridge University Press.

———, 1991. Post-Ipomoean modernism: The Duna example. In *Big Men and Great men: Personifications of Power in Melanesia,* eds. M. Godelier and M. Strathern, pp. 234–55. Cambridge: Cambridge University Press.

Monro, G., 1980. Review of edible pandanus in Papua New Guinea. Manuscript. High Altitude Experimental Station, Tambul, Western Highlands Province, PNG.

Morren, G., 1977. From hunting to herding: Pigs and the control of energy in Montane New Guinea. In *Subsistence and Survival: Rural Ecology in the Pacific,* eds. R. Bayliss-Smith and R. Feachem, pp. 273–315. New York: Academic Press.

Naroll, R., 1956. A preliminary index of social development. *American Anthropologist* 56:687–715.

Neumann, K., 1992. *Not the Way It Really Was: Constructing the Tolai Past.* Honolulu: University of Hawaii Press.

Nihil, M., n.d. Alternating ontologies: The dynamics of Anganen ritual and ceremonial exchange in time and space. In *Blurred Boundaries and Transformed Identities,* eds. C. Ballard and J. Clark. Canberra: Canberra Anthropology Monograph Series. In press.

O'Brien, P., 1972. The sweet potato: Its origin and dispersal. *American Anthropologist* 73:342–56.

Ortner, S., 1984. Theory in anthropology since the sixties. *Comparative Studies in Society and History* 26:126–66.

Parkinson, A., 1974. Malaria in Papua New Guinea 1973. *Papua New Guinea Medical Journal* 17:8–16.

Pawley, A., 1992. Kalam pandanus language: An old New Guinea experiment in language engineering. In *The Language Game: Papers in Memory of Donald C. Laycock,* eds. T. Dutton, M. Ross, and D. Tryon, pp. 313–34. Canberra: Department of Linguistics, Australian National University.

Peterson, N., 1975. Hunter-gatherer territoriality: The perspective from Australia. *American Anthropologist* 77:53–68.

Ploeg, A., 1969. *Government in Wanggulam.* The Hague: Martinus Nijhoff.

Poole, F., 1994. Ethnohistorical and mythological traditions of places of origin, paths of migration, and formations of communities among the Bimin-Kushusmin, West Sepik (Sandaun) Province, Papua New Guinea. In *Migration and Transformations: Regional Perspectives on New Guinea,* eds. A Strathern and G. Stürzenhofecker, pp. 179–208. Pittsburgh: University of Pittsburgh Press.

Pupu, N., 1988. The role of *kamongos* in Enga. *Enga Nius,* March. Wabag: Department of Enga.

Raich, H., 1967. Ein weiteres Fruchtbarkeitsidol aus dem westlichen Hochland von Neuguinea. *Anthropos* 62:938–39.

Rappaport, R., 1968. *Pigs for the Ancestors: Ritual in the Ecology of a New Guinea People.* New Haven, Connecticut: Yale University Press.

Rosaldo, R., 1980. Doing oral history. *Social Analysis* 4:89–99.

Rose, C., 1982. Preliminary observations on the pandanus nut (*Pandanus juilianetti martelli*). In *Proceedings of the Second Papua New Guinea Food Conference*, part one, eds. R. Bourke and V. Kesavan, pp. 160–67. Port Moresby: Department of Primary Industry.

Sahlins, M., 1963. Poor man, rich man, chief: Political types in Melanesia and Polynesia. *Comparative Studies in Society and History*, 5:285–303.

———, 1981. *Historical Metaphors and Mythical Realities: Structure in the Early History of the Sandwich Islands Kingdom*. Ann Arbor: University of Michigan Press.

———, 1985. *Islands of History*. Chicago: University of Chicago Press.

Scaglion, R., and K. Soto, 1994. A prehistoric introduction of the sweet potato in New Guinea? In *Migration and Transformations: Regional Perspectives on New Guinea*, eds. A. Strathern and G. Stürzenhofecker, pp. 257–94. Pittsburgh: University of Pittsburgh Press.

Schieffelin, E., and R. Crittenden, 1991. *Like People You See in a Dream: First Contact in Six Papuan Societies*. Stanford, California: Stanford University Press.

Schwab, J., 1995. The Sandalu bachelor ritual among the Laiapu Enga (Papua New Guinea). Edited by Philip Gibbs. *Anthropos* 90:27–47.

Sillitoe, P., 1978. Big men and war in New Guinea. *Man* 13:352–72.

———, 1979. *Give and Take*. Canberra: Australian National Unviersity Press.

Sinnett, P., 1975. *The People of Murapin*. Institute of Medical Research, Papua New Guinea, Monograph Series no. 4. Oxon: E. W. Chussey, Ltd.

Sorenson, E., 1972. Socio-ecological change among the Fore of New Guinea. *Current Anthropology* 13:349–83.

———, 1976. *The Edge of the Forest: Land, Childhood, and Change in a New Guinea Protoagricultural Society*. Washington, D.C.: Smithsonian Institution Press.

Spooner, B., 1972. *Population Growth: Anthropological Implications*. Philadelphia: University of Pennsylvania Press.

Strathern, A., 1969. Finance and production: Two strategies in New Guinea highlands exchange systems. *Oceania* 40:42–67.

———, 1970. The female and male spirit cults in Mount Hagen. *Man* 5:572–85.

———, 1971. *The Rope of Moka: Big-Men and Ceremonial Exchange in Mount Hagen, New Guinea*. Cambridge: Cambridge University Press.

———, 1975. Why is shame on the skin? *Ethnology* 14:347–56.

———, 1979a. Men's house, women's house: The efficacy of opposition, reversal and pairing in the Melpa Amb Kor cult. *Journal of the Polynesian Society* 88:37–51.

———, 1979b. Gender, ideology and money in Mt. Hagen. *Man* 14:530–48.

———, 1989. Melpa dream interpretation and the concept of hidden truth. *Ethnology* 28:301–15.

———, 1994. Lines of power. In *Migration and Transformations: Regional Perspectives in New Guinea*, eds. A. Strathern and G. Stürzenhofecker, pp. 231–56. Pittsburgh: University of Pittsburgh Press.

Strathern, A., and M. Strathern, 1971. *Self-decoration in Mt. Hagen.* London: Duckworth.

Strathern, M., 1972. *Women in Between. Female Roles in a Male World: Mount Hagen, New Guinea.* London: Seminar Press.

Strauss, H., and H. Tischner, 1962. *Die Mi-Kultur der Hagenberg-Stämme.* Hamburg: Cram de Gruyter.

Stürzenhofecker, G., 1993. Times enmeshed: Gender, space and history among the Duna. Unpublished Ph.D. diss., University of Pittsburgh.

———, 1994. Duna in Between: Scales of Variation in Montane New Guinea. In *Migration and Transformations: Regional Perspectives in New Guinea,* eds. A. Strathern and G. Stürzenhofecker, pp. 209-230. Pittsburgh: University of Pittsburgh Press.

———, 1995. Dialectics of history: Female witchcraft and male dominance in Aluni. In *Papuan Borderlands: Huli, Duna and Ipili Perspectives on the New Guinea Highlands,* ed. A. Biersack, pp. 287-314. Ann Arbor: University of Michigan Press.

Swadling, P., 1986. *Papua New Guinea's Prehistory: An Introduction.* Port Moresby: National Museum and Art Gallery.

Swadling, P., and G. Hope, 1992. Environmental change in New Guinea since human settlement. In *The Native Lands: Prehistory and Environmental Change in Australia and the South-west Pacific,* ed. J. Dodson, pp. 13-42. Melbourne: Longman Cheshire.

Talyaga, K., 1975. *Modern Enga Songs.* Port Moresby: Institute of Papua New Guinea Studies.

———, 1982. The Enga yesterday and today: A personal account. In *Enga: Foundations for Development,* eds. B. Carrad, D. Lea, and K. Talyaga, pp. 59-75. Enga Yaaka Lasemana, vol. 3. Armidale, Australia: Department of Geography, University of New England.

———, 1984. Geneology of the Tiyane, Waiwa and Tuanda clans of Aparnage and Alipis villages. Porgera Gold Mine: Socio-economic Impact Study, Interim Report.

Taylor, J. L., 1971 [1939]. Hagen-Sepik patrol 1938-1939: Interim report. *New Guinea and Australia, the Pacific and South-east Asia,* 6:24-45.

Terray, E., 1972. *Marxism and "Primitive" Societies.* New York: Monthly Review Press.

Trigger, B., 1976. *The Children of Aetaentsic: A History of the Huron People to 1660.* Montreal: McGill-Queen's University Press.

———, 1990. Maintaining economic equality in opposition of complexity: An Iroquoian case study. In *The Evolution of Political Systems: Sociopolitics in Small-Scale Societies,* ed. S. Upham, pp. 119-45. Cambridge: Cambridge University Press.

Tumu, A., A. Kyakas, P. Munini, and P. Wiessner, 1989. *A View of Enga Culture.* Madang, PNG: Kristen Press.

Upham, S., 1987. A theoretical consideration of middle-range societies. In *Archaeological Reconstructions and Chiefdoms in the Americas,* eds. R. Drennan and C. Uribe, pp. 345-68. New York: University Press of America.

Upham, S. (ed.), 1990. *The Evolution of Political Systems: Sociopolitics in Small-Scale Societies.* Cambridge: Cambridge University Press.

van der Dennen, J., 1995. *The Origin of War.* Groningen, Netherlands: Origin Press.

Vansina, J., 1965. *Oral Tradition: A Study in Historical Methodology.* London: Routledge & Kegan Paul.

————, 1985. *Oral Tradition as History.* London: James Curry.

Waddell, E., 1972. *The Mound Builders: Agricultural Practices, Environment and Society in the Central Highlands of New Guinea.* Seattle: University of Washington Press.

————, 1975. How the Enga cope with frost: Responses to climatic perturbations in the central highlands of New Guinea. *Human Ecology* 3:249-73.

Waiko, J. 1982. Be Jijimo: A history according to the tradition of the Binandere people of Papua New Guinea. Unpublished Ph.D. thesis, Australian National University.

————, 1986. Oral traditions among the Binandere: Problems of method in a Melanesian society. *Journal of Pacific History* 21:21-38.

————, 1993. *A Short History of Papua New Guinea.* Oxford: Oxford University Press.

Walker, D., and J. Flenley, 1979. Later Quaternary vegetation history of the Enga Province of upland Papua New Guinea. *Philosophical Transactions of the Royal Society of London* 286:265-344.

Watson, J., 1965a. The significance of recent ecological change in the central highlands of New Guinea. *Journal of the Polynesian Society* 74:438-50.

————, 1965b. From hunting to horticulture in the New Guinea highlands. *Ethnology* 4:295-309.

————, 1968. *Pueraria:* Names and traditions of a lesser crop of the central highlands of New Guinea. *Ethnology* 7:268-79.

————, 1971. Tairora: The politics of despotism in a small society. In *Politics in New Guinea,* eds. B. R. Lawrence and P. Lawrence, pp 224-75. Nedlands: University of Western Australian Press.

————, 1977. Pigs, fodder and the Jones effect in post-Ipomoean New Guinea. *Ethnology* 16:57-70.

Weiner, A., 1976. *Women of Value, Men of Renown: New Perspectives in Trobriand Exchange.* Austin: University of Texas Press.

————, 1992. *Inalienable Possessions: The Paradox of Keeping-While-Giving.* Berkeley: University of California Press.

White, J., and J. O'Connell, 1982. *A Prehistory of Australia, New Guinea and Sahul.* Sydney: Academic Press.

Wiessner, P., and W. Schiefenhövel (eds.), 1996. *Food and the Status Quest: An Interdisciplinary Perspective.* Oxford: Berghahn Books.

Wiessner, P., and A. Tumu, 1994. Ain's cult revisited. Unpublished paper prepared for Society for Oceanists conference, Basel, Switzerland.

Wohlt, P., 1978. Ecology, agriculture, and social organization: The dynamics of group composition in the highlands of New Guinea. Ph.D. diss, University of Minnesota. Ann Arbor: University Microfilms.

————, 1986. *Subsistence Systems of Enga Province.* Wabag: Department of Enga, Division of Primary Industry, Subsistence Unit.

Wolf, E., 1982. *Europe and the People Without History.* Berkeley: University of California Press.

Wormsley, W., and M. Toke, 1985. *The Enga Law and Order Project: Final Report.* Wabag: Enga Provincial Government.

Yen, D., 1974. *The Sweet Potato and Oceania: An Essay in Ethnobotany.* Honolulu: Bishop Museum Bulletin 236.

Young, D., 1986. Pastoral responses to tribal fighting in Enga. *Catalyst* 16:7–26.

———, 1995. Resolving conflict for Gutpela Sindaun: An analysis and evaluation of traditional and modern methods of achieving peaceful intergroup relations among the Enga of Papua New Guinea. Unpublished Ph.D. thesis, Macquarie University.

Young, M., 1971. *Fighting with Food: Leadership, Values and Social Control in a Massim Society.* Cambridge: Cambridge University Press.

Index

Page numbers in bold indicate maps. Portions of entries found in parentheses are either glosses of terms in Enga or English, or are equivalent terms or synonyms for the main entry. The appendixes and notes have not been indexed.

480

Apakasa, 169
appearance, 227, 244. *See also* attire
Apulini tribe, **20-21,** 107, 134, 169; and Aeatee
cult, 311, 315; in Great Ceremonial War, 283;
and Kepele ancestral cult, 203; marriage
among, 82; migration, **128,** 133; salt springs,
158; Sangai bachelors' cult participation, **222,**
235, 237; and Tee cycle, 299, 305, 330, 345-46
Atone Enga, 55, 86, 248; Sangai bachelors' cult,
222. *See also* Kandepe Enga
attire, 253; Pendaine Lambu, 336-37; in Sangai
bachelors' cult, 215, 218; warriors', 270, 280
Auwini tribe, **20-21, 137**
Awaini tribe, **20-21;** in Great Ceremonial
Wars, 278, 282-88; salt springs, 158; in Tee
cycles, 329-30. *See also* Itapuni-Awaini versus
Malipini-Potealini Great Ceremonial War
axes, 93-94, 258, 349; as bridewealth payments,
303; in Tee cycle, 296, 335, 338; in war reparations, 258
Ayakali, Pambene, 94

bachelors' cults, 215-44; models of behavior,
362; origin traditions, **222;** praise poetry, 26,
39; representation of women, 366. *See also*
cults; magic; Sangai bachelors' cult
Ballard, C., 191
bananas, 63
basket work figures (*yupini*), 199, 204, 207. *See
also* Kepele ancestral cult
beta pingi (payment for children's injury or illness, 84
Biersack, Aletta, 230
"big-man" societies, 377
big-men (*kamongo*), 160, 177, 231-32, 266; abilities, 252-53; in ancestral cults, 359; arranging war reparations, 252; competition
among, 342, 347; cult ownership, 196, 233,
363-64; distributing wealth, 195; and egalitarian ethic, 217; elite circles, 238, 310; European influence on, 349-50; goals, 364;
kamongo andake, 340; limitations, 253-54,
370, 372-73; organizing Tee cycle, 240, 297-
98, 308-9, 333-35; personal ambitions, 152;
polygynous marriages, 236-37; requirements
and responsibilities, 230, 259, 382; senior
bachelors as, 219. *See also* great war leaders;
leadership
Bipi, 74
Bipi tribe, **20-21,** 82; and ancestor cults, 192-93,
198; female courtship, 242; and introduction
of sweet potato, 113-14; migration, 136, **137,**
140, 141; origin tradition, 74-75; population
growth, 116-17; in warfare, 146
Blong, Russell, 32, 70-71
boasting, 80
body oil, 296
boundary maintenance, 43, 85, 153; physical
means (warfare), 355; social means, 149, 246,
355, 357; and war reparations, 263-64
Bowers, N., 117
breadfruit, 127
breast milk, 206, 218
Brennan, Paul, 16, 41, 52-53, 54, 93, 319
bridewealth, 82-84, 360, 362, 375; cultural variation in, 266; Godelier's model, 377; payments in pearl shell, 303-4; for servants, 341;
in Tee cycle, 161-62, 163, 172, 176, 302; and
war reparations, 248, 259
"bridge of the sweet potato vines" ritual, **104,**
105-9, 203-4
Brookfield, Harold, 112, 374
Bulmer, Sue, 22
burial of ritual experts, 204
Burton, John, 93-94
Bus, G. A. M., 298

cane, 95
cannibalism in myth, 185
cassowary, 296, 338
central Enga, 244, 356, 382, 383; bachelors' cults,
220, **222;** competition and warfare, 358; exchange systems, 304-5; female courtship, 242;
Great Ceremonial Wars, 291, 298-302; Kepele
ancestral cult, 202-3; migration, 127-33, **128;**
pearl shell trade, 303-4; Sangai bachelors' cult,
221, **222,** 224, 225-29; social change, 363; subsistence, 57-58, 110-11, 243; systems of exchange, 304-5; Tee cycle in, 254, 265, 294; warfare, 129-33, 266, 366; war reparations,
163-64, 247, 252; Yainanda cult, 182-83
ceremonial attire, 336-37. *See also* attire
ceremonial exchange, 17, 117; networks of, 98;
and reparations to allies, 85-89. See also *Tee
Ceremonial Exchange Cycle*
ceremonial grounds: sacred stones on, 183; use
in ritual, 286, 287, 329; use in Tee cycle, 335,
337
chains of finance, 164-65, 174-75, 177, 361, 368
change. *See* social change
charisma, 227
children: growth payments for, 84; neglect of,
117; payments for illness or injury of, 84; ritual cure for poor growth of, 182

Mbowamb. *See* Melpa

Meane, Tumbuli, 86-87

meat sharing, as cause of conflict, 144, 146

mediation: by big-men, 253; role of oratory, 260-61; war reparations, 250-51

medical beliefs and practices, 117

Meggitt, Mervyn, 70-71, 78, 85, 175; on central Enga, 143; on competition, 342, 351; on land and warfare, 119-20, 148-50, 151; on Sangai bachelors' cult, 216; on Tee cycle, 298, 325-26; on war reparations, 251

Melpa, 183

Melpa (Mbowamb), **2,** 163, 303, 361, 379; ritual sphere, 183; similar to Enga, 1-2; ties to eastern Enga, 194; transmission of cults, 195

mena sapya (sides of pork), 296

mena yae pingi (distribution of pork), 296-97, 305, 307, 330. *See also* pigs and pork

Mendi, **2,** 60, 95, 361, 364, 379, 382; Kepele ancestral cult, 199; similar to Enga, 1-2; ties to eastern Enga, 194; trade with Enga, 98; transmission of cults, 195

men's houses, during Great Ceremonial Wars, 269

menstrual pollution, 117, 217-18, 227, 239, 318; changes in beliefs about, 367; and Female Spirit cult, 318

metaphor, in oratory, 261

metaphorical legends, 26, 39

methodology. *See* research methodology

migration, 34-36, 36, 86-88, 145; as catalyst for change, 354-55; in central Enga, 129-33; clans encouraging immigration, 125; cult transmission, 197; in eastern Enga, **122,** 126, 127; encouraging through affinal kin, 140; in middle Lagaip valley, 135-40; not related to warfare, 136; and trade, 136; in upper Lagaip valley, 134-35; and warfare, 119, 125-37, 140-42. *See also* population

millenarian cults, 185, 383. *See also* cults

Mioko, Yakapusa, 276

Mitchell, William, 372-73

mobility, 117

Modjeska, Nicholas, 152, 374, 375-76, 378

Moka exchange system, 163, 175-76, 303

Molopai, 74

Molopai myth, 193, 198

molopai (rainbow python), 202, 207-8; as religious symbol, 193-94

Monaini tribe, **20-21,** 107, 108; causes of war, 147-48; in Great Ceremonial Wars, 134, 166; migration, **137;** and Sangai bachelors' cult, **222**

Monaini versus Yanaitini Great Ceremonial War, **274;** conclusion, 322; costs, 275; origins, 273; and Tee networks, **306,** 308

Mondatepa tribe, **20-21, 137,** 141

mondo. See sweet potato

moral codes, 181

Morren, George, 67

mote boys' initiation, 194, 199, 205-8; variations of, 202, 208

mother, symbolic separation from, 206-7

motokea, 93

Mountain Ok, 379

Mount Hagen, 176

mourning, during Great Ceremonial Wars, 270

Mulapini tribe, **20-21, 128, 137**

Muramuni Enga, **15,** 53

murder, revenge for, 146-48

myths, 26-27

narrative. *See* oral history, narratives

neighbors: conflict and cooperation among, 150, 151-52; problems between, 146

Nembo, Danny Kili, 6

nemongo. See magic

Nenae, 164

Nenaini tribe, **20-21,** 87-88, **122,** 172

Nenge tribe, **20-21**

Nete, **2,** 52

net goods, 94

networks of exchange. *See* exchange

Neumann, Klaus, 5

oral history, 3, 9, 25-42; chronology, 9, 27, 31-33; colonialism's effects on, 7; estimating population size, 33-34; factualness, 41; narratives, 36-38; narrators, 9; origin traditions, 34-36; seminar, 9; of social change, 41-42; tracking tribal dispersal, 33; writing down, 354. *See also* interviewing; research methodology

oratory, 260-61

origins of Enga, 14-16, 19, **22;** tribal origins, **50-51.** *See also specific tribes*

origin traditions, **22,** 23-25, 34-36, **50-51;** of ancestor cults, 179; of bachelors' cults, **222;** oral history, 34-36; of Sangai bachelors' cult, 219, 220-29, 232-43; of tribes, 179

Pakaini tribe, **20-21.** *See also* Yakani tribe

Pakena, Pyakole, 278

Pakiala, 302-3

Pakiala, Maua, 293

Pandame tribe, **20-21**
pandanus, 65-66, 182; as cause of war, 144; lowland, 127
Pangium edule, 127
Papaiyakali legend, 190-91. *See also* Dindi Gamu
Papu, Kepa, 251
Papua New Guinea: climate and geography, 19; introduction of sweet potato, 102; location of Enga, 2; traditional religious beliefs, 18
patrilineal clans, 357; obligations and rights of members, 362; social structure, 78-79, 99-100. *See also* descent
Pauakaka tribe, **20-21**, 168
peace: and Aeatee cult, 312; after the Great Ceremonial Wars, 323; making, 150, 152; and marriage ties, 262-63; negotiation through song, 254. *See also* war reparations
pearl shell, 95, 247, 249, 349; in Tee cycle, 296, 302-4; use in Female Spirit cult, 319-20; in war reparations, 259
Peke, 342, 343, 344
Pembe, 23, 82-83
Penale, 52
Pendaine. *See* Lambu, Pendaine
penge (bamboo containers for sacred fluid), 218, 226, 227. *See also* Sangai bachelors' cult
Peter, Alo, 105-6
phratries. *See* tribes
Piandane tribe, **20-21**, 137
pig husbandry, 66-68, 112, 115, 173; gender of caretaker, 236-37; of Lambu (son of Pendaine Lambu), 341; and marriage, 272; sweet potatoes as fodder, 112, 114; and war reparations, 257-58. *See also* pigs
pigs and pork, 66-68, 164-65, 292, 336, 374-76, 378; in Aeatee cult, 313; consumption of, 115; counting system for, 331; cure for poor growth, 182; as currency, 356; in Great Ceremonial Wars, 272, 286; Great War pig kill, 287; in Kaima ritual, 184; in Lambu Tee cycle, 337-38; *lome nyingi* (payment of live pigs), 272; in Lyaini-Sakalini versus Pumane-Aiyele Great Ceremonial War, 278; pork feasts in war reparations, 329; production of, 359-60, 382; protein gap, 375; relation to shifts in subsistence, 365, 367; in ritual, 115, 184-85, 206, 212; *saandi pingi* (initiatory gifts), 294, 296, 307; *tee pingi* (main gifts), 296; use of fat, 209, 210; in war reparations, 200, 252, 253, 256-58, 262; *yae pingi* (distribution of pork), 296-97, 305, 307, 330, 339;

yuku pingi (initiatory gifts from hosts to owners of fight), 271-72. *See also* Lambu family; pig husbandry
Pilisa, Iki, 240
Pima tribe, **20-21, 137**
plants: male, 229; men's and women's crops, 73; wild foods, 65
PNG. *See* Papua New Guinea
poetry, 65; in Sandalu, 238; in Sangai bachelors' cult, 219. *See also* magic; praise poetry
Pokalya cult network, cult houses, **188**
Pokalyanda fertility cult, 73
Polaoanda (Male Spirit cult), 316-18
political organization, 17, 369-71, 379-80; complexity, 355; Kepele ancestral cult, 212
politics: and ritual, 218; speech and metaphor in, 261; and warfare, 146-48
pollen analysis, 22, 60-61; introduction of sweet potato, 102
pollution. *See* menstrual pollution
polygyny. *See* marriage
Polynesia, 102
population, 17; as catalyst to change, 354-56; density, 249; distribution and size, 49-52, 55-56, 117, 150, 153; in eastern Enga, **122,** 123-24, 125-26; and ecology, 379; in Great Ceremonial Wars, 266; growth, 116-18, 119, 350-51, 355; in Kandep, 141-42; settlement patterns, 365; as social problem, 199; in western Enga, 358-59. *See also* migration
Porgera valley, 58-59, 201, 221. *See also* western Enga
pork. *See* feasting; pigs and pork
Portuguese traders, and sweet potato, 102
Pote, Sipisipi, 80
Potealini tribe, **20-21,** 270, 333; in Great Ceremonial Wars, 276, 308-9; Kepele ancestral cult, 202; migration, **128,** 132, 133; Pokalyanda (Aeatee) fertility cult, 73; and Tee cycle, 330. *See also* Malipini-Potealini versus Itapuni-Awaini Great Ceremonial War
Potepa tribe, 175
Poul, Leme, 9-10, 168, 273, 300-301
power: changes in, 380; nature of, 370; separation of secular and ritual, 370
practice theory, 43-44, 380-81
praise poetry, 218, 219; in bachelors' cults, 26, 39; and Sangai bachelors' cult, 230-32
prehistory, 19-23; introduction of sweet potato, 102; pollen evidence in, 22, 60-61; "time of darkness," 23, 70-71
prestige, 298, 326